Popular Culture
in Late Imperial China

STUDIES ON CHINA

A series of conference volumes sponsored by the Joint Committee on Chinese Studies of the American Council of Learned Societies and the Social Science Research Council.

Popular Culture
in Late Imperial China

EDITED BY

David Johnson
Andrew J. Nathan
Evelyn S. Rawski

CONTRIBUTORS

Judith A. Berling · James Hayes · Robert E. Hegel
David Johnson · Leo Ou-fan Lee · Victor H. Mair
Andrew J. Nathan · Susan Naquin · Daniel L. Overmyer
Evelyn S. Rawski · Tanaka Issei · Barbara E. Ward
James L. Watson

UNIVERSITY OF CALIFORNIA PRESS

Berkeley · Los Angeles · London

University of California Press
Berkeley and Los Angeles, California
University of California Press, Ltd.
London, England
© 1985 by
The Regents of the University of California
Printed in the United States of America
First Paperback Printing 1987

1 2 3 4 5 6 7 8 9

Library of Congress Cataloging in Publication Data
Main entry under title:

Popular culture in late imperial China.

Based on a conference sponsored by the
Committee on Studies of Chinese Civilization of
the American Council of Learned Societies.
Includes index.
1. China—Civilization—1644–1912.
2. China—Popular culture.
I. Johnson, David G. (David George) II. Nathan,
Andrew J. (Andrew James) III. Rawski, Evelyn
S. (Evelyn Sakakida). IV. American Council of
Learned Societies. Committee on Studies of
Chinese Civilization.
DS754.14.P66 1984 951'.03   83-18012
ISBN 0-520-06172-1

CONTENTS

ACKNOWLEDGMENTS

The conference in which this book originated was sponsored by the Committee on Studies of Chinese Civilization of the American Council of Learned Societies, which also helped defray the costs of publication. Additional support and meeting facilities were provided by the East-West Communications Institute of the East-West Center, Honolulu. Administrative assistance was given by the East Asian Institute of Columbia University and by the Department of History, University of California, Berkeley.

The conference proposal was written at a planning meeting in January, 1979, attended by Myron L. Cohen, Leo Ou-fan Lee, Donald J. Munro, Daniel L. Overmyer, and the editors. Commentators at the conference were Godwin C. Chu, Wolfram Eberhard, Perry Link, John McCoy, Donald J. Munro, G. William Skinner, Tu Wei-ming, and Eugen Weber, whose contribution was especially valuable because he was the only participant who was not a China specialist. Daniel Kwok, Y. W. Ma, and Michael Saso, of the University of Hawaii, also took part in a number of sessions. Godwin Chu and Meg White were warm hosts on behalf of the East-West Communications Institute.

Barbara Ward died not long after completing the final version of her chapter. She had just published several important essays and had major projects under way. The loss to scholarship was great, but those who knew the energy, wit, and sheer delight she brought to every gathering will also understand our deep sense of personal loss.

PREFACE

One of the principal purposes of this book is to help bring the study of non-elite culture into the mainstream of academic discourse about traditional China. No one believes that we can understand China by studying only the privileged and the educated. But they produced most of the documents, and so they have received, and still receive, attention from historians far out of proportion to their numbers. This overemphasis on the elite has led to grave distortions in our vision of Chinese history and culture, distortions that can only be remedied by serious, systematic study of the world beyond the boundaries of the ruling class.

Such study is not as problematic as it is often assumed to be. We can seldom hope to form more than the dimmest conception of the attitudes and values of the illiterate majority, but, as the essays in this book suggest, by late imperial times there were many people who could read, and even write, and yet were not members of any elite. From this broad and variegated group came the producers or consumers of virtually all the surviving documents directly relevant to the study of popular culture. Many such texts make an appearance in the papers that follow: scriptures, for example, and edifying tales; almanacs, handbooks, and the like; explanations in plain language of the orthodox ideology of the *Sacred Edict*; accounts of the miracles of local gods; scripts of plays; even a novel written to popularize a new religion. These materials were written, but at the same time were not too far removed from the illiterate realm. Some were designed to be read aloud; others were used by those who could read them as the basis of instruction or advice to those who could not. Such materials are the foundation of any attempt to reconstruct non-elite mentalities in premodern times.

In addition to their importance as source materials, these stories, scriptures, plays, and so on are often extremely interesting and enjoyable in their own right. They frequently have a more direct appeal than the complex, sophisticated writings of the intellectual and political elites. The mental and emotional world revealed in many of the public writings of the late imperial ruling class has a certain formal, self-conscious, subdued character that makes all the more attractive the unselfconscious, vigorous, colorful, and straightforward qualities of village plays, popular ballads, tales derived from storytellers' performances, and the like. Many students of China feel an immediate sympathy with the world of popular culture, and find working in the field a stimulating and even liberating experience. We hope our readers will sense something of this.

Popular culture comprises an enormous range of phenomena, from domestic architecture to millenarian cults, from irrigation techniques to shadow plays. This book does not pretend to cover, or even to touch upon, more than a few of these phenomena. We have narrowed our focus in two ways: first, by confining our attention to the late imperial period (about 1550 to 1920), and second, by concentrating on values and their communication (to adapt a phrase from the title of the conference at which these papers were first presented).

Popular culture was transformed in Sung and Yuan times, thanks to the advent and spread of commercial printing, and is being transformed again today as radio, movies, and especially television make deeper and deeper inroads. Why, then, did we choose to focus on the late imperial period? To begin with, we felt that the mass media brought such profound changes in their train that popular culture in the modern period was appropriately the subject of a separate book. We therefore decided to concentrate on the best-documented and most accessible period in the premodern epoch, which of course is the most recent one. This was also the most highly differentiated stage of traditional Chinese civilization, and illustrates the premodern processes of cultural communication and integration at their most intricate. Evelyn Rawski shows in her opening essay that this final phase of imperial history began around the middle of the sixteenth century and extended down to the early twentieth century. That epoch was set apart from what went before by new relations between landlords and tenants, an intensification of economic activity, new educational institutions, new developments in commercial printing, and a more open and competitive social order.

People are alive today whose parents and grandparents lived under Ch'ing rule and who themselves experienced late imperial popular culture—which outlived the political institutions of the empire by many years. This was another reason for choosing the late imperial period as the focus of this book: it allowed us to use the findings of anthropologists and others who have lived among people to whom the subjects of this book are, or were, living realities. Because so much that we need to know about popular culture is left unsaid in the surviving documents, this kind of eyewitness evidence is of the highest value. Of course, the use of contemporary data to illuminate the past requires care. James Hayes, for example, shows that many of the books he has collected in Hong Kong were first printed in the late Ch'ing, and, by citing nineteenth-century missionary sources, he demonstrates that the social conditions governing the circulation and use of these texts have not changed significantly since that time. Barbara Ward argues that colonial administrators in Hong Kong have preserved the traditional diversity of Chinese opera in a way that the regimes in mainland China did not permit. Moreover, she focuses her report on festival performances, which she maintains are less changed from late Ch'ing times than any other type. And James Watson places his Hong Kong field data in the context of the historical evolution of the T'ien Hou cult, as reconstructed from documentary sources.

Just as we chose to work within a clearly delimited historical period, so too we focused on a restricted group of themes. These, as already noted, fall under the general heading of values and their communication. It is impossible to comprehend behavior without understanding the values, ideas, and beliefs—the mentalities—of those who are acting. And to understand values and the like one must study how they moved from person to person and group to group, and how they changed as they moved. Of course, many other aspects of non-elite life are eminently worth studying—demography, material culture, and economic conditions come immediately to mind—but we believe that focusing on values and their communication offers an especially effective way of understanding late imperial China.

At the beginning of our period, the population of China had already passed the 100 million mark, and by the last quarter of the eighteenth century it was approaching 300 million.[1] At that time France, the largest nation in Europe, would have ranked third among the provinces of China, and England would have been one of the smallest, surpassing only remote Yunnan, Kweichow, and Kwangsi.[2] Demographically, China was not a France or an England—it was a Europe. But while Europe was divided into a multitude of nations growing ever more distinct from each other linguistically, economically, socially, and culturally, China was a single polity, and had been since the late sixth century (with interruptions during the Five Dynasties and Southern Sung periods). A direct consequence of these two facts was that Chinese culture in the last centuries of imperial rule was both extremely diverse and highly integrated. The diversity is easy to understand—it was an obvious function of China's great size. There were many varieties of popular culture, non-elite subcultures as it were, reflecting differences of power, prestige, education, and wealth, and of region, dialect, and occupation. Elite culture, too, displayed significant internal variations. And, of course, popular and elite cultures were very different from each other. But—and this is much harder to account for—these diverse elements were

---

[1] Ping-ti Ho, *Studies on the Population of China, 1368–1953* (Cambridge, Mass.: Harvard University Press, 1959), pp. 264, 281.

[2] Ho, *Studies*, p. 283; Pierre Goubert, *The Ancien Régime: French Society 1600–1750*, trans. Steve Cox (New York: Harper Torchbooks, 1974), pp. 33–34; E. A. Wrigley, *Population and History* (New York: McGraw-Hill [World University Library], 1969), pp. 78, 153.

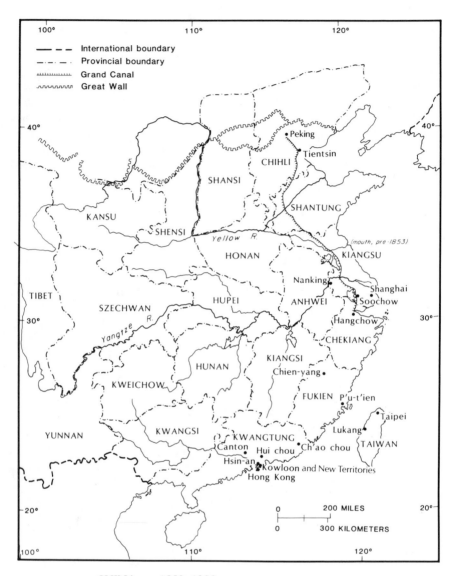

MAP I. CHINA, ca. 1550–1920

integrated into a single complex cultural system. The intellectual and spiritual world of the scholar or official in late imperial times was not utterly alien to the peasant or laborer, nor was the reverse true. There were common elements in the mental worlds of all Chinese. We are far from satisfied with our account of the nature of those elements, but we take it as axiomatic that they existed. If they had not, the whole idea of Chinese culture dissolves—"China" is reduced to the semantic triviality of "Asia."

How can we account for the integration of this extraordinarily diverse culture? We start from the conviction that the sharing of values, ideas, assumptions, and points of reference across great social, geographic, and economic distances is the result of specific, identifiable human actions. Hence, one of our main concerns has been with the agents and mechanisms by which verbal and symbolic structures were transmitted. We have also sought to understand, from the very beginning, how beliefs and attitudes were modified as they were presented to different kinds of audiences, and how the mentalities of the various social groups differed from each other. All the papers in the body of this book are concerned in one way or another with these issues.

The book begins with two essays that are meant to set the stage for what follows. Evelyn Rawski's chapter offers a characterization of the late imperial period, with special emphasis on the interplay of economic and cultural factors. The developments that she describes in education and, particularly, in the printing industry, are fundamental to a proper understanding of the nature of the era. In the second introductory chapter, David Johnson develops a general approach to the study of popular culture. He outlines the systems of communication (oral and written) and the structure of dominance in late imperial China. He proposes a new taxonomy of social groups based on the position of individuals in both these structures and derives from it a systematic definition of the term "popular culture." He suggests that the groups thus defined had their own characteristic collective mentalities and outlines some of the features of each. Johnson's chapter is not so much a program for the book as a comment on the other papers and on the study of popular culture in general.

The main body of the book opens with an account by James Hayes of the many kinds of writings that were intended for non-elite audiences. He pays particular attention to the individuals he calls "specialists"—school teachers, letter writers, experts on ceremonial, entertainers, and the like—who in most cases were the only people in rural communities able to use written materials. They functioned as intermediaries between illiterate villagers and townspeople on the one hand and the educated classes on the other. It was they who did most of the work of popularizing elite literary and intellectual culture. Hayes draws on his long experience of life in Hong Kong's New Territories to provide a new and vivid picture of some of the most important ways in which ideas and values moved from the upper to the lower strata of late imperial Chinese society. Robert Hegel focuses on a closely related topic: the way in which a story—in this case the system of legend and history concerning the early T'ang general Li Mi—changes when presented to different audiences. Hegel stresses the close connection between the audience of a work and its content, an idea that is fundamental to this book, since it applies not only to fiction and drama, but also to religious teachings, ideas about medicine and the natural world, and any other widespread narrative construct or system of ideas. He concludes by underscoring the common elements in the versions of the Li Mi story he has discussed, what he calls an essential unity of ideology. This is a theme that is central to the book.

Over the past two decades, Tanaka Issei has carried out extensive studies of local drama in the late imperial period, and in his chapter he provides a summary of his findings. Tanaka identifies the three major settings of local dramatic performances: the market town, the village, and the lineage hall. He suggests that in each of these venues the theater was dominated by representatives of a different social stratum. As a consequence, both the plays presented and, if the plays were the same, significant details in their scripts, tended to differ from setting to setting. In the second of this volume's two papers on the theater, that most important of the popular arts, Barbara Ward provides a systematic description of the regional operas she spent many years observing in Hong Kong, especially the type she calls "festival operas," which she believes have more in common with Ch'ing popular drama than any other type. She also puts forward a stimulating and provocative interpretation of the nature of Chinese theater that speaks directly to one of the main themes of this book. Where Hegel and Tanaka pursue the way in which the performance context, or the author's sense of his audience, served to generate variations in the material presented, Ward emphasizes the elements common to all drama. "The large majority of Chinese operas," she writes, "relied on the same stylized role categories and made use of the same popular stories . . . that formed the shared repertoire of storytellers, puppeteers, ballad singers, and other entertainers all over China. There is no question but that at least from toward the end of the first half of the Ming dynasty onward the messages relayed by these traditional media to the Chinese populace were essentially the same"—a conclusion similar to Hegel's. Thus, Ward stresses the essential unity of traditional drama, while Tanaka emphasizes its diversity. Ward recognizes the conflict between these positions and tries to resolve it, but is not entirely successful. Clearly, identifying the common elements in the cultural diversity of late imperial China is a major conceptual problem.

With Judith Berling's paper we find ourselves in the region where entertainment and instruction meet. Berling describes and analyzes an early seventeenth-century novel that was written to spread the doctrines of the Three Teachings religion, which had been founded in the late sixteenth century. The novel is a perfect example of how men who wished to persuade or instruct had to use means that would appeal to the people they hoped to reach. The author of

The Romance of the Three Teachings was writing for men who were literate but were neither officials nor scholars—it is not surprising that he wrote a novel to get his message across. Since it had to depict improper behavior in order to expose and reform it, the novel provides an unusually revealing account of the tensions, anxieties, and conflicts that were part of life in the lower Yangtze region in the early seventeenth century.

The Romance of the Three Teachings belongs to a large class of writings that uses the techniques of popular fiction and song to popularize religious teachings. One of the most important genres in that class was the *pao-chüan*, the subject of Daniel Overmyer's essay. Overmyer begins with a description of the various types of *pao-chüan* and a brief account of their history. He then provides a full and systematic treatment of their teachings. Overmyer stresses the important role played by women in the audience of *pao-chüan*, discussing in considerable detail the *Liu Hsiang pao-chüan*, the main concern of which is with the "courage, freedom, and salvation of women." Susan Naquin also writes of popular sectarian religion in late imperial times. But where Overmyer is largely concerned with the values taught by sectarian scriptures, Naquin concentrates on explicating the methods used by different kinds of White Lotus sects to propagate their beliefs. She demonstrates that there were two main types of White Lotus sect in the mid-Ch'ing period. In one, written scriptures and their communal recitation played a central role; in the other, whose members seem to have been villagers with little or no education, short chants or mantras, transmitted orally, were the characteristic means by which doctrine was propagated. The teachings of the two types of sect also differed considerably, as Naquin shows; yet they both accepted the basic ideas of White Lotus religion. Thus, Naquin's paper too speaks to the issue of themes and variations that was addressed in differing ways by Hegel and Ward.

The Chinese state was in effect a theocracy: the emperor was the Son of Heaven, intermediary between the human and divine worlds. As a consequence, the civil authorities were extremely sensitive about the religious beliefs of the people, and constantly intervened in the world of popular religion. The sects discussed by Overmyer and Naquin were often criticized and sometimes violently attacked by local and central government officials. James Watson shows that ordinary community-based popular cults, which were very different from the White Lotus-type sects, were also subject to close scrutiny and frequent manipulation by the authorities. He describes in detail the process by which "Aunt Lin," a goddess known initially only to the people of a small coastal town in Fukien, grew more and more popular, and ultimately was transformed through governmental patronage into T'ien Hou, Empress of Heaven, one of the most important deities in the popular pantheon. The cult of Aunt Lin was then reimposed, in this altered form, on the very communities among which it had first appeared. In the process, Watson develops the argument that T'ien Hou, like all important religious symbols, meant different things to different people. He concludes, in contrast to Ward and Hegel, that the integration of Chinese culture was made possible by the ambiguity of its symbols.

Besides attempting to modify the content of indigenous popular cults, the authorities devised various ways of directly propagating orthodox values. Victor Mair writes about a characteristic method: the composition by scholars or officials of explanations of the meaning of the so-called *Sacred Edict*, a set of sixteen brief maxims or commandments composed by the K'ang-hsi emperor (r. 1662–1722). Since few people could understand easily the meaning of the original text, which was written in a compressed, literary style, explanations written in simpler language were prepared. In addition, a regular program of twice-monthly lectures was instituted in settlements of all sizes, at which the sixteen commandments were explained to the people in plain language, since they would have been incomprehensible to most people if simply read aloud. These lectures were often based on the written explanations just mentioned, the texts of which still survive. Mair has discovered that there were also unofficial lecturers on the *Sacred Edict*, more akin to storytellers than to preachers, who told stories that were intended, officially at any rate, to illustrate the meaning of the sixteen commandments. His paper provides unusually detailed information on the ways in which orthodox ideology was transmitted to the people at large, and how it was modified in the process.

In the paper that concludes the main part of the volume, Leo Lee and Andrew Nathan focus on journalism and fiction in the period of transition from traditional popular culture to modern mass culture. They show that the problem of accommodating popular tastes while inculcating approved values and providing socially useful information is an even more serious problem in the age of mass communication than it was under the Ch'ing and earlier. At the same time, they provide another illustration of the interdependence of values and communication.

We have tried in this book to concentrate on topics of special importance to the study of Chinese popular culture, and to come to grips with some of the major conceptual problems that arose in the course of research, writing, and discussion. But many significant areas of research have been barely touched upon or ignored entirely, and difficult conceptual problems remain to be solved. Evelyn Rawski provides an overview of these topics and problems in the concluding chapter. What kinds of texts were easiest to read for the moderately educated person? How is the meaning of a text to be defined? What is the nature of cultural integration? Rawski's discussion of these and other issues leads naturally to the identification of promising areas for future research, among which are the interrelationship of popular religion and drama; the role of ritual and ritual specialists in popular culture; the whole range of cultural specialists discussed by Hayes; women, their culture and their role in the integration of Chinese culture; domestic architecture and other aspects of material culture;

and so on. As Rawski's paper makes clear, Chinese popular culture is an exceptionally interesting and important field that is just beginning to be explored. We hope this book will prompt others to venture into it, and will provide them with some useful guidance when they do.

—The Editors

PART I

Introductory
Perspectives

ONE

Economic and
Social Foundations of
Late Imperial Culture

Evelyn S. Rawski

This essay focuses on two questions. In answer to the first—Why do we study the late Ming and Ch'ing as one historical unit?—we argue that this era, the late imperial period (sixteenth through nineteenth centuries), was substantively different from its predecessors and was characterized by considerable continuity in key institutions and socio-economic structure. In investigating this continuity, we discuss three major phenomena: economic growth and change, which led to shifts in the composition and character of the elite; an expansion of the educational system, produced in part by economic growth; and the onset of large-scale printing, stimulated by prosperity and expanded education. These three factors all have direct bearing on a second question, the concern of many papers in this volume: namely, the degree to which Ming and Ch'ing citizens shared ideas, values, assumptions, and frames of reference. The final section of this essay briefly considers the relationship of long-run economic and social trends with the forces of cultural integration and diversity.

THE LATE IMPERIAL ECONOMY

Despite profound differences of opinion on the contours of the historical landscape, Chinese, Japanese, and American historians seem agreed on one thing: that Chinese society underwent significant changes in the course of the Ming dynasty, changes that produced the political, social, and economic institutions of late imperial China.

One major economic development during the Ming dynasty was the monetization of silver. This trend was reflected in the sixteenth-century Single Whip fiscal reforms, which simplified tax levies and commuted them to money payments. Monetization was based on an expanded marketing system that drew regions situated along the coast and the Yangtze River into long-distance and even international trade. What was new was not the existence of such trade but its magnitude, made possible by a shift in the sixteenth-century focus of trade from Central Asia to the southeast coast. As Owen Lattimore notes, the shift to water was critical: "Even a small sailing ship could in one voyage carry from Canton to London more cargo, in a shorter time and at a higher profit, than could be moved by a succession of caravans plodding from ancient or medieval China to the markets of the Mediterranean."[1] Ming junks went not to London but to ports in Japan, the Spanish colony of Manila, and Southeast Asia, but the effect was still the same: a large expansion, in the sixteenth and early seventeenth centuries, in the volume of trade accompanying the shift of focus from China's inner frontiers to the southeast coast.

The influence of the foreign trade was first felt in the flow of Japanese and Mexican silver into China. According to William Atwell, who compares domestic silver production with silver imports, foreign trade accounted for the bulk of the new supplies of silver entering China's economy in the late sixteenth and early seventeenth centuries. He concludes that "Japanese and American silver may well have been *the* most significant factor in the vigorous economic expansion which occurred in China," an expansion that ended in the 1630s when Spanish efforts to restrict the Manila trade and Japanese efforts (after 1638) to bar the Portuguese from trade in Japan succeeded in substantially reducing trade volumes and in bringing a deflation to China.[2] While this deflation was probably important in stimulating the crises at the end of Ming, China's involvement in the world economy suffered only a temporary setback. In subsequent centuries its involvement increased and deepened.

The economic upsurge of the sixteenth century, which G. W. Skinner identifies as the ascending phase of the second great macrocycle in Chinese history, brought increased commercialization of agriculture, further growth in rural and urban handicraft production, and more rural markets in the Southeast Coast, Lower Yangtze, and areas in North China adjoining the Grand Canal. The growth of rural markets occurred in sixteenth-century coastal Fukien and sixteenth-century Ningpo. In Fukien, cash cropping in sugar cane and expanded production of cotton and porcelain appeared in response to new opportunities for trade with the Portuguese, Japanese, and Spanish. In the Lower Yangtze the sixteenth century saw further development of handicrafts, particularly cotton weaving, which was a rural industry. The size of the handicraft sector is revealed indirectly in the development of specialized regions for cotton cultivation along the Grand Canal in North

---

[1] Owen Lattimore, cited in William S. Atwell, "Notes on Silver, Foreign Trade, and the Late Ming Economy," *Ch'ing-shih wen-t'i* 3.8: 30(1977), n. 59.

[2] Atwell, "Notes on Silver."

China: we know that cotton grown here was sold to traders from the Lower Yangtze for spinning and weaving in Kiangnan.[3]

Thus, the sixteenth century saw developing markets and commercialization of agriculture in three macroregional cores: the North China core along the Grand Canal, and the cores of the Lower Yangtze and the Southeast Coast. Although we know less about the Lingnan regional economy, the onset in the sixteenth century of Portuguese trade at Macao and the increase in numbers of private academies suggest that this region also experienced growth and prosperity.

The creation of rural markets outpaced population growth and altered the hierarchy of central places. According to Skinner,

> the regional city systems that developed in the medieval era were immature and uneven: capitals and market towns were only very imperfectly meshed into an integrated system, and the urban population as a whole was concentrated in the largest cities. By contrast, city systems of the late imperial era were more mature and more fully fleshed out: capitals and market towns were better integrated into a single hierarchical system, and the total urban population was more evenly distributed throughout the hierarchy.

Integration of the urban hierarchy and increased ties between towns and villages facilitated what James Liu calls the "radiating diffusion" of urban culture into rural areas and was thus an important factor in shaping the contours of Ming-Ch'ing popular culture.[4]

Market development and economic growth also prompted relaxation of direct government controls over the economy. The Ming founder had continued the Yuan practice of registering certain households for special service as salt producers, soldiers, or artisans, but this system collapsed in the sixteenth century and was replaced by commuted payments in money. Goods obtained for Imperial Household use with corvée labor in early Ming were now acquired

---

[3] For a detailed exposition on macroregions, which will be referred to throughout this essay, see G. William Skinner, "Regional Urbanization in Nineteenth-Century China," in *The City in Late Imperial China*, ed. G. William Skinner (Stanford: Stanford University Press, 1977). Also G. William Skinner, "Urban Development in Imperial China," ibid., p. 28; Yoshinobu Shiba, "Ningpo and Its Hinterland," ibid., pp. 399, 401; Mark Elvin, "Market Towns and Waterways: The County of Shang-hai from 1480 to 1910," ibid., pp. 470–471; E. S. Rawski, *Agricultural Change and the Peasant Economy of South China* (Cambridge: Harvard University Press, 1972), pp. 64–88; Kataoka Shibako 片岡芝子, "Min-matsu Shin-sho no Kahoku ni okeru nōka keiei" 明末清初之華北 に於ける農家經營 [The peasant economy of North China in late Ming and early Ch'ing], *Shakai keizai shigaku* 社会経済史学 25.2–3:77–100(1959); Mark Elvin, *The Pattern of the Chinese Past* (Stanford: Stanford University Press, 1973), pp. 269–284.

[4] Skinner, "Urban Development," p. 28, referring to T'ang–Sung as the medieval period and Ming–Ch'ing as the late imperial era. James T. C. Liu, "Integrative Factors Through Chinese History: Their Interaction," in *Traditional China*, ed. James T. C. Liu and Wei-ming Tu (Englewood Cliffs, N.J.: Prentice-Hall, 1970), p. 14.

through subcontracts to private firms using wage labor. Government direction of water-control projects was similarly replaced by local financing and management.[5] This tendency for the central government to retreat from direct participation and control of the economy continued in Ch'ing times.

Agricultural productivity increased during the late Ming. The effects of economic development on agriculture can be seen most markedly in the emergence of rights of permanent tenure and multiple ownership of land in the rice-producing regions of South and Central China. Whether or not one agrees with the Japanese scholarship that identifies this development with dissolution of manorial controls on rural peasants and tenants, it is clear that these rights, which are first cited in sixteenth-century Fukien gazetteers, represent an improvement of the tenant's position with respect to the landlord. In the eighteenth and nineteenth centuries, permanent tenure appeared in Kiangsu, Kiangsi, and other rice-producing regions of China.[6]

Government retreat from economic intervention, increased social mobility resulting from flourishing markets, and improved tenancy rights are signposts of a cumulative process familiar to us from European examples: the replacement of direct controls over individuals by the indirect controls of the market. Of course, neither the late Ming nor the Ch'ing economy was dominated by the market. The contract, which appears in Ming and Ch'ing times for a wide variety of transactions, was still not ubiquitous, and broad regional variations in the importance of contractual obligations versus those of status undoubtedly persisted. The significance of these developments, however, lies not in their statistical frequency but in their function as signs of a gradual and long-term trend toward the triumph of the market economy.

In the Lower Yangtze core, North China core, and other regions where

[5] Ping-ti Ho, *The Ladder of Success in Imperial China* (New York: Columbia University Press, 1962), chap. 2; Michael Dillon, "Jingdezhen as a Ming Industrial Center," *Ming Studies* 6:39–41 (1978); Tsing Yuan, "The Porcelain Industry at Ching-te chen 1500–1700," *Ming Studies* 6:47–48 (1978). Skinner, "Urban Development," p. 25, notes that this was part of a long-term trend, beginning in the T'ang, "whereby the degree of involvement in local affairs—not only in marketing and commerce but also in social regulation . . . and administration itself—steadily declined, a retrenchment forced by the growing scale of empire."

[6] Elvin, *The Pattern of the Chinese Past*, chap. 15, and Mi-chu Wiens, "Lord and Peasant: The Sixteenth to the Eighteenth Century," *Modern China* 6.1:3–39 (1980), rely on Japanese and Chinese scholarship; neither studies the regional distribution and first appearance of permanent tenancy and multiple landownership. Oyama Masaaki 小山正明, "Min Shin shakai keizaishi kenkyū no kaiko" 明清社會經濟史研究の回顧 [Retrospective on research in Ming–Ch'ing socio-economic history], *Shakai keizai shigaku* 社会経済史学 31.1–5:281–293 (1966) surveys the voluminous Japanese literature on permanent tenancy. Recent Chinese works include Fu I-ling 傅衣凌, "Kuan-yü Ming-mo Ch'ing-ch'u Chung-kuo nung-ts'un she-hui kuan-hsi ti hsin ku-chi" 關於明末清初中國農村社會關係的新估計 [A new estimate of social relations in late Ming and early Ch'ing villages], *Hsia-men ta-hsüeh hsüeh-pao* 廈門大學學報 2:57–70 (1959); Li Wen-chih 李文治, "Lun Ch'ing-tai ch'ien-ch'i ti t'u-ti chan-yu kuan-hsi" 論清代前期的土地占有關係 [On land occupancy relations in early Ch'ing], *Li-shih yen-chiu* 歷史研究 5:75–108 (1963).

commercial agriculture was practiced, peasants were subjected more intensely than before to the full influence of the market. On one hand, market participation brought increased productivity, stimulated handicraft production, and encouraged improved conditions for tenants. Increased participation in marketing and the emergence of lower level rural markets meant improvements in communications between town and village, as peddlers, peasants, landlords, and others came together in the periodic markets. The increased flow of trade and heightened market participation thus surely influenced the shape of Chinese culture in both rural and urban places.[7]

Those who produced for the market were exposed to the risk of price fluctuations. Bountiful harvests could now have negative consequences for individual farmers, as the price for a crop fell; bad harvests, when prices soared, could benefit the producer whose crop had not been damaged. Exposure to market forces made the economic calculations of individual households much more complex, and tied household welfare to forces operating above the level of the village. Market participation raised the value of knowledge concerning conditions in the larger world. The risks and benefits of market participation must have also sharpened the competitive environment in which villagers lived. The impact of market participation on peasant mentality lies behind Elvin's observation that "society became restless, fragmented and fiercely competitive."[8]

Economic growth affected Chinese social structure in several ways. It stimulated a trend toward increased social stratification, which can be discerned at various levels of Chinese society. Scholars believe that village society became more highly stratified during the Ming and Ch'ing. Wage labor increasingly replaced the labor of serflike households. Absentee landlordism increased and a new group of managerial landlords emerged. Village society now included absentee landlords, managerial landlords, self-cultivators, tenant farmers, and farm laborers. Among the literati, differentiation was reflected in several spheres. In elite lineages we find the more successful branches sloughing off poorer descent lines by excluding them from genealogies and lineage benefits. We also find tension between the rurally based small landowner and the new absentee landlord, whose interests did not coincide. Rural rent-resistance movements sometimes found the rural landlord at odds with his urban counterpart. Differentiation also characterized elites who aspired to leadership of county society. One recent work asserts that there was no cohesive county elite, but at least two, if not more, distinct elite strata, that did not intermarry: a local elite group, which cultivated marriage alliances with similar families within the

[7] G. William Skinner, "Chinese Peasants and the Closed Community: An Open and Shut Case," *Comparative Studies in Society and History* 13.3:270–281 (1971).

[8] Elvin, *The Pattern of the Chinese Past*, p. 235; Wiens, "Lord and Peasant," pp. 8, 15; Oyama, "Min Shin," p. 283; Li Wen-chih, "Lun Ch'ing-tai," pp. 92–93, 95–96, 106; Fu I-ling, "Kuan-yü," pp. 58, 62–70.

county and maintained strong community ties, and a group of more ambitious families, who were oriented toward the larger bureaucratic elite world outside the county boundaries, whose marriages cemented bureaucratic alliances, and who normally devoted little attention to the local community.[9]

Stratification was probably most marked in the Lower Yangtze core, where absentee landlordism was a prominent development during the late Ming and Ch'ing periods. In advanced economies like the Lower Yangtze core, reliance on contractual rather than personal frameworks of control enabled richer landowners to respond to the economic and cultural opportunities offered by an urban milieu, and they began to move out of villages into towns and cities. Urban residence altered patterns of elite investment and consumption. Landlords residing in towns began to invest their surplus funds in pawnshops, commerce, and urban real estate, ventures that promised higher profits than land investments but that also entailed higher risk. Urban-based landlords and scholar families confronted a more insecure financial future than did their rural relatives, not only because of their greater involvement in the marketplace, but because their expenditures tended to soar once they had moved to town. Towns offered improved access to books and an intellectually dynamic urban culture, but they frequently also offered irresistible diversions from the narrow path of examination studies in the form of wine, women, and song. One man's reaction to urban life, Chang Ying's paean to rural tradition, *Heng-ch'an so-yen* (Remarks on real estate), written at the close of the seventeenth century, tells us a great deal about the dangers of urban life for the Chinese elite.[10]

Elite insecurity and anxiety were the byproducts of another Ming development linked with economic growth—namely, the emergence of a fluid and flexible status system, largely free of effective legal barriers to status mobility.

---

[9] On village stratification, see *Ming and Qing Historical Studies in the People's Republic of China*, ed. Frederic Wakeman, Jr. (Berkeley: Center for Chinese Studies, 1980), pp. 96–103; on elite differentiation, see Jerry Dennerline, *The Chia-ting Loyalists: Confucian Leadership and Social Change in Seventeenth-Century China* (New Haven: Yale University Press, 1981), chaps. 3, 4; Mori Masao 森正夫, "Jūnana seiki no Fukken Neika-ken ni okeru Kō Tsū no kōso hanran (2)" 十七世紀の福建寧化県における黄通の抗租反乱 [The anti-rent rebellion of Huang T'ung in seventeenth-century Ninghua county, Fukien], *Nagoya daigaku bungakubu kenkyū ronshū* 名古屋大学文学部研究論集 21:13–35 (1974).

[10] The extensive Japanese secondary literature on the subject of absentee landlords and local elites is reviewed by Linda Grove and Joseph W. Esherick, "From Feudalism to Capitalism: Japanese Scholarship on the Transformation of Chinese Rural Society," *Modern China* 6.4:397–438 (1980); see Fu I-ling, *Ming Ch'ing nung-ts'un she-hui ching-chi* 明清農村社會經濟 [Ming Ch'ing village society and economy] (1961; reprint ed., Hong Kong: Shih-yung shu-chü 實用書局, 1972), pp. 64–65; Fu, *Ming-tai Chiang-nan shih-min ching-chi shih-t'an* 明代江南市民經濟試探 [Exploration of the Kiangnan urban economy in the Ming] (Shanghai: Jen-min ch'u-pan she 人民出版社, 1963), chaps. 2, 3. A translation of *Heng-ch'an so-yin* is included in Hilary J. Beattie, *Land and Lineage in China: A Study of T'ung-ch'eng County, Anhwei, in the Ming and Ch'ing Dynasties* (Cambridge: Cambridge University Press, 1979), pp. 140–151.

The economic boom of the sixteenth century stimulated expansion of the school system and thus increased the number of examination candidates competing for degrees. As competition for examination degrees sharpened, so did the anxiety among households with elite status, who saw threats to the perpetuation of their status through their children and grandchildren in the improved chances for upward mobility among persons of lower status. Nor was this the only source of anxiety for such households. The emergence of commercial opportunities and the relative downgrading of landed investment signaled the growing complexity of the relationship between wealth, derived from commerce as well as land, and elite status.

Many descendents of older families might, like Fang I-chih, view money making with disdain, but few could ignore the implications of the new social conditions, which saw rich merchants partaking in such traditionally elite activities as book collection, patronage of the arts, and the creation of elaborate gardens and mansions. Partible inheritance divided the family estate in each generation upon the death of the head of the household. If the succeeding generation failed to win degrees or spent too long pursuing degrees, the family's prospects of maintaining high status were poor. One common response to this dilemma is evident in P. T. Ho's case studies of mobility: specialization by sons whereby one made money in order to permit another to pursue studies. Whether this strategy succeeded, however, depended on individual talent and political and economic conditions. There can be little doubt that the psychic pressures on elite households were intensified with the increased competition for examination degrees.[11]

Our view of late Ming and Ch'ing society rests on the socio-economic developments described above. The growth of trade stimulated commercial agriculture and handicrafts and spurred expansion of rural markets. Greater integration of the central place hierarchy and growing market participation facilitated the flow of ideas as well as goods between city and country, while the trend to urban residence among some elites, notably in the Lower Yangtze core, stimulated urban culture.

Economic growth also sparked competition. The regional club (*hui-kuan*) appeared when advances in the economy lured merchants outside their own local systems to penetrate new markets. These merchants found that they could best pursue their interests in a sharply competitive urban setting by forming native-place associations. Later, these associations also accommodated degree candidates and officials who shared native-place ties, and formed foci for regional competition in an urban setting. Competition in some rural areas was organized around lineages, which also expanded in the late seventeenth century.

---

[11] Willard J. Peterson, *Bitter Gourd: Fang I-chih and the Impetus for Intellectual Change* (New Haven: Yale University Press, 1979), chap. 4; Ho, *The Ladder of Success*, pp. 267–318.

Lineages were used to advance collective interests in a locality, or to enhance elite control in regions where the penetration of the commercial economy had weakened traditional mechanisms of social control.[12]

The competitive environment that gave rise to these collective strategies also produced the anxiety and psychic tension described above—anxiety regarding personal status, the security of household fortunes, and, on the part of the traditional elite, the perpetuation of their preeminence.

As noted, these significant changes in the social and economic order began in the late Ming. But they did not end with the demise of the Ming house in 1644; indeed, there are grounds for arguing that the change of dynasties did not affect these fundamental socio-economic trends. As Jonathan Spence and John Wills note, commercial growth, urbanization, and the increasing numbers of examination candidates resulting from the improved access to education were important secular trends that suffered "only brief interruption" from the Ch'ing conquest.[13]

In the Lower Yangtze core, despite instances of spectacular resistance to the Ch'ing armies, most regions surrendered peacefully to the changing order. The social order of the Lower Yangtze survived the interregnum and such Manchu attacks on gentry privilege as the Kiangnan tax case of 1661. The Lower Yangtze economy also recovered quickly in the late seventeenth century. The Southeast Coast, especially Fukien, was hard hit by the Ch'ing policy banning maritime trade and evacuating the coastal population during the campaigns against Koxinga, but conditions improved in the eighteenth century as Fukienese migrated to Taiwan, opened up land for cultivation, and developed marketing links between Taiwan and Fukien ports. Lingnan benefited from the misfortunes of the Southeast Coast, receiving a large stream of immigrants from Swatow and southern Fukien, and profiting from Canton's role as China's entrepot for foreign trade before 1840. The late seventeenth century saw North China begin another cycle of growth, which continued until the rebellions of the 1850s. The Upper Yangtze and Middle Yangtze regions, where civil war (particularly in Szechwan) had been very fierce, also received large groups of new settlers in early Ch'ing who helped rehabilitate the local economy. For

---

[12] On *hui-kuan*, see G. William Skinner, "Introduction: Urban Social Structure," in *The City in Late Imperial China*, pp. 538–46; Ho Ping-ti 何炳棣, *Chung-kuo hui-kuan shih lun* 中國會館史論 [An historical survey of *landsmannschaften* in China] (Taipei: Hsüeh-sheng shu-chü 學生書局, 1966); on lineages, see Rubie S. Watson, "The Creation of a Chinese Lineage: The Teng of Ha Tsuen, 1669–1751," *Modern Asian Studies* 16.1:69–100 (1982), and Dennerline, *The Chia-ting Loyalists*, pp. 98–103.

[13] *From Ming to Ch'ing: Conquest, Region, and Continuity in Seventeenth-Century China*, ed. Jonathan Spence and John Wills, Jr. (New Haven: Yale University Press, 1979), p. xvii; Frederic Wakeman, "Introduction," in *Conflict and Control in Late Imperial China*, ed. Frederic Wakeman, Jr. and Carolyn Grant (Berkeley: University of California Press, 1975), p. 2.

many of China's macroregions, the eighteenth century was a period of peace and prosperity comparable to the sixteenth century.[14]

EDUCATION

Prosperity stimulated expansion of the school system in Ming China. Although we cannot estimate the rates of school attendance, a variety of anecdotal and circumstantial evidence indicates that the sixteenth century brought increased access to education in many regions. The community schools (*she-hsüeh*) of the Ming, like their Ch'ing counterparts, were charitable elementary schools established in towns and villages on local initiative with the state's blessing. One study shows that there were 3837 *she-hsüeh* in 472 Ming administrative units, or an average of slightly more than eight schools per unit. These schools provided education for only a small proportion of the school-age population. In Ming and Ch'ing times, most boys were educated in lineage schools, village schools (where tuition had to be paid), and private schools in the households of the well-to-do. Since the records that would enable us to evaluate the extent of private schooling are rare and scattered, quantitative estimates of the rate of school attendance are at best speculative. Elsewhere I have calculated that there were enough private and charitable schools by the late Ch'ing to teach basic literacy to between one-third and one-half the males of school age.[15]

Anecdotal and circumstantial evidence supports the contention that education expanded during the Ming and Ch'ing periods. Education was the key to prestige, power, and wealth, because it carried the prospect of entry to official careers for highly trained young men, as well as more modest social and economic advantages for men of lesser education. The civil service examinations were the primary means of recruitment into the bureaucracy, and they attained heightened significance as the hereditary (*yin*) privilege was gradually restricted, first to cover only one son and subsequently to encompass only

[14] On the Ch'ing conquest of Kiangnan, see Frederic Wakeman, Jr., "Localism and Loyalism During the Ch'ing Conquest of Kiangnan: The Tragedy of Chiang-yin," in *Conflict and Control*, pp. 43–44; and Hilary Beattie, "The Alternative to Resistance: The Case of T'ung-ch'eng, Anhwei," in *From Ming to Ch'ing*, pp. 250–251, 256, 262. On the Kiangnan tax case and the coastal evacuation, see Lawrence D. Kessler, *K'ang-hsi and the Consolidation of Ch'ing Rule, 1661–1684* (Chicago: University of Chicago Press, 1976), pp. 33–45. Migration to Taiwan is treated in Johanna Meskill, *A Chinese Pioneer Family: The Lins of Wu-feng, Taiwan, 1729–1895* (Princeton: Princeton University Press, 1979). Tilemann Grimm, "Academies and Urban Systems in Kwangtung," in *The City in Late Imperial China*, pp. 475–498, identifies three periods of regional prosperity: the sixteenth, late eighteenth–early nineteenth, and late nineteenth centuries. Skinner discusses the timing of various macroregional cycles in his essays in *The City in Late Imperial China*, pp. 16–17, 27, 219.

[15] Wang Lan-yin 王蘭蔭, "Ming-tai chih she-hsueh" 明代之社學 [Ming community schools], *Shih-ta yüeh-k'an* 師大月刊 5.4:42–102 (1935); Evelyn Rawski, *Education and Popular Literacy in Ch'ing China* (Ann Arbor: University of Michigan Press, 1979), pp. 24–41, 81–95, 183–193.

officials of the third rank and above who had served in office for a specified term.[16]

As hereditary privilege narrowed, the groups who were eligible to take the examinations expanded. The examinations were open to all but a very small number of males from certain ethnic groups and occupations. Former slaves, members of families of prostitutes, entertainers, and lictors, and the "mean people" (*chien-min*) were excluded until 1729 from taking the examinations, but according to P. T. Ho these groups represented less than one percent of the total population.[17]

If the lure of examination success was a primary cause of the Chinese "profound reverence" for schooling, there were also considerable rewards for literacy in everyday life: innumerable government notices, regulations, and documents to read, fill in, and file, and written contracts for business transactions of all kinds—buying and selling real estate, renting land, borrowing money, and selling children. The Ming and Ch'ing police security (*pao-chia*) and tax collection (*li-chia*) systems required record keeping; so did the water-control organizations that passed into local control in the late Ming. Lineages, undergoing expansion in the late seventeenth century, also required written records of corporate property management and membership.[18] Literacy was thus essential "not only for scholarship and official administration, but for successful farm management and commerce, and it was extremely useful if not essential for those wishing to assume a greater than ordinary influence in the affairs of their neighborhood or village."[19] Families used literacy as a defense against being cheated. P. T. Ho cites a family of agricultural tenants in East China who, bilked by a villager over a land deal, sent a son to school, "for without an educated man the family could not defend itself against local sharpers in the future."[20] The incentives for education extended to farmers and traders as well as potential officials.

Educational expansion had several consequences for late imperial society. The structure of the examination system, which had quotas at different administrative levels and regional quotas at the higher level examinations, ensured that the educated elite were scattered through China's various regions: because there was a unified curriculum, one could assume homogeneity in elite values regardless of locality, and this was an important element in sustaining a unified empire over such great distances under premodern conditions of transport and communications. The significance of China's written language as a

---

[16] Ho, *The Ladder of Success*, pp. 149–153.

[17] Ibid.; Chung-li Chang, *The Chinese Gentry: Studies on Their Role in Nineteenth-Century Chinese Society* (Seattle: University of Washington Press, 1955), pp. 10–11.

[18] Rawski, *Education*, pp. 9–11.

[19] Myron Cohen, in the introduction to Arthur H. Smith, *Village Life in China* (1899; reprint ed., Boston: Brown, 1970), p. xv.

[20] Ho, *The Ladder of Success*, p. 314.

factor working for integration of elite culture cannot be overestimated.

Educational expansion was accompanied by stiffer competition among candidates sitting for the civil service examinations, and the resulting frustration was important in stimulating creativity in urban culture. The sixteenth century, which witnessed great economic growth, was also a period of intense intellectual development, particularly in the cities of the Lower Yangtze core. The frustrations engendered by examination competition and the dangers of factional politics within the bureaucracy had turned many educated youths away from the orthodox career route to contemplate purposeful activity in other realms. Willard Peterson describes the *wen-jen* (man of culture) model in the late Ming:

> For such men, who were only minimally involved in government, or not at all, arts were more than a pastime or entertainment.... Seen in the best light, such "men of culture" eschewed ambitions of wealth and standing as officials in order to devote themselves to literature and art.... Some men put their efforts and trust into literature and books, calligraphy and painting, collecting and appreciating, as other men might put theirs into moral philosophy or politics.[21]

The *wen-jen* model·had existed in earlier dynasties, but its importance increased in late Ming, and it became highly relevant for the men born under the Ming who lived as adults under the Manchus. For the K'ang-hsi generation of scholars, ambivalence regarding official careers was intensified by the pressure of the loyalist ideal to avoid holding office under the conquerors. Then, too, as Lynn Struve shows, Manchu policy in the seventeenth century provided few openings for young Han Chinese. The thwarted political ambitions of many in this generation were deflected toward the sphere of culture.[22]

The fruits of deflected literati energy appear clearly in the seventeenth-century novel, studied by Robert Hegel. Hegel describes the rise of the novel as a serious literary form, a vehicle for political protest and examination of substantive issues confronting intellectuals. Fiction was not escapist, but rather expressed Confucian ideals that were no longer realized in office holding.[23]

If, as Hegel demonstrates, fiction appealed to a narrow circle of wealthy, well-educated readers, the repercussions of the elite search for meaning in private activities were far broader. While some literati pursued fiction and drama (which had a more socially varied audience than fiction), others turned to religion and the reform of popular mores.

The intellectual ferment of the late sixteenth and seventeenth centuries

[21] Peterson, *Bitter Gourd*, p. 32; see pp. 5, 8 as well.

[22] Peterson, pp. 32–33; Lynn Struve, "Ambivalence and Action: Some Frustrated Scholars of the K'ang-hsi Period," in *From Ming to Ch'ing*, pp. 321–365.

[23] Robert E. Hegel, *The Novel in Seventeenth Century China* (New York: Columbia University Press, 1981), chaps. 1–3.

included a revival of Buddhism, led by four great monks. One of them, Chu-hung (1535–1615), the subject of a study by Chün-fang Yü, displays many of the characteristics just cited. Born into an elite family in Hangchow prefecture, Chu-hung studied for the examinations and spent his first thirty-two years in pursuits appropriate to a member of the leisured class. His decision to renounce this way of life and become a monk was spurred by repeated failures in the examinations, and the successive loss of several close family members.[24]

Chu-hung's major accomplishments included the promotion of lay Buddhism. In view of his Confucian education and social background, it is not surprising that he strove to accommodate Buddhism to Confucianism, and acquired a following that included many men from elite backgrounds similar to his own. Chu-hung's tolerance of Confucian ideals, his counsel that believers should first fulfill their filial obligations, and his opinion that officials could carry out all their duties (including execution of criminals) without repudiating their Buddhist commitment, reflected tendencies of late Ming Buddhism that helped promote expansion of the faith: emphasis on moral action in this life, and the belief that individuals could find salvation while fulfilling their social roles within society.[25]

Chu-hung's propagation of Buddhism stopped short of organization. He was afraid of potential involvement with heterodox sects such as the White Lotus societies studied by Daniel Overmyer and Susan Naquin, and attacked many practices linked with Buddhist sectarianism. He disapproved of lay associations with female members, believing that women should practice their faith at home. He criticized monks who acted as geomancers, mediums, pharmacists, or healers of female diseases, and he regarded the use of the planchette in "spirit writing" as superstitious.[26] On these matters Chu-hung's attitude was entirely orthodox, which helps explain why Buddhist sectarian movements were not led by monks but by lay believers.

Chu-hung's social background was similar to those of other religious leaders in the sixteenth century. His contemporaries, Lin Chao-en (1517–1598) and Yuan Huang (1533–1606), who were both active in promoting variant forms of syncretism, also came from prominent families, were educated for official careers, and were extremely knowledgeable not only about Confucianism but about Taoism and Buddhism as well. This broad knowledge seems to have been quite common among educated men of the period.[27] Although Yuan was a *chin-*

---

[24] Chün-fang Yü, *The Renewal of Buddhism in China: Chu-hung and the Late Ming Synthesis* (New York: Columbia University Press, 1981).

[25] Ibid., chap. 4.

[26] Ibid., pp. 46, 76–78, 185–186.

[27] Judith Berling, *The Syncretic Religion of Lin Chao-en* (New York: Columbia University Press, 1980), chaps. 3, 4; *Dictionary of Ming Biography, 1368–1644*, ed. L. Carrington Goodrich and Chaoying Fang (New York: Columbia University Press, 1976), II, 1632–1635; Yü, *The Renewal of Buddhism*, p. 94.

shih who served in office, Lin, like Chu-hung, redirected his efforts toward religion after the death of members of his immediate family. Yuan, like Chu-hung, resided in the prosperous Lower Yangtze delta, which was the center not only of the Ming Buddhist revival but of the seventeenth-century advances in fiction. Lin Chao-en's home province, Fukien, was in the heyday of its trade with the Portuguese, Japanese, and Spanish in the sixteenth century, and might well have been prosperous enough to constitute another intellectual center in the empire. Lin's home county, P'u-t'ien, was a center of illegal trade, as was Chin-chiang (Ch'üan-chou prefecture), the native place of Lin's famous contemporary, the iconoclast Li Chih (1527–1602).[28]

The same motives that directed some intellectuals into *wen-jen* activity thus drew other literati into religion. This religious revival should be seen as another product of the late Ming educational expansion and should be linked to the *wen-jen* effort not only in terms of the social background and education of religious leaders (and some followers), but also as an alternative in the quest for sagehood.

Earlier we noted the beginnings of a long-term trend in the economy away from direct controls over individuals and toward the indirect controls of the market, one of the essential elements in the complex sequence of transformations to be found in societies undergoing modernization. In the cultural realm we find a parallel trend, reflected in the morality books (*shan-shu*), which stress the internalization of values and moral autonomy. We may interpret the Ming emergence of morality books in several ways. In their emphasis on man's ability to exert control over his destiny, morality books can be viewed as an expression of economic changes that created opportunities to quickly raise or depress individual fortunes. Further, since these books specify behavior appropriate to various social strata, we might also see them as guides to new social roles for the upwardly mobile.[29] Alternatively, the assumption in these books that moral action was linked to material success may be interpreted as a response to the anxiety produced by enhanced social mobility in the core regions of the Lower Yangtze and Southeast Coast. By drawing on religious beliefs, morality books provided modes of coping with the psychic uncertainties linked with social change. Finally, we may cite status anxiety on the part of the older elite as a motivation for writing morality books, which were seen as a means of halting the moral decline brought about by the rise of new groups to social and economic prominence. The morality books of the late Ming and early Ch'ing represent the private complement to vigorous government efforts in the same

[28] Berling, chap. 4; *Dictionary of Ming Biography*, II, 1632–1635, and I, 807–818; Yü, chap. 2; on the Southeast Coast in the sixteenth century, see John Wills, Jr., "Maritime China from Wang Chih to Shih Lang: Themes in Peripheral History," in *From Ming to Ch'ing*, pp. 201–238.

[29] Yü, *The Renewal of Buddhism*, pp. 136–137. According to W. L. Idema, "Storytelling and the Short Story in China," *T'oung Pao* 59:34–35 (1973), late Ming novels also reveal a new emphasis on the power of individuals to shape their own destinies.

direction, highlighted by the *Sacred Edict* lectures discussed by Victor Mair in chapter 11 of this book.[30]

Morality books were very popular during the sixteenth century. Both Yuan Huang and Chu-hung enthusiastically advocated one particular text, the *Ledger of Merits and Demerits According to the Immortal T'ai-wei* (*T'ai-wei Hsien-chün kung-kuo-ko*), a Taoist work dating from the late twelfth century. Yuan Huang testified that his whole life changed after a Ch'an monk presented him with this book; Chu-hung was so taken with it that he had it reprinted and distributed for free.[31] Chu-hung later wrote his own morality book, the *Record of Self-Knowledge* (*Tzu-chih lu*), which was modeled on the *Ledger of Merits and Demerits*. What was new in the *Record*, and especially striking when compared to earlier Sung morality books, was the nature of the sanction, which was no longer supernatural, but the working of an impersonal karmic law. Individuals could affect their fate by their own actions. Not only did human beings now have power over their own destinies, but they were to be judged by the more subtle criterion not of action but of wish or motivation.[32]

Late Ming morality books commonly made this distinction between behavior and motivation. The new emphasis on moral internalization was the product of contemporary religious, intellectual, and social developments. Wang Yang-ming's emphasis on the potential of every man to become a sage encouraged a belief in universal sagehood that paralleled the post-Sung Buddhist focus on the potential of all sentient beings to achieve salvation. Neo-Confucian and Buddhist optimism coincided with the increased social mobility resulting from prosperity, educational expansion, and large-scale printing.[33]

Educational expansion and increased social mobility thus had multiple effects on Chinese culture and society. Those climbing the social ladder and those afraid of downward mobility turned to religion for solace and as a tool of social control. The literati and government assigned a high priority to the inculcation of moral and ethical values; social mobility enhanced the receptivity of the commoner population to such attempts. The extension of education enhanced the circulation of written materials in Chinese society. Before we turn to the consequences of the attempt to indoctrinate citizens with appropriate values, we must survey the condition and distribution of the publishing industry, whose expansion was also a byproduct of the sixteenth-century surge.

---

[30] Hegel, *The Novel*, pp. 106–107, offers a somewhat different explanation. He identifies elite emancipation from traditional roles as a source of confusion and anxiety that stimulated examination of the conflicts between the claims of self and society in the seventeenth-century novel.

[31] Yü, *The Renewal of Buddhism*, pp. 118–124.

[32] Ibid., pp. 106–118.

[33] Ibid., pp. 113–116.

THE PUBLISHING INDUSTRY

The Ming period brought four advances in printing technology: the innovation of color printing (*t'ao-pan*), used to produce multicolored illustrations, maps, or texts; the improvement and increased use of woodcut illustrations; the use of copper movable type; and the production of woodcut facsimiles of earlier editions.

Despite these advances, the dominant technology remained unchanged from earlier times. Chinese printing relied on a very simple and inexpensive process, woodblock printing or xylography. Matteo Ricci furnishes a good description of this technique:

> The text is written in ink, with a brush made of very fine hair, on a sheet of paper which is inverted and pasted on a wooden tablet. When a paper has become thoroughly dry, its surface is scraped off quickly and with great skill, until nothing but a fine tissue bearing the characters remains on the wooden tablet. Then, with a steel graver, the workman cuts away the surface following the outlines of the characters until these alone stand out in low relief. From such a block a skilled printer can make copies with incredible speed, turning out as many as fifteen hundred copies in a single day.[34]

This printing method incurred almost no capital costs. There were no foundries for casting type, no machines for printing or binding. The tools could be packed up and carried on a workman's back, and the major costs were instead raw materials (paper, ink, woodblocks) and labor. Woodblock printing could begin on a shoestring, without large printings. Ricci noted:

> Their method of printing has one decided advantage, namely, that once these tablets are made, they can be preserved and used for making changes in the text as often as one wishes.... Again, with this method, the printer and the author are not obliged to produce here and now an excessively large edition of a book, but are able to print a book in smaller or larger lots sufficient to meet the demand at the time.... The simplicity of Chinese printing is what accounts for the exceedingly large numbers of books in circulation here and the ridiculously low prices at which they are sold.[35]

Of course, Ricci was evaluating Chinese printing in terms of the European situation. Books were considerably more expensive in Europe in the first centuries of European printing. European presses used movable type, which was obviously superior for an alphabetic language with a limited number of symbols but less advantageous for Chinese, where the number of unique characters used in a book might reach into the thousands.

[34] Louis J. Gallagher, *China in the Sixteenth Century: The Journals of Matthew Ricci, 1595–1610* (New York: Random House, 1953), pp. 20–21.
[35] Ibid., p. 21.

Movable-type printing required greater skill and education than the wood-block method. A printer was a skilled metalworker who had been trained through apprenticeship in the craft. The early printers were also quite well educated; they had to be, to know enough Latin to set texts correctly.[36] In China, literacy was not required because the texts, written on thin sheets of paper, were pasted onto the blocks. Carving might require some skill, but the other operations such as the inking and pulling of sheets could be done by virtually anyone. A local gazetteer of Ma-kang, a printing center in the Pearl River delta of Kwangtung, notes that "women and children can all do it; the men only carve the text on the blocks, according to the handwritten manuscript. The rest is done with female labor. Because of their cheapness, the books go everywhere."[37] Unskilled female labor was used in other printing centers such as Fo-shan (Kwangtung) and Hsü-wan (Kiangsi).[38]

Movable-type printing also called for a larger capital investment than xylography. Early sixteenth-century European death inventories show that the major items of equipment in printers' workshops were one or more presses and sets of type, the latter usually valued at several times the value of the press.[39] These costs were all absent in the Chinese industry.

Operating costs were also greater in Europe. Paper had been the one primary component of printing that Europe lacked. Lucien Febvre and Henri-Jean Martin observe, "What use would it have been to be able to print with movable type if the only medium was skin, which takes ink poorly, and when only the costliest skin, that of the calf, was flat and supple enough to be used under the press?"[40]

Paper, invented in China, entered Europe in the twelfth century and spread gradually from Italy to other countries in western Europe. By the fifteenth century, paper was available for printing, but its cost remained high because European manufacture relied on rags. Economies of scale, most marked when fixed costs are a high proportion of total cost, were limited in Europe by the high cost of rag paper. Rags were the essential raw material of European paper-making from the fourteenth to the nineteenth centuries, and the limited rag supply constrained the potential expansion of the paper industry. As printing developed, the demand for paper soared, and the scarcity of rags became more acute. In the sixteenth and seventeenth centuries, the paper cost accounts in

[36] B. A. Uhlendorf, "The Invention of Printing and Its Spread Till 1470 with Special Reference to Social and Economic Factors," *The Library Quarterly* 2.3:230–231 (1932).

[37] *Shun-te hsien-chih* 順德縣志 (1853 ed.), 3.50a.

[38] Nagasawa Kikuya 長澤規矩, *Wa Kan sho no insatsu to sono rekishi* 和漢書の印刷とその歴史 [The printing of Japanese and Chinese books and their history] (Tokyo: Yoshikawa kōbunkan 吉川弘文館, 1952), pp. 87–88; Yeh Te-hui 葉德輝, *Shu-lin ch'ing hua* 書林清話 [Chats on books] (3rd ed., N. p., 1920), 7.13b–15a.

[39] Lucien Febvre and Henri-Jean Martin, *The Coming of the Book: The Impact of Printing 1450–1800*, trans. David Gerard (London: New Left Books, 1976), pp. 110–111.

[40] Ibid., p. 30.

many cases for more than half the total cost of a book. Paper was one material that had to be supplied to printers by publishers, no doubt because of its expense.[41] In China, where paper could be made from bamboo fibers, tree bark, and other plant fibers, the cost of ink, wood, and paper was a relatively minor component of total printing costs.[42]

Potential economies of scale in European publishing were further limited by the small market for books and by the production technology. Febvre and Martin conclude that while setting up a print shop was relatively inexpensive, the capital requirement for publishing was very high. Printers and booksellers might have wished to maximize the number of copies in an edition, thus lowering the cost of printing each copy, but the small size of the market limited actual output, since "there was absolutely no point in a publisher printing more copies of a particular book than the market could absorb within a reasonable period of time. To ignore this meant many unsold copies or, at the best, tying up a substantial capital sum in a commodity that sold all too slowly."[43] An indication of how slowly a book could sell is provided by Florence E. de Roover, who studied an Italian travelling merchant named Girolamo di Carlo di Marco Strozzi. In 1476, Strozzi commissioned the printing of two Florentine histories in the vernacular. He sent 550 of the 600 copies of each title printed to Florence for sale. It took seven years, until 1483, before "almost all" had in fact been sold.[44] According to Febvre and Martin, the search for retail outlets was "the constant and central preoccupation of publishers" through the early period of European printing.[45]

In order to spread risk and minimize the danger of publishing a title that would not sell, European publishers and printers generally produced several titles concurrently; that is, they never concentrated all their efforts on one edition, but tried to print several at one time. This meant that each title took a long time to produce and that the type for a particular page was set, printed, and then broken up for use in another page. Although metal movable type was capable of producing any number of copies, the actual size of editions was very small. Into the 1470s, an edition of several hundred copies was considered good; in the 1480s, the number of copies printed rose to an average of 400–500 an edition, and in the early sixteenth century to 1500 copies. Through the sixteenth and seventeenth centuries, the only works that regularly exceeded 2000 copies were religious titles or textbooks, and in the eighteenth century most

[41] Ibid., chap. 1 and pp. 112–113.

[42] Rawski, *Education*, pp. 120–121; Sung Ying-hsing, *T'ien-Kung K'ai-Wu: Chinese Technology in the Seventeenth Century*, trans. E-tu Zen Sun and Shiou-chuan Sun (University Park: Pennsylvania State University Press, 1966), chap. 13.

[43] Febvre and Martin, *Coming of the Book*, p. 217.

[44] Florence Edler de Roover, "New Facets on the Financing and Marketing of Early Printed Books," *Bulletin of the Business Historical Society* 27:222–230 (1953).

[45] Febvre and Martin, *Coming of the Book*, p. 216.

print runs continued to fall below 2000 copies. Febvre and Martin note that the dissemination of popular works such as Luther's German Bible came not from large printings but from repeated printings, often by different printers.[46]

The advantages of metal movable type for expanding the scale of production were thus largely unrealized by European publishers and printers in the early period of printing. When good sales of a particular book stimulated a new edition, the type had to be reset, in contrast to the Chinese woodblock, which, once carved, could be stored for future printings.

Technically, a woodblock carved of the standard wood, pear or jujube, could be used to print 16,000–26,000 copies. We know very little about the actual size of printings in China. Government-sponsored editions ranged from several hundred up to several thousand copies of a title. The size of editions put out by commercial firms is unknown to us. W. L. Idema has complained that our evidence shows that the technical maximum was rarely attained, except perhaps in the case of "readily sold works, like basic schoolbooks and almanacs."[47] From the viewpoint of cost, however, the size of a "run" was less important in China, where blocks were preserved for future use, than in Europe, where the entire book would have to be reset for a new printing. We do know that printing firms sold engraved blocks to one another. An individual who printed his own work, like Yuan Mei, the eighteenth-century poet, regarded his inventory of printing blocks as a capital asset, leaving them to his heirs as a source of future revenue.[48]

There were thus important limits to the expansion of European printing from the fifteenth to eighteenth centuries on both the supply and demand side that did not exist in China during the same period. The cost of training, equipment, and raw materials (notably paper) was higher in Europe than in China. It was the Chinese industry and not the European one that profited from scale economies in this era. The limited demand for books was a greater problem for the Europeans too. Europe's population was smaller, and the size of its premodern elite correspondingly limited. In the mid-fifteenth century, when Latin was still the educated language throughout Europe, publishers sold in an international book market, but the Reformation was followed by a retreat into national vernaculars, and book markets shrank into boundaries corresponding to those of the newly developing nation states. The aristocratic society of Europe was more decisively divided into rural and urban sectors than was China's, with the result that literacy and book purchases were largely confined to the urban population. Elizabeth Eisenstein notes that many rural areas in

[46] Ibid., pp. 217–220; D. F. McKenzie, "Printers of the Mind: Some Notes on Bibliographical Theories and Printing-House Practices," *Studies in Bibliography* (University of Virginia) 22:14–16 (1969).

[47] W. L. Idema, *Chinese Vernacular Fiction: The Formative Period* (Leiden: Brill, 1974), pp. lvi–lviii.

[48] Arthur Waley, *Yuan Mei: Eighteenth Century Chinese Poet* (Stanford: Stanford University Press, 1970), pp. 108–109, 200.

Europe remained untouched by printed literature until the advent of the railroad, and concludes that the large peasant populations and the persistence of local dialects in rural areas make it probable that only a very small portion of the population of Europe was affected by the initial advent of printing.[49]

We have already noted why Ming and Ch'ing publishing costs were lower than their European counterparts.[50] On the demand side, we can cite demographic, linguistic and social structural reasons why conditions favored the Chinese industry. China, of course, had a larger population, estimated at 150 million in the late Ming, and since the elite in China made up roughly the same proportion of the population as the elite in Europe, the Chinese book market was much larger than the European market.[51] Moreover, educational expansion in late Ming and Ch'ing times increased the demand for books.

The Chinese book market was not subdivided by dialect or different vernaculars, since the written language was standardized and uniform throughout the empire. The regional quotas in the civil service examinations, which produced an unusually broad dispersion of the literate population, ensured that a demand for books and written materials could be found in every region. Nor were literacy and book purchase confined to cities and towns: how could they be, when the rural and urban sectors were less sharply differentiated than in Europe? In China one could find literati residing in both country and town, and publishing took place in both locales as well.[52]

A comparison of Chinese and European publishing and printing indicates that Chinese technology and market conditions were more favorable to expansion of the industry. We have earlier observed that the technical advances in Ming printing did not play a leading role in stimulating expansion; it was, rather, the increase in education and the economic prosperity of the sixteenth century, continued in subsequent periods under the Ch'ing, that was responsible for the effect.

Who were the publishers, and how did the structure of the publishing industry influence the impact of printing on popular culture? Xylography permitted extreme decentralization of China's printing industry: as long as

[49] Elizabeth Eisenstein, *The Printing Press as An Agent of Change: Communications and Cultural Transformations in Early Modern Europe* (Cambridge: Cambridge University Press, 1979), I, 62; Febvre and Martin, *Coming of the Book*, pp. 178–197, 224–239.

[50] Thomas F. Carter, *The Invention of Printing and Its Spread Westward*, rev. L. C. Goodrich (New York: Columbia University Press, 1955), pp. 1–6; Sung, *Chinese Technology in the Seventeenth Century*, (cited n. 42), chap. 13.

[51] P. T. Ho, *Studies on the Population of China 1368–1953* (Cambridge, Mass.: Harvard University Press, 1959), p. 264; Roger Mols, "Population in Europe, 1500–1700," in *The Fontana Economic History of Europe*, ed. Carlo M. Cipolla (Glasgow: Collins, 1974), pp. 2, 38. This estimate includes areas such as Poland, Russia, and the Balkans that were not fully part of a European book market.

[52] Frederick W. Mote, "A Millennium of Chinese Urban History: Form, Time, and Space Concepts in Soochow," *Rice University Studies* 59:35–65 (Fall 1973); Skinner, "Chinese Peasants and the Closed Community."

one could find carvers, one could print. Most studies have concentrated on what may be the smallest (in terms of volume) if most illustrious sector of the industry—namely, the government and literati publishers—and have neglected the part of the industry producing more humble materials such as elementary primers, almanacs, and religious pamphlets.

Government agencies, private individuals, institutions, and commercial firms all published books. The government had long been a large publisher of official documents, historical records, and Confucian texts. Its concern for the authenticity of the Confucian classics was a primary stimulus in the development of the printing industry. All levels of agencies, from the Imperial Household down to the county *yamen*, acted as publishers and printers.[53] However, although Ming and Ch'ing emperors sponsored notable compilations of religious and secular texts, the government was not the major source for expanded publications during our period.

The publishing activities of literati, institutions, and commercial firms all increased in the late Ming, as the expansion of education raised the demand for textbooks at all levels. The demand for advanced texts was met most prominently by academies (*shu-yuan*) and bibliophiles such as Huang P'ei-lieh, Mao Chin, and Pao T'ing-po, who collected and reproduced rare texts, thus stimulating what became the major field of Ch'ing historical scholarship. These were books of fine quality, clearly intended for a small and wealthy readership. It was the literati, particularly those residing in the Lower Yangtze core, who also published collections of drama, short stories, and fiction in editions of high quality intended for a limited urban audience.[54]

The demand for educational texts and fiction was also met by commercial firms. Some were famous, like the Huangs of She county, Anhwei, known for their skilled woodcut illustrations, and the Lius of Chien-yang, Fukien, who were prominent printers during the Yuan and Ming dynasties. Our information about the business organization of these firms is very sketchy. Whether the close connection of bookstores with publishing that existed in Ch'ing times was a new development or a continuation of Ming conditions is not clear. The appearance of bookstore–publishers with regional branches in Ch'ing is another organizational advance that might have previously appeared in Ming times.[55]

[53] K. T. Wu, "Ming Printing and Printers," *Harvard Journal of Asiatic Studies* 7:203–225 (1943); Liu Kuo-chün 劉國鈞, *Chung-kuo shu shih chien-pien* 中國書史簡編 [Concise history of Chinese books] (Peking: Kao-teng chiao-yü ch'u-pan she 高等教育出版社, 1958), pp. 75, 77, 83–87; Sun Yü-hsiu 孫毓修, *Chung-kuo tiao-pan yuan-liu k'ao* 中國雕板源流攷 [History of Chinese printing] (Shanghai: Commercial Press, 1926), pp. 13–22.

[54] Cheuk-woon Taam, *The Development of Chinese Libraries under the Ch'ing Dynasty, 1644–1911* (Shanghai: Commercial Press, 1935), pp. 15–17; Liu Kuo-chün, *Concise History*, pp. 13–22; Hegel, *The Novel*, pp. 11, 50, 120, 185.

[55] Wu, "Ming Printing," pp. 209, 234–35; Ts'un-yan Liu, *Chinese Popular Fiction in Two London Libraries* (Hong Kong: Lung Men, 1967), pp. 38–39.

Commercial firms published books varying widely in quality. There were expensive editions of fiction, history, and Confucian texts, and other, presumably cheaper, editions with blurred type and poor editing. The poor editing of cheaper Confucian texts drew official ire, as in this seventeenth-century proclamation from Soochow:

> Unscrupulous individuals usually reproduce . . . [literary collections] for profit, with blocks poorly cut and the texts defective because of omissions and mistakes. . . . Distant book-dealers have been frequently deceived, and students, in turn, have also been misled.[56]

While a strong demand for all scholarly aids appeared in late Ming times, the greatest demand stimulated by the educational expansion was for elementary primers, since there were many more students attending school for one or two years than the number continuing on to advanced examination preparation. The late Ming and early Ch'ing brought a proliferation of primers, including rhymed works and glossaries (*tsa-tzu*).[57]

Commercial firms engaged in many other kinds of printing for the market. Popular encyclopedias, filled with homely advice as well as arithmetic aids, contract forms, and information useful for daily life, were printed in greater numbers than before. There were almanacs, identified by C. K. Yang as the most popular literature in traditional China, and other products that fall outside the realm of the printed word, such as the numerous religious prints intended for use in private homes. In Chekiang, according to Clarence Day, these paper gods (*ma-chang*) were used in "practically every kind of religious ceremonial" by rich and poor alike. *Ma-chang* were woodcut illustrations, frequently with a few characters written on them and sometimes with longer inscriptions, printed on cheap paper and frequently burned during religious rites. The production of religious prints goes back to the earliest period of Chinese printing and no doubt continued to flourish in every subsequent era, yet we know very little about this industry despite the probability that it constituted one of the most widespread forms of printing during the traditional period. Paper money, used for religious offerings, was a related product in widespread use, whose manufacture also deserves more study.[58]

If the printing activities of commercial firms seemed to be more closely oriented to the practical concerns of a poorly educated consumer, it does not

---

[56] Cited in Wu, "Ming Printing,", pp. 230–231.

[57] Chang Chih-kung 張志公, *Ch'uan-t'ung yü-wen chiao-yü ch'u-t'an* 傳統語文教育初探 [A preliminary study of traditional language education], 2nd ed. (Shanghai: Chiao-yü ch'u-pan she 教育出版社, 1964), pp. 11–12 (preface), 11–20, 28–30.

[58] C. K. Yang, *Religion in Chinese Society* (Berkeley: University of California Press, 1961), p. 17; Rawski, *Education*, pp. 114–115; Clarence B. Day, *Chinese Peasant Cults: Being a Study of Chinese Paper Gods*, 2nd ed. (Taipei: Ch'eng Wen, 1974), pp. 3–5; Ching-lang Hou, *Monnaies d'offrande et la notion de tresorerie dans la religion chinoise* (Paris: Collège de France, 1975).

follow that the products of literati printing affected only the educated elite. The printing and distribution of religious pamphlets was seen as an act of piety, worth a specific number of "merits" in the *Record of Self-Knowledge* and other morality books. Such pamphlets must have been widely distributed, for nineteenth-century missionaries found them everywhere.[59]

Printing touched other sectors in the society. Lineages engaged in publishing, for example, and the late seventeenth century saw an increasing number of genealogies being printed. Also, charitable organizations began to publish reports of their activities, as indicated by the documents of Shanghai charitable institutions dating from the early nineteenth century.[60] And Buddhist sectarian groups managed to transmit their scriptures despite government repression, as Overmyer and Naquin show in chapters 8 and 9 of this book.

In comparison with earlier periods, the late Ming and Ch'ing witnessed an increase not only in the volume of printing but in the printing activities of literati, institutions, and commercial firms. The educated elite dominated publishing as creators and consumers, but the expansion of publishing reflected a spread of literate culture that affected a much broader social spectrum. By late Ch'ing times, and probably earlier, even illiterates lived in what was basically a literate culture. This is very evident in James Hayes's study (chapter 3 of this book) of the written materials to be found in twentieth-century villages in the New Territories.

Did the expansion of the publishing industry alter the geographical distribution of printing centers? Most secondary literature on printing focuses on the Lower Yangtze printing centers that dominated the national deluxe book market during Ming and Ch'ing. In fact, with the exception of the late developing Yun-Kwei macroregion, each region had its own printing centers. As one sixteenth-century scholar wrote,

> There are three regions printing books: Kiangsu, Chekiang, and Fukien. Szechwan imprints were the best in Sung, but recently are very scarce. Peking, Canton, Shensi, and Hupei/Hunan all print books ... but they are not as flourishing as the three. For quality Kiangsu is best, for quantity Fukien is first, and Chekiang is second in both. Kiangsu is the most expensive, Fukien the cheapest, Chekiang is in between.[61]

In the sixteenth century, outstanding printing centers were thus sited in seven of the eight Chinese macroregions. At the same time, there was a national market in elite books. The center of official printing was the capital city, so the Ming capitals of Nanking and Peking and the Ch'ing capital of Peking stood at

---

[59] Mrs. E. T. Williams, "Some Popular Religious Literature of the Chinese," *Journal of the Royal Asiatic Society, China Branch*, n.s. 33:11–29 (1900–1901); Yü, *Renewal of Buddhism*, p. 235.

[60] See chart, pp. 60–61, in Taga Akigorō 多賀秋五郎, *Sōfu no kenkyū* 宗譜の研究 [Research on genealogies] (Tokyo: Tōyō Bunko 東洋文庫, 1960); Rawski, *Education*, pp. 121–122.

[61] Hu Ying-lin (1551–1602), cited by Liu Kuo-chün, *Concise History*, p. 78.

the apex of government publishing, which could be found at every administrative level in every region.[62]

Literati printing was concentrated in the cities of the Lower Yangtze, where many of the most active scholar-printers and writers lived. Nanking, the most important metropolis in the region during the Ming, and Soochow, which replaced Nanking as the central metropolis during the late Ming, attracted large numbers of writers and scholars. Li Yü, the seventeenth-century dramatist, poet, and essayist, spent much of his life in Nanking, the site of his famous bookstore, the Mustard Seed Garden. The littérateur Feng Meng-lung, a native of Soochow, may well have owned a printing concern in that city, where he and Ling Meng-ch'u, the short story writer and scholar, were closely tied to publishing circles. Soochow was also the home of Huang P'ei-lieh, who reprinted many Sung texts in facsimile editions. Other Yangtze centers included Ch'ang-shu, where Mao Chin and his son Mao I published about 600 titles, and Hangchow, where the book collectors studied by Nancy Swann also engaged in printing.[63]

Throughout the Ming and Ch'ing, Chien-yang County, Fukien, was the area producing the largest volume of commercially printed books. Ma-sha chen and Shu-fang chen ("Booktown") in Chien-yang were known for low-quality imprints. Large centers of commercial printing were also located in the Middle Yangtze and Lingnan macroregions during the Ch'ing. According to Nagasawa Kikuya,

> For size of printings, Kiangsi and Kwangtung are the greatest, Kiangsi's printing is in Chin-hsi county's Hsü-wan; Kwangtung's is in Shun-te county's Ma-kang. Both have prospered from large numbers of printings.[64]

Hsü-wan and Ma-kang were rivals of Chien-yang, producing cheap editions of poor quality with female and child labor. There were similar printing centers in Nan-ch'ang, Kiangsi; Ch'ang-sha, Hunan; and Fo-shan, Kwangtung. Canton was also a major printing center during the Ch'ing.[65]

In contrast to the centers cited above, the commercial firms in the Lower

---

[62] Liu Kuo-chün, *Concise History*, pp. 77, 86–88; Nagasawa Kikuya, *Printing History*, pp. 86–87. The recent discovery in a grave in Shanghai of fifteenth-century song books and drama produced in Peking indicates that Peking also had a commercial printing sector: Wang Ch'ing-cheng 汪慶正, "Chi wen-hsüeh, hsi-ch'ü ho pan-hua shih shang ti i-tz'u chung-yao fa-hsien" 記文學、戲典和版畫史上的一次重要發現 [A major discovery in the history of literature, drama and printed illustration], *Wen-wu* 文物, 11:58–67 (1973).

[63] *Dictionary of Ming Biography*, vol. I, pp. 930–931 and 450–453; *Eminent Chinese of the Ch'ing Period*, ed. Arthur W. Hummel, (Washington, D. C.: U. S. Government Printing Office, 1943–1944), vol. I, pp. 340–341 and 565–566; Nancy Lee Swann, "Seven Intimate Library Owners," *Harvard Journal of Asiatic Studies* 1:363–390 (1936); Wu, "Ming Printing," pp. 239–243.

[64] Liu Kuo-chün, *Concise History*, pp. 78–79; Wu, "Ming Printing," pp. 232–236; Nagasawa, *Printing History*, p. 87.

[65] Nagasawa, *Printing History*, pp. 87–88; Sun, *History of Chinese Printing*, pp. 38–39.

TABLE I. Regional Origins of Ming–Ch'ing Books

Macroregion	Ming		Ch'ing	
	No. of books	*Regional percentage of Ming total*	*No. of books*	*Regional percentage of Ch'ing total*
Lower Yangtze	88	49.2	51	42.8
North China	36	20.1	39	32.8
Southeast Coast	14	7.8	0	0
Northwest China	11	6.1	3	2.5
Upper Yangtze	8	4.5	3	2.5
Middle Yangtze	7	3.9	7	5.9
Lingnan	7	3.9	7	5.9
Yun-Kwei	7	3.9	5	4.2
Outside empire	1	0.6	4	3.4
Total	179	100.0	119	100.0

SOURCE: Pei-ching t'u-shu-kuan, eds., *Chung-kuo yin-pen shu-chi chan-lan mu-lu* [Catalogue of the exhibit of Chinese printed books] (Peking: Chung-yang jen-min cheng-fu wen-hua pu, she-hui wen-hua shih-yeh kuan-li chü, 1952), items #349-720, pp. 57-94.

Yangtze cities specialized in high-quality, expensive books, although Nanking, Soochow, and Hangchow also published other kinds of materials. The Li Kuang-ming chuang in Nanking, for example, was the largest publisher of elementary primers in the Ch'ing, while the Sao-yeh shan fang, run by the Hsi family in Soochow, was reputed to be the single largest Ch'ing commercial publisher. Some Lower Yangtze bookstore–publishers had regional branches. Liu Ts'un-yan informs us of one such store, the Shan ch'eng t'ang, which had branches in Soochow, Hangchow, Chekiang, and Fukien.[66]

During the Ming and Ch'ing, publishing centers emerged in every region at the same time that the Lower Yangtze cities dominated the national elite book market. Analysis of the regional origins of several extant collections of Ming and Ch'ing books shows both aspects of the regional distribution of the industry. Table 1 presents the regional origins of several hundred Ming and Ch'ing editions exhibited at the Peking Library in 1952. This exhibition emphasized nonfiction and included histories, poetry, books on agriculture and technology, local gazetteers, collected writings of scholars, and religious texts. Every region was represented in the exhibition. Peking was the single largest publishing center represented, with fifty-eight titles; Nanking was second, with twenty-eight, Soochow third, with twenty-three, and Hangchow was represented by seven books.

[66] On the Li Kuang-ming chuang, see Chang Chih-kung, *Preliminary Study*, illustration 3; on the Sao-yeh shan t'ang, Sun Yü-hsiu, *History of Chinese Printing* p. 35; Ts'un-yan Liu, *Chinese Popular Fiction*, pp. 38–39.

The Peking Library exhibition reveals the importance of Peking as a center of government printing. Analysis of collections of fiction show the primacy of the Southeast Coast and Lower Yangtze centers. Of the ten texts out of twenty-four extant Ming and Ch'ing editions of *Romance of the Three Kingdoms* (*San kuo chih t'ung-su yen-i*) whose regional origins can be identified, six were printed in Fukien, three in Soochow, and one in Nanking.[67]

Canton's primacy in the Lingnan book market emerges from Liu Ts'un-yan's analysis of the regional origins of Chinese popular fiction held by two libraries in London. The more than 130 books held by these libraries were published by 90 bookstores, 56 of which have been located. Of the latter, 28.5 percent were in Canton; 9 percent in Fo-shan; and 5 percent in Hong Kong, so a total of 42.8 percent of the books in the collection came from the Lingnan macroregion. As Liu explains, the dominance of Kwangtung imprints in a collection that includes imprints from the Lower Yangtze, Southeast Coast, and North China stems from the fact that Canton is the marketing center for the region in which Hong Kong is located.[68] The contrast between this collection and the regional distribution found by Sun K'ai-ti in his survey of Japanese and Chinese collections, in which Southeast Coast and Lower Yangtze books dominated, underlines the regional flavor of the London holdings.

Long-distance trade was probably limited to books intended for a well-educated and wealthy readership. Fiction, histories, and the titles of the books in the collections we have analyzed were mostly read by men belonging to a small elite. The high prices of books of quality permitted merchants to bear the cost of long-distance transport and still show a profit. The long-distance book trade was dominated by merchants from the major printing centers of the Lower Yangtze and Kiangsi. We find Soochow merchants bringing Soochow imprints to Canton, and purchasing cheaper Ma-kang editions there to take back to sell in Kiangnan. Merchants from Soochow, Hu-chou, and Kiangsi dominated Peking's famous book quarter, Liu-li-ch'ang, from the eighteenth until the late nineteenth century.[69]

As the prestige and price of a printed work declined, so did the distance it was traded. If we could find the information needed to study this subject, we could trace a hierarchy of markets and production centers, reaching from the central metropolis of a macroregion down to the central or intermediate market town,

[67] Pei-ching t'u-shu-kuan 北京圖書館, eds., *Chung-kuo yin-pen shu-chi chan-lan mu-lu* 中國印本書籍展覽目錄 [Catalogue of the exhibit of Chinese printed books] (Peking: Chung-yang jen-min cheng-fu wen-hua pu, she-hui wen-hua shih-yeh kuan-li chü 中央人民政府文化 部, 社會文化實業管理局, 1952); Sun K'ai-ti 孫楷第, *Chung-kuo t'ung-su hsiao-shuo shu-mu* 中國通俗小說書目 [Catalogue of Chinese popular fiction] (Peking: Tso-chia ch'u-pan she 作家出版社, 1957), pp. 20, 24–37.

[68] Ts'un-yan Liu, *Chinese Popular Fiction*, pp. 39–42.

[69] *Shun-te hsien-chih*, 3.50a; Wang Yen-ch'iu 王冶秋, *Liu-li-ch'ang shih-hua* 琉璃廠史話 [Historical chats about Liu-li-ch'ang] (Peking: San-lien shu-tien 三聯書店, 1963), pp. 21, 41; Yeh Te-hui, *Chats*, 9.26b 32b.

depending on the population density and degree of economic advance of the specific region. When we study items such as almanacs, which Ricci noted "are sold in such quantities that every house has a supply of them," or paper gods, which seem to have been for sale in villages, we are likely to be dealing with objects printed at centers only a step or two higher in the central place hierarchy.[70] Further research is needed before we can discuss production of this most popular kind of printed material and the mechanisms that facilitated its dissemination, such as book fairs and peddler's networks.

SOCIO-ECONOMIC DEVELOPMENT AND ITS IMPACT ON CULTURE

The development of the economy, expansion of education and functional literacy, and penetration of printed culture into rural villages fundamentally influenced Chinese popular culture. We have already described some of these influences.

Increased participation in marketing opened broader horizons for peasants and increased the value of literacy for everyday life while providing households with the funds to pay for schooling. The commercial economy also exposed individuals to a keener competitive environment, in which potential losses loomed as large as the potential profits. Enhanced social mobility was thus linked with increased uncertainty: these dual tensions are reflected in late Ming fiction and morality books in the new stress on the importance of individual action in determining one's fate and the assumption that material rewards would flow from virtuous action. A mentality resembling that of the market-place emerges in the "ideology of merit making" to be found in these books: one can think of the ledgers of merit and demerit that appear during this period as spiritual account books, with "target saving"—that is, the belief that achievement of a specified total of meritorious deeds will automatically bring good fortune. Chün-fang Yü provides such a testimonial from Yuan Huang, who ascribed his success in winning the *chü-jen* and *chin-shih* degrees and acquiring a long-desired son to the accumulation of a targeted number of good deeds.[71]

The ideology of merit making may thus be interpreted as a response to the uncertainty produced by heightened social mobility. The notion of spiritual accounting reveals the penetration of a commercial mentality and rationality into the ethical-religious sphere.

Economic advance and educational expansion changed elite culture. In the Lower Yangtze, the most advanced, urbanized, and one of the most densely populated regions in late Ming China, the movement of large landlords out of

[70] Gallagher, *China in the Sixteenth Century*, pp. 82–83.

[71] Yü, *Renewal of Buddhism*, pp. 121–124; see Philippe Ariès, *The Hour of Our Death* (New York: Knopf, 1981), pp. 103–104, 154, on the thirteenth-century European parallel to this Chinese development.

villages into towns and cities stimulated urban culture. The Lower Yangtze's largest cities, such as Nanking, became centers of intellectual and artistic life, as young men, frustrated by the increasingly difficult competition for examination degrees, sought gratification in private pursuits. A shift from public to private activity did not, however, mean abandonment of Confucian values and goals, and the rise of elite concern about declining morals, itself a product of social change, stimulated production of fiction and works on morality during the late Ming and early Ch'ing.

Educational expansion affected cultural development in several other ways. By enabling more people than ever before to read at least simple materials, this phenomenon encouraged broader use of written communications in society. Educational expansion, most significant at elementary levels of schooling, brought primers into the sphere of popular knowledge as a consequence of the unified curriculum and unified written language. We can explore the implications of this development by briefly examining the primers and their content.

The Ming and Ch'ing elementary curriculum rested on three primers: the *Trimetrical Classic* (*San tzu ching*), *Thousand Character Classic* (*Ch'ien tzu wen*), and the *Hundred Names* (*Pai chia hsing*). The *Trimetrical Classic* was the primer with which many boys began their studies. Originally written in Sung times, this text existed in many versions in Ming and Ch'ing. It consisted of approximately 356 lines of three characters each and contained 500 different characters after repetitions were eliminated. Its famous opening lines present a Mencian tenet: "Men at their birth are naturally good. Their natures are much the same; their habits become widely different. If foolishly there is no teaching, the nature will deteriorate."[72] The primer blended factual and historical information with strictures on the reciprocal obligations of parents and sons, teachers and students, elders and juniors.

The oldest of the primers was the *Thousand Character Classic*. Compiled in the sixth century, it consisted of a thousand different characters organized into eight-character couplets. The information presented was very similar to that in the *Trimetrical Classic*: there were names of seasons, plants, animals but also names of dynasties, heroes worthy of emulation, and hortatory sections on the conduct proper for a Confucian gentleman: modesty in demeanor and dress, caution in speech, mental self-discipline, and humility. Like the *Trimetrical Classic*, the *Thousand Character Classic* was designed for ease in chanting (and hence memorization); the characters introduced were those commonly found in the classical texts to be studied later, and its lines used common easy constructions. In Ming and Ch'ing times many versions of this text were in circulation.

The third primer, the *Hundred Names*, consisted of four hundred family

---

[72] The translation is taken from Herbert A. Giles, *Elementary Chinese: San Tzu Ching* (Shanghai: Kelly and Walsh, 1910). The description of these primers draws heavily on Chang Chih-kung *Preliminary Study*, pp. 6–27, 154–159.

surnames, but since some names were more than one character in length, the book actually contained more than four hundred characters.

Together these three primers provided the beginning student with knowledge of about two thousand characters and constituted the vocabulary acquired by boys in well-to-do households before they enrolled in formal studies with a tutor. The three primers—known as the *"San, Pai, Ch'ien"*—were also used in village and charitable schools, where they could be read in a year. As the Ming scholar Lü K'un wrote,

> When first entering the community school, those eight *sui* and below should first read the *Trimetrical Classic* in order to practice reading and hearing; the *Hundred Names* for daily use; and the *Thousand Character Classic* also has principle.[73]

It would be difficult to overestimate the penetration of these three texts into Ming and Ch'ing culture. The *Thousand Character Classic* and the other texts appeared not only in Chinese but in Mongolian–Chinese and Manchu–Chinese editions. The absence of character repetition and its general popularity made the *Thousand Character Classic* a useful ordering system for all kinds of things. The Taoist ordination list was "numbered" using the characters (in sequence) from the *Thousand Character Classic*; carpenters put together furniture that had been disassembled for shipping using the same system. Ichisada Miyazaki tells us that the cells in Nanking's provincial examination hall were arranged in lanes, each lane being identified by a character taken in serial order from the *Thousand Character Classic*. Since each cell in a lane was given a number, the system permitted identification of every cell in the entire compound. The same system was used for business account books and pawn tickets. Even though the character would be changed each month, no two tickets from the same pawnshop could bear identical code numbers for more than eighty-three years.[74] The widespread use of the *Thousand Character Classic* for such practical purposes testifies to its popularity among persons of diverse social groups and occupations, including artisans, clerks, merchants, monks, and scholars. Chang Chih-kung's work shows the equal popularity of the *San tzu ching*, revealed in the numerous primers bearing this title: *Geographical San tzu ching* (*Ti-li STC*), *Western Studies San tzu ching* (*Hsi-hsüeh STC*), and so on.[75]

Testimony on the penetration of the three primers into Ming-Ch'ing society

---

[73] Cited in Chang Chih-kung, *Preliminary Study*, p. 25.

[74] Yoshitoyo Yoshioka, "Taoist Monastic Life," in *Facets of Taoism: Essays in Chinese Religion*, ed. Holmes Welch and Anna Seidel (New Haven: Yale University Press, 1979), p. 235; H. A. Giles, "Thousand Character Numerals Used by Artisans," *Journal of the Royal Asiatic Society, China Branch* 20:279 (1885); Ichisada Miyazaki, *China's Examination Hell: The Civil Service Examinations of Imperial China*, trans. Conrad Schirokauer (New York: Weatherhill, 1976), p. 44; T. S. Whelan, *The Pawnshop in China* (Ann Arbor: Center for Chinese Studies, University of Michigan, 1979), pp. 42–43; Chang Chih-kung, *Preliminary Study*, p. 8.

[75] Chang Chih-kung, *Preliminary Study*, pp. 19, 159.

thus comes from school regulations, personal reminiscences, and documentation of the practical applications listed above. This evidence supports the conclusion that the elementary curriculum was known throughout the Ming and Ch'ing empire and among varied social groups.

What was taught in the primers? Primers serve religious causes in many premodern cultures—this was true in Protestant Europe, where religion was the primary motivation for education, true in Catholic Europe, and the Islamic world.[76] In China, the *Trimetrical Classic* and *Thousand Character Classic* were vehicles for what we might identify as Confucian doctrines: faith in the perfectibility of human nature, stress on education as essential to development of man's goodness, presentation of roles (Three Bonds, Five Relationships) central to Confucian society, and the values appropriate to a *chün-tzu*, or perfect man: *jen* ("human-heartedness"), *i* ("righteousness"), *li* ("rites"), *chih* ("moral knowledge"), and *hsin* ("good faith"). The texts also presented values that fit into the economic climate of late imperial China: diligence, perseverance, and ambition. In the words of the text, "Make a name for yourselves, glorify your father and mother, shed lustre on your ancestors, and enrich your posterity," for "diligence has its reward." [77]

The values transmitted in elementary schooling were thus consonant with not only the Confucian orientation of Chinese society but with the heightened social mobility of late Ming and early Ch'ing times. The values and the primers in which they were expressed were not new: as we have noted, the *Trimetrical Classic* and *Thousand Character Classic* go back to Sung and earlier. The difference lay in the economic and social changes described above. Educational expansion brought more boys into the schools, where they memorized the primers; the printing boom produced a larger number of "*San, Pai, Ch'ien*" and many other primers conveying the same values to beginning students. Values taught in the classroom were further reinforced in the larger society, through imperially sponsored programs such as the village lectures (*hsiang-yüeh*) and literati efforts to promote morality education among ordinary citizens.

Since education was viewed as a vital instrument of moral indoctrination, it was the focus of imperial, official, and literati attention. This is true in most societies, but the connection between public order and inculcation of values (as opposed to simple coercion) was perhaps more explicit in China than in many other premodern cultures. The school curriculum and the textbooks came under intense scrutiny: the unification of the elementary curriculum was thus the product of informal and formal regulation. Officials and literati frequently espoused production and distribution of the proper primers, and we have Ch'ing records of officials providing free texts to charitable schools in their

[76] Lawrence Stone, "Literacy and Education in England, 1640–1900," *Past and Present* 42 : 79 (1969); Jack Goody, "Restricted Literacy in Northern Ghana," in *Literacy in Traditional Societies*, ed. Jack Goody (Cambridge: Cambridge University Press, 1968), pp. 222–223.

[77] Lines 345–348, 353 in H. A. Giles's translation of *San tzu ching, Elementary Chinese*.

districts.[78] But education was very broadly construed to include oral transmission of values to the populace. This was the intent of the Ch'ing *Sacred Edicts*
studied by Victor Mair and of their predecessors, the *Sacred Edicts* issued in 1388
and 1399 by the Hung-wu Emperor, Ming T'ai-tsu (see chapter 11). As Kung-
chuan Hsiao has observed, these edicts were "the substance of the Confucian
ethic reduced to the barest essentials." Six in number, the commandments of
the Ming *Sacred Edicts* were identical to those promulgated in 1652 by the Shun-
chih Emperor, the founder of the Ch'ing: "Be filial to your parents; be respectful
to your elders; live in harmony with your neighbors; instruct your sons and
grandsons; be content with your calling; and do no evil." The Hung-wu
Emperor ordered that these maxims be posted on school walls and inscribed on
stone tablets erected before Confucian temples and examination halls. In
addition, they were read aloud to villagers six times a month.[79]

The *Sacred Edicts* attempted to transmit core Confucian values to those who
had not attended school and were illiterate. What was presented was a simplification of the lessons found in the elementary primers, not to mention the
Confucian classics themselves. The public lecture was supplemented by other
practices designed to promote virtue: the honoring of the aged, chaste widows,
and filial sons. Then there was the negative reinforcement for good behavior,
embodied in an elaborate penal code that supported the Confucian family
system.[80]

Government efforts to inculcate values were matched by literati efforts in
both the secular and religious spheres. Individuals endowed charitable schools;
created vernacular, rhymed primers to teach normative values more easily;
sponsored lay Buddhist and other religious associations; and wrote, printed,
and distributed religious pamphlets and morality books. Each of these activities, affecting the dissemination of social values, was important in the period
we are studying.

The growing integration of late imperial Chinese culture was a product not
only of conscious official policy but of the increased integration of markets and
hence of rural and urban places. The enhanced communications network
helped bring the value systems of the elite and peasant tradition into closer
congruence. The final triumph of imperially sanctioned values can be seen in
their acceptance by groups who explicitly rejected orthodoxy. The White Lotus
sectarians studied by Susan Naquin (chapter 9, below) expressed in their
mantras the same core values found in the *Sacred Edicts*, although these ethical
principles were now set in the context of religious salvation and rebirth after
death.

---

[78] Kung-chuan Hsiao, *Rural China: Imperial Control in the Nineteenth Century* (Seattle: University of
Washington Press, 1960), p. 241; Rawski, *Education*, pp. 49–52.

[79] Hsiao, *Rural China*, p. 186; *Dictionary of Ming Biography*, vol. I, p. 389.

[80] Hsiao, *Rural China*, chap. 6; T'ung-tsu Ch'ü, *Law and Society in Traditional China* (Paris:
Mouton, 1961).

Cultural integration produced the social stability desired by the elite and the state. As James Liu concludes, "It was this closely knit economic, social, and intellectual web that made it possible for the government of such a vast empire to confine its formal structure mainly in the cities, while utilizing the social structure for rural control." [81]

Of course, cultural integration marched hand in hand with increased social differentiation and social tension, which were engendered by the same socioeconomic conditions that produced integration. Economic advance brought greater social mobility and social stratification; increases in trade and marketing heightened awareness of the differences separating regional and ethnic cultures. The new emphasis on striving, expressed in fiction and morality books, reflects the competitive milieu that confronted ambitious Chinese during late Ming and Ch'ing times. It was natural that culture became not only a shared language, but a vehicle for communicating power relationships, as demonstrated in James Watson's essay in this volume (chapter 10) on the T'ien Hou cult in Kwangtung, and that cultural symbols conveyed a multitude of meanings that were different for different individuals in the society.

Cultural integration and cultural diversity: these were concomitant developments of the late imperial period. The importance of each factor shifts with our focus. On the macrosocietal level, when we consider the premodern communication and transportation technology of Ming and Ch'ing, we must count the cultural unity of the empire as a major achievement. China also appears to have arrived at a greater degree of cultural homogeneity than many premodern European countries—for example, France, not to mention the disunited and atomized states in Germany and Italy. Several essays in this volume begin from this perspective to investigate why and how this cultural integration was achieved.

In seeking to understand how late imperial society functioned at the family, village, and local level, both cultural integration and cultural diversity emerged as extremely important topics for analysis and study. Research on syncretic movements, heterodox and orthodox cults, and analysis of drama and fiction provides us with clues to the values embedded in Chinese culture at various times and places and gives us glimpses of the dynamic interaction between the socio-economic context and the ideas and norms guiding individual behavior. We are at the beginning of a relatively unexplored but fascinating field.

[81] Liu, "Integrative Factors," pp. 14–15.

TWO

Communication, Class, and Consciousness in Late Imperial China

David Johnson

In most of the chapters of this book the leading role is played not by specific individuals, or institutions, or notable events, but by texts—novels and plays, lectures and handbooks, scriptures and sermons—almost all of which were directed at people who were neither highly educated nor particularly powerful. These materials are given so much attention because they help us understand better what the great mass of Chinese who were not part of the national elite thought and felt about themselves and the world around them. Values can be embodied in nonverbal symbols, and exemplified in behavior, but to be communicated with any precision, or to be explained, they must find expression in words. For this reason, historians concerned with beliefs, attitudes, ideas, and the like, as we are in this book, naturally begin by studying the verbal forms that were contrived to express them.

However, without knowing who wrote the tract or guidebook or ballad we are interested in, it is extremely difficult to interpret it properly, to understand what it is actually saying. Then, too, adequate assessment of the social and historical significance of any text requires that we know how widely it circulated, how many people it influenced, and who they were. Finally, if we are concerned with the impact of an entire system of thought, as opposed to a specific text, we must take account of the differences among versions of that

Earlier drafts of this paper were written while I was a Senior Fellow in Columbia University's Society of Fellows in the Humanities, and during a year supported by a grant from the American Council of Learned Societies. I am grateful to both those exemplary organizations. The discussions at the Honolulu conference of an early version of this paper had a substantial impact on my thinking that I am glad to acknowledge formally. I am particularly indebted to my co-editors, Andrew Nathan and Evelyn Rawski, whose criticisms of the work at every stage were invaluable. I am also grateful to the following persons, who were kind enough to read and comment on the final draft: James Watson, Myron Cohen, Roger des Forges, and Gilbert Rozman.

system prepared for different audiences or produced by members of different classes. In short, the study of values involves the study of communication and social structure as well. One of the chief aims of this book is to develop a better sense of the interrelationships of these three aspects of Chinese culture in the late imperial period, especially in the broad reaches of society beyond the confines of the ruling class. My purpose in this essay is to present a preliminary analysis of how the structures of communication and dominance affected consciousness in the Ming–Ch'ing era.

I

The verbal forms that imagination and intellect create take on social meaning only when they pass from person to person. Conversations, storytelling, gossip, preaching, letter writing, the reading of books—such activities go on constantly, and the manifold connections between people that they create can be seen as a network of enormous complexity involving virtually every member of a culture. Certain features of this network in late imperial China are obvious enough. To begin with, it had oral and literary components, and the oral component was itself subdivided by dialect. But here we already are moving from the obvious to the obscure. How serious a barrier to communication in the Ming–Ch'ing period were dialect differences? How many mutually unintelligible dialects were there? How large were the groups that spoke them? (Obviously, dialects spoken by only a few people will be of little significance to our understanding of the culture as a whole.) If dialect differences did constitute important barriers to communication, further questions arise: How common was the ability to speak both dialects in regions that lay along dialectal boundaries? If the transition between dialect areas was rather abrupt, and bilingualism rather uncommon, individuals who were bilingual would have been of great importance in cultural interchanges between regions. Were they more likely to be found in certain kinds of occupations or social roles than in others? Did they come predominantly from a certain class? How often were civil and military officials bilingual in this sense? The answers to these questions will have a considerable impact on our understanding of (among other things) the spread of legends and cults, and the nature of the relationship between officialdom and the people.

Dialect differences also have a direct bearing on our understanding of what appears to be the relatively high degree of cultural integration on the sub-elite level in Ming and Ch'ing times. Such sharing of values and ideas across social and geographic boundaries comes about in general through a combination of two processes. In one, myths, legends, stories, songs, and the like pass from person to person by word of mouth, the values embedded in them thus diffusing slowly until they are familiar to large numbers of people. In the other, certain values are deliberately inculcated by a dominant social group, or a priestly class, to further its own interests, to bring salvation to the people, or both. In such cases, the values almost always have their roots in written texts of some kind, for texts are by far the most effective means of ensuring continuity and uniformity in an ideology.

Many of the essays in this book provide evidence of the inculcation of values from above. But we know too that things like the Mid-Autumn Festival, the legend of Liang Shan-po and Chu Ying-t'ai, and the cult of the Stove God are found in very similar forms in many regions of China. Since at first glance such matters seem unlikely to have been of much concern to officials or priests, it appears that diffusion was also at work, as we would expect. But we do not yet know how difficult it was for oral messages to move from one dialect area to another. The more difficult it was, the more important must have been the role of literate intermediaries even in the spread of popular festivals and cults. If the barriers of dialect were very great, we can predict that the most widespread elements of popular culture will be the ones most likely to carry an ideological burden, the legacy of the participation of educated middlemen in the process of transmission.

Although Ming–Ch'ing oral culture was naturally compartmentalized and parochial, it goes without saying that in any dialect area every native could speak the dialect. By contrast, while individuals who could read and write were to be found everywhere in China, in any particular region they formed only a small minority of the population.[1] Furthermore, there were wide variations in degree of literacy. But differences in literacy did not automatically lead to the breakdown of communication. A man of modest education could, if he was able to write at all coherently, communicate in writing on at least some subjects with any other literate person. And a sophisticated scholar could "write down" to a humble audience and make himself understood, though he may have found the exercise demeaning, and have failed to reach his readers.

It follows that only those persons who could write as well as read were part of the network of written communications, since those who could not write would have been unable to originate or transmit written messages. Hence the image of a communications network is probably more appropriate to the oral realm than to the world of writing. Ability to communicate reciprocally in writing had considerable influence on individual consciousness, of course, but far more important was access to the literary tradition, the great body of texts that had accumulated over the centuries. The consciousness of an individual whose access to that tradition was very limited is certain to have been different from that of someone with unlimited access to it. Such access depended on an individual's education, class position, and native intelligence, for taken together they determined the texts he encountered, the time he could spend

---

[1] Evelyn S. Rawski, *Education and Popular Literacy in Ch'ing China* (Ann Arbor: University of Michigan Press, 1979), pp. 8–20.

on them, and his ability to understand them. Therefore the appropriate figure for thinking about the literate realm is not a network, but a hierarchy. Comparatively few people were able to read and comprehend everything in the literary tradition, a few more were able to read everything except the most difficult texts, and so on down through the degrees of difficulty or accessibility. The result is strongly reminiscent of diagrams of social stratification, as it should be, since class position and education (which were strongly interrelated) largely determined how well a person could read and understand the texts of the literary tradition. In fact, the most meaningful subdivisions of the literate realm were related to class, as those of the oral realm were to geography.

The boundaries of these subdivisions did not form the kind of barriers that were created by the boundaries between dialect areas, because they only operated in one direction: the incomprehension was not mutual. A poorly educated person could not understand the abstruse texts studied by the scholar, but the scholar could read with ease—if not pleasure—books written by unsophisticated hacks. Surmounting the barriers within the literate realm was therefore essentially a matter of producing written versions of complex texts that could be understood by "the common reader." One of the *Sacred Edict* popularizations discussed in Victor Mair's essay, Liang Yen-nien's *Illustrated Explanation of the Sacred Edict*, seems to have been prepared for such a purpose (see below, pp. 330–335). *The Romance of the Three Teachings*, the novel that is the subject of Judith Berling's study (see chapter 7), was written to make the ideas of the Ming religious innovator Lin Chao-en accessible to a wider literate audience. We can assume, too, that at least some of the texts used by the local specialists who figure in James Hayes's essay (see chapter 3) were the result of the conscious simplification of complex ideas for readers of limited educations. There was in fact considerable interest on the part of educated men in making available to less educated readers the content of texts and systems of texts that otherwise would have been inaccessible to them. The importance of such "translation" work can hardly be overstated. It plays a large role in this book, and should be a high priority for future research. I shall return to it below.

But if we think of the literate population as arranged in a hierarchy, where shall we place the lines dividing the various strata? The gradations between different levels of literacy were infinitely fine. Moreover, comprehension itself could exist in varying degrees, from complete understanding to "getting the gist." There were also specialized literacies in the less-educated strata, though we know next to nothing about them (see below, pp. 63–64). It appears, therefore, that the distinctions we make are liable to be somewhat arbitrary, and that in any case the boundaries between groups of literates will not be sharp. Still, two points are reasonably clear. First, we can assume that a man who had passed the *yuan* examination (that is, a *sheng-yuan*), or had completed his studies in preparation for it, could read virtually everything in the literary tradition. Second, there must have been a substantial number of individuals whose limited schooling had made it possible for them to grasp the meaning of many texts but not to write easily or well. Such persons had some access to the literary tradition and hence had transcended the confines of local oral culture, but were unable to use writing to order and record their thoughts. The distinction between those literates who could not write, or at any rate habitually did not, and those who did, is one of the most significant within the literate realm, perhaps as important as the distinction between those who did and did not have full access to the literary tradition. This distinction ought therefore to be included in any model of the literate realm. But since I have no idea how many of these moderately literate but nonwriting individuals there may have been, for the time being I can do no more than note their probable importance, and hope that future research will throw enough light on the subject to allow them to be brought into the model.[2]

Up to now, I have tried to show where the most important divisions within the oral realm and the literate realm lay, and how they affected the process of communication and hence the formation of consciousness. I shall turn now to the most basic division of all: that separating the oral and the written realms themselves.

The illiterate could not transcend the world of folk tales, sermons, legends, gossip, and hearsay—a rich and varied realm, but still confining. The teachings of the ritual scriptures, the adventures of the heroes of *The Romance of the Three Kingdoms*, the latest edict against heterodox religion, even a letter from home— all these had to be explained to him by someone who could read. Communication in the oral realm took place in a complex network of face-to-face encounters, and if a message was irrelevant to present interests and concerns it was forgotten, and ceased to exist. A message that was not forgotten was changed in the process of telling and retelling until eventually many different versions of it came to exist. Each telling was in effect a re-creation, for a new audience, and the most successful of these took on lives of their own. Thus there were two double barriers around the typical illiterate. He could not understand oral messages in dialects different than his own, or any written message; and he could not communicate with others if circumstances required either that he use another dialect, or the written word.

But the oral and literate realms were not mutually inaccessible. Just as stories and beliefs could move from one dialect area to another with the assistance of bilingual intermediaries, so they could move across the gulf separating the oral and the literate realms, although the process was very complex and involved intermediaries of many different types. The entire system of intercommunications between the illiterate and the educated is of absolutely central importance to the understanding of Chinese history from at least Sung times on, and

---

[2] For some further remarks on this topic, see below, p. 44.

deserves the close attention of students of all aspects of Chinese cultural history. The transformation of texts into oral forms that were accessible to the illiterate masses was probably the most important part of this process. Later chapters provide many examples of it: officials (and a storyteller) explaining the *Sacred Edict*; members of the Lo and Hung-yang sects reciting their scriptures to groups of peasants; village fortune tellers, geomancers, and experts on ceremonial expounding to their clients or friends the information in the handbooks and encyclopedias they owned; actors presenting to small-town audiences undoubtedly composed largely of illiterates plays that had been written by men with great command over the written language.[3]

It also happened that oral compositions of various kinds were reduced to writing, and thus entered the literate realm. A large number of important literary genres are believed to have originated in this way: *tz'u* poetry, *chu-kung-tiao* ballads, and *pien-wen* stories, among others. Of course, important changes must have been introduced into the sung or spoken originals as they were being made into reading matter (just as the oral version of a written text would have been very different from its original), but nevertheless the movement from oral to written did take place.

We are interested in more than the simple transposition of verbal material from one medium into another, though. Our basic concern is with the movement of beliefs, ideas, values, and the like from group to group, and this could take place in subtler ways. For example, Wang Ken, in one of his public lectures, could well have explained to his audience things that he had heard during discussions with Wang Yang-ming. Here we see how the ideas of a highly educated man could have become part of the consciousness of people with much less education, without ever having been written down. And, of course, elements of oral culture could also find their way into the consciousness of an educated man without being written down. He would have absorbed a great deal of such material when he was a child, and throughout his life would have continued to be exposed to it, since every person was able to participate fully in the oral culture of his native region. Yet it is not quite correct to say, as Peter Burke does, that the educated man was "bi-cultural," though he was indeed familiar with both literate and oral culture.[4] For when he heard a local legend, or a pious tale, it would have meant something rather different to him than to a peasant. Each of them would have had a different stock of ideas and values with which the new idea had to be integrated and against which it was assessed. Those elements of oral culture that the educated man learned as a child would no doubt have struck deep roots, but he would have come to distrust or even despise many of them as he grew up and underwent the

---

[3] Not discussed in later chapters but of considerable importance in the transfer of written material into the oral realm was the person who read aloud to small groups of illiterate kinfolk or friends.

[4] *Popular Culture in Early Modern Europe* (London: Temple Smith, 1978), p. 28.

indoctrination of a classical education. Even if he remained sympathetic to certain aspects of oral culture, his peers may not have been, and this would have encouraged him to maintain an emotional distance from such material or even to repress it entirely.

2

In the preceding pages I have tried both to trace the most common paths followed by stories, proverbs, sermons, histories, and all other creations of language as they moved throughout China in late traditional times, and to describe the barriers they encountered. The patterns thus formed have their own fascination, but it is the messages that are really important, for the words in which people express their ideas and feelings are the best evidence of their consciousness, and consciousness is what we seek, finally, to understand in this book.

But what *does* a text reveal about "consciousness"? If we are honest with ourselves, I think we must admit that while we regard some texts as evidence of the consciousness of their authors, we assume that others somehow represent or embody the consciousness of entire groups. Texts that are technically sophisticated or intellectually complex, that are unconventional or idiosyncratic, that display a marked authorial self-consciousness, and that have been written by well-known intellectual or literary figures—in such texts we unthinkingly assume that it is the consciousness of the author that is being revealed. But texts that are anonymous, that deal in familiar ways with traditional subjects, that are uncomplicated either artistically or intellectually, that seem to have been composed quite unselfconsciously, and that have a function as simple and obvious as a catechism's or a riddle's—these we tend to take as evidence for the mentality not of an author, but of an entire group.

Now certain extremely original works are probably reliable evidence only of their authors' mentalities, while at the other extreme, traditional materials such as myths and legends really do reflect the values of groups rather than particular individuals, because after having been passed down from generation to generation they have become collective creations. But most texts—oral and written—can tell us something about the consciousness of both the person who created them and of larger groups as well.

Group consciousness, or collective mentalities, is a subject of major concern for this book, and the concept therefore demands especially careful consideration. I believe that in the ordinary course of reading and reflection we tend to assume that texts such as the sectarian scriptures discussed by Overmyer, or *The Romance of the Three Teachings*, treated by Berling, provide evidence about the mentality of one or both of two kinds of groups: first, the people who belonged to the same social group as the author; and second, the text's audience. Both these assumptions require careful scrutiny.

That every consciousness is unique and that therefore strictly speaking one can never extrapolate from an authorial mentality to that of a group is one of those truisms we all cheerfully ignore every day, and rightly so. The important problems arise when we try to decide whom to include in the group to which the author belongs, whose values and attitudes his work helps us understand. Should it be others of the same economic class? Or should it be those of the same occupation or profession? Those of the same educational and cultural level? Those of the same city or region? No final answer is possible to this sort of question; certain problems seem to require that we define these groupings in one manner, other problems in another. But in general we ought to be guided by the factors that shape individual consciousness most strongly. I believe two types of factor are most important: those relating to position in the systems of communication I outlined above (including access to the literary tradition), and those relating to position in what I call the structure of dominance. I shall discuss both of them at some length below.

The other group whose collective mentality is believed to be revealed, or reflected, or in some way expressed by a text, is its audience. Much confusion exists here. To begin with, we must distinguish between actual audience—sometimes called the public of a work—and intended audience: the person or persons for whom the author was consciously writing. Information about the actual audiences of most texts in Ming–Ch'ing times is of course virtually impossible to obtain, but we can sometimes make reasonable assumptions. For example, the fifteenth-century *shuo-ch'ang tz'u-hua* discovered in the coffin of the wife of an official must have been read by her, and by other women of the same class[5]; the folk plays collected by Sydney Gamble and his associates were presented to village audiences in Ting hsien[6]; folk tales collected in Shansi circulated among the illiterate peasants there; texts such as the unpretentious editions of the Four Books with explanatory notes, discussed by Sakai Tadao in his article on Ming morality books,[7] can be assumed to have had wide circulation in the non-elite part of the population; and so on. But we will have little information on how many copies of a text were printed at one time, and how many times it was reprinted. We will probably not know how much it cost, and hence who could not afford to buy it.[8] Nor will we know as much as we should

[5] See David T. Roy, "The Fifteenth-Century *Shuo-Ch'ang Tz'u-Hua* as Examples of Written Formulaic Composition," *CHINOPERL Papers* 10:97–128 (1982). See also W. L. Idema, *Chinese Vernacular Fiction: The Formative Period* (Leiden: E. J. Brill, 1974), pp. xxxv ff.

[6] See *Chinese Village Plays*, ed. Sidney S. Gamble (Amsterdam: Philo Press, 1970). The Chinese texts, which should be consulted in conjunction with Gamble's renderings, can be found in *Ting-hsien yang ko hsuan* 定縣秧歌選 [Ting hsien rice-planting songs], ed. Li Ching-han 李景漢 and Chang Shih-wen 張世文 (Taipei: Tung-fang wen-hua shu-chü, 東方文化書局, 1971; reprint of 1933 ed.), 4 vols.

[7] "Confucianism and Popular Educational Works," in *Self and Society in Ming Thought*, ed. Wm. Theodore de Bary (New York: Columbia University Press, 1970), p. 336.

[8] For some interesting speculations about these questions and related matters, see Idema, *Chinese Vernacular Fiction* (cited n. 5), pp. xliv–lxiv.

about what proportion of the population in a given region would have been educated enough to read and comprehend it, although here at least we can draw on Evelyn Rawski's pioneering book.[9] Our ignorance of such matters makes it virtually impossible to speak with confidence of the actual audience of any written text in Ming–Ch'ing times. We should therefore be cautious about assuming that a particular text influenced or embodied the consciousness of a particular social group. We can make such judgments only in cases where we are very sure that the material was genuinely popular among the members of that group, and hence met their expectations or needs in some important way, or affected their way of looking at the world.

There remains the notion of intended audience, which is the sense usually carried by the term "audience" in discussions of Chinese literature. Sometimes, in the preface or elsewhere in a work, the author will identify explicitly the people he hopes to reach.[10] In other texts, such as personal letters or official documents, the intended readers are perfectly obvious. But usually it is necessary to guess. To do so intelligently it is essential to understand the structure of the networks of oral and written communication. No one could have intended a written text for an illiterate audience (except for the rare cases where a text was composed especially for oral delivery). Nor would an erudite, highly allusive disquisition on statecraft or literary theory have been aimed at an audience of readers who had not gone beyond the village school. Nor would a text that contains expressions peculiar to Cantonese have been intended for readers in Peking.

After we have drawn obvious inferences such as these—and they can be extremely helpful—we must bring to bear more subtle methods. Here the distinction between literature intended to entertain, and literature intended to instruct or enlighten must be kept in mind. The ideological or doctrinal burden of the latter frequently makes it obvious whom the author is addressing. And since the particular concern of the authors of entertainment literature was to please their readers, their conception of the mentality of their audience will be clearly visible in their writings as well. But here we arrive at the essential problem raised by the notion of intended audience. Even if we can identify with precision the group at which a writer was aiming, his work will inform us not about the mentality of that group but about the author's conception of it. Hence, the most important thing to know about the intended audience of a given text is whether its members belonged to the same social group as the author, or whether, on the contrary, the author expected his work to find its readers among a group significantly different from his own.

If author and audience occupied roughly similar positions in the networks of

[9] See note 1.

[10] A number of examples are provided in Sakai's "Confucianism and Popular Educational Works" (cited n. 7), p. 334, and in Victor Mair's essay in this book.

communication and the structure of dominance, a text can teach us about the mentality of the audience because the author's mentality will resemble or reflect it. But what if an author is attempting to cross social boundaries to reach his audience? If a highly educated man who occupied a secure position in the ruling elite wrote a novel for a non-elite reading audience, could we use the novel as evidence of non-elite mentality? It goes without saying that we could, if we knew that it had in fact been extremely successful among such readers. But if, as will usually be the case, we have little information about actual readership, and know only who the author had hoped would read the book, then everything will depend on how well he understood their mentality. And obviously we cannot routinely assume that an author was intimately familiar with the mentality of people of a social class different from his own.

Unfortunately, most of the premodern Chinese texts with which the historian and literary critic have to deal are either anonymous or attributed to men of whom we know nothing. If these texts are to teach us something about specific social groups, we must be able to guess fairly accurately the group or class to which their authors belonged. It is relatively easy to do this in a limited way. We can be sure that certain works were written by highly educated men, even if they are anonymous, because, for example, they employ a vocabulary and make allusions and in general are written in a style only an educated person could command. And of course we know that the author of any written work belonged to the literate minority. But although such knowledge is useful, it is also limited, and we naturally are impatient to say more. Sometimes this impatience leads to circular reasoning: unexamined intuitions (our own or those of other scholars) tell us that a certain text was not written by or for highly educated readers; we identify a number of what seem to us characteristic features in it; and then, when we encounter these features in another text, we take them as evidence of its popular provenance. We can never eliminate this circularity entirely: we know too little about authors and audiences. There will never be a way of definitively placing a text by an unknown author in a particular social context; we will always have to rely on intuition in the end. But the greater one's knowledge of late imperial society and the more sophisticated one's appreciation of the factors influencing consciousness, the truer to historical reality one's intuitions are likely to be. The first step toward these ends should be to develop a better sense of the entire range of social groups that were likely to have had distinctive mentalities. In what follows, I shall first try to show why I believe that position in the systems of communication and in the structure of dominance influenced consciousness profoundly. I shall then show that the careful application of these two criteria allows us to identify significant social groups. Each of those groups had a characteristic collective mentality, but I shall not attempt to describe them systematically—that is impossible at this stage, even for the best-studied groups. I shall simply offer some common-sense suggestions that I hope will serve to make our intuitions more reliable.

3

The consciousness that is more or less revealed by any utterance or text was shaped in part by the entire range of verbal structures that the speaker or writer had encountered. His consciousness was also influenced, in a negative sense, by the information and ideas that for one reason or another could *not* reach him. An illiterate seventeenth-century Nan-p'ing storyteller, for example, would have been steeped in Fukienese oral culture, but his knowledge of the oral culture of the Wu-speaking area to the north, or the Yueh-speaking region to the south, would have depended on that material having been translated into Min by bilingual intermediaries. In the same way, his knowledge of the content of written texts could only have been indirect and mediated by one or more literate middlemen, who would certainly have introduced changes in the original text.

A man who could write, but who had received only a limited literary education, would have remained unacquainted with a good deal of the literary tradition. As a consequence, he would not have made certain kinds of literary allusions, would have been limited to a certain range of vocabulary, and would probably have avoided certain genres. These and many other characteristics of his writing will reveal his lack of familiarity with the full literary tradition.

The writings of a scholar-official, especially if they were aimed at other scholar-officials, will reveal the fact of his classical education and subsequent reading as surely as the storyteller's performance or the imperfectly educated person's letter will reveal *their* characteristic limitations. The entire range of extant writings from all periods of Chinese history was, in theory at least, open to the classically educated man, and under ordinary circumstances he would have encountered a much greater variety of verbal material than either of the other two persons we have been imagining. In addition, not only the content of the literatus's consciousness, but also his very style of thought, differed greatly from that of an illiterate peasant. That a person could, and did, write down his ideas had a profound effect upon their complexity and abstraction. The habit of writing also encouraged the development of intellectual self-awareness, thanks to the process of revision and correction that is part of all composition, and to the opportunity it affords for close study of one's own words. As Ibsen has it, "To write: that is to sit/in judgement over one's self." This subject is too complex to pursue here, but it deserves serious study.[11]

---

[11] Jack Goody's *The Domestication of the Savage Mind* (Cambridge: Cambridge University Press, 1977), a stimulating meditation on the impact of the invention of writing on preliterate consciousness, unfortunately has little to offer the student of traditional cultures such as China's that were characterized by the coexistence of literate and nonliterate traditions. The Ibsen passage can be found in Robertson Davies, *The Manticore* (New York: Penguin Books, 1976), p. 73.

Thus, the dialects a person understood and the texts he could comprehend determined to a considerable degree what he knew and how he expressed it— that is, both the content and the style of his consciousness. These in turn shaped his own writings and utterances, and hence were revealed in them. Whether he was one of the creative few or the imitative many, when he put his thoughts or feelings into words he could not help but draw heavily, both consciously and unconsciously, on what he had earlier heard and read. This is why it is possible, in theory at least, to reconstruct the influences on a person's thought, or, more accurately, the sources of a particular text. Each individual was constantly engaged in fashioning out of what he had heard and read a more or less coherent view of the world. This weaving together by each person of the almost infinite variety of verbal material he had encountered in his life was in itself a process of cultural integration, perhaps the most fundamental one. Although each of these personal syntheses was, by definition, unique, those produced by individuals located in a particular segment of the systems of communication naturally shared many features of both form and content. Here we see the direct, necessary connection between communication and consciousness.

Consciousness is not shaped by words alone, however. What a person reads and hears has to be integrated with what he has learned about the world simply by living in it. After all, would we not expect the writings of two classically educated men, one wealthy and powerful, the other eking out a precarious existence as the tutor of rich merchants' sons, to reveal somewhat different attitudes and values? And would we not expect a well-to-do farmer to enjoy somewhat less heartily than his tenants a village play that excoriated greedy landlords? Many social, economic, and psychological factors interact to produce such differences in consciousness, of course, but I believe most of them are directly related to a person's position in what I shall call the structure of dominance. There are many sorts of domination, and hence "structure of dominance" can mean a number of things. This is one of the term's strengths, since in the real world a person perceives his situation as a whole, and not in analytically convenient categories like wealth or prestige. So I will not offer a detailed explication; the meanings I attach to the term will become clearer as we proceed.[12]

The influence upon consciousness of position in the structure of dominance is

---

[12] The use of the terms "domination" and "subordination" in speaking of class relationships appears to go back to the writings of Antonio Gramsci, though I first encountered them in books by Raymond Williams and George Rudé, two contemporary British Marxist scholars. (See below, pp. 47, 49, and n. 22.) Gramsci's conception of dominant and subordinate classes is also fundamental to Carlo Ginzburg's brilliant reconstruction of the mental world of a late-sixteenth-century northern Italian miller: *The Cheese and the Worms*, trans. John and Anne Tedeschi (Baltimore: Johns Hopkins University Press, 1980), pp. xiv, 129–130.

an exceedingly complex problem that can only be treated adequately when the discussion is rooted in concrete historical particulars. All I hope to do in this brief and all too schematic discussion is provide an explicit conceptual basis for further investigations. Before I begin the discussion proper, however, I should like to examine a crucially important phenomenon that at first glance seems intimately related to this topic, but which in fact is quite separate from it. I refer to the dissemination throughout Chinese society of values deemed appropriate by the ruling elite, what Eugen Weber has called "official culture." [13]

One of the leading characteristics of Ming–Ch'ing culture is the extraordinary degree to which values and beliefs favorable to ruling class interests permeated popular consciousness, as many of the essays in this book demonstrate. This was in part the achievement of Chinese officials and other members of the ruling elite who had worked for centuries to replace "corrupt" or "superstitious" elements in popular culture with ideologically acceptable ones. Thus, worship of the Hangchow tidal bore became connected with veneration of Wu Tzu-hsu, who had himself been transformed at an early stage by Confucian historians from a martial hero into a paragon of loyalty and self-sacrifice;[14] midsummer sacrifices to river and fever gods in central and south China were partially transformed into worship of "the loyal Ch'ü Yuan";[15] and local legends were rewritten to bring them into line with conventional morality.[16] James Watson's essay in this volume vividly recounts the appropriation and promotion of the T'ien Hou cult, and others, by the Ch'ing authorities. "The state intervened in subtle ways," he writes, "to impose a kind of unity on regional and local-level cults" (see below, p. 293).

This process can be observed in many times and places. Keith Thomas's *Religion and the Decline of Magic*[17] shows how the representatives of orthodox Christianity worked to root out ancient practices and beliefs in the English countryside, for example, and the transformation in medieval Europe of pagan sacred places such as springs and grottoes into Christian pilgrimage centers and cathedral sites, complete with appropriate legends and miracles, is

---

[13] In remarks delivered at the ACLS Conference on Values and Communication in Ming–Ch'ing Popular Culture, Honolulu, January, 1981. Weber's superb *Peasants Into Frenchmen: The Modernization of Rural France, 1870–1914* (Stanford: Stanford University Press, 1976), will richly repay study by anyone interested in the relationship between the subordinate classes and centralizing state authority.

[14] See my "The Wu Tzu-hsü *Pien-wen* and Its Sources, Part II," *Harvard Journal of Asiatic Studies* 40.2 (December 1980).

[15] See Wolfram Eberhard, *Chinese Festivals* (Taipei: The Orient Cultural Service, 1972), pp. 77–104.

[16] I have discovered a number of examples of this kind of elite manipulation of popular lore in my researches on the origin and early development of the city god cults, which will appear in a forthcoming issue of the *Harvard Journal of Asiatic Studies*.

[17] New York: Scribner's, 1971.

well known.[18] As Northrop Frye has written, "The central mythical area [that is, the body of "stories" that illustrate the chief concerns of a society and that are regarded as uniquely important or serious by its members] is an area of special authority, which means that people in authority take it over."[19] The central myths (in Frye's sense) of a culture, thus appropriated and reinterpreted, become the core of a system of beliefs, values, and ideas that is gradually diffused through the whole society. Such systems invariably contain elements that justify the existing order of things, but to regard them merely as conscious contrivances of a ruling class intent on securing its own privileges and power is to see only part of their significance. It is true that there is indoctrination, but there also is a desire to be indoctrinated—that is, to believe what it is proper to believe. The values and beliefs of a dominant class take on the radiance of truth in the eyes of ordinary people. As George Rudé has written in his *Ideology and Popular Protest*, "The people become willing partners in their own subjection."[20]

This sentence appears at the conclusion of Rudé's brief account of Antonio Gramsci's idea of "hegemony." Although his summary does not convey Gramsci's full meaning, nevertheless it contains an important point. He writes that for Gramsci, hegemony is "the process whereby the ruling class imposes a consensus, its dominion in the realm of ideas, by largely peaceful means. This happens through its control of the media of indoctrination in that part of the state he terms 'civil society': through the press [for Ming–Ch'ing China, we should say rather "publishing, especially of drama and fiction"], church and education."[21]

Gramsci's distinction between the private institutions of "civil society"[22] and the public institutions of the State has little relevance for China, where a single elite controlled all national institutions. But this very fact made possible a hegemony of startling strength and scope. Nor is this all. "Control of the media

---

[18] For a provocative overview of this process in the early medieval period in Europe, see Jacques Le Goff, "Clerical Culture and Folklore Traditions in Merovingian Civilization," in his *Time, Work, and Culture in the Middle Ages*, trans. Arthur Goldhammer (Chicago: University of Chicago Press, 1980), pp. 153–158. Peter Burke argues that there was a "reform of popular culture" in early modern Europe, a "systematic attempt by some of the educated ... to change the attitudes and values of the rest of the population, or as the Victorians used to say, to 'improve' them." *Popular Culture in Early Modern Europe* (cited n. 4), p. 207.

[19] *The Secular Scripture: A Study of the Structure of Romance* (Cambridge, Mass.: Harvard University Press, 1976), pp. 6–7, 27.

[20] New York: Pantheon Books, 1980, p. 23. Part One of this book is particularly stimulating.

[21] *Ideology and Popular Protest*, p. 23.

[22] He speaks of "civil society" as "the ensemble of organisms commonly called 'private,'" as opposed to the public institutions of the state; "the so-called private organisations, like the Church, the trade unions, the schools, etc." See Antonio Gramsci, *Selections from the Prison Notebooks of Antonio Gramsci*, ed. and trans. Quintin Hoare and Geoffrey N. Smith (New York: International Publishers, 1971), pp. 12, 56 n.

of indoctrination" by the ruling class was unusually complete in Ming–Ch'ing times, because China had become by that time a grammatocracy: the learned ruled. The ruling class was composed, by law and custom, of men who had achieved great skill in writing and deep familiarity with the literary tradition. Moreover, since the purpose of almost all advanced education was preparation for the civil service examinations, and since those examinations tested ideological soundness (among other things), intellectuals tended to develop variations on received tradition and the dominant ideology rather than radical alternatives to them. Even elementary education was in most cases strongly ideological, although since it was less exclusively in the hands of the ruling elite, it was possible for divergent forms to appear.[23] Finally, the officials were responsible for the protection and, if possible, the improvement of public morals. They had—and used—the power to censor the books, plays, and so on that the people under their administration were likely to come in contact with, and to punish anyone involved in the performance or dissemination of material they believed to be subversive of public morality.

Here we have a method for producing not only cultural integration, but cultural integration based on a particular ideology; cultural integration that is not the natural result of the interaction of people with each other and with their traditions, but the willed product of a particular class. This is a useful reminder that while systems of communication are part of the cultural landscape, which, like the physical landscape, changes very slowly, they can, like rivers and hills, be made to serve specific social purposes by groups that can mobilize and deploy resources sufficient to the task. A part—sometimes a very significant part—of the things a person heard and read in Ming–Ch'ing times contained values and ideas agreeable to the ruling class because those books or plays or whatever had been produced by members of that class or influenced by them. That is why it is proper to treat this topic under the rubric of communication. But it is also true that this process cannot be understood without a clear sense of the hierarchy of dominance and subordination. Hence it supplies a natural transition to the next part of the discussion.

I shall argue in what follows that position in the structure of dominance *in itself* has a decisive effect upon consciousness, an effect both analytically and historically separate from the effects of position in the systems of communication. As I have said, this is an enormously complicated subject, probably too complicated to be considered a single "problem," certainly too complicated to yield simple answers. Nevertheless, it is impossible to deny that consciousness is influenced by position in the structure of dominance. To suggest why this is so, I shall turn once more to Gramsci, and to several contemporary British Marxist historians and theoreticians who have been influenced by him.

Gramsci believed that earlier Marxist theoreticians had seriously under-

[23] Rawski, *Education and Popular Literacy* (cited n. 1), pp. 49, 128–139.

estimated the importance of popular consciousness. Rather than accepting the prevailing notion that the intellectuals were a separate social group, Gramsci insisted that "all men are intellectuals," even though they do not all "have in society the function of intellectuals." [24] Every person has his own "'spontaneous philosophy' ... contained in: 1. language itself, which is a totality of determined notions and concepts and not just words grammatically devoid of content; 2. 'common sense' and 'good sense';[25] 3. popular religion and, therefore, also in the entire system of beliefs, superstitions, opinions, ways of seeing things and of acting, which are collectively bundled together under the name of 'folklore'." [26] "Common sense is not a single unique conception, identical in time and space. It is the 'folklore' of philosophy, and, like folklore, it takes countless different forms." These depend upon "the various social and cultural environments in which the moral individuality of the average man is developed"; they are responses to "certain specific problems posed by reality." [27]

Gramsci's fragmentary ideas on this subject are summarized and interpreted eloquently by Raymond Williams in his *Marxism and Literature*: "What is decisive is not only the conscious system of ideas and beliefs [the expression or projection of ruling class interest known as "ideology" in conventional Marxist political theory], but the whole lived social process as practically organized by specific and dominant meanings and values." The concept of ideology ignores "the relatively mixed, confused, incomplete, or inarticulate consciousness of actual men in [a particular] period and society"[28]—what Rudé, also paraphrasing Gramsci, calls "those less structured forms of thought that circulate among the common people, often contradictory and confused and compounded of folklore, myth, and day-to-day popular experience." [29] Williams states that Gramsci's approach

of course does not exclude the articulate and formal meanings, values, and beliefs which a dominant class develops and propagates. But it does not ... reduce consciousness to them. Instead it sees the relations of domination and subordination, in their forms as practical consciousness, as in effect a saturation of the whole process of living ... of the whole substance of lived identities and relationships, to such a depth that the pressures and limits of what can ultimately be seen as a specific economic, political, and cultural system seem to most of us the pressures and limits of simple experience and common sense. ... [Hegemony] thus constitutes a sense of reality for most people in the society, a sense of absolute

[24] *The Prison Notebooks*, p. 9.
[25] The translators gloss these terms usefully: "Broadly speaking, 'common sense' means the incoherent set of generally held assumptions and beliefs common to any given society, while 'good sense' means practical empirical common sense in the English sense of the term" (p. 323, n. 1).
[26] *The Prison Notebooks*, p. 323.
[27] Ibid., pp. 419, 324.
[28] Oxford: Oxford University Press, 1977, p. 109.
[29] *Ideology and Popular Protest* (cited n. 20), p. 23.

because experienced reality beyond which it is very difficult for most members of the society to move, in most areas of their lives.[30]

E. P. Thompson, perhaps the most impressive of the British Marxist historians, supplies a telling example of the impact of subordination on consciousness:

> Defoe's fictional cloth worker, called before the magistrate to account for default, [says]: "not *my Master*, and't please your Worship, I hope I am *my own Master*." The deference which he refuses to his employer, overflows in the calculated obsequiousness to "your Worship." He wishes to struggle free from the immediate, daily humiliations of dependency. But the larger outlines of power, station in life, political authority, appear to be as inevitable and irreversible as the earth and the sky. Cultural hegemony of this kind induces exactly such a state of mind in which the established structures of authority and even modes of exploitation appear to be the very course of nature.[31]

I accept the basic propositions just outlined—that consciousness is strongly influenced by the existential realities in which each person is immersed, and that the most fundamental of these realities are bound up with the relations of dominance and subordination—and in what follows I shall try to show that they provide a powerful analytic perspective for the study of late imperial Chinese society. A point of definition needs to be made first, though. I will be speaking of collective mentalities, not of class consciousness in the Marxist sense. My concern is with characteristic beliefs and values that members of a particular social group held, not with their consciousness that they constituted a group with common interests that they could act collectively to defend or promote. I have cited the remarks of Williams, Rudé, and Thompson not because I subscribe to their theoretical position *in toto*—as should be obvious from the first half of this paper—but because they provide the most persuasive account I have seen of the way in which position in the structure of dominance affects consciousness.

4

The main features of the structure of dominance in rural China in late imperial times are well known.[32] In every village there were some families and

---

[30] *Marxism and Literature*, pp. 109–110.

[31] "Patrician Society, Plebian Culture," *Journal of Social History* 7.4:387–388 (Summer 1974).

[32] It is important to point out that we know much more about Chinese social structure in the eighteenth and especially the nineteenth centuries than earlier in the Ming–Ch'ing period, and my account naturally reflects this imbalance. Since my analysis is essentially synchronic, this leaves the impression that nineteenth-century conditions prevailed through the whole period. Of course this was not the case at all, as Evelyn Rawski's historical introduction makes clear. But I do not believe that this weakens my argument; the approach outlined in this essay can be employed regardless of the size of the various social groups.

individuals who either were landless or whose landholdings were too small to support them. To stay alive, such people rented additional land, worked as laborers of one kind or another, handicrafted small items or engaged in other cottage industries, and in more desperate times borrowed, begged, and even— as Elizabeth Perry has described in considerable detail—stole.[33] Such people obviously were profoundly dependent upon the persons from whom they rented land and borrowed money, or for whom they labored, or to whom they sold the things they made. It is impossible to say with confidence what proportion of the rural population this most dependent and vulnerable group represented. Its size certainly varied with both period and region. But most scholars agree that by the late nineteenth and early twentieth centuries, the group was very large. In a recent survey, Joseph Esherick concludes that in the 1930s, 40 percent to 80 percent of the rural population, depending on province, was not self-sufficient.[34] This was the massive foundation of the entire structure of dominance.

Those who owned more land than they could cultivate themselves, and who either hired laborers or rented out their land, or both, were the most dominant people in the village world. This group included both the "rich peasants" and the "village landlords" of Chinese Communist class analysis, and may have constituted 10 percent of China's rural population in the 1930s.[35]

A number of other elements in the structure of dominance in the countryside could be mentioned here, for that structure was exceedingly complex—some tenant farmers, for example, had virtually permanent tenure of large tracts of land and were therefore quite prosperous—but one group merits special attention because it lies near the boundary dividing the obviously dependent from the obviously prosperous. That group was composed of people who never accumulated much in the way of surplus, but either owned enough land or had sufficient income from other secure sources to deserve to be called independent

[33] *Rebels and Revolutionaries in North China, 1845–1945* (Stanford: Stanford University Press, 1980), chap. 3.

[34] "Number Games: A Note on Land Distribution in Prerevolutionary China," *Modern China* 7.4:404, table 7 (October 1981). The national total was 68 percent. Obviously, Esherick's figures are far from ideal for my purposes, since they are (as he admits) based on inadequate data, and also concern what may well be an atypical period. But I have turned up nothing better, or even comparable, in the secondary literature on late Ming and Ch'ing social history. When considering Esherick's conclusions, readers ought also to bear in mind the following passage by one of the greatest living European historians of rural life:

> In no case could a holding of less than twelve *hectares* assure its occupant of the slightest trace of economic independence [in the Beauvais in the seventeenth century]. As our documents amply illustrate, the great majority of the peasants—three quarters or more—remained well below that level. Were they, then, condemned to suffer hunger, or even starve to death? The answer is most definitely in the affirmative.

And Pierre Goubert goes on to demonstrate this chilling conclusion most effectively. See "A Regional Case Study of the Seventeenth-Century Peasantry," in *The Peasantry in the Old Regime: Conditions and Protests*, ed. Isser Woloch (New York: Holt, Rinehart & Winston, 1970), p. 37.

[35] Esherick, "Number Games," pp. 405, 408 n. 11.

or self-sufficient. According to Esherick, they made up 22 percent of the rural population in the 1930s.[36] In practice, it is extremely difficult to say where dependency ends and self-sufficiency begins, and obviously there will always be some borderline cases that we cannot with confidence place in either category. Nevertheless, the distinction I have in mind is fundamental. It is the distinction between, on the one hand, those who were dependent directly on members of their own community, people they probably saw every day, whose faces were familiar and whose habits they knew, and on the other those who were free of such dependency, who were able, in the words of Pierre Goubert, "to feed their families from that portion of the harvest left at their disposal."[37] The lowest stratum of self-sufficient families probably led fairly insecure lives, since a few bad harvests would have impoverished them. But to be thus vulnerable to the uncontrollable and unpredictable vagaries of nature has, to my mind, profoundly different psychological consequences than dependency on members of one's own community. It is true that these self-sufficient people were subordinate in law to the gentry and officials, and in fact to the local magnates, but this subordination too was of a different quality than that of those whose very survival was in the hands of others. For these reasons, I have placed this transitional group with the less dependent of the two great divisions of rural society, with the landlords rather than the impoverished.[38]

The relations of dominance and subordination in rural China are summed up effectively in Jing and Luo's *Landlord and Labor in Late Imperial China*:

> The [village] landlord class had the right to concern themselves with local affairs. They were frequently the organizers of calamity relief, and other such matters. They were also the arbiters of all forms of dispute, whether within the lineage or within the village. Their word could often carry the force of law. . . . These broad powers deeply influenced the lives of the owner-peasants and poor peasants in the village. Those peasants, including the long- and short-term laborers, who depended for their livelihood in whole or in part on working for the landlords had no option but to tremble before their power and do exactly as they were told.[39]

[36] Ibid.

[37] "A Regional Case Study" (cited n. 34), p. 35.

[38] Note that Jerome Blum, in his magisterial survey *The End of the Old Order in Rural Europe* (Princeton: Princeton University Press, 1978), while emphasizing the great range of variation in the structure of peasant societies, seems in practice to favor a three-part model similar to the one just outlined. There were peasants who were "prosperous"; those with "middling" holdings that were "just about large enough or productive enough to support the household"; and those who had "so little land that they had to find other sources of support" (p. 105). Blum does not stress the distinction between the first two groups and the third, however.

[39] Jing Su and Luo Lun, *Landlord and Labor in Late Imperial China*, trans. Endymion Wilkinson (Cambridge, Mass.: Council on East Asian Studies, Harvard University, 1978), p. 210. A vivid description of the conditions in which the most dependent part of the rural population lived can be found in Part I (pp. 8–19) of P'eng P'ai, *Seeds of Peasant Revolution: Report on the Haifeng Peasant Movement*, trans. Donald Holoch (Ithaca: China-Japan Program, Cornell University, 1973 [Cornell East Asia Papers, number 1]). The report describes the organization of peasant unions in Kwangtung in the 1920s.

Above the village landlords in the structure of dominance were the families that owned large amounts of land but worked none of it themselves, preferring instead to rent it out with the assistance of resident managers and agents. These absentee landlords resided in market towns and larger cities, living on their rents and on income from various commercial enterprises. Thus they belong more to urban than to rural society, though naturally they were influential wherever they owned land.

Towns and cities had their own structures of dominance, quite distinct in the lower levels from that of the countryside. (For a brief but vivid glimpse of urban social structure in late Ming, see pp. 193–194 of Judith Berling's essay, below.) There was an impoverished class of laborers, scavengers, peddlers, and the like, and of course a well-to-do stratum composed of those who employed others in their workshops and stores. Between these two were the employees, a group that was characteristically urban, and that must have been fairly large, including as it did a broad variety of workers, from unpaid apprentices to powerful managers. Since employees could be dismissed at any time, they were profoundly dependent in the sense I am giving the word, though some were far more comfortable financially than others. (These last are a group that deserves special study.) The relations of dominance and subordination that bound employer and employee together were frequently articulated through the guilds. This can be seen with particular clarity in the case of apprentices. Peter Golas, discussing Ch'ing guild regulations, writes,

> In general, the ideal held out to the apprentice was total submission to those above him.... [He was required] to address associates with kin terms appropriate to their status and seniority.... When his period of apprenticeship was over, he still carried the same obligations toward his master as a son toward his father.[40]

On the upper levels of the structure of dominance in both town and country was the group known as the gentry. Their dominance was not only due to the practical realities of wealth and power; it also was legally defined and enforced. Their degrees and titles brought specific legal privileges, including exemption from various taxes, special treatment in all phases of legal proceedings, and the right to wear distinctive insignia of rank.[41] Intertwined with these legal privileges were many customary privileges and other benefits of gentry status, which all in all placed the members of this tiny group in a position indisputably superior to everyone else in Chinese society.

Although there has been considerable debate over details, most scholars now agree that in Ming and Ch'ing times the core of the gentry group was composed of active and retired officials, and those qualified to hold office: civil and military *chin-shih* and *chü-jen, kung-sheng* by examination and purchase, and, in

[40] "Early Ch'ing Guilds," in *The City in Late Imperial China*, ed. G. William Skinner (Stanford: Stanford University Press, 1977), p. 566.

[41] Chung-li Chang, *The Chinese Gentry: Studies on Their Role in Nineteenth-Century Chinese Society* (Seattle: University of Washington Press, 1955), pp. 32–43.

Ming, *chien-sheng*.[42] Within this group, the officials occupied the more dominant position, and were of course the most powerful group in Chinese society. Both T'ung-tsu Ch'ü and Chung-li Chang have demonstrated that in Ch'ing times the holders of *sheng-yuan* and *chien-sheng* degrees shared in the legal privileges of the gentry group, but occupied a distinctly lower position in the structure of dominance.[43] The *sheng-yuan* (and *chien-sheng* in Ch'ing) were thus a transitional group, placed by law and custom above the people at large, but below the gentry proper.[44] In the eyes of the magistrate, retired officials, and holders of higher degrees in a county, they were subordinate, but from the perspective of the commoners, they were very exalted, with flagstaffs outside their houses and vermilion plaques above their gates.[45] As Philip Kuhn points out, "such lower degree holders . . . might easily dominate community life in poor and backward rural areas."[46]

The *sheng-yuan–chien-sheng* group helps to show that in the lower reaches of the structure of dominance, wealth and power were the prime determinants of position, while at the top, these were rank and legal privilege, tied to achievement in the examinations. The *sheng-yuan* occupied an anomalous position, because they were located in the part of the structure where one type of determinant began to be replaced by the other. Their examination achievement conferred prestige, but did not necessarily bring dominance.[47] (The very wealthy merchant who had not purchased a degree also occupied a rather anomalous social position, and for similar reasons.) In sum, the decisive division in this part of the structure of dominance was that between those who had legal privileges due to official rank or examination status on the one hand, and the rest of the population on the other.

Women participated so little in the nondomestic side of life that they cannot readily be made part of the structure of dominance whose outlines I have been sketching. But if we consider each household as an arena in which the relations of dominance and subordination were played out, it is clear that in any given

---

[42] Philip Kuhn, *Rebellion and Its Enemies in Late Imperial China* (Cambridge, Mass.: Harvard University Press, 1970), pp. 3–4; Ping-ti Ho, *The Ladder of Success in Imperial China* (New York: Columbia University Press, 1962), pp. 24–41; Jing and Luo, *Landlord and Labor* (cited n. 39), p. 11.

[43] *The Chinese Gentry*, pp. 6–8; T'ung-tsu Ch'ü, *Local Government in China under the Ch'ing* (Cambridge, Mass.: Harvard University Press, 1962), pp. 173–175.

[44] Ho, *Ladder of Success*, p. 35.

[45] T. C. Lai, *A Scholar in Imperial China* (Hong Kong: Kelly and Walsh, 1970), p. 2.

[46] Kuhn, *Rebellion and Its Enemies*, p. 4.

[47] The image of the impoverished *hsiu-ts'ai* (the popular term for holders of the *sheng-yuan* degree) as an object of contempt and scorn, common in novels of social protest such as *Ju-lin wai-shih* and *Lao Ts'an yu-chi*, and also present in *The Romance of the Three Teachings* (see below, p. 202), has been very influential, but it would be good to have more objective evidence on the subject. (Cf. Ho, *Ladder of Success* [cited n. 42], pp. 36–37.) Just how common was it for *sheng-yuan* to be poor and despised in a given region and period during Ming and Ch'ing times? Scholars who consign them to a somewhat ignominious role may well have unconsciously adopted a high-gentry point of view.

social group, the women can be regarded as a separate and subordinate subgroup—since women seldom achieved dominant positions in the Chinese family. This suggests that in any social group, the women and men will have had mentalities at least somewhat divergent in character. (Note the provocative remarks of James Watson on the differences between male and female religiosity in his essay, pp. 320–321 below.) This is a fact of great significance for our understanding of the inner workings of Ming–Ch'ing culture, as I shall try to demonstrate below.

The main elements of the structure of dominance in late imperial China were therefore as follows. At the bottom were all those who could not support themselves and their families independently of wealthier or more powerful individuals: peasants with tiny plots of land or none at all, poor laborers in the cities, and the like, together with hereditary tenants, bondservants, slaves, and others whose legal status placed them below ordinary commoners. At the top was the small group of people who possessed the ranks and titles that brought legal privileges. Between them came all those who possessed at least enough land (or other property) to be self-sufficient, and perhaps a great deal more, but who enjoyed none of the legal privileges of the gentry, and hence were by no means exempt from the anxieties and resentments engendered by dependence, though they were spared its most degrading consequences. In both this and the most dependent group there were urban as well as rural components, and the members of the middling group who lived in cities—craftsmen, shop-keepers, and so on—were subdivided in a number of ways, as the guild system indicates. Finally, there were the women, almost always subordinate to their husbands and parents-in-law, and barred from participation in nondomestic life.

The perception of dominance and subordination depended greatly upon the context in which a person was acting. A village boss would have been utterly inconsequential in the prefectural capital. But he knew this. People understood in their bones the entire range of relations of dominance and subordination, even if they usually experienced only a few of them. The village landowner, untitled, perhaps illiterate, who did not fear the officials or gentry, who did not feel that he must defer to even a *hsiu-ts'ai*, must have been rare indeed. This is why position in the hierarchy of dominance influenced people's consciousness, and it follows that the members of each important subdivision in that hierarchy must have tended to develop a characteristic consciousness or collective mentality.

5

We have seen that both position in the structure of dominance and location in the networks of communication influenced consciousness. But these two aspects of existence were not separate; every person experienced the effects of both simultaneously. Furthermore, position in one system affected position in the other. To identify social groups with real significance for consciousness, we must therefore consider both position in the hierarchy of dominance and position in the systems of communication. For example, in the oral realm, dialect was crucial, but so too was whether one was dependent (in the sense employed here) or self-sufficient. In every dialect, stories told by persons who were poor agricultural laborers or sharecroppers would necessarily have expressed different values and attitudes than those told by people whose livelihoods were secure. Similarly, the consciousnesses of two prosperous farmers, one illiterate and the other (by some quirk of biography) classically educated, must have differed considerably.

The three most important strata in the hierarchy of dominance and subordination were the dependent, the legally privileged, and, lying between those two extremes, the self-sufficient commoners; the three most significant subdivisions in the realm of communications—leaving aside the dialect groupings—were the illiterates, the classically educated, and those who were literate in varying degrees but not classically educated. If we combine these categories, we obtain nine distinct social-cultural groupings, as shown in Figure 1.

FIGURE 1.   Chief Social-Cultural Groups of Late Imperial China

DOMINANCE

	Greatest		Least
Greatest	Classically educated/ legally privileged	Classically educated/ self-sufficient	Classically educated/ dependent
	Literate/ legally privileged	Literate/ self-sufficient	Literate/ dependent
Least	Illiterate/ legally privileged	Illiterate/ self-sufficient	Illiterate/ dependent

EDUCATION/ LITERACY

Ideally, a third axis, perpendicular to the other two, would be included, on which the different linguistic regions would be arranged, further subdivided into rural and urban elements. If this were done, the lines dividing the various dialects, and the rural and urban segments, would probably be very faint in the top tier, especially in the classically educated/legally privileged group, and extremely strong in the bottom tier, especially in the illiterate/self-sufficient and illiterate/dependent groups. For while Min-speaking scholar-officials must have exhibited certain attitudes and beliefs that differed from those of their Wu-speaking colleagues, I believe those differences were insignificant when compared with the differences in the mentalities of poor peasants in the two regions. In addition, rural oral culture probably differed substantially from urban oral culture, while literati culture was probably much the same in country or city.[48] However, we still know very little about differences in the oral cultures of different linguistic regions, and much work is necessary before we can assess the real importance of these differences. Close study of regional dramatic traditions, at least some of which must have corresponded with linguistic regions, appears to be one promising way to approach this problem.[49] Another is the comparative study of proverbs from different regions, which R. David Arkush has proposed,[50] and of folk tales. But until these and related studies are undertaken, there is little we can say about the cultural differences of linguistic regions that goes beyond traditional stereotypes.

We are on firmer ground, conceptually at least, if we confine ourselves to the nine social-cultural groups in Figure 1. Some of them—such as the classically educated/dependent—were probably historically insignificant (though it would be unwise to take this for granted). Others—such as the classically educated/legally privileged and the illiterate/dependent—were very important and have long been recognized as such. And still others—such as the illiterate/legally privileged and the classically educated/self-sufficient—were very significant but have hardly been studied. In what follows I shall discuss briefly each of these groups, pointing out some of their more significant characteristics.

There was a very close relationship between position in the two systems—at least for men. This was true because education and access to the literary tradition were almost always dependent on wealth, wealth in turn was closely related to position in the structure of dominance, and entry into the highest reaches of the structure of dominance was impossible without a classical edu-

---

[48] F. W. Mote, in "The Transformation of Nanking, 1350–1400," while deprecating the idea of a *general* urban–rural dichotomy in Chinese culture, believes that "among the lower ranks of society, there probably were much more clearly identifiable urbanites and ruralites, and no doubt the distinction between city and country must have had greater meaning in their daily lives [than in the lives of the elite]." Again, "there certainly were attitudes and characteristics [of consciousness] associated with the city" (*The City in Late Imperial China* [cited n. 40], pp. 117, 106).

[49] See Colin MacKerras, "The Growth of Chinese Regional Drama in the Ming and Ch'ing," *Journal of Oriental Studies* (University of Hong Kong) 9.1:58–91 (1971).

[50] In his "Economic Calculation and Social Morality as Seen in Chinese Peasant Proverbs," paper presented at ACLS–NEH Conference on Orthodoxy and Heterodoxy in Late Imperial China (Montecito, California, August 20–26, 1981), p. 5.

cation. Since everyone wanted to rise in the hierarchy of dominance, or at least to maintain their position, families educated sons to the limits of their resources. Only the sons of the truly impoverished received no schooling at all. Furthermore, learning itself was an essential aspect of dominance in traditional China. In the orthodox view, dominance was legitimated by learning; the learned deserved to rule. And, in practice, the people at large paid deference to the learned, not merely because they were usually wealthier or more powerful than ordinary people, but also because they were masters of writing in a culture where the written word had almost magical potency and were experts on the rules of ritual in a society where virtually everyone agreed on the great importance of knowing and following the proper forms of behavior.

The members of the legally privileged group, the gentry, were by definition classically educated. This is one of the most familiar groups in the structure of power and education whose outlines I am sketching. There is no need to stress the importance of this group or describe its leading characteristics, since it is by far the best-studied segment of late imperial society.

What of the other two groups in the top tier of the diagram: the classically educated/dependent and the classically educated/self-sufficient? Very few who were well educated enough to compete in the *yuan* examinations would have been as low in the structure of dominance as poor peasants or coolies. We read of impoverished scholars, of course—poor village schoolmasters and the like— but most men with classical educations must have come from well-to-do families, or at least have had patrons who were comfortably off (in village terms). Truly poor youths who acquired classical educations, such as the Li Yung (1627–1705) who provides one of Ho Ping-ti's fascinating illustrations of social mobility, must have been as rare as saints—and, indeed, some of Ho's brief biographies have more than a little of the hagiographic about them.[51] The bulk of this group must therefore have been made up of men who had grown up in easy circumstances and received good educations, but who for one reason or another had later become impoverished. However, I doubt that there were many such men, and feel quite sure that the classically educated/dependent group was rather insignificant. There may well have been large numbers of men with classical educations who regarded themselves as poor, and were so re-garded by their wealthier friends, but such "poverty" was usually of an entirely different order than the poverty of the landless peasant or urban laborer.

The middle group in the top tier of the chart, the classically educated/self-sufficient, played a very important role in the integration of Chinese culture, and is worth the closest study. One of the most interesting things about this group of highly educated commoners is how large it was. Since virtually everyone who undertook the classical curriculum did so in the hope of passing the literary examinations, the number of classically educated men must have been roughly equal to the number of candidates (*t'ung-sheng*) for the *yuan*

---

[51] *The Ladder of Success* (cited n. 42), pp. 280–283.

examinations (for the *sheng-yuan* degree), plus those who had at one time been *t'ung-sheng* and had then abandoned the examination life. Since the *yuan shih* was only a preliminary or qualifying examination, it was felt to be improper for older men to compete in it, and in fact Chung-li Chang presents evidence that suggests that very few men passed the *yuan* examination after the age of thirty.[52] Chang estimates the life expectancy of members of the gentry at a little under sixty years.[53] If we assume that life expectancy was the same for the pre-gentry (a convenient name for those who had classical educations but did not have gentry status), we can conclude that the number of former *t'ung-sheng* was about double that of active *t'ung-sheng* (fifteen years of active candidacy, then an average thirty more years of life). Chang's estimated number of *t'ung-sheng* in a "locality"—1000 to 1500—should therefore be tripled, since he is obviously relying on estimates of *active* candidates for the preliminary examinations.[54] Since "locality" must refer to *hsien* and *chou*, of which there were roughly 1400 in Ch'ing times,[55] this gives a total of between 4,200,000 and 6,300,000 *t'ung-sheng* and former *t'ung-sheng* at any given time in Ch'ing before the late nineteenth century. This conclusion finds support in another calculation based on Chang's data. He states that only one or two percent of the candidates succeeded in passing the *yuan* examinations (though it is not at all clear how he arrived at this figure).[56] In the pre-Taiping era, the national quota for *sheng-yuan* was about 25,000,[57] and at any given time there would therefore have been between 1,250,000 and 2,500,000 active candidates. Tripling these numbers yields a total of active and former candidates of between 3,750,000 and 7,500,000, nicely bracketing the first estimate. I believe therefore that it is safe to say that there were at least 5,000,000 classically educated male commoners in Ch'ing times—roughly 5 percent of the adult male population at the start of the nineteenth century, and 10 percent in the early eighteenth century.[58] There

[52] Miyazaki Ichisada, *China's Examination Hell: The Civil Service Examinations of Imperial China*, trans. Conrad Schirokauer (New Haven: Yale University Press, 1981), p. 19; Chang, *The Chinese Gentry* (cited n. 41), p. 95.

[53] *The Chinese Gentry*, p. 97.

[54] Ibid., p. 92.

[55] Ch'ü, *Local Government* (cited n. 43), pp. 1–2.

[56] *The Chinese Gentry*, p. 11.

[57] Ibid., pp. 78–79.

[58] Using the age and sex ratios given in Rawski, *Education and Popular Literacy* (cited n. 1), pp. 183–184, and taking age 15 as the beginning of adulthood, there would have been something fewer than 110 million adult males in the early nineteenth century, when the population was around 300 million and half that many ca. 1700. F. W. Mote has estimated the number of *sheng-yuan* candidates in Ch'ing times at "twenty to thirty million." This figure is much too high (as he himself suspected), because he neglected to allow for the fact that many men sat for the examinations more than once. See "China's Past in the Study of China Today—Some Comments on the Recent Work of Richard Solomon," *Journal of Asian Studies* 32.1 : 108–110 (November 1972). The situation in Ming times is less clear, though before late Ming the number of *sheng-yuan* seems to have been much smaller than in Ch'ing. See Ho, *Ladder of Success* (cited n. 42), pp. 172–179.

would in addition have been a small number of women who had classical educations and yet were not members of gentry households. Thus (in Ch'ing, at any rate) there was a rather substantial number of classically educated commoners. Such people were probably to be found in virtually every small town, and in many villages. One of the status terms that appears in Ch'ing population registers is "farmer-scholar" (*keng-tu*). It clearly refers to someone who was both educated and a farmer, and although I do not know what level of scholarly attainment was necessary before this distinction was bestowed on a person, it seems reasonable to assume that it must have been fairly high. Indeed, another translation of *keng-tu* could be "classically educated commoner." [59] Whether or not they had received official recognition, classically educated commoners would certainly have been among the cultural elite, and probably the social elite as well, in market towns or villages. Some served as community leaders and lineage managers. Others were religious innovators, such as Lin Chao-en (1517–1598), whose doctrines *The Romance of the Three Teachings* was written to promote—probably by another classically educated commoner. (See Judith Berling's essay, pp. 189–190, 196, below.) Lo Ch'ing (fl. early sixteenth century, the author of several widely circulated popular scriptures and founder of the sect known as the *Lo chiao*, may also belong in this category, although it is just as likely that he should be placed in the literate/self-sufficient group. (See Daniel Overmyer's essay, pp. 231 ff., below.) The Buddhist and Taoist clerical elites should also be placed here, for they too were highly educated, and had a substantial influence on the values and beliefs of the people at large. Still other members of this group became teachers (a fact that has perhaps received too much emphasis), ritual experts, private secretaries, calligraphers, letter-writers, physicians, diviners, geomancers, and so on—the indispensable local experts and specialists that play such an important part in James Hayes's essay in this volume (see especially pp. 93–96, 98–99). Such men—classically educated commoners, elite monks and priests—almost certainly wrote most of the texts prepared for non-elite readers, from morality books (*shan-shu*) to inexpensive chapbook fiction, from encyclopedias for daily use (*jih-yung lei-shu*) to letter-writing guides. The role that these men played in the popularization of complex ideas and beliefs, and above all in the spread of Confucian elite values, was very great; their importance as the shapers of non-elite consciousness can hardly be exaggerated.

By now it should be obvious that to think of the classically educated in Ming–Ch'ing times as a homogeneous group is a serious error. Some classically educated men enjoyed gentry status, while others were ordinary commoners. All had undergone the same kind of indoctrination, and had the same degree of

---

[59] I first learned of the *keng-tu* status in a brief presentation made by James Lee, of the California Institute of Technology, at the 1982 meeting of the Association for Asian Studies (AAS), in San Francisco.

access to the literary tradition, but only a few had passed the examinations. The rest remained to one degree or another subordinate and vulnerable. Some of these men must have continued to identify with the gentry and to espouse their values, but many others must have been led by their experiences and situations in life to have greater sympathy for commoners than the typical gentry man had—after all, they were commoners too. These highly educated but disillusioned men were probably more willing to listen sympathetically to, and even advocate, ideas or beliefs that were not quite respectable than full-fledged members of the gentry were, for whom even the appearance of dissent from orthodox values could have had extremely serious consequences. Obviously, the classically educated were not a coherent group with a characteristic collective mentality. Indeed, although most Ming or Ch'ing texts written in classical Chinese by men who appear to have undergone advanced literary educations will probably exhibit the conventional ruling-class world view (see below, p. 69), some may well reveal a mentality ambivalent or even antagonistic toward the ruling elite and its values.[60] (There may have been a similar cleavage between the core of the privileged group and the *sheng-yuan* and *chien-sheng* on its fringes.)

The next tier in the diagram—again divided into three groups—comprises individuals who were at least functionally literate and perhaps quite well read, but not classically educated. If membership in the gentry had been dependent solely upon passing examinations, the first of these groups—the literate/legally privileged—would have had little actual social meaning. But gentry status could also be purchased in late Ming and Ch'ing.[61] Now it seems likely that the typical degree purchaser was a man from a comfortable background who had received a standard classical education, but was simply not talented enough at memorization and composition to be able to pass the examinations. This is by no means proven, however, and if it turns out that a large number of the men who bought their way into the privileged elite had not been classically educated, this group will have considerable significance.

We can be more certain about another characteristic of the literate/legally privileged group: it included a substantial number of women. While it is true that an upper-class woman was subordinate to her husband (and his parents) both in law and custom, it is also true that in many ways she shared her husband's (or father's, or son's) position in the extradomestic hierarchy of dominance. But women seldom received classical educations, and hence the wives of men with gentry status were likely to be moderately educated at best, and quite possibly illiterate. Thus the women of the privileged group usually

---

[60] I am assuming that *t'ung-sheng* would almost always have been capable of writing good classical Chinese.

[61] Ho, *Ladder of Success* (cited n. 42), pp. 46–47; Chang, *The Chinese Gentry* (cited n. 41), pp. 11–12, 102–111, and *passim*.

had less access to the literary tradition than the men, and this inevitably created important differences in their views of the world. For one thing, gentry women must have remained much closer to the main currents of non-elite culture: they had not been taught to prefer the monuments of the great literary tradition, the subtleties of classical scholarship, the systems of the approved philosophers. These literate, well-to-do women must also have formed a significant audience for popular written literature.[62] Such women were entertained by the *Hsin-k'an shuo-ch'ang Pao Lung-t'u tuan Ts'ao kuo-chiu kung-an chuan* and the other printed fifteenth-century *tz'u-hua* mentioned earlier (above, p. 41), and edified by the *Liu Hsiang pao-chüan* and other popular religious texts discussed by Daniel Overmyer in his essay (below, pp. 228–230). Upper-class women whose families were especially wealthy are likely also to have been among the purchasers of the elegantly printed editions of unsophisticated novels and moralistic tracts that have puzzled literary historians from time to time.[63] It is not surprising, therefore, that—in my experience, at any rate—one of the hallmarks of true popular literature in China is the heroine who initiates actions, who is one of the moving forces of the plot, and who is not submissive but who, on the contrary, struggles against the restrictions of conventional domestic morality.

At the same time, upper-class women probably played an important role in the perpetuation of both religious beliefs and oral literature such as legends and ballads. This was not some kind of "women's culture" (though of course there almost certainly was *that* too), but was in fact an important part of what we call Chinese popular culture. And the things women believed, the maxims they knew, the stories they told, and so on must have been very familiar indeed to their sons and husbands. Upper-class mothers (who, as I have said, would seldom have been well educated) naturally instilled elements of nonclassical and even folk culture into the consciousness of their sons, and when those boys grew up, their wives and concubines helped ensure that they did not forget what they had learned at their mother's knee. And precisely the same point can be made of the servants who surrounded such men throughout their lives.

Thus, it is clear that the legally privileged group contained an important segment that was not classically educated, and that this contributed profoundly to the steady infusion of non-elite values and beliefs into the consciousness of gentry men. In short, the fact that classically educated men usually married women who had substantially less education created one of the basic mechan-

---

[62] See Joanna Handlin, "Lü K'un's New Audience: The Influence of Women's Literacy on Sixteenth-Century Thought," in *Women in Chinese Society*, ed. Margery Wolf and Roxane Witke (Stanford: Stanford University Press, 1975), pp. 16–19.

[63] See Idema, *Chinese Vernacular Fiction* (cited n. 5), pp. 93–94. On p. lxi he mentions "the problem of the nicely executed but simply written works of the first three quarters of the 16th century, which I think might have been designed for some of the not very highly-literate groups within the social elite." This is not to disparage Idema's excellent book, which is central to the whole subject.

isms of cultural integration in China, one whose effects ran directly counter to the effects of that other important agency of cultural integration, gentry hegemony. One of the great challenges facing students of traditional China is to do justice to this largely hidden dimension of elite culture.

The second group in this tier of the diagram—the literate/self-sufficient— must have been rather large and heterogeneous, and was also very significant. (It is possible that at least some of the "farmer-scholars" mentioned above ought to be placed here.) Since we know so little about literacy rates in the non-elite segments of Ming–Ch'ing society, there is no way to estimate the size of this group, but I would suggest that the proportion of functionally literate adult men in a village must have been comparable to, though somewhat smaller than, the proportion of "middle" or "rich" peasant households in the preceding generation, and similarly for the rural population of a region in general. Families that were living right at the edge of subsistence could not have afforded to send children even to the village school; but every family that was able to accumulate a little surplus probably tried to give at least one of their sons some education. In the early twentieth century, therefore, anywhere from roughly 15 to 45 percent of the adult men in the rural population, depending on province, could have been functionally literate.[64] There must have been some women in this group, but I believe that the wives of moderately educated men were seldom as well educated as their spouses (since people tended to marry within their class, and in every class except the lowest the men would have been better educated, on balance, than the women). Therefore, the number of literate women in the middle region of the structure of dominance was probably rather small. An illustration is provided by the brief glimpse of a woman's ballad-reading circle given in James Hayes's essay. Village women would gather to listen to someone chant ballads from printed booklets or broadsheets "especially designed for women to read or sing" (below, p. 89). This makes sense only if most of the listeners were illiterate.

In the larger towns and cities, many of the shop owners and some of the craftsmen were probably literate in varying degrees short of a full classical education, and they too belong in this category.[65] The importance of specialized occupational literacies of various kinds has been stressed in recent reports by participants in a large-scale study of popular literacy in Chinese

[64] The percentages of rich and middle peasants in various provinces in the 1930s are given in Esherick, "Number Games" (cited n. 34), p. 404, table 7. These figures are roughly consistent with Rawski's estimates; see *Education and Popular Literacy* (cited n. 1), p. 23.

[65] Information on the literacy rates in various occupations in sixteenth- and seventeenth-century England, which provides a good starting point for thinking about urban literacy in Ming–Ch'ing China, is presented in David Cressey, *Literacy and the Social Order: Reading and Writing in Tudor and Stuart England* (Cambridge: Cambridge University Press, 1980), pp. 130–141. This book should be read by anyone concerned with the interrelations of social and cultural stratification in the premodern period.

history that has been organized at the Chinese University of Hong Kong, including Thomas Lee, David Faure, and Alice Ng. Just how specialized literacy could be is vividly suggested by a vocabulary book (*tsa-tzu*) described by Faure and Ng. It consists entirely of the names of fish, arranged in rhyming couplets to facilitate memorization, and of numerals. It was probably used by apprentices in the fish trade when they were learning to keep accounts, write receipts, and so on.[66] Of course, a person who knew only the characters for three hundred kinds of fish was not literate in any meaningful sense of the word. But the example points up the importance of literacy in all but the simplest kinds of commercial endeavors. We do not yet know what the literacy rates were in Chinese cities in the Ming–Ch'ing period, but they certainly were greater than rural literacy rates.[67]

All in all, the literate/self-sufficient group made up a substantial portion of the literate population. These yeomen and burghers were peculiarly well situated to mediate between elite and folk culture. They lived close to the illiterate peasants and town workers, often earned their livings in similar ways, and probably enjoyed similar entertainments. Yet they could read, and hence were able to have direct access to at least part of the realm of the written word. They closely resemble the *ch'u-shih* who form "the central and best developed class of characters in [*The Romance of the Three Teachings*]," according to Judith Berling. It is true that some of them are *hsiu-ts'ai* (i.e., *sheng-yuan*), but "the bulk of the *ch'u-shih* in the novel do not seem to have competed in the government examinations or studied in government schools. The term seems to connote simply 'gentlemen' in the sense of members of the local (nonnational [i.e., not legally privileged]) town elite. They may have a modicum of education, but they are not elites by virtue of scholarly achievement" (see below, p. 194). The "literate men with interests in land and commerce, [who] were eager to co-operate with state authorities in the standardization of cults," and who assisted in the construction of state-approved temples, of whom James Watson writes in his essay, can probably also be placed in the literate/self-sufficient category (see below, pp. 293, 314). We also see men from this group in James Hayes's essay, sharing with their illiterate neighbors information about proper ritual forms and lucky days found in books they owned and could read (see below, p. 102). The reciters of the *Sacred Edict*, discussed in Victor Mair's essay, who read stories to fascinated village audiences, should probably be included in this group, too. Though they of course were itinerants and not "yeomen" or "burghers," they probably did as much to bridge the gap between the learned and illiterate as their more respectable counterparts.

[66] This information, and other preliminary findings of the Chinese University of Hong Kong project, were presented in papers by Lee, Faure and Ng, and others (Bernard Luk and Yue-him Tam) at a panel on popular literacy at the 1982 annual meeting of the AAS.

[67] Rawski, *Education and Popular Literacy* (cited n. 1), p. 17.

Since the typical members of this group were comfortably off but not wealthy, it is unlikely that they constituted a market for expensive books. But they certainly must have purchased less costly reading matter, such as cheap editions of the classics with simple commentaries, almanacs, shorter (and therefore less expensive) *pao-chüan* and *shan-shu*, ballad broadsheets and pamphlets such as the "wooden-fish books" of Kwangtung (some of which were specially prepared for women, as we have seen), and so on.[68] This group must also have formed the backbone of the audience for what W. L. Idema has called "chapbooks."[69] According to Idema, these novels were written in "a dreary, repetitive, and monotonous 'novelese,'" quoted very few documents written in the literary language (these appeared frequently in novels aimed at a more sophisticated audience), and contained "few if any historical or literary allusions, besides the most obvious."[70] Note too that their "subject matter followed the popular theatre," that they were almost all anonymous, and evidently aimed at non-elite readers, and that they were frequently published in what were obviously cheap editions.[71] Clearly such books were intended for people very similar to those in the literate/self-sufficient group that I have been discussing. These novels, and all the other inexpensive texts aimed at non-elite reading audiences, have hardly been studied, since they were despised by the Chinese scholars who taught the teachers of our teachers, and their contempt has been passed on from generation to generation. Moreover, these books are difficult to find, for the book collectors who were interested in such "trash" were rare indeed. But in the aggregate, such works must have been far and away the most widely circulated literature in late imperial China. It was the only kind of text that many people ever read. The cumulative impact of these writings on Chinese culture was very great, for not only did they give order and direction to the ideas and beliefs of the moderately educated people who read them, but they probably influenced significantly a great variety of oral material, ranging from the rules of propriety to the adventures of Judge Pao, that circulated among the illiterate everywhere in China. These texts, standing as they did on the boundary between the written and the oral, played a crucial role in the complex process by which elements of elite literary culture were translated into terms that the illiterate could comprehend.

---

[68] See James Hayes's and Susan Naquin's essays, pp. 82–92, 272–273, below. On "wooden-fish books" see Leung Pui-chee 梁培熾, *Hsiang-kang ta-hsueh suo ts'ang mu-yü shu hsu-lu yü yen-chiu* 香港大學所藏木魚書叙錄與研究 [Wooden-fish books: critical essays and an annotated bibliography based on the collections in the University of Hong Kong] (Hong Kong: Centre of Asian Studies, University of Hong Kong, 1978). See also *Cantonese Ballads from Germany*, ed. Wolfram Eberhard (Taipei: The Orient Cultural Service, 1972 [Asian Folklore and Social Life Monographs, vol. 30]).

[69] *Chinese Vernacular Fiction* (cited n. 5), pp. xi–xii.

[70] Ibid., p. xi.

[71] Ibid., pp. liii, lxi, 119.

The final group in the second tier of the diagram—the literate/dependent—could not have contained very many people, at least among the rural population. We can say, though, that since the poorest peasants were unable to educate their children, any poor peasant who was functionally literate probably had come down in the world since he was of school age. Such a person was not likely to have had a benign view of the prevailing order of things. Slipping from a comfortable position in the world to the edge of the abyss breeds both anxiety and rancor. It seems probable therefore that this group may have produced more than its share of rebels and members of millenarian cults. Their literacy enabled such people to see beyond the village horizon (if they chose), while their experiences would have made them resentful of the status quo. They could not have afforded even to *rent* books, but many kinds of pamphlets and broadsides appear to have been given away and posted in public places, and we can be sure that not all of them were uplifting moral tracts. One possible example of what these literate underdogs actually read has recently come to my attention. It is a manual of the Heaven and Earth Society (*T'ien ti hui*), first discovered in 1811 and recently republished, which is discussed by David Faure in an interesting paper.[72] In an insightful section called "The written word in a semi-literate tradition," Faure demonstrates that texts such as this manual were part of both the written and oral realms. Other probable examples are provided by some of the White Lotus texts discussed by Susan Naquin and Daniel Overmyer in their articles in this book. This is an area where vigorous research is almost certain to produce important results fairly quickly, in my opinion, but at the moment we know all too little.

This brings us to the final three groups in the diagram: the illiterate/legally privileged, the illiterate/self-sufficient, and the illiterate/dependent. By definition there could have been no adult men in the first of these groups, but there must have been a certain number of women. They, like their moderately educated counterparts, would have helped make oral culture part of the consciousness of men of the scholar-official class, first as mothers, then as wives.

The second group may have been fairly large—although our ignorance of class-specific literacy rates makes it impossible to be sure. For example, the wives of literate merchants and well-to-do farmers were probably usually illiterate, and hence belong in this category. Then, too, many of the so-called "middle" peasants were probably illiterate, either because they had never gone to school or because in the long years of toil following their schooling they had forgotten the little they had once learned.

But by far the most important of these three categories was the illiterate/dependent, the bottom dogs of traditional China, the familiar "il-

---

[72] "The Heaven and Earth Society in the Nineteenth Century," presented at the Montecito Conference on Orthodoxy and Heterodoxy in Late Imperial China (see n. 50).

literate masses," both rural and urban. They could easily have made up half the rural population in late imperial times, and thus were the largest of all the social groups I have been discussing. Not only were they the foundation of the structure of dominance, they also were by far the most important reservoir of traditional folk culture, in its various regional versions.

It is important to note that the illiterates were no more a single homogeneous social group—or audience—than the classically educated were. There were, of course, the differences between dialect-based subcultures (although, as I have said, we do not yet have a clear sense of how significant such differences were), and there were other important distinctions within the group as well. To begin with, many illiterate women were found in the middle and even upper ranges of the hierarchy of dominance. It seems unlikely that the oral lore transmitted by such persons was identical in what we might call ideological content to that current among grindingly poor peasants, nor could the two groups have been receptive to exactly the same ballads or plays. It seems probable to me, however, that these materials had a good deal in common, in light of the fact that women of all classes were subordinate to their husbands and in-laws. Second, not all illiterate men were poor agricultural laborers or coolies. Some undoubtedly owned enough land to support their families; others owned considerably more than that. The mentality of such landowning illiterates would have differed substantially from that of the truly poor, even though the world of the written word was equally closed to all of them. There were, in short, a number of differing oral cultures, quite apart from the dialect groups.

6

These, then, are the nine social groups whose existence in Ming–Ch'ing times is suggested by my assumptions about the main factors that shape consciousness and about the specific character of late imperial society. I trust that my comments on their leading characteristics will help "to make our intuitions [about texts and their social contexts] more reliable," as I said earlier I hoped they would. There is not space enough here to pursue in detail this discussion of collective mentalities—nor would my knowledge be equal to the task if there were. But the mode of analysis advocated in this essay—the simultaneous deployment of communications and class criteria in the identification of social groups and the interpretation of texts—has some other applications and implications that are worth discussing in conclusion.

To begin with, it must now be clear why scholars have in the past found it so difficult to frame satisfactory definitions of "popular culture" and "elite culture." After all, at least three very different kinds of people are included in what is ordinarily thought of, in a vague way, as "the elite": classically educated men with the legal privileges of gentry status; the less well educated wives and mothers of such men; and classically educated commoners. If, in an effort to limit the scope of the term, we define "elite" as "ruling class," then we exclude commoners to whom the whole literary tradition was open and who may have been extremely creative writers and thinkers. If we define "elite" in terms of education or mastery of the literary tradition, narrowing it in a different way, then we must include in it some men who were of little consequence socially or politically. And, of course, the term "popular culture" presents even harder problems: under it are subsumed four or five groups—or more, it we take regional differences into account. I am not arguing that the terms "popular culture" and "elite culture" should be abandoned—in fact, they are probably indispensable. But if we use these terms without a full awareness of the complex social realities that they denote, they will only create confusion.

Thus, if we limit the discussion to verbal structures made by and for the members of a single group, it is obvious that we can use the medium of communication—spoken versus written, unsophisticated versus learned literary styles—as a means of making a preliminary estimate of their origins. But we cannot stop there. Texts written by classically educated men for classically educated readers will exhibit a range of viewpoints, not simply because each consciousness is unique, but because highly educated men did not all occupy similar positions in the structure of dominance: some belonged to the legally privileged gentry, while the bulk were pre-gentry commoners. It will not do to assume that any text in classical Chinese was written by a man who was a member of the legally privileged elite. On the contrary, we should expect any large sampling of classical texts from the Ming–Ch'ing period to exhibit various viewpoints.

The same argument can be made for oral material, although here the discussion must of necessity be largely hypothetical, since so little material prepared by and for illiterates has survived and is accessible. Still, we know that successful storytellers, actors, ballad singers, preachers, and other performers of oral literature who intended to entertain or instruct, were very sensitive to the expectations and aptitudes of their listeners, whether or not they were of the same class, and certainly adjusted their "texts" to fit their audiences. Their performances have vanished, but it may be that careful research will enable us to identify not only regional groupings (and perhaps also urban and rural groupings) in Chinese folk tales, ballads, and the like, but also at least two class-related groupings: the oral literature of the most dependent segment of the population, and of those who were at least self-sufficient—laborers' tales and landlords' tales, coolies' ballads and masters' ballads.

Texts read by and prepared especially for moderately educated readers can be approached in the same manner, for as a group they extended across a very large part of the structure of dominance. But since I very much doubt that yeomen wrote what yeomen read, we here confront the problems discussed in the first part of this essay (above, pp. 42–43). When an author is trying to reach an audience in a social group other than his own, we must know something about his text's actual readership before we can use it as evidence of the target group's mentality. Otherwise, it can only be used as evidence of its author's conception of the mentality of his intended audience. Yet even in such an unpromising situation, the methodology I have outlined above can be helpful. If we are dealing with a popular text of some complexity, such as *The Romance of the Three Teachings* discussed by Judith Berling in chapter 7, or the *Liu Hsiang pao-chüan* translated and analyzed below by Daniel Overmyer, both of which were written by individuals with a substantial command of the resources of written Chinese, it is probably safe to assume that the authors either belonged to the gentry or were classically educated commoners. Very often the subject matter of the text itself will be enough to enable us to decide which of the two it was, for I take it as an axiom in the interpretation of Ming and Ch'ing literature that members of the legally privileged, classically educated elite almost always were committed to the philosophical-religious orthodoxy that can be called Neo-Confucianism, if that term is construed in its broadest sense. They had been thoroughly imbued with a characteristic world view during their pursuit of examination degrees, and, as officials, were members of a quasi-priestly class, one of whose chief duties was the rectification of ideological deviations and the extirpation of heresy. Naturally there were exceptions, but in general I believe we will usually be on safe ground if we assume pre-gentry or non-gentry background in any classically educated author in late imperial times who advocated new or unusual religious ideas (especially if they were strongly colored by Buddhism or Taoism), or expressed disapproval of the present condition of women, or advocated the equalization of property, or supported any other doctrine that tended to undermine the existing social and political order.

Of course, dependency and powerlessness did not invariably engender resentment and antagonism in those who experienced them—far from it. Few poor people had much hope of improving their lot, so they usually tried to come to terms with the conditions in which they lived. In this endeavor they received the constant encouragement of the ruling class, one of whose major concerns it was to make the people "willing partners in their own subjection." It would be naive to expect only outrage and despair in the lowest reaches of the structure of dependence. Deference and resignation, expressed in terms partly imposed from above and partly inherited from countless earlier generations of poor and vulnerable forebears, were far more common.

Yet consciousness of the sheer fact of subordination (or dominance) is always present in one form or another, since it is near the very heart of a person's life experience. That is why we can frequently detect a "social viewpoint" in stories and novels. How are commoners regarded by the author? From what class does the hero come? How does the hero treat characters from various classes? How frequently are representatives of various social groups seen, and how important are they to the action of the plot? Even if the protagonist is an official or scholar, as is so often the case, a story may still have a point of view that is non-elite (as in the story so ably translated by H. C. Chang as "The Clerk's Lady").[73] Moreover, the position of a person in the systems of communication largely determined the manner in which he expressed his attitude toward his lot in life, whatever that attitude may have been. In short, the members of each group defined above had a characteristic sense of where they stood in the great structure of dominance and subordination, and also a distinctive style in which they expressed the ideology that reflected that sense. A group's mentality thus had a characteristic *combination* of content and style—which follows directly and necessarily from the fact that consciousness is shaped both by experience and by words. This, finally, is why the methodology presented above provides a rationale for linking a text and its context, something that is essential for the proper interpretation of any document.

The method of analysis developed in this essay has the additional advantage that it can be combined very effectively with G. William Skinner's regional systems analysis. It is clear, for example, that a wealthy region was liable to have a higher literacy rate and general educational level than an impoverished one, and that in consequence their verbal and intellectual cultures would have differed noticeably. That "women poets were particularly abundant in Kiangsu and Chekiang" in late Ch'ing surely reflects the fact that in those wealthy provinces a higher proportion of women were literate.[74]

Furthermore, in a given region the periphery was likely to have had a higher proportion of poor, and therefore uneducated, people than the core. Thus, the educational level of the bitterly poor Huai-pei area, which was largely peripheral in Skinner's terms, was very low.[75] Moreover, the communication networks were denser in the cores of regions than in their peripheries.[76] A person living in a core area was exposed to a greater variety and volume of messages, both oral and written, than someone living in a remote peripheral area. It seems probable, therefore, that there were systematic differences between "core" and "peripheral" mentalities at all levels of education and literacy. The more frequent occurrence of shamanic healing in the peripheries of certain regions than in their cores in the late nineteenth and early twentieth centuries, reported by Donald Sutton in a recent paper, is an example of such differences.[77] This line of analysis also leads directly to the conclusion—which Skinner regards

---

[73] *Chinese Literature: Popular Fiction and Drama* (Edinburgh: Edinburgh University Press, 1973), pp. 184–204.

[74] Mary B. Rankin, "The Emergence of Women at the End of the Ch'ing: The Case of Ch'iu Chin," in *Women in Chinese Society*, ed. Wolf and Witke (cited n. 62), p. 41.

[75] Perry, *Rebels and Revolutionaries* (cited n. 33), p. 38.

[76] Skinner, *The City in Late Imperial China* (cited n. 40), pp. 216, 281–282.

[77] "Pilot Surveys of Chinese Shamans, 1875–1945: A Spatial Approach to Social History," *Journal of Social History* 15:39–50 (Fall 1981).

with some suspicion but which is borne out by the virtually unanimous testimony, intentional and unintentional, of twentieth-century Chinese urban intellectuals—that there were important differences between urban and rural mentalities.[78] It is interesting to note in this connection that of the two types of White Lotus sect discussed in Susan Naquin's essay, one—the "sutra-recitation" type—was predominantly urban, while the other—the "meditational" type—was largely rural, and that the former made greater use of texts and had a higher proportion of literate members than the latter. (See below, chapter 9.)

The social-cultural analysis employed in this essay also helps us understand more clearly the ways in which ideas and values moved in Ming–Ch'ing China, which is one of the main concerns of this book. Everyone recognizes that the bonds of sympathy on which all persuasion or entertainment depends develop much more quickly between people who occupy similar positions in the structure of dominance and whose cultural levels are comparable.[79] This is usually what we mean when we say of an author or storyteller or preacher that he understands his audience. Having shared their life experiences and education, and thus knowing their needs and expectations, such a person is far better able to reach them than someone to whom their lives are unfamiliar, and whose education has been unlike theirs. Hence, the movement of values or beliefs from one group in Figure 1 to another, quite distant one must almost always have involved the mediation of some of the groups lying in between. If we want to understand how, for example, a Buddhist conception moved, over the course of centuries, from a classical Chinese translation of a Sanskrit text into the consciousness of the average peasant—that Yama was the king of Hell, for instance—the figure will suggest some of the paths that it may have followed on its journey. The same is true for elements of folk religion that became part of elite religious behavior—such as the making of offerings to the *t'u-ti*, the ubiquitous earth gods.

Another, far more important point about the movement of ideas and values in Chinese society follows directly from my main assumptions. It is that as a system of thought, or a religious revelation, or any other creation of the human verbal imagination, spread through Chinese society, it must have come to exist

[78] *The City in Late Imperial China*, pp. 253–269. But see also F. W. Mote's position on this issue, summarized in n. 48, above.

[79] An amusing example of what happens when would-be teachers try to bridge too broad a cultural gap is provided in Judith Berling's essay, when the monk Inner Light tries to explain to a village audience what is meant by "prajñā-pāramitā" (one villager assumes it is a dialect word) and "contemplating the self-existent." (See below, pp. 199–200.) The *Sacred Edict* storytellers who appear in Victor Mair's essay obviously understood their village audiences far better (below, pp. 354–355). P'eng P'ai gives an engrossing account of the difficulties he had in the 1920s, as the educated son of a local landlord, in reaching the peasants with his ideas about peasant unions, and what he did to overcome them. *Seeds of Peasant Revolution* (cited n. 39), pp. 19–26, especially p. 22.

in a number of versions, each produced by or for an important social-cultural group. The principal beliefs and dominant ideas that clustered around the most fearsome and fascinating aspects of human existence—the systems of traditions, precepts, information, and inspiration that we call religion, law, medicine, historiography, science, and the like—were always formulated and transmitted in ranges of related texts (oral and written), from peasant proverbs and tales to learned treatises and sophisticated narratives. To appreciate the true importance for Chinese history of a complex system of thought, such as Neo-Confucianism (or of a less elaborate grouping of ideas, such as the teachings of Lo Ch'ing, or even of a single concept, such as the notion that there is a deity named Ma-tsu), it is essential to study all the versions of it that were produced. These can be treated diachronically or synchronically. Tracing the divergence and amalgamation over time of subtraditions within larger traditions gives what I believe to be the truest picture of the development of Chinese intellectual and religious history. And studying the similarities and differences in the versions of a mature system of thought current in a given era—such as Buddhism in the Sung—is the only way to comprehend what it really meant for Chinese then.

The variations in a system of thought, a story cycle, a religious idea, and so on, are important for another reason: they provide the key to the mentalities of the major social-cultural groups. By studying the verbal material that was specific to a given group, and discovering what the versions of various ideas or systems of thought intended for that group had in common, both in form and content, we will gradually achieve a deeper understanding of that group's collective mentality. And as in time our conception of the whole range of collective mentalities becomes clearer, our comprehension of what they had in common will improve as well, until at last we begin to see what made them all Chinese.

PART II

THREE

Specialists and Written Materials in the Village World

James Hayes

In the old, central part of the industrial town of Tsuen Wan in the New Territories of Hong Kong, in the streets adjoining the market, can be found a number of letter writers. They cater to people who have private business correspondence to attend to or who wish to send a letter to a government department but cannot write or cannot write in the approved style.[1]

I owe the three editors of this volume my appreciative thanks for the care they took before, during, and since the conference in helping me to discern the specialists' role in traditional Chinese society, especially as that role has persisted, owing to the on-going need for specialists' services, in Hong Kong. I am also much indebted to Barbara Ward, who helped me shape this essay; Lynn White III, for obtaining materials I could not find in Hong Kong; Ramon Myers, for his usual incisive and helpful observations; and to Richard J. Smith, who shares my obsessions with the subject matter and himself makes no small contribution to the wider study. My special thanks go to my late father-in-law, Wong Kwan-pui 黃君沛, who died in October 1979, aged 81. It was he who furthered my understanding of the link between the great poets of T'ang and Sung and the common people, and the extent of their attachment to their culture. He was not in good health, but took a great interest in my attempts to learn, and gave valuable assistance and tolerant, kindly encouragement, which are keenly missed.

In this essay, I have not discussed medical specialists and their texts. This is a substantial omission, given the wealth of printed and manuscript material available on the Hong Kong book market. Though I have collected such items for the Kwangtung Archive at the Center of Asian Studies, University of Hong Kong, this field is a specialized one in which I am not qualified to write, and its place in the literature of popular culture must be left to others to determine.

The interested reader is referred to three other works by the author on the subjects discussed in this essay: "Popular Culture in Late Ch'ing China: Printed Books and Manuscripts from the Hong Kong Region," *Journal of the Hong Kong Library Association* 7 : 57–72 (1983); the Chinese book lists to go with it are published in *Journal of the Hong Kong Branch, Royal Asiatic Society* (hereafter *JHKBRAS*) 20 : 168–83 (1980) (published 1983). My book, *The Rural Communities of Hong Kong: Studies and Themes* (Hong Kong: Oxford University Press, 1983), contains both old and new material from fieldwork.

[1] Information derived from a survey undertaken in 1981 by staff of the District Office, Tsuen Wan, New Territories Administration. The types of letter most in demand, after family letters to

The men who find full- and part-time employment in this way are the survivors of an old tradition of service. They are a direct link with the specialists in letter writing and social protocol who, until comparatively recently, could be found in every market town and village in the Hong Kong area. They are also part of the larger body of specialists described in this essay, who played a major role in transmitting vital elements of Chinese culture from one generation to another and ensuring that diverse elements in the Chinese cosmos maintained harmonious relationships.

This essay concerns such men and their stock of written materials, both printed and handwritten. It has been prepared in the face of considerable disadvantages. In the seventy years since the fall of the Ch'ing, and especially in the last forty years, events unfavorable to the preservation of records include the Japanese military occupation of Hong Kong from 1941 to 1945[2]; the massive postwar redevelopment of the New Territories by the Hong Kong government; and the modernization or replacement of many old houses by their private owners in places not affected by general redevelopment. In Southeast China as a whole, the stock of written material must surely have been reduced by the wars and the local disturbances of 1911–1949, and by the upheavals and destruction that have accompanied political action at various times since 1949.[3] Finally, everywhere in the region, climatic conditions and the ravages of insects must have ruined or destroyed many books and papers.[4]

Handwritten materials are, of course, no less vulnerable to these hazards than printed books, and to me it is significant that they have survived at all.

China, were those to the Hong Kong government's housing department on various aspects of its work in housing large numbers of the population.

[2] The Japanese wartime occupiers are blamed for all manner of destruction, ranging from the Hong Kong government's prewar files and records, to private documents of all kinds and even to large and venerable trees in the villages. They are overconvenient scapegoats for losses of all kinds of valuable material, though I suspect that little could be laid directly at their door. Indirectly, however, the fears they engendered did lead to much destruction, as recorded in note 4 below.

[3] See, for instance, Lo Hsiang-lin, "The Preservation of Genealogical Records in China," in *Studies in Asian Genealogy*, ed. Spencer J. Palmer (Provo: Brigham Young University Press, 1972), pp. 50–51, 55.

[4] As my friend and former senior colleague K. M. A. Barnett (Hong Kong Administrative Service 1933–1969, District Commissioner, New Territories 1954–1958) wrote to me with special reference to the wartime Japanese occupation of Hong Kong, "many New Territories families were afraid to retain written records. In the Clearwater Bay area, the *zrukpoo* (*tsûk-pó*; in Mandarin, *tsu-p'u*) of the Lraw (Lōh) and Lreonq (Leūng) clans were buried and I was present when the Zrukzeorng (*tsûk-cheúng*; in Mandarin, *tsu-chang*) of the Lraw clan dug up his to find that damp and vermin had shredded it. With the *zrukpoo* were several $100 banknotes and I was able to get the bank (Hong Kong and Shanghai) to replace them, because the numbers could be made out; but the notes resembled red lace." (Romanization is in Barnett-Chao system of Cantonese, with Meyer-Wempe form in parenthesis.) A vivid description of adverse conditions in a matshed government office in the New Territories, with their effect upon the records, is given in a long minute by Cecil Clementi to the Honourable Colonial Secretary of Hong Kong dated 6 July 1906 (Colonial Secretary's Office (CSO) 1624/06 in the Public Records Office, Hong Kong).

Their endurance can only be attributable to the great store their owners set by them. In considering them, and the specialists to whom they belonged, this essay represents no more than a preliminary notice of a very wide and potentially important field of enquiry. If these handbooks can be collected in sufficient numbers and variety, they will represent a new body of research material that has much to add to our conception of traditional Chinese society in the countryside and its social and political organization. It is with great satisfaction that I can report that intensive collecting work of this kind is being undertaken by a group of my friends in the Chinese University of Hong Kong.[5]

I obtained the material for this essay from fieldwork and discussions with old residents as well as from general collecting, and it has seemed useful to provide an account of the base area in which I made local investigations. I chose my workplace, the former small market center of Tsuen Wan with its surrounding villages, for the quite practical reasons detailed below.

TSUEN WAN AND THE NEW TERRITORIES

Tsuen Wan is located in the western New Territories, close to present-day urban Kowloon. The district includes neighbouring Kwai Chung and the adjacent inhabited islands of Tsing Yi and Ma Wan.[6] At the 1911 census of the colony of Hong Kong the Tsuen Wan district had a population of 2982 persons,[7] of which 2249 were Hakka and 530 were Punti. With the exception of those residing in the market village, all were rural dwellers living in a score of isolated, self-managing communities of one or more lineages, with populations ranging from several tens to several hundreds. The villages had their own institutions: among them ancestral halls (one or more for every settled lineage, however small), community temples in the four geographical parts of the subdistrict, a dozen schools, and a considerable number of landholding trusts.

[5] The collection effort began in 1978 with a survey of historical tablets: see *JHKBRAS* 19:192–194 (1979). I began the quest for manuscript handbooks and am continuing the search in areas where I have village friends. However, this search has been greatly extended and more intensively conducted by Dr. David Faure and his colleagues at the Chinese University of Hong Kong, with the help of two of my fellow district officers, Dr. Patrick Hase in Shatin and Mr. Chan Sui-jeung in Sai Kung. Material is coming in fast for photocopying, and some has been bound and deposited in the public library at Hong Kong's city hall.

[6] *A Gazetteer of Place Names in Hong Kong, Kowloon and the New Territories* (Hong Kong: Government Printer, n.d. but 1960), pp. 148–154; for miscellaneous information on old Tsuen Wan, see my notes in *JHKBRAS* 16:282–283 (1976); 17:168–179, 183–198, 216–218 (1977); 19:204–216 (1979). See also my article "Chinese Clan Genealogies and Family Histories: Chinese Genealogies as Local and Family History," in *Asian and African Family and Local History* (Salt Lake City: Corporation of the President of the Church of Jesus Christ of Latter Day Saints, 1980), vol. 11.

[7] *Sessional Papers 1911* (Papers presented to the Legislative Council of Hong Kong, 103) (21, 26, and 36). Closer investigation of the census returns increases these numbers, since the population of certain villages listed on 29 under Au T'au District and on 35 under Tai Po District would have to be added.

In this area, in late Ch'ing, the villagers depended for their livelihood upon a farming economy based on two annual rice crops and upon coastal fishing from small boats and stake nets operated from the shore. They supplemented their income by cutting grass and firewood to sell in Hong Kong and Kowloon, and many families also made bean curd and bean stick to sell in the urban areas. There were some rural industries, such as distilling, fruit preserving, preparing fish paste and soya sauce, manufacturing lime for the building industry, and making incense powder. In the market street, there were general shops and a number of specialists, including persons who built and repaired houses, made agricultural tools, and rendered various other services to the local population.

All these villages were fairly typical of settlements in the New Territories, but there was nonetheless a considerable diversity of settlement in the Hong Kong region. Tsuen Wan was one of the smaller and later settled subdistricts, not to be compared with those around the larger market centers of Yuen Long and Tai Po in the northern New Territories, or with the coastal market centers and boat anchorages of Cheung Chau and Tai O. At the 1911 colony census, these places had land and boat populations of 3964 and 2248, and 4422 and 5413 respectively, while the total recorded resident land population of the whole New Territories (excluding New Kowloon) was given as 80,622.[8] Many of the men were working abroad or on ocean-going steamships.

THE CATEGORIZATION OF RELEVANT MATERIALS

From the stock of materials that has come to my notice from the New Territories and elsewhere, the books and miscellaneous papers potentially accessible to families in the local villages and market towns of the Hong Kong region fall into three main categories: various types of books and handbooks; books provided for and by specialists; and written materials providing the cultural and social context of daily life. As I shall attempt to show, this last set of materials constituted a fund of original sources remarkable for its richness and intensity. Together, these three categories of written materials constituted the corpus of "literary" influences that, in varying degrees of presence and effect, attached themselves to Chinese rural and town life in late Ch'ing Kwangtung.

BOOKS AND HANDBOOKS

The following items fall under the heading of books and handbooks:
1. Genealogical records
2. Handbooks of family and social practice
3. Almanacs

---

[8] *Sessional Papers 1911:* 103 (26 and 38). The floating population of Tai O is included in the Lantau figure.

4. Collections of couplets for every occasion
5. Educational texts, including classics, primers and other aids to literacy
6. Guides to letter writing, simple and literary
7. Guides to contract forms
8. Encyclopedias of daily use containing a wide range of materials drawn from the preceding categories
9. Ballads
10. Popular poetry
11. Novels and stories relating to behavior and its relevance to good or bad fortune
12. Morality books (including books about the deities worshipped in the popular religion)

Although much of this material was printed, there is increasing evidence that a good deal was also kept in manuscript. I shall now briefly describe the various types listed here.

1. Genealogical Records

Many Kwangtung lineages had lineage records (*chia-p'u*), mostly kept in manuscript. The Tsuen Wan subdistrict of the New Territories is a fairly typical case. Among its fifty long-settled lineages, which today vary in size from several tens of persons to between six to seven hundred, more than half have genealogies. Twelve more state that they possessed them until the time of the Japanese occupation, 1941–1945, but that they either lost or destroyed them before or during that time. All but two of these genealogies, both those extant and those only recalled, are in manuscript and many of them are clearly old, at least in origin. The longest handwritten record consists of 136 pages and the shortest consists of about 10.[9]

These records were normally kept by elders in the various branches of the lineage, and were not available for everyday consultation. However, their existence was probably known to all, which is why, in 1901, E. H. Parker, the British sinologue-consul, was able to state (with a pardonable degree of exaggeration) that "the commonest Chinaman can trace his descent back by memory for from 200–500 years, or even more by referring to his 'genealogy' book at home."[10]

The genealogy's main purpose was to serve as a basic reference to enable families to organize themselves in venerating the ancestors. These records brought together all kinds of information on lineage members and lineage property. The genealogies contain a greater or lesser number of names and descent lines and provided a varying range of material about (mostly) male persons in past generations. Information on ancestral halls and lineage land,

---

[9] "Chinese Clan Genealogies and Family Histories," pp. 4–5.
[10] E. H. Parker, *John Chinaman and a Few Others* (London: John Murray, 1901), p. 70.

the location and geomantic data of the main tombs, worshipping practices and requirements, schools, academic or purchased degrees, the official ranks or titles held by members in past generations, and the rules governing conduct within the lineage all had their place in a genealogy.[11] Thus, genealogies served to heighten the general awareness of the lineage as an institution and to strengthen the family ethic. Naturally, the vast amount of information to be found in the large printed productions of wealthy clans is not usually matched in the smaller, hand-copied works possessed by local lineages, but contents do vary considerably and one cannot generalize with complete accuracy.

Many genealogies contain rules for the behavior of lineage members. These were considered to be of such importance for the continuance of the lineage that in some families they were given special attention, published separately, and included in printed collections of material on the subject. A famous early example was the *Family Instructions for the Yen Clan* (*Yen-shih chia-hsün*) published as early as the sixth century.[12] A more recent instance is the *Maxims for Family Management* (*Chih-chia ko-yen*) of Chu Pai-lu (Chu Yung-ch'un) of the early Ch'ing, sometimes condensed into a one hundred character essay whose text I have seen repeated in scrolls and paintings to this day. Ssu-yü Teng, the translator of the Yen *Instructions*, has listed other types of material in his introduction to that work.[13]

It is hard to exaggerate the importance of this general body of material for the ancestral cult. This material serves to inculcate ethical values and obedience in families and individuals and, by extension, to encourage and maintain conformist attitudes toward all levels of government, in its private or public forms.[14] This powerful function helps to explain the numbers of genealogies of all types that were produced, some of which are still available today though the social circumstances have changed vastly.

However, expressing rules of conduct was not the only reason for compiling the genealogies. There is detectable in all instances a strong drive towards the well-being of the living that also helps to explain the survival of the practice.

---

[11] Hsien-chin Hu, *The Common Descent Group in China and its Functions* (New York: Viking Fund, 1948); and Hui-chen Wang Liu, *The Traditional Chinese Clan Rules* (New York: J. J. Augustin, 1959), especially pp. 7–13 and chap. II.

[12] Ssu-yü Teng, *Family Instructions for the Yen Clan, An Annotated Translation with Introduction* (Leiden: Brill, 1966).

[13] Ibid., p. x.

[14] These attitudes were perhaps most powerfully and economically expressed in the texts of grave tablets to the deceased. I have one from the Tsuen Wan district, dated in the Hsien-feng reign (1851–1862), which, in its 120 characters, serves as the epitome of the kind. Emphasis on the family and the duty of submission to parental authority was, as Sir George Staunton stated in 1810, a "vital and universally operating principle of the Chinese government," which "continues to this day [to be] powerfully enforced, both by positive laws, and by public opinion." From his *Ta Tsing Leu Lee; being The Fundamental Laws, and a Selection from the Supplementary Statutes of the Penal Code of China* (reprint ed. Taipei: Ch'eng-wen, 1966), pp. xviii–xix.

This tendency can be illustrated by an interesting and, I think, little known offshoot of the genealogy, one that was common, and in some cases can still be found, among ordinary families, land and boat dwellers alike. The phenomenon consists of a red cloth square marked with black ink characters giving the date and time of birth of all family members. This cloth was drawn up for a man and woman at the time of their marriage, with children's names and other details about them being added as they were born. I have heard such cloths described as genealogies (*kang p'ó*; in Mandarin, *keng-p'u*) by several families possessing them, and colloquially as *mēng tsź p'ó* (in Mandarin, *ming-tzu p'u*) or as name registers.[15] However, their main purpose was undoubtedly to assist with the drawing up of horoscopes for marriage and other occasions when such data were required. In the present context, their interest lies in their being found in very ordinary families, and in the possibility, too, that they might be seen as very modest genealogies and, in small clans of late settlement, as potential beginnings of genealogies proper.

2. *Handbooks of Family and Social Practice*

Handbooks containing descriptions of family and social practices are variously titled *chia-li* and *li-i*. They usually comprise two main sections, dealing with the rites and procedures connected with marriage and with death, respectively, usually entitled *hsi-shih* and *sang-shih*. These are otherwise included in books under the heading *chiao-chi*, with "*ta-ch'eng*" and similar additions to complete their titles.

Printed guides of this kind were quite common. The later books specify both the old and newly introduced practices; the former grow progressively more complex and tedious as we go back in time, according to their compilers.[16] Manuscript versions are also common, and families had their own handwritten guides. They were generally available in even small villages and, in the hands of a few persons, were used to draw up the necessary cards and documentation for occasions such as marriages, deaths, and so on. A detailed investigation of the handwritten books would show whether they were merely copied from the printed handbooks or whether they described local and particular family practices. From a random reference in one of the local village books on how to greet a *chü-jen*, or senior degree holder—rather an unlikely event, I would have

---

[15] Those seen have come from Hong Kong Island, Lantau, and Tsuen Wan.

[16] The wording of the 1842 preface to Ch'en Ch'in-sheng's 陳琴生 *Chia-li t'ieh-shih chi-ch'eng* 家禮帖式集成 (earlier preface 1770) by an unknown writer implies this. A new style guide to ceremonies prepared during the early period of the Chinese Republic is more forthright. It states that many people are still using the old-fashioned and troublesome forms of ceremony of the Ch'ing dynasty, and that because ceremonial is so important, the government is now trying to formulate a (new) standard system for weddings, funerals, and social intercourse, with the aim of getting rid of extravagance, deceit, and superstition. These, it is clearly implied, are characteristic of the old forms! *Kuo-min jih-yung pai-liao ch'üan shu* 國民日用百料全書 [Encyclopedia of daily use for the people of the (Chinese) Republic] (Shanghai: Kuang-i shu-chü 廣益書局, 1930), *chüan* 4, p. 1.

thought—it would seem that a certain amount of indiscriminate copying from printed books was being done! Written material was used in connection with all kinds of family occasions: funerals, weddings, birthdays in later life, and the celebrations that took place one month after the birth of a male child. Papers drawn up on these occasions list the persons attending and note the presents or amounts of money they have given. I have seen examples from the rural community of Tsuen Wan. The printed eulogies sometimes prepared for the funeral services of men and women in elite and merchant families as well as some rural leaders also fall into this category.[17] Such documents are occasionally found in second-hand book stalls, but as they are privately printed productions for distribution rather than sale they are usually kept at home, where they readily fall victim to the hazards that beset all printed materials in times of rapid change.

3. Almanacs

Kulp states, "Among all the printed books of the village at the present time, the almanac is the most important."[18] Almanacs are undoubtedly among the commonest books to be found in local towns and villages, and I have seen them frequently in shops and old houses. My local informants' estimates of their distribution and availability varied; some said that "practically every family bought one annually," others that "only a few households would purchase them." Some said that copies would often be given free by shopkeepers to their regular customers at the lunar new year. Most added that, whether bought or provided, the almanacs would be made available to others, and that their simpler contents were therefore generally known to all.[19] The almanac's main purpose was, of course, to indicate lucky and unlucky days.

In his major mid-nineteenth century work, *The Middle Kingdom*, S. Wells

[17] These are described as *foô mān* or *noî sz lûk* in Cantonese.

[18] Daniel H. Kulp II, *Country Life in South China, The Sociology of Familism* (New York: Columbia University Press, 1925), pp. 278–279. In Kwangtung the almanac is known by the name *T'ung shìng*. Strictly speaking, it should be *T'ung shue*, but this has been changed in popular usage because the correct character carries the same sound as that meaning "to lose" (sc. at gambling), which would never do, especially at the start of a new year.

[19] The informants were mostly Tsuen Wan villagers. An idea of the contents of the almanac is given in Adele M. Fielde, *Pagoda Shadows, Studies of Life in China* (Boston: Corthell, 1884), p. 79; Mrs. J. G. Cormack, *Everyday Customs in China* (Edinburgh: Moray Press, 1935), chap. 1; Juliet Bredon and Igor Mitrophanow, *The Moon Year: A Record of Chinese Customs and Festivals* (Shanghai: Kelly and Walsh, 1927), pp. 13–17; Robert K. Douglas, *China*, 2nd ed., rev. (London: Society for Promoting Christian Knowledge, 1887), pp. 299–310. The almanac was also used to choose a lucky date for beginning a child's education; see Irene Cheng, *Clara Ho Tung: A Hong Kong Lady, Her Family and Her Times* (Hong Kong: Chinese University of Hong Kong, 1976), pp. 66–67; and K. M. A. Barnett, "The Measurement of Elapsed Time in Hong Kong: The Chinese Calendar; Its Uses and Value," in *Some Traditional Chinese Ideas and Conceptions in Hong Kong Social Life Today*, ed. Marjorie Topley (Hong Kong: Hong Kong Branch, Royal Asiatic Society, 1967), pp. 36–53, especially 48–50.

Williams states that the almanac

> is annually prepared at Peking, under the direction of a bureau attached to the Board of Rites, and, by making it a penal offence to issue a counterfeit or pirated edition the government astrologers have monopolized the management of the superstitions of the people in regard to the fortunate or unlucky conjunctions of each day and hour.... [passages omitted in original]. Two or three editions are published for the convenience of the people, the prices of which vary from three to ten cents a copy. No one ventures to be without an almanac, lest he be liable to the greatest misfortunes, and run the imminent hazard of undertaking important events on black-balled days.[20]

Despite these remarks, the copies to be found in Hong Kong market towns and villages are not the authorized, officially prepared editions described by Wells Williams, but are copies that were compiled and published annually in Canton, Fo-shan, or Hong Kong itself. Besides including the usual astrological forecasts and information on charms and such matters as the "Twenty-four Examples of Filial Piety," Chu Pai-lu's *Maxims for Family Management* (mentioned above), and the Hundred Family Names, the local almanacs could also contain practical advice. An example of the latter is the "Manual for Apprentices in Trade" included in a Fo-shan almanac of 1905 translated in full by Lien-sheng Yang in his article, "Schedules of Work and Rest in Imperial China."[21] Kulp also styles the almanac "the village textbook in science."[22]

4. Couplets

The large number of printed editions devoted to couplets (*tui-lien* or *lien-yü*), the wide range of subject heads, the inclusion of sections about them in all guides and encyclopedias, the frequency with which collections of couplets are encountered in handwritten village books, and their common use in religious houses, temples and shrines, homes, and boats and shops testify to the importance of couplets as an item in the inventory of written materials used in everyday life. After describing the origins of the couplet in the late T'ang and Five Dynasties, a local schoolmaster friend of mine wrote this for me, knowing my interest:

> Later [couplets] were used for celebrations, sorrows, for the presentation of gifts and in ever-widening uses. There is no rule governing the number of characters or whether the style shall be simple or complex. A good couplet not only delights the

---

[20] S. Wells Williams, *The Middle Kingdom, A Survey of the Geography, Government, Literature, Social Life, Arts, and History of The Chinese Empire and its Inhabitants*, rev. ed. (London: W. H. Allen, 1883), vol. II, pp. 79–80.

[21] Lien-sheng Yang, *Studies in Chinese Institutional History* (Cambridge, Mass.: Harvard University Press, 1963), pp. 36, 38–42. In a Hong Kong book shop, I found a similar woodblock-printed work, issued separately in a cheap edition, undated but from about the same period.

[22] Kulp, *Country Life in South China* (cited n. 18), p. 279.

spirit but encourages virtue. A virtuous couplet educates society and creates benefits for the individuals as it continues the tradition.

The village handbooks I have seen from Tsuen Wan contain lists of couplets for use on many different occasions. One typical example contains 313 couplets of four, five, seven, or eleven characters to the line, seven being the most common. The major groupings are for use at the lunar new year (110), at weddings (56), at funerals (20), in various temples and shrines (37), for a new house (24), for schoolrooms (16), and for shops (12), with other couplets for use on the opera and puppet stages, at raising the roof beam in a new house, and at the opening of new ancestral halls. Handwritten books from elsewhere in Tsuen Wan and other subdistricts of the New Territories repeat this wide variety and help to make clear the widespread use and popularity of couplets in the Hong Kong region. The books collected so far come from villages, but there is every reason to think that they were present in the market towns, with perhaps some printed ones available there also.

The relationship between printed and handwritten collections of couplets is close, as their contents are often similar or identical to each other, but my village friends agree that it is more likely that the handwritten ones were transmitted from older copies than taken directly from the printed compilations. Moreover, the former often contain couplets for specific local use: for example, for display in community temples in each locality and in worshipping village heroes there (described as *hsiang-i yung-lieh shih*).[23]

5. *Educational Texts and Aids to Literacy*

From the number and variety of copies still to be found today, it seems that the Four Books and Five Classics were readily available in cheap red paperback editions, without annotation. These were obviously intended to be learned by rote under the teacher's instructions and bawled out by memory in the famed "backing the book" procedure (whereby the pupil turns his back on the master and recites from memory). There were also annotated printed editions for the

---

[23] Couplets often embody local traditions and history. A good example is given by another schoolmaster, born in 1895, who wrote as follows: "One day when I was young, my attention was attracted by a pair of vertical scrolls which were posted on the gate of the Wai San Tong Family Temple at Ping Shan [near Castle Peak, New Territories of Hong Kong]. The characters on the scrolls read: 'Watch for the dragon which rose from the blue water circling this gate: Listen for the deer which barked in this land at Ping Shan.' I had an uncle then and I asked him if these characters really meant what they said, or if they were just some classical allusions used here for literary style's sake. 'The scrolls', he said, 'were written by . . . a scholar holding the literary degree of *chü-jen*.' Then he began the following story. . . ." See the article in the New Territories Weekly *Hsin-chieh chou-k'an* 新界週刊, 24 March 1962, in which the writer proceeded to explain the meaning of the legend behind the couplet.

An interesting collection of couplets from buildings of the Ch'ing period in the Sha T'ou Chen subdistrict of Nan-hai County of Kwangtung is given at pp. 101–110 of the 36th anniversary bulletin of the Nam Hoi Sha Tau Association, Hong Kong, published by the association in 1964.

benefit of more advanced students and a similar range of editions of such other important educational texts as the *Trimetrical Classic*, the *Thousand Character Classic*, and the *Hundred Names*. More practical primers and word lists were prepared at different times, including the comprehensive modern editions from the later Ch'ing and early Republican periods. These, too, came in very cheap editions. Practically all the copies of the texts in these genres were printed in Canton or Hong Kong. Such productions are well covered in Evelyn Rawski's recent work, and the texts, though not the word lists, were given a good deal of attention by nineteenth-century Western writers in China.[24] My informants have said that such texts, being mainly for school use, could be bought in the Tsuen Wan market street and, of course, in Hong Kong.[25]

6. *Guides to Letter Writing*

Judging by the number of books old and new to be found on the subject, this type of guide was very popular. It was also necessary, in that letters follow a variety of proper forms depending upon the age, sex, and relationship to the writer of the person being addressed. Reverend Hardy recalls an incident mentioned by the Abbé Huc that illustrates this point rather aptly. While residing in South China, Huc was about to send a messenger to Peking. Knowing that the local schoolmaster came from Peking, Huc asked him whether he wished to send a letter to his mother. Huc expressed surprise when a boy was instructed to write the letter, and in response the schoolmaster said, "For more than a year [this boy] has been studying literary composition, and he is acquainted with a number of elegant formulae; how then could he not know how a son should write to a mother?"[26]

[24] Evelyn Sakakida Rawski, *Education and Popular Literacy in Ch'ing China* (Ann Arbor: University of Michigan Press, 1979), pp. 46–52, 125–139, and Wells Williams, *The Middle Kingdom*, I, 526–541, 572–577.

[25] The Tsuen Wan market street was not very large. Around 1911 it had about thirty miscellaneous undertakings of which one was a general shop selling simple books for children, mainly of an educational type. However, Hong Kong seems to have been a flourishing book center. The colony census of 1891 listed 57 printers and 122 book binders: "Occupations in Victoria and Villages," *Sessional Papers 1891*, Table XV, p. 394.

[26] Rev. E. J. Hardy, *John Chinaman at Home, Sketches of Men, Manners and Things in China* (London: T. Fisher Unwin, 1907), p. 205. Many letter forms in Chinese and English translation can be found in S. Wells Williams, *Easy Lessons in Chinese or Progressive Exercises to Facilitate the Study of that Language Especially Adapted to the Cantonese Dialect* (Macao: Office of the Chinese Repository, 1842), pp. 210–220. See also James Summers, *A Handbook of the Chinese Language Parts I and II Grammar and Chrestomathy* (Oxford: University Press, 1863), part II, pp. 32, 89–91. Translations of other model letters, to and from a go-between for the marriage of a child, and to and from scholars by purchase and examination, are given by Mrs. Arnold Foster, *In The Valley of the Yangtze* (London: London Missionary Society, 1899), pp. 45–46, 62–63. The passion for letter-writing manuals was carried into the English language in such ports as Shanghai and Hong Kong, where smart boys desiring employment with Western firms made much use of them; see Carl Crow, *400 Million Customers* (New York: Pocket Books, 1945), pp. 72–77.

These books included many letter forms for use between relatives on both the male and female side and across three generations, between friends, and between business associates. The subject matter covered births, marriages, deaths, birthdays. Specimen letters from and to sons studying away from home were supplied, as were samples on borrowing money, asking for employment, entering apprenticeship, and many more topics of a most varied nature. The guides also provided the titles of address to be used for the recipients and by the writers. The female side is more prominent in these books than might be expected.

A typical example of a letter-writing guide is the "revised and newly augmented" guide entitled *Hsin-tseng ch'ih-tu ch'eng-hu ho-chieh*. It was published in Canton in 1895, but apparently first issued in 1886, and consists of 167 double pages of woodblock text. My copy has been marked throughout in red ink, indicating careful study. The earliest Kwangtung work I have found in my collecting to date is the *Chiang-hu ch'ih-tu fen-yun ts'o-yao ho-chi*, in various printings, and with preface dated 1782.[27] Similar material is also available in appropriate sections of the encyclopedias and general guides.

Letter forms had apparently been both highly stylized and elaborate in this period and earlier, and the first years of the Chinese Republic saw a reaction against these tendencies. As with the guides to *chia-li*, compilers of new guides to letter writing contrasted their simpler and more straightforward styles with the complicated format of earlier times.[28]

Besides these popular guides, there are the many pieces, mainly letters, written by famous scholars and writers across the ages (*ch'ih tu*, "sample compositions"). These are literary productions, full of allusions and written in elegant style. They are often difficult to understand, but usually contain explanatory notes. Despite their highly literary nature, these pieces were none-theless part of the popular culture, since some teachers used them in their schools, even if merely asking their better pupils to learn an essay here and there by heart. Thus, some of the writers' names and portions of the more famous prose and poetry became widely known at a humble level.

7. Guides to Contract Forms

Blank contract forms covering a variety of situations are to be found in different types of handbooks, but publications also exist in which all these forms were brought together. I have one such, *Shu-ch'i pien-meng*, dated 1895 and

[27] Much of its contents appear in a later work, *Kai-liang tseng-kuang hsieh-hsin pi-tu* 改良增廣寫信必讀 [Improved, expanded primer for correspondence], available in Canton, Hong Kong, and Shanghai imprints with Hsüan-t'ung and early Republican dates, but I had not until recently connected this with the earlier work described in the text that was used by S. Wells Williams as the basis for his *Tonic Dictionary of the Chinese Language in the Canton Dialect* (Canton: Office of the Chinese Repository, 1856), pp. xi–xii.

[28] See the foreword (undated but, like the *hsu*, probably 1913), entitled "Principles for Editing the Improved Edition," to the *Kai-liang tseng-kuang hsieh-hsin pi-tu*. While much of the earlier content was carried forward, replacements and additions in the new style also appeared.

printed in Shanghai, which includes no less than 84 different forms. This book was reissued under the same title in 1923, with some rearrangement of the contents. Other Shanghai book companies published new and larger collections in the 1930s.

There was a great need for widespread knowledge of these forms. Judging by the volume and variety of documents becoming available, most social and economic transactions in Ch'ing China were apparently documented in writing.[29] In many such cases the writers of these contracts were not parties to the transactions, although, like the middlemen introducing buyer and seller, they were paid for their trouble. My enquiries show that they were likely to be fellow villagers and clansmen, or fellow townspeople, who in drawing up their documents would be guided by local custom and earlier examples.[30] Thus, both the guides (to an unknown extent) and certainly the earlier documents (which were usually passed on to the new purchaser) helped to spread essential knowledge in this vast and vital field. Sometimes account books for certain properties carry the text of the purchase document for ease of reference, and I have found blank forms scribbled in notebooks and on empty spaces in genealogies and other books, indicating widespread use.

8. Encyclopedias of Daily Use (General Handbooks)

The printed handbooks that served as encyclopedias of daily use were apparently quite common in the late imperial and early Republican periods. Their purpose was to provide the rudiments of what was deemed to be useful knowledge across a wide range of activities. None dated earlier than the Ch'ien-lung reign have come to my notice through collecting in local book stores, but we know from library collections that they existed in the early part of our study period.[31] The Ch'ien-lung publication Ch'ou-shih chin-nang, in six ts'e (preface

---

[29] See Fu-mei Chang Chen and Ramon H. Myers, "Customary Law and the Economic Growth of China During the Ch'ing Period," Ch'ing-shih wen-t'i 3.5 and 3.10 (November 1976 and November 1978) for examples. Upon reflection, it seems obvious that the variety and complexity of Chinese economic and social relationships must have been based on a large stock of written material even at the ordinary levels of society, from the baby girl handed over to a religious house (with a red deed of disposal to prove it) to the sworn brotherhood between men of different clan names (with a document to show it) to the complex divisions of family property or the sale of land (again, with documentary proof and—a feature of all deeds—witnesses to prove the genuineness of the transaction in case things went wrong).

[30] James Hayes, The Hong Kong Region 1850–1911: Institutions and Leadership in Town and Countryside (Hamden, Conn.: Archon-Dawson, 1977), pp. 124–135.

[31] Ch'iu K'ai-ming has described and analyzed sixty-five Ming encyclopedias and reference works from the Ssu-k'u Catalogue in "Ha-fo ta-hsueh Ha-fo Yen-ching hsueh-she t'u-shu-kuan ts'ang Ming-tai lei-shu kai-shu" 哈佛大學哈佛燕京學社圖書舘藏明代類書概述 [An annotated catalogue of Ming encyclopedias and reference works in the Chinese-Japanese Library of the Harvard-Yenching Institute at Harvard University], Ch'ing-hua hsüeh-pao 清華學報, new series 2.2:93–115 (June 1961). He has done the same for another forty-six recorded in the Ssu-k'u Catalogue in "Ssu-k'u shih-shou Ming-tai lei-shu k'ao" 四庫失收明代類書考 [Ming encyclopedias and reference works unrecorded in the Ssu-k'u ch'üan-shu tsung-mu], Journal of the Institute of Chinese Studies of the Chinese University of Hong Kong 2.1:43–58 (September 1969).

dated 1771), seems to have served its purpose so well that it was still being reprinted by Shanghai book publishers at the end of the nineteenth century. I have acquired editions from three separate publishing houses from about that time, adding substance to contemporary complaints about book pirating![32] Another production, very similar in size and style, the *Ying-ch'ou pien-lan*, in eight *ts'e* (1896 preface), published by a fourth Shanghai house the following year, does not seem to have (or does not acknowledge) an earlier version. There are yet others of the kind. All these works carry the full range of subjects that can be found in similar guides produced under new titles in the Republican period. That period also saw a fresh wave of guides, apparently inspired by the constitutional change. Revision of certain sections of these traditional works was made necessary by the existence of new social and literary attitudes among the young and western-educated elite, which in turn influenced parts of the Chinese population in the cities.[33] Each major Shanghai publishing house produced its own, and revised and usually enlarged editions came out every few years.[34]

9. *Ballads*

Wolfram Eberhard has produced an interesting book on a collection of ballads that has been in the ownership of the Munich State Library since 1840. He describes them as follows:

> All these ballads are in the form of poems with seven words per line. Occasionally, a line has more than seven words, and in such cases, two words are pronounced as if they were one single word so that the rhythm is not disturbed. The ballads are printed in or near Canton by publishers which are otherwise known. Most of them are of the same small size which is still used today for ballads; they are printed on low quality paper in wood-cut print, which is often smeared and hard to read. The size of such ballad books is often quite small, consisting of two or three pages only. Some longer ballads are published in a set of small short booklets; sometimes, two very short ballads are printed together in one booklet. All this is still done with ballads in Taiwan.[35]

From the number of ballad books that can still be found in Hong Kong, and from the well-thumbed condition of many of them, it would seem that such

---

[32] See a high official's statement on the subject printed at the front of *Ts'e-hsueh pei-tsuan* 策學備纂, a general encyclopedic compilation in thirty-two *chüan*, printed in Shanghai by the Tien-shih-chai 點石齋 in 1900.

[33] The most common revisions are in the sections dealing with marriage and death, which usually contain both old and new styles of address, format, and rites for readers to follow according to their family's wishes.

[34] See the list of Chinese books in *JHKBRAS* 20 : 168–183 (1980).

[35] Wolfram Eberhard, *Cantonese Ballads (Munich State Library Collection)* (Taipei: Orient Cultural Service, 1972), p. 1. Leung Pui-chee, *Wooden-Fish Books: Critical Essays and an Annotated Catalogue Based on the Collections in the University of Hong Kong* (Hong Kong: Centre of Asian Studies, University of Hong Kong, 1978), is an exhaustive examination of that category of Cantonese ballad known as *mûk-ūe-shue* (in Mandarin, *mu-yü-shu*) "wooden-fish books".

books were extensively distributed and widely used. Indeed, one of the Canton publishers also set up business in the British colony.[36]

Ballads were especially favored by women. Kulp states that in Phenix Village (northeast Kwangtung) "the women like to gather in a reading circle and listen to one of their number 'sing' ballads. These ballads are in simple and rhythmic popular language, especially designed for women to read or sing."[37] In late imperial China, ordinary men and women led a virtually separate social existence, even in the villages, it seems. Writing in the 1920s, Cheng Tien-fang could state (again, with special reference to Kwangtung),

> There is no social life between men and women in the village. The custom and the ethical teaching of the Chinese are that men and women, unless they are members of the same family, should keep apart as much as possible; so even the male and the female members of the same class never join together in a party, a feast, or a celebration. In making calls, extending congratulations or consolations, the men visit the men and the women visit the women.[38]

The same division is reflected in the written forms of social intercourse listed in the handbooks.

10. Popular Poetry

Kulp uses the term "popular poetry" to refer specifically to the *Three Hundred Poems of the T'ang* and the *"Thousand Poets" Anthology* (a Sung collection). Judging by the copies I have seen, cheap editions of T'ang poetry were commonly available in nineteenth-century Canton, locally printed and seemingly widely distributed, and cheap editions of this poetry have a good circulation even today. In Tsuen Wan and elsewhere in the New Territories of Hong Kong, old men say that these were among the remembered books of their boyhood, and verses are still to be seen on the walls of many of the surviving old ancestral halls, houses, and schools. There was, as noted by Lin Yutang, a strong connection between popular poetry and the couplets described in subsection 4 above, since "in the 'T'ang poems' . . . in a verse of eight lines, the middle four lines must perforce be in the form of two couplets. And [he adds] good lines of poetry should be popular because every perfect line should have a melody and inevitableness of expression besides the thought, like a proverb."[39]

[36] For an account of Wu-kuei T'ang see Leung, *Wooden-Fish Books*, pp. 253–256.

[37] Kulp, *Country Life* (cited n. 18), p. 279.

[38] Cheng Tien-fang, *Oriental Immigration in Canada* (Shanghai: Commercial Press, 1931), pp. 17–18. This separation was reflected in the design and layout of mission churches in China. J. A. Turner, *Kwang Tung or Five Years in South China* (London: S. W. Partridge, c. 1894), p. 38, writing of the Wesleyan chapel at Tsang Sha, Canton, states that "a partition runs down the middle, to screen off the women from the view of the men, according to Chinese ideas of propriety."

[39] Lin Yutang, ed., *The Wisdom of China and India* (New York: Random House, 1942), p. 1092. This explains why so many couplets by T'ang and Sung poets are listed under the heads for use on various occasions in, e.g., Wang Yen-lun 王言論 et al., *Jih-yung pai-k'o ch'üan-shu* 日用百科全書, 2 vols. (Shanghai: Commercial Press, 1919–1920), vol. I, *p'ien* 15, pp. 20–30.

11. *Novels and Short Stories*

Novels and short stories were said to be common, at least in the larger towns and cities. Wells Williams refers to them as "the chief type of books found along the street,"[40] presumably referring to those sold by the hawkers who appear, along with other types of workers, in the earlier Western books and pictures describing Chinese trades.[41] However, I have not found any novels and short stories in my enquiries in the villages so far, though they are plentiful enough in the second-hand book stalls and shops in the city. Elderly villagers do mention the titles of famous books such as the *Romance of the Three Kingdoms, Water Margin, Journey to the West*, the *Investiture of the Gods* and similar great novels.[42] But where they may have existed these books seem to have become casualties of war, climate, and change, being (in cheap printings) more fragile and probably less treasured than the handbooks.

The villagers make no mention of other novels, particularly of those purport-

[40] Wells Williams, *The Middle Kingdom*, vol. I, p. 692.

[41] George Henry Mason, *The Costume of China, Illustrated by Sixty Engravings with Explanations in English and French* (London: Printed for W. Miller, 1800), includes itinerant booksellers. See also M. Bertin and M. Breton's *China: Its Costumes, Arts, Manufactures etc. Translated from the French* (London: J. J. Stockdale, 1812), vol. II, p. 10: "China has its booksellers' shops and warehouses like those of Europe: the subject of this [print] is a stall or pedlar bookseller; he does not deal in classical books, but in tales and songbooks for the lower orders." See also Jules Arène, *La Chine Familière et Galante* (Paris: Charpentier et Cie., 1876), pp. 5 ff; and Rawski, *Education and Popular Literacy* (cited n. 24), pp. 11–12.

[42] By way of comparison, an interesting list of twenty-three books from which Peking storytellers took their stories is included at appendix 7, p. 475, in Sidney D. Gamble, *Peking: A Social Survey* (New York: George H. Doran, 1921). Three articles by Stewart Culin (all made available to me by Lynn White III) on the life of the ordinary Chinese in the United States in the 1880s provide useful information on their reading material, customs, and amusements. These are as follows: "Popular Literature of the Chinese Laborers in the United States," *Oriental Studies: A Selection of Papers Read before the Oriental Club of Philadelphia, 1888–1894* (Boston: 1894), pp. 52–62; "Customs of the Chinese in America," *Journal of American Folk-Lore* 3.10:191–200 (July–September, 1890); and "The Gambling Games of the Chinese in America," *Publications of the University of Pennsylvania*, Series in Philology, Literature and Archaeology, 1.4:1–17 (1891). The first of these indicates that "romances, dramas and song books constituted the greater part of the Chinese literature current among the Chinese laborers in the United States, and that the remainder came from the 'folk literature,' including books on divination and other means of fortune telling, fhe 'white pigeon lottery,' use of the abacus, medicine, school texts, history and dictionaries, and letter-writing guides" (including the book cited n. 27). See also Alvin P. Cohen, "Notes on a Chinese Workingclass Bookshelf," *Journal of the American Oriental Society* 96.3:419–430 (July–September 1976).

Besides handbooks, two "libraries" have been discovered by the History Project team. One (1981) belonged to a "rich peasant" type of villager in the small outlying village of Hoi Ha in North Sai Kung. The other (1982) came from a family in the market village of Hoi Pa, Tsuen Wan. There are more than three hundred books in the first collection, and more than one hundred in the latter. The Hoi Ha books have been catalogued by Dr. Patrick Hase with a view to publication, and the Hoi Pa collection was presented to the Urban Services Department by its owner; see the illustrated accounts in the English and Chinese language press in Hong Kong for 27 May 1982.

ing to be set in the home province of Kwangtung. Those seen in the book stalls are usually set in a particular time and place, a device that adds to the realism of the tale for the audience. One early twentieth-century printed collection of short stories in my possession, the *Su-hua ch'ing-t'an*, set in different provinces of China, contains the following from places in Kwangtung: brothers quarrelling and going to court over their deceased father's land (see the tale "Seven *Mou* of Fertile Land"); how forecast bad fortune could be altered by good deeds (this story, entitled *Ch'iu Ch'iung-shan*, involves a famous Ming scholar from Hainan island, Ch'iu Chün [1420–1495]); how brothers should not allow bad friends to turn one against the other, and the part played by a loyal wife in reconciling them (see the tale "The Test of Brothers' Love"). Another woodblock collection of stories set entirely in various counties of Kwangtung, *Hsun huan chien*, is mainly concerned with showing how various bad deeds involved their authors in ill fortune, and how good deeds resulted in good fortune or a return to it.[43] (Time has not allowed a check on how many of these stories, if any, are familiar to my informants and others, but it is a task worth the effort. It may, incidentally, be the case that some of these books—especially those with local settings—should be classified as *shan-shu*, or morality books, their purpose being so obviously to edify and improve behavior.)

12. *Morality Books*

The class of books called morality books, which includes books about the deities of the popular religion, was probably in greater supply than the various guides to daily life or even cheaply printed novels. Books and pamphlets stemming from the popular religion, Taoism, and Buddhism, were printed and distributed by monasteries, temples, and religious specialists. Their production was often underwritten by wealthy men and women who turned to religion in their later years as a means of acquiring merit. From various entries in older European and American accounts of China it would appear that such works were plentiful.[44] They were usually distributed by itinerant book sellers, of a type who long predated the nineteenth-century Chinese colporteurs of bibles and tracts for Western missions.

Besides those devoted to Buddhist and Taoist teachings and doctrines, a type of morality book specifically related to the more popular gods, whose images are still to be found in local temples. This type told of the history and miracles attributed to these gods, usually cautioning readers to behave well and perform meritorious deeds. Such books are today often found in local book shops and

---

[43] I have only *chüan* 3–4 of this work.

[44] See Hardy, *John Chinaman* (cited n. 26), p. 206; Fielde, *Pagoda Shadows* (cited n. 19), p. 280; Wells Williams, *The Middle Kingdom*, vol. I, p. 577; and Samuel Beal, *Buddhism in China* (London: Society for Propagating Christian Knowledge, 1884), pp. 4, 96–97, 186ff., 247–248. On the reception of Christian tracts, see Hannah Davies, *Among Hills and Valleys in Western China, Incidents of Missionary Work* (London: S. W. Partridge, 1901), pp. 68, 210, 275; and W. T. A. Barber, *David Hill, Missionary and Saint* (London: Charles H. Kelly, 1903), pp. 115–116.

stalls selling old books.[45] It is also likely that, as occurs nowadays, broadsheets were occasionally issued by temple keepers or trustees giving the same type of information. I imagine that, owing to its importance in the popular religion, this type of literature was still to be found in many villages and small towns in Kwangtung.

SPECIALISTS AND WRITTEN MATERIALS FOR SPECIALISTS

The large class of people I am calling specialists played, if I am not mistaken, a particularly important role in Chinese society. An example comes from the work of the Catholic missionary Charles Rey, who prepared his study of the Hakka language after many years' service in the countryside near Swatow in northeast Kwangtung. Rey chose to draw on the specialists and their lore for some of his chapters, and it is no surprise to find in his pages geomancers, diviners, blind fortune tellers, and the like (as well as the occasional charlatan) conversing with their clients or themselves serving as the subjects of discussion. We are here receiving the very stuff of rural life from an acute observer close to the people.[46]

In the Hong Kong region such persons are to be seen to this day and were very likely found throughout the land in late Ch'ing and Republican times. They could be engaged to exercise their skills on behalf of groups or individuals over a very wide range of situations. If recent observation, augmented by information from books and informants, is any reliable guide, some pursued their specialist occupations full time, and others combined them with their principal means of livelihood.

Two main groups of specialists played a crucial role at the local level— namely, those expert in protective rituals and the manipulation of the forces thought to influence human fate, and those knowledgeable in performing social rites and in the forms of polite intercourse. According to elderly informants from Tsuen Wan, their fellow villagers and townspeople knew well enough how to practice the trades or occupations that supplied them with their livelihood, but they were not so well versed in ritual and ceremonial matters. Yet the former were held to be of crucial importance to safety and well-being in this life as well as the next, while the latter were deemed essential for maintaining a Chinese-style existence.[47]

---

[45] Two typical instances are compilations concerning T'in-haû (T'ien Hou) and Kam-fa (Chin-hua), two popular deities of South China. For titles, see *JHKBRAS* 20:183 (1980).

[46] Charles Rey, *Conversations Chinoises: prises sur le vif avec Notes Grammaticales: Langage Hac-Ka,* reprint of 1937 ed. (Taipei: Chinese Association for Folklore, 1973), pp. v, 244, 414ff., 540ff., 588ff.

[47] Richard J. Smith of Rice University comments, "By late imperial times *li* had come to embrace all forms of sacred and secular ritual, as well as the entire body of social institutions, rituals and regulations, conventions and norms, that governed human relations in China." See his essay "The Cultural Role of Ritual in Ch'ing China" presented to the ACLS–NEH Conference on Orthodoxy and Heterodoxy in Late Imperial China: Cultural Belief and Social Divisions (Montecito, California, 1981).

Specialists Dealing with Human Fate

The group of specialists dealing with human fate is perhaps best introduced by an extract from the autobiography of the Republican scholar and official Monlin Chiang, who makes the following statement about his father's beliefs:

> He believed in *feng shui*, the spirits of wind and water and in fortune telling and therefore—with a sort of fatalism—that a man's life was predetermined by supernatural forces. However, he also believed that by virtuous conduct and clean thinking one could make these forces respond by bestowing blessings upon oneself as well as one's family; thus the predetermined course of life would gradually shift its ground to a better course.[48]

This credo is probably fairly typical for a person of the educated class, but by my observation it might also apply to many of the older generation of villagers today, who had a need to consult specialists in all matters concerning fate and the future.

The written materials dealing with crises and the manipulation of fortune necessarily constitute a very large corpus, given the frequency of disease, the uncertainty of the elements, and the universality of belief in the existence of malevolent spirits and of good and bad influences.[49] Indeed, it was these factors that, taken together, dictated the requirement for one or another of the services offered by the main group of specialists. I wish now to consider this subject under a number of principal heads—namely, *feng-shui*, or geomancy; the preparation and varied use of charms; and divination and fortune telling.

Feng-shui, or Geomancy   The Hong Kong countryside is dotted with graves, and I am told that it was usual to engage geomancers in selecting the place of a coffin burial, and practically obligatory when placing the formal, horse-shoe-type masonry grave of the second, or urn, burial. Lineages and individuals attached the greatest practical importance to *feng-shui* as affecting their good

---

[48] Monlin Chiang, *Tides from the West*, reprint of 1947 ed. (Taipei: China Cultural Publishing Foundation, 1957), p. 29. This attitude towards predeterminism was apparently common all through the long Confucian period. See C. K. Yang's "The Role of Religion in Chinese Society," in *An Introduction to Chinese Civilization*, ed. John T. Meskill (Lexington, Kentucky: D. C. Heath, 1973), pp. 662–663.

[49] See, for instance, J. J. M. de Groot, *The Religion of the Chinese* (New York: Macmillan, 1910), p. 32. "It is a doctrine of the Chinese nation, a dogma, an axiom, an inveterate conviction, that spirits exist, keeping up a most lively intercourse with the living—as intimate almost as that among men. In every respect that intercourse bears an active character. It brings blessing, and evil as well, the spirits thus effectually ruling mankind's fate. From them man has everything to hope, but equally much to fear. As a natural consequence, it is around the ghosts and spirits that China groups her religious acts, with the sole intent to avert their wrath and the evil it brings, and to insure their good-will and help." There is also Mrs. Cormack's two chapters on "The Influence of the Spirit World" and "Spectres and How to Deal with Them", in *Everyday Customs* (cited n. 19), pp. 231–256, and her statement, p. 231, "All who have lived in China and studied the people know how strong and real this influence is. . . . It is a fact that they are bound about with superstitious fear of spirits, spectres and demons, and that they believe these are constantly all about them."

and bad fortune in this life and the hereafter.[50] There was a degree of specialization in this field. Some geomancers concentrated on the *feng-shui* of graves (*yin-chai*), others on the *feng-shui* of houses and buildings (*yang-chai*). Some were specialists in urban as opposed to rural geomancy, and others concentrated on siting wells. The services of all were in frequent demand in the Hong Kong region—and no doubt beyond—not only for such relatively simple concerns as siting, resiting, or rebuilding, but also for correcting *feng-shui* or even for harming or counteracting that of another family or lineage, for the manipulative potential was as strong here as it was in the realm of charms.[51]

Feng-shui emphasized the siting of graves of apical ancestors and the location of ancestral halls, since the good fortune of the living and future descendants was held to depend upon it. Take, for instance, the situation where an ancestral hall was to be rebuilt or resited. In the past, such an event could take place not only when the ruinous state of the old building required a reconstruction, but also when a geomancer advised moving the site or altering the dimensions and orientation of an existing building in order to improve family fortunes. Two such cases, typical of many of the kind, have come to my notice recently, and may serve as examples for present purposes. They are contained in manuscript papers, one in a genealogy[52] and another in a private family notebook entitled *A Record of Correcting Feng Shui* (*Hsiu-kai feng-shui chi*).[53] The former, dated about 1925, refers to a reduction in the dimensions and the re-orientation of an existing building, by a lineage long resident on Tsing Yi Island in the Tsuen Wan subdistrict of the New Territories. The second, from Shun Tak (Shun-te) County, dated 1907–1908, relates that a particular Ho clan had built an ancestral temple in 1450, and for the next 300 years their descendents did not have good fortune. The temple was moved to another location in 1808 by three of the writer's great-grandfathers, but despite this and other measures involving the redirection of an adjacent stream, the family's fortunes were still not sufficiently improved. A further reconstruction was planned in the writer's time, on the advice of another geomancer.

Geomancers' names and places of origin are often mentioned on grave

---

[50] See Stephen D. R. Feuchtwang, *An Anthropological Analysis of Chinese Geomancy* (Vientiane: Editions Vithagna, 1974); M. Freedman, "Geomancy," in *The Study of Chinese Society, Essays by Maurice Freedman*, ed. G. William Skinner (Stanford: Stanford University Press, 1979), pp. 313–333.

[51] Hugh Baker cites an excellent example of "*feng-shui* fighting" in appendix II of his *Chinese Family and Kinship* (London: Macmillan, 1979). The activities of *feng-shui hsien-sheng* and their cousins the *yin-yang hsien-sheng* are recounted by R. F. Johnston in his *Lion and Dragon in Northern China* (London: John Murray, 1910), pp. 118–120, 264–270.

[52] The genealogy of the Chan (Ch'en) lineage of Chung Mei, Tsing Yi, Hong Kong, of which copies are now available in the Chinese Library of the University of Hong Kong and in the Library of the Genealogical Society of Utah (Church of Jesus Christ of Latter Day Saints).

[53] The original notebook is included in the collection of Kwangtung material in the Centre of Asian Studies, University of Hong Kong.

tablets, and local investigation can assist in identifying these people. Generally, my enquiries into geomancers operating in our area showed that they fell into two groups: sought-after itinerants with good reputations from other places, and local persons, usually of the class of schoolmasters and minor local gentry. The latter undertook the work out of interest and the need to have something to do, and, of course, in cases involving requests from their friends and relatives, out of reciprocity and obligation.

Geomancy generated a very large body of writings. To the corpus of published handbooks on all the ramifications of *feng-shui* must be added the perhaps even larger stock—much of it probably now destroyed—of handwritten material. It is certain that over a lifetime's practice, most specialists would have prepared their own notes, some copied from rare or standard works and their own teachers' writings, and others based on their own studies and experience. Some of this material would have been passed on to their disciples in turn. Such papers—individual notebooks or even a complete stock of handwritten and printed works—come onto the market occasionally, but, as with all specialist materials, the numbers that appear in this way provide a guide not to their real extent, but only to their nature and content.

The reason we cannot estimate the numbers of such manuscript books in existence is that those addressing these different skills were mostly not for general circulation. They were private property, and the information they contained was probably closely guarded. Meant for the specialists' own use, they were very likely handed on or allowed to be copied only when a pupil had satisfied his master. In this they strongly resemble the sacred texts of the White Lotus "sutra recitation" sects discussed in this volume by Susan Naquin. Indeed, ordinary people, including family members, probably stood in some awe and even fear of these books.[54] This category of books also includes the specialists' written statements of personal advice produced for individuals and families. These, too, were private and confidential papers that their owners would keep carefully—especially as it was believed that, in the wrong hands, favorable prognostications could be reversed by other specialists.[55] The extent

[54] The family of one of my acquaintances, a seventy-year-old *naăm-mōh-lő* from Ham Tin, Pui O, Lantau Island, burned all his books and papers after his death, before I learned of the event.

[55] This applies especially to astrological forecasts for individuals and ancestral graves, which are usually in manuscript because of their highly individual purpose. Forecasts in fortune telling can be brief or detailed. If the former, they are called *shiù paai* and if the latter *taaî paai*. These records are usually kept confidential, for if another person gets to know the details and is ill-disposed, it is thought that he or she can bring bad luck, illness or even death to the original person by doing something harmful in *feng shui* such as cutting a tree near his or her house, digging a ditch, erecting a pillar, and the like (I am indebted to my friend Anthony Siu Kwok-kin of Hong Kong for this information). Grave descriptions, again, are private documents of concern to individuals, branches, and even whole lineages. They are detailed papers drawn up by a geomancer with regard to the geomantic properties of a particular grave or graves. I have seen only a few during my collecting, but have every reason to think that many more existed.

to which these books and papers were understood by the bulk of their clientele (or in some cases even by the specialists themselves) was, of course, quite another matter, but one of less importance than their existence, transmission, and execution. For the mass, the value of these books lay more in the comforting protection given by, or the promise of continued or new prosperity to be acquired through, the specialists' knowledge and expertise.

The Knowledge, Writing, and Preparation of Charms Even more than geomancy, an expertise regarding charms was probably one of the most sought-after specialist contributions to everyday life. This knowledge was especially demanded in times of crisis, in view of the general belief in malevolent spirits and baleful influences emphasized above. As Mrs. Arnold Foster noted, "the Chinese make a very wicked use of charms. When they hate any one, and wish some evil to happen to him, they get certain kinds of charms which are supposed to be able to cause his death, or, at any rate, to make him ill. . . . Another plan is to buy hurtful charms from a temple."[56] She also mentioned that charms could be counteracted by the use of other charms, bringing in the manipulative action referred to above.[57] A later missionary, J. L. Stewart, described the charms emanating from Taoist priests: "They are made up of ordinary characters, usually greatly distorted or symbolized, with, at times, the image of a god depicted above and his signature below."[58] He also states that Buddhist charms and formulas were often "made from old Sanscrit characters, meaningless in their original but mystic enough to deceive the multitude."[59]

Charms of the former sort are frequently encountered in the handbooks kept by village specialists of the kind known locally as *naām-mŏh-ló*. Some boxing masters of the type known as *Maû-shaan sz-foô* (in Mandarin, *Mao-shan shih-fu*)[60] also hold such items, though in their case the charms are also written on crepe or cloth and worn on the body like sashes or breast pieces, for protection. It is more than likely that such charms have come down from earlier specialists, being transmitted from teacher to pupil through the generations.[61]

---

[56] Mrs. Arnold Foster, *In the Valley of the Yangtze* (cited n. 26), pp. 99–100.

[57] Ibid., p. 100.

[58] James Livingstone Stewart, *Chinese Culture and Christianity* (New York: Fleming H. Revell, 1926), p. 180. Charms formed a regular part of the contents of the almanacs.

[59] Ibid., p. 250.

[60] See Michael R. Saso, *The Teachings of Taoist Master Chuang* (New Haven: Yale University Press, 1978), pp. 128–132.

[61] One *naām-mŏh-ló* who performs protective rites in Tsuen Wan uses a handwritten book left to him by his teacher and dated in the Kuang-hsu reign. At Sheung Ling Pei village, Tung Chung, Lantau Island, the seventy-year-old village representative gave me (1980) a folded slip of red paper, personally copied by him from an older version twenty-five years before, which was used at dedication ceremonies at temples and shrines of the kind known locally as *hoi kwong shān tsẑ* (in Mandarin, *k'ai-kuang shen-tzu*). The first part of the text invited many village deities to the

The provision of charms was an important service for communities as well as for individuals. Specialist practitioners were often called upon by communities when they were thought to be imperiled by evil forces that made themselves felt through the sickness and death of animals and humans. At such times of general alarm, it was the duty of the village leaders to find specialists who could perform protective rites for the community as a whole and bring it back to stability and health. A notable part of these proceedings, known locally as *tán foō*, is the preparation of charms and the placing of them, with due ceremony, at each location for which protection is desired.[62] When they have to be extended roughly every six months, the later rites are known as *nuĕn-foō*, "warming" or renewing the charms.

Judging by the material that is coming to light today, the ritual and charm-writing specialists could be found in most subdistricts and even in many of the larger villages. In an age when communications were limited and slow, the need for a good distribution of personnel was linked not only with the convenience of having specialists at hand, but also with the desirability of having the rituals performed in the local dialect. Specialists in the New Territories were often Hakka or Hoklo as well as Cantonese-speaking.

The persons who prepared charms and carried out protective rituals were undoubtedly of lesser status than the geomancers, considered above, and the diviners, described in the next section. Many seem to have been townspeople and villagers of modest education and social status, though known to all and well-established enough in their occupations. However, both government and the elite society tended to frown on these arts. The provisions of the law enabled officials to deal severely with persons who deluded and excited the multitude or

ceremony, and the second sent them off to their home Heaven (I am grateful to Professor Tanaka Issei for this explanation). Religious specialists had many gods and spirits to deal with in each locality. The village representative of Ha Kwai Chung, Tsuen Wan subdistrict of the New Territories, told me that he had gone round the area when his village was resited in 1964 and had summoned forty-six gods to take up their communal abode in a new shrine (at which, however, there was no outward sign-posting of their presence).

[62] Such ceremonies are described in chapter 13, "Occasional Protective Rites," of my book, *The Rural Communities of Hong Kong: Studies and Themes* (Hong Kong: Oxford University Press, 1983). Great importance is attached to them by village communities.

Other common forms of communal action were the processions to drive away pests or disease from the fields and those connected with the rain-making ceremony in time of drought. Specialists and lay people joined in the action. In a letter dated July 7, 1877, the English missionary David Hill described a rain-making procession at Kuang-chi, Hupeh: "The people have been praying for rain. From neighbouring temples they form processions carrying a great unsightly idol in their midst, with one or two men carrying burning incense and a priest screaming forth some incantation. Those forming the procession are farmers chiefly; each carries a long bamboo branch in his hand, to which is attached a triangular sheet of paper with their prayer written on it. This consists in almost every case of four characters: 'Save the lives of the people, Quickly let rain descend.'" Barber, *David Hill*, p. 140.

subverted good order and discipline in any way.[63] This could apply to geoman-cers and fortune tellers and diviners just as much as to writers of charms.

Divination and Fortune Telling   Divination and fortune telling are other fields of activity for specialists of this group. This is because of the traditional belief that the human being's fate is linked to cosmological influences, and that human life and activities are dominated by them. Stewart states that divination had its origin in the *Book of Changes,* and describes the various accessories, both ancient and modern, needed for it. He adds that the ancient plan of divination forms the seventh division of another of China's oldest classics, the *Book of Documents.* He also condemns the whole, commenting that "the use of stalks and the tortoise shell and the choosing of lucky days thus sanctioned, has paved the way for various superstitions, magic and astrology." [64] Stewart fails to mention either the superior origin and status of the early practitioners,[65] or to accept how widespread and compelling these practices have been ever since the earliest times. However, he differentiates usefully between recourse to specialists for divination and the means whereby individuals can secure advice in the temples, it being the usual practice for written "fortunes" to be made available there in conjunction with the divining blocks (*kaaù pooî* or *shing pooî*) or use of the bamboo cylinder and its slips (*k'aù ch'im*).[66]

All classes in traditional Chinese society required assistance from specialists in fortune telling and divination. These services were always sought in connec-

---

[63] For some of the legal provisions see Staunton, *Ta Tsing Leu Lee* (cited n. 14), pp. 175, 179, 273, 310, and 548–549. See also Derk Bodde and Clarence Morris, *Law in Imperial China Exemplified by 190 Ch'ing Dynasty Cases Translated from the Hsing-an hui-lan* (Philadelphia: University of Pennsylvania Press, 1967), pp. 272–273, 288–290. The existence of double standards in these matters is demonstrated by the differences between public and official attitudes on the one hand and actual practice on the other, for almost everyone, no matter what his social standing, availed himself of the services of the three main types of expert mentioned. (See Parker, *John Chinaman* [cited n. 10], p. 284; and J. O. P. Bland and E. Backhouse, *China under the Empress Dowager* [Peking: Henri Vetch, 1939], pp. 119–120, 123, for the example of the Censor Wu K'o-tu in 1878.) We should perhaps look for a dividing line between those whose expertise was grounded in study, and those at a much lower level of education who were considered to be deluding and cheating the masses. Otherwise, it is hard to explain the existence of the imperially appointed experts who compiled the official almanac, and the strictures against others, such as those who prepared the unofficial but widely circulated almanacs to be found in the provinces.

[64] Stewart, *Chinese Culture* (cited n. 58), pp. 123–129, 218.

[65] See, e.g., Jacques Gernet, *Ancient China from the Beginnings to the Empire* (London: Faber and Faber, 1968), pp. 65, 115.

[66] Stewart, p. 128. I have used Cantonese romanization for the divining blocks and bamboo cylinder used in Hong Kong, since Stewart calls the first "Kwa" (*Kua*) and does not give a term for the other. A most interesting translation of fortune-telling slips for use in Man Mo (Wen-wu) temples has just been published in Hong Kong. See S. T. Cheung, *Fortune Stick Predictions Man Mo Temple* (Hong Kong: Tung Wah Group of Hospitals, 1981) taken from a traditional work. My teacher and friend, Francis S. Y. Sham, has compiled a similar work for Kuan Yin temples, which was also published by the Tung Wah Group of Hospitals, 1983.

tion with marriage, as it was a requirement that the horoscopes of a prospective couple be ascertained and exchanged through the go-betweens handling the negotiations. In ordinary families, the red cloth (*mêng tsz̀ p'ó*) listing the names of family members and their astrological details was, as stated earlier, considered essential, since it provided the basic facts with which to cast horoscopes and thereby gauge the suitability of the marriage partners. In another widespread usage, fortune telling was used to determine the cosmological reasons for sickness and ill-health in order to effect cures.[67]

The arts of divination were also utilized to decide who ought not to be present at ceremonies to pacify spirits, or at marriages, capping ceremonies, and other rituals. It was the usual practice to advise persons of specified ages whose horoscopes were for various reasons unsuited to the occasion to keep away from such events, for fear of bringing harm to themselves and of nullifying the effectiveness of the ritual.[68]

In short, timing was everything in life's pursuits, and even in death's domain. All the many activities for which a lucky start and auspicious stages were desired required prior divination, so there was plenty of work for these people.[69] Thus the related documents, where they can be found, serve to emphasize the importance laid upon fortune telling and indicate the huge size of the clientele for specialists of this group.

We find that many of the practitioners of fortune telling and divination came from the respectable classes. Like the geomancers, many appear to have been scholars who dabbled in such matters in their leisure time, practicing them within their families or circle of personal relationships, producing manuscripts, and publishing new books or commentaries on old works. The profusion of books on these subjects, each of which has had a long history and a great following, may perhaps be explained in this way. Respectability is further evidenced by

[67] See Edward H. Hume, *Doctors East Doctors West: An American Physician's Life in China* (London: George Allen and Unwin, 1949), p. 77.

[68] In *In the Valley of the Yangtze*, Mrs. Arnold Foster writes, "They sometimes say that a certain animal is to be feared [caused by the presence of unsuitable or hostile influences] or avoided at the time of some wedding or funeral. This means that those born under that animal are not to be present at it" (p. 68). This advice is, to my knowledge, still followed in arrangements made for the periodic protective rites held in various communities, or those held for specific reasons on irregular occasions. See, generally, Theodora Lau, *The Handbook of Chinese Horoscopes* (New York: Harper & Row, 1979).

[69] A tablet inside the T'ien Hou temple in Sai Kung Market, New Territories of Hong Kong, records its reconstruction in 1916. "The T'ien Hou temple is situated in the direction of south-east. The demolition of the main building began on the 15th day of the fourth moon of the fifth year of the Republic of China (1916) at 6:15 P.M. auspicious time. The scaffolding was erected on the 18th day of the fourth moon at 6 P.M. auspicious time. The main beam of the main building was placed in position on the 25th day of the fourth moon at 8:20 A.M. auspicious time. . . . The divine image of the God of Earth (T'u Ti) was placed in position on the 30th day of the seventh moon at 10:15 A.M. auspicious time. The rededication ceremony was performed on the 16th day of the eighth moon at 2:15 A.M. auspicious time."

inclusion in, for example, K'ang Hsi's *Imperial Encyclopaedia* (*Ch'in-ting ku-chin t'u-shu chi-ch'eng*), which covers these topics on the section on arts, occupations, and professions (XVII), and provides biographies of famous practitioners.[70] In the case of the diviners and fortune tellers, I am not, of course, suggesting that all were of the same social level, but, since their practice was a literate one, for which a basic knowledge of Chinese systems of astrology and cosmology was required, it was likely to have an enhanced status, especially in the eyes of ordinary folks.[71]

Specialists Dealing with Social Rites and Protocol

I turn now to the second main group, the village specialists performing services connected with social rites and protocol. These included the ceremonies connected with all the events of the family and the individual's life cycle, including the ancestral rites. They also took in the community rites undertaken by leaders in the local temples for the benefit of all residents and for departed village heroes.

There was a great demand for guidance and instruction in ceremonial matters from all classes. The Chinese attached extreme importance to propriety and hence to the formulas relating to such matters. A London Missionary Society worker wrote, in 1908,

> It is indeed true that a very great deal of time and trouble is taken to make the scholars familiar with the laws of propriety. Every schoolboy seems to know how to conduct himself on all occasions. To see them saluting guests in their homes, or

[70] Lionel Giles, *An Alphabetical Index to the Chinese Encyclopaedia Ch'in Ting Ku Chin T'u Shu Chi Ch'eng* (London: British Museum, 1911) under the appropriate heads. A letter-writing compilation published in 1895 but probably considerably older, being described as *Tseng-hsin hsiang-chu*—newly augmented with detailed commentary—includes medicine, astrology, divination, geomancy, physiognomy, writing, art, and printing in *chüan* 4, *chi-i lei* (accomplished arts). The book opens with a list of the occupations encompassed in its title: (*Tseng-hsin hsiang-chu*) *San-pai liu-shih hang ch'ih-tu* (增新詳註)三百六十行尺牘. A useful reminder that these professions or practices could be combined is given in C. Campbell Brown, *A Chinese St. Francis or The Life of Brother Mao* (London: Hodder and Stoughton, 1911), p. 199, which deals with Fukien province in the late nineteenth century. The father of one convert was "geomancer, doctor, idol medium and fortune-teller" in one.

[71] See Holmes Welch's comment on a fortune teller at the Ling Yin Ssu in Hangchow in 1948. Seated at a table with his various aids around him, he seemed "a man of education and varied talent. Divination could be a respected profession in China" (caption of one of the photographs between p. 131 and p. 132 of *The Buddhist Revival in China* [Cambridge, Mass.: Harvard University Press, 1968]). It would be interesting to know if Professor Skinner's theory of "the export of specialized human talent as a maximization strategy pursued by territorial based social systems in late Imperial China" can be applied at the micro (or local) level with the various specialists described here. More research is needed, especially on the geomancers. See G. William Skinner, "Mobility Strategies in Late Imperial China: A Regional Systems Analysis," in *Regional Analysis*, ed. Carol A. Smith (New York: Academic Press, 1976), pp. 327–364.

engaging in any of the many social duties at such times as the New Year Festival, gives one the impression ... that a well-bred lad just knows exactly what to do and exactly when to do it.[72]

Such instances could be multiplied endlessly, and they help to explain the wealth of published handbooks on letter styles and forms of address for all occasions, and the wide range of couplets available, the highest concentration being for use in connection with births, marriages, and deaths. It is significant, however, that the compilers of letter forms and correct address could claim that these were as much needed by scholars as by unlettered people. Without this book, one states in the preface, "even scholars would not know where to turn for advice"; and in another the writer adds that they "do not necessarily know the details of all ceremonies."[73] Is this fact, one wonders, or defensive sales talk?

Certainly the whole group of teachers, letter writers, and other guardians of social etiquette were in universal demand. Elderly village informants from Tsuen Wan state that social ceremonial was closely observed by rural people in the prewar period. As one of them put it, "the correct forms of address (*ch'ing foo*; in Mandarin, *ch'eng hu*) were taken very seriously, and the divisions between generations and grades of relationship were very clearly known and reflected in both spoken and written address." One added that, in his village, persons invited to both "red" and "white" occasions would get cards delivered by hand. This rule applied irrespective of whether they lived in or near the village or in other settlements. Needless to say, statements vary, but on the whole both the written and verbal evidence point to a high degree of ceremonial in even the smaller, newer settlements. One important point must be made in passing. My informants stress that where help was given with writing letters and cards it was usually free of charge, since most transactions were said to have been conducted on the basis of mutual reciprocity and the inculcation of the keen sense of obligations due and favors owed that lived in every villager's head.

Besides the family use stated above, the handbooks used by the specialists can also tell us much about the identity and social ties of a particular village or subdistrict, thus furthering our understanding of local society in Ch'ing times. The local productions usually include material on community rites that indicate factors making for group cohesion. They provide the text of prayers to be said at local temples and give couplets suitable for use in particular temples. One of the Tsuen Wan handbooks gives the prayers to be said at the twice-yearly worship by leading elders at the T'ien Hou temple for persons killed in

[72] Rev. Bernard Upward, *The Sons of Han, Stories of Chinese Life and Mission Work* (London: London Missionary Society, 1908), pp. 42–43.

[73] The first is from a manuscript compilation *Chi-li lu* 吉禮錄, subtitled *Chia-ch'ü pien-lan* 嫁娶便覽, apparently from Canton and dated *kuei-hai* year (1923). The second is from a work printed in Canton, *Hsin-ting t'ieh-shih chien-yao* 新訂帖式簡要, revised edition 1920.

armed clashes with neighboring villages in the 1860s.[74] And, as if to show that both the fighting and the worship were common occurrences, another from an adjoining district lists similar prayers without mentioning a temple.[75]

Who were the persons who owned the handbooks and knew the written formulas that guided village practice in social events and community affairs? According to informants, in some settlements it was the village schoolmaster, and in other places it was a villager with intellectual curiosity and ability above the norm. Some local examples may serve to illustrate each type of person. In the Hong Kong region in late Ch'ing, schoolmasters could be local or could come from outside. Many were from the same village or belonged to other villages in the *hsiang*. The local ones were more likely to be effective transmitters and helpers in social requirements than the outsiders because of their strong connection with other local families through marriage and permanent settlement. Some were merely teachers, but others held managerial posts in their lineages, villages, or *hsiang*s. The other type of transmitter was the capable villager who was not a teacher. The owner of one of the Tsuen Wan handbooks is a sixty-four-year-old villager of Sheung Kwai Chung.[76] He belongs to a small lineage that has settled in this and several other villages of the Tsuen Wan subdistrict in the last 300 years. A respectable man who was educated at the local village school but received no higher education, he lives in a house little different from others in the village, and has no more property than the other land-owning families, but he is the kind of man who takes on community chores and is looked up to as a leader. His father, from whom the handbook descended, was a similar kind of man, and an uncle was a teacher.[77] Knowledgeable informants report that it was the superior villager of this type who linked the teachers and specialists of the senior generations with contemporary villagers. People in this role were, in truth, themselves specialists through their education

[74] These handbooks have no page numbering. They are in the process of being prepared for library storage and use. This particular book came from a member of the Tsang lineage of Sheung Kwai Chung (*Gazetteer of Place Names*, 150). The village war in question is described in my note, "A Village War," *JHKBRAS* 17:185–186 (1977).

[75] This handbook came from the Cheung lineage presently of Tai Uk Wai, Tsuen Wan, but before its removal for a reservoir in 1956 resident at Kwan Uk Tei near Tai Lam Chung (*Gazetteer*, p. 156).

[76] See note 74.

[77] My informant's great uncle, Tsang Kwong-yuk (*tzu* Long-ue) (1851–1933), is also worth mentioning. He came from a tiny offshoot of the main (Sheung Kwai Chung) village, called Yau Ma Hom, where his grandfather had settled in the Chia-ch'ing period. He possessed a superior house and, as is usually the case with persons of ability, was the manager of some lineage trusts. He had outside employment as a clerk in the *yamen* of Kowloon City Deputy Submagistracy and the two positions combined to give him a high local status. It is fascinating that when the family's ancestral hall was recently rebuilt, the decoration included historical representations of all famous members of the ancient Wu-ch'eng Tseng lineage, beginning with Tseng Ts'an (B.C. 505–436), who was a leading disciple of Confucius and including Tseng Kuo-fan (1811–1872) and ending with this man!

and community service, forming part of what C. K. Yang, as late as the end of the 1940s, described as the "small percentage of literates" that "served adequately ... [the] traditional literacy needs" of the village population.[78]

What is less clear is who performed the rites and prayers listed in the handbooks owned by such persons. The most I have been able to glean from Tsuen Wan people is that some of the schoolmasters of their acquaintance and certain respected village elders would attend at weddings, funerals, and other occasions when the saying of prayers and the making of offerings required the presence of masters of ceremony. Generally, these people would come from the village community, but if there was no one available, an expert was called from another village or from outside. This happens more often nowadays in Tsuen Wan than before, usually when villages have reopened their resited or rebuilt ancestral halls.[79]

WRITTEN MATERIALS PROVIDING THE CULTURAL AND SOCIAL CONTEXT TO DAILY LIFE

Alongside the varied corpus of written materials there existed in both town and country an equally extensive body of ancillary writing whose importance for villagers, citizens, and researchers alike lies in the fact that it created the cultural environment in which Chinese lived. It is fair to say that the written character was all around them. We may categorize these writings as being of a permanent, semipermanent, or ephemeral nature. There were the shop signs and those written materials that formed part of the more or less permanent structure or decoration of public and private buildings. The semipermanent genre included the scrolls and couplets written on perishable materials that I have already touched upon briefly. The last group comprised notices, bills, public accounts, and so on, posted on walls and other external parts of buildings, the true *ephemera*, together with those to be found inside ordinary people's homes. I shall consider the permanent stock first, before turning to the *ephemera*.

The Chinese written language was a feature of the internal and external decoration of practically all institutional buildings and superior dwelling houses. In the Hong Kong region, such inscriptions and decorative materials are a major part of village life even today. If one looks at any of the surviving older and larger buildings of the types mentioned, there are always couplets painted on, or cut into, the pillars. Most local temples have couplets chiseled on granite pillars or inscribed on vertical wooden posts. Couplets and inscriptions

---

[78] C. K. Yang, *Chinese Communist Society: The Family and the Village*, paperback ed. (Cambridge, Mass.: MIT Press, 1965), p. 182. Most village teachers' salaries were the bare minimum. J. Campbell Gibson notes that in the Chiu Chau (Ch'ao-chou) area of northeast Kwangtung, teachers supplemented their incomes by writing letters, telling fortunes, providing the calligraphy on hanging scrolls, and even preparing documents for lawsuits. See Gibson, *Mission Problems and Mission Methods in South China* (Edinburgh: Oliphant, Anderson and Ferrier, 1902), pp. 132–133.

[79] Two brief accounts of the reopening of ancestral halls in Tsuen Wan District are given in appendix 2, "Moving Ancestors," of my *Rural Communities of Hong Kong* (cited n. 62).

can also be found on other large religious buildings, and often on the entrance gateways and pavilions inside their grounds.[80] Even street and village shrines have them in abundance. In all save the last the inscriptions are complemented by the inscribed presentation boards to be found hanging inside the structures. There was, too, an important, because extensive, stock of written decoration to be found on the walls of ancestral halls, schools, temples, and also on the better houses. As stated above, this form mostly comprised verses from T'ang poetry. Also in this category are the many decorative examples of Chinese art symbols used in the decoration of houses, with their direct link to specific written characters and auspicious meanings.[81]

Besides the buildings themselves, in every town and market of any size practically every shop had its painted signboard and its inscribed lantern. James Scott's animated description of Cholon (Saigon) in the 1880s, "to all intents and purposes, Chinese," can serve as an indication of what was to be seen in every town in China:

> the frontage, with the narrow, deep houses, the huge red and black and yellow lanterns, the gay swinging signboards, are all suggestive of the Middle Kingdom. Cornchandler, restaurant-keeper, greengrocer, apothecary, tailor, shoemaker, gold and silversmith, iron monger, furniture dealer, pastrycook—everyone has his name over the door in letters of gold, and pendent signboards painted red, blue, gold, or black, according to taste, recommending his wares; by day, the clerks sitting naked to the waist languidly fanning themselves; by night, the place brilliantly lighted up with lanterns of all sizes and colours, setting forth the Hong name, and the goods to be sold.[82]

Certainly this is all very reminiscent of South China and old Hong Kong.

I turn now to the *ephemera*. To the array of decoration on buildings and the multifarious shop signs must be added the placards and notices plentifully plastered on buildings. Notices of accommodation to sell or rent vied with advertisements for efficacious pills and the services of bone setters and herbal doctors. Notices about the forthcoming celebration of religious services or performances of various kinds of opera were abundant, together with the statements about subscriptions and expenditures posted in public view for all to see.

---

[80] Some examples of this type of permanent decoration in Hong Kong can be found in T. C. Lai, *Chinese Couplets*, 2nd ed. (Hong Kong: University Book Store, 1970), pp. 7, 17, 28, 37, 40, 54, *passim*. Many others are to be found in the close-ups of buildings photographed in Ernst Boerschmann's *Picturesque China, Architecture and Landscape* (London: T. Fisher Unwin, c. 1920).

[81] See the supplement of 160 "Chinese Art Symbols" by Francess Hawley Seyssel in W. M. Hawley, *Chinese Folk Designs* (reprint ed. New York: Dover, 1971). Many of those listed appear on the older houses and in household and personal items in the Hong Kong region. C. A. S. Williams, *Outlines of Chinese Symbolism and Art Motives*, 3rd rev. ed. (1941; reprint ed. New York: Dover, 1976), contains useful summaries of information bearing on this subject. See also Schuyler Cammann, "Types of Symbols in Chinese Art," in *Studies in Chinese Thought*, ed. Arthur F. Wright (Chicago: University of Chicago Press, 1953), pp. 195–231.

[82] James George Scott, *France and Tonking, A Narrative of the Campaign of 1884 and the Occupation of Further India* (London: T. Fisher Unwin, 1885), pp. 319–320.

In the towns—I have no information about the villages—the district government added its contribution to the visual accumulation of the written character. It was usual, writes Wells Williams, for the commands of government to be printed in large characters, chopped with an official seal and exhibited in public places,[83] while important legal settlements or pronouncements were carved on stone tablets and put in prominent places or inside well-used public buildings for the people to see and read. It was also official practice for persons convicted of petty offences to sit in the cangue—a heavy wooden board worn across the shoulders and with an aperture for the head—with their name, age, place of residence, offence and sentence pasted on the frame for all to see.[84] Persons sentenced as part of their punishment to parade through the streets also bore placards to the same end, a practice apparently followed by the people's own local apparatus of punishment in the villages.[85] Hardy illustrates another, more severe form of public exposure, with men strung up in wooden frames, again, it appears, accompanied by the cataloging of offences.[86]

One cannot leave this subject without mentioning the placards used to excite popular feeling, especially in towns and cities where the population was dense, against officials, missionaries, foreigners in general, and so on, in war and peace. Wakeman gives examples in his account of Kwangtung in the mid-nineteenth century, as does Archdeacon Moule, describing the contents of a placard directed against him in Chuki (Tz'u-ch'i), near Hangchow: "The valiant inhabitants of Chuki, whose stubborn resistance to the T'aip'ing marauders is bruited throughout the world, will never allow this foreign barbarian intruder (the Missionary Mo) to obtain a foothold in their city."[87]

Besides the *ephemera* to be seen in the streets, there were those to be found in the homes. The people's liking for art is mentioned by Kulp who, in his account of a village in northeastern Kwangtung, refers to "the ubiquitous evidences of art appreciation" and gives a chapter to the subject.[88] This was, and is, especially noticeable at the New Year. Brush-written couplets for doorways and lintels, together with New Year pictures, are then much in evidence, and can be seen in the streets of towns and market centers before the event. The pictures (*nien-hua*) are of all kinds; they include subjects such as historical tales from *The Romance of the Three Kingdoms* and *Water Margin*, representations of longevity and

[83] Wells Williams, *The Middle Kingdom*, vol. I, p. 469.

[84] Ibid., vol. I, p. 509. The cangue is described by E. Bard, *Les Chinois chez Eux* (Paris: Librairie Armand Colin, 1904), p. 179. See also Charles Commeaux, *La Vie Quotidienne en Chine sous Les Mandchous* (Paris: Librairie Hachette, 1970), p. 165 and the note at p. 250; T. L. Bullock, *Progressive Exercises in the Chinese Written Language*, 3rd ed., rev. by H. A. Giles (Shanghai: Kelly and Walsh, 1923), which, contrary to Bard, states that the cangue was usually taken off at night.

[85] Wells Williams, *The Middle Kingdom*, vol. I, p. 511; Hayes, *The Hong Kong Region*, p. 146.

[86] Hardy, *John Chinaman* (cited n. 26), p. 232.

[87] Archdeacon Moule, *New China and Old, Personal Recollections of Thirty Years* (London: Seeley, 1891), p. 150; Frederic Wakeman, Jr., *Strangers at the Gate: Social Disorder in South China 1839–1861* (Berkeley: University of California Press, 1966).

[88] Kulp, *Country Life* (cited n. 18), chap. IX.

male children, and other traditional art motives, as well as (nowadays) modern Western art and pictorial broadsheets. The representations of male children are a perennially popular subject and, as a People's Republic catalogue of wood-block pictures dated 1956 has it, "reflect the hopes of the people for an abundance of posterity and a happy life." Their main purpose is to help create that background atmosphere of joyful ease and comfortable feelings that means so much to Chinese people of all degrees of education, especially on happy family occasions and at major festival times.[89]

In this general connection, one must take into account the highly developed sense of the importance of the written word. As Lyall, with his forty-two years' service in China, wrote, "Though few Chinese can read, they have the highest regard for learning."[90] We know that this extended to characters and the paper on which they were written, for there were countless societies dedicated to retrieving discarded scraps of written paper for burning and reverential disposal. In the 1860s, Doolittle described this reverence for written materials as "a national characteristic,"[91] and Evelyn Rawski has noted that it extended deep into the religious system, which "used written materials at the humblest levels."[92] Even today in old villages written strips of paper seeking after good fortune are to be found posted on houses and farm buildings, on agricultural tools, on trees and shrines and on and inside the houses.

[89] This prevailing sentiment comes across strongly in the contents of the fortnightly magazine *Hsiang T'u* 鄉土, which contains a rich store of both general and local material on festivals, folklore, and customs, with special reference to northeastern Kwangtung and occasionally Fukien. (It was published in Hong Kong by the Hsin-ti ch'u-pan she from January 1957 for an as yet unknown length of time.) The feeling can also be glimpsed in the many interesting and varied short contributions on the cultural background in the monthly issues of *China Reconstructs*.

[90] L. A. Lyall, *China* (The Modern World Series) (London: Ernest Benn, 1944), p. 96.

[91] Rev. Justus Doolittle, *Social Life of the Chinese, with some Account of their Religions, Government, Educational, and Business Customs and Opinions, With Special but not Exclusive Reference to Fuchau* (New York: Harper Brothers, 1865), vol. 2, pp. 167–170. See Hayes, *The Hong Kong Region*, pp. 96, 233, n. 44; Rev. H. J. Stevens, *Cantonese Apothegms Classified, Translated and Commented Upon* (Canton: E-shing, 1902), pp. 9–10, 30–31.

[92] Rawski, *Education*, p. 142. Auspicious couplets and red papers such as those pasted up at the lunar New Year were, as Johnston records for Wei Hai Wei, "regarded by the common people (who can rarely read them) as equivalent to powerful charms." See R. F. Johnston, *Lion and Dragon*, p. 194. This attitude extended towards the almanac itself, of which Kulp, in *Country Life in South China* (cited n. 18), has this to say: "When people cannot read the instructions and advice, they simply select those days under which most of the text occurs, for they consider the large sections or the sections printed in red ink as particularly felicitous for important occasions" (p. 186). Precisely the same thing was said to me this year (1980) by elders of a village in the Tsuen Wan subdistrict, in the course of discussing the extent to which people bought and used the almanac up to twenty years ago. Mrs. Arnold Foster states, in *In the Valley of the Yangtse* (cited n. 26), that "some of the Chinese classics are supposed to keep away evil spirits if you put them under your pillow at night ..." (p. 98). This talismanic usage was extended to superseded paper currency. "Those who are building, fasten one of these notes to the main beam of the house, from a conviction that this species of talisman will preserve their families from every kind of misfortune" (Bertin and Breton, *China*, vol. II, p. 105).

Entertainers as Cultural Specialists

This section would not be complete without a brief mention of entertainers. Though not operating directly through the medium of the written character, they were another group of specialists who contributed much to the cultural context of village and town life. As discussed by Barbara Ward in this volume (chapter 6), the populace depended heavily upon them for visual and oral transmission of historical "facts" and cultural values. Through such frequent and regular activities as village, lineage, family, and association plays, whether full-scale operas or puppet shows; through story telling by villagers or itinerant professionals; through ballad singing by other professionals, often blind persons, who visited homes and teahouses; through the round of activities over the extended lunar New Year period, including guessing games, lantern riddles, and New Year pictures, residents of all ages were instructed as well as entertained.[93]

Various forms of entertainment provided a cultural indoctrination of immense strength. As one Republican educationalist has said in his autobiography, "Moral ideas were driven into the people by every possible means—temples, theatres, homes, toys, proverbs, schools, history and stories—until they became habits in daily life."[94] This social indoctrination and its results were noticed by European observers such as John Francis Davis, who in the 1830s observed that "the Chinese lower classes were better educated or at least better trained than in most other countries."[95]

BOOKS VERSUS SPECIALISTS

It is necessary to make some assessment of the relative importance of books and specialists among the same "lower classes." From my own observations in Hong Kong villages before their modernization, I am fairly pessimistic about the presence of books in many village houses and town dwellings at that time. In ordinary villages, the older houses then to be seen were perhaps well over a hundred years old. Their earth floors, dark and narrow interiors, and spartan furnishings—hardly more than board beds, gate legged or trestle tables, and

---

[93] See Hayes, *The Hong Kong Region*, p. 55, notes p. 216; Monlin Chiang, *Tides from the West* (cited n. 48), p. 34; and Douglas, *China*, pp. 264–265 on New Year entertainments. Blind storytellers or legend chanters were popular: "A woman, at her best, in good training, can recite some hundred books, no book taking less than an hour to repeat, most of them three and four hours and some from six to nine" (Mary Darley, *Cameos of a Chinese City* [Chien-ning, Fukien], [London: Church of England Zenana Missionary Society, 1917], p. 114). On the theater, see Barbara E. Ward, "Readers and Audiences: An Exploration of the Spread of Traditional Chinese Culture," *ASA Essays in Social Anthropology* (Oxford: Association for Social Anthropologists, 1973), vol. II, pp. 181–203.

[94] Chiang, *Tides from the West* (cited n. 48), pp. 8–9.

[95] John Francis Davis, *The Chinese, A General Description of the Empire of China and its Inhabitants* (London: Charles Knight, 1836), vol. II, pp. 29–30.

rough benches and stools—reflected the poor and simple lives of their inhabitants.[96] It is not for nothing, one supposes, that the older generations in Tsuen
Wan emphasize that before the war it was still "very poor," despite the receipt
of overseas remittances (the money seems often to have gone into building new
houses) and the opportunities for selling produce in urban Hong Kong that
were utilized by some families.

Yet I believe that, where it prevailed, poverty alone (as contributing to
illiteracy) was not mainly responsible for the lack of books that may have
characterized many, even most, rural settlements in our region. Educational
requirements apart, books may not have been needed by most villagers for
instruction or recreation, or the social, economic, and religious pursuits of daily
life, or in crises or special occasions. I am left with the impression that, even
where available, the various printed handbooks cited earlier could not, and
very probably did not, take the place of specialists and their large stock of
handwritten materials. At all levels, and despite the existence of inexpensively
printed popular guides and practical encyclopedias over many centuries, there
was probably a far greater reliance on specialists in the workings of Chinese
society and their writings and collected materials than one would infer from the
high standards of cultural life and the degree and geographical extent of general
literacy adduced by Dr. Rawski.[97]

As I see it, the very complexity of society and the general sophistication
perhaps encouraged this reliance on the experts, and it may be argued that this
phenomenon was clearly linked to the nature of the society itself. T. D. Selby
became very much aware of this through his missionary travels. He wrote, in
1900,

> Chinese life is verily complex and the division of labour carried out to peculiar and
> inscrutable lengths. A Chinaman who heard a missionary denouncing idolatry
> went home, not to weigh the arguments that had been urged against image-
> worship, but to count up the number of trades that would be more or less affected,
> if the missionary's message was heeded. He put down a hundred and seventy, and
> came back the next day to ask if he was not correct in the list he had so
> industriously compiled.[98]

Selby was probably thinking of the town of Fo-shan, near Canton, when he
wrote this—his mission had a chapel there—but he would have been the first to

---

[96] There was, of course, a considerable variety in the types of houses, and standard of housing,
to be found in the 600–700 villages of Hong Kong's New Territories, and no doubt elsewhere in
Kwangtung. (See, for instance, the rather more favorable statement given in Stewart Lockhart's
report [1899] after visiting many of the larger villages of the region.) But I am here talking of the
larger number of poorer, smaller, more remote villages that were more typical of the mass. (The
report is printed in *The Hongkong Government Gazette*, 8 April 1899. Lockhart states that there were
423 villages, but I know the figure to be considerably higher.)

[97] Rawski, *Education and Popular Literacy* (cited n. 24), p. 140.

[98] Thomas G. Selby, *Chinamen at Home* (London: Hodder and Stoughton, 1900), p. 178.

agree that it is a complexity also to be found in the villages. When I first saw the apparently long-established poverty of many of the villages of the southern district of Hong Kong's New Territories in the mid 1950s, I was surprised that, in these circumstances, there was so little self-sufficiency. Even the smallest village called in masons and carpenters to build houses, and itinerant black-smiths came yearly to make and repair agricultural tools—as in former days did the weavers who wove cloth and made clothes. Later, as my acquaintance grew, I saw how this diversity extended to many aspects of social and cere-monial life, and the popular religion with it, and noted that there was a cash economy to service it, with land transactions eking out the deficiency on major occasions. It was, eventually, no surprise to learn of the full range of specialists living in the villages and marketing centers and to see how they served the mass, which by one means or another managed to pay for their services in cash or in kind. Though poor, this was a sophisticated society. My impression, too, is that this would have been even more the case at, say, the end of the Ch'ing, as there has been a decline in village life and rural institutions in the New Territories extending over several generations.

The wonder is, perhaps, that the mass had such diverse needs. Its expecta-tions with regard to family ritual and ceremonial were indeed high, because of the ingrained Confucian ethic and the intensity of social life in settlements where all were neighbors and many were relatives. Great emphasis was placed on social obligations and reciprocity, and, as we know from many sources, the cost was steep in relation to normal farm income.[99] The answer, to at least one Chinese anthropologist, writing at a time when it could still be evaluated from life (1923), was that the average peasant was the "earnest imitator of the life patterns established by the gentry-scholar class."[100] If so—and I would cer-tainly agree on the basis of my observation and study—this would help to explain how, across a wide range of incomes, the services of specialists were sought by all and to the same ends. Only the extent and the cost varied, according to means. No doubt there were expensive, fashionable practitioners in all occupations to meet the needs of the rich, and others to cater for the humbler but no less insistent needs of the poor. From such abstruse specialist concerns such as geomancy, fortune telling, and the complicated rituals of the popular religion, with their combined concern for creating favorable influences and averting or neutralizing adverse ones, to the more prosaic requirements of social and community life, specialists were at the core of Chinese society. And

---

[99]John Lossing Buck, *Land Utilization in China* (Shanghai: Commercial Press, 1937), pp. 467–470. For a New Territories example (1950) see D. Y. Lin's "Report of a Trial Survey of the Economic Conditions of 60 Families in the New Territories," referred to in Thomas R. Tregear, *Land Use in Hong Kong and the New Territories* (Hong Kong: Hong Kong University Press, 1958), pp. 61–65 and the appendix.

[100]Sing King Su quoted in Shu-ching Lee, "China's Traditional Family, Its Characteristics and Disintegration," *American Sociological Review* 18:272 (1958).

these arts all relied, to a greater or lesser degree, on the written word in the hands of a relatively few people who kept everything moving along and helped to ensure transmission of the culture, taken in its broadest sense.

CONCLUSION

Having completed this cursory survey of specialists and their materials in the context of the cultural background and with special reference to rural life in late imperial China, my tentative conclusion is that the specialists were the leaven in the loaf—the means whereby, among the mass of the people, the core elements of Chinese civilization and society as we know them were continued and enriched. Despite the estimated degree of literacy in the society taken overall, and the large production (perhaps not so widespread distribution) of printed material, I am left with the impression that, especially at the lower levels, this was an "entertained" rather than an entertaining society, and that it was also a "facilitated" rather than a facilitating society, owing to the widely observed reliance on specialists of all kinds.

The manuscript productions to be found in the villages and their long co-existence and perpetuation side by side with printed books, in some places replacing and substituting for them, is evidence for the uniformity of the Chinese cultural heritage and for how highly its written basis was valued, how widely it was spread, and how deeply it penetrated. Since there is no reason whatever to think that this genre is unique to Kwangtung—Shih-ch'ing Wang has catalogued material of similar and related kinds on Taiwan[101]—it clearly constitutes a major new source of evidence for understanding the means by which Chinese culture penetrated into many parts of the rural population at least by the nineteenth century, if not earlier. Though not yet sufficiently explored, the study of handwritten books in the village world, and the unveiling of the true dimensions of the specialists' effects, have important implications for the nature of Chinese society and, in time, can directly contribute to a re-evaluation of the situation in late imperial times.[102] Perhaps, among other possibilities, this pursuit holds the key to the mysterious, lingering strength of the traditional Chinese state until well into the twentieth century.

[101] Shih-ch'ing Wang, "Contracts and Other Old Documents as Sources for Family History and Genealogy in Taiwan" in *Asian and African Family and Local History*, vol. 11, World Conference on Records, Salt Lake City (Corporation of the President of the Church of Jesus Christ of Latter Day Saints, 1980). Also his three volumes of *Taiwanese Historical Documents in Private Holdings*, Nos. 2, 4, and 5 of Source Materials Series (in Chinese) (Taipei: National Book Company, 1977, 1978, 1980).

[102] Generally speaking, handwritten and handcopied manuals and notebooks do not appear to have been used or collected until recently. As one of my Chinese friends, a schoolmaster, has said, the main reason for this neglect is that persons with scholastic interests did not consider such materials to be of any importance. Hence, they have been generally disregarded in China. It would be of considerable interest to know whether this has also been the case among Japanese scholars of China.

It was perhaps the richness of Chinese life and its powerful unifying forces, visible to those with eyes to see, that led the late Professor F. S. Drake of the University of Hong Kong, in his obituary notice of Arthur De Carle Sowerby (1885–1954), the great naturalist from Shanghai, to reflect upon "the spaciousness of the closing years of Imperial China—an experience that leaves its mark upon all that have had it."[103] As I read the situation at ground level, the specialists and their materials represented an enormous but still mainly unrecognized social and cultural force in the society of late imperial China, and contributed more fully than we know to this spaciousness, supplying both unity and diversity.

[103] *Journal of Oriental Studies* (University of Hong Kong) II : 145 (1955).

FOUR

Distinguishing Levels of Audiences
For Ming–Ch'ing Vernacular Literature:
A Case Study

Robert E. Hegel

The differences in values among audiences of different cultural levels in late imperial China are a complex and elusive subject. First, we must identify audiences of these varying cultural levels at least by the texts intended for them, and then we must compare and contrast the texts themselves in terms of discernible ideological differences in their content. Neither is a simple task. In neither can we totally avoid hypothetical propositions and speculation, although at least we can minimize their use. Consequently, this essay is admittedly as much an explanation of approaches to this sort of study as it is an analysis of cultural differences within a society; the reader must bear in mind that my conclusions at each stage are tentative.

For this case study I have chosen a series of vernacular novels and plays written during the Ming and Ch'ing periods. But the number of texts examined here is too small to be any more than suggestive of the conclusions reachable after further study. Likewise, I have tried to avoid literary works and approaches through which the differences in values presented might be related more to temporal or geographical variation than to cultural level within society.[1] This

---

[1] Geographical and temporal differentiation may account for variations in the values expressed in these texts in addition to those related to social level of intended audience. However, given the relative continuity of linguistic style through nearly all vernacular literature—usually essentially a variety of Northern Chinese rather than Wu (central), Min (southeastern) or Yueh (southern) dialects—it is often nearly impossible to identify the geographical origins of specific texts. Likewise, single stories may be altered by the conventions of the genre, rather than the time in which they appear, at least among popular works. I discuss the temporal setting of these works below; they probably originate from only two regions of China, the Peking area (the early Ming plays and the Peking opera), and the Lower Yangtze. I believe that the effect of genre or literary form on values expressed in the works addressed here is slight. However, one would need to examine a much larger body of texts before this could be ascertained; see the texts mentioned in notes 5 and 6 below. For insightful comments on such questions, see Patrick Hanan, *The Chinese Vernacular Story* (Cambridge, Mass.: Harvard University Press, 1981), pp. 8–15.

problem, too, is difficult, and one not fully solved by this single paper. But I believe that the conclusions reached below are reasonable, given our present state of knowledge of elite versus popular culture in late imperial China; they await the rejection, verification, or revision that only further research can occasion.

AUDIENCES: SOME PRELIMINARY CONSIDERATIONS

Evidence for distinguishing audiences for China's vernacular literary artifacts is sparse at best. There are no known data on numbers of copies printed for any given work, and often little explicit evidence exists to indicate its intended audience. Consequently, students of Chinese culture customarily have often had to use rather problematic evaluations of styles of language to identify the intended readers for specific works.[2] Obviously, literary works written in a heavily connotative and allusive version of the classical style were intended for the best educated segment of society, the cultural—and usually social—elite; oral narratives, *chantefable* literature in a mixture of prose and verse (now called *shuo-ch'ang wen-hsueh*), and drama—in the vernacular—must have been designed for hearing by the illiterate masses; and between these two levels was a third, written vernacular literature intended to be read by more general audiences. But who were these "general audiences"? Presumably, they included upper-class women and young people, merchants, lower-level governmental functionaries, and shopkeepers and the like who were literate but not extensively trained in aristocratic literature. However, while this division is suggestive of the true situation, it is misleading: style of language in itself is insufficient as a criterion for determining audience. Styles of the vernacular, in particular, are not yet sufficiently understood to serve reliably: vernacular literature consists of a variety of levels of linguistic complexity, of dialectical differentiations, and of generically shaped written media. Vernacular written narratives and theatrical pieces include works written for both China's cultural elite and its illiterate and disadvantaged masses.

[2] David Johnson's recent articles on popular literature discuss the problems of language and audiences for popular literature; see "The Wu Tzu-hsü *Pien-wen* and Its Sources: Part I," *Harvard Journal of Asiatic Studies* 40.1:95, esp. n. 1 (1980), and "Chinese Popular Literature and Its Contexts," *Chinese Literature: Essays, Articles, and Reviews* 3.2:225–234 (July 1981) in particular. The most intelligent and persuasive discussions of education and literacy—and of the two types "functional" and "general"—appear in a research report presented at the Association for Asian Studies meeting in Chicago, 2 April 1982, by Thomas H. C. Lee and Bernard H. Luk of the Chinese University of Hong Kong. Proof that audiences were not mutually exclusive is easily found. For example, poorly educated Chinese have read, probably with less than total comprehension and esthetic appreciation, *Sui T'ang yen-i*, which is demonstrably an elite novel. See below and Alvin P. Cohen, "Notes on a Chinese Workingclass Bookshelf," *Journal of the American Oriental Society* 96.3:425 (1976). Cohen's "workingclass readers" accumulated this book collection in the 1950s; given the limitations on educational opportunities in twentieth-century China available to working people of the late imperial period, his findings are of limited relevance here, but they do confirm my observation that audiences overlap considerably in reality.

Since we are as yet unable to determine audience on the basis of linguistic medium within vernacular literature, I have tried below to use only non-linguistic evidence, of types both intrinsic and extrinsic to the texts themselves. Such data include biographical information on authors, the social milieu in which certain forms circulated, literary form, and such internal features as function of verse and generic conventions. While this hodgepodge of information is less complete than one might hope, still it may serve to support (or to throw into question) the yet more hypothetical constructs upon which earlier generalizations about Ming–Ch'ing cultural levels have been based. This evidence suggests a range of audiences for vernacular literature and drama extending from the cultural elite, through the literate non-elite, to the illiterate masses. By "audience" I mean the social stratum or group for which a particular work was *intentionally* produced; a determination of *real* audiences would require evidence that is not readily available—if it exists at all.

THE BASIC TALE OF LI MI'S CAREER

For this case study in audiences and values I have chosen a portion of a story complex circulated among all levels of Chinese society through many centuries.[3] This is the tale of Li Mi (581–618), an unsuccessful contender for the realm, from the cycle of tales concerning the fall of the Sui and the founding of the T'ang centering on Li Shih-min (600–649). The texts addressed here are the only extant and available Ming and Ch'ing vernacular versions of Li Mi's fall: a trilogy of early Ming plays, a popular chronicle and a modified *chantefable* narrative from the middle of the sixteenth century, a pair of seventeenth-century historical romances, an eighteenth-century military romance, and a late Ch'ing Peking opera. The tale of Li Mi meets the needs of this study because his fictional development originated in elite writing and spread to mass forms. Ming–Ch'ing vernacular literature more commonly draws source material from elite written works than vice versa,[4] and it guarantees that more levels of audience will be represented in the various versions of the tale. (Li Mi's development thus proceeded quite differently from that of the upright magistrate Pao Cheng, the central figure in a long story cycle,[5] or Wu Sung, like Li

---

[3] The story complex is a concept used effectively by Hanan in his *Chinese Vernacular Story*, pp. 7–8.

[4] Hanan, *Chinese Vernacular Story*, pp. 13, 21, 24, 55.

[5] The *kung-an* 公案, or crime-case tales, were apparently popular throughout Ming and Ch'ing China; Magistrate Pao 包公 was the favorite subject. Pao Cheng 包拯 lived during the Northern Sung period. By the Yuan period there were plays about him; see George Hayden, "The Courtroom Plays of the Yüan and Early Ming Periods," *Harvard Journal of Asiatic Studies* 34:192–220 (1974), and also his *Crime and Punishment in Medieval Chinese Drama* (Cambridge, Mass.: Harvard University Press, 1978); and Ching-Hsi Perng, *Double Jeopardy: A Critique of Seven Yüan Courtroom Dramas* (Ann Arbor: University of Michigan Center for Chinese Studies, 1978). For textual and other studies of relevant Ming prose narratives, see Wolfgang Bauer, "The Tradition of the 'Criminal Cases of Master Pao' Pao-Kung-An (*Lung-t'u kung-an*)," *Oriens* 23–24 (1970–1971),

Mi a military hero of secondary importance, in the larger *Shui-hu* cycle.[6]) Likewise, all versions agree in their outline of the same events, leaving differences only on significant details, particularly the reasons why characters behave the way they do. This range of variations, of course, speaks directly to differences in values from version to version, the final subject of this study.

Since the story complex concerning the T'ang founding is based on recorded fact, the historical record may serve as the standard version of Li Mi's tale. In order to ascertain the degree of historicity in each literary or dramatic version, the relevance of which will be addressed later, one must compare these fictional accounts with references to Li Mi that are to be found in *Chiu T'ang shu* [The old T'ang history] and *Hsin T'ang shu* [The new T'ang History]—his biography is in each—and in the chronologically arranged *Tzu-chih t'ung-chien* [The comprehensive mirror for aid in governing], in the sections that record the years of

and Y. W. Ma, "The Textual Tradition of Ming *Kung-an* Fiction: A Study of the *Lung-t'u kung-an*," *Harvard Journal of Asiatic Studies* 35:190–220 (1975), Ma's "Themes and Characterization in the *Lung-t'u kung-an*," *T'oung Pao* 59:179–202 (1973), and, in particular, Patrick Hanan, "*Judge Bao's Hundred Cases* Reconstructed," *Harvard Journal of Asiatic Studies* 40.2:301–323 (1980). For the Ch'ing novels in this series—*Lung-t'u kung-an* 龍圖公案 [Judge Pao's cases], 1775; *San-hsia wu-i* 三俠五義 [Three swordsmen and five knights], 1879 (Shanghai: Shanghai wen-hua 上海文化, 1956, with a foreword in this edition by Chao Ching-shen 趙景深); and *Ch'i-hsia wu-i* 七俠五義 [Seven swordsmen and five knights], 1889—see Liu Ts'un-yan, *Chinese Popular Fiction in Two London Libraries* (Hong Kong: Lung Men, 1967), pp. 292–293, and Susan Blader, "*San-hsia wu-yi* and its Link to Oral Literature," *CHINOPERL Papers* 8:9–38 (1979). A selection of these tales is "retold" in Leon Comber's *The Strange Cases of Magistrate Pao* (Rutland, Vt.: Tuttle, 1964). A recent publication of *chantefable* texts relevant to this cycle is *Ming Ch'eng-hua shuo-ch'ang tz'u-hua ts'ung-k'an* 明成化說唱詞話叢刊 [Anthology of *Chantefables* from the Ch'eng-hua era of the Ming Period] (Shanghai: Shanghai po-wu kuan 上海博物館, 1973); of the sixteen pieces reprinted here, eight narrate Magistrate Pao adventures. They were discovered in a fifteenth-century tomb; see the report by Chao Ching-shen 趙景深, "T'an Ming Ch'eng-hua k'an-pen 'Shuo-ch'ang tz'u-hua'" 談明成化刊本說唱詞話 *Wen-wu* 文物 11:19–22 (1972).

[6] On the *Shui-hu* story complex, see Richard G. Irwin, *The Evolution of a Chinese Novel: Shui-hu-chuan* (Cambridge, Mass.: Harvard University Press, 1953); Hu Shih, "*Shui-hu chuan* k'ao-cheng" 水滸傳考證 [Researches on the *Shui-hu chuan*], *Hu Shih wen-ts'un* 胡適文存 [Extant works of Hu Shih] (Taipei: Yuan-tung t'u-shu kung-ssu 遠東圖書公司, 1971), vol. I, pp. 500–547; C. T. Hsia, *The Classic Chinese Novel* (New York: Columbia University Press, 1968), chap. III, esp. pp. 76–82. William O. Hennessey translates an early version, the *Hsuan-ho i-shih* 宣和遺事 (see the Taipei, Shih-chieh shu-chü 世界書局 edition of 1958) in his *Proclaiming Harmony* (Ann Arbor: University of Michigan Center for Chinese Studies, 1982); Sidney Shapiro provides the best translation of the novel form in his *Outlaws of the Marsh* (Bloomington and Beijing: Indiana University Press and Foreign Languages Press, 1981). Available editions include *Shui-hu ch'üan-chuan* 全傳, ed. Cheng Chen-to 鄭振鐸 [The complete *Shui-hu chuan*], a variorum edition based on the 100-chapter edition with the last twenty chapters added from late Ming recensions (Peking: Jen-min wen-hsueh 人民文學, 1954); *Shui-hu chuan*, the 1610 edition with 100 chapters (Peking: Jen-min wen-hsueh, 1975); *Chin Sheng-t'an ch'i-shih-i-hui-pen* 金聖歎七十一回本 *Shui-hu chuan* (The 71-chapter version edited by Chin Sheng-t'an, 1641) (Shanghai: Chung-hua shu-chü 中華書局, 1934). Plays in this story complex are collected in *Shui-hu hsi-ch'ü chi* 戲曲集 [Collected *Shui-hu* plays], ed. Fu Hsi-hua 傅惜華, et al. (Shanghai: Chung-hua shu-chü, 1962); the latest oral version, a Yangchow *p'ing-hua* 評話, was recorded in the 1950s; see Wang Shao-t'ang 王少堂, narrator, *Wu Sung* 武松 (Nanking: Kiangsu wen-i ch'u-pan-she 江蘇文藝出版社, 1959).

his prominence. The first two of these works enjoyed at least limited circulation in Ming–Ch'ing literati circles; the latter, in its abridged editions, was among the reference books most readily available to students and scholars. (There also existed a sizable body of unofficial historical writing concerning the Sui and the T'ang, but this circulated only among wealthy book collectors.[7])

A summary of the relevant segments of these histories will make comparisons clearer. Li Mi was a member of the aristocratic elite of northwest China, a protégé of the high minister Yang Su. When Sui imperial control began to falter, Li Mi readily joined the rebel force led by Yang's son. Unfortunately for him, the younger Yang soon fell, and Li Mi turned to brigandage in the year 613. It is at this point that the popular narratives begin to follow the outline of events provided by the orthodox histories (which concur on these events): initially, Li Mi joined forces with the outlaw Chai Jang, who relinquished leadership to him. Later, when Chai repented his action, Li had him summarily executed. By 616 he was in control of a coalition of rebel bands in the Loyang region. Li Mi's army was subsequently involved in action against the regicide Yü-wen Hua-chi. Their forces arrayed against each other, and Li taunted the traitor for his treachery in destroying the Sui emperor Yang, who had so trusted and supported him. Demoralized, Yü-wen lost the battle and, soon afterward, his life. This left three major contenders, Li Yuan, Wang Shih-ch'ung, and Li Mi. His troops lacking uniforms, Li Mi traded grain to Wang for cloth despite the opposition of his advisors; thus resupplied, Wang attacked and soundly defeated Li Mi, his military strength enhanced by the latter's bad strategy in combat. The question of loyalty here becomes of supreme importance to the orthodox historians: his earlier arrogance thoroughly crushed, Li Mi tried to commit suicide out of shame for being unworthy of his generals' respect. One of their number, Wang Po-tang, prevented him from doing so, vowing eternal allegiance. Li Mi thus decided to surrender to the T'ang to give his generals— and himself—another chance for glory. Initially the T'ang emperor Li Yuan treated him well, as he did all surrendered contenders, even marrying Li Mi to a young woman of the empress's family. However, the quality of his reception

---

[7] Informal sources of Sui and T'ang history include *Ch'ang-shih yen-chih* 常侍言旨 [Oral directives of the constant attendant] by Liu Ch'eng 柳珵 (late eighth century); *Tz'u Liu-shih chiu-wen* 次柳氏舊聞 [Old tales after (the versions recorded by) Mr. Liu] by Li Te-yü 李德裕 (787–850); the anonymous *Ta T'ang ch'uan-tsai* 大唐傳載 [Current anecdotes on the great T'ang]; *Sui T'ang chia-hua* 隋唐嘉話 [Fine tales about the Sui and the T'ang], by Liu Su 劉餗 (fl. mid-eighth century); *Kuo shih pu* 國史補 [Supplement to the history of the state], by Li Chao 李肇 (fl. 820); and *Chin-luan mi-chi* 金鑾密記 [Secret tales from the palace], by Han Wo 韓偓 (fl. 900). All these collections of material appear in *T'ang tai ts'ung-shu* 唐代叢書 [A T'ang period collection], comp. Ch'en Lien-t'ang 陳蓮塘 (n.p.: Lien-yuan-ko 蓮元閣, 1869), first collection. For a discussion of them, see Evangeline D. Edwards, *Chinese Prose Literature of the T'ang Period, A.D. 618–906* (London: Probsthain, 1937). Ch'u Jen-huo 褚人穫 utilized the last three of these works—and others—as source material for his historical novel; see Robert E. Hegel, *The Novel in Seventeenth-Century China* (New York: Columbia University Press, 1981), pp. 239–240.

soon declined. Before long, Li Yuan ordered Li Mi to pacify an area the latter had formerly occupied, but Li Yuan rescinded the order once Li Mi was on his way. Suspicious of the motivation behind the emperor's shift of plans, Li Mi decided to strike out on his own again. Failing in his efforts to dissuade him from rebellion, the faithful Wang Po-tang stood by Li Mi to the death as they rode straight into a T'ang ambush. Li Mi was captured and executed; he was 37 years old at the time.

It is ironic that this historical Li Mi should have been so keenly aware of the obligations to be observed by others and yet be loath to stand by his own commitments. His battlefield lecture to Yü-wen Hua-chi, Wang Po-tang's impassioned vows to serve his lord to the end—even the debt Li owed to the T'ang emperor for a bride and high position—made no impression on this obviously headstrong individual. To the orthodox historians these are mere empty gestures; they identify him as no different from a brigand. Unquestionably, to the historians, Li Mi was the sole cause of his own downfall. Able to recognize talent in others and in possession of many other leadership skills, he all too often ignored even the most sincere advice.[8] As a consequence, he fell far short of the qualities considered essential for a serious contender for the throne. Now let us consider various vernacular versions of the tale in order to compare the values offered audiences of distinguishable cultural levels in Ming and Ch'ing China.

FICTIONAL AND DRAMATIC VARIATIONS

The earliest vernacular texts that preserve fictionalized versions of the tale of Li Mi are a cycle of fourteenth-century *tsa-chü* plays. This form was commercially very successful during the Yuan period; it grew to prominence in northern urban theaters playing to audiences of a variety of social levels. Its arias frequently utilize allusions to classical literature and may not have been completely intelligible to all segments of a listening audience, but the import of each aria was normally summarized in prose afterward. Prose portions must have been intelligible to listeners regardless of educational background. From its

---

[8] Sources for the life of Li Mi include *Chiu T'ang shu* 舊唐書, *chüan* 53 (see the Chung-hua 中華 edition, Peking, 1975, vol. 7, pp. 2207–2224); *Hsin T'ang shu* 新唐書, *chüan* 84 (Chung-hua edition, Peking, 1975, vol. 12, pp. 3677–3686); and *Tzu-chih t'ung-chien* 資治通鑑, *chüan* 184–186. See Li Tsung-t'ung 李宗侗 and Hsia Te-i 夏德儀 et al., eds., *Tzu-chih t'ung-chien chin chu* 今注 (Taipei: Shang-wu 商務, 1966), vol. 10, pp. 401–536, on the last two years of Li Mi's life. Readers may wish to consult modern scholarly studies of the period. Woodbridge Bingham, *The Founding of the T'ang Dynasty: The Fall of Sui and the Rise of T'ang* (1941; reprint ed., New York: Octagon, 1971), and C. P. Fitzgerald, *Son of Heaven: A Biography of Li Shih-min, Founder of the T'ang Dynasty* (1933; reprint ed., Taipei: Cheng Wen, 1970) are pioneering Western works; more recent studies include Arthur F. Wright, *The Sui Dynasty* (New York: Knopf, 1978) and the relevant volume of *The Cambridge History of China*, Denis Twitchett, ed., *Sui and T'ang China, 589–906*, part I (Cambridge: Cambridge University Press, 1979), pp. 158–159, 161–162, 165–166.

social context, then, this type of theatrical was originally intended for audiences that included the poorly educated and the illiterate, in particular.[9] The same conclusion may be safely advanced concerning the Li Mi plays.

Given the number and variety of short *tsa-chü* plays concerning T'ang heroes composed during the Yuan and early Ming, the events surrounding the T'ang conquest must have been popular among theater audiences by that time. Extant plays capture moments in what could only have been a long cycle of fictionalized stories on the founding of the T'ang, the interlocking adventures of a number of larger-than-life heroes—and villains—as popular legend grew to fill the gaps left by the spare biographical sketches in the histories. In them, Li Mi had become an unmistakable villain.

For ease of comprehension in a form that combines singing with dialogue, all characters appeared on the *tsa-chü* stage in stereotyped roles. The moral attributes of each were predictable. Moral ambiguity had no easy means of expression in this tightly structured form, but heroism and villainy were the stock-in-trade. The actions and motivations signifying truancy on the part of Li Mi include virtual sacrilege, the destruction of a shrine in honor of a paragon of loyal service, and Li's failure to comply with an agreement made with a deity. The transposition of Li Mi's perfidy from the rational political to the fantastic religious realm marks a considerable distance between the scholarly historical record and popular historical drama. In none of these plays is Li Mi the central male character (*cheng-mo*); instead he is relegated to a secondary (*wai*) role in each. Their focus is on other characters: Wang Po-tang, Ch'in Shu-pao, and the advisors whose integrity and wisdom are tested by his presence.

Uncanny elements loom large in all these early plays. Li Shih-min is a strong and capable leader here, but he is also foolhardy. In *Lao-chün t'ang* [The temple of Lao-tzu], by Cheng Te-hui, fl. fourteenth century, Li Shih-min disregards the doom foretold by an advisor to go hunting not far from Li Mi's camp. Even though he actually intends to spy on Li Mi, when a white stag appears his predatory instincts drive him perilously close to his adversary. Li Mi's general Ch'eng Yao-chin then singlehandedly chases him into a temple; there another general, Ch'in Shu-pao, prevents Ch'eng from killing Shih-min. Li Mi resolutely imprisons this rival despite advice to the contrary, and even detains the T'ang emissary sent to plead for his release. This act convinces Li Mi's officers, including Ch'in Shu-pao, Wei Cheng, and Hsu Shih-chi, that he is a petty man by comparison with Li Shih-min; Li Mi's rule is therefore unjust while the T'ang clearly has Heaven's mandate. Consequently, they falsify Li Mi's proclamation of amnesty to include Li Shih-min and his officer, who then escape.

<hr />

[9] For a general survey of Chinese theatricals, see William Dolby's excellent *A History of Chinese Drama* (London: Paul Elek, 1976), esp. pp. 40–70, and the essays in Colin Mackerras, ed., *Chinese Theater: From Its Origins to the Present Day* (Honolulu: University of Hawaii Press, 1983). Recent studies of the *tsa-chü* in particular are Chung-wen Shih, *The Golden Age of Chinese Drama* (Princeton: Princeton University Press, 1976) and James I. Crump, *Chinese Theater in the Days of Kublai Khan* (Tucson: University of Arizona Press, 1980).

Mention of Li Mi's destruction is made at the end of the play as Li Shih-min pardons Ch'eng Yao-chin for the attempt on his life. "We were serving different masters then," the prince concludes.[10]

A somewhat later play in the same form, *Wei Cheng kai-chao* [Wei Cheng alters the proclamation], written during the early Ming, begins with declarations of loyalty by Li Shih-min's lieutenants, one of whom predicts disaster. "I do not believe in this *yin-yang* prognostication business," Li Shih-min declares, but he takes a sizable force with him to spy on Li Mi's stronghold. Ch'in Shu-pao challenges him and refuses steadfastly when Shih-min tries to win his allegiance. It is this same general Ch'in who prevents Ch'eng Yao-chin from slaying their captive in the temple, giving as his excuse the T'ang prince's obvious virtue and the orders Li Mi had given them—to capture, not to kill, Li Shih-min. When the latter is imprisoned, Wei Cheng takes full responsibility for changing the proclamation to free him. The play ends with Hsu, Wei, and Ch'in being feted when they submit to the T'ang.[11]

Ssu-ma t'ou T'ang [Four riders submit to the T'ang] is another anonymous early Ming play in this sequence. Here, when Wang Shih-ch'ung petitions Li Mi to borrow food grains and fodder, Li Mi readily agrees, despite Hsu Shih-chi's opposition, because Wang is Li's nephew. Overjoyed by this turn of events, Wang is further encouraged when he learns that Li Mi has destroyed a temple dedicated to the Duke of Chou, the sagely advisor to the Chou dynasty founder in the eleventh century B.C. As a consequence, spirit soldiers will aid in punishing Li Mi for his sacrilege. A brief battle ensues; Li Mi realizes that his defeat is proper retribution. Wang Po-tang chides him for his errors of judgment when Li Mi decides to join the T'ang—the worst of which was imprisoning Li Shih-min, who will bear him a grudge. Lacking any alternative, Li Mi, Wang Po-tang, and two other Wei generals surrender. Li Mi's initial reception in the T'ang capital is warm. But Li Shih-min is vindictive and shames Li Mi repeatedly. The latter cannot tolerate these affronts, however, and rebels soon afterward. He and his faithful Wang Po-tang flee through the mountains. In desperation, Li Mi prays for an omen in the temple of the Mountain Spirit—a deity whom he had offended by misusing a divine sword! Helpless, Li Mi leaps to his death into a gorge; Wang Po-tang spurns offers to join the T'ang and commits suicide to follow his lord.[12]

The long middle-Ming historical narrative *Sui T'ang liang-ch'ao chih-chuan*

---

[10] The text of *Lao-chün t'ang* 老君堂 can be found in *Yuan ch'ü hsuan wai-pien* 元曲選外編 [A further selection of Yuan plays], ed. Sui Shu-sen 隋樹森 (Peking: Chung-hua 中華, 1959), pp. 530–544; the quotation is from p. 543. Cheng Te-hui 鄭德輝 is also known as Cheng Kuang-tsu 光祖; he served as a minor official in Hangchow.

[11] The text of *Wei Cheng kai-chao* 魏徵改詔 can be found in *Ku-pen Yuan Ming tsa-chü* 孤本元明雜劇 [Old editions of Yuan and Ming *tsa-chü* plays], ed. Chao Yuan-tu 趙元度 (Peking: Chung-hua hsi-chü 中華戲劇, 1958), vol. 3, pp. 2061–2096; the quotation is from act 1, p. 2065.

[12] The text of *Ssu-ma t'ou T'ang* 四馬投唐 can be found in *Ku-pen Yuan Ming tsa-chü*, vol. 3, pp. 2127–2167. In passing, this play notes that Li Mi killed his bride before rebelling; see p. 2151. Hsu Shih-chi is known here as Hsu Mao-kung 徐懋功.

[Chronicles of two courts, Sui and T'ang], ca. 1550, recounts the fall of the Sui and most of the history of the T'ang. While shifting from one contender to another, this work gives Li Mi much fuller characterization, a function in part of its much greater length compared to the short *tsa-chü* plays. Despite its attempt to appear like the standard histories, its anonymous author ignored the historians' more rationalistic explanation of Li Mi's fall to elaborate on legendary and fantastic elements of his tale. These elements are common in the theater pieces above and were probably current in the oral tradition.

Here, as Li Shih-min cowers under the altar in the Lao-tzu temple, a dragon whirls in the air over the T'ang prince's head; Ch'in Shu-pao prevents Ch'eng Yao-chin from killing him because he recognizes the dragon as an omen identifying the "True Ruler" (*chen-chu*). Li Mi becomes more violent in this version: he would execute Li Shih-min for spying; Wei Cheng barely succeeds in dissuading him from doing so. Li Mi spurns the T'ang emperor's offer of land in return for his son and has the T'ang envoy beaten. Again, Wei Cheng falsifies Li Mi's edict to justify releasing Li Shih-min; he, Hsu Shih-chi, and Ch'in Shu-pao lament that they are obligated to serve this petty contender and vow to join the T'ang as soon as possible. Li Mi is distraught to find his prisoners gone; further angered by Hsu's insistence that he should have allied with the T'ang, Li Mi decides to behead the conspirators within his ranks.

Finally, Li Mi relents and releases Wei, Ch'in, and Hsu. When Wang Shih-ch'ung requests food grains, Li Mi discovers that his granaries are ominously infested with scaly winged rats. He fulfills his agreement only to be attacked by the duplicitous Wang Shih-ch'ung. The campaign goes badly for Wang until in a dream the Duke of Chou offers spirit soldiers to help Wang gain revenge for Li Mi's destruction of the shrine to the duke. As a consequence, the tide turns against Li Mi, who begins to perceive demons all around him. Convinced that Heaven has withdrawn its favor for his cause, Li Mi attempts suicide. Wang Po-tang stops him and takes the initiative in submitting to the T'ang. The T'ang emperor, for his part, can only stifle his anger against Li Mi for the good of the realm. (Note the significant alteration of Li Yuan's personality here.) Despondent because of the shame he feels over being repeatedly rebuked by Li Shih-min, Li Mi gladly accepts Wang Po-tang's advice to wait for an opportunity to rise in rebellion. He explains this to his bride, who spits in his face because of his disloyalty; in a rage Li Mi cuts her down, after which he can only flee with Wang Po-tang and a handful of retainers. Together Li Mi and his trusted lieutenant die in a hail of T'ang arrows, fit punishment for their treachery.[13]

Identifying the audience for which *Chronicles of Two Courts* was written is no

[13] *Sui T'ang liang-ch'ao chih-chuan* 隋唐兩朝志傳, attributed to Lin Han 林瀚 (ca. 1550, extant ed., Soochow, 1619), chaps. 31–38, 4:1b–51b. This is a rare work; the one known copy, a photocopy of which was used for this study, is to be found in the Sonkeikaku Library 尊經閣文庫 in Tokyo.

easy task. The anonymous compiler of this popular chronicle[14] (ostensibly based on a text written by Lo Kuan-chung in the fourteenth century and revised by Lin Han in the sixteenth) strove for completeness of narrative and enough verisimilitude to pass for historical veracity. To this end he makes careful lists of all persons of prominence involved in any action and identifies the years in which the events of each *chüan* occurred; each chapter concludes with a commentary (*p'ing*) apparently modeled on the remarks (*tsan*) appended to biographies in orthodox histories. Chapter 38 of *Chronicles of Two Courts* contains a final note on the differences between Li Mi and Hsiang Yü, adapted, it would seem, from the T'ang dynastic histories[15]—even though it is of little relevance to the character as developed here. A "poem on history" (*yung-shih shih*) by the unidentified poet styled Li-ch'üan that lauds Wang Po-tang for his unswerving loyalty, as did the historians, is also to be found here.[16] *Chronicles of Two Courts* presents Li Mi's fall rationalistically as a product of his own actions—but only to a limited degree. Li Shih-min has Heaven's mandate; there is no way that Li Mi might gain it unless Li Shih-min should prove unworthy of the mantle. As proof of its sanction, Heaven sends Shih-min a protecting dragon and Mi rats and bad dreams. Basic loyalty is superfluous to this tale, Princess Tu-ku's clamor notwithstanding; Li Mi's tragedy, such as it is, rests in his attempt to challenge his destiny. Once he fails, *Chronicles* forgets Li Mi, never to refer to him again.[17] This rambling prose text thus transposes into reading matter the legendary figure of Li Mi and his hopeless fate adapted from the oral tradition, particularly the stage.

An outgrowth, or even a continuation, of the earlier *p'ing-hua* historical narratives of the Yuan and early Ming, such popular chronicles seem to have been intended, like the *p'ing-hua*, to provide both entertainment and instruction for those whose level of literacy was insufficient to read more formal works of history. Both of these vernacular forms use poetry—even by the same poets—in the same way; both Yuan *p'ing-hua* and Ming popular chronicles are generally highly episodic. In these respects and in use of language, the popular chronicle seems to represent an evolutionary stage between China's first works of lengthy historical fiction and the highly developed historical romance of the seven-

---

[14] The term "popular chronicle" has been used by students of Chinese fiction writing in English to distinguish these early works from later and more mature historical novels such as *Sui T'ang yen-i* and from military romances, imaginative fiction parading as history. See C. T. Hsia, "The Military Romance: A Genre of Chinese Fiction," in *Studies in Chinese Literary Genres*, ed. Cyril Birch (Berkeley: University of California Press, 1974), pp. 339–390, esp. pp. 339–346.

[15] *Sui T'ang liang-ch'ao chih-chuan*, 4:51b; compare *Chiu T'ang shu*, 7, 2225, and *Hsin T'ang shu*, 12, 3687.

[16] *Sui T'ang liang-ch'ao chih-chuan*, 4:51.

[17] That loyalty was of some concern to the author can be seen in the frequent discussions of that virtue between the characters here; see *Sui T'ang liang-ch'ao chih-chuan*, 5:4b–5, 5:13, 5:30, 6:28b, 6:33, etc.

teenth century.[18] Subsequent observations will confirm that it is correct to identify this work as having been designed for audiences who were literate but not well educated.

Of approximately the same age as *Chronicles of Two Courts* is *Ta T'ang Ch'in-wang tz'u-hua* [Prince of Ch'in of the great T'ang, a *tz'u-hua*], dating in its present form from around 1550.[19] This has been termed the earliest extant *ku-tz'u*, or drumsong text, although its modern editors acknowledge the considerable distance between a transcription of oral performances and this written version.[20] The confusion over the nature of the work relates to its mixture of prose and verse and the function of the latter here. In contrast to developing novelistic practice, here the verse sections of five-, seven-, and ten-syllable lines

[18] For a discussion of the *p'ing-hua* 平話, see Wilt L. Idema, *Chinese Vernacular Fiction: The Formative Period* (Leiden: Brill, 1974), pp. 69–120; Chang Cheng-lang 張政烺, "Chiang-shih yü yung-shih-shih" 講史與詠史詩 [The retelling of history and verse about history], *Bulletin of the Institute of History and Philology (Academica Sinica)* 10:601–645 (1948); James I. Crump, "*P'ing-hua* and the Early History of the *San-kuo chih*," *Journal of the American Oriental Society* 71:249–256 (1951). Liu Ts'un-yan 柳存仁 discusses *Chronicles of Two Courts* in his "Lo Kuan-chung and His Historical Romances," in *Critical Essays on Chinese Fiction*, eds. Winston L. Y. Yang and Curtis P. Adkins (Hong Kong: Chinese University Press, 1980), pp. 99–108. Hsia, "Military Romance," p. 350, identifies Hsiung Chung-ku 熊鍾谷 (fl. 1550), to whom most such chronicles are attributed, as an author of works for popular audiences.

[19] The problems involved in identifying the sequence of these narratives and their textual interrelations with the various versions of *T'ang shu yen-i* 唐書演義 [The history of the T'ang, a romance], ca. 1553, by Hsiung Chung-ku, the publisher from Chien-yang 建陽, Fukien, are numerous and quite complicated. I hope to address them on another occasion, but for present purposes it is justifiable to consider *Prince of Ch'in* as the older. Relevant observations concerning these works and their textual relations may be found in Sun K'ai-ti 孫楷第, *Jih-pen Tung-ching so-chien Chung-kuo hsiao-shuo shu-mu* 日本東京所見中國小說書目 [Chinese fiction seen in Tokyo, Japan: A bibliography] (Hong Kong: Shih-yung 實用, 1967), pp. 32–42; Cheng Chen-to, "Chung-kuo hsiao-shuo t'i-yao" 中國小說提要 [Notes on Chinese fiction], in his *Chung-kuo wen-hsueh yen-chiu* 中國文學研究 [Studies in Chinese literature] (Hong Kong: Chung-wen shu-chü 中文書局, 1961), vol. I, pp. 351–353; Liu Ts'un-yan, *Chinese Popular Fiction*, pp. 100, 255–262; Hsia, "Military Romance," pp. 359 ff; Idema, *Chinese Vernacular Fiction*, p. xxxvi, n. 47. Although this work, like several other *tz'u-hua* recently discovered (see n. 5), was meant to be read, it also reflects the oral genre "to a large extent," as P. D. Hanan puts it in "*Judge Bao's Hundred Cases* Reconstructed." Liu Ts'un-yan, "Lo Kuan-chung," esp. pp. 88–99, notes significant parallels between this and other works attributed to Lo Kuan-chung 羅貫中.

[20] Sun K'ai-ti, "Tz'u-hua k'ao" 詞話考 [Studies of *tz'u-hua*], 1933, in his *Ts'ang-chou chi* 滄州集 [Selected essays by Sun K'ai-ti] (Peking: Chung-hua 中華, 1965), pp. 99, 103; the unsigned explanatory note prefacing the reprinted version, Chu Sheng-lin 諸聖隣, *Ta T'ang Ch'in-wang tz'u-hua* 大唐秦王詞話 (Peking: Wen-hsueh ku-chi k'an-hsing-she 文學古籍刊行社, 1955; hereafter *Ta T'ang*); Cheng Chen-to 鄭振鐸, *Chung-kuo su-wen-hsueh shih* 中國俗文學史 [A history of Chinese popular literature] (Peking: Wen-hsueh ku-chi k'an-hsing-she, 1959), vol. 2, p. 385; Idema, *Chinese Vernacular Fiction*, pp. xxxvii, 119, considers that it may be an "experimental novel." Yeh Te-yun 葉德均, *Sung Yuan Ming chiang-ch'ang wen-hsueh* 宋元明講唱文學 [Chantefable literature of the Sung, Yuan, and Ming] (Shanghai: Ku-tien wen-hsueh 古典文學, 1957), pp. 40–49, discusses the development of the (hypothetical) *tz'u-hua* form. His explanation, he admits, is full of inconsistencies. David Roy, "The Fifteenth-Century *shuo-ch'ang tz'u-hua* as Examples of Written Formulaic Composition," *CHINOPERL Papers* 10:124, n. 6 (1982), concludes that *tz'u-hua* in these titles designates only "doggerel verse employed for narrative or descriptive purposes."

in *shih* format, as well as the *tz'u* poems, not only record descriptions of scene, costume, and the like, but also share the burden of narration with prose. Even some dialogue is set in verse. Clearly, *Prince of Ch'in* owes these formal features in part to the *chantefable* tradition, and for this reason it is only natural that it exhibit values common to theatrical works for mass audiences. I will return to its intended audience shortly, after observations on its content.

The prince of the title is Li Shih-min. The narrative records his rise to prominence and his eventual unification of the empire as its ruler. All other characters are of secondary interest; Li Mi becomes a strikingly contrasting foil to the prince. W. L. Idema has rightly praised the work's central conflict— between Li Shih-min's filial duty to his father (Li Yuan, the T'ang founder) and the responsibility he owes his own loyal followers, attracted to him by his personal virtue. This conflict gives the work a kind of coherence lacking in the structurally much cruder *Chronicles of Two Courts*. Furthermore, the struggles of the prince for power are given tragic and ironic dimensions through the repeated poetic interludes devoted to life's transience.[21]

Several scenes contrast sharply with this rationalistic tendency, however. While Li Mi is portrayed in *Prince of Ch'in* as a contender who fails through his own arrogance and perfidy, supernatural forces also conspire to seal his doom. The Duke of Chou from the eleventh century B.C. sends flying rats to destroy Li Mi's grain stores; Hsi Wang Mu, the mythical "Queen Mother of the West," confiscates his magically potent sword—because he had broken the three interdictions limiting its use.[22] This latter episode has all the flavor of folklore; it contradicts the historically sanctioned descriptions of Li Mi's disaster as having been self-made. Li Shih-min is no less the victim of capricious forces beyond his ken. Before a big battle with another contender for power, his trusted advisor Li Ching warns that disaster will befall if the prince goes sightseeing, hunts, or practices with his bow. The T'ang forces are victorious and the enemy is besieged. To while away the time, Li Shih-min wishes to visit the nearby tombs of Han period worthies, on Mount Pei-mang. A seer, Li Chun-feng, again foretells doom if he refuses to believe in *yin-yang* prognostication—and if he is not back by noon. Just as he is about to return, a deer scampers past. Li shoots it, and follows the wounded animal to a tomb. On its wall in bas-relief is a deer with an arrow in its leg. An ominous verse beside it suggests that disaster is imminent.

As noon approaches, Li Shih-min sees a city and rides over to inspect it. Its commander, Li Mi, orders out his generals to attack. Ch'eng Yao-chin ap- proaches; the prince wounds him in the leg with another arrow and then flees. Although his prayers in the Lao-tzu shrine bring him temporary safety, Shih-

---

[21] This is in contrast to the often hackneyed poems on history (*yung-shih shih* 詠史詩) to be found in other early vernacular historical narratives; verse here having this greater significance is also quite moving. See Idema, *Chinese Vernacular Fiction*, pp. xxxvi–xxxviii. I refer to verse passages introducing *chüan* 3, for example.

[22] See *Ta T'ang*, chap. 16, 1.364–368.

min guarantees his own betrayal: Ch'eng has a woodcutter climb a tall tree to survey the area for the prince. This man does perceive a dragon hovering over the prince but pretends that he sees nothing. So fearful of discovery is Li Shih-min that he shoots the hapless man in the throat, thus giving away his where-abouts. Ch'eng captures him with Ch'in Shu-pao's help. With the Prince in Li Mi's prison, the narrator chides him again, in verse, for his lack of faith in prognostication—even as a star heralds his future regal station.[23]

Fairy-tale innocence concerning causation appears regularly here. In chapter 9, when Li Mi fails to exterminate the flying rats in his granaries, he has a group of the rats driven past him. He observes that one is gold in color and bigger than the rest. Ch'in Shu-pao shoots it, which causes all the rats to disappear, leaving behind a note predicting fire; this is the proclamation of the king of the rats. A spider web suddenly appears and then reappears across the door of the storehouse. Exasperated by it, Li Mi orders the web burned. A miraculous wind springs up, carrying sparks inside and even to Li Mi's treasuries of precious metals, all of which are consumed by the fire.[24] Later the contender Wang Shih-ch'ung wins the general Shan Hsiung-hsin over to his side by getting him drunk and putting his own concubines in Shan's bed. After committing the offense of sleeping with Wang's concubines, Shan must join Wang or die; he chooses the former alternative. When Li Mi begins to worry why Shan has not returned, he gullibly sends three lone envoys to inquire of Wang about him—thus proving himself a total fool compared to the wily Wang, who springs his trap for Li Mi with diabolical glee.[25] Likewise, Li Mi follows the most unreasonable advice of an otherwise undistinguished retainer to rebel against the T'ang when reliable Wang Po-tang knows full well that such a course is suicidal. Here, when Li Mi's time is up he no longer functions in any capacity as a worthwhile ruler, forgetting even the basics of military strategy.[26] But then Li Shih-min's reason had deserted him as well. Through this inconsistent blend of innocent absurdity and intellectual rationalism,[27] we

---

[23] *Ta T'ang*, chaps. 2–5, 1.82–132. In addition to his prescience, Li Ching 李靖 can also command storms like Chu-ko Liang 諸葛亮 in *Romance of the Three Kingdoms*; see *Ta T'ang* 1.165–168.

[24] *Ta T'ang*, chap. 9, 1.229–232.

[25] *Ta T'ang*, chaps. 9 and 10, 1.235–243, 1.245–249. This bedroom deception was already seen in chap. 1, 1.48–49, in which Li Shih-min tricks his father Li Yuan into rebelling against the Sui. It is this latter ruse, developed perhaps with details borrowed from the former, that appears in subsequent historical fiction.

[26] See *Ta T'ang* 1.340–355.

[27] For the loss of Li Mi's sword, see *Ta T'ang* 1.366–368; his receipt of the weapon from Hsi Wang Mu is not narrated here. Likewise, the circumstances of the Duke of Chou's revenge are related in detail, but the crime meriting this punishment, Li Mi's destruction of the shrines dedicated to this model minister, is not narrated here. Presumably, all these events appeared in earlier, genuine *chantefable*, versions of the tale. Perhaps the compiler of the present edition, Chu Sheng-lin, felt that it was unnecessary to do so, as it would have been if these stories were still common in the oral tradition of the middle Ming. His lapse, then, demonstrates all the more clearly the popularity of the T'ang founders story cycle.

can find confirmation of what the structure of the work reveals. *Prince of Ch'in* is a hybrid narrative structurally indebted to popular *chantefable* literature for oral performance and to a growing body of fictionalized historical narratives in prose. At least in its earlier form as a pure *tz'u-hua*, its intended audience must have been basically unlettered despite the flashes of self-conscious literary sophistication in its later version; in its present form it must fall near the socially lower end of the audience spectrum, for a literate but non-elite audience.

Scholars of diverse backgrounds and leanings have divided mature Ming and Ch'ing novels into two general categories, those written by identified scholar-novelists for other highly educated readers and those composed anonymously by literate but less well educated men for culturally less sophisticated readers. Modern Chinese editors term the former "classical fiction" (*ku-tien hsiao-shuo*) and have reprinted some of these works in carefully prepared punctuated and even annotated editions. The other works have often been considerably altered to rid them of "feudal ideas" and "superstitious beliefs"; such novels are called "popular reading materials" (*t'ung-su tu-wu*). W. L. Idema uses the terms "literary novels" and "chapbooks" to distinguish the two types, and although C. T. Hsia objects strenuously to Idema's criteria for this distinction, he still finds the categorization useful. The reason for this disagreement is a difficulty in deciding upon defensible criteria. Idema, following the Chinese lead, tends to view anonymous works as generally falling into this second category, particularly historical fiction and "swordsman novels" (*wu-hsia hsiao-shuo*).

Style of language is an important criterion for Idema, which Hsia easily renders dubious in its reliability.[28] Idema also uses the cost of production as a criterion—that is, in his view expensive, large-format editions with many high-quality illustrations were meant for wealthy purchasers; cheap editions were meant for the less affluent. While this is a self-evident truth, Hsia again throws its relevance into question by observing that the wealthy were not necessarily the more culturally sophisticated, nor were works produced in rich format only those of greatest art. Furthermore, later editions might be considerably less expensive than the first (with the result that subsequent audiences may be different from that originally intended by the novelist). While Idema searches for objective criteria for the categorization of old China's novels, C. T. Hsia insists that only on the basis of artistic complexity can works for different

---

[28] While the literary novels tend toward inventive use of vernacular language, chapbooks utilize a simplified classical style devoid of literary polish, according to Idema, *Chinese Vernacular Fiction*, pp. xi–xii. Hsia, however, illustrates exceptions to this rule: a "chapbook" in northern colloquial and a pair of presumably elite works written in elegant forms of the classical style; see Hsia, "The Scholar-Novelist and Chinese Culture: A Reappraisal of *Ching-hua yuan*," in *Chinese Narrative: Critical and Theoretical Essays*, ed. Andrew H. Plaks (Princeton: Princeton University Press, 1977), pp. 267–270, esp. notes 4–5. I do not believe that these exceptions invalidate Idema's general rule, but this is a point that needs further consideration.

audiences be distinguished.[29] Neither approach is without merit; used together they can reveal the audiences we seek to establish.

It seems generally true that highly literate members of the social elite who acknowledged their role in the production of vernacular fiction were usually writing specifically for their peers. These works were normally very well printed and often lavishly illustrated. Moreover, literati novels are generally distinguishable by certain obtrusive literary conventions and by the relative complexity of motivations they attribute to their characters. Foremost in the first category is an aggregation of characteristics now often described as the "storyteller's manner." These novels, like the fully developed *hua-pen* short story of the seventeenth century, engage the reader in a fictive dialogue with the narrator, who frequently interrupts the narrative to elucidate the meaning to be drawn from plot and characterization. By contrast, works for non-elite readers merely present action to be appreciated on its own terms without this further distancing device. Literati novels also provide commentary at the ends of chapters to continue this dialogue from a somewhat different perspective: the commentator may not in fact be other than the novelist himself, but this new stance allows discussion on matters of structure, narrative skill, and historical veracity, for example, that are inappropriate to the perspective of the storyteller. The pace of action is deliberately slowed in mature novels for the elite by frequent insertion of verse, usually attributable to the narrator or "quoted" by him from earlier, characteristically anonymous, sources. Such poems describe character, setting or moral evaluation of events.[30] Literati novelists, or, as Hsia terms them, scholar-novelists, utilized the novel form to meet specific intellectual needs: social and political commentary, philosophical exploration, self-expression, and even their own and their friends' enjoyment.[31] More popular works seem to have entertainment of less educated readers as their primary function.

[29] See Idema, *Chinese Vernacular Fiction*, p. lxi; Hsia, "Scholar-Novelist," p. 269, n. 6. In a recent study of two late Ming *ch'uan-ch'i* 傳奇 plays, Cyril Birch compares them on six values—the musical, lyric, mythic, mimetic, comic, and spectacular. He discovers that the play designed more specifically for elite audiences emphasizes the earlier values on this list over the later ones; the more popular play presents more comedy and spectacle by comparison. Such observations do not conclusively distinguish works for different audiences, but they do reinforce my assertions below. See Birch, "The Dramatic Potential of Xi Shi: *Huanshaji* and *Jiaopaji* Compared," *CHINOPERL Papers* 10:129–140 (1982).

[30] For a discussion of the "storyteller's manner" in Ming and Ch'ing fiction, see Idema, *Chinese Vernacular Fiction*, pp. 70, 122; and Hanan, *Chinese Vernacular Story*, pp. 20–22. Andrew H. Plaks describes the use of ironic distance between novelist and events narrated most perceptively in his "Full-length *Hsiao-shuo* and the Western Novel: A Generic Reappraisal," *New Asia Academic Bulletin* 1:163–176 (1978), esp. pp. 171–173. See also Plaks's recent "*Shui-hu chuan* and the Sixteenth-Century Novel Form: An Interpretive Reappraisal," *Chinese Literature: Essays, Articles and Reviews* 2.1:3–53 (January 1980), and my discussions of literati fiction in *Novel*.

[31] Hsia, "Scholar-Novelist," pp. 269–271.

Textually related[32] versions of the tale of Li Mi appear in two literati novels of the seventeenth century, *Sui shih i-wen* [Forgotten tales of the Sui, 1633] by the poet and dramatist Yuan Yü-ling (1599–1674) and *Sui T'ang yen-i* [Romance of the Sui and the T'ang, ca. 1675, first edition 1695], by the scholar-publisher Ch'u Jen-huo (ca. 1635–ca. 1705). Both authors considered the writing of novels a serious literary endeavor. To Yuan Yü-ling, no literatus should be without such classics of popular fiction as *Hsi-yu chi* [Journey to the West].[33] He re-edited at least one earlier historical novel, but it was on *Forgotten Tales* that he lavished his attention. In his preface to that work Yuan relates, in pseudo-jocular vein, that he wishes to supplement standard historiography by describing the early life of a famous figure while he was still in youthful obscurity. What Yuan presents is a dramatic view of maturation, imbued with sensitivity and good humor, but replete with strident warnings about the state of society and the monarchy.[34] Ch'u Jen-huo was a publisher and a compiler of anthologies. In the former capacity he produced an edition of a sixteenth-century novel of myth and adventure, *Feng-shen yen-i* [Investiture of the gods], that is still considered the standard today. Ch'u's publishing venture produced editions of highest quality; his *Romance* is a first-rate example of the xylographic printer's art. Its format is large; he used high-quality paper and engaged an artist who signed his illustrations for the work. As a compiler Ch'u demonstrates his devotion to reading broadly; he regularly cites hundreds of works in his own anecdote collections. The same scholarly tendency is visible in his *Romance of the Sui and the T'ang*: here Ch'u copied, often verbatim, segments from dozens of works of fiction and informal history concerning the Sui and early T'ang. Clearly he was writing for readers as well versed in historiographical sources as he was himself—that is, other literati. Furthermore, the overall structure of the novel is experimental and keyed to contemporary literary trends—among the elite.[35] His work, like Yuan's, could only have been intended for an elite audience of sophisticated readers.

Li Mi appears as a peripheral character in these two literati novels. *Forgotten Tales* concentrates on the early career of the warrior Ch'in Shu-pao, while the *Romance* sets its sights, more broadly, on the rise and fall of political forces over a

[32] While textual problems are not of central concern here, they may not be disregarded. Ch'u Jen-huo acknowledged in his preface to *Sui T'ang yen-i* that *Sui T'ang liang-ch'ao chih-chuan* formed the basis for his own work. To its spare framework he grafted nearly all of *Sui shih i-wen*, either verbatim or in outline, and major portions of another late Ming novel, *Sui Yang-ti yen-shih* 隋煬帝艷史 [The merry adventures of Emperor Yang of the Sui], and a variety of shorter prose narratives. For details, see Hegel, *Novel*, appendix I, pp. 239–240.

[33] See Yuan's *T'i-tz'u* 題辭 in an edition of *Hsi-yu chi* 西遊記, ostensibly edited by Li Chih 李贄, quoted in Sun K'ai-ti, *Jih-pen*, p. 77.

[34] See Hegel, *Novel*, pp. 112–139, esp. pp. 129–130.

[35] See Robert E. Hegel, "*Sui T'ang yen-i* and the Aesthetics of the Seventeenth-Century Suchou Elite," in *Chinese Narrative*, ed. Plaks, esp. pp. 126–139, 141–142, 145–153. Liu Ts'un-yan discusses illustrations in novels in his *Chinese Popular Fiction*, pp. 25–29.

two-hundred-year period.[36] *Forgotten Tales* introduces into the tale a test of the hero's loyalty: with Li Mi firmly in power, his ambitions grow to encompass the empire. Wang Po-tang dissuades his lord from attacking the T'ang; Li Yuan's armies are simply too strong to be defeated, he argues. Consequently, Ch'in Shu-pao and the strategist Wei Cheng take a proposal of alliance to the T'ang court on Li Mi's behalf. Impressed by his valor, Li Shih-min invites Ch'in to shift his allegiance to their side. Reluctantly Ch'in refuses; he must fulfill his commitments to Li Mi.[37]

Ch'u Jen-huo's concern in *Romance of the Sui and the T'ang* was to demonstrate the workings of Heaven in the rise of the T'ang. To this end he introduced a new element into the Li Mi tale. When the various Wei generals debate ways to help him escape from Li Mi's prison, they dismiss the alternative of changing the pardon as too simplistic to be convincing. Instead, the jailor and his attractive daughter ferry Li Shih-min to safety on the pretext of transferring him to another prison.[38]

More like rationalistic history and yet still mysterious are the explanations in these elite versions of the tale. That is, Yuan Yü-ling's concern has been with the nature of the hero, his maturation and the means by which he might properly establish himself in the eyes of the world. To become a behavioral model deliberately constructed for society's leaders, the hero Ch'in Shu-pao must develop a keen sensitivity to those qualities demonstrative of moral greatness and the capacity to rule. Li Mi falls short in both of these areas in contrast to Li Shih-min. The novelist even set himself the task of fabricating a plausible biography of Ch'in's early life to *supplement*, not to supplant, the histories[39]; thus his view of Li Mi comes closer to that of the historians than of the professional dramatists and popular chroniclers of the Ming. Given Ch'u Jen-huo's emphasis on the larger motive forces behind historical change, the role of Heaven and the inherent weaknesses of political institutions, he was unwilling to leave any of his major characters stereotyped as good or wicked. Li Mi is not a villain in *Romance*. Nor is Li Shih-min pure moral exemplar—like most other emperors in this novel, he falls prey to the temptations of the flesh. As a consequence, he neglects his official duties and his state suffers thereby.[40] Fantasy can be found here, but Ch'u Jen-huo's Li Mi falls through his own inadequacies—to which Heaven responds.

---

[36] These essential differences are never so clearly demonstrated as in their treatment of Ch'in Shu-pao; see Robert E. Hegel, "Maturation and Conflicting Values: Two Novelists' Portraits of the Chinese Hero Ch'in Shu-pao," in *Critical Studies on Chinese Fiction*, ed. Yang and Adkins, pp. 115–150.

[37] *Sui shih i-wen* 隋史遺文, by Yuan Yü-ling 袁于令 (Taipei: Yu-shih yueh-k'an she 幼獅 月刊社, 1975), chap. 49, pp. 338–342.

[38] *Sui T'ang yen-i* 隋唐演義, by Ch'u Jen-huo (Shanghai: Ku-tien wen-hsueh 古典文學, 1956), chap. 51, pp. 389, 392–393.

[39] See *Sui shih i-wen*, "*Sui shih i-wen hsu*" 序, pp. 3–5.

[40] See Hegel, "Aesthetics," pp. 124–159.

The one extended narrative that corresponds most closely to the theatrical recreations of Li Mi's fall is *Shuo T'ang yen-i* [Tales of the T'ang], later retitled *Shuo T'ang ch'ien-chuan* [First series], when sequels began to appear a century after it was written. This work may be safely considered a novel for a less well educated, non-elite readership, on the basis of these characteristics: this anonymous early eighteenth-century novel is textually indebted to older fiction and drama concerning the Sui and the T'ang, but in its action-packed pages is to be found a certain amount of innovative content. Among this new material is a new character, the fourth son of Li Yuan, named Li Yuan-pa. Historically, this person died as a small child; here he is pure prodigy. At the age of twelve he is bigger and far stronger than a normal man. He can defeat any number of soldiers in personal combat; the hyperbole with which he is described far surpasses the only occasionally extravagant descriptions in literati novels.

In its version of Li Mi's later career, *Tales of the T'ang* has Li Mi lead the allied forces to punish the regicide solely in order to obtain the imperial insignia with which he may legitimize his own claim to the throne. Ch'eng Yao-chin heads the expedition, having won that honor by virtue of his magical—in addition to his military—prowess. Li Mi's forces are initially successful until Li Yuan-pa singlehandedly holds the entire allied army at bay, demanding the insignia and their surrender to the T'ang. When one leader objects to the second demand, Yuan-pa tears the man limb from limb with his bare hands.[41]

Because of this one act, subsequent military action against the T'ang in *Tales of the T'ang* is motivated in large part by a thirst for revenge. All complexities of characterization to be found in the literati novels are swept aside in this adventure novel to leave a disproportionate supply of the more gross motivations for human behavior. Fear, greed, revenge, blind rage—while it cannot be said that *Tales of the T'ang* endorses these feelings as just cause for action (all characters fail when their exploits are so motivated), because it presents raw emotion in crude form, the reader might more readily respond to these expressions and to pure physical strength than to the intricacies of conflicting moral obligations and refined strategy. Even Li Mi is made more immediate by the exposure of his physical lusts here: upon his defeat of the regicide he gladly trades treasure for the Empress Hsiao, with whom he has become infatuated.[42] By contrast with characters in the literati novels, the simple heroes and villains of *Tales of the T'ang* are far more easily understood. From their different approaches, C. T. Hsia and W. L. Idema both conclude that this work was

---

[41] *Hsiu-hsiang Shuo T'ang yen-i ch'üan-chuan* 繡像說唐演義全傳 [Complete tales of the T'ang, illustrated] (Shanghai: Chin-chang t'u-shu-chü 錦章圖書局, ca. 1915), hereafter *Shuo T'ang*, chap. 42, 2:16. This edition is the complete 68-chapter version; other recent editions are condensed to 66 or even 64 chapters. Li Yuan-pa 李元霸 is introduced in chap. 35, 2:10b.

[42] *Shuo T'ang*, 2:16b. Li Yuan-pa is miraculously destroyed by Heaven here, apparently because he cursed it for breaking a thunderstorm over his head!

intended for less sophisticated reading audiences than *Forgotten Tales* and *Romance of the Sui and the T'ang.*[43]

From at least the Yuan, local and regional dramatic forms flourished all over China. The primary point of difference among them was in the musical traditions they incorporated, although of course they differed in dialect of performance as well. Some story material was nearly universally shared among these different traditions. The best known and most important form in recent centuries developed in the Peking area, called *p'i-huang hsi* (drama using music in the *hsi-p'i* and *erh-huang* styles) or *ching-hsi* (Peking opera). Here, on a simple stage, actors perform in conventional role categories, each with its appropriate costuming, makeup, stage properties, and style of singing. Conventions of makeup and gesture are particularly complex but symbolize the character's level of moral and aesthetic refinement. While the form is obviously designed to delight the eye, northern audiences of all social classes went, as common terminology has it, to "hear the play" (*t'ing-hsi*), music being the most important element. Experience at the theater might have been required to appreciate fully its art, but literacy was not a prerequisite. We may safely conclude that these commercial entertainments were designed to appeal to audiences consisting in large part of the unlettered masses. Because it was a performer's, not a playwright's, art form, texts of plays were fluid entities until by happenstance or by scholarly effort they came to be recorded. Texts now current represent nineteenth- or twentieth-century stage versions.[44]

The compilers of Peking operas presented further new elements in the downfall of Li Mi. In *Shuang t'ou T'ang* [A pair shift allegiance to the T'ang], the central character is Wang Po-tang in a *lao-sheng* (distinguished and upright older male) role. At his introduction, Wang has just returned from a mission to capture the advisors Hsu Shih-chi and Wei Cheng; they had deserted Li Mi to join the T'ang. True to his vows of sworn brotherhood with them, Wang would rather lie to his lord than to bring them harm. Li Mi sees through Wang Po-

---

[43] Here again Hsia's criterion is art. His proof lies in the total failure of *Tales of the T'ang* to present the superior strategic planning of historical military advisors in any convincing manner. Instead, this military romance makes such characters into wizards—as they are in the plays and the *chantefable* of the Ming. However, here the characters are altered to fit role categories of the developing military-romance genre: they are provided with astral origins, masters from whom they learn their skills, and lifelong friends; see Hsia, "Military Romance," pp. 359–362. Likewise, *Tales of the T'ang* is almost certainly an adaptation of the literati novels discussed above; see Hsia, "Military Romance," pp. 379–389, esp. n. 55. No early edition, to my knowledge, had the artistic quality—or, presumably, the high price—of *Forgotten Tales* or *Romance*.

[44] For detailed descriptions of Peking opera, see Dolby, *History*, pp. 157–196, 216–230; Colin P. Mackerras, *The Rise of the Peking Opera, 1770–1870* (Oxford: Clarendon Press, 1972); and Mackerras's *The Chinese Theatre in Modern Times From 1840 to the Present Day* (Amherst: University of Massachusetts Press, 1975). In addition to these excellent historical surveys, noteworthy among older works is L. C. Arlington, *The Chinese Drama* (Shanghai, 1930; reprint ed. New York: Benjamin Blom, 1966) and *Famous Chinese Plays*, trans. and ed. Arlington and Harold Acton (Peking: Henri Vetch, 1937).

tang's lie that they outran him, however. Among his essential lieutenants, only Wang remains in Mi's camp—the others have defected to Li Shih-min. For that reason, one should not be suspicious of his sole loyal follower, Wang suggests, to which Li Mi replies prophetically, "If I misjudge your good heart, may I die in a hail of arrows!" Wang Po-tang suggests that they surrender to the T'ang, giving up glory and independence to guarantee survival. Every enterprise has its rise and its fall, Wang declares.

For his part, Li Shih-min in this play wants revenge for being imprisoned. While hunting he downs a goose but cannot locate it. Li Mi and Wang Po-tang find the dead bird; the latter uses it as an introduction to the T'ang commander. Li Shih-min here declares his willingness to forgive and forget; it is his father's anger that needs assuaging. To assure his loyalty, the emperor awards Li Mi with a princess for wife. But when Li Mi tries to enlist her aid in his rebellion, she refuses and he slays her and all of her maids—an act he here justifies as karma from a previous life. Wang Po-tang had earlier refused to swear allegiance to the T'ang in order that he might continue to serve Li Mi personally; now he reprimands his lord sternly for his treachery. Wang even laments that his fate is to serve such a perfidious leader. Nevertheless, Wang distracts their pursuers to allow Li Mi a last chance for freedom. Failing in that, he dies together with his lord in a hail of arrows. Wang's reward is forthcoming, however; Li Shih-min orders a formal funeral for him—but not for Li Mi.[45]

Loyalty within the social hierarchy has been displaced by other, lateral obligations in this version of the tale. Here oaths of brotherhood and commitment to an individual supplant loyalty to a cause or to a state. It is true that Wang's ties to Li Mi bring him to his death, but clearly he places a higher priority on protecting his friends than he does on truthfulness to his lord—he maintains his pretense that they evaded his pursuit until Li Mi is finally convinced. Li Mi's trust is thus ironic in the context of the play and reveals the considerably simpler view of human motivations presented here. Again, as in *Tales of the T'ang*, this play emphasizes immediacy of appreciation by its frequent references to fate or karma and simple cause-and-effect relationships. The demands of the theater account for certain variations from the tale as presented in literati fiction, but the degree of attention to the more concrete obligations to individuals rather than merely to some abstract cause or nebulous political entity can only have been the result of conscious choice on the part of the dramatist. Personal considerations and higher forces take precedence over public concerns here; this fact is certainly essential in understanding the values presented in art forms such as this.

From this brief overview, it is obvious that the fall of Li Mi appeared in vernacular narratives intended for a range of audiences—from novels written

---

[45] The text appears in *Kuo-chü ta-ch'eng* 國劇大成 [A compendium of the national opera], ed. Chang Po-ch'in 張伯謹 (Taipei: Kuo-fang-pu yin-chih-ch'ang 國防部印製廠, 1969), vol. 5, pp. 359–372; the quotation is from p. 361.

for the highly cultured members of the well-to-do social elite to plays designed for audiences specifically including the illiterate masses. If we take these groups as poles of a spectrum, then the other three popular narratives fall between them: the modified *chantefable Prince of Ch'in* near the plays and *Chronicles of Two Courts* nearer the elite novels, when formal features are considered. Its anonymous authorship and emphasis on fast-paced action suggest a less sophisticated readership for *Tales of the T'ang*, thus placing it with *Prince of Ch'in* near the play end of this continuum. These relationships may be represented as follows:

| Elite | : | Non-elite | |
| Highly literate | : Moderately literate | | Primarily illiterate |

Forgotten Tales *Romance*   *Chronicles* *Prince* *Tales*   Ming plays *A Pair*

During discussion of these versions of the Li Mi tale, I have approached them in chronological order, concentrating on the differences between them, particularly on how each successive version builds on its predecessors. By implication, I have suggested as one criterion the degree of rationality versus fantastic or supernatural elements in motivations ascribed to central characters such as Li Mi, Wang Po-tang, Ch'in Shu-pao, and Ch'eng Yao-chin. This approach can be used again to array these works along a spectrum; their positions along a continuum of motivation explanations parallels that for intended audience. None of these works occupies a position at one of the poles of this scale. However, to the extent that this criterion confirms other evidence submitted above, the differences of motivations attributed to characters provide an avenue for further investigations of values presented to specific audiences.

Rational explanations of motivations		Dependence on supernatural explanations for motivations

Forgotten Tales *Romance* *Chronicles* *Prince*   *Tales* Ming plays *A Pair*

CORRELATIONS OF CONTENT AND VALUES
WITH DIFFERENT AUDIENCES

By concentrating on dissimilarities among the different versions of Li Mi's fall, we have overlooked the significant overlaps in story material. Table I presents a hypothetical "complete" tale of Li Mi's fall by listing in a single chronological sequence all of the incidents from these seven sources (taking the Ming play cycle as a single entry), noting the ones that occur in more than a single version. Sixty separate incidents appear when the texts are compared. When sources provide dissimilar accounts of the same incident, these cases have been designated as subcategories of the numbered entries (e.g., 29a, 29b, 29c). For easy comparison I have grouped these works by intended audience as identified above. "History" here means the standard histories *Chiu T'ang shu* and *Hsin T'ang shu* and the chronological history *Tzu-chih t'ung-chien*. While it is possible that less formal but still reliable sources may have been used by some of the writers involved, I have not taken such works into account here; these three histories by themselves serve adequately to make clear distinctions between the various popular versions.

Even at first glance, Table I presents a considerable degree of overlap between the vernacular versions of Li Mi's fall for different audiences. All versions vary appreciably from the historical record, inserting speeches, battles, and even characters that have little or no basis in the official histories. Clearly, all Ming–Ch'ing writers of historical fiction and drama, like their counterparts in other cultures and eras, were motivated to flesh out the bare facts with dramatic detail. Mere reference to a behavioral model (of the negative sort) like Hsiang Yü would not suffice; writers for all audiences felt the need to exemplify their understanding of this historical character in concrete ways by showing (either literally or figuratively) the events and forces that contributed significantly to Li Mi's fall. Table I also shows that a certain number of incidents from the tale of Li occur only in vernacular works for non-elite readers and for illiterates, including Ming and Ch'ing plays, while others are present only in the elite works, *Forgotten Tales* and *Romance*. Thirty-seven of the total of seventy-eight incidents and variations occur only in the more popular works, 47 percent of the total. In the elite novels there are nine unique incidents, or 12 percent of the total. The rest are shared by one or more works from each of these two major categories. It is through these differences in the tale that we may seek differences in values presented to separable audiences.

First, it would appear either that writers for non-elite literate and illiterate audiences were the more innovative in incorporating new incidents into the tale, or that literati novelists were less willing to present legendary or irrational materials to elite audiences. I suspect that both observations are accurate to a certain extent; regardless of the sources for these accretions to the tale, major categories of vernacular literature are distinguishable on this basis. After all, the

TABLE 1. Incidents in the Fall of Li Mi from History and Vernacular Literature

Number	Incident	Original sources — Histories	Elite novels — Forgotten Tales	Elite novels — Romance of the Sui and the T'ang	Non-elite narratives — Chronicles	Non-elite narratives — Prince of Ch'in	Non-elite narratives — Tales of the T'ang	Plays — Ming plays	Plays — A Pair
1.	Li Mi joins Chai Jang, becomes primary leader (A3ᵃ)	X	X	X	X		X	X	
2.	Li Mi executes Chai (E3)	X	X	X	X				
3.	Subordinates flee Li Mi to join T'ang (C3)			X					
4.	Wang Po-tang dissuades Li Mi from attacking T'ang, urges alliance (A3, F)		X						
5.	Ch'in Shu-pao and Wei Cheng take letter to T'ang (A3, F)		X						
6.	Ch'in Shu-pao refuses invitation to join T'ang forces (A2)		X						
7.	Li Mi gloats over T'ang response (G1)		X						
8a.	Li Mi leads expedition against the regicide (A3, E2)ᵇ						X		
8b.	Li Mi participates in the attack (A3)	X	X	X	X				
9.	Regicide's deserters join Li Mi (A2)		X		X				
10.	Li Mi obtains imperial insignia (E1)						X		
11.	Li Yuan-pa takes insignia, forces surrender (A3, G1)						X		
12.	Li Mi obtains Empress Hsiao (G5)						X		
13.	Li Mi desecrates the Duke of Chou shrine (G1)					X			X
14a.	Li Shih-min makes war on Wang Shih-ch'ung (A3 [plays], E6)				X	X	X		X
14b.	Wang Shih-ch'ung makes war on T'ang (E6)					X	X		
15a.	Li Mi supplies Wang Shih-ch'ung with food grains (D)ᶜ	X	X						X
16.	Drunken Shih-min follows stag/heron to Mi's camp (G6 [plays], C2)				X	X	X	X	X
17.	Li Mi declines to have Shih-min pursued (F [*Chronicles*], E1)				X	X			
18.	Ch'eng Yao-chin pursues (E7 [plays], E5 [*Chronicles, Romance*], E6 [*Tales*], G2 [*Prince*])				X	X	X	X	X
19.	Ch'in Shu-pao rejects Li Shih-min's offer (A2)								X
20.	Ch'eng chases Li Shih-min into the shrine				X	X	X	X	X

ᵃFor explanations of A1, A2, A3, etc., see Table 3.

ᵇThe subdivisions of a single entry (8a, 8b; 14a, 14b; etc.) indicate alternative versions of what is essentially the same incident in the tale of Li Mi as a whole.

ᶜI have located the two versions of this incident, 15a and 15b, in different sections of the table to clarify the plot relations: in two sources the incident is a consequence of others; in the non-elite narratives it is the cause of a number of other incidents.

TABLE 1. (*continued*)

Number	Incident	Original sources — Histories	Elite novels — Forgotten Tales	Romance of the Sui and the T'ang	Non-elite narratives — Chronicles	Prince of Ch'in	Tales of the T'ang	Plays — Ming plays	A Pair
21.	The deity hides Shih-min (C2)			X		X			
22.	Dragon portends Shih-min's future (C2)			X					
23a.	Dragon protects Shih-min (C2)			X	X		X		
23b.	Shih-min shoots woodsman (E1)					X			
24.	Ch'in Shu-pao protects Shih-min (C3, E7 [plays, *Prince*, *Tales*], E4 [*Chronicles*, *Romance*])			X	X	X	X	X	
25.	Li Mi to execute Shih-min (E6 [*Tales*], A3, E1)			X	X	X	X		
26.	Li Mi imprisons Shih-min (A2 [*Tales*], F, G2)			X	X	X	X	X	
27a.	Wei Cheng tricks Mi to treat Shih-min well (C3, E4)					X			
27b.	Jailor's daughter dreams of way to save Shih-min (C2)			X					
28.	Wei Cheng, Hsu Shih-chi, Ch'in Shu-pao drawn to Shih-min (C3)			X	X	X		X	
29a.	Li Mi's declaration altered by Wei Cheng (C3, E3, E4)			X	X				
29c.	Declaration altered by Wei and Hsu Shih-chi (C3, E3, E4)						X		
29c.	Declaration altered by Wei, Hsu, and Ch'in Shu-pao (C3)					X		X	
30a.	Wei Cheng takes responsibility (B)							X	
30b.	Ch'in Shu-pao gives Shih-min a horse					X			
31a.	Li Mi imprisons Hsu and Wei (G4)			X	X		X		
31b.	Li Mi exiles Wei Cheng (G4)					X			
32.	Hsu and Wei flee to T'ang (E3, C3)						X		
33.	Wang Po-tang allows Hsu and Wei to escape (B)								X
34.	Wang Po-tang lies to Li Mi (B, E3)								X
35.	Ch'in and Lo Ch'eng to be executed for failing to catch Hsu, Wei (G4)						X		
36.	Ch'in, Lo, Ch'eng desert Li Mi after dismissal (E3)						X		
15b.	Li Mi supplies Wang Shih-ch'ung with grain (F, B [*Prince*])				X	X			
37.	Li Mi distributes grains to the hungry (E2)		X				X		
38a.	Li Mi's grain ruined by rats (C2)			X	X	X	X		X
38b.	Mi's treasury destroyed by fire (C2)					X			
39a.	Mi defeated by Wang Shih-ch'ung (G3, C2 [*Tales*, *Prince*], F [*Prince*, *Romance*])	X	X	X	X	X	X	X	
39b.	Shan Hsiung-hsin's treachery (G7)					X			

TABLE I. (*continued*)

Number	Incident	Original sources — Histories	Elite novels — Forgotten Tales	Elite novels — Romance of the Sui and the T'ang	Non-elite narratives — Chronicles	Non-elite narratives — Prince of Ch'in	Non-elite narratives — Tales of the T'ang	Plays — Ming plays	Plays — A Pair
40.	Li Mi hallucinates demons (C1)				X				
41.	Li Mi loses hope over desertions (C2)								X
42.	Wang Po-tang suggests new strategy			X					
43.	Mi expresses contrition [*Forgotten*], attempts suicide (E5, C2)	X	X	X	X				
44.	Wang Po-tang vows loyalty (D7)	X							X
45a.	Wang Po-tang suggests surrender (A1 [*Chronicles*], E1 [*Tales*], E1, G2 [*A Pair*])				X		X		X
45b.	Jao Chün-su suggests surrender (F)					X			
46.	Li Mi leads surrender (E1)	X	X	X			X	X	X
47.	Wang Po-tang, Li admit retribution (C1, C2)					X			X
48.	Wang Po-tang tries to win Li Shih-min's favor (A1, E1)								X
49a.	Mi shamed in argument with Li Shih-min (G1)					X		X	X
49b.	Mi shamed by Shih-min's snub (G1)		X		X	X			
50.	Li Mi accepted by Li Yuan (A3)		X	X	X	X	X		X
51.	Wang reaffirms loyalty to Mi		X				X		X
52.	Mi given a T'ang bride	X		X	X	X	X	X	X
53a.	Li Mi waits the time to rebel (E5 [*Romance*], E5, F [*Chronicles*])			X	X				
53b.	Ts'ai Chien-te provokes rebellion (G2, G3)					X			
54a.	Mi slays his bride E6, C2 (*A Pair*), E6, G7			X	X	X	X		X
54b.	Li Mi sent on mission, recalled (F)	X	X						
55.	Mi rebels (E1 [history], E5 [plays, *Romance*], G1 [*Forgotten*], F, G2 [*Prince*])	X	X	X	X	X		X	X
56.	Wang Po-tang objects to revolt (A3, C2)	X				X		X	X
57a.	Li Mi prays for omens, gives up hope (G2)								X
57b.	Li Mi destroys own astral body (C1, C2)					X			
58.	Wang Po-tang tries to protect Li Mi (A1)					X	X		X
59a.	Mi shot by T'ang forces	X	X	X	X	X	X		X
59b.	Mi commits suicide (E5)							X	
60a.	Mi's followers recruited by T'ang (C3)				X	X		X	
60b.	Hsu and Wei mourn Mi, then join T'ang (A2)		X	X			X		

illogical and supernatural are most often seen in works toward the less well educated and uneducated end of the scale of audiences. Incidents to be found in works for non-elite audiences include numbers 10–12, 33–34, 39b, 47–48, 49a, 56, and 57a, 57b, and 58; among them the fictional elements that were utilized by two or more anonymous creators of non-elite works—and by neither of the literati novelists—are numbers 49a, 56, and 58. (In number 58, the Peking dramatist probably used *Tales of the T'ang* as his source, although all four incidents could well have been in circulation among storytellers before the seventeenth century; in the other two cases the source substantially predates the literati novels.) The incidents in question go beyond mere use of the supernatural; they compose a scene that pits Li Mi against Li Shih-min—both haughty in their positions of authority—in a confrontation of will and of literary skills, a moving speech by Wang Po-tang in which he attempts one last time to dissuade Li Mi from rebellion against the T'ang, and Wang's final effort to shield his master's body from the weapons of their foe. All of these scenes portray either unmitigated heroism or the highest villainy; they are immediate and highly dramatic, and likely to appeal to culturally less sophisticated audiences for that reason.

Incidents that occur only in elite works, the literati novels, are numbers 3–7, 22, 27b, and 42. The first group here serves to clarify the moral contrast between Li Mi and the T'ang leaders: they demonstrate the awareness on the part of Li Mi's lieutenants that he is unworthy to rule in contrast to Li Shih-min; they also give testimony to the moral uprightness of these men. Ch'in Shu-pao, as one example, honors his obligation to serve Li Mi when a personally more satisfactory alternative is presented. Incidents 21–22 illustrate Ch'u Jen-huo's preoccupation with the workings of higher powers in the establishment of dynasties (from *Romance of the Sui and the T'ang*); only the first is shared with the *chantefable Prince of Ch'in*. In incident 42, Wang Po-tang illustrates his diligent service to his chosen lord by proposing a new military strategy in an effort to bolster Li Mi's courage after defeat. The reasons behind these acts are complex; the acts demonstrate a keen awareness of moral responsibility, of moral order in the universe. One might go so far as to see here concerns for the political role of the literatus in society, not as one who has to beware of the world's "great men," as in the less morally complex works, but as interpreter of the times, the fate of the realm, and the responsibility of ministers to the throne to maintain social order (which function they were trained to perform). As a consequence, we may conclude that these works are more appropriate for a relatively sophisticated audience. Furthermore, they are somewhat less emotionally dramatic and more thought-provoking than the comparatively straightforward, action-oriented mass and general works, presumably meant to appeal to an audience accustomed to relating intellectually, on a philosophical level, to works of more formal literature, poetry and classical prose.

TABLE 2.   Historical and "Original" Material in Various Versions
of the Fall of Li Mi

Source	Number of incidents	Shared with histories Number	Shared with histories Percentage	No known source Number	No known source Percentage
Histories	13	(13)	(100)		
Forgotten Tales	19	9	47	7	37
Romance	31	9	29	4	13
Total elite novels	50	18	36	11	22
Chronicles	31	8	26	7	23
Prince	34	5	15	19	56
Tales	30	5	17	8	27
Total "general" works	95	18	19	34	38
Ming plays	22	7	32	15	68
A Pair	18	6	33	4	22
Total plays	40	13	33	19	48

Needless to say, the differences between these two sets of scenes are small and, perhaps, are distinguished in a manner that is insufficiently objective for a genuinely convincing argument. Likewise, nearly half of the total number of incidents in the complete tale are shared by works toward both poles of the spectrum. Thus, these findings are only suggestive, not definitive, in themselves. However, tabular arrangement of these data does tend to confirm the intended audiences tentatively identified for each work thus far. First, let us compare the amount of material ultimately derived from recorded history, the dynastic histories and *Tzu-chih t'ung-chien*, to which all writers might have had access (leaving aside the question of unofficial, privately compiled histories) with that for which there is no extant source, presumably oral and original material.

On the basis of the relative degrees of rational versus fantastic or supernatural explanation given for the causes of actions and events, in Table 2 I have arranged these works tentatively along a spectrum of intended audiences. The table confirms that the arrangement, in general, is valid: elite novels have a relatively high degree of historicity compared with written works for non-elite audiences. Conversely, the intellectually less complex narratives demonstrate a higher degree of "originality" than do the elite novels. Of course, this originality must include on the one hand elements from folklore and oral narratives as well as from vernacular written sources now lost and, on the other, genuine innovations to the story. Presumably, the first of these two untraceable types of material accounts for the large amount of apparent originality in the plays composed for oral performance before mass audiences. The same can be said for *Prince of Ch'in*, an adaptation of an oral work. The high percentage of incidents common to the plays and the histories paradoxically may confirm this observation: since popular theater tended to present stories already familiar to listening audiences, anonymous dramatists probably adhered more closely to the factual record than the more imaginative writers for non-elite readers. Certainly relationships between plays and popular written narratives warrant much further study. The literati novelists were probably the only ones among these writers who could have access to unofficial historical sources concerning Li Mi, and yet reference to these works becomes irrelevant for present purposes. That is, the elite novels have more material in common with recorded history than do more popular works when only the best known histories are considered. Table 2 thus reinforces our separation of these works into different portions of the audience spectrum.

In order to determine whether writers consistently explained their characters' actions differently for elite audiences than for non-elite audiences, I have recorded in Table 3 the motivation behind each act or incident when—and only when—causation was made clear in the texts. Similarities between works for different audiences can be interpreted as evidence of cultural integration across different levels of society; differences would indicate values and interests distinguishable by social group and class.

In total, these texts mention twenty-three different reasons behind the actions they narrate. To limit the effect of my subjective reading on this analysis, I have avoided imputing motivation when none was made explicit in a text. I have grouped these rationales into seven categories for convenience. This analysis is preliminary, of course; the classification scheme could well be improved by reference to social scientific work beyond the range of this study. Table 3 lists these various motivations in their separate categories and indicates the frequency with which each was cited in the texts. Designations derived from this list appear following the incidents in Table 1 above. In Table 3, I have again grouped the texts to facilitate comparisons between those intended for elite and non-elite audiences. Column 1 is history, columns 2 and 3 are the literati novels designed for sophisticated readers, columns 4 and 6 the prose narratives intended for non-elite reading audiences, column 5 the *chantefable*, and columns 7 and 8 are the plays. The reader will notice that no one explanation of characters' motivations is offered consistently in any one text; all twenty-three are cited in nearly every version of the tale, although some rationales are cited more frequently than others. And yet even here patterns emerge that serve to distinguish elite works from works for non-elite audiences.

Commitment to a state or to a cause such as righteous government is most often offered as motivation in both elite and non-elite works. Self-preservation, too, occurs as a frequent rationale for action in both types of works. But blind chance, sometimes identified as Heaven's favor, serves as a very common rationale in the non-elite works, including the plays and *Prince of Ch'in*. The appearance of this rationale in *Romance* is a function of the novelist's preoccupation with ultimate causes and is not shared with the other elite novel, *Forgotten*

Tales. A corollary, recognition of Heaven's favor, is a common rationale for action in less intellectual works but not in the literati novels. Strategic planning and acting on advice in matters of strategy (F in Table 3) is cited in the histories, in *Prince of Ch'in* and *Chronicles*, and in the literati novels; a desire for personal honor and glory motivated the historical Li Mi—but only his counterparts in works for more general audiences.

Using Table 3, we can compile lists of motivations and rationales of greater interest to one or another audience:

1. Rationales more often offered to readers among the literate elite:
   a. Shame concerning failure or errors (E5)
   b. Strategic planning and advice concerning strategy (F)
2. Rationales more often offered to non-elite audiences:
   a. Personal devotion to one's leader (A1)
   b. Altruism; personal devotion to friends (B)
   c. Heaven's favor, or chance (C2)
   d. Recognition of Heaven's favor (C3)
   e. Personal revenge for humiliation (E6)
   f. Desire for personal honor and glory (G2)

These lists again suggest that elite readers are more concerned with greater issues—for example, those affecting a political, social, or military group. Shame, which is cited often, also involves an awareness of the views of other people. Works of fiction and drama for the less well educated, on the other hand, are concerned to a greater extent with the individual: devotion to a leader, a friend, one's reputation, one's status, and comfort. Non-elite literature also addresses matters far beyond the human being's feeble reach, such as Heaven's inscrutable mandate for a ruling house to succeed. One might infer that writers for non-elite audiences focused on action that fell more within the experience of common people; matters of political or military planning might not be of interest, but attention is given to events that put even the elite in their place—the acts of Heaven itself. Likewise, the second group of rationales for behavior are more readily and immediately comprehensible—they require neither strong commitment nor penetrating contemplation on the part of an audience. Consequently, they confirm our intuition that relatively uneducated readers and illiterate listening audiences are less likely to respond to the concerns of another class in society, but are more inclined to respond to supernatural references and to the acts of individuals.

Certain motivations are common to both the elite and non-elite versions of Li Mi's tale. Pride and arrogance (G1) motivate individuals in the histories and the vernacular narratives; figures in all renditions may choose an unwise course of action (G3). Self-preservation (E1) is similarly of importance to all audiences. Surprisingly, the need for commitment to higher causes, either the state or the principle of just government, motivates the actions of characters in all

TABLE 3. Frequency of Motivations and Rationales Cited as Causes
for Events in the Fall of Li Mi

Motivation or rationale	Original sources — Histories	Elite novels — Forgotten Tales	Elite novels — Romance	Non-elite narratives — Chronicles	Non-elite narratives — Prince	Non-elite narratives — Tales of T'ang	Plays — Ming plays	Plays — A Pair
A. Loyalty								
1. Personal devotion	1	1	1	1		2		3
2. Obligation to repay favors	2	3	1			2	1	
3. Commitment to a state or cause	2	5	3	5	3	4	3	2
B. Altruistic allegiance to friends					1		1	2
C. Fate								
1. Retribution		1		2	2		1	1
2. Heaven's favor or chance			7	3	7	3	1	3
3. Recognition of Heaven's favor (of a "true ruler")			3	3	4	3	4	
D. Family obligations					1			
E. Personal interests and needs								
1. Self-preservation	2	2	4	2	1	3	1	3
2. Self-justification		2	1			2	1	1
3. Self-righteous condemnation of unworthiness in another	2		1	1		3		1
4. Preparation for a later shift of loyalties			3	3	1	1	1	1
5. Shame at failure or error	1	1	3	3				
6. Revenge for humiliation				2	3	4		1
7. Acting on orders					1	1	2	
F. Strategy and strategic advice from a trusted person	1	4	1	3	4			
G. Personal shortcomings								
1. Pride, arrogance	1	2	1	2	1	1	2	1
2. Desire for power and glory	1			2	2		1	2
3. Bad choice or poor strategy	1	1	2	1	2		3	
4. Disobedience			1	1	1	2		
5. Desire for physical pleasure						1		
6. Disbelief in omens					1		1	
7. Deliberate betrayal of trust					2			1

versions of the story. That a principle so essential to the preservation of this
Confucian political ideal appears generally is probably a function of deliberate
didacticism, an approach shared by writers regardless of intended audience.
Historical fiction, if we can reasonably generalize from such a small amount of
material, served to integrate Ming–Ch'ing society by emphasizing values of

primary interest to the state, while on less crucial questions it could allow for the preferences of distinct audiences within the general population. Beyond this point lies pure speculation about values keyed to intended audiences. Further studies on other groups of related texts are needed to test these few tentative conclusions.

In summary, then, investigation of the various vernacular versions of the fall of Li Mi has provided a workable, albeit cumbersome, means of distinguishing works intended for different audiences. Nonlinguistic criteria have included extrinsic evidence concerning how and among what strata of society a work circulated as well as biographical information about known authors and the significant anonymity of others. Intrinsic evidence has ranged among formal features—the type and use of verse and the conventional narrator—that define genres and thereby suggest audiences, and has included relative degrees of rationalism, historicity, and apparent innovation within each text. This evidence is not intended to question the usual division of Chinese society during the Ming and Ch'ing into elite, non-elite, and folk audiences; instead it demonstrates that the body of vernacular texts consists of material designed for all of these audiences.

To reiterate, the audiences for vernacular literature constitute a spectrum of overlapping designations, though we cannot place the works under consideration along this spectrum with absolute certainty. Nor do the values more common to the extremes in this body of texts appear as distinctly different as we might expect. This fact, among others noted above, again demonstrates the essential unity of ideology as presented to different strata of Ming–Ch'ing society, a unity that transcended differences of literary form and intended audience. This point, of course, confirms the didactic function of even the most commercial literature originating in the Confucian content of the formal learning that ultimately finds expression in all forms of fictionalized history.

FIVE

The Social and Historical Context of Ming–Ch'ing Local Drama

Tanaka Issei

The music-dramas that were performed in villages and small market towns all across China constituted an important part of Ming–Ch'ing popular culture. In this essay I shall try to show that the specific social milieu in which such plays were performed—in particular, the social position of the sponsors or organizers—helped determine which plays were presented, and even worked to shape the language of a given performance. Troupes adapted their presentations to meet the demands of sponsors and audiences; moreover, there was a hierarchy of troupes that reflected the level of talent and training of their members and the social and economic position of their patrons, and the status of a troupe had its own effect on the content of its performances.

The popular drama of early Ming times was gradually transformed into literary drama for the upper classes, but in Ch'ing there was a resurgence of popular drama in the form of regional dramatic traditions. This appropriation by the ruling class of the creations of popular culture, followed by the appearance of new popular cultural forms, is a leading characteristic of Chinese history, and is another major concern of this essay.

Village plays can be classified on the basis of their organizers or sponsors. The oldest type, dating from the Sung and Yuan periods, probably consisted of plays sponsored by groups of villages that were linked together by a shared market, or by cooperative agricultural activities such as irrigation. Such plays were performed at temples in large villages or small towns that served as market centers for the surrounding settlements. They were sponsored and organized by professional promoters, called *pao-t'ou jen*, who belonged to local secret societies. The plays were held during the annual festival on the local god's birthday, and during the rites designed to propitiate orphan souls.[1] Plays also served to attract

---

[1] Tanaka Issei 田仲一成, *Chūgoku saishi engeki kenkyū* 中國祭祀演劇研究 [Ritual theaters in China] (Tokyo: Tōyō bunka kenkyūjo 東洋文化研究所, 1981), pp. 36–64, 292.

people to the fairs that were held on such occasions.[2] Thus, they had both ritual and economic functions. The population in many market towns was too large and varied to be controlled successfully by the local landowning elite, influential though they were. Idlers, beggars, gamblers, fortune tellers, herb sellers, and the like, many of whom were not residents and had connections with secret societies, gathered in such places and presented performances of dramas that the landowner elite considered licentious or rebellious.[3] So, in fact, plays that were presented in conjunction with temple fairs in local market centers probably reflected the attitudes and values of the common people rather than those of the landowners.

Plays were also performed in smaller villages that were not market centers. As with the market-center plays, these plays were performed during the annual festival in honor of the village god and as part of the prayers for a good harvest;[4] they were also given during the rites aimed at controlling the orphan souls of the community and protecting the community from flood and drought.[5] These performances also had an economic function, but one that had to do with maintaining the productivity of the village rather than promoting the exchange of commodities. The small temples where these plays were performed served as meeting places, and the villagers assembled there every two or three years to discuss the community regulations and to renew their pledges to obey them. These regulations were especially concerned with the proper management of common resources, such as streams, ponds, and woods, and included such prohibitions as those against unrestrained felling of trees,[6] contaminating drinking water,[7] allowing livestock to damage crops,[8] and theft.[9] Plays were performed during village assemblies as a means of solemnizing the agreement in the presence of the gods. Those who violated the agreement were often required

---

[2] *T'ang-yin hsien chih* 湯陰縣志 (1738), *chüan* 7, "hui chi" 會記. (The relevant passage is reproduced in *Chūgoku saishi engeki kenkyū* [hereafter *CSEK*], p. 266, n. 30.)

[3] Ch'en Hung-mou 陳宏謀, *P'ei-yuan-t'ang ou-ts'un kao* 培遠堂偶存稿, *chüan* 21, "Shan-hsi, Ch'a-chin shih-hui chü-tu hsi" 陝西, 查禁市會聚賭檄 (1745); text in *CSEK*, p. 330, n. 79.

[4] *Hu-nan sheng-li ch'eng-an* 湖南省例成案, "hsing-lü" 刑律, *chüan* 10, "Hsiao-yü chien-su pao-chia, ch'eng-hsiung shih-ch'iang ch'ing-sheng t'un-chi ko-k'uan" 曉諭健訴保甲, 逞兇恃強輕生囤積 各款 (1743); *Fu-yü hsuan-hua lu* 撫豫宣化錄, "Ch'üan-yü ko ch'ung chieh-chien i yü min ts'ai-shih" 勸諭各崇節儉以裕民財事 (1725); texts in *CSEK*, p. 263, n. 8.

[5] Ch'en Lung-cheng 陳龍正, *Chi-t'ing ch'üan-shu* 幾亭全書 (1614), *chüan* 24, "T'ung-shan-hui chiang hua" 同善會講話; text in *CSEK*, p. 264, n. 9.

[6] *Chin-li Huang-shih chia-p'u* 錦里黃氏家譜 (1769), *chüan* 1, "ssu-tien" 祀典; *Ming-chou Wu-shih chia-chi* 茗洲吳氏家記 (manuscript of the Wan-li period), *chüan* 7, "t'iao yueh" 條約; texts in *CSEK*, p. 325, n. 58; p. 319, n. 27.

[7] *Chen-hsi Chiao-ho-ts'un Ch'en-shih tsung-p'u* 鎮西蛟河村陳氏宗譜 (1898), *chüan* 1, "Feng-ch'ih pei-chi" 鳳池碑記; text in *CSEK*, p. 264, n. 11.

[8] *Lu-yang Hsing-shih tsung-p'u* 盧陽邢氏宗譜 (1791), *chüan* 2, "Ch'ung-shen chin-yueh" 重申 禁約; text in *CSEK*, p. 264, n. 10.

[9] *Po-yang Chu-shih tsung-p'u* 白洋朱氏宗譜 (1884), *chüan* 5, "Ssu-ku-yuan chin-yueh" 嗣古原 禁約; text in *CSEK*, p. 264, n. 12.

to pay for a "penalty play," and at that time to renew their oath to obey the regulations.[10]

These dramatic performances were organized by the entire village community, and therefore plays of the kind favored by poorer peasants and tenant farmers were often selected for performance. But the landowners of the village, in rotation, raised funds, built the stage, and selected the troupe of actors.[11] It can be said, therefore, that both the common people and the landowners influenced this kind of village theater, in contrast to the theater of the market centers, which was dominated by non-elite elements.

A third type of village theater was that organized by lineages or other groups of kinfolk. Most villages were composed of several surname groups, and we can regard such groups as subdivisions of the village community. Lineages usually held some land in common, the income from which was used for both ritual and practical purposes, and they also frequently had ancestral halls, in which the spirits of the forebears of the lineage were enshrined. The rituals performed in the ancestral hall were important events, which contributed to the spiritual unity of the lineage. Up to the sixteenth century, these rituals were carried out in orthodox Confucian fashion. In this way, the landowning elite within the lineage hoped to maintain its authority in the lineage. But after the sixteenth century, probably because of the great popularity of plays performed in village temples, theatrical performances began to be included in the rituals of some South Chinese lineages. Elaborate performances were staged at the ancestral hall on important festival days such as the Lantern Festival, Ch'ing-ming, and the spring and autumn festivals (*ch'un-ch'i, ch'iu-pao*).[12] Theatricals on such occasions were organized by the entire lineage, but at other times smaller units within the lineage sponsored performances. The first of the latter sort to appear were those performed in conjunction with funerary rites.[13] Later, lineage branches sponsored plays to help celebrate marriages, the coming of age of sons, success in the civil service examinations, and the like.[14] These plays were offered

---

[10] *Huai-ning Chan-shih tsung-p'u* 懷寧詹氏宗譜 (1768), *chüan* 17, "Wang-chia-shan chin-yueh" 旺家山禁約; text in *CSEK*, p. 326, n. 59.

[11] *CSEK*, pp. 280–292.

[12] *Lan-feng Shen-shih chia-p'u* 蘭風沈氏家譜 (1832), *chüan* 1, "Ssu-tsu yuan-liu chi" 祀祖源流記 (1784); *Ch'ang-hsiang Shen-shih tsung-p'u* 長巷沈氏宗譜 (1893), *chüan* 34, "tsung-yueh" 宗約 (1741); *I-men Ch'en-shih tsung-p'u* 義門陳氏宗譜 (1920), *chüan* 3, "Shih-hui-shan wei pen sheng-tsu hsien she-li ssu-ch'an pei-chi" 釋慧山爲本生祖先設立祀產碑記 (1796); *Shih-ts'un Ts'ao-shih tsung-p'u* 史村曹氏宗譜 (1848), *chüan* 1, "Ssu-tsu yen-chü chou-yeh kuei-shih" 祀祖演劇晝夜規式; texts in *CSEK*, p. 264, notes 15–17.

[13] Chou Hsuan 周旋, *Wei-an wen-chi* 畏菴文集 (Ch'eng-hua period [1465–1487]), *chüan* 10, "Shu-kao" 疏稿; text in *CSEK*, p. 265, n. 22.

[14] *T'ung-an hsien chih* 同安縣志 (1616), Ch'ing-pai-t'ang kao 淸白堂稿 ed., "Feng-su chih" 風俗志; Feng Shih-k'o 馮時可, *Feng Yuan-ch'eng hsuan-chi* 馮元成選集 (early seventeenth century), *chüan* 26, "Li-shuo" 禮說; *Ta-kang Chao-shih tsu-p'u* 大港趙氏族譜 (1779), "Ssu-kuei" 祀規; *Fang-ts'un Hsieh-shih tsu-p'u* 芳村謝氏族譜 (K'ang-hsi period [1662–1722]), "Ju-chu wen" 入主文; texts in *CSEK*, p. 265, n. 22; p. 264, n. 18; p. 533, n. 1.

to the spirits of the ancestors in gratitude for their blessings. In both lineages and branches, the dramatic performances were under the control of the wealthier and more powerful kinsmen, while the poorer relatives had very little voice in the matter. Hence, lineage-centered drama was probably the most conservative of the three types.

Each of the three types of sponsoring group—market center, village, and lineage—tended to employ a different sort of theatrical troupe. There were three ranks of troupes. The lowest-ranking troupes did not reside permanently in a particular town, but traveled from market to market. This type of troupe is probably the oldest, appearing as early as the Northern Sung.[15] Such troupes frequently had connections with secret societies, and could perform, under the protection of professional promoters, even when the local authorities tried to prevent them. This type of troupe was favored by these promoters, who most commonly organized dramatic performances in market towns and at temple fairs.

Troupes of the middle rank usually earned their living by performing for rich citizens in the local city (*chen*, for the most part), but would also tour nearby villages during the spring and autumn festival seasons. Their services were in demand by village leaders who were reluctant to hire the itinerant troupes for fear that they would cause disruptions. Since the middle-ranking troupes lived in the local city, they were under the control of the landowners and local officials, and were thus more attractive to the conservative village elders.

The highest-ranking troupes stayed permanently in the local city, protected and patronized by wealthy landowners and merchants and the local officials.[16] Such troupes were well trained and skillful, and were far beyond the reach of ordinary villagers. Wealthy lineage leaders residing in the local cities preferred to employ troupes of this sort.

The itinerant and semi-itinerant troupes were less technically skilled than the others and had little prestige, but they played a leading role in the development of popular drama. For example, in mid-nineteenth century Canton the highest ranking troupes were called collectively *wai chiang pan* ("troupes from beyond the river"), and their guild hall was in the city of Canton. The middle- and low-ranking troupes were known as *pen-ti pan* ("local troupes"), and their guild hall was in a suburban market called Fo-shan *chen*. During the Taiping rebellion, the actors belonging to the Fo-shan *chen* guild hall joined the Taipings, and after the war their guild hall was destroyed by the

---

[15] One type of traveling troupe in that period was called "river market musicians" (*ho-shih yueh-jen* 河市樂人); *CSEK*, pp. 29–30. See also Li Hsiao-ts'ang 李嘯倉, "Sung Chin Yuan tsa-chü yuan-pen t'i-chih k'ao" 宋金元雜劇院本體制考 [On the structure of Sung, Chin, and Yuan *tsa-chü* and *yuan-pen*], in his *Sung Yuan chi-i tsa-k'ao* 宋元伎藝雜考 [Studies on Sung and Yuan dynasty performing arts] (Shanghai: Shang-tsa ch'u-pan she 上雜出版社, 1953).

[16] Feng Meng-chen 馮夢禎, *K'uai-hsueh-t'ang jih-chi* 快雪堂日記, in his *K'uai-hsueh t'ang chi* 集, *chüan* 49, 56, 57, 59, 60, 61; see *CSEK*, pp. 356–363.

local authorities in retaliation for this action. The Canton guild hall of the *wai chiang pan* troupes, on the other hand, was not touched, since their members had not joined the rebels. Yet the low- and middle-ranking (itinerant and semi-itinerant) troupes quickly recovered, and went on to develop a new form of popular drama, Cantonese Opera (*Yueh chü*), while the high-ranking troupes, despite the patronage of the rich and powerful, gradually lost their influence and finally disappeared.[17] This imbalance of creative importance between high-ranking troupes and the others is characteristic of the local theater through the entire Ming–Ch'ing period.

We have seen that the relative influence on dramatic productions of the local elites and of the poorer part of the community varied as the setting changed from small market town to individual village temple to lineage ancestral hall, and that different kinds of acting troupes tended to be employed in each setting. What effect did these differences have on the types of play presented? It is not possible to give a final answer to this question, but a number of significant clues are provided by three late-Ming texts.

We can gain some sense of which plays were performed in market towns from a play called *Yung t'uan yuan*, written by Li Yü in about 1630. A scene in this play depicts a procession in a market town during the celebration of the Lantern Festival.[18] In the procession appear peasants and merchants from in and around the town costumed as characters from various plays. The heroes and heroines who were portrayed in this manner were presumably favorites with the citizens of such towns. Therefore, Li Yü's procession probably provides a glimpse of the taste of the non-elite segment of local society, especially when we recall that market town plays were usually controlled by non-elite groups. I have arranged the characters that appear in the procession in six categories, following a classification scheme for drama proposed by Lü T'ien-ch'eng, a famous late-Ming drama critic and near-contemporary of Li Yü, in his *Classification of Drama* (*Ch'ü p'in*).[19] In the scene, each character is identified in a phrase or two. I have translated one of these identifying remarks in each category. For convenience, I include the title of the best-known play in which the character appears and performs the actions described, but it is not certain that the plays actually presented by troupes of itinerant actors at temple fairs and the like in late-Ming times were identical to the texts we now have.

Lü T'ien-ch'eng's first category, "Loyalty and Filial Piety" (*chung hsiao*), contains plays portraying the loyalty of a faithful subject or the self-sacrifice of a filial child. One hero of this type appears in the procession scene: Kuan Yü, identified by the phrase "Admire Yun-ch'ang's lofty virtue, traveling alone a

[17] Yü Hsun-ch'ing 兪洵慶, "Ho-lang pi-chi" 荷廊筆記, in *Fan-ou hsien hsu chih* 番禺縣續志 (1910), *chüan* 44; text in *CSEK*, p. 614, n. 2.
[18] Li Yü 李玉, *Yung-t'uan yuan* 永團圓, "Hui hsin" 會釁; text in *CSEK*, p. 394, n. 53.
[19] *CSEK*, p. 334.

thousand *li*" (*Ku-ch'eng chi*). The second category, "Fidelity" (*chieh-i*), comprises plays depicting a faithful wife or husband. One character of this type appears: Liu Yao-ch'i, identified by the phrase "Master Yao-ch'i, truly young" (*Pai-t'u chi*). The third is named "Love" (*feng-ch'ing*), and contains plays on romantic themes. Characters from seven such plays appear, among whom is Ch'en Miao-ch'ang, identified by the comment, "The priestess Miao-ch'ang, clinging closely to the youth Pi-cheng" (*Yü-tsan chi*).[20] The fourth, "Knights Errant" (*hao hsia*), contains plays about daring and principled martial heroes. Seven of this kind of character are portrayed, including Yü-ch'ih Kung, identified in the phrase "The escape of the 'Little Prince of Ch'in'; Yü-ch'ih Kung's bravery" (*Chin-tiao chi*).[21] The fifth of Lü T'ien-ch'eng's six categories is named "Renown" (*kung ming*), and contains plays in which the resourcefulness and patience of the hero are praised. The heroes of three such plays are represented in the procession scene, including Lü Meng-cheng, identified by the phrase "Ah! See the colored ball, shining like a star; the scholar living in a miserable hovel" (*P'o-yao chi*).[22] The last category, "Immortals and Buddhas" (*hsien fo*), contains plays with a strong supernatural element. Nine characters from such plays are in the procession, including Tung-fang Shuo, identified as "Tung-fang Shuo, who can steal the peach [of Heaven]" (*P'an-t'ao chi*).[23]

A number of points can be made about this list. To begin with, only five of the twenty-eight heroes and heroines in the procession scene are from plays of the most didactic types (the first, second, and fifth categories). This is all the more interesting in view of the fact that Lü T'ien-ch'eng believed that these were the most common kinds of village drama.[24] On the other hand, twenty-three of the twenty-eight characters can be associated with plays about romantic love, martial prowess, and the supernatural. Such plays were regarded with suspicion by the authorities, who feared that they would have a bad effect on the morals of the people. At times they went so far as to demand that "licentious"

[20] The other six are Wang Chao-chün 王昭君 (*Ho-jung chi* 和戎記), Hung-niang 紅娘 (*Hsi-hsiang chi* 西廂記), Tu Li-niang 杜麗娘 (*Mu-tan t'ing* 牡丹亭), Ch'ien Wan-ch'ien 錢萬錢 (*Wang-hu-t'ing chi* 望湖亭記), Chih-nü 織女 (*T'ien-ho p'ei* 天河配), and Hsi-shih 西施 (*Huan-sha chi* 浣紗記).

[21] The other six are Chang Fei 張飛 (*San Kuo chi* 三國記), Chao K'uang-yin 趙匡胤 (*Feng yun hui* 風雲會), Li Ts'un-hsiao 李存孝 (*Yen men kuan* 雁門關), Ch'ao Kai 晁蓋 (*Shui-hu chi* 水滸記), Li K'uei 李逵 (*Shui-hu chi*), Shih-erh kua-fu 十二寡婦 (*Yang-chia-chiang chuan* 楊家將傳).

[22] The other two are Hsueh Jen-kuei 薛仁貴 (*Pai-p'ao chi* 白袍記) and Chu Mai-ch'en 朱買臣 (*Yü ch'iao chi* 漁樵記).

[23] The other eight are Lao-tzu (drama unknown), Yen Tzu-ling 嚴子陵 (drama unknown), T'ang Hsuan-tsung 唐玄宗 (*T'ien-pao i-shih* 天寶遺事), Ta-mo 達摩 (drama unknown), T'ang San-tsang 唐三藏 (*Hsi-yu chi* 西遊記), Kuan-yin p'u-sa 觀音菩薩 (*Hsiang-shan chi* 香山記; this is a dramatic version of the story that in *pao-chüan* form appears in Overmyer's essay, chap. 8), Chung-k'uei's younger sister (*Chung-k'uei chia-mei* 鍾馗嫁妹), and "seven red ghosts and eight black ghosts" (*Ch'i-hung chi* 七紅記).

[24] *Ch'ü-p'in* 曲品 (1610), *Chung-kuo ku-tien hsi-ch'ü lun-chu chi-ch'eng* 中國古典戲曲論著集成 [Anthology of writings on classical Chinese drama], vol. 6 (Peking: Chung-kuo hsi-chü ch'u-pan she, 1959), *chüan* B, p. 223.

and "heterodox" plays such as *Hsi-hsiang chi* and *Yü-tsan chi,* which as we have seen are among those represented in the procession, be suppressed.[25] They probably had good reason for their concern, because most of the theaters in small market towns were dominated by people with close ties to secret societies. This may account for the fact that plays about martial prowess were popular in such places. In any case, Li Yü's play suggests that the dramas presented in small market towns and at temple fairs, performed by low-ranking troupes of itinerant actors, and less under the control of local elites than the plays presented in individual villages or for lineages or other groups of kinfolk, were far more likely to be about romantic love, adventure, and the supernatural than about exemplars of loyalty, filial piety, chastity, and the like.

Evidence on the nature of plays performed in villages is found in an encyclopedia for daily use entitled *Ao t'ou tsa tzu,* compiled by Tseng Ch'u-ch'ing and printed around 1630. This work contains thirty-five couplets (*tui-lien*) under the heading "couplets for thanksgiving plays."[26] Judging by the subject matter of some of them, these couplets were probably pasted on the posts at the front of the stages that were constructed at the village temples on the occasion of communal ceremonies such as the spring and autumn festivals, prayers for rain, the birthday of the chief local god, and so on. Thirty of them clearly refer to characters in plays, and presumably were pasted up when those plays were to be performed. The couplets give us some sense, therefore, of the kinds of plays that were presented in late-Ming times at important ritual occasions in the villages.

If we classify the characters to whom the couplets refer in Lü T'ien-ch'eng's six categories, we obtain a very interesting result. There are ten characters from plays of the "Renown" type, including Hsueh Jen-kuei: "The groom whose great achievements are worthy of praise, with three arrows takes T'ien shan. The wearer of the white gown, whose merit is exceptional, singlehandedly assists the nation" (*Pai-p'ao chi*).[27] There are seven from plays of the "Loyalty and Filial Piety" type, including Su Wu: "Leaning on his staff of command, he watches over the flocks of sheep; can his brave heart ever have submitted to dogs and pigs? He ties his silken letter to the foot of a wild goose; venerable and praised, his portrait is hung in the Unicorn Hall" (*Mu-yang chi*).[28] There are nine from plays of the "Fidelity" type, including Wang Shih-p'eng: "Old Mr. Ch'ien with clear eyes searches for a man of talent in this imperfect world. The

---

[25] See the remarks of T'ao Shih-ling 陶奭齡, quoted in *CSEK*, p. 388, n. 2.

[26] *CSEK*, pp. 335–352.

[27] The other nine are Han Hsin 韓信 (*Ch'ien-chin chi* 千金記), Ts'ao Pin 曹彬 (*San hsing chao* 三星照), Pan Chao 班超 (*T'ou-pi chi* 投筆記), Su Ch'in 蘇秦 (*Chin-yin chi* 金印記), Liu Chih-yuan 劉知遠 (*Pai-t'u chi* 白兔記), Lü Meng-cheng 呂蒙正 (*P'o-yao chi* 破窰記), Chu Mai-ch'en (*Yü-ch'iao chi*), Hsueh Teng-shan 薛登山 (drama unknown), and Yang Cheng-ch'ing 楊正卿 (drama unknown).

[28] The other six are Su Ying 蘇英 (*Ying-wu chi* 鸚鵡記), K'ai Wen 凱文 (drama unknown), Yang Hsien 楊顯 (drama unknown), Chiang Shih 姜詩 (*Yueh-li chi* 躍鯉記), Liu Yin 劉殷 (drama unknown; Liu Yin was one of the twenty-four exemplars of filial piety), and Liu Hsi 劉錫 (*Ch'en-hsiang t'ai-tzu* 沉香太子).

river bears up the chaste one, for Lord Heaven supports a top graduate's wife" (*Ching-chai chi*).[29] There are only four couplets that refer to characters from plays of the "Love" type. These include Liang Shan-po and Chu Ying-t'ai: "As sworn brothers they delight each other; from this their fates are twined together. They were not united as man and wife; this is the occasion of their annual meeting" (*Tung-ch'uang chi*).[30] And there are no couplets referring to characters in plays of the "Knights Errant" and "Immortals and Buddhas" types.

It appears that the types of plays selected for presentation in villages on ceremonial occasions were very different from those preferred by audiences in market towns. Twenty-six of the thirty characters are from plays of the first three categories, which concern exemplary heroes, loyal subjects, filial children, chaste wives, and the like. Only four are from plays about romantic love, and none are from plays about martial prowess or the supernatural—while twenty-three of the twenty-eight characters in Li Yü's festival procession are from plays of these types. It is particularly notable that there is no couplet alluding to characters from *Shui-hu chuan*. This is consistent with my argument that plays presented in the villages, which were usually performed by middle-ranking troupes, reflected the more conservative and conventional taste of the village elite, who had control over the selection of the plays as well as of the troupes.

An anthology of excerpts from plays, compiled in about 1600, entitled *Yüeh-fu hung-shan*, provides some evidence of the kind of dramatic material that was performed under the auspices of lineages or other kin groups.[31] This work was evidently used by lineage leaders when they were planning the entertainment for family occasions such as birthdays, weddings, celebrations of success in the examinations, and so on. At such times it was customary in well-to-do families to present a selection of scenes from various plays, rather than an entire play. In *Yüeh-fu hung-shan*, one hundred excerpts from sixty-six different plays are classified according to their contents under sixteen headings. The sixteen headings are listed below, together with the number of excerpts of each type that were included, an example in each category of the phrase used in the anthology to identify the play, the name of the play, and the act in which the action of the excerpt takes place, where this can be discovered.[32]

---

[29] The other eight are Ts'ai Po-chieh 蔡伯喈 (*P'i-p'a chi* 琵琶記), Yang-shih 楊氏 (*Sha-kou chi* 殺狗記), Wu Lun-ch'üan 五倫全 and Wu Lun-pei 五倫備 (*Wu Lun-ch'üan-pei chi* 五倫全備記), Meng Tao 孟道 (drama unknown), Wen Chün 文俊 (drama unknown), Yü-hsiao-nü 玉簫女 (*Liang-shih yin-yuan* 兩世姻緣), Wen Hsien 文顯 (drama unknown), and Li Yen-kui 李彥貴 (*Mai-shui chi* 賣水記).

[30] The other three are Wang Jui-lan 王瑞蘭 (*Pai-yueh t'ing* 拜月亭), Ch'en San 陳三 (*Li-ching chi* 荔鏡記), and Fu Ch'un-ch'ing 傅春卿 (drama unknown).

[31] Patrick Hanan, "The Nature and Contents of the *Yüeh-Fu Hung-Shan*," *Bulletin of the School of Oriental and African Studies* 26.2:346–361 (1963) (Hanan's translations of the names of the sixteen categories have been used below, with one exception); *CSEK*, pp. 498–500.

[32] Unlike the previous two texts, *Yüeh-fu hung-shan* actually supplies the title of each play listed. I have provided the act number where possible.

1. "Birthday Congratulations." (In each excerpt, the birthday of an elder is celebrated.) Total: eight. Example: "The eight immortals go to the peach [garden] for the great celebration [in honor of the birthday of the Heavenly Empress]." Play: *Sheng-hsien chi* (act unknown).

2. "Husband and Wife." (In each excerpt, the hero and heroine are married in the presence of family members.) Total: five. Example: "Councillor Ts'ai is married in the Niu mansion." Play: *P'i-p'a chi* (act 19).

3. "Birth of a Son." (In each excerpt, the birth of an heir is celebrated.) Total: five. Example: "Li San-niang gives birth to her son in a mill." Play: *Pai-t'u chi* (act 27).

4. "Instruction." (In each excerpt, a parent admonishes a child to be virtuous and successful.) Total: seven. Example: "Kuan Yü of Han admonishes his son." Play: *T'ao-yuan chi* (act unknown).

5. "Encouragement." (In each excerpt, women encourage their husbands or sons.) Total: five. Example: "Ch'in Hsueh-mei destroys her loom to instruct her son." Play: *San-yuan chi* (act 26).

6. "Parting." (In each excerpt, a man sets out on a long journey in the hope of rising in the world, leaving wife or mother behind.) Total: ten. Example: "Pan Chao leaves his mother to join the army." Play: *T'ou-pi chi* (act 8).

7. "Longing." (In each excerpt, a husband or wife thinks about his or her absent spouse.) Total: nine. Example: "Ch'ien Yü-lien and her mother-in-law think about the absent one." Play: *Ching-chai chi* (act 22).

8. "Announcement of Success." (In each excerpt, a wife receives word of her absent husband's success in the examinations.) Total: six. Example: "Kao Wen-chü reports that he has passed the examinations." Play: *Mi-lan chi* (act 12).

9. "Making Inquiries." (In each excerpt, the hero searches out a reliable friend or adviser.) Total: three. Example: "Sung T'ai-tsu visits Chao P'u on a snowy night." Play: *Huang-pao chi* (act unknown).

10. "Enjoying Scenery." (In each excerpt, the hero enjoys the beauties of nature.) Total: eight. Example: "Wang Shang makes an excursion to West Lake with many singing girls." Play: *Yü-ch'ueh chi* (act 12).

11. "Feasting." (In each excerpt, the hero attends a banquet, where he and his friends exchange poems.) Total: nine. Example: "The hegemon of Ch'u holds a banquet in his camp at night." Play: *Ch'ien-chin chi* (act 14).

12. "Chance Encounter." (In each excerpt, the hero and heroine meet by chance and fall in love.) Total: four. Example: "Chiang Shih-lung has an unexpected encounter in the wilderness." Play: *Pai-yueh t'ing* (act 19).

13. "Love." (In each excerpt, lovers meet or communicate despite many obstacles.) Total: five. Example: "Ts'ui Ying-ying communicates her love in a beautiful letter." Play: *Hsi-hsiang chi* (act 9).

14. "Loyalty, Filial Piety, Fidelity." (In each excerpt, a loyal, filial, or faithful person is depicted.) Total: seven. Example: "Mother Liu searches the dressing case." Play: *Chin-wan chi* (act 29).

15. "Doing Good in Secret." (In each excerpt, a person does a secret act of kindness and is rewarded by Heaven.) Total: four. Example: "P'ei Tu gives back the belt at Hsiang-shan." Play: *Huan-tai chi* (act 9).

16. "Glorious Reunion." (In each excerpt, long-separated family members are reunited.) Total: three. Example: "Su Ch'in returns home wearing brocade." Play: *Chin-yin chi* (act 40).

The *Yueh-fu hung-shan* list probably provides a reliable picture of the kind of material that was considered suitable for family- or lineage-sponsored performances. It is notable that the sixteen subjects, taken together, reflect a highly conventional view of life: children are admonished to be virtuous and hard-working; wives and mothers exhort their husbands and sons to strive for success, and wait patiently at home while they are away; men leave their homes to make their way in the world, and eventually send letters reporting success back to their anxious families; filial children and loyal friends are held up as models of virtue; the successful man secures his position by cultivating patrons and friends, and does not neglect to enlist Heaven on his side. Certainly there must have been a didactic or moralistic intent behind the selection of such scenes for presentation at important family occasions, in addition to the simple desire to entertain the people gathered there. In fact, the selection process can be seen as a way of editing or anthologizing popular drama to bring it into line with the moral and educational aims of the influential members of the lineage or family. Drama became part of a system of family education.

We can see, then, that plays presented at temple fairs, or in small market towns, were much more likely to concern subjects that aroused elite disapproval, such as romantic love, martial prowess, or the supernatural, than were plays performed at village temples or ancestral halls. Moreover, the fact that dramatic performances sponsored by lineages or other kin groups were liable to consist of individual acts or scenes, rather than entire plays, made it possible to exercise even closer control over the material presented. I would suggest, therefore, that of the three types of setting for local drama in Ming and Ch'ing times, the small market town was the most hospitable to plays that went against the taste of local elites, and the ancestral hall the least, with the village temple somewhere in between.

Since the specific setting clearly influenced the choice of plays to be presented, it is reasonable to ask whether it may also have affected their content. Were modifications made in the script of a play to make it more suitable for a given setting? This is a difficult question, since many such changes could have been made orally and never written down. Even such textual variations as have been preserved in written form cannot be infallibly connected to specific performance contexts, since there is no way to prove that a given version of a play was used by a given type of troupe or in a given setting.

However, the thesis that a given play could be varied in content as it was presented to different audiences would be strengthened if we found that there were apparently class-related differences among texts of those plays that exist in multiple written versions. To see whether this is the case, I have examined seventeen editions of the famous play, *P'i-p'a chi*, the most popular drama of Ming times. There are, in fact, differences among these texts that may be supposed to reflect the tastes of audiences—or of editors—of different classes.

P'i-p'a chi is set in the Han dynasty, and concerns Ts'ai Po-chieh and his wife, Chao Wu-niang. When they have been married only a month, Ts'ai has to travel to the capital to take the civil service examinations, leaving his family behind. He passes the examinations and receives an official post, but the letters he writes to his family are not delivered, so they are unaware of his success. At the same time, Prime Minister Niu, believing Ts'ai to have a promising career ahead of him, compels him to marry his daughter. Then famine strikes the region of Ts'ai's home. His wife and parents are destitute, since the money he has been sending them has also not been delivered. His wife struggles to find food for her parents-in-law, but cannot get enough, and the aged couple weaken and die. Then Ts'ai's wife sets out for the capital to look for him, supporting herself by playing the lute (*p'i-p'a*) and singing in the streets. Eventually she finds her husband, only to discover that he has another wife. But Miss Niu, when she learns what has happened, voluntarily takes the position of secondary wife, and thus the play ends happily.

The early texts of *P'i-p'a chi* that I have studied fall into three groups. The first group (group I) contains eight texts, all published (or in one case copied) in Soochow or Chia-hsing.[33] Group II contains three texts, two of which were

---

[33] The eight texts of the first group are:

I.1. *Hsin-k'an chin-hsiang Ts'ai Po-chieh P'i-p'a chi* 新刊巾箱蔡伯喈琵琶記. 2 *chüan*. Printed in Soochow in the Ming Chia-ching period (1522–1556). Reprinted by Sung-fen shih 誦芬室, ca. 1930. This is the oldest extant text of *P'i-p'a chi*.

I.2. *Hsin-k'an Yuan-pen* 元本 *Ts'ai Po-chieh P'i-P'a chi*. 2 *chüan*. Ch'ing manuscript copy by Lu I-tien 陸貽典 of an edition printed in Soochow before 1550. Reprinted in *Ku-pen hsi-ch'ü ts'ung-k'an ch'u-chi* 古本戲曲叢刊初集 [Collection of plays in old editions, first series], (Shanghai: Commercial Press, 1954).

I.3. Selected songs from *P'i-p'a chi*, in Hsu Ying-ch'ing 徐迎慶 and Niu Shao-ya 鈕少雅, eds., *Hui-tsuan Yuan-p'u nan-ch'ü chiu-kung cheng-shih* 彙纂元譜南曲九宮正始. 1 *chüan*. Printed in Soochow ca. 1630 from a text probably earlier than 1550. Reprinted Peking, 1936.

I.4. Selected songs from *P'i-p'a chi*, in Chiang Hsiao 蔣孝, ed., *Chiu-pien nan chiu-kung p'u* 舊編南九宮譜 10 *chüan*. Printed in Soochow in the Ming Chia-ching period. Reprinted in *Hsuan-lan-t'ang ts'ung-shu* 玄覽堂叢書.

published in Chien-an, Fukien.[34] Group III contains six texts, all but one published in Nanking.[35] Comparison of these seventeen texts discloses many differences between them. The differences are of six general types. Below I will present one example of each type.

1. Coarse language or broad humor is toned down. In act 33, Li Wang, the servant of Prime Minister Niu, attempts to avoid going to the country home of Ts'ai Po-chieh to get Ts'ai's wife, as he had been ordered to do, because he fears that if the two wives are brought together, a bitter struggle for the position of senior wife may ensue. In the group I texts, Li Wang says, "[I'm worried that when I bring the little wife here,] this wife

---

I.5.　Selected songs from *P'i-p'a chi*, in Shen Ching 沈璟, ed., *Nan-ch'ü p'u* 南曲譜. *22 chüan.* Printed in the Ming Wan-li period (1573–1619). Reprinted in *Hsiao yü p'u* 嘯余譜, 1662. Presently in the collection of the Naikaku Bunko.

I.6.　Selected acts from *P'i-p'a chi*, in "T'i-yueh chu-jen" 梯月主人 (pseud.), ed., *Wu-yü ts'ui-ya* 吳歈萃雅. *4 chüan.* Printed in Soochow in the Ming Wan-li period. Presently in the collection of the Naikaku Bunko.

I.7.　Selected acts from *P'i-p'a chi*, in Ling Ch'u-ch'eng 凌初成, ed., *Nan-yin san-lai* 南音三籟. *4 chüan.* Printed in Chia-hsing, ca. 1600 (rpt. Shanghai: Shanghai ku-chi shu-tien 上海古籍書店, 1963).

I.8.　*Ch'ü-hsien ts'ang* 瞿仙藏 *P'i-p'a chi. 4 chüan.* Printed in Chia-hsing, ca. 1600, by Ling Ch'u-ch'eng. Reprinted by Ch'an-yin lu 蟬隱盧, Shanghai, ca. 1930.

[34] The three texts in the second group are:

II.1.　*San-ting* 三訂 *P'i-p'a chi*, revised by [Chu] "Ch'ung-huai" [朱] 冲懷 (pseud.) of Ku-lin 古臨. *2 chüan.* Printed by Yü "Hui-ch'üan" 余會泉 (pseud.) in Chien-an, Fukien, ca. 1600. Presently in the collection of Professor Uemura Kōji. This is the oldest text in this group, although not the oldest printed copy.

II.2.　*Ch'ung-chiao* 重校 *P'i-p'a chi. 4 chüan.* Printed by Chi-i t'ang 集義堂 in Chien-an, Fukien, ca. 1600. Presently in the collection of the Hōsa Library 蓬左文庫.

II.3.　*Ch'ung-chiao P'i-p'a chi*, collated by Ch'en Pang-t'ai 陳邦泰 in the Ming period. *4 chüan.* Printed by Chi-chih chai 繼志齋 of Chin-ling (Nanking), 1598 (copy in Naikaku Bunko).

[35] The six texts of the third group are:

III.1.　*Yuan-pen ch'u-hsiang nan* 元本出相南 *P'i-p'a chi*, critically edited by Wang Shih-chen 王世貞 and Li Chih 李贄 in the Ming period. *3 chüan.* Printed by Ch'i-feng kuan 起鳳館, Nanking, ca. 1590. Presently in the collection of the Seikadō Library.

III.2.　*Li Cho-wu hsien-sheng p'i-p'ing* 李卓吾先生批評 *P'i-p'a chi*, critically edited by Li Chih in the Ming period. *2 chüan.* Printed by Jung-yü t'ang of Hu-lin 虎林容與堂, Nanking, Ming Wan-li period (1573–1619). Reprinted in *Ku-pen hsi-ch'ü ts'ung-k'an ti-san-chi* 古本戲曲叢刊第三集 [Collection of plays in old editions, third series], Peking, 1965.

III.3.　*Ch'en Mei-kung* 陳眉公 *p'i-p'ing P'i-p'a chi*, critically edited by Ch'en Chi-ju 繼儒 in the Ming period. *2 chüan.* Reprinted in Liu Shih-heng 劉世珩, *Hui-k'o ch'uan-ch'i* 彙刻傳奇, Nanking (?), 1919.

III.4.　*Yuan Liao-fan hsien-sheng shih-i* 袁了凡先生釋義 *P'i-p'a chi*, collated by Wang T'ing-no 汪廷訥 in the Ming period. *2 chüan.* Printed by Huan-ts'ui t'ang 環翠堂, Nanking, ca. 1600. Presently in the collection of the Faculty of Letters, Kyoto University.

III.5.　*P'i-p'a chi. 2 chüan.* Contained in *Liu-shih chung ch'ü* 六十種曲, printed by Mao Chin's Chi-ku ko 毛晉汲古閣, Nanking, ca. 1630 (rpt. Peking: Wen-hsueh ku-chi ch'u-pan she 文學古籍出版社, 1955).

III.6.　*Chu-ting* 硃訂 *P'i-p'a chi*, critically revised by Sun K'uang 孫鑛 in the Ming period. *2 chüan.* Printed in Nanking ca. 1630. Presently in the collection of the Seikadō Library.

will contend with her to see who will be the senior. If there's a big fight, Li Wang sure won't get a reward!" But the texts of groups II and III have: "[I'm worried that when I bring the little wife here,] my lady (*fu jen*) will contend with her to see who will be the senior. And then how can she not blame Li Wang?" (See Table 1.) Here the more formal "my lady" is substituted for "wife" (or "woman": *niang-tzu*), the reference to the possibility of an actual fight is quietly elided, and Li Wang is made to speak of being blamed rather than of not getting a reward. The total effect of the group I texts is broader and coarser.

2. Local dialect is changed into standard language. In act 3, when a maid of the Niu family says to another maid that they ought to go out and enjoy themselves, in the group I texts an expression from Wu dialect is used ("*hsieh tzu*," in one case modified into the Northern dialect equivalent, "*tse ke*"). This is eliminated from the group II and III texts and replaced with a nondialect phrase. (See Table 2.)

3. Realism is replaced by moralism. In act 21, the heroine, Chao Wu-niang, describing her despair when she was unable to get food for her husband's parents, in the group I texts says, "Many times I wanted to sell myself," while in the group II and III texts she says "Many times I [wanted to] kill myself." (This sentence reads very awkwardly, probably a sign of careless revision of the original.) (See Table 3.)

4. Anti-establishment criticism is muted. In act 2, Ts'ai Po-chieh's mother, attempting to dissuade him from leaving home to take the examinations, in the group I texts says, "Listen! True felicity is in the fields and gardens. Who cares about being a nobleman today?" This is changed in the group II and III texts to "Who cares about petty noblemen?" thus removing the faint hint of social criticism seemingly contained in the original phrasing. (See Table 4.)

5. Stricter attention is paid to the correct use of status terms. In act 31, near the end of the play, when Ts'ai's wife, the daughter of Prime Minister Niu, declares that she intends to go to Ts'ai's home to mourn for his parents, in all but one of the group I texts she refers to herself as "the wife of their child." But the group II and III texts rather pedantically change this to "the junior wife of their child," making clear the precise status she then had. (See Table 5.)

6. Natural sentiments are replaced by rigorous ethics. In act 23, when Chao Wu-niang is advised by her father-in-law to forget about Ts'ai Po-chieh, who has apparently abandoned them all, and to take another husband, in the group I (and group II) texts she replies, "I'm afraid he would be just as bad as Po-chieh." But in the group III texts she declares that it is not proper to remarry. Here the group III texts replace a rather cynical and disillusioned remark, quite natural under the circumstances, with a highly moralistic one that is much less convincing. (See Table 6.)

TABLE 1

Text I.1	娘子又要	爭大	小	厮打時節，	不賞李旺了
I.2	〃 〃 〃 〃	〃 〃	〃	〃 〃 〃 〃 ，	〃 〃 〃 〃 〃
I.3ª					
I.4					
I.5					
I.6					
I.7					
I.8	〃 〃 〃 〃	〃 〃 爭	〃	〃 〃 〃 〃 ，	〃 〃 〃 〃 〃
II.1	夫人 〃 〃 和他 〃 〃	〃 ，	到那 〃 〃 ，	可 〃 埋冤李旺
II.2	〃 〃 〃 〃 〃 〃 〃 〃	〃 ，	〃 〃 〃 〃 ，	〃 〃 〃 〃 〃
II.3	〃 〃 〃 〃 〃 〃 〃 〃	〃 ，	〃 〃 〃 〃 ，	〃 〃 〃 〃 〃
III.1	〃 〃 〃 〃 〃 〃 〃 〃 〃 〃	，	〃 〃 〃 〃 ，	〃 〃 〃 〃 〃
III.2	〃 〃 〃 〃 〃 〃 〃 〃	，	〃 〃 〃 〃 ，	〃 〃 〃 〃 〃
III.3	〃 〃 〃 〃 〃 〃 〃 〃	，	〃 〃 〃 〃 ，	〃 〃 〃 〃 〃
III.4	〃 〃 〃 〃 〃 〃 〃 〃	，	〃 〃 〃 〃 ，	〃 〃 〃 〃 〃
III.5	〃 〃 〃 〃 〃 〃 〃 〃	，	〃 〃 〃 〃 ，	〃 〃 〃 〃 〃
III.6	〃 〃 〃 〃 〃 〃 〃 〃	，	〃 〃 〃 〃 ，	〃 〃 〃 〃 〃

ªWhere no mark appears, no such character exists in the text.

TABLE 2

Text I.1	今日能勾得在此閑戲歇子
I.2	〃 〃 〃 〃 〃 〃 〃 〃 〃 〃 〃
I.3ª	
I.4	
I.5	
I.6	
I.7	
I.8	〃 〃 〃 〃 〃 〃 〃 〃 〃 則個
II.1	〃 〃 　 〃 來 〃 花園遊嬉
II.2	〃 〃
II.3	〃 〃 　 〃 〃 〃 〃 〃 〃
III.1	〃 〃 〃 彀 〃 〃 〃 〃 〃 〃 〃
III.2	〃 〃 〃 〃 〃 〃 〃 〃 〃 〃 〃
III.3	〃 〃 〃 〃 〃 〃 爭 〃 〃 〃 〃
III.4	〃 〃 〃 〃 〃 〃 〃 〃 〃 〃 〃
III.5	〃 〃 〃 〃 〃 〃 〃 〃 〃 〃 〃
III.6	〃 〃 〃 〃 〃 〃 〃 〃 〃 〃 戲

ªWhere no mark appears, no such character exists in the text.

TABLE 3

Text I.1	幾	番	要	賣	了	奴	身	己
I.2	”	”	”	”	”	”	”	”
I.3ᵃ								
I.4								
I.5								
I.6								
I.7								
I.8	”	”	”	”	”	”	”	”
II.1	”	”	拚	死	”	”	”	”
II.2	”	”	”	”	”	”	”	”
II.3	”	”	”	”	”	”	”	”
III.1	”	”	”	”	”	”	”	”
III.2	”	”	”	”	”	”	”	”
III.3	”	”	”	”	”	”	”	”
III.4	”	”	”	”	”	”	”	”
III.5	”	”	”	”	”	”	”	”
III.6	”	”		”	”	”	”	”

ᵃWhere no mark appears, no such character exists in the text.

TABLE 4

Text I.1	何	必	當	今	公	與	侯
I.2	”	”	”	”	”	”	”
I.3ᵃ							
I.4							
I.5							
I.6	”	”	”	”	”	”	”
I.7	”	”	”	”	”	”	”
I.8	”	”	”	”	”	”	”
II.1	”	”	區	區	”	”	”
II.2	”	”	”	”	”	”	”
II.3	”	”	”	”	”	”	”
III.1	”	”	”	”	”	”	”
III.2	”	”	”	”	”	”	”
III.3	”	”	”	”	”	”	”
III.4	”	”	”	”	”	”	”
III.5	”	”	”	”	”	”	”
III.6	”	”	”	”	”	”	”

ᵃWhere no mark appears, no such character exists in the text.

TABLE 5

Text					
I.1	他	孩	兒	的	妻
I.2a	,,	,,	,,	,,	,,
I.3	,,	,,	,,	,,	,,
I.4	,,	,,	,,	次	,,
I.5	,,	,,	,,	,,	,,
I.6	,,	,,	,,	,,	,,
I.7	,,	,,	,,	,,	,,
I.8	,,	,,	,,	,,	,,
II.1	,,	,,	,,	,, ,,	,,
II.2	,,	,,	,,	,, ,,	,,
II.3	,,	,,	,,	,, ,,	,,
III.1	,,	,,	,,	,,	,,
III.2	,,	,,	,,	,,	,,
III.3	,,	,,	,,	,,	,,
III.4	,,	,,	,,	,,	,,
III.5	,,	,,	,,	,,	,,
III.6	,,	,,	,,	,,	,,

aWhere no mark appears, no such character exists in the text.

TABLE 6

Text			
I.1	只 怕		再 如 伯 嗒
I.2	,, ,,		,, ,, ,, ,,
I.3a			
I.4			
I.5			
I.6			
I.7			
I.8	,, ,,	嫁 了 人 呵	,, ,, ,, ,,
II.1	,, ,,		,, ,, ,, ,,
II.2	,, ,,		,, ,, ,, ,,
II.3	,, ,,		,, ,, ,, ,,
III.1	那 些 個	不 更 二 夫	
III.2	,, ,, ,,	,? ,, ,, ,,	
III.3	,, ,, ,,	,, ,, ,, ,,	
III.4	,, ,, ,,	,, ,, ,, ,,	
III.5	,, ,, ,,	,, ,, ,, ,,	
III.6	,, ,, ,,	,, ,, ,, ,,	

aWhere no mark appears, no such character exists in the text.

There are consistent differences between the group I texts on one side, and the group III texts on the other, with the group II texts usually agreeing with those of group III. The differences exhibit a definite pattern: passages in the group I texts that are realistic, cynical, spontaneous, and even somewhat vulgar, are made more didactic, more moralistic, and more "respectable" in the group II and III texts. When we recall that the group III texts are later than the group I texts, it is difficult to resist concluding that the group III texts derive from a version or versions of *P'i-p'a chi* that had been edited to conform better to elite values, either because of audience demand, or editorial preference.[36] If even the script of a classic play like *P'i-p'a chi* was liable to be changed for ideological reasons, it is likely that less famous works were modified even more drastically.

In the preceding pages I have presented a typology of Chinese local drama based on the sponsorship of performances. But my subject has a historical dimension as well. Local drama was affected by changes in the world of Chinese drama as a whole in Ming and Ch'ing times, and the balance of importance between popular and literary drama in that world was affected by larger social and economic developments. We can understand the evolution of Chinese local drama in Ming and Ch'ing times only in the context of the general relationship between local culture and local power. Folk songs, dances, plays, and other forms of popular culture are the creation of the common people, and develop vigorously as long as the villagers live in conditions of approximate equality. But when local power begins to be concentrated in a few hands—that is, when landownership becomes concentrated—the old popular culture is appropriated by the landowning class, and is transformed under their influence into more elegant and literary forms. Then, when the power of this class is weakened or broken by the resistance of the common people and conditions in the villages become more egalitarian again, popular culture recovers its vitality and expresses itself in new forms, beginning the cycle once more.

This pattern can already be seen in the ancient epoch of the *Poetry Scripture* (*Shih ching*). The folk songs (*kuo feng*) flourished during the time when all villagers participated equally in the village festivals. But as the gap between rich and poor in the villages emerged and widened, the old village festivals were replaced by clan rituals of the wealthy families, and the folk songs were replaced by banqueting songs (*ta ya* and *hsiao ya*) and by ritual songs performed in the clan ancestral shrine (*sung*).[37]

---

[36] *CSEK*, pp. 398–437. See also Tanaka Issei, "A Study on *P'i-p'a chi* in Hui-chou Drama: Formation of Local Plays in Ming and Ch'ing Eras and Hsin-an Merchants," *Acta Asiatica* 32:34–72 (1977).

[37] *CSEK*, pp. 498–499; Matsumoto Masaaki 松本雅明, *Okinawa no rekishi to bunka* 沖縄の歴史と文化 [History and culture of Okinawa] (Tokyo: Kondō shuppan sha 近藤出版社, 1971), pp. 223–224.

The same pattern is visible also in the development of drama during the Ming–Ch'ing period. In early Ming, village and market-town drama flourished, as it had under the Yuan. In the north it was what is known today as "Yuan drama," and in the south was what is called "southern drama" (*nan hsi*). The predominant themes of works in these dramatic traditions were romantic love, martial heroism, and the supernatural—just the themes that were preponderant in the plays whose chief characters were depicted in the festival procession in Li Yü's *Yung t'uan yuan* (see above, pp. 147–148). In mid-Ming and after, landownership became more concentrated and local society became more differentiated. As the influence of local elites in the rural areas grew, the development of local drama was constrained. Landlords and others were anxious to prevent the spread of unconventional, dissenting, and heterodox values, and were especially concerned to eliminate them from local drama. Since they were in control of the plays that were presented in most villages and lineage temples, they were in a position to prevent the presentation of material of which they did not approve. Thus, the popular local drama of early Ming was gradually appropriated by local elites and transformed into the more conservative clan drama. This development reached its climax with the appearance of a new, highly sophisticated kind of drama called *ch'uan-ch'i*.

The *ch'uan-ch'i* plays were so called because they were based on the T'ang novellas in the literary language known as *ch'uan-ch'i*. (For example, the Ming plays *Han tan chi* and *Nan ho chi* are based on the T'ang *ch'uan-ch'i Chen chung chi* and *Nan ho t'ai-shou chuan*.) Ming literati found such stories, written for the elite of that time, congenial in both ideology and sentiment, and greatly favored the plays that were based on them. Many *ch'uan-ch'i* plays were written, but they were never a popular entertainment form. The patrons and audiences of *ch'uan-ch'i* were officials, literati, and other powerful, well-educated persons. This fact is reflected in the subject matter of the plays, which usually depict the vicissitudes of official life or present political commentary and criticism.

At the same time, however, changes were taking place on the lower levels of society. Late Ming times saw the emergence and spread of popular resistance to local landlord power. The riots and disturbances of the time helped greatly weaken the landlords' authority in the countryside. Accordingly, popular local drama began to flourish again. New regional drama of all kinds, including the famous Peking opera, developed prodigiously. Thus, the profound creativity of the common people when released from the hegemony of the landowning class was demonstrated once again.

SIX

Regional Operas
and Their Audiences:
Evidence from Hong Kong

Barbara E. Ward

It is often said that the popular theater was one of the most significant of the media that disseminated Chinese culture and values. Unfortunately, though understandably, most writers on traditional Chinese drama have been more interested in the plays themselves, the players, and the techniques of acting than in their audiences. Provocative hints can be gleaned here and there, but there is not much hard evidence. In its absence, it seems appropriate to examine the audiences for present-day traditional theaters and tap the long memories of surviving fans of late Ch'ing opera to throw a little light backwards in time upon this crucial but relatively little documented subject.

Surprising though it may seem, Hong Kong is one of the best places to look for data for such a re-creation. Hong Kong is useful in this context not only because of its accessibility but also because of the virtually uninterrupted and vigorous survival there of at least three forms of Chinese regional opera—Cantonese, Ch'ao Chou, and Waichow—in a traditional setting. This somewhat unexpected concomitant of the British colonial presence requires a few words of explanation.

It was a common paradox of British colonialism that it often permitted (and sometimes actually encouraged) the untrammeled continuance of certain indigenous cultural practices that a native government might have tried to

Most of the research on which this paper is based was carried out at intervals between 1950 and 1981 as part of an on-going longitudinal study of socio-economic change in Hong Kong. Financial assistance has come from various sources, to all of which I am permanently indebted. These sources include H. M. Treasury (the so-called Hayter Committee), UNESCO, the Chinese University of Hong Kong, the London-Cornell Project, Cornell University, the Smuts Memorial Fund (Cambridge University), and Clare Hall (Cambridge University). In 1975, the Principal and Fellows of Newnham College (Cambridge University) awarded me a Gibbs Travelling Fellowship and earmarked it for theater research. I also thank the Chinese University of Hong Kong for a generous grant for research on the sociology of Cantonese opera.

control or even eradicate. No British government ever felt itself politically threatened by Chinese opera performances, but from time to time in the past Chinese governments certainly have felt so and reacted accordingly; the control exercised over the theater in China since 1949 needs no discussion here. Chinese opera in Hong Kong is not, and to the best of my knowledge has never been, censored.

It is probably also significant here that Hong Kong has lacked a strong reformist public opinion of the kind that might have tried to influence the government to act against certain popular religious practices. Here, too, one surmises that the colonial paradox may have helped to secure preservation and continuity. In nearly all their colonies, British administrators left local religious practices severely alone except when such practices appeared to them to pose a clear political threat or to prejudice public order, or when what the British deemed to be the "principles of natural justice" were at stake. Thus, in Hong Kong the rituals of secret societies are rigorously suppressed but popular religious festivals meet with indulgence from officials. Far from wishing to decry these festivals as superstitious, wasteful, or simply old-fashioned, these officials tend to consider them interesting and enjoyable and wish to control them only insofar as they impede traffic, constitute fire hazards, or lead otherwise to the commission of public nuisances or law breaking. As most large-scale popular religious festivals include a set of performances of Chinese operas, this policy has contributed indirectly to the survival of old-style theater in what, in terms of reaching a mass audience, was probably always its most significant traditional setting—one that does not now exist on the mainland and is greatly reduced in Taiwan. In Hong Kong the number of festival performances was actually higher in the early 1980s than it was in the early 1950s.

The following discussion is divided into four sections. The first outlines the current status of Chinese opera in Hong Kong with particular though not exclusive reference to its role in religious festivals. The second considers questions of continuity and discontinuity—between secular and religious occasions, between the present and the past, and among social classes, geographical regions, and rural and urban milieux. The third section attempts to describe and analyze present-day audiences in Hong Kong, and the fourth touches briefly on the question What were the messages conveyed by this mass medium?

TRADITIONAL DRAMA IN PRESENT-DAY HONG KONG

The Numbers and Occasions of Performance

Hong Kong today contains more than 5 million people living on just under 400 square miles of land, most of which is steep, barren mountainside. Every year in this small area about 200 temporary theaters are erected for theatrical performances, most but by no means all of them in rural areas. Very nearly all these temporary theaters are built in connection with festivals of the popular religion. I do not know how many of the temporary theaters are used by more than one regional type of opera troupe before being dismantled, but the number may be in the region of 50 or 60. Taking the higher figure, we have a total of about 280 sets (or runs) of festival-opera performances a year. Assuming further that each run includes nine different full-scale operas, we then have an estimated total showing of around 2520 festival operas a year. Of these, the large majority (more than 65 percent) are performed by Cantonese troupes, the next largest proportion (about 25 percent) by Ch'ao Chou troupes, and the smallest proportion (about 10 percent) by Waichow troupes.[1] At a very rough estimate, then, about 1600 Cantonese operas, 650 Ch'ao Chou operas, and 400 Waichow operas are performed annually in temporary "matshed" theaters[2] on ritual occasions in town and country. A corresponding estimate of the numbers of operas performed in major city theaters on secular occasions shows them to be far fewer: Cantonese operas about 90, Ch'ao Chou operas about 50, Waichow and Peking operas about 10 each. If we add to these the secular performances given in the amusement parks and assume nightly shows throughout the year (almost certainly a gross exaggeration), we can add 730 more performances, mostly Cantonese. Thus, at an outside guess there may be a total of just under 900 purely secular shows a year, nearly all of them in permanent city theaters.

Not only are the numbers of festival operas larger than all the rest, but so are their audiences. The fact that the matshed theaters are seldom enclosed areas and that seating is usually free means that it is impossible to give accurate figures, but it also means that audiences can be very large indeed. In densely populated or easily accessible areas, with a good troupe and well-known star performers, as many as three or four thousand people may be present at a time.

---

[1] Cantonese opera (Mandarin: Yueh chü 粵劇, not to be confused with Shao-hsing 紹興 opera, also called Yueh chü but written differently 越劇) has much in common with Peking opera, especially its domination by the two styles *erh-huang* 二黃 and *hsi-p'i* 西皮. On the other hand, its orchestral accompaniment is more varied, and over the last sixty years there has been a constant striving for modernization and change. Cantonese operas, performed in the Cantonese dialect, are normally presented as whole plays lasting several hours. Ch'ao Chou opera originates from the city of Swatow in northern Kwangtung and uses the Swatow dialect. It has more in common with the opera of Fukien Province than with Cantonese opera. The same is true of Waichow opera, commonly referred to in Hong Kong as "Hoklo," which is performed in the Hokkien dialect spoken in the city of that name in Kwangtung, farther north, and on the coast. There has been little study of regional opera by non-Chinese writers, but an introduction to the subject is now available: Colin Mackerras, *The Chinese Theatre in Modern Times* (London: Thames and Hudson, 1975), especially part two.

[2] Figures for 1975 by kind courtesy of the Royal Hong Kong Police. Temporary theaters are constructed of China fir, bamboo, and tin sheeting. (The last has replaced the traditional palm leaf matting that gave all such temporary constructions their familiar English name of "matsheds".) For reasons connected with crowd control and fire hazards, matshed theaters have to be licensed by both the R.H.K.P. and the Fire Services Department. Some matshed theaters can seat more than 3000 people, but the theaters vary in size. The average theater probably accommodates 1000 persons. See B. E. Ward, "Temporary Theatres in Hong Kong" (manuscript).

Decried by many of the elite and modern-educated as old-fashioned, dirty, noisy, vulgar, and connected with superstition, the festival performances nevertheless remain the backbone of local regional opera without which even Cantonese opera would probably have hardly survived the years since the demise of Hong Kong's two regular opera houses in the early 1960s.

CONTINUITIES AND DISCONTINUITIES

Secular and Sacred Occasions

Two preliminary points must be clearly understood about all the opera performances discussed in this paper: first, no matter where or on what occasion they are performed, all are professional shows; second, the essential differences between what I am calling "festival" operas and secular ones lie less in the performances as such than in the occasions on which they are given.[3] Each point needs some elaboration.

In view of the fact that several studies[4] made in other parts of China describe operas performed by villagers themselves or by other amateurs or actors who at most could be called semiprofessional, it is necessary to make it clear that none of the performances discussed in this paper are "folk" performances in that sense. Whether in town or country, on ritual or secular occasions, or in temporary or permanent theater buildings, the operas presented to mass audiences in Hong Kong today are professional shows, and according to my informants the same could be said of Kwangtung province in general in the early years of this century too.[5] It is important to note also that the same troupes

[3] In outline form, the main types of live professional opera that can be seen in Hong Kong today, according to sponsorship and place of performance, follow:
  1. Community sponsored, normally in matshed theaters: festival performances; Cantonese, Ch'ao Chou, Hoklo.
  2. Privately sponsored, in restaurants, private dwellings: Cantonese, others (very uncommon at the present time).
  3. Officially and municipally sponsored, in public auditoria, matshed theaters (occasionally), and public parks (open-air shows): commercial performances; mainly Cantonese, some Ch'ao Chou, occasional Hoklo, some visiting troupes and puppets.
  4. Entrepreneurial sponsorship, in opera houses (now defunct), adapted cinemas, public auditoria, amusement-park theaters, and matshed theaters (occasionally): commercial performances; mainly Cantonese, some Ch'ao Chou, occasional Hoklo, visiting troupes (various).

[4] See William Dolby, *A History of Chinese Drama* (London: Paul Elek, 1976), chap. 11, especially pp. 229–230; also S. D. Gamble, ed. *Chinese Village Plays* (Amsterdam: Philo Press, 1970). Dolby's volume contains a comprehensive bibliography of Chinese works on regional drama.

[5] Hong Kong troupes today are distinguished according to quality (first, second, third class, etc.) but villagers who are willing to pay the high fees required can hire the very best actors. Third- and fourth-class troupes are more likely to be seen in the city amusement parks than anywhere else. The evidence about past practice is conflicting. On the one hand, there are the phrases *lok heung paan* 落鄉班 (literally: "go down to the countryside troupes") and *kwoh shan paan* 過山班 (literally "cross the mountains troupes"), terms that might suggest that these were inferior troupes that acted only

of professional (though not necessarily full-time) actors perform on both festival and secular occasions. Moreover, most of the same plays also appear on both, though festival performances invariably include certain ceremonial playlets that may or may not find a place in secular programs.

Most secular performances are organized commercially. A few are charity shows, and some are put on under some kind of official (usually municipal) sponsorship. The more prestigious employ well-known actors and have rather short runs—a week being considered daringly long. Most of them take place in permanent theaters (at present usually in cinemas adapted for the occasion or in one of the municipal auditoria) with a box office for tickets and reservations. There is a strong tendency for their audiences to come from the middle and upper classes. The less prestigious are usually performed in small, ill-equipped permanent theaters in one or another of the local amusement parks, often night after night. These shows commonly employ third- or fourth-rate actors and musicians, charge—very cheaply—for entrance, do not normally accept reservations, and cater mainly to lower-middle- and lower-class audiences.

Unlike the secular shows, the primary object of the festival performances is neither commercial nor artistic; it is to please a deity or deities. Presented in a specially constructed temporary theater and organized by a specially selected local committee, which normally does not sell tickets for admission, a set of festival plays is conceived of as an offering of live entertainment to a particular god or set of gods. The occasions for such offerings are normally the annual celebrations of a temple god's so-called birthday, the annual rituals for the "hungry ghosts" in the seventh lunar month, or the less frequent but also

---

in rural areas. On the other hand, one reads and hears of the Red Boats, which traveled the whole delta region in the late Ch'ing and Republican periods carrying the famous as well as the less famous actors. Some informants have told me that all Cantonese troupes, without exception, used to go down to the countryside from time to time, because there was never enough work in Canton itself to keep them busy all year round. Whatever the situation elsewhere, in the delta region at least people in rural Kwangtung often had the chance to see good professional drama from the provincial capital and the drama center at Fo-shan. See B. E. Ward, "The Red Boats of the Canton Delta: A Chapter in the Historical Sociology of Chinese Opera," in *Proceedings of the International Conference on Sinology* (Taipei: Academia Sinica, 1981). Since about 1970, a troupe of talented employees of Radio Television Hong Kong has been giving regular open-air performances in public parks in Kowloon and on Hong Kong Island, under the sponsorship of the Urban Services Department. This troupe has also performed in City Hall. Its performances are in Cantonese and the operas presented are in the Cantonese style with some adaptations (for example, the introduction of Peking-style painted faces). Since 1978, a troupe of apprentice actors under the auspices of the Cantonese Opera Artists Association (the professional association that includes Cantonese opera actors, musicians, acrobats, costume specialists, and stage hands) has also taken part in providing free public entertainment. These semiprofessional performances are not included in the numerical estimates cited in the text. There are also amateur performances in Hong Kong, attended mainly by relatives and friends of the performers. There is plenty of amateur interest in performing in Hong Kong, especially in singing, but this is mainly an urban phenomenon. The gulf between the talented amateur and the good professional is usually very wide, but exceptionally gifted and persevering amateurs do and did sometimes cross it and become professionals.

regularly recurring Taoist rites known in Cantonese as *ta chiu* (Mandarin: *ta chiao*). The religious role of the operas as part (socially the most important and certainly the most expensive part) of the offerings that are presented to the gods on such occasions is clearly acknowledged in the Cantonese term *shan kung hei* (literally: "god revere plays"), by which festival performances are usually known.

The position of the stage for festival performances is an important indicator of their role as offerings. Like the permanent stages that can still be seen in some temple complexes in China, the temporary stage is frequently constructed directly opposite the main entrance to a temple in such a way that the players face (usually northwards) directly towards the images. Sometimes these are brought out in front of the temple's entrance "in order to allow them to see." In places where, for topographical or other reasons, the stage cannot be erected in front of the temple in this way, one of the following two solutions to the ensuing problem may appear. The more usual one is for a sort of temporary temple or shrine (Cantonese: *shan p'aang*) to be constructed for the images. Such a shrine is always placed facing the stage, and the images are brought out of the temple in procession and ritually installed not long before the first performance. The temporary shrine then becomes the focus of the religious rituals connected with the festival.

Sometimes, however, the temple proper remains the focus of the rites, but an image of the god is brought out in the same way and installed, not in a temporary matshed shrine, but in what I have elsewhere called a sort of "royal box"—a small platform or shelf built high above the heads of the human audience under the matshed roof, facing the stage.[6] In either case, the images remain in their temporary abodes for the duration of the whole set of festival performances and are ritually escorted home again to their places in the temple only after the last play is over and the closing rites completed. There can be no doubt but that this placement indicates the religious significance of the plays as offerings. This is a theme that most human members of festival audiences are well aware of and willing to explain, sometimes with a hint of disbelief and amusement, sometimes in all apparent seriousness. One is reminded of the accounts of the drama festivals in sixth-century Athens, when pride of place was given to the image of Dionysius, which was escorted to the central place in the front row and returned later to its usual abode in the temple in processions not unlike those that can be seen to this day in Hong Kong.

A typical run of Cantonese festival operas stretches over five consecutive nights and four days. The opening performance is an evening one starting at 7:30 or 8:00 P.M. and continuing until midnight or later. The second performance begins at 2:00 P.M. the following day and finishes at about 5:30 or 6:00 P.M., to be followed by the third performance that same evening—and so on for

---

[6] B. E. Ward, "Not Merely Players: Drama, Act, and Ritual in Traditional China," *Man* n.s. 14.1:18–39 (1979); "Red Boats." Also see chap. 5.

five evening and four afternoon shows. Each show includes one long play—a love story; a fighting drama; a tale of filial piety, ministerial loyalty, or good (or bad) officials; or a story based on legend. Usually the plot is known to the audience. Normally the play has no specifically ritual content; it is purely for entertainment. Apart from the conventions that all must end happily and that each of the entertainment operas in a single run of festival performances must be different, the program is quite flexible. The choice of play is usually left to the organizer of the troupe. There is no set order in which certain titles must appear; words, music, and movements can vary quite widely even for operas with the same name, basically similar plots, and performed by the same players; and there is usually much scope for improvisation. These are the operas the audiences come to see. At commercial or other secular performances, they are usually the only operas presented.

At festival performances, however, there are certain obligatory additions to the program. These are usually very short items that differ from entertainment plays in a number of ways, the most significant of which probably is their predictability. Some are obligatory at all festival performances, some are merely common, and some appear only in special circumstances. Each has its own fixed music, which is heavily dependent upon percussion and wind instruments. Most of these playlets are mimed without either sung or spoken words, and when spoken words do occur they follow a fixed "text," often in somewhat archaic language. Action is highly formalized and consists mainly of a series of set routines of posture and movement. Titles are unvarying and plots simple and fixed. Everyone in the audience knows most of these pieces by heart, and knows, too, when to expect them in the program. Though some of them may be much enjoyed, their importance is not primarily for entertainment but for their symbolic meaning. Most are believed to have at least a degree of ritual efficacy. For this reason and because of their repetitive and predictable nature which contrasts strongly with the flexibility of the entertainment plays, I refer to these plays as "ritual plays."[7]

---

[7] Current Cantonese has several terms for ritual plays, of which one of the most frequently heard is *lai hei* 例戲 ("regulated plays"). For an important discussion of their content and role in Cantonese drama, see Alan L. Kagan, "Cantonese Puppet Theater: An Operatic Tradition and Its Role in the Chinese Religious Belief System," Ph.D. thesis, Music, Indiana University, 1978. Ch'ao Chou and Waichow festival performances also include ritual plays. In Hong Kong, all opera troupes place a shrine to their own patron deities backstage, no matter what the occasion for the performance. Here incense is regularly offered on behalf of the troupe as a whole and by individual actors on their own behalf. Each regional opera has its distinctive patron god(s). See the articles by B. E. Ward already cited, and an important study by Tanaka Issei 田仲一成, *Chūgoku saishi engeki kenkyū* 中國祭祀演劇研究 [Ritual theaters in China] (Tokyo: Tōyō bunka kenkyūjo 東洋文化研究所, 1981). The archaic language referred to, known as "stage Mandarin" (in Cantonese, *hei t'oi koon wa* 戲抬官話), is said to have been based on Kweilin pronunciation and to have been the normal pronunciation used for all Cantonese operas before the early years of this century. The use of Cantonese apparently spread quickly after the revolution of 1911. Elderly informants mention being unable to understand everything they heard from the stage when they were children.

For the purposes of this paper, it is unnecessary to perform a detailed analysis of the role and meaning of the ritual plays. Their broadly auspicious nature is well-known to their audiences, though few are able to explain the plays' symbolism in any but the most general terms, and—with the exception of the longest and most spectacular (which, incidentally, have the least religious significance)—most people appear to take little interest in their performance. As with many other rituals, the important thing is that they be done and done properly; there is no assumption that congregational participation and understanding are necessary adjuncts to a performance or have any effect upon its efficacy.

Present and Past

It is commonly assumed in Hong Kong today that festival performances are "more traditional" and commercial and other ones "more modern." It would follow that festival performances would be the more likely to provide useful clues to past practice, but the matter is not so simple. Let us take, for an example, the fact that in present-day Hong Kong commercial and other shows require tickets for admission whereas festival performances typically do not. It does not follow that charging for admission is a modern phenomenon. A delightful poem of the thirteenth century entitled "A Peasant Unfamiliar with the Theater" and written in the first person describes how

I came to town to buy some spirit money and incense.
As I walked down the street I saw a colorful paper notice;
Nowhere else was there such a bustling throng.
I saw a man leaning with his hand against a wooden gate,
Shouting loudly, "Step right up, step right up,"
Warning that latecomers would find the place full and no more benches.
. . . .
He demanded two hundred in cash and then let me pass.[8]

Six hundred years later—and one hundred years ago—at the popular theaters of the late Ch'ing dynasty (there were more than twenty such theaters in Peking alone), one paid "seat money" varying in price according to place and degree of comfort, or bought a "tea ticket" for a whole box seating about a dozen people.[9]

The broad distinction between different levels of commercial theater is not new either. Dolby's description of nineteenth-century theaters distinguishes between "play establishments" (or "emporia") and "play gardens." At the former, select groups of elite and wealthy customers held banquets accompanied by plays, dancing, singing, and music; the latter were the main popular theaters, at which, though tea was served, wine and meals were unavailable,

---

[8] Chung-wen Shih, *The Golden Age of Chinese Drama: Yuan Tsa-chü* (Princeton: Princeton University Press, 1976), pp. 198–199.

[9] Dolby, *History*, p. 191.

and the large audiences composed people of every social class. Private entertainment somewhat similar to that described for the "play establishments" continues to this day in the big hotel restaurants and tea houses of Hong Kong, though the range of possible entertainers is now vastly extended and includes contemporary popular singers, variety shows of all kinds, jazz, discos, and ballroom dancing. Certain well-known opera stars may still be invited to sing on such occasions, but the engagement of a whole opera troupe is hardly ever heard of now.[10]

Much more significant for the history of Chinese opera is the current distinction between different types or grades of commercial performance proper referred to already: on the one hand, the performances that take place in one or another of the handful of prestigious central locations, and, on the other hand, those that appear in the small, cramped theaters in the amusement parks or, occasionally, in temporary matsheds. Admission to the former is expensive, performances are relatively few, and the theater management commonly imposes upon the audience a number of behavioral constraints based upon westernized middle-class norms. These performances are usually widely advertised, seats are booked in advance, and the numbers of people who can see them are necessarily few and preponderantly middle- and upper-class. In short, the performances are restricted (though by different means and rather less rigorously) to much the same kinds of wealthy audience as frequented the nineteenth-century "play establishments." Needless to say, such performances are always given by well-known troupes with star players.

The audiences at the amusement-park theaters are much more mixed and, except in size and class composition, resemble those of the "play gardens" described by Dolby. Although the presence of the better known troupes and star players is not unknown in them, most performances are of inferior quality. However, despite their small capacity, the amusement-park theaters cater to a great many more people than the prestigious central theaters, because their tickets are cheap, their performances frequent, and their location within easy reach of some of the most densely populated areas of mass housing. Moreover, their patrons are not forbidden to walk about, smoke, eat, talk, take photographs, make sound recordings, or share their seats with their small children. For these reasons, and because in any case the other amusement-park attractions appeal more to the lower than the upper classes, it is not surprising that these theaters reach down to a mass audience in a way that the grander commercial shows do not. At the same time, it is likely that some kind of polarization of class interests is occurring, since proportionately fewer people from the upper and educated classes who used to frequent the old opera houses

---

[10] Dolby, *History*, pp. 154–196. In 1951–1952 I saw Cantonese opera being performed at a private party on board two Chinese junks lashed together on the waterfront on Hong Kong Island. However, only a few actors were employed.

go to the amusement-park theaters of the present day. (It is also certainly true that the formal theater manners today demanded in, say, Hong Kong's city hall were unknown in the old-style Chinese theaters at any level.) However, it is important to realize that, except for being required to buy tickets, the amusement-park audiences in contemporary Hong Kong are similar to those one sees at festival performances, and, with the exception of the obligatory presence of the ritual plays at the latter, so are the performances they see. In other words, the distinction between "more traditional" and "more modern" does not correspond to that between "commercial occasion" and "festival occasion," but rather cuts clean across it.

One may ask further about the performances as such. If the restricted audiences who pay a great deal to see the shows that are put on from time to time in the centrally located theaters are new in the sense that they behave in a more "modern" way, does it follow that the performances they come to see are also "modern"? Certainly some of these performances are innovative, with new plots, new types of costume, more adventurous music, Western lighting effects and scenery and so on, but a good many others, especially when the older and most famous stars take part, exhibit a marked traditionalism. What seems to be happening is that these high-class shows before restricted audiences are often occasions for the appearance of a more self-consciously artistic approach to Chinese opera—an approach long ago made familiar by Mei Lan-fang and others with regard to Peking opera, but less widely adopted for most forms of regional opera outside the People's Republic. As a generalization, that statement is far too sweeping to fit all the facts (particularly, as we shall see, with regard to Cantonese and Ch'ao Chou opera), and in any case it requires a paper in itself. Moreover, the distinction is not clearcut, since most of the same actors (and many of the same plays) who appear in, say, a high-class secular performance at the city hall also play in matshed theaters at religious festivals and every now and then in the amusement parks too. Nevertheless, I would argue that the self-consciously artistic opera is a feature of the current scene in Hong Kong, which, though it does not invalidate the use of all aspects of the high-class commercial shows as pointers to the past, does make them less useful in many respects than the much less prestigious lower class commercial shows and the festival operas. It is these performances that carry on, albeit in a reduced way, the traditions of Hong Kong's two or three big commercial opera houses, which, as we already know, are now defunct.[11]

[11] The big commercial opera houses were specialist houses, not adapted cinemas or multipurpose public auditoria. It is said that from the mid-1920s to mid-1950s (with the exception of the period of Japanese occupation) they played to full houses every night. They were the real counterparts of the "play gardens" described by Dolby. Dolby notes the same lack of clearcut differentiation discussed here: "The major troupes would tend to monopolize the bigger theatres, and the lesser troupes to stick to the smaller, less savoury theatres, but the divisions were not rigid. Troupes would move around the various theatres" (*History*, p. 189).

Social Class

Enough has been said about the class composition of the opera audiences in the "play gardens" to make it clear that at least by the middle and late Ch'ing period they were remarkably like the Elizabethan audiences of the late sixteenth and early seventeenth centuries at the Globe in London. There, a complete cross-section of social classes, courtiers, groundlings, and all in-between enjoyed the same spectacle (though no doubt interpreting it in different ways, and being affected by different aspects), and even when the occasion or place of performance restricted the audience (say, at a royal reception or private banquet) the same plays and players would usually appear.

This continued to be the case in Hong Kong up to about the mid-1950s, when two of the old opera houses were still in operation, when neither the new high-class shows nor television had been developed, and when cinema and radio programs still included great chunks of Cantonese every day. The differentiation noted in the preceding section has been developing over the last twenty years or so, but it is still at an early stage and what the future will bring is still uncertain.[12] As Dolby puts it,

> the drama of the rich and the drama of the poor have not been very rigidly divided and have been the more easily able to replenish and renew each other. As we have seen, from Song times and earlier, the street, market and village actors and vulgar popular plays moved readily into the palace and back again, while in turn palace taste and distaste could rapidly affect the grass roots drama.[13]

At first sight that conclusion may appear to be denied by the argument put forward by Professor Tanaka Issei in chapter 5 above. Professor Tanaka's meticulous textual research into different versions of the same operas reveals that certain verbal variations can be correlated with the social class of their audiences and, particularly, their sponsors. The thesis that drama was influenced by the demands of sponsors and audience can be supported by a great deal of evidence, but it does not follow that the general thesis that "the drama of the rich and the drama of the poor have not been very rigidly divided" is therefore invalid.

Exact adherence to a script was not demanded of Chinese opera actors in the past. Indeed, scripts were often regarded more as guidelines than as texts, while at least some regional conventions positively required verbal as well as musical invention on the part of the singers. In other cases there was no script at all, merely a scenario.[14] It is obvious that such flexibility would have allowed for the appearance of almost innumerable variations, in much the same way as the

---

[12] There are signs of a marked increase in interest in Cantonese opera among young people in Hong Kong.

[13] Dolby, *History*, p. 184.

[14] Bell Yung, "The Role of Speech Tones in the Creative Process of the Cantonese Opera," *CHINOPERL News* 6: 157–167 (1975); see the B. E. Ward articles cited.

flexibility of English pantomime today allows performers to ad-lib as they themselves judge appropriate for the audience of the moment. But (and this is the nub) in much the same way, too, this feature also allows for the general process of borrowing and counterborrowing that every writer on Chinese opera describes, and that also applies to pantomime. In short, the structure of Chinese opera in performance explains both the possibility of variation and the process of homogenization. Whether one concentrates on the former or the latter depends upon the focus of one's interest.

In any case, whatever the verbal differences between versions of the "same" opera performed in private and in public or before different kinds of more or less restricted audience, two countervailing facts are important: the first, discussed immediately below, is that the plots of the operas and, with them, the sets of values they embodied were universally distributed; the second is that, just as in Hong Kong today so all over China in the Ming and Ch'ing dynasties, the overwhelming majority of opera performances took place in public (whether in such commercial establishments as the "play gardens" or in connection with religious festivals), in front of unrestricted audiences as mixed as and very much larger than those of sixteenth-century England.

Region

All the historical evidence indicates that the comments about the relative unimportance of class differences apply to regional differences too. To quote Dolby once more,

> Local and national forms merged, adapted to new conditions and borrowed and appropriated from each other. . . . The total result was a dazzling kaleidoscope. . . . Vogues for a local kind of drama or music could rapidly have nationwide consequences.[15]

Script writers everywhere learned from one another. There was no concept (still less a law) of copyright or ownership in a particular plot or version of a text, and, in any case, all the stories used were drawn from a single great shared repertoire of history, legend, and fiction. As a result, the same plots appeared virtually everywhere and cross-fertilization constantly occurred. The distinctiveness of the various regional styles lay mostly in their music and partly in such matters as costume and choreography. Characterization in the sense made familiar in modern realistic drama was not a feature of Chinese opera, all varieties of which relied on very similar stylized role categories. By the middle of the Ming dynasty at the latest, China had developed opera as its own distinctive mass medium, and the existence of regional differences in music and style did not detract from the China-wide nature of its messages.

The evidence from Hong Kong supports this argument. In addition to the

---

[15] Dolby, *History*, p. 101.

three regional styles performed by locally based troupes, which are the main focus of this paper, opera-goers in contemporary Hong Kong have the chance to see performances of Capital (Peking) opera fairly often and a number of other regional styles when they are performed by visiting troupes from time to time. Though only a very small proportion of the three hundred or so regional styles of Chinese opera, the styles that are represented provide at least some opportunity for comparison. Also, experience suggests that regional differences are much greater in music (especially singing) than in anything else, although differences in costume, choreography, and general presentation are also distinctive enough to be diagnostic. In narrative content, however, in the values and attitudes that are expressed in it, and in the broad outlines of characterization there is marked similarity.

Urban and Rural

The current image of Hong Kong is essentially urban and westernized. Can anything that comes out of the high-rise concrete environment of one of the most densely populated townscapes in the twentieth century be used to illuminate the predominantly rural past of premodern China?

To this objection there are a number of possible rejoinders. The rural nature of much of Hong Kong itself must not be forgotten, nor must the fact that until little more than twenty years ago its countryside was still dominated by traditional rice farming. Of course, today even the most remote New Territories settlements are thoroughly in touch not only with the town but also, through emigration, with Europe, in a way that makes most of their inhabitants a good deal more cosmopolitan in outlook than most Hong Kong urban dwellers. In short, many of Hong Kong's villagers today can be said to be more urbane (as well as, often, richer) than most of the town dwellers. The rural-urban dichotomy has become blurred.

Leaving aside its purely modern aspects (such as electricity, good roads, access by air to Europe, and so on), however, it is possible to wonder to what extent this blurring of the so-called dichotomy is really a new phenomenon in the context of traditional theater and its audiences, and, for that matter, in a number of other contexts as well. The sociological model that distinguishes sharply between village and town is essentially a Western one and G. William Skinner's marketing studies, together with the work of C. K. Yang and Martin C. Yang, make it abundantly clear that in the late imperial period spatial separation and differences in size and productive function did not mean that Chinese villages were cut off from towns, for they depended economically, administratively, maritally, educationally, ritually, medically, and for various kinds of sociability—including entertainment—upon local market towns and often upon higher urban centers too.[16] What is needed, therefore, is an analysis

[16] G. William Skinner, "Marketing and Social Structure in Rural China, Part I," *Journal of Asian Studies* 24.1:32–43 (1964).

of the relative degrees to which different contexts of activity brought villagers and townspeople in different areas of China into contact with one another.

Three points are relevant here. First, Skinner and others have made it very clear that market-day contacts were by no means restricted to market matters. It is also important to remember that villagers' contacts with towns were not necessarily confined to market days. In many parts of China emigration to town or even overseas is a long-established tradition. And it is apposite to recall that China's inland communications were at least as good as and often much better than those of any other part of the world before the railway age.

Second, contacts between villages and towns were by no means only one-way. Though more villagers went to towns, nevertheless some townsmen also went to villages, and not seldom. In addition to such people as *yamen* servants, tax and rent collectors, and the like, certain types of petty craftsmen and traders made their rounds in traditional China in much the same way as their counterparts in nineteenth- and twentieth-century England. Again, just as in England, entertainers—storytellers, jugglers, and, most important in this context, troupes of professional opera players—also toured the villages. The professional theater in China was an urban phenomenon just as it was in Western countries, but, like the circus in Europe and North America or the showboats on the Mississippi River, it was an urban phenomenon that also went down to the country.

Finally, it is no denigration of the market model to point out that despite the care Skinner has taken to build in its nonmarket aspects, the model unavoidably tends to draw attention away from matters that occur outside the market framework. Theatrical performances did just that. In describing the occasions that are here called "religious festivals," earlier Western writers often use the term "temple fairs." It is important not to allow the use of this term to confuse the issue. Although fairs have economic connotations, they are quite distinct from markets. Whereas market cycles are short, as is required by their primarily economic function, and continue throughout the year, each market day being but a single day, fairs are usually annual occasions, linked to a ritual calendar and lasting for several days. Moreover, fairs may or may not be held in market centers, and even when they are, the fact that they may overlap with one of the regular market days is strictly coincidental. So much is obvious, but there is another relevant point. Skinner's market model persuades us that each standard market area was typically discrete. This was not true of temple festival areas, which, though organized by local committees and focused on particular temples, nonetheless often drew participants and probably always drew opera audiences from much further afield.

This is certainly true of temple and other festivals in Hong Kong today. Besides opera, such festivals provide a number of other attractions, which draw in townspeople and country people alike, and, indeed, the general patterns of these festivals are basically similar wherever they are located. For example, they all include a main day for special worship with all the colorful panoply and often excitement of the Taoist or Buddhist rituals performed on such days; they often include at least some period for especially good eating, drinking, and gambling; and they are times for meeting old friends and relatives, renewing networks, catching up on gossip, and settling personal and business affairs. In short, festival days are holidays, understandably popular in the sense that people enjoy them, flock to them, take time off to visit them. Nor, as I have argued above, is interest confined only to the festival in one's own village or area. Any festival within fairly easy reach may be visited by anyone who can afford to go. Some are based upon town temples and some on village temples, while still others take place in any convenient open space, whether in town or country, like the playgrounds in Kowloon today or the dry river beds described by Robert Fortune writing about Anhwei province in the 1840s.[17] In every case, the matshed theaters with their brave flags and elaborate red and white announcement boards, their colored lights and amplified music, stand four-square in front of temporary or permanent temples where incense smokes continually, Taoist and Buddhist priests gesture and chant, and scores of small processions come bearing personal or group offerings of whole roast pigs, fruit, flowers, cakes, red-colored eggs, wine, and tea, led by the clamor of dancing lions and unicorns and followed by great, tall, red and multicolored paper shrines. Tea houses, temporary and permanent, do a roaring trade; dozens of small booths sell foodstuffs and drinks; and there are possibly scores of tiny stalls where one can buy religious paraphernalia and toys for children. Even those town and country people who experience their festivals separately have similar experiences.

To argue thus is not, of course, to deny that there were any differences between villages and towns in China, but it is to claim that in certain areas and in some of the most widespread and typical theatrical contexts such differences were unimportant. I am convinced that this was true for most parts of the Canton Delta area in the late Ch'ing and probably earlier, and I suggest that it is inherently likely to have been true in a good many other parts of China as well—for example in all of Skinner's core areas.[18] In practical terms this must have meant that in such areas very large numbers of people, town and country folk alike, watched the same players performing the same operas and mixed in the same or same kinds of audiences.

[17] Robert Fortune, *A Journey to the Tea Countries of China* (London: John Murray, 1842), pp. 74–76, and *A Residence Among the Chinese* (London: John Murray, 1872), pp. 256–257, quoted in Dolby, *History*, p. 186.

[18] G. William Skinner, "Cities and the Hierarchy of Local Systems," in *The City in Late Imperial China* ed. G. William Skinner (Stanford: Stanford University Press, 1977), pp. 275–351, and his "Urban and Rural in Chinese Society," pp. 153–274 in the same volume.

AUDIENCES IN CONTEMPORARY HONG KONG

In this section I concentrate upon festival performances, following my previous argument that (together with those in the amusement-park theaters) they are the most nearly like those of the late Ch'ing period and possibly even earlier. I first give a little more detail about seating and organization and then briefly discuss the audiences for each of the three local types of regional opera in turn.

Seating

At most festival performances admission and seating are free; the sides and back of the auditorium are open, and members of the audience come and go at will. Nonlocal spectators are assumed to be members of families who have made or will make offerings in the temple, at which time they also contribute a larger or smaller amount of *heung yao ts'in* (incense and oil money). The heads of the families of local spectators (or the better-off among them) are in any case likely to have contributed or promised quite substantial sums in addition. The common explanation is that to see a festival opera one does not need to pay, since the plays are for the gods' delight. If humans see them too that is a kind of bonus, a sharing in the offering, not unlike sharing the pork, cakes, and other foodstuffs that are offered in the temple on the main day of the festival and later divided up among all contributors for their own consumption.

The idea that the operas are offerings to the gods is made still more explicit in the practice of performing "dawn plays".[19] These take place overnight, starting some time after the end of the evening show and continuing until dawn. They are usually played by junior members of the troupe, only sketchily costumed and scarcely made up, before rows of almost empty seats where a few beggars and visiting peddlers who have nowhere else to sleep are lying down. Whether or not dawn plays are performed at any given festival is a matter of local custom. Asked about them, informants nearly always evince a knowing interest and have no hesitation in explaining that they are provided for the sake of the divine, not the human, audience.

Duration, Timing, and the Size of Audiences

Sets of festival operas run for varying periods of time, the most common being the "five nights and four days" described earlier—nine regular performances in all (all different, of course), starting two or three evenings before the main day of the festival and continuing with one afternoon and one evening show each day. If dawn plays are also performed, the total number of plays is greater. Usually the whole troupe packs up and the matshed builders start dismantling the stage and theater immediately after the end of the last evening performance and the very brief ritual playlet that marks the completion of the series.

---

[19] Cantonese: *t'in kwong hei* 天光戲 .

Some runs are shorter than the usual five nights and four days—for two or three days only ("three nights and two days")—and some are longer. Very long runs—for, say, two or three weeks—tend to be in town, correlated with dense population, and are more likely to occur with Cantonese operas. A fairly recent practice, however, is for a single matshed to be used in sequence by different regional opera troupes. Throughout the 1970s, for example, the festival for T'ien Hou (who is Ma Tsu, Queen of Heaven) at Sai Kung in the New Territories was celebrated first by a week or more of Cantonese opera after which a Ch'ao Chou troupe took over the stage for five nights and four days of Ch'ao Chou opera. In more than one of the most thickly populated newly developed areas of urban Kowloon, runs of Waichow operas are regularly followed in a rather similar way by runs of Cantonese opera.

In general, evening performances are much better attended than afternoon ones, which, except on the main day of the festival, are usually given by the troupe's second-rate actors and musicians before an audience of women and children. At afternoon performances the seats are rarely full. Evenings or the afternoon of the main festival day bring on the first-rank musicians and star performers, and attract the biggest and most varied audiences. The most popular plays, the best stars, and the largest attendance appear on the eve of the main day and on the afternoon and evening of that day. Then the seats are completely taken up, rows of extra seats are set out (usually in front), and several rows of standing spectators—mainly men—crowd the back and sides of the auditorium.

The afternoon performance on the main day is usually preceded (or interrupted) by a secular community ceremony on the stage: speeches are made; awards in the form of specially embroidered silk banners are presented to the leading players, the impresario, locally significant government officers, and other dignitaries; and the all-important "draw" for lucky numbers connected with certain temple offerings is made.[20] The ceremony is often preceded or followed by one or more of the short ritual playlets. In marked contrast to the

[20] At most temple festivals in Hong Kong, groups known in Cantonese as *fa p'aau ooi* 花炮會 [firecracker or fireworks associations] bring offerings in procession. These include tall red and multicolored shrines made of bamboo and paper and hung with figurines. Each shrine houses a small glass-sided box containing an image of the temple god. Each is numbered, and, after being presented before the temple, is stood outside it beside the others in a elaborately colorful display. Each association then buys a great many numbered tickets for the lottery. At the ceremonial meeting on stage, local dignitaries are invited to draw lucky tickets up to the total number of shrines. In this way, the images are redistributed among the shrine associations for the coming twelve months, at the end of which they will be mounted in new paper shrines and brought back for re-presentation and redistribution. In most places the draw is a recent substitute for an older custom, in which numbered slivers of bamboo were shot out of small firecracker rockets and scrambled for by the young men of the shrine associations. Such more exciting but often dangerous goings-on were abandoned after the 1967 riots and the ensuing government ban on fireworks of all kinds. For a description of the shrine associations, see C. Fred Blake, *Ethnic Groups and Social Change in a Chinese Market Town* (Honolulu: University Press of Hawaii, 1981), pp. 94–97.

intent concentration with which the largest audience of the whole festival follows the presentation of banners and, especially, the "draw", little attention is paid to these.

The audience on that afternoon and the immediately preceding and following evenings is greatly swollen by the presence of a mass of nonlocal visitors who come to make offerings in the temple. Even in tiny villages with a few hundred inhabitants, a famous temple and a good Cantonese opera troupe can attract as many as two or three thousand persons on such occasions. In larger centers with famous temples there are likely to be at least twice that many.[21] Not all of them watch the operas, but an appreciable number do so for at least part of the time.

Ethnicity and Opera Going

The size and composition of the audiences vary not only at different performances in each run of festival operas and from place to place, but also with the kind of regional drama being performed. Not surprisingly, in preponderantly Cantonese-speaking Hong Kong, Cantonese opera attracts the largest audiences. Locally sponsored Cantonese festival operas in town, where nowadays the matshed theaters are usually erected in the playgrounds of multistory housing estates or on cleared building sites or reclamations, can play for three weeks or more to full houses. Ch'ao Chou and Waichow performances appeal (in that order) to smaller audiences. Few Cantonese enjoy them or try to do so, but Cantonese operas are intelligible to a much wider following, since Cantonese is not only the native language of the majority but also the *lingua franca*. Thus, whereas the audiences for Ch'ao Chou and Waichow operas show a strong preponderance of Ch'ao Chou and Waichow speakers respectively, the audiences for Cantonese operas are a good deal less ethnically homogeneous.[22] With the exception of the cultured elite, who regard the Capital Opera of Peking as the only style worth discussing, the majority of the opera-going public in Hong Kong consider Cantonese opera to be "the real thing"; Ch'ao Chou and Waichow operas appeal to minority interests.

Waichow operas and their audiences. In Hong Kong, as in other places where there are large numbers of immigrants, there is a tendency for certain immigrant ethnic groups to be more or less class specific. This not to say that all members of a particular ethnic group can be placed in a particular social class, but simply that a large majority can be so placed. Waichow opera takes its name from the city of Waichow in northeastern Kwangtung. The Hokkien

---

[21] The matsheds constructed for the *chiao* 醮 at Fanling in 1980 and in the Lam Tsuen Valley in 1981 had seats for 2200 and 3200, respectively. Both occasions brought several hundred emigrants back from overseas (the majority from the British Isles) for a stay of several weeks.

[22] To the best of my knowledge, the large Hakka-speaking population of Hong Kong is not served by a distinct Hakka opera troupe. Hakka speakers support Cantonese opera as a rule, but Hakka originating from the Hokkien dialect areas, especially those from Waichow city, also attend performances given by the Waichow troupes.

language in which it is performed is one of the Min dialects spoken in Hong Kong by immigrants from that area and the coast. Commonly referred to in Cantonese by the rather derogatory term *Hoklo*, these people are predominantly working and lower-middle class. The audiences for Waichow operas, therefore, tend to be homogeneous as to both ethnicity and class. They are also relatively small in size, and usually drawn from tightly knit communities who, in putting on their distinctive operas for their own pleasure (and that of their usually equally distinctive temple gods), are also making a symbolic gesture of ethnic solidarity and assertion, whether consciously or not.

There are two professional Waichow troupes in Hong Kong. At certain times of the year, especially but not only in the seventh month of the lunar calendar, they are in continuous demand.[23] The occasions are all strictly religious, and taken together they attract virtually the whole of the Hokkien-speaking population. The opera performances that go with them divide neatly and nightly into two halves. The former, which runs from 7:30 or 8:00 P.M. until shortly before midnight, is always a "military" play (in Mandarin, *wu hsi*), usually a long sequence from *The Romance of the Three Kingdoms*. Here Kuan Kung, Ts'ao Ts'ao, and their companions posture endlessly about the stage, marching and countermarching their flag-waving armies back and forth. There are few female roles, and little or no singing takes place. These are curiously archaic performances, full of stylized but unpolished movement, more like pageants than operas. There are no acrobatics. The audience is intent, following every move, and unusually silent. The seats are full, about half the spectators being males of all ages. An onlooker can have no doubt but that they are gripped by the drama. As soon as it is over people relax, cough, stand up, move about, talk, laugh—and most of them go away.

At midnight the second half of the program begins. Instead of masculine fighting to the sound of *sona*, cymbal, and drum, there now comes a feminine "civil" play (in Mandarin, *wen hsi*). There is no fighting, little speaking, and only light percussion with a great deal of singing accompanied by strings and the flute. The plot, dominated by a woman singer, usually hangs on a theme of filial piety and motherly devotion. The audience is now much smaller. Perhaps a score or so will see the whole play through. The rest come and go, chat or listen as they feel inclined, discuss the singing or the latest gossip, nibble snacks, swallow soft drinks, and fidget. On the next night the sequence is repeated with different stories but the same two types of play, and the same two types of audience.[24]

[23] The seventh lunar month is marked by the so-called Hungry Ghost Festivals celebrated by all Chinese ethnic communities in Hong Kong but most elaborately by Hokkien and Ch'ao Chou speakers.

[24] The similarity between the second kind of Waichow performance described here and the refined, somewhat feminine charms of Ming *k'un-ch'ü* opera lends force to the argument that *k'un-ch'ü*, so beloved by the literati, was probably always a minority interest.

Ch'ao Chou operas and audiences.   To the best of my knowledge there were few if
any festival performances of Ch'ao Chou opera in Hong Kong before World
War II. Today the Ch'ao Chou are the second largest ethnic group in the
territory and, while evincing a strong preference for residential concentration,
are to be found almost everywhere. Ch'ao Chou people in Hong Kong exhibit
the usual immigrant propensities for occupational specialization, but their
large numbers and the fact that their specialties include several types of highly
successful business activity have allowed them to spread right across the local
spectrum of socioeconomic class. Unlike the Hokkien speakers, they maintain a
highly conspicuous ethnic profile and display their solidarity not only on
occasions of specifically Ch'ao Chou significance but also at a number of
festivals that until quite recently were organized by local Cantonese or Hakka
interests alone. The result is that Hong Kong now has many Ch'ao Chou
festival performances every year in addition to a number of municipally and
entrepreneurially sponsored shows that are well advertised and attract considerable attention.

   Ch'ao Chou performances have a mannered sophistication allied with realistic facial expression that contrasts strongly with the archaism of the
Waichow military plays on the one hand and the many-sided and innovative
Cantonese opera on the other. One aspect of their sophistication is that,
unusually among regional styles, the music and libretti of several Ch'ao Chou
operas have been published. These books include the texts of several performances that have been polished to near perfection by a group of talented
artists and now exist in more or less definitive forms for which their audiences
have developed a high degree of informed critical appreciation. It is not
unknown for members of the audience at a Ch'ao Chou performance to follow
their copies of the score, like students at a concert of classical European music.

   Such detailed connoisseurship is made easier by the fact that the Ch'ao Chou
repertoire (at least as it is to be seen in contemporary Hong Kong) is somewhat
limited. Cantonese informants give two different but not unconnected explanations. The first is musical. The distinctive Ch'ao Chou opera music most
commonly heard in Hong Kong is often described by Cantonese in an unkind
phrase that implies (among other things) that it is squeaky. The point here is
that it is not appropriate for fighting plays. Most Ch'ao Chou plots are, in fact,
rather light comedies. This characteristic is said to be linked also with the rather
special types of players who are employed. In the past these are said to have
been mostly boys in their teens and below; today they are mainly women and
girls. Both then and now the number of adult male actors was small, with the
result that there was a heavy preponderance of "civil" plays—the light comedies mentioned above. It is as if the Ch'ao Chou script writers had taken a
Waichow program and, discarding the first half altogether, concentrated upon
polishing and refining a lighter, much gayer version of the second. Cantonese,
who enjoy fighting plays and like their stage heroes to be men, tend to sniff at
Ch'ao Chou opera and call it (literally) "child's play."

The audiences for Ch'ao Chou performances are, of course, composed almost exclusively of Ch'ao Chou residents, together with other Min (mainly Hokkien) speakers, and perhaps some visitors from Taiwan and the Nanyang. The Cantonese, who in any case cannot understand the dialect, usually dislike Ch'ao Chou opera, and it is noticeable that when a set of Ch'ao Chou performances follows a set of Cantonese shows the organizers remove a good many rows of seats. Women in the Ch'ao Chou audiences and the men who know and love their own plays follow intently, but it is my impression that younger males, who often speak Cantonese better than Ch'ao Chou, tend to stay away. Like many young people in Hong Kong today, they are likely to declare that they dislike all traditional opera and prefer the cinema and television.

In terms of social class, Ch'ao Chou audiences can be roughly divided into three categories: first, there are the middle-aged and elderly of both sexes and the younger women and girls—from middle, lower-middle, and working classes, with a majority from the lower end of the range; second, there are sometimes a few educated middle- and upper-middle-class young people—often in couples— some of whom bring their scores and follow them carefully; finally, around the outskirts of the audience, looking on from time to time, talking, eating, gambling, and lounging about in a holiday mood but not really taking much interest in the show, are the vast majority of lower and lower-middle class males, young and not so young. They are there for all sorts of reasons, the operas being only one of them.

Cantonese opera.   Casual conversation with people in most walks of life in Hong Kong leads one to believe that Cantonese opera is declining in popularity and is now watched only by the old, the late middle-aged (especially women), the very poor, and people in New Territories villages who have no other forms of entertainment. This quite commonly expressed view is simply not borne out by observation. Given a well-known troupe, an evening performance in the urban areas attracts crowds several thousand strong, filling every seat in the matshed theater, and standing five or six deep down the sides and twenty or more deep at the back. Outside the urban areas, too, evening performances are well attended, and the audiences include males of all age groups as well as working females who have been unable to leave their jobs in the daytime, together with the women and children who have already watched the afternoon shows. Bus and ferry companies may run special services for such performances; minibuses and taxis do good business; tea houses, food hawkers, and peddlers are all fully occupied. Cantonese opera audiences are invariably the largest and the most heterogeneous.

Broadly speaking, these audiences are mainly working and lower-middle class, but there may well be a good many middle-class people there (nurses, primary school teachers, lower clerks in government service, and the like) and if the players are famous and the venue easily accessible it is not unusual to see small groups of upper-middle- or even occasionally upper-class types who have come because they are opera fans. At evening shows the sexes are fairly evenly balanced, and literally all age groups are represented (from one-month-old babies to great-grandparents in their nineties). Despite the common view that all young people dislike Chinese opera, about half the people present are likely to be under 25 years of age.[25]

In most places, but especially the smaller, more remote ones and where seating is free, an evening audience comprises a solid core of local residents with their personal friends and kinsmen—mainly women and girls, babies, small children, and older men—who pack the front seats whenever possible and fill the central area. The outer edges (sides and back) are the domain of the middle-aged and younger men, who tend to move about more than the women. Except at the more riveting moments of the play, they are relatively easily distracted by conversation or invitations to go and eat or drink or gamble, and they more often sit on the outside seats, or stand, shifting their place from time to time, moving in and out of the auditorium. Children, especially boys, run up and down the aisles, press themselves right up against the front of the stage gazing raptly upwards, or climb up onto it in order to watch from the wings or investigate the dressing rooms backstage. Except at moments of great dramatic tension or greatly admired song, everyone eats, chats, discusses the unfolding plot and the latest gossip, takes flash photographs, and makes tape recordings; there is almost constant movement and little silence. The total professionalism of the leading actors is the more marked as they continue the performance regardless of the din and confusion in front of them. No wonder the habitues of festival shows find the austerities of city hall performances somewhat daunting!

Despite the sprinkling of middle-class people, the general standard of education in these predominantly lower-middle and lower-class audiences is low, though nowadays the large majority are likely to be literate. Lack of school education does not necessarily connote lack of knowledge about Cantonese theater, however. Not only has each mature adult seen many operas before, but everyone is also familiar with radio, television, and cinema, and, as in the days before any of those media existed, most people still know the majority of the stories in the repertoire.

CONTENT: CULTURE AND VALUES

Readers accustomed to evaluating plays in terms of plot construction and characterization may need to be reminded that the large majority of Chinese operas relied on the same stylized role categories and made use of the same popular stories based on history, legend, and fiction, that formed the shared repertoire of storytellers, puppeteers, ballad singers, and other entertainers all

[25] Evidence based upon informal counts made in 1980–1982. This is but one of a number of signs of a marked recrudescence of interest in Cantonese culture in contemporary Hong Kong.

over China. There is no question but that at least from toward the end of the first half of the Ming dynasty onward the messages relayed by these traditional media to the Chinese populace were essentially the same. The pertinent questions here are What were those messages? and With what degree of success were they transmitted?

Plots: The Historical and Literary Tradition

Chinese writers divide the plays of the traditional theater into *wu hsi* and *wen hsi*—the former being concerned with brigands, battles, and affairs of state, the latter with love stories and social and domestic matters—but the division is not absolute and both styles can be intermingled. Fighting plays usually require large and varied casts, elaborate costumes, and complicated choreography. Typically, plots are drawn from the *San kuo chih yen-i* (*The Romance of the Three Kingdoms*) and *Shui-hu chuan* (*Water Margin*). Other sources are the famous tale *Hsi-yu chi* (*Journey to the West*), known more familiarly in English as *Monkey*, and a large number of other historical and quasihistorical chronicles and legends. Several of the *wen hsi* derive from tales known at least since the T'ang dynasty, and from early Yuan plays, and Ming courtly drama (*K'un-ch'ü*). Domestic novels like *Hung-lou meng* (*The Dream of the Red Chamber*) and *Chin P'ing Mei* (*Golden Lotus*), and so on, and ghost stories, Taoist and Buddhist legends, and folk tales have also all been used over and over again. It is clear that the total number of plots available in the common repertoire was very great, and that it covered virtually every aspect of traditional history, folklore, and literature. It cannot be said too often that these were the same stories as those told by the storytellers to the nonreading public and read (albeit surreptitiously) by the scholars. Lin Yutang put the matter in a nutshell nearly fifty years ago:

> Apart from teaching the people an intensive love of music the theatre has taught the Chinese people . . . a knowledge of history truly amazing, crystallizing, as it were, the folklore and entire literary and historical tradition in plays of characters that have captured the heart and imagination of the common men and women. Thus any amah has a livelier conception than I have of many historical heroes from her intimate knowledge of Chinese plays, as I was prevented from attending the theatres in my childhood . . . and had to learn it all piecemeal from the cold pages of history books.[26]

It follows, of course, that just as the plots of Chinese operas recapitulated the common repertoire of the Chinese historical and literary tradition so they repeated at the same time the major themes of Chinese morality, for the plots invariably turned upon points of good and evil. Moreover, by presenting these values *on the stage*, represented in human form by characters with whom the audiences could identify or from whom they dissociated themselves, the operas almost certainly achieved an impact greater than that of either the spoken or

---

[26] Lin Yutang, *My Country and My People* (London: Heinemann, revised ed., 1939), pp. 251–252.

the written word alone. Again Lin Yutang expresses the point clearly:

> Practically all the standardized Chinese notions of loyal ministers and filial sons and brave warriors and faithful wives and chaste maidens and intriguing maid-servants are reflected in the ... plays. Represented in the form of stories with human characters, whom they hate or love as the case may be, they sink deep into [the people's] moral consciousness. Ts'ao Ts'ao's hyprocrisy, Min Tzu's filial piety, Wenchün's romance, Inging's passion, Yang Kweifei's pampered tastes, Ch'in Kwei's treason, Yen Sung's greed and cruelty, Chuko Liang's strategy, Chang Fei's quick temper, and Mulien's religious sanctity—they all become associated in the Chinese minds with their ethical tradition and become their concrete conceptions of good and evil conduct.[27]

Lin Yutang is here distilling in English the considered opinion of generations of Chinese writers on the theater.

Experience among the Hong Kong audiences described above bears Lin out. Villagers of the small fishing settlement of Kau Sai, for example, stage nine major performances of Cantonese opera and five dawn plays every year in connection with the so-called birthday of their tutelary divinity. The program includes three or four fighting plays and five or six domestic dramas. The former draw rather larger crowds, but the latter are almost as eagerly followed, especially when the top singers are billed to appear. Looking at the audience from the stage, one sees a tightly packed carpet of upturned faces and, except at moments of greatest dramatic excitement or most popular singing, hears a constant buzz of talk. If one listens to the talk, one soon discovers that the major topic is the play itself. There is criticism of the acting, singing, costumes, and so on, but the greater part of the conversation is about the play: "What is happening now?" "Who is that?" "What's going to happen next?" Though usually quite well known, the plots are exceedingly complicated and usually very long; people need help in understanding. But they also make moral comments: "That's a terrible thing to do; she'll surely be punished for that!" "That's not fair, the judge didn't listen; but then he's been bribed!" "Aiya! She's putting poison in the wine!" (Very occasionally a spectator is really carried away: "Look out! He's behind you with a sword!") In short, the fact that the plots may have been seen many times and that music, singing, and acting style are indeed of great importance does not mean that audiences like this are without a most lively interest in the stories themselves and their moral implications.

Heightened Occasions and Total Theater

The village of Kau Sai is isolated on a small island. Until about 1950, when one villager acquired his first radio, the only kind of professional entertainment the people knew were the operas performed at their own temple festivals and

---

[27] Ibid.

four or five others within easy reach. On my reckoning, the average fishing family in Kau Sai watched twenty or more entertainment operas a year, sometimes more. By the age of 40, many persons must have seen nearly a thousand, and as they saw nothing else, the effect cannot have been small.

Even today, when four families have members living in England and several residents have visited them there, when local travel is swift and easy and almost everyone has long experience of the cinema, and when every house has color television, the contrast between the color, excitement, and glamor of festival days and the drab monotony of everyday life has to be seen to be believed. Thirty years ago, when I first lived in the village, it was overwhelming. Suddenly, almost overnight, a single strip of less than twenty houses along the water's edge is transformed into a fairground with stalls and gambling pitches, temporary tea houses spring up from nowhere, hawkers arrive with exotic wares to sell, the population zooms up to several thousand, and the matshed theater towers over all with its flags and colored lights and blaring loudspeakers. If the operas are the highlight of the fair, the festival in its turn highlights the operas. In 1975 an old informant in Hong Kong recalled for me what must have been essentially similar but even larger scale occasions in Shun Tak County, Kwangtung, to which his father had taken him as an excited ten-year-old nearly seventy years before:

> My father liked Cantonese opera very much. He used to take me to all the nearby temple festivals to see the plays. In those days, of course, all the actors were men and they used to travel in the Red Boats on the river. The crowds were very big, so I used to go right up to the front near the stage in order to see properly. Sometimes I even climbed up onto the stage and watched from the side. My father bought me water chestnuts on sticks to eat, too, and once or twice a wooden sword. Of course I remembered all the stories, and later I read them too.

Furthermore, although it is hard to suggest any way in which it could be measured, the sense of heightened occasion is not merely secular. The temple *fair* is a *temple* fair. The cycle of events is anchored in religion. It builds up through the rituals of the "birthday" eve to a crescendo of offerings, processions, and feasting on the main day itself, and the plays are part of the offerings. It is noticeable that whatever his or her individual verbal professions of belief or disbelief, no one in Kau Sai fails to take part in temple worship on the main day, no young man absents himself from the rituals on the preceding day, and every family with a new baby (even in England) is at pains to register the fact properly with the appropriate gift of red-colored eggs to their local deity. It is, to say the least, probable that the messages put across in enjoyable operatic performances that themselves play a ritual role on such highly charged religious occasions will stick.

There is still one more consideration. As I have demonstrated elsewhere, Chinese opera is "total theater." A good performance both bombards and woos the audience with almost every possible combination of color, movement, sound, and sense, and caters to several different levels of understanding at the same time. At its best (judged in local terms, which may or may not be the same as Western or modern ones), Chinese opera engenders a high degree of audience participation, too easily missed by outsiders, who are often misled by the lack of handclapping applause or the rush to get away to bed or the tea house before the final curtain. Here is yet another reason for us to expect that the content of such performances will remain memorable long after the event. And, in any case, the event is likely to be experienced all over again next year, if not before.

Not only scholars and writers like Lin Yutang and the players themselves have been aware of the influence of opera performances. Successive Chinese governments have constantly sought to control opera in the interests of public order and conformity. As Mackerras says in his study of the rise of Peking opera, this impulse indicates that they well knew that "the theatre was more than a place for enjoyment and relaxation; it was also a major social force, the influence of which extended deeply into the lives of the people."[28] Ch'ing governments seem to have been especially harsh towards dramatic performances, and there is a good deal of evidence that they were wise to be suspicious. The fact that the drama was a major vehicle for the inculcation of values did not at all guarantee that the values so inculcated were necessarily either orthodox or politically innocuous. The contrary might just as easily be the case. Certainly throughout the period of anti-Manchu sentiment that was a very real possibility. It was not by accident that players insisted on wearing Ming-type costumes on stage, and there were good grounds for the continued suppression of Cantonese opera after the Taiping rebellion. But, as Dolby points out, it seems that the complete suppression of the theater "would have entailed grave and possibly perilous disruptions—worse even than the evils it was deemed to provoke."[29] In any case, it was not done.

That suppression was ever contemplated at all, however, shows that Chinese governments of the day, like their successors in the People's Republic of China and like their Elizabethan and Jacobean counterparts faced with a rather similar situation in England, were convinced of the importance of the theater as a moral force. The evidence from Hong Kong indicates that they were right.

For the great mass of the population of Ming and Ch'ing·China, the entertainment media, especially the festival operas, were the most significant source of information about the believed-in historical past, the values and manners of the elite, attitudes and relationships between and among people of different status, and ideas of good (which usually triumphed in the end) and evil

---

[28] Colin Mackerras, *The Rise of the Peking Opera 1770–1870* (Oxford: Clarendon Press, 1972), p. 218.

[29] Dolby, *History*, p. 141.

(which was usually routed). In short, what the Chinese theater disseminated was the major part of what ordinary people in the matshed audience knew about the vast complex of Chinese culture and values—both orthodox and heterodox—of which (as they also knew) the one small corner of their own everyday experience was only a minute fraction. For all but the (predominantly male) 5 percent or so who actually carried the high culture, the theater was the literal embodiment of Chinese culture and values. It was a superbly successful teacher.

SEVEN

Religion and Popular Culture:
The Management of Moral Capital in
The Romance of the Three Teachings

Judith A. Berling

Between 1612 and 1620, a Nanking publishing house of some repute published a novel entitled *San-chiao k'ai-mi kuei-cheng yen-i* [The romance of the three teachings clearing up the deluded and returning them to the true way]. No trace of this work is found in Chinese bibliographies and catalogues except as a work "not seen"; we know of its existence thanks to the work of Sawada Mizuho, who discovered a copy in the Tenri University Library.[1] The novel was not a success among those who collected and catalogued fiction; whether it had a more popular readership we will probably never know. Although we cannot identify its audience, this novel is an important source for the study of popular literary culture. The author, P'an Ching-jo, by his own report, was self-consciously outside the national elite, and was deliberately aiming at a popular audience. The novel depicts the world of the local elite in the highly commercialized, urbanized region of Southeast China, and the religious content was inspired by an actual movement in that region. P'an Ching-jo portrays the mentality and distinctive religious attitude in the middle-level popular culture of the region in a way that deepens our understanding of the significance of

---

[1] Sawada Mizuho 澤田瑞穂 "Sankyō shisō to heiwa shōsetsu" 三教思想と平話小説 [Colloquial novels and Three Teachings thought], *Biburia* 16:37–39 (1960). Some years later, he published a second essay discussing the evidence on publication, date, and authorship in his book *Bukkyō to Chūgoku bungaku* 仏教と中国文学 [Buddhism and Chinese literature] (Tokyo: Kokusho kankōkai 国書刊行会, 1975), pp. 163–167. There is to date no scholarship on the novel in Western languages.

The Tenri University copy is eight hundred Chinese pages long, plus prefatory material; the body contains one hundred chapters divided into twenty *chüan* of forty pages each. The prefatory material is written in elegant classical Chinese, and one preface is carved in running script. The rest of the novel is in large, standard woodblock characters, with no illustrations. There is no indication in the text that the novel was sponsored or edited by a group as an act of religious merit; it was either privately funded or an outright commercial venture.

religious developments in the late Ming, and of their specific cultural and social base. P'an Ching-jo's work is not a historical record of the documented attitudes of a specific religious organization; he calls it a *yen-i*, which generally designates historical novels.[2] However, compared with its contemporaries, this novel is highly realistic. It is situated in the present (the late Ming) and centered in the region in which it was published. It deals not with the great events of history like *The Romance of the Three Kingdoms (San kuo yen-i)*, but with the day-to-day problems of relatively ordinary people. Despite the inclusion of some fantastic and supernatural motifs, the overwhelming focus is on ordinary human characters and not larger-than-life heroes, as in *Water Margin (Shui-hu chuan)*, or monsters and gods, as in *Journey to the West (Hsi-yu chi)*. *The Romance of the Three Teachings* portrays the impact of social forces and historical changes on the everyday lives of real people in the present world: in this sense it echoes the realism of *Golden Lotus (Chin P'ing Mei)* and foreshadows that of *The Scholars (Ju-lin wai-shih)*.[3] P'an Ching-jo's work does not rank among the best of the Chinese novels. However, it is a valuable resource for studying the mentality of popular culture in Southeast China during the late Ming.

THE ROMANCE OF THE THREE TEACHINGS
AS POPULAR CULTURE

The Author

According to the novel, the ancestors of author P'an Ching-jo had participated in T'ai-tsu's invasion and occupation of Nanking, and at least one was a master of Taoist spiritual arts (15.21a–21b).[4] P'an appears briefly in the novel, described as "about fifty and a military degree holder from the capital"

[2] Andrew H. Plaks has drawn attention to the close links between history and fiction in the Chinese tradition. He writes, "Because the *yen-i* category sits astride the watershed between history and fiction, it is in a position to deal with the private lives of public figures ... as well as the public affairs of men who would otherwise not come up for extensive historical scrutiny." From "Towards a Critical Theory of Chinese Narrative" (p. 320) in *Chinese Narrative: Critical and Theoretical Essays*, ed. Andrew H. Plaks (Princeton: Princeton University Press, 1977), pp. 309–352.

[3] Ian Watt has argued that the realism of the early English novel (time as the sequence of daily events, specific settings, easy plots devoid of heavy allegory and fantastic motifs) reflected the bourgeois life in eighteenth-century British cities. *The Rise of the Novel: Studies in Defoe, Richardson, and Fielding* (Berkeley: University of California Press, 1962). I am making similar claims for this novel, but the claim has to be qualified. This novel has allegorical and fantastical elements that Watt would consider prenovelistic; however, the Chinese genre is not precisely comparable to its Western counterpart. This is a very early Chinese novel, and it falls somewhere between *Pilgrim's Progress* and *Robinson Crusoe* in its treatment of realistic moral issues.

[4] Sawada Mizuho also relied on this passage to develop the background of the author; *Bukkyō to Chūgoku bungaku*, p. 166. The parenthetical reference is to the novel. See n. 1, above. The citation 15.21a–21b means *chüan* 15, folio 21, *recto* and *verso*. Subsequent references to the novel are given parenthetically in the same form.

(1.15b). In all probability he was a military officer stationed in the Nanking area. He cuts a rather imposing figure:

> Thick eyebrows and piercing eyes.
> Broad back with high shoulders.
> Long ears frame the sea of his mouth.
> Hemp robes make him look like T'ai-kung going to meet Wen Wang.
> . . . .
> His whole countenance dignified and imposing,
> He wears a square soldier's turban
> And a six-cloud pattern embroidered jacket. (1.15b)[5]

On meeting him, a gentleman laments that P'an must bear the disgrace of military status: "With his virtuous appearance and great talent, how could he be in the inferior military? Today when civil virtues are ascendant and military power is slight, one who has followed the scorned path must be hard put to avoid sighs of dejection" (1.15b–16a). Despite his education and worthy appearance, P'an is not a member of the elite, since he does not have the all-important *chin-shih* degree from the civil service examination system; the *chin-shih* was by far the most important route to high status. The military degree and military office were viewed by the elite—and most of society—as second-rate and marginal.

The marginality of military officers is a recurring theme in the novel. One officer becomes so enraged that a mere stable hand can treat military men with insolence that he is about to have him beaten to death; he is restrained by the argument that respect can be gained only by emulating the virtues and courtesies of the civil elite (14.12a–13a). Another officer is scorned by his civilian counterpart in the county because he hires opera players for his birthday party; the civil officer cannot endure such vulgar entertainments. The civil officer is persuaded to stay and view the drama on the grounds that it is a local custom to present a play to wish the host a long and happy life (15.30b–31a). The passage is surprising, since other writings of the period suggest that even very eminent families had plays performed within their households. Eminent patrons might worry about the level of vulgarity in the themes and language of the drama, and the style in which it was performed,[6] but in this story it is the very performance of the play that had to be defended. The author is satirizing what he perceives to be an excessively straitlaced attitude among some members of the official class who were suspicious of all forms of popular entertainment. He is correct to the extent that although the elite may have enjoyed popular amusements such as

---

[5] T'ai-kung and Wen Wang were moral exemplars from the golden age of the early Chou dynasty who appear in popular dramas as sage heroes. The poem has a theatrical flavor, and establishes P'an's imposing figure as though he were a heroic character in an opera.

[6] See Tanaka Issei's discussion of these issues in the first half of his paper in this volume, chap. 5.

fiction and drama, many of them condescended to anyone whose cultural tastes were limited to this sphere.

Author P'an Ching-jo is quite conscious of the marginal status of the military and of the disdain some members of the elite have for unrefined and vulgar (i.e., popular) tastes. Yet as a military man writing a work of popular fiction, he claims the highest moral purposes for his work. He writes in the *fan-li* (general principles), which precedes the novel,

> This tale stresses only the constant principles of human relationships taught by Confucians in order to unite Buddhists and Taoists with the strictly orthodox teaching. It uses their doctrines ... to purge depravity, encourage the good, and transform the wicked in order to aid the orthodox teaching.

He defends his use of popular motifs as consistent with this moral purpose:

> This tale includes popular (*su*) tunes because I want people to be able to understand it. Yet in the vulgar is hidden something subtle; even the coarse places are pure and sincere. This is not the work of a clumsy artisan.

The novel uses not only popular songs, but simple language; it is a combination of simple classical Chinese with *kuan-hua*, the standard vernacular of official business. Although far removed from the spoken dialect of the Nanking area, *kuan-hua* was a useful *lingua franca* for those whose lives involved extensive travel across dialect lines. In addition, proverbs and sayings rather than literary or classical allusions illustrate the morals. Frequent recapitulation keeps the reader from losing the thread of the story. Lest the reader miss the crucial points, the author highlights them by adding circles beside each character in the passage. In a variety of ways, P'an Ching-jo has worked to make the novel easy to understand.

P'an defends both his realism (treatment of familiar, everyday situations) and his inclusion of fantastic elements:

> Although the matters discussed in the tale are sometimes trivial and annoying, one meets more than half of them in a lifetime. If the discussions are correct, it will really serve to clear up delusions. This is like saying that good medicine is bitter to the mouth. If some of the stories are fantastic, that is also to cure delusions. This is like saying that wine cures drunkenness.

The stories in the novel are meant to give the readers a model of self-improvement through moral self-examination.

> If people can lessen their empty boasting, listen to admonishment, examine their daily conduct, not go too far or fail to go far enough, then naturally the whole mind will be clear, the body will be comfortable, and they will progress toward enlightenment.

While many fictional works bow perfunctorily to proper morals before moving on to the real business, this novel is about moral self-examination in real-life situations. The didacticism is central to the enterprise. P'an Ching-jo is writing as a teacher, to reform the world. He is claiming for himself the elevated moral function of elite scholars who write essays and commentaries on the Classics. As we shall see, P'an believes that the Classical discussions of the elite are ineffective as moral education for ordinary people. In writing this novel, he is showing that he can educate them more effectively by using the techniques of fiction. As he says in the general plan, "this is not the work of a clumsy artisan."

It may be useful at this point to compare this novel to the literary *pao-chüan* (precious scrolls), which include didactic tales of karmic retribution.[7] While some of the themes and values of the literary *pao-chüan* overlap with those in *The Romance of the Three Teachings*, the two genres are quite distinct:

1. Literary *pao-chüan* did not coalesce as a separate genre until the late nineteenth century, two hundred fifty years after P'an Ching-jo's novel was published.
2. The novel is much longer than a *pao-chüan*.
3. While both alternate prose and verse, the prose sections of the novel are longer and more expansive than in *pao-chüan*; poetry is brief and serves occasionally to summarize the moral of an episode or to set the mood of a scene.
4. The novel is set in the present, while the literary *pao-chüan* are set in the distant past.
5. The novel deals with ordinary people, while the *pao-chüan* are about families of high officials or very wealthy merchants.
6. The novel treats a wide range of characters in a series of relatively brief episodes, while the literary *pao-chüan* (as reported by Overmyer) develop a dramatic plot around the figures in one family.
7. The novel is less pious and puts less emphasis on leading an explicitly religious life than the literary *pao-chüan*. The Three Masters inculcate moral and religious attitudes by stressing their practical and utilitarian benefits in real-life situations. The *pao-chüan* emphasize religious piety, see values in black-and-white terms, laud those who suffer for virtue, and teach that the Buddha will ultimately reward the faithful. It would be an exaggeration to say that the novel is secular, but its teachings have a strong this-worldly and practical bent.

The Social Perspective

The social perspective of the novel reflects conditions in the region through which the characters travel. The story begins and ends in the fictional town of

---

[7] See Daniel Overmyer's paper in this volume, chap. 8, especially his fourth category of *pao-chüan*. In my description of the genre I am heavily indebted to Overmyer and to an examination of the text he provides as the model for the fourth category.

Ch'ung-cheng li (Orthodox Town), which is located in Mo-ling County, a real place just south of Chin-ling (Nanking), where the novel was published. The Three Masters, protagonists of the novel, first journey by boat along the waterways of the region. On the way to Wu-lin (modern Hangchow), they visit the island called Mt. Tung-t'ing in Lake T'ai in Kiangsu; then they continue on to Chia-shan just across the border in Chekiang, and then go south to Ch'ung-te. In Wu-lin, they learn that the person they are looking for has gone north, so they head back to Chin-ling, on to Wei-yang in central Kiangsu, west to T'ien-ch'ang in Anhwei, and then farther west to Hsiu-chou, Anhwei. From there they leave the familiar Lower Yangtze region and head through the unfamiliar north toward Peking, passing through Te-chou in Shantung; they go to Ching-chou in southern Hopei, and to Hsin-ch'eng, which is a southern gateway into the capital, Peking. They stay only briefly in the capital, for, as outsiders to the national elite, they are intimidated by its grandeur. They arrange to take an ocean-going boat back to Fukien. From there they make their way to Ch'ung-cheng, with an intermediary stop in P'u-t'ien, Fukien.

The main action of the novel is centered precisely in the Lower Yangtze core, a flourishing urbanized region where waterways teemed with traders. As Evelyn Rawski discusses in her paper, although some of the changes go as far back as the Sung, the development of this region was greatly stimulated in the sixteenth century when the Southeast became the focus of maritime trade. The economies of the Southeast and the Lower Yangtze core were stimulated by the influx of silver and growing domestic and overseas markets for goods. Economic growth was accompanied by urban growth and increasing integration of town and rural markets into the urban hierarchy. Urbanization stimulated cash crops, handicraft industries, and specialization in luxury goods, giving rise to a highly competitive atmosphere with a high degree of social mobility. Urban patterns and opportunities, such as luxury consumption, entertainment, education, economic specialization, and written contractual agreements gradually displaced older village patterns of social interaction based on stable and long-term networks of personal obligations.[8]

The journey of the Three Masters follows the commercial waterways of the Lower Yangtze core and the maritime shipping route between Peking and Fukien. The towns and cities they visit in their journey reflect the urban life of this region. The towns are depicted as flourishing commercial centers: shopkeepers know all the gossip and loud marketplace squabbles give them plenty to gossip about. Inns, tea houses, brothels, and gambling dens provide lodging and urban pleasures for all travelers. In this urban setting young wastrels dissipate family fortunes in whoring and gambling: sycophants sponge off the rich; phoney literati while away their days in poetry while all goes to ruin about

---

[8] I have relied heavily on Evelyn Rawski's essay in this volume, chap. 1.

them; con artists, hustlers, and pettifoggers ply their trades. The towns of the novel are peopled with entrepreneurs, from wealthy salt dealers to lowly *pao-tzu* peddlers and fruit vendors and a wide range in between: silversmiths, traveling and stationary wine merchants, innkeepers, jewel dealers, sandal weavers, coffin makers, medicine shop owners, signmakers, butchers, and so on. The towns also contain an underclass including thieves of necessity and professional thieves, beggars, kidnappers, boatmen, fishermen, prostitutes, runaway servants, boat haulers, and local bullies. Rich or poor, all are struggling to get ahead in the competitive urban environment.

Rawski has noted that one facet of this period was the collapse of government controls of the economy and the shift to local financing and management.[9] This may account for the minor and relatively negative role of government in the novel. Government is discussed only at the local level, and is represented by two magistrates, a military officer, and *yamen* runners and functionaries. It is not a major force in the rectification of social problems.

The central and best developed class of characters in the novel, however, are the *ch'u-shih*. Ordinarily this term designates local scholars, usually possessors of the *chin-shih* degree living in their home communities while they are not serving in official posts. However, in this book the term carries a less exalted sense; aside from the two magistrates, no one in the novel has a degree beyond the *hsiu-ts'ai*. In the late Ming, *hsiu-ts'ai* were not ranked among the national elite: they were commoners.[10] The bulk of the *ch'u-shih* in the novel do not seem to have competed in the government examinations or studied in government schools. The term seems to connote simply "gentlemen" in the sense of members of the local (nonnational) town elite. They may have a modicum of education, but they are not elites by virtue of scholarly achievement.

Local elite status in late traditional China was the result of wealth, education, power, or ability sufficient to put one in a leadership role. Leadership meant organizing religious festivals or markets, sponsoring drama performances, or playing a significant role in local organizations such as a lineage

[9] See Rawski's essay in this volume, chap. 1.

[10] They are not "commoners" in the sense of poor peasants, but are depicted as those who wear cotton as opposed to official robes. Ping-ti Ho has noted the great social distance between *hsiu-ts'ai* and holders of higher degrees in *The Ladder of Success in Imperial China: Aspects of Social Mobility, 1368–1911* (New York: Columbia University Press, 1962), pp. 26–43. T'ung-tsu Ch'ü argues from concrete usages in Ch'ing documents of the terms *shen-chin* 紳衿 and *shen-shih* 紳士 (translated variously as "gentry," "ruling class," "scholar-officials," "gentry-officials," but clearly designating the social elite) that the term did include lower-degree holders, in *Local Government in China under the Ch'ing* (Cambridge, Mass.: Harvard University Press, 1962), p. 318, n. 22. Philip Kuhn has stressed that *hsiu-ts'ai* are in an intermediate position, part of the local as opposed to the national elite. *Rebellion and Its Enemies in Late Imperial China* (Cambridge, Mass.: Harvard University Press, 1970), pp. 3–4. The debate on this issue is discussed and evaluated by Paul S. Ropp, *Dissent in Early Modern China: Ju-lin wai-shih and Ch'ing Social Criticism* (Ann Arbor: University of Michigan Press, 1981), pp. 11–15, esp. pp. 21–26. See also David Johnson's paper, chap. 2 of this volume.

merchant guild or a religious society.[11] The first group of "gentlemen" in the novel certainly fits the profile of local elite:

But our story goes that in Ch'ung-cheng li there were a dozen households of gentlemen (ch'u-shih). It was their habit to spend leisure time sitting in the temple, but they did not understand at all the abstruse principles of the Way. Now when word spread that a Master of the Three Teachings had arrived, they went to the temple to have a look. One of these gentlemen was called Hsin Te (Goodhearted), with the sobriquet Pen-hsü (Originally Void). He was a loyal, generous, sincere, and honest gentleman. Another was named Hsiao Hsien (Sighing Leisure), with the sobriquet Wu-shih (Easygoing); he was an openhearted, non-opinionated gentleman. Another was named Lin Se (Stingy) with the sobriquet Pi-fu (Niggardly); he was a stingy and greedy gentleman. Another was called Fei Yung (Spendthrift) with the sobriquet Pu-ching (Reckless; literally No Management); he was an extravagant gentleman who was fond of winning. Another was named Wu Ming (Dim) with the sobriquet Ta-liang (Big Light); he was a narrow man with a shallow sense of right and wrong. (1.4b)

These "gentlemen" are active in local temple activities; they spend their leisure time there, collect for the renovation of the temple (1.8b), sponsor the lectures of visiting teachers (1.7a), and organize major ritual occasions. They are not sophisticated either religiously or culturally; they understand neither the Way nor the literature of the Classical tradition. They are educated, but are not notable for their learning. They are the elite only in their tiny corner of the world.

It is mainly through the eyes of "gentlemen" such as these that the novel views the life of the late Ming. They view government (represented by the yamen) with some distaste, seeing it as corrupt and unnecessarily harsh.[12] On the other hand, they view with alarm the disorderly elements of society (young bullies, riffraff, runaway servants, religious charlatans). They feel responsible as the local elite to sponsor educational lectures and as family heads to manage property and reduce family tensions, but they lack the confidence and know-how to meet these responsibilities in a changing world. They are frightened because they do not get the respect they feel their position merits from wives, servants, children, neighbors, relatives, and friends. The old (village-based) patterns of relationship are breaking down, and new ones have not yet emerged to fit the urbanized world. This local elite lacks the prestige, connections, and broad responsibilities of the national elite; they are concerned with problems at the ground level and close to home.

[11] On the local elite, see James Hayes, The Hong Kong Region, 1850–1911: Institutions and Leadership in Town and Countryside (Hamden, Conn.: Archon Books, 1977), and Hilary J. Beattie, Land and Lineage in China: A Study of T'ung-cheng County, Anhwei, in the Ming and Ch'ing Dynasties (Cambridge: Cambridge University Press, 1979), pp. 1–22.

[12] For the institutional realities that created tension between yamen and the local community see John R. Watt, "The Yamen and Urban Administration," in The City in Late Imperial China, ed. G. William Skinner (Stanford: Stanford University Press, 1977), pp. 353–390.

Didactic Content

The moral content of *The Romance of the Three Teachings* was inspired by the Three Teachings Religion of Lin Chao-en (1517–1598), the temples of which dotted the region depicted in the novel.[13] Although a scion of a very eminent family of P'u-t'ien, Fukien, Lin Chao-en burned his student cap before the official school after receiving his *hsiu-ts'ai* degree in order to seek the true Way and embody it in his life and actions. Thereafter, he considered himself a commoner. After ten years he had a vision of an enlightened Master (in one version, Confucius himself), who taught him a step-by-step method of yogic self-transformation combining elements of Taoist and Buddhist meditation techniques with Confucian views of moral cultivation. Not only did this method provide a concrete program for cultivating sagehood, but at every stage the results were actually experienced in body and mind. The pupil knew exactly what he had achieved. One of the first signs of progress was the ability to heal illness; Lin was instructed by the Enlightened Master to use healing as a sign of the power of his Way. His fame as a healer attracted thousands of followers. Among these was the commander Ch'i Chi-kuang (1528–1587), who may appear, under another name, in *The Romance of the Three Teachings*.[14]

In his early years, Lin Chao-en was a modest teacher in the traditional Confucian mold. However, during the early 1560s he became famous because of his deep involvement in philanthropic activities and ritual services for the homeless souls of those killed during several years of Japanese pirate raids. This philanthropic and priestly activity led him to assume the role of religious teacher. After this he expanded his "school" to include halls and curricula for all social classes; he taught and healed along the roads to audiences including the poor; he wrote simple tracts in the vernacular to reach a broader audience with his writings. Although no good figures are available, his followers probably numbered in the thousands. Shrines proliferated and publications multiplied. Lin Chao-en's Religion of the Three Teachings included merchants and some modest religious seekers whose names made their way into the local gazetteers. Lin Chao-en attempted—no one knows how successfully—to reach a popular audience, people similar to the characters of the novel.[15]

[13] The *Lin-tzu nien-p'u* 林子年譜 [Chronological biography of Master Lin], ed. 1610 by Lin Chao-k'o 林兆珂, now preserved in the Hōsa Bunko, Nagoya, Japan, includes a listing of the Three Teachings Shrines erected by 1610, twelve years after Lin's death. There were more than twenty shrines established in P'u-t'ien County, and ten more centers (several with multiple shrines) stretching as far as Nanking. None of the shrines listed are in towns visited in the journey of the Three Masters (except for Nanking).

[14] The military officer An Pien 安邊 (Pacifier of the Borders) is said to have campaigned against the Japanese pirates (14.3a). Ch'i Chi-kuang's success against pirates in Fukien was the start of his rise to fame. See Ray Huang, *1587, A Year of No Significance: The Ming Dynasty in Decline* (New Haven: Yale University Press, 1981), pp. 156–186.

[15] Further information on Lin's life, writings, and his religious organization can be found in Judith A. Berling, *The Syncretic Religion of Lin Chao-en* (New York: Columbia University Press, 1980).

THE STORY AND STRUCTURE OF THE NOVEL

The basic plot of the novel is as follows: Lin Chao-en goes to call on his friend and disciple Tsung K'ung (Honors Confucius), whose sobriquet is Ta-ju (Great Scholar); Scholar is a *hsiu-ts'ai* like Lin himself. Scholar has gone off with his friend the Taoist (*Tao-shih*) Yuan Ling-ming (Originally Enlightened; I will call him Spirit Power because his *ling-ming*, spiritual or ritual clarity, is the source of his ritual prowess) to visit the Hun-yuan miao (Temple of the Undifferentiated Origin) in Ch'ung-cheng. Lin's presence there attracts a Buddhist monk from Mount O-mei in Szechwan, who is called Pao-kuang (Precious Ray; I will call him Inner Light, since it is his meditative vision that he wields as a weapon in the novel). The gentlemen in the town ask Lin Chao-en to stay and lecture, but since he has other obligations he leaves the Masters of the Three Teachings—Scholar, Spirit Power, and Inner Light—to lecture in his place.

The public lectures of the Three Masters go completely over the heads of the local audience. In the wake of the lectures it becomes clear that a group of young men in the town are no-goods who spend all of their time drinking, gambling, and womanizing. The poor among them sponge from their richer friends, while the affluent filch cash from their parents. Scholar invites them to lunch with the goal of reforming them, but the delinquents grow so wild they knock over an ancient stele and thus release a long-confined fox spirit (*yao*), who begins to cause trouble by stealing wine and women, assuming various guises to seduce local youth of both sexes. While the Three Masters try in vain to capture the fox spirit, one of the young delinquents so upsets his father that the old man suffocates to death in a box he is trying out as a coffin (he is convinced he will die impoverished because of his wastrel son). A visiting Buddhist monk named Chen-k'ung (True Emptiness, but in this case Really Empty!) feels sorry for the old man; in an act of excessive compassion he ritually opens a crack in Hell to retrieve the old man's soul. The crack allows ten thousand deluded souls to escape the darkest reaches of Hell. Chen-k'ung retreats into a meditative trance and does not reemerge until the mess has been cleared up at the end of the novel. The deluded souls, now abroad in the world, find a place for themselves in the minds of persons who share their delusions; the invading souls exaggerate the character flaws of their victims until they are caricatures of themselves.[16]

[16] "Delusion" is not a fully adequate rendering of the Chinese term *mi* 迷 as used in this novel. The Chinese have no notion of radical sin or evil, and believe that every human being is born with a good nature, which can be obscured or forgotten in the course of living but can never be fully destroyed. *Mi* in its lightest form is simply confusion or error, a departure from innate wisdom. However, this confusion has a clouding effect, and tends to obscure the heart and mind so that correct decisions become more difficult in the future. The clouding of the moral nature through confusion distorts the person's self-image and gives rise to one or more character flaws. Wrong or confused thinking inevitably leads to wrong actions, so that delusion has a social side; it is visible in

The Three Masters are chagrined at the moral ineffectiveness of their teaching. They set out to seek instruction from Lin Chao-en, vowing that on their journey they will cure the victims of delusion and capture and return the escaped souls to Hell. They are accompanied by Chih-ch'iu (Seeker), a reformed young man of the village formerly known as Hsin Fang (Mind Amok).[17] Seeker represents Everyman: he comments on the situations they meet and slowly learns to control his unsteady heart, which is profoundly shaken by lust. On their journey, the Three Masters gradually learn to diagnose and cure delusions.

In the end they conquer all the deluded souls and the fox spirit and place them in the charge of a spirit general. They return to Ch'ung-cheng, where they finally catch up with Lin Chao-en and discuss with him the proper disposition of the souls. The souls are given a last chance to repent and be blessed by a *chiao* ritual of renewal.[18] The temple is repaired, a new bell cast and donated, a Three Teachings Hall constructed, and the town is healthy and happy once again.

POPULAR PEDAGOGY

When the Three Masters are asked to lecture on the Way, each chooses to lecture on a great Classic from his tradition. After all, the norms and truths of the Way are recorded in the Classics; hence the Classics are the basis of all education. However, their audience in Ch'ung-cheng was quite diverse; the entire populace had been mobilized to participate in this event. All families—rich and poor—contributed money or materials to repair the temple and build a Three Teachings Hall for the lectures. When it was completed,

> The faithful men and women of the town all came to celebrate: old and young, loud and quiet, worthy and ignorant. There was a troop of women: Aunty Chang from Father's side, Aunty Li from Mother's side, Madam Wang—fat and thin, dressed in black cotton or hemp, tall and short, flower-footed and big-footed, painted and powdered—each in a class by herself. They were all coming and going, pressing and crowding: altogether it was quite lively. (1.8b)

---

the personal interactions of an individual. The opposite of *mi* in the novel is *cheng*: true, orthodox, or upright attitudes that issue in correct actions. *Cheng* is correct in the sense of "on target," not distorted. Often in the story characters with opposite delusions are brought together to help them both see the folly of their attitudes and their behavior; the interaction of the two distorted extremes points up the correct middle way, the mature and balanced view.

[17] An allusion to *Mencius* 6A:11: "They let the mind run amok and do not know enough to seek for it."

[18] On the *chiao* ritual, see Michael Saso, *Taoism and the Rite of Cosmic Renewal* (Pullman, Wash.: Washington State University Press, 1972).

Scholar opened the ceremonies by asking the audience to vow to accept and follow the Way they were about to expound, and then he went first.

He selected the *Great Learning*, lecturing on the phrase, "The Way of the *Great Learning* lies in manifesting bright virtue." [19]
A villager asked, "Why is it called the *Great Learning?*"
Scholar replied, "It is the learning of the great man." [20]
The villager asked, "Is that a great man who wears a hat, or a big fat man?"
Scholar smiled and said, "It refers to a gentleman of virtue." (1.10a)

Scholar went on to explain the phrase "manifesting bright virtue." The crowd discusses how people can manifest bright virtue if they do not even recognize their errors. For instance, some people (they mean Stingy) think they are a model of frugality, while in reality they are just plain stingy. Scholar discourses on the need for moderation, even in frugality, but Stingy can only see the dangers of spending too much. He thinks that Scholar's ideas are very strange (1.10a–11b).

After Scholar, the Buddhist, Inner Light, has his turn:

Inner Light ascended the dharma-seat, opened the *Heart Sutra* and lectured on *prajñā-pāramitā* (the perfection of wisdom).
A villager asked, "What sort of thing is *prajñā-pāramitā* that people are not aroused by it?" [21]
Inner Light smiled and replied, "This is a Sanskrit term."
Another villager said, "I thought it was a local dialect! Please explain it clearly for us."
Inner Light said, "This is when the mind has achieved wisdom; it is like a boat reaching the other shore. One is saved from birth and death."
Easygoing asked, "What do you mean by contemplating the self-existent?" [22]
Inner Light replied, "When the mind of selfish desires is aroused, that is not the original true nature. Only in a sage or Buddha is the true nature always so clear that they can look into the pure self-existent. In the same way, when people have no guilt or shortcoming and are not deluded by greed or passion, their hearts will not be agitated or fearful, but peaceful and unaroused. This is called the self-existent. Once wrong thoughts arise, it is as though the mind goes out [after the object of desire] and is not present. When present, it is agitated and uneasy. How

[19] The first line of the *Great Learning*, which was singled out by the Neo-Confucian Chu Hsi as one of the Four Books that were to have the first place in the Confucian curriculum.
[20] Chu Hsi's standard commentary on the first line. See Chu Hsi 朱熹, *Ssu-shu chi-chu* 四書集註 (Hong Kong: T'ai-p'ing shu-chü 太平書局, 1968), p. 1. Scholar is starting at the beginning of the basic Confucian curriculum.
[21] The villager is responding to the sutra's litany about the absence of sensory and mental stimulation in the state of perfected wisdom.
[22] Seeing into the self-existent (*kuan tzu-tsai*, 觀自在) is a name of Avalokiteśvara, the bodhisattva whose practice of perfected wisdom is discussed in the sutra. The villager hears the name, but not knowing about the bodhisattva, asks rather about the meaning of the term.

could this be the self-existent? If people can look into this self-existent, they will obtain the *prajñā* oar of the raft of dharma and cross the river of *pāramitās* to the shore of the Way. These are the principles of manifesting the nature and enlightening the mind." (1.11b–12a)

Rustic complains that he already has too much to worry about. "My mind is busy all day planning for my family until I cannot even sleep at night. How can I also work at seeing some self-existent?" Others, however, are willing to try.

> Inner Light said, "Close your eyes and think: the self-existent is before me. Sort out the ways in which it permeates the myriad things."
> Dim closed his eyes briefly, then opened them and said, "I looked before and behind, but I saw no self-existent. I only saw the rise and fall of kindness and hatred, a crowd of conflicting and confusing things."
> The villagers all began to laugh. (1.12b)

The section ends, "How could the villagers understand the broad and deep teachings of the Buddha? But they dared not argue. Each believed, saluted, praised, and withdrew" (1.13a).

Spirit Power, the Taoist, had no more success, since—inevitably—when the people heard about the Tao they laughed and laughed (1.13b).[23]

Despite their polite praise, the crowd did not understand even the simplest sayings from the Classics of the three religions, and the technical language was utterly foreign to them. It was not only the "ignorant" folks from the countryside; even the "gentlemen" Stingy and Dim failed to get the message. The depth of the failure of the Three Masters became only too apparent when they could not reform the young delinquents. The abstract doctrines and Classical phrases of the high traditions were not effective as popular pedagogy; the officials confronted similar problems in their lectures on the *Sacred Edict*.[24]

In the course of the story, the Three Masters gradually develop more effective methods of moral instruction. They learn to use persuasion and gentle satire. Persuasion in this novel does not entail rational debate over the meaning of universal ethical constructs or passages from the Classics, but rather making the deluded see the unfortunate long-term consequences of their actions. Satire demonstrates how ridiculous their actions make them look, how they are "losing face," embarrassing themselves and their families through their foolish actions. Both gentle persuasion and satire appeal to enlightened self-interest based on the doctrine of moral retribution. When reason fails, extraordinary measures are invoked; Spirit Power may use his ritual powers to visit the dream world and instruct people in their dreams, or Inner Light may use his meditative vision to see and dramatize the spiritual forces at work in a given situation.

---

[23] Allusion to chapter 41 of the *Tao te ching* 道德經: "When the worst student hears about the Way / He laughs out loud. / If he did not laugh / It would be unworthy of being the way." Cited from *Lao Tzu, Tao Te Ching*, D. C. Lau, trans. (Harmondsworth, Eng.: Penguin, 1963), p. 102.

[24] See Victor Mair's paper in this volume, chap. 11.

Scholar defends this cooperation:

> We Confucians have established a life-line of ancient and eternal principles for human relationships, but because our orthodox way (*cheng-chiao*) cannot transform every spot in the world, Buddhism and Taoism provide some principles to aid us. (13.35a)

The spiritual arts and magical exploits always support the rational message of the story; they provide a convenient way to dramatize in powerful terms the effects of moral delusions. They are teaching aids, both for the characters in the novel and for the reader.

The Deluded World of The Romance of the Three Teachings

The Romance of the Three Teachings is about curing the delusions in the world. Despite the rhetorical bow to the glories of the Ming at the opening of the work, it is clear even before the ten thousand souls escape from Hell that there is plenty of delusion around. There is something rotten in late Ming society, as shown in the lament of the Ch'ung-cheng townsmen over the loss of the good old days:

> "Today and yesterday are different times. Is it only civilian and military that have changed?[25] Customs change often and sharply. When people first sat down together, they discussed filiality, brotherly love, official service, love for the people and true government. But today when we open our mouths, we praise the family with money, the family with power, the family with officials: how much their land earns, or what they will leave to their sons."
>
> A teacher nodded and said, "It is not only that old customs and names have been lost. In the beginning of the Way, the employers came to the gate to salute and invite the teacher; today it is often the teacher who goes around to the gates seeking students. With sweet talk he courts his employer as though he doesn't know how to teach...."
>
> A lifelong silk merchant said, " ... Even the feelings of the world are in disorder. In former times the poor bought cotton and the rich bought silk. Today rich families save their money by buying cotton, while the poor buy silk on credit to put on airs."
>
> A tailor said, "It is true that ancient times were better. In the old days silk clothes were lined, while gauze clothes were unlined. Today everything is money and power. Those with linings act as though they have none [to hide their wealth], while those without act as though they have them [to pretend they are wealthy]."
>
> The gentlemen and townsmen all began to laugh, each sighing for the Way. (1.16a–16b)

This group perceives their world as one in which customs have changed; money and influence have replaced traditional virtues as the standards of behavior; teachers are mere employees and no longer command the respect they once enjoyed; conspicuous consumption buys the appearance of wealth; frugality

---

[25] This passage immediately follows Virtue's lament that P'an must suffer the disgrace of military status, cited above.

helps the prosperous to accumulate savings; money is a source of envy and social display.

The Three Masters in their travels cure the delusions of a variety of people who have been affected by the decline of traditional virtues and rise of greed. The length and episodic structure of the novel allows for a wide range of incidents. The following list provides a very rough idea of the range and relative balance of issues treated:

Money: its power and its dangers (42 incidents)
Proper and wicked uses of religious beliefs, rites, and practices (37)
Tensions in the practice of business (25)
Ambition: its strategies and dangers (23)
Marital conflicts and jealousies (19)
Corruption in local government (14)
The use and abuse of education (12)
General personality flaws (12)
Nonmarital family quarrels (11) and feuds (2)
Quarrels in public places (10)
Criminal acts (8)

Money and Self-Image

The novel portrays a world in which people are trying to get rich, stay rich, or pretend that they are rich. The obsession with money gives rise to many delusions and affects people's views of themselves.

Traditionally, men of learning and virtue were respected in China as the embodiments of the highest values of the society. Now a virtuous *hsiu-ts'ai*, who has demonstrated considerable learning by passing the first of the arduous government examinations, is disconsolate:

> Spirit Power saw that this scholar's mournful eyebrows were locked into a frown and that his good countenance was full of shame. His body looked like a rain-drenched chicken, and his appearance was like a dog in a house observing mourning. (4.11b)

He is scorned by neighbors and friends because of his poverty. In another incident even poor boatmen with no education treat a poor student with utter contempt (19.24a). Learning counts for nothing; money and status are everything.

Other characters, although quite comfortably wealthy, are plagued by profound insecurities. They work ceaselessly and obsessively, fearing they will never have enough (14.25b). They worry that the property they have amassed will be destroyed by flood or fire (11.20a–23a).

Everyone dreams of money; it is the panacea, the key that opens all doors. The poor have grand plans about what they could do with a little money.

They saw a poor man (*min-jen*) who said, "I am called Chi Tso (Lucky Aid). A month ago I came up with a plan for my family, and I figured out that I needed a hundred *liang* for it. In half a month, I was not able to figure out how to get even fifty *liang*. In the next ten days I couldn't figure out how to get even twenty or thirty. In the next few days I couldn't even figure out how to get five or seven *liang*, so now I don't even have that much. My mind seems either to lose by going too far or not going far enough."

Inner Light smiled and said, "You shouldn't think about five or seven *liang* of silver. You have a job before you. Clean yourself up and get through the day."

Lucky Aid said, "But if there's no money, even when I'm cleaned up, my mind cannot be at ease." (15.7b)

Lucky Aid has grand plans, but no strategy for building up his nest egg.

Money breeds extravagance, and town culture provides many temptations for those who wish to spend their money: singsong houses, gambling dens, wine shops, and the like. The wealthy enjoy a life of leisure and pleasure. Seeing that, the ambitious are sometimes tempted to pursue their romantic dreams of personal success or adventure; they abandon their family obligations to make their names or fortunes in the world (13.5a; 16.21a).

On the other hand, money also breeds avarice. Stingy has become a laughing-stock for his tightfistedness. When the town plans to install an image of the Three Teachings, he recommends a paper drawing; bronze, wood, or clay are too expensive (1.15a). He won't call a doctor when he is ill, for the medicines are too expensive (2.13b). He gives his grown son no spending money, forcing him to steal from the family coffers. Although he is quite prosperous, he thinks of himself as in imminent danger of destitution, and so he is stingy.

The Corruption of Human Relationships

The pervasive influence of money not only warps one's self-image; it also distorts relationships with others. An extremely rich man named Fu Jao (Wealthy) disdains the traditional polite arts, so his relationships are all defined and distorted by his money:

His fields stretch for a hundred *ch'ing*[26] and he occupies another thousand scattered plots. But he does not practice poetry or literature or study courtesy and ethics. He spends all his time surrounded by flatterers. Local people of little pride cultivate friendships with him; if it is not idlers it is false and sycophantic friends. (4.16a–16b)

Wealthy treats the Three Masters with such arrogant lack of courtesy that

---

[26] A standard *mou* was 6000 square feet, and a *ch'ing* was 100 *mou*, or a little more than 15 acres. However, the measurements varied from region to region. See Ray Huang, *Taxation and Governmental Finance in Sixteenth-Century China* (Cambridge: Cambridge University Press, 1974), pp. 40–41.

Spirit Power cannot resist needling him by asking how many local gentry and notables he knows. Wealthy sweats and squirms and tries to evade the question by asking them to discuss the relative importance of wealth and titles (*kuei*).[27] Spirit Power sees that because the man is scorned by the local gentry, he hopes to hear that wealth is more important. He and Inner Light play along, saying what he wants to hear until "he regained his composure and his arrogant manner faded" (4.18a). Then Scholar moves in:

> Spirit Power's saying that titles are not as good as wealth is too vague, and Inner Light's statement that the wealthy can easily acquire titles is too simple. As I see it, wealth and titles are mutually opposed. The wealthy honor titles, and men with titles honor wealth. But the arrogance and lawlessness of the wealthy earn them the scorn of the highly placed, while the elite's dissatisfaction with their position [they also covet money] earns them the contempt of the rich. Each is inferior in some sense, so they are mutually opposed.
>
> I have met many wealthy people, but in the end none achieved filiality towards his parents, respect for his elders, refinement in literature, and understanding of proper behavior. If you had these, both the eminent and humble would respect you. The local people would look up to you and friends and relatives would love you. How could they offer you empty veneration?" (4.18a–18b)

The last point strikes home; Wealthy realizes that he is surrounded by flatterers and sycophants. As he orders his fawning friends away, one grovels and weeps that he cannot survive without "the abundant sea of Wealthy's liberality." Spirit Power attempts to cure this man of his self-abasement. He has endured countless public humiliations from Wealthy in the hope of getting a few paltry gifts from him. Spirit Power warns the fawner that he will never discover an honest way to make a living until he breaks out of this degrading relationship (4.20a–20b).

When people use friendship to get ahead it is easy to become bitter about human relationships. One man complains about a friend who took money and gifts from him and then absconded, spreading lies about his benefactor (8.2a–2b). Another man pretends to comfort troubled friends by playing chess with them, while in reality he fleeces them to replenish the family fortune he lost gambling (6.21a–22b). Religious charlatans, quack doctors, fortune tellers, and geomancers all feign sympathy and interest while profiting from the hopes and fears of innocent people.

Suspicion of people's motives in this competitive urban setting leads to a breakdown of traditional networks of mutual support and generosity. One man confesses that he failed to help a poverty-stricken student so that he could compete in the exams (11.15b). A *pao-tzu* peddler defends his lack of charity

---

[27] *Kuei* means "honorable" or "high-class," but in this passage it refers to the honor or status that results only from holding official position, or having an official title.

towards a beggar:

> You three say I did not give that beggar a *pao-tzu*, but you don't understand that I worked hard to make these *pao-tzu*. Why should I let him eat them for no reason? One can always feel sorry for the poor, but a few *pao-tzu* can hardly do the trick. This door of charity cannot be closed. If you three give him a *pao-tzu*, that is just one instance of humaneness. You do it once and move on. I sell *pao-tzu* here all day long. How could I keep it up? (14.23a)

In the city charity is difficult, for the poor keep coming. Unlike the small village where the lines of responsibility can be drawn in terms of a hierarchy of relationships and obligations, in town there is a vast human sea of "the poor." The relative impersonality and scale of town life contribute to the breakdown of human relationships.[28]

Moreover, the competitive atmosphere of the urban setting makes a travesty of the traditional ideal of harmony. Inns are so competitive that workers sent out to "invite" guests engage in violent tugs-of-war with the luggage of the customers (16.23a). Petty thefts and street incidents lead to quarrels and fist-fights (16.7b). During these squabbles onlookers laugh or cower, but there seems to be no effective mechanism for mediating the disputes. Theoretically, a system of elders and mutual security teams (*pao-chia*) should handle it, but it is not functioning in these towns; in fact the system seldom functioned effectively. The Three Masters advise avoiding the police and the *yamen*, since any justice there will be gained only at the cost of exorbitant graft and considerable human suffering (4.26b–27a); the *yamens* are so corrupt that an honest official can barely survive (10.25a ff).[29] New mechanisms are needed for resolving disputes.

The Battleground of the Family

If the marketplaces and the streets are noisy with squabbles, things are just as bad at home. In the story, wives pit brother against brother, each wanting for her husband and children the maximum slice of the family's pie. They care little for the ideal of a cooperative extended family.[30] Seeker naively tries to resolve

---

[28] Keith Thomas has argued that in England after the decline of the manorial system the breakdown of the traditional network of mutual assistance gave rise to guilt that spawned popular witchcraft accusations; people believed that those refused help were angered and took their vengeance in curses. *Religion and the Decline of Magic* (New York: Scribner's, 1971), pp. 555–567. Thomas's discussion of forces emanating from the lower levels of society that helped to give rise to a new conception of religion in eighteenth- and nineteenth-century England suggests many questions that it would be useful to ask about late traditional China.

[29] On the failure of the *pao-chia* system, see Kung-chuan Hsiao, *Rural China: Imperial Control in the Nineteenth Century* (Seattle: University of Washington Press, 1960), pp. 43–83, 184–258. On the forces contributing to corruption, see John Watt, "Yamen and Urban Administration."

[30] See Margery Wolf, *Women and the Family in Rural Taiwan* (Stanford: Stanford University Press, 1972), esp. pp. 32–41.

such a case, sweetly explaining to the women the ideal of family harmony. One wife hits him, asserting, "Principle or no principle, I want to divide the family (*fen-chia*)!" (15.32b).[31]

The marital system is viewed by many as a way to get ahead (8.24b–25a). Some families in regions famous for beautiful women make a business of marketing their daughters as concubines. Spirit Power asks a salt dealer how such parents can "sell them like so much meat." The man replies,

> You don't understand. Wei-yang is a prosperous area, a hub and destination for many; this is how our daughters come to be sought for by outsiders. Some [of these women] are in hiding [presumably runaway wives or servants], evading the law or doing business. Some are not raised by their own families. I hear it has become a custom for poor families with too many daughters to adopt some out. These other families raise them and train them in music and the arts, regarding them as assets they can sell as concubines. There are also hard-hearted parents who seek only wealth through their daughters, and thus ask the matchmakers to marry them far away. They really have the heart to destroy basic values! (10.2a–2b)

Scholar adds that those who purchase such overpriced concubines are also to blame for depriving some poor man of a bride who would enable him to carry on his family line.

In a competitive world it is tempting to break off an engagement if a better match comes along (8.27a–29a). However, the bride may feel degraded if she is married to a horrid man whose only virtue is his money. In one episode such a woman resists the marriage, and nags her boorish husband unmercifully (8.31a). One group of young women is so angry about being paraded before matchmakers as potential concubines that they form a secret sisterhood to meet at night and seek their own romantic trysts in defiance of their parents (10.10b).

People who marry to get ahead are almost never satisfied with what they have, and town life and travel provide plenty of opportunities for roving eyes. This is not limited to men. One wife, attracted to a fisherman she sees, agrees on the spot to help him murder her husband (17.27b–28a). Another falls for a young student, and thereafter cannot stomach her ugly and stupid husband (1.29a). A husband and wife fantasize about each other's deaths, dreaming that the second marriage will be sweeter (17.34b–36a).

Parents get little respect when they fail in their parental obligations; how can children be filial if they have not known parental love (12.21a)? Husbands get little respect when they are stupid and foolish. One man defends his lifelong habit of beating his wife:

> When I tell my old lady to make me clothes, they are too short; when she makes me shoes, they are too small. Yet she scolds me, saying it's not the clothes and the

---

[31]On the volatile process of family division, see Maurice Freedman, *Lineage Organization in Southeastern China* (London: Athlone Press, 1958), pp. 18–27.

shoes, but that I am too tall and my feet are too large! Can I let her say that
without beating her? (13.29a)

The wife is insolent in part because the husband is crude and violent. Like other
couples in the novel, they are caught in a vicious cycle of vituperation, jealousy,
nagging, and violence until their home becomes a battleground.

Distorting Education

The obsession with wealth and status has also warped people's views of
education. Some err by thinking that social display is more important than
education; they are willing to spend more on weddings than to educate their
sons (9.8b–9a). This is a misplaced investment in a world where official position
is still the only source of real eminence.

On the other hand, the prosperity of the region provided more people with
the means to pursue an education.[32] Many of the newly literate class are quite
romantic about their learning and laughably unrealistic about its limitations.
One fellow describes a friend who read histories on the rice-drying floor:

> His wife told him to see that the cows did not eat the rice, but when she went into
> the house the cow started eating it. The man put down his book and ordered the
> cow not to eat the rice. How could the cow obey his order?
>
> The wife came out, picked up a stick, and beat the cow until it went away. The
> man laughed and said, "I understand the rituals of the Duke of Chou, and I study
> the writings of the sages. But I don't see how you get those animals to fear an old
> woman." (9.5a)

Li Wei-i (Only One Principle) is so fond of his learning that he spends all his
time reading histories while enjoying the lakeside scenery (7.37b–38a). He
introduces the Three Masters to Yu Meng-hsin (Very Stupid), whose parents
want him to succeed so much that they locked him in a room for three years to
encourage him to pursue his studies. Recently they saw him nodding his head,
so they assume he has made some progress.

> The old man unlocked the door and let Stupid out. See how arrogantly he surveys
> the group just like a graduate stuffed with learning! The old man said, "Son, you
> have studied for three years in that room. Yesterday I saw you nod as you read the
> histories. You must have understood some truth. We have invited these teachers
> to examine you and to see the obedient and educated son we have raised."
>
> Stupid happily said, "I have indeed understood something."
>
> The old man asked, "What did you understand?"
>
> Stupid smiles, "Three years ago I thought these histories were hand-copied;
> now I realize they are printed. So I nodded."
>
> When the group heard this they laughed, and the old man laughed too. He

---

[32] On the expansion of literacy, see Rawski's paper in this volume, chap. 1.

said, "Son, you were behind closed doors for three years and have gained such a clever insight! Indeed your parents have not educated you in vain." (7.39a–39b)

The man is ready to send servants to the local officials to sign Stupid up for the next official examination. He really believes his son will be a great official.

The Three Masters realize that although the boy is stupid, the father is even more deluded in believing he can succeed. He long ago dismissed the teachers who refused to tutor his untalented son. "Magpies can be taught to speak, and monkeys can be taught to dance. How could a human being be unable to learn to read?" (8.1a). Inner Light explains that it is one thing to learn the basics and quite another to master the high degree of literary skills needed to compete in the government examinations (8.1b).

THE ANSWER: RELIGION AS THE MANAGEMENT
OF MORAL CAPITAL

Although they sigh for the good old days, the Three Masters learn that they cannot cure delusions simply by citing ancient books or mouthing old values. Delusions arise from the everyday struggles and tensions of life; the forces of money, competition, conflict, and social aspiration have to be faced directly if religion is to be relevant in the lives of real people.

Theologically, the novel centers on the tension between humanity (jen) and righteousness (i), on the one hand, and profit (li) and desires ($yü$) on the other.[33] The stories of the religious professionals in the novel dramatize the dynamics of this tension in the human soul in traditional religious terms: their spiritual and ritual powers depend directly on a pure heart free of cupidity and lust. When the heart-mind is pure, the inner light leads to wise discernment and the power of the spirit can conquer all evil forces.

Jen and *i* are defined in concrete and practical terms. *Jen* is generosity, charity, and tolerance toward the less fortunate. *I* is honesty, decency, and simple courtesy. *Jen* and *i* are also treated as moral capital, earned and saved like money. Moral capital (accumulated merit) is just as important as a legacy for one's descendents as land or money. In fact, the successful long-term management of property depends on the management of moral capital; the two cannot be separated.

This view is summed up in the story of Chin I-ch'u (Gold Digger). Gold Digger suddenly became wealthy when he discovered a cache of gold in his back yard. Later he dreamt that some men demanded repayment with interest of the "borrowed" money. Since his assets in the spirit world (moral merit) were insufficient to cover the debt, they took his children hostage until he could pay off. When he awoke his children had indeed contracted a mysterious illness.

---

[33] The tension goes back to *Mencius* 1A:1. Expressed more generally as pure mind versus desires, it is a common theme in all Chinese religion.

Spirit Power sends his spirit to the other world and asks a red-robed official why Gold Digger is being punished. He is told,

> Money in this life is related to the fortunes of one's ancestors. When this poor man suddenly came up with a fortune, people misunderstood and told him that fate (*ming-yun*) had brought it. How could they know it was the result of his grandfather's accumulated merit (*chi-te*)? Since his grandfather accumulated merit but died before he could enjoy its benefits, it flowed down to his grandson. If he had understood his sudden reversal of fortune, he would have been careful to continue diligently accumulating good deeds. Then the humanity (*jen*) could be handed down from generation to generation, and the wealth could have been preserved always. But he did not think about his sudden reversal of fortune, and acted recklessly and arrogantly. He will be able to preserve his life, but he has exhausted the merit of his grandfather. If his wickedness gets worse, his grandfather's merit may not be able to compensate, and he will gradually sink back into poverty. (19.3a–3b)

Gold Digger's success was not due to fate or even to his own efforts; it was the result of the deeds of his grandfather. The grandfather's good deeds are a kind of capital, a moral collateral behind the money Gold Digger unearthed. Gold Digger's debt is in the spirit world, but he is paying in the real world through the sickness of his children.

Spirit Power is given a chance to examine the account (*chang-pu-tzu*) that details Gold Digger's debt:

1. The grandfather buried five thousand ounces of gold.
2. The grandfather lacked sufficient merit to hand it on to his son.
3. The father had no moral base for receiving it.
4. Gold Digger was poor without resenting it, and he was able to maintain what was allotted to him. Thus he could receive his grandfather's legacy with three-fold profit.
5. After he dug up the gold, he agitated his Earth and Wood components and injured his moist life force.[34] His faults were many. This is the first reason to press for payment.
6. After digging up the gold, he lent money at a high profit, so that [the borrowers] were trapped in poverty. This is the second reason to press for payment.
7. After digging up the gold, he became arrogant. He abused his servants until they moaned that he had destroyed their hope [of living long enough] to continue their lines. This is the third reason to press for payment.
8. After digging up the gold, he was no longer grateful for the support of Heaven and Earth, for the rulers who govern water and soil, for the shining of sun and moon, or for the nurturance of his parents. All day long he savored

---

[34] Earth and Wood are two of the five phases (*wu-hsing* 五行). Gold Digger used a hoe (Wood) to disturb the soil (Earth) when he dug up the gold; subsequently he disturbed his inner moral balance (the harmony of the five phases in his internal microcosm) by behaving recklessly and to excess.

fine food and wine and indulged his passions and excesses. This is the fourth reason to press for payment.

9. After he dug up the gold, he fiddled with weights and measures, cheated, and lent money [at high interest] under the false pretext of concern for the orphaned and cold. He is truly a silkworm who feeds on fields and property! This is the fifth reason to press for payment.

10. After digging up the gold, he was wealthy without being humane [i.e., generous]. He did not get along with his relations and did not aid the unfortunate. He overstuffed his mouth and belly until he harmed his life. This is the sixth reason to press for payment. (19.4a–4b).

The indictment is not vague or abstract, nor is it a general list of the good and bad deeds of his life. It outlines how the wealth he found has ruined him; he became a usurer, a cruel master, an ungrateful son, an indulgent lecher, a dishonest businessman, and a skinflint. He has misused and abused the blessing he received, and thus has exhausted the moral capital that serves as collateral for this wealth.

Nor is this a purely individual matter. Gold Digger's sins affect not only himself, but his descendents. When Spirit Power asks, "Why not simply kill him and spare his children?" the official replies, "First, his years are not lived out, and second it would be wrong to hand his wickedness down to his children in the form of property" (19.4a). The Chinese view (embodied in the concept of face) is that the actions of an individual affect the reputation of the group; in this view good or bad deeds are family property, not the isolated acts of an individual. This reinforces the Chinese view of the self as part of a larger nexus of human relations.

The final point of the story is that Gold Digger can confess his faults and vow to change his behavior, thus beginning the task of rebuilding the account of merit (19.5a). The story is not simple theodicy, an explanation of why he and his children must suffer. He is challenged to take responsibility for his actions and to learn to manage his moral capital as carefully as he has managed his money.

Religion as the management of moral capital thus involves taking responsibility: learning to manage one's life and human relationships so as not to exhaust moral collateral. In one episode, two families are seeking to avert a feud by resolving the conflicts between them. They discover that their quarrel has been inflamed by a troublemaker called Two-edged Sword (Liang-mien Tao), who has been feeding each side with false reports of the vile schemes and plots of the other. The Three Masters explain that there are three methods for handling the situation: (1) using rituals and charms to exorcise the demon in Two-edged Sword; (2) going to the *yamen* to have him arrested; and (3) taking care of it themselves. The last and preferable course involves writing down the real facts, getting Two-edged Sword to comment on them, and then judging his claims against the evidence before a panel of representatives of neutral lineages

(8.10a–11a). In recommending the latter course, the Three Masters suggest a strategy in which these people will not be subject to the whims of the gods (as in the case of ritual) or decisions of the officials (as in going to the *yamen*). They will circumvent the priests and officials and handle matters on their own.[35] They will use their literacy by putting the facts in writing and will develop organizational and mediational skills in the informal hearing. They will become the main actors and shapers of their own lives.

The view of religion as management of moral capital is one result of the development of Ming morality books (*shan-shu*) and ledgers of merit and demerit (*kung-kuo ko*). Originally, morality books served to illustrate the workings of moral retribution according to the Buddhist law of karma, with special emphasis on piety—the hideous punishments for sacrilege and the great rewards for acts of devotion to the Buddha. By the Ming, morality books had taken on another character entirely. While they were still illustrated with tales of saintly paragons and depraved sinners, devotional values were overshadowed by very practical moral teachings, geared to the workaday activities of people in all walks of life.[36] Ming morality books had a new theological understanding of retribution. Earlier morality books had depicted karma as the fruit of many lifetimes; one's karmic burden was great and could not be wiped out simply by good deeds during one lifetime. The believer had to perform acts of great devotion to entrust himself to the compassion of the bodhisattvas whose superhuman powers would aid the karma-burdened sinner. In the Ming, morality books no longer stressed the karmic burden of multiple incarnations or the compassion of the bodhisattvas. They had become a practical science of moral cultivation. One started with a clean slate (no karmic debt) or with the legacy of one's immediate forebears, and from that point recorded good and bad deeds to earn (or repay) blessings and avoid calamities.[37] Acts of piety and devotion counted, but only as good deeds, not as a special category with special spiritual merit.

There is an accounting mentality behind Ming morality books; one earns or pays for life's blessings with the "cash" of good deeds. The deeds are classified and sometimes assigned weighted values, as taught by Chu-hung (1535–

---

[35] I am grateful to David Jordan for suggesting to me that anticlericalism may be an important key to interpreting the novel's attitude toward rituals. His suggestion led to the larger thesis concerning the rejection of intermediating authorities. Arthur P. Wolf has developed the thesis that the attitude of worshipers towards the gods reflects their attitude toward bureaucratic authorities as influenced by their social position in the culture. See his "Gods, Ghosts, and Ancestors," in *Religion and Ritual in Chinese Society*, ed. Arthur P. Wolf (Stanford: Stanford University Press, 1974), pp. 131–182.

[36] See Sakai Tadao 酒井忠夫, *Chūgoku zensho no kenkyū* 中国善書の研究 [Researches on Chinese morality books] (Tokyo: Kokusho kankōkai 国書刊行会, 1960), *passim*.

[37] See Wm. Theodore deBary, "Individualism and Humanitarianism in Late Ming Thought," in *Self and Society in Ming Thought*, ed. W. T. deBary and the Conference on Ming Thought (New York: Columbia University Press, 1970), p. 176.

1615).[38] They can be earmarked for a specific goal; Yuan Huang (1533–1606) vowed three thousand good deeds for a son and ten thousand for a *chin-shih* degree.[39] As a person kept his daily ledger, he could see the gradual accumulation of savings toward his goal.

The Romance of the Three Teachings makes even more explicit the analogy of accounting behind the morality books, and it develops the accounting system a step further. The story of Gold Digger goes beyond a simple classification and numerical weighting of good deeds as general moral capital. It analyzes the mismanagement of wealth in moral terms. Conversely, it teaches that moral management forms the basis of property management.

Gold Digger's misuse of his wealth created enemies: the borrowers ruined by his exorbitant interest rates; the servants he abused; his parents, whom he scorned; the poor, whom he cheated; his relatives, whom he refused to help. These people—among whom he and his children had to live—would be out to get him. He had not developed a base of human good will, which would allow him to maintain his wealth without incurring dangerous resentment. It was not just the gods who were angry; the abuse of wealth had surrounded the family with resentments that would eventually lead to its downfall.

In sum, the management of moral capital has two sides. First, it is a lesson in management: (1) taking the initiative in shaping one's life and responsibility for one's actions, and (2) analyzing the long-term effects of one's actions in order to plan and act more effectively. This management side reinforces the enterprising actions of groups and individuals in the competitive urban milieu of the Lower Yangtze region. Second, it is practical morality: (1) recognizing the necessity of maintaining good will in the network of human relationships, and (2) curbing rampant greed, including desire for selfish (individualistic) and quick profits at the expense of human relations. There is a positive value put on management and enterprise, but they must not controvert the basic values of society.

Examples of Proper Management

In the competitive, rapidly changing, urbanized Lower Yangtze core region, various areas of life required management and responsible moral reflection. The Three Masters try to make people see sounder moral approaches to the management of life's problems.

Responsible management of education in the novel means seeing it as a major investment with short-term and long-term payoffs. The ultimate goal of

---

[38] See Yü Chün-fang, *The Renewal of Buddhism in China: Chu-hung and the Late Ming Synthesis* (New York: Columbia University Press, 1981), pp. 120–121. Yü gives a brief history of morality books and discusses Ming developments; she stresses the "greater premium on moral internalization and ethical intention" (p. 113) in the Ming books. I would go on to argue that the Gold Digger story moves beyond quantification-plus-intention to the analysis of mismanagement of blessings previously earned.

[39] Sakai Tadao, *Chūgoku zensho no kenkyū*, p. 320 ff.

education in Chinese society was passing the examinations and gaining an official position. But since very few achieved that coveted prize, it was important to understand the less exalted uses of education.[40] One use was illustrated in the story about conflict resolution through written evidence and mediation discussed in the last section. Literacy is a tool for managing property and conflict more effectively.

Members of the national elite in the late Ming were bitter and angry about the extreme competitiveness and over-refined pedanticism of the government examinations.[41] However, according to this novel, many of the poor believed they could achieve high office through education. Pa Kao (Reaching High) had longed to be an official ever since he saw one in full regalia. When told that success in the examinations requires "a firm foundation in fate," he retorts, "Common households produce great officials!" Spirit Power informs him that the foundation is not wealth, but "accumulated virtue and skillful means." He advises him to "teach his sons to read early in life." Then he may be able to live in the wonderful surroundings of the official (15.6b–7a). Reaching High must recognize that fulfilling his ambition is a long-term project based on the accumulation of moral capital and investment in the education of his sons. What he cannot gain for himself he may be able to achieve indirectly through his sons by means of a long-term investment in education.

Another area requiring moral management is sexuality. The novel depicts the deterioration of family life as a result of the exploitation and distortion of sexual relationships: selling daughters as concubines; wasting wealth on prostitutes and concubines and thus poisoning wives with jealousy; compromising patriarchal authority by indulging in boorish behavior. Husbands and fathers must curb their greed and manage their sexual desires to maintain peace and respect in the family.

Town life also gave restless women opportunities for illicit sexual relationships that threatened the legitimacy of the family line. The wife of Li Tung (Shaken) was seduced by a fox spirit disguised as her husband. Religious rites failed to capture the fox. Ultimately, the husband and wife themselves defeated him by making a temporary vow of celibacy, which gave her a way of distinguishing the fox from her husband (3.13a). The moral is not that sexual management means celibacy. Rather, husband and wife were willing to curb their desires to the point of abstention in order to resolve the crisis that was destroying their marriage. Moreover, the husband demonstrated his faith in his wife by agreeing to the vow; he believed her when she said that she was deceived and was not intentionally unfaithful. He was willing to cooperate to unmask the villain.

[40] G. William Skinner, "Social Mobility Strategies in Late Imperial China: A Regional Systems Analysis," in *Regional Analysis*, ed. Carol A. Smith (New York: Academic Press, 1976), *I: Economic Systems*, pp. 327–364, esp. pp. 336–343.

[41] See Paul Ropp, *Dissent in Early Modern China*, pp. 91–119.

Respect, affection, and cooperation of husband and wife defeated the threat of infidelity.[42]

Another aspect of the management of moral capital is work. Work is the cure for the ills of poverty. The poor in the novel moan that the wealthy locals or their rich relatives refuse to help them and treat them with contempt. The Three Masters tell them that the man of character can bear poverty as long as he has the Way. But, one poor man asks, what about the real sufferings of cold and hunger? Scholar replies,

> Your insight is penetrating. When people fear they will freeze or starve, they apply themselves to seek food and clothing. If they cannot find a way, they face real misery; the mind is injured and the body may perish. But if you know this truth, then Heaven and Earth which gave you life will not let you starve or freeze. You must obey your natural instincts with a calm mind, and you will know that you must cultivate virtue and find a livelihood which suits the specific talents you were allotted. Then body and mind will be healthy. But to envy the rich and the "haves" is a great mistake which leads to death; you will try so hard to get ahead that you will work yourself to death before your time. (19.28a–28b)

Hard work for survival is instinctual; people somehow find a way to survive. But bemoaning one's poverty is another matter; self-pity saps the energy and warps the mind. One must work to survive and then, if one has built up a supply of merit, it will serve as a base for future prosperity.

Work is essential even for the wealthy; the idle rich are no different from a horse or a dog (6.24b), simply feeding all the time. Work is a basic part of being human. Given the value placed on work, it is not surprising that the Three Masters argue that the mental labor of the gentleman (*chün-tzu*) is just as much work as the physical labor of the little man.[43] Scholar describes the work of the Three Masters: "We wander around the mountains and seas endlessly preaching and teaching. What is that if not using both body and mind to work?" (18.17b). He does not defend their role as teachers on the basis of their wisdom or their value as moral models; they work at traveling, talking, persuading others.

Last, but by no means least, the novel deals with the management of property. It not only criticizes the waste of property in licentious pleasures and

----

[42] This is particularly striking because of the increasingly rigid ideal of female chastity from the Sung dynasty on; widows were not to remarry and wives were to die rather than yield to another. An unfaithful wife could be summarily divorced, and was sometimes executed by her husband. This, at least, was the elite ideal; there is reason to doubt that it extended very far down the social scale. In any event, Li Tung's trust of his wife is all the more impressive since it turns out that she is carrying the illegitimate twins of the fox spirit.

[43] Reference to *Mencius* 3A:4. "Those who labor with minds govern others; those who labor with strength are governed." This passage is often cited to prove the Confucian elite's class prejudice and their disdain for physical labor.

lavish social display, it also criticizes excessive frugality. In the competitive urban world of the novel, there are many opportunities for families to develop their property. It thus becomes crucial that grown and married sons be actively involved in the management and development of the family's fortune. Fathers who hold too tightly to the purse strings are doing their families a great disservice. In confronting one family head who is opposed to dividing his property among his sons, Spirit Power feigns agreement to show him the folly of his views:

> Certainly you are right in not wanting to divide it. If you divide it into three portions, they would fill out, and then there would be a lot of wealth to manage. You might forget your former livelihood with all that money to spend! Not only would your own portion shrink, but the sons would quarrel over it after your death. Better not to divide! One person can maintain the property a long time. . . . But if you don't divide it, you had better cultivate your health to live a thousand years. Still, you could give one son a thousand ounces of gold and have him draw up a written guarantee (*pao-kuan wen-chüan*). . . . With a written guarantee, years later when there are many descendents, they will not go hungry, and will be unable to encroach on each other against your wishes. If they do, the contract will order the officials to punish them and adjudicate, so that two-thirds (after court costs) of the property will be assigned to the management of two households. (19.21b–22a)

The last point alarms the old man, since he doesn't want some unknown and probably corrupt official deciding the division of his property.[44] The passage seems to suggest that the financial position of the family will be strengthened through division, since each son will work to preserve and expand his share. If that is the implication, it runs counter not only to the ideal of the extended family, but also to the growth in the late Ming and early Ch'ing of large unified lineages under centralized management.[45] However, well-organized, large lineages attempted to deploy the talents of all adult male members in such a way as to maximize lineage prosperity and strength. The stingy fathers of *The Romance of the Three Teachings* may be criticized for being too conservative and for ineffective utilization of communal property and resources. Proper manage-

[44] On the bitter disputes involved in dividing property, see Freedman, *Lineage Organization*, and n. 26, above. Jonathan K. Ocko describes a number of lawsuits involving division of family property in "Family Disharmony as Seen in Ch'ing Legal Cases," presented at "Orthodoxy and Heterodoxy in Late Imperial China: Cultural Beliefs and Social Divisions," A.C.L.S. Conference at Montecito, California, August 20–26, 1981. The written management guarantee in the passage may reflect the late Ming growth of large lineage organizations with written guidelines for handling lineage properties and for handling internal disputes. See Charlotte Furth, "The Orthodox Family and Its Discontents: The View from Household Instructions," also presented at the "Orthodoxy and Heterodoxy" conference.

[45] See Fu-mei Chang and Ramon H. Myers, "Customary Law and the Economic Growth of China during the Ch'ing Period," *Ch'ing-shih wen-t'i* 3.10:4–27 (1978) for examples of growth of cooperation within lineages.

ment involves the use of both property and manpower for the benefit of the lineage in the long run.

In all of these examples, the individual is encouraged to take a broad and long view, considering not only him- or herself, but the nexus of human relationships in the present and future. The fierce competition of late Ming society provided a drive toward unbridled "individualism" and sharp rivalry. The novel articulates a counterview, which balances work and enterprise with a recognition of the need for success to be grounded in the long-term interests of the family and in the good will of the people who make up the world in which the family lives and does business.

The Romance of the Three Teachings *and Late Ming Religion*

The Romance of the Three Teachings is a work of literature; we must exercise caution in moving from it to the actual historical realities of late Ming popular culture. However, because the picture it paints of late Ming society in the Lower Yangtze region is generally corroborated by historical evidence, and because it reflects actual religious movements of the period, we can draw some cautious conclusions. The novel helps to illumine the mentality behind some of what we know of late Ming religion, and to highlight its social significance.

The Romance mentions the religion of Lin Chao-en with sufficient specificity to demonstrate that the author was familiar with the writings and practices of the religion. However, the Three Masters modestly decline to discuss any of the technical aspects of Lin's meditative system, claiming that they are only proficient in its basic ethical teachings (8.27b–28a). This is not a serious distortion of the popular teachings of the religion. Lin's writings confirm that basic ethical training and vows to Heaven geared to the circumstances and livelihood of the student were the core of religious training until the student proved himself ready for further instruction.[46]

The Three-in-One Religion and the lay Buddhist movement of Chu-hung are examples of lay religious movements largely independent of religious professionals. *The Romance of the Three Teachings* describes the building of a Three Teachings Hall at the initiative of the local lay elite with the cooperation of the entire community. The novel encourages grass-roots cooperation and discussion in the resolution of all sorts of disputes, and discourages resorting to religious professionals, fortune tellers, government officials, or professional go-betweens. This suggests that the popularity of the lay syncretic organizations may have stemmed from an interest in self-help organizations. It ties these movements more explicitly to the contemporary developments of merchant guilds, brotherhoods, and laborers' organizations.[47] It suggests that the syn-

---

[46] See Berling, *The Syncretic Religion of Lin Chao-en*, p. 110.

[47] See Daniel Overmyer's paper in this volume, chap. 8, for a discussion of how millenarian Buddhist organizations reflect the same trend.

cretism of these groups may be rooted in the diverse backgrounds of persons now banding together to pursue common goals and seeking a common ideological vision. Perhaps because the leadership and organizational skills of the local elite had long been developed largely in temple-related activities, virtually all the new organizations had some religious dimension.[48] However, their concerns are also secular, and some (like merchant guilds and boatmen's associations) became increasingly secular over time.[49] However, religion is perceived as the vehicle through which to promote group interest (and self-interest) within the guidelines of accepted values.

In a broader sense, *The Romance of the Three Teachings* makes explicit some of the values implicit in the thought of Wang Yang-ming (1472–1529), especially as developed by the popularizing T'ai-chou branch of his disciples. Wang Yang-ming's notion of innate good-knowing (*liang-chih*) meant that moral truth was already present in the minds of all people. Further, his identification of knowledge with action helped him to break out from under the weight of tradition and an overrefined scholasticism. In the Wang Yang-ming school, the Confucian ideal of sagehood was no longer confined to the profoundly learned and deeply reflective scholar who embodied the most rarified of cultural ideals. Dynamic action in the world and moral activity in daily life were also manifestations of the sagely Way. These two ideas paved the way for the popularization of Neo-Confucianism; disciples of Wang Yang-ming literally took to the streets to teach the universal applicability of the Way of the sages.[50]

If Wang Yang-ming's identification of knowledge with action and his affirmation of dynamic action in daily life implicitly bring all forms of honest work under the umbrella of the sagely Way, *The Romance of the Three Teachings* makes it explicit. Self-cultivation in *The Romance* is self-improvement through morally responsible activity, including work. Wang Yang-ming's notion of *liang-chih* seemed to obviate the need for a formal classical education as a prerequisite to sagehood, although Wang himself stressed the importance of learning. His iconoclastic follower Li Chih (1527–1602) went further to argue that novels are better than the Classics or history as a means for learning about real values.[51] P'an Ching-jo seems to have taken Li Chih at his word; he wrote a novel about the moral struggles of everyday life as his way of transforming the world. Moreover, the story suggests that the Classics are ineffective as the direct basis of popular pedagogy; to teach real people, religion must deal with the problems of real life in terms accessible to the people.

Finally, as we have seen, *The Romance of the Three Teachings* espouses a view of religion as the management of moral resources that both reflects and develops

[48] See Hayes, *The Hong Kong Region, passim.*

[49] See David E. Kelly, "Sect and Society: The Evolution of the Lo Sect among Grain Tribute Fleet Boatmen, 1700–1850," presented at "Orthodoxy and Heterodoxy in Late Imperial China."

[50] See deBary, "Individualism and Humanitarianism," pp. 171–179.

[51] See deBary, "Individualism and Humanitarianism," p. 196.

the Ming morality book movement. By making explicit and developing the analogy of management of moral capital, *The Romance* reveals the mentality behind the morality book movement and its deep roots in the highly commercialized urban culture of the Southeast. We see here the seeds of a religiously based work ethic not unlike the Calvinist ethic in the West.

The Romance valorizes work as a vehicle of self-improvement and self-cultivation. It espouses realistic and carefully planned strategies for getting ahead that would work through the family and network of human associations. It encourages family cooperation in property matters, especially giving adult sons an opportunity to work for the family's future. The novel deals with the costs of competition and risk, and gives advice for dealing with sudden successes and failures without abandoning traditional values. It encourages the saving and earning of money so long as obligations to family and neighbors are not forgotten. It seeks a balance between the individual and family obligations, wealth and traditional values, self-interest and generosity.

The religious attitude of the novel, then, affirms basic Chinese values while at the same time encouraging behaviors and strategies suited to coping with a highly competitive urban world. Viewing religion as the management of moral capital stresses the practical and concrete side of religion, and adapts ancient values to the perceptions, attitudes, and concerns of a particular segment of late Chinese popular culture.

EIGHT

Values in Chinese Sectarian Literature: Ming and Ch'ing *Pao-chüan*

Daniel L. Overmyer

"For every household there is a road to Ch'ang-an." — (Chin-kang ching k'o-i pao-chüan)

INTRODUCTION

Of the many different types of Chinese vernacular literature one was developed primarily in popular religious sects. These voluntary associations first appeared in their late traditional form in the Yuan dynasty (1271–1368). They were characterized by a predominantly lay membership and had their own forms of leadership, hierarchical organization, scripture texts, mythology, and rituals. The earliest extant texts related to these groups are Buddhist in origin and orientation, though with some Taoist and Confucian elements. These books date from the first half of the Ming dynasty (1368–1644).

However, from the beginning, sectarian groups were subject to strong influence from a popular religious tradition that emphasized healing, divination, exorcism, and other pragmatic values and rituals. In texts we have from the mid-sixteenth century, these pragmatic values are more in evidence, together with mythological themes of Taoist origin.[1]

The generic name for Ming and Ch'ing sectarian scriptures is *pao-chüan*, "precious volumes," though several other terms are used as well. In style, these texts alternate between prose and seven- or ten-character rhyming verse. The verses sum up each prose section and introduce the next. The typical *pao-chüan* begins with pictures of deities or characters important in it, short verses invoking blessings on the emperor and realm, one or more prefaces, and a table of contents. The text itself opens with the title of the first chapter, a "psalm of praise while offering incense," and a prose section. There are one or two *chüan*, with in some cases twenty-four or more divisions (*fen*) or sections (*p'in*). At the

---

[1] For a recent description of the sectarian context of these books, see my article, "Alternatives: Popular Religious Sects in Chinese Society," *Modern China* 7.2:153–190 (April 1981). See also my book, *Folk Buddhist Religion: Dissenting Sects in Late Traditional China* (Cambridge, Mass.: Harvard University Press, 1976).

end there may be a note on the reprinting, and a list of donors with amounts contributed by each. Variations occur in this structure, but enough constants remain for a book of the *pao-chüan* type from any period to be quite easily recognizable.

Needless to say, this continuity of structure does not necessarily mean similarity of content. The *pao-chüan* form was employed by those who wished to communicate religious teachings or moral lessons at a popular level. Though such writers were aware of and consciously followed the *pao-chüan* type, any discussion of the "development of *pao-chüan* literature," of course, reflects our perspective, not that of participants in the tradition.

There are different subtypes of *pao-chüan*, which can be roughly distinguished by content and/or date of production. The earliest texts containing the term *pao-chüan* in at least some versions of their titles are vernacular discussions of orthodox Buddhist teachings and hero tales. However, their structure does not fully conform to that outlined above. The dates of extant texts of this type are unclear, but we know that they appeared in some form before 1500, because they are quoted in early sixteenth-century *pao-chüan*. They were composed by Buddhist monks.

The second type of *pao-chüan* was begun by the sectarian leader Lo Ch'ing (1443–1527), who used this form to expound his own doctrines. In the process he quoted a variety of earlier Buddhist scriptures. The third type first appears later in the sixteenth century, clearly indebted to Lo Ch'ing in style and orientation, but exhibiting different religious content. Many of these late Ming books are centered on the myth of a mother creator, which is not a part of Lo Ch'ing's teachings. Lo Ch'ing's books are a mosaic of quotations from other texts, but *pao-chüan* of the third type rarely employ quotations. They establish the characteristic style and content of sectarian texts from the Ming on. It was this type that was used by the "*sütra*-recitation sects" discussed by Susan Naquin in this volume.

The fourth type of *pao-chüan* has a more literary character, and is dominated by long stories about the struggles and victories of moral persons who in the end attain salvation. There is no doubt that the majority of these stories were first published as *pao-chüan* in the late nineteenth century. They represent a stage when this genre was losing contact with sectarian history, and becoming a form of didactic literature concerned as well with entertainment. Many of these books were produced by local publishers as commercial ventures. Not every story *pao-chüan* is late, however. In some cases the story line goes far back in the history of Chinese drama and vernacular literature; in others the story *pao-chüan* itself first appeared long before the nineteenth century, as in the case of the *Hsiang-shan pao-chüan* and the *Liu Hsiang pao-chüan* discussed below. The values of this type of *pao-chüan* are similar to those of the moralistic seventeenth-century novel discussed in this volume by Judith Berling. However, this one-hundred-chapter novel is of course very different in form, and appears to be more Confucian in its orientation than these story *pao-chüan*.

By the nineteenth century, another form of text was employed for the exposition of mythology and ethical injunctions, believed to be composed by direct revelations from deities and spirits through *fu-chi*, spirit writing with the planchette. Popular religious sects continued to be active, but now some of their books appeared in the *fu-chi* form, with scores of ethical injunctions from specific deities. This spirit-writing tradition began during the Sung dynasty (960–1279), and was practiced by both literati and commoners. By the seventeenth century, this method was used to produce books of moral teachings.

Scattered references to a sectarian use of spirit writing appear before the nineteenth century, but they refer to it as a source of divination and medical prescriptions, not as a means of composing books. The earliest sectarian book I have yet encountered, which is a collection of *fu-chi* revelations, is the *Yü-lu chin-p'an* [Golden basin of the jade dew], published in 1880, but with references in the text to revelatory activity earlier in the century. I call this text "sectarian" because it is used as revered scripture by popular religious groups in Taiwan, and because its teachings are based on the late Ming sectarian myth of a saving mother deity. From the *Yü-lu* on, if not before, *fu-chi* texts became important carriers of sectarian teaching, and still play this role in Taiwan.

Though doctrinal content varied, the ethical values of sectarian literature remained fairly constant from the Ming dynasty on. They were a combination of popularized Buddhist and Confucian principles within a framework of karmic retribution. That is to say, the explicit ethical injunctions of these texts are basically orthodox and traditional. In this orientation, *pao-chüan* and *fu-chi* texts are agreed. It could be argued, however, that some of the implicit values of these books are not in full accord with established family-centered principles. The earlier *pao-chüan* in particular assume the equality of men and women, rich and poor, noble and humble in the perspective of a socially transcendent principle, such as the "Limitless," or the "Venerable Mother" of mankind. We need to remember that the texts we are discussing are the literary expression of voluntary associations that cut across family lines.

A utopian theme in some late Ming *pao-chüan* encouraged some of these associations to try to create their own states or safe areas, in the name of Maitreya, the future Buddha, using military force if necessary. However, in the *fu-chi* texts eschatological tension is resolved, for in them Maitreya has already come, and the third age of the world has dawned. The chief sign of this new dispensation is direct revelations from the gods.

With the exception of the egalitarianism and utopian hope of late Ming *pao-chüan*, values in Chinese sectarian literature are quite conservative. In Taiwan today, this literature continues to be a bearer of traditional principles, ideas, and language in a rapidly changing world. As an expression of popular attitudes and beliefs, such writings should be given serious consideration in our attempts to understand China, past and present.

This paper is a discussion of the values expressed in *pao-chüan*—that is, what they represent as important and worthwhile in the proper living of human life.

For the most part, such values are explicitly stated in ethical injunctions and comments concerning rewards or punishments to be sought or avoided. In addition, there are implicit values in these texts, ones not clearly stated but nonetheless assumed to be important. This paper attempts to deal with both the explicit and implicit values.

Since this study is about values, it does not deal extensively with the history, language, and style of these popular texts, which I have discussed in earlier studies, and which in the case of *pao-chüan*, Sawada Mizuho has dealt with at length. However, since for the most part these books are as yet little known, I have in each case included some information about the text itself and its basic ideas or story line.

This article summarizes the values of two presectarian books of the *pao-chüan* type to indicate the immediate textual background of Lo Ch'ing's writings. There follows a section on the social context of this literature, and a more detailed discussion of values in the second, third, and fourth types of *pao-chüan* mentioned above, sectarian and literary, each illustrated by a representative text.

SECTARIAN *PAO-CHÜAN*: THE TEXTUAL BACKGROUND

The earliest extant text related to a Chinese popular religious association is the *T'ai-p'ing ching* [Scripture of great peace], which was used by proto-Taoist groups in the second century A.D.[2] Anna Seidel has discussed other Taoist texts that reflect the ideas of popular movements.[3] Though there were a number of predominantly lay associations in the first centuries of Chinese Buddhist history, I have not yet come across clear evidence that they produced their own texts. Popular Manichaean groups, however, possessed texts with distinctive titles, as described by a report in the early twelfth century.[4]

In a recent article, I have suggested that the characteristic early modern

[2] Max Kaltenmark, "The Ideology of the *T'ai-p'ing ching*," in *Facets of Taoism: Essays in Chinese Religion*, ed. Holmes Welch and Anna Seidel (New Haven: Yale University Press, 1979), pp. 19–52.

[3] Anna K. Seidel, "The Image of the Perfect Ruler in Early Taoist Messianism: Lao-tzu and Li Hung," *History of Religions* 9.2–3:216–247 (November 1969/February 1970).

[4] Samuel N. C. Lieu, *The Religion of Light: An Introduction to the History of Manichaeism in China* (Hong Kong: Centre of Asian Studies, University of Hong Kong, 1979), pp. 29–30. In a recent study, E. Zürcher describes Buddhist texts from the sixth century A.D. that were evidently produced in China. They include language about the coming end of the world that is similar to that of late Ming *pao-chüan*. One text criticizes monks and asserts that they will be the last of eight categories of people to be saved. Though the social origin of these books is unclear, there is enough evidence to permit Zürcher to say that "we are dealing with beliefs and movements that (1) primarily belong in the sphere of *lay* religion, and (2) are operating on a local scale." E. Zürcher, "Prince Moonlight: Messianism and Eschatology in Early Medieval Chinese Buddhism," *T'oung Pao* LXVIII, 1–3 (1982), pp. 39–44, 47. Hence, it is possible that the production of texts by predominantly lay groups began in the sixth century.

form of sectarian association appeared in the White Lotus school (Pai-lien tsung) during the Yuan dynasty. The popular wing of this school blended Buddhism together with a variety of Taoist practices aimed at health, sexual vitality, and long life. An early fourteenth-century account by a Buddhist monk named Yu-t'an P'u-tu (d. 1330) describes adherents' beliefs in some detail, and in the process mentions the names of two scriptures composed by this group, the *Chen-tsung miao-i kuei-k'ung chi* [The returning to emptiness collection of the excellent purport of the true school] and the *Ta-mo hsueh-mai chin-sha lun* [The golden sand discourse of the blood tradition of Bodhidharma]. P'u-tu's discussion is based in part on these texts, particularly the *Chen-tsung miao-i ching*. His account stresses circulation of the vital force, prognostication, medicinal practices, and anticlerical attitudes.[5]

The oldest extant texts of the early modern sectarian tradition were written by a lay Buddhist named Lo Ch'ing in the first decade of the sixteenth century. These books became scriptures of the Lo chiao (sect) or Wu-wei chiao. Lo Ch'ing's texts in turn were based on early Ming Buddhist penance texts, amplifications of *sūtras*, and stories of religious heroes. Some of the books he quotes are called *chüan* or *pao-chüan*, but they appear to have been composed by orthodox monks to amplify Buddhist teachings and thus are not carriers of sectarian teachings per se.

Lo Ch'ing cites a variety of sources in his books, including such *sūtras* as the *Heart*, *Diamond*, *Nirvāna* and *Hua-yen* (*Avatámsaka*). The values of these *sūtras* are of course those of orthodox Mahāyāna Buddhism, with its combination of wisdom and compassion. They are all concerned in various ways with liberation from the sufferings of birth and death through the attainment of enlightenment.

I have two of the presectarian *pao-chüan* quoted by Lo Ch'ing, the *Hsiang-shan pao-chüan* and the *Chin-kang ching k'o-i pao-chüan*, both in Ch'ing editions. The copy of the *Hsiang-shan pao-chüan* in my possession is of an edition published in Ch'ien-lung 38 (1773), at Hangchow.[6] This edition, in one *chüan* with 130

---

[5] Overmyer, "Alternatives."

[6] The original text of this edition is owned by Yoshioka Yoshitoyo 吉岡義豊, who published it in *Dokyō kenkyū* 道教研究 [Taoist studies], vol. 4, ed. Yoshioka and Michel Soymie (Tokyo, Henkyōsha 辺境社, 1971). The title given is *Kuan-shih-yin p'u-sa pen-hsing ching* 觀世音菩薩本行經 [The *sūtra* of the deeds of the bodhisattva Kuan-yin (Avalokitésvara)]. In the Ch'ing colophon it is called *Hsiang-shan pao-chüan* 香山寶卷. Yoshioka lists twelve editions printed in the Ch'ing and early Republican periods (pp. 118–119), while Li Shih-yü 李世瑜 in his *Pao-chüan tsung-lu* 寶卷綜錄 [A general bibliography of *pao-chüan*] (Shanghai: Chung-hua shu-chü 中華書局, 1961), pp. 56–57, lists ten, in twenty-one reproductions, including six in manuscript, all dating from 1850 to 1934. The titles given by Yoshioka are all called *ching* 經, and begin with Kuan-yin or Kuan-shih-yin, but give *Hsiang-shan pao-chüan* as an alternate title. In the *Pao-chüan tsung-lu*, all but two of the texts listed have the name Hsiang-shan in their titles, with the most frequently reprinted title being the *Ta-ch'eng fa-pao Hsiang-shan pao-chüan* 大乘法寶香山寶卷 [The Fragrant Mountain *pao-chüan*, dharma jewel of the great vehicle].

leaves, begins with a picture of Kuan-yin robed in white, seated, and attended by two acolytes. There follow an homage to the emperor ("10,000 years to the present emperor, 10,000 times 10,000 years!"), and an undated preface by a monk named Hai-yin. The preface, in classical Chinese, praises the breadth and unfathomable wonder of the Buddhist Way, which brings benefit, protection, and blessings for unending *kalpas* (eons).

The text itself begins by listing its editor and compiler, distributor, reviser and transmitter, all described as Buddhist monks. The editor is given as the Ch'an Master P'u-ming of T'ien-chu (in modern Chekiang). The introduction gives the date of P'u-ming's work as Sung Ch'ung-ning 2 (1103).

The *pao-chüan* opens with an introduction describing its origin and purpose, and then proceeds to the story of a young princess named Miao-shan, who, after a long struggle, becomes enlightened and discovers that in fact she is Kuan-yin. This story in effect provides mythic background for the cult of Kuan-yin of 1000 eyes and arms, who sees and aids all.

Elsewhere, I have summarized the story on which this text is based, and discussed antecedents going back to the beginning of the twelfth century.[7] In 1978, Glen Dudbridge published a whole book on this topic, *The Legend of Miao-shan*, in which he demonstrates that though the story did not become well known until about 1100, there are references to it as early as 667. Though the *pao-chüan* version was subject to some later modifications, Dudbridge notes corroborative external evidence for the 1103 date provided by the text itself, and concludes that, "What emerges is ... a sense of internal preservation through a tradition." Thus, he discusses the *Hsiang-shan pao-chüan* in his category of texts composed before 1500.[8]

At the level of values, this book portrays a contest between two different understandings of filial piety, traditional Chinese and Buddhist, this-worldly and transcendental. Princess Miao-shan is the third daughter of a king with no sons, who tries to force her to marry in order to provide him with a son-in-law and descendents. She, however, decides to become a nun, for which after much bitterness she is eventually executed. However, she is resurrected by the gods and proceeds to heal her father of a loathsome illness by donating her own eyes and arms to make medicine for him. In the end she saves her whole family and is revealed to be the bodhisattva Kuan-yin. Thus, though at one level she is unfilial because she refuses to obey her parents' injunction to marry, at another level this disobedience becomes an essential precondition for her own enlightenment, which in turn gives her the power to deliver others. The highest value in this text is salvation through rebirth in Amitābha's Pure Land. The chief proximate values are devotion to the symbols and teachings of Buddhism, courage in maintaining religious ideals, compassion, service, and forgiveness.

[7] Daniel L. Overmyer, "*Pao-chüan*: Types and Transformations" (unpublished paper, 1978), pp. 7–14.

[8] Glen Dudbridge, *The Legend of Miao-shan* (London: Ithaca Press, 1978), pp. 10–50.

At the level of practice, this *pao-chüan* encourages celibacy, meditation, recitation of Amitābha's name, and vegetarianism. Perhaps the most important implicit value is that women also can be saved in this present life, and can even become religious heroines of the highest order. We shall see that this theme continued to be influential in *pao-chüan* literature.

The most important *pao-chüan* source for Lo Ch'ing—he cites it regularly—is the *Chin-kang ching k'o-i pao-chüan* [The precious volume amplifying the *Diamond sūtra*], which may go back to Sung times.[9] The *Chin-kang k'o-i* is in one *chüan* with thirty-two divisions (*fen*). After three leaves of introductory discussion it proceeds to quote Kumārajīva's translation of the *Diamond sūtra*, one section at a time. Following each quoted portion there is a prose explanation, called *pai*. This is followed by a short question, called *wen*, which in turn is succeeded by an answer, *ta*, in paired lines of seven character verse. Whereas the *sūtra* is in Buddhist classical Chinese, the amplification contains many vernacular constructions. It is thus not surprising that the majority of Lo Ch'ing's citations are from the amplification, not the *sūtra*.

This book is based on a combination of Ch'an and Pure Land Buddhism, with an emphasis on attaining enlightenment through realizing the Buddha-nature within. This nature is in turn equated with Amitābha and the Pure Land of the West, though in some passages a more literal spatial imagery seems still to be present. The key to transcending the insubstantiality and fleetingness of life is to attain a nondual perspective, based on the inner potential for attaining Buddha cognition that is shared by all beings. Thus, all are promised deliverance.

The basic teaching of the *Chin-kang k'o-i* is indicated by the following passages:

... the illusory body does not last long, the floating world is not firm. (p. 130a)

* * *

Some follow the wrong path of spiritual discipline and do not examine the meaning [of this text]; they do not recognize that the enlightened *bodhi* nature is complete in each [being]; everyone is able to understand the good roots of wisdom. Do not ask about degrees of enlightenment; stop differentiating between those who remain in the household life and those who leave it, do not adhere to [the difference between] clergy and laity. One needs only to understand that in the mind there is fundamentally neither male nor female; why must one cling to outer form? (p. 130b)

* * *

[9] There is an 1835 edition of this text in *Hsu Tsang-ching* 續藏經 129:129b–144, edited by a monk named Chien-chi 建基. This book appears to have been composed by a monk named Tsung-ching 宗鏡, whose name is in an introductory section. In his *Zōho Hōkan no kenkyū* 增補寶卷の研究 (Tokyo: Kokusho kanko kai 国書刊行会, 1975), pp. 101–102, Sawada Mizuho 澤田瑞穗 discusses a Ming edition of this book, written by Tsung-ching of the Sung. I have not been able to determine Tsung-ching's dates. *K'o-i* 科儀 here refers to a text that amplifies and explains a *sūtra*.

Do not seek afar off for the Buddha on Spirit Vulture Peak (Ling-shan), for this
peak is in your own mind. Everyone possesses a Ling-shan pagoda. . . . (p. 131a)

*   *   *

Question: "Where does the Tao mind manifest itself?"
Answer: . . .
    Everyone possesses the Pure Land of the West;
    Do not in error devote yourself to what has already appeared [in the
outer realm].
    If superior beings and good people see into their natures,
they stand
    side by side with Amitābha Buddha. (p. 132a)

*   *   *

Every step and everything is the Way.
Amitābha never lived in the West.
The dharma body fills all the 3000 worlds. (p. 133a)

*   *   *

Poverty, wealth, nobility and humble position are all like a dream.
When one awakens from this dream he returns [to true understanding]. (p. 133b)

*   *   *

In the dharma there is neither high nor low. Therefore, sentient beings in the
minds of the Buddhas constantly attain the Way, apart from "self" and "other."
And, the Buddhas in the minds of sentient beings with every thought realize the
true. So, to recite the Buddha's name does not block meditating, and meditating is
no obstacle to reciting the Buddha's name, to the point that one recites without
reciting and meditates without meditating . . . [and] thoroughly understands the
Pure Land of mind only (*wei-hsin Ching-t'u*). (p. 140a)

*   *   *

For every household there is a road to Ch'ang-an. (p. 140a)

*   *   *

Here it is made clear that all can attain deliverance directly and easily,
because such deliverance is simply a matter of insight into the true nature of
one's own mind. Buddhahood consists essentially of a detached attitude, an
attitude that brings acceptance and peace. This being the case, conventional
Buddhas depicted in images and mythology are simply symbols of what we have
the potential to become. This perspective is egalitarian; there is no justification
for distinctions based on social or religious status, wealth or sex. There is no
need to adopt a celibate life style in a monastery, to worship Buddhas imagined
to be in some other realm, or to spend years in arduous meditation.

Lo Ch'ing seized upon these teachings with great enthusiasm and much
repetition. It is instructive to realize that this father of the early modern

sectarian scriptural tradition was strongly influenced by a text with such an egalitarian point of view, made to order for a lay leader speaking to ordinary people.

The chief value of the *Chin-kang k'o-i* is salvation as spiritual freedom; it is a doctrinal text that contains very little discussion of ethics. Of course, Buddhist morality is assumed, but the emphasis is on going beyond the duality and merit-building this morality implies. Thus, the texts that formed the immediate background of the sectarian *pao-chüan* tradition were sober popularizations of orthodox Buddhism, with an overriding emphasis on spiritual deliverance. Lo Ch'ing continued this emphasis, but was more concerned to put forward a doctrinal position of his own, distinguished from a variety of competing points of view.

THE SOCIAL CONTEXTS OF *PAO-CHÜAN* LITERATURE

The immediate social context of *pao-chüan* literature from Lo Ch'ing on is that formed by the popular religious sects discussed in my 1976 book and in articles and papers mentioned in the notes for this chapter. For the most part, members of these groups were from the middle to lower levels of prestige, wealth, and literacy. The majority were lay persons, though a few were Buddhist monks. We have noted that the earliest *pao-chüan*, such as the *Hsiang-shan* and *Chin-kang k'o-i*, were written by such monks, and that monks edited and commented on Lo Ch'ing's scriptures. Historical accounts of the Lo chiao and other sects frequently mention monk participants, though their level of literacy is not always clear.[10]

During the late Ming, some sects received high-level support from court eunuchs, officials, and the wives of officials, as Sawada Mizuho has emphasized. Some of the *pao-chüan* from this period were printed in an elaborate style by the Nei-ching ch'ang, a government office for printing Taoist and Buddhist texts. However, as the Ch'ing government consolidated its control, the sects were more effectively suppressed, and thus cut off from support by the wealthy and powerful. During the eighteenth and nineteenth centuries, some of these groups were forced to operate in a clandestine manner, for the mere possession of their own scriptures could lead to arrest and punishment. Hence, production of *pao-chüan* declined, and many of the books that remained were confiscated and burned.[11] Susan Naquin's work has done much to clarify the social situation of the sects in this period,[12] and to indicate their changing relationship to the *pao-*

---

[10] Overmyer, *Folk Buddhist Religion*, pp. 113–115, 162–176; Daniel L. Overmyer, "Boatmen and Buddhas: The Lo chiao in Ming Dynasty China," *History of Religions* 17.3–4:284–288 (February/May 1978); Overmyer, "*Pao-chüan*," pp. 15–21.

[11] Sawada, *Hōkan*, pp. 35–38.

[12] Susan Naquin, *Millenarian Rebellion in China: The Eight Trigrams Uprising of 1813* (New Haven: Yale University Press, 1976), pp. 31–49. See also Professor Naquin's essay in this volume.

chüan tradition. One suspects that the decline in the production of these books, discussed by Sawada Mizuho, is related to the transition between the two types of sects that Naquin discusses in her contribution to this volume (chapter 9). The "Trigram" groups did not emphasize scripture texts, in part because *pao-chüan* were less readily available and possession of them was so dangerous.

The question of audience arises naturally here. For whom were these books written? Who recited and distributed them? There is some internal evidence bearing on these questions, particularly in the lists of donors of contributions for the expenses of printing that are appended to *pao-chüan*. The basic fact to keep in mind is that all *pao-chüan* were written not for an educated clergy, but for lay people at a variety of social levels. These books began as popularizations of Buddhist *sūtras* and hero stories. From Lo Ch'ing on, *pao-chüan* were written in the vernacular. Later texts incorporated more and more popular deities, themes, and tunes; terms and characters from operas also appeared in them.[13] These books were recited in small group settings, from a sectarian worship service, to a room in the women's quarters, to the corner of a busy market. Thus, their audience included nonliterate persons, as Susan Naquin indicates.

Perhaps the most distinctive internal evidence regarding audience in *pao-chüan* is their frequent direct address to "pious men and women," and their denial of the validity of sexual distinctions in the quest for salvation. This is particularly true for Lo chiao texts, but later sectarian scriptures also promise salvation to the "sons and daughters of the Venerable Mother beyond life and death." The point is that here women are included; they are an integral part of the religion, as was the case to some extent in orthodox Buddhism as well.

Nor were women slow to respond. Historical accounts emphasize the presence and equality of women in popular sects from the thirteenth century on. By the nineteenth century, some *pao-chüan* texts were produced specifically with women in mind, and women had a role in their preaching and distribution (*hsuan-chüan*).[14] So it was that in China as well as Europe there was, in the words of Keith Thomas, an "association of women [with] small religious sects." As Thomas writes,

> Women seem to have played a disproportionate role in the history of mysticism and spiritual religion. Almost all the mediaeval sects from Manichaeans to the Waldenses, the Donatists to the Cathars, received to a marked degree the support of women, and welcomed them, sometimes as influential patronesses, but more often ... as active members on a basis of practical equality ... it is hardly surprising that women were attracted to those groups or that form of religion which offered spiritual equality, the depreciation of educational advantages, and

[13] Overmyer, *Folk Buddhist Religion*, pp. 182–183; Sawada, *Hōkan.* pp. 50–51.
[14] Overmyer, "Alternatives"; Overmyer, *"Pao-chüan"*, pp. 31–38; Sawada, *Hōkan*, pp. 65–66, 81–85.

that opportunity to preach or even hold priestly office which they were otherwise denied. . . .

The same factors must have operated among the women of the Civil War sects (that is, the Baptists, Quakers etc. of seventeenth century England).[15]

These factors operated among Chinese women as well. I have discussed before the pious lay donors of Lo sect texts, who by their contributions hoped to gain merit for all.[16] In his *Hōkan no kenkyū*, Sawada Mizuho has a chapter on the spread, printing, and distribution of *pao-chüan* that discusses in some detail evidence provided by lists of donors at the end of some texts. He begins with the example of the *Mantra of the spiritual influence of Kuan-yin* [*Kuan-yin ling-kan chen-yen*], a short verse invocation of only fifty-four characters published in the Ming Hung-chih period (1488–1506). Fourteen donors of thousands of copies of this broadsheet are listed for a period of about one hundred and seventy years, beginning with a Yuan censor from Chi-nan, who contributed a thousand copies in gratitude for a pardon. Other donors included pious women, a provincial inspector, a military officer, and a eunuch. Sawada points out the *pao-chüan* were longer and more difficult to reprint than this short text, so that those who produced them had to rely on wealthy contributors, as had been the case with Chinese Buddhist texts from the beginning.

Sawada also discusses two *pao-chüan* published in 1584 by the West Ta-ch'eng sect in Shun-t'ien prefecture of Chihli. The printing of this text was supported by a number of Ming officials, aristocrats, and their wives, while the prefaces for both texts were written by Chiang Chien-yuan, Marquis Who Pacifies the West, Chief Military Commissioner of the Vanguard Army.

Sawada provides evidence of high-level support for *pao-chüan* printing from a variety of other texts as well, including those of the Hung-yang sect, which were also published through connections with officials and eunuchs. Some of these officials were associated with the Nei-ching ch'ang, so it seems likely that the Hung-yang chiao texts were printed there as well.

Sawada then suggests that severe investigation of the sects during the Ch'ing made it impossible for them to maintain such powerful connections, and that funds for publishing *pao-chüan* in the eighteenth century had therefore to come from more donors with less money. He discusses a K'ang-hsi period (1662–1722) text, which provides a list of forty-seven donors from Ho-chien fu in Chih-li, none of them officials or wealthy people. Fifteen of these contributors were women. Sawada describes in addition a Ch'ien-lung period (1736–1795) text reprinted in 1909 to which is appended a fifty-six-page list of the names of more than 1600 donors from Hopei and Shansi. The largest contribution listed is five silver dollars, with others as small as twenty-five cents.

---

[15] Keith Thomas, "Women and the Civil War Sects," *Past and Present* 13:42–62 (April 1958).
[16] Overmyer, *Folk Buddhist Religion*, pp. 115–116.

From the mid-Ch'ing on, many *pao-chüan* were printed or reprinted by morality book publishers, usually "on demand" from those who wished to gain merit by distributing such texts. Both Sawada and Li Shih-yü provide long lists of the names and locations of these book shops, most of them located in East China—Shanghai, Hangchow, Soochow, Ningpo, and so on. Of course, local sects continued to publish their own books as well. Sawada goes on to describe the mass reprinting of more than two hundred *pao-chüan* in Shanghai during the Republican period.[17] All this evidence, of course, tends to support Evelyn Rawski's thesis that functional literacy was widespread in the Ming and Ch'ing periods.[18]

The audience for *pao-chüan* thus ranged from officials and eunuchs to sect members and a variety of ordinary folk. Perhaps variations in this audience explain in part the differences of *pao-chüan* style and content. For example, as there are no explicitly sectarian references in the *Chin-kang k'o-i*, its audience may have been adherents of a monastery, clerical and lay, some with enough education to understand the relatively abstract language of this text. Lo Ch'ing's many references to Buddhist scriptures indicate that he must have had a teacher learned in Buddhism; no doubt these references were appealing to the monks among his followers as well. Later sectarian texts do not quote scriptures in this way.

In texts of the Hung-yang sect, mentioned above, there is praise for saints who in fact were eunuch supporters of the sect at court. However, the clearest evidence of the role of audience is the attention given to women in a number of *pao-chüan*. As Sawada emphasizes, women played a substantial part in the printing and dissemination of these books from the beginning, until by the late nineteenth century the special role of *pao-chüan* reciter (*hsuan-chüan che*) was often filled by women, many of whose listeners were female as well. From the early twentieth century there is even evidence for the recitation of these texts in brothels on festival days.[19] In other words, it appears that by this time women had come to play a very important role in the *pao-chüan* tradition, and, as we shall see below, this role is reflected in the texts. On the other hand, some spirit-writing texts in the nineteenth and early twentieth centuries were produced and distributed by local officials and military men. The influence of this social setting can be seen in the conservative Confucian values of these books and in their very traditional injunctions to women.[20] In sum, it is obvious that *pao-chüan* were influenced by their immediate social contexts, an issue that could be

---

[17] Sawada, *Hōkan*, pp. 70–80; Li Shih-yü, *Pao-chüan tsung-lu*, "Introduction," pp. 10–13.

[18] Evelyn Sakakida Rawski, *Education and Popular Literacy in Ch'ing China* (Ann Arbor: University of Michigan Press, 1979). See also her article in this volume.

[19] Sawada, *Hōkan*, pp. 85–86.

[20] For a discussion of spirit-writing texts and their values, see David K. Jordan and Daniel L. Overmyer, *The Flying Phoenix: Aspects of Chinese Sectarianism in Taiwan* (Princeton, N.J.: Princeton University Press, 1985).

examined in more detail in a study of the relationship of particular texts to the history of the sects that produced and used them.[21]

VALUES IN THREE TYPES OF *PAO-CHÜAN*, SECTARIAN AND LITERARY

The first of the four types of *pao-chüan* literature mentioned at the beginning of this essay comprises texts such as the *Chin-kang k'o-i* discussed above. In this section, I discuss one major text from each of the latter three types, beginning with the *P'o-hsieh hsien-cheng yao-shih chüan* [The key to refuting heresy and making truth manifest], c. 1509, by Lo Ch'ing.

Lo Ch'ing was a literate lay Buddhist (*chü-shih*) from Chi-mo County near the eastern tip of Shantung who served for a time in a garrison near Peking. Military service was an hereditary occupation in his family. Autobiographical passages in the texts he wrote tell us that he meditated and practiced religious austerities for thirteen years before reaching enlightenment, after which he "preached the dharma to save others," and wrote his texts "to enable you to escape suffering in the realm of birth and death, and obtain eternal salvation, never to return." Some of Lo's disciples evidently worked among grain canal boatmen, because it is chiefly in their ranks that his religion spread to Chekiang, and from there all over China. We do not know with whom Lo studied, or where he obtained the many texts he quotes, but judging from the contents of his work his source may have been a Ch'an monk. In any event, it is Lin-chi monks who later commented on his scriptures. Statements by Lo Ch'ing and his followers, as well as evidence from external sources, indicate that the Lo sect was an independent tradition, conscious of its own integrity, at first distinct from other popular sects. However, with the rise of many other groups in the late sixteenth century, there was some blending of more radical traditions with the Lo chiao, at the levels of both organization and teaching. Though this group began as popular Buddhism, in the history of sectarian movements it appears as an important "ancestral" tradition, whose beliefs and scriptures were appropriated by later groups, often with different interpretations. Lo Ch'ing served as a model to later sectarian leaders who wanted to teach and gain adherents through texts they themselves wrote. Partly because

---

[21] However, the relative importance of female protagonists in *pao-chüan* may also be related to female roles in earlier Chinese literature, particularly in Yuan operas. In several of these dramas, particularly those by Kuan Han-ch'ing 關漢卿, women have the most interesting and important parts, and are exemplars of moral courage. On this see, for example, "Injustice Done to Tou Ngo" in *Six Yüan Plays*, trans. Liu Jung-en (Harmondsworth, Eng.: Penguin, 1972), and other opera texts in Yang Hsien-yi and Gladys Yang, trans., *Selected Plays of Kuan Han-ching* (Peking: Foreign Languages Press, 1958). See also Wang Shih-fu, *The Romance of the Western Chamber*, as translated with this title by T. C. Lai and Ed Gamarekian (Hong Kong: Heinemann Educational Books [Asia], 1973). For this information I am indebted in part to Jennifer Parkinson, a graduate student in the Department of Asian Studies, University of British Columbia.

of this association, the Lo sect was proscribed in the late sixteenth century as just another heretical religion (*hsieh-chiao*), though it continued to exist until the twentieth century.

Lo Ch'ing, or Lo Tsu (the Patriarch Lo), wrote five *pao-chüan*, commonly called the *wu-pu liu-ts'e*, "five books in six volumes," because one of them was in two *chüan*. Sect adherents wrote commentaries on these texts in the late sixteenth and mid-seventeenth centuries, and the works were reprinted as late as the nineteenth century. I have described these books in some detail elsewhere,[22] and have summarized the teachings of one of them, the *Cheng-hsin ch'u-i wu hsiu cheng tzu-tsai pao-chüan* [The precious book concerning the (truth) which is self-existent, needing neither cultivation nor realization, which rectifies belief and dispels doubt].[23]

The *P'o-hsieh* text is in two *chüan*. I have two editions, first the text alone, collated and verified by Lo Wen-chü in 1615. This edition has only the first *chüan* in eleven sections (*p'in*). It is elegantly decorated, with pictures of saints and Buddhas, dedicatory verses, and an appeal for long life for the emperor. There follows a table of contents with chapter titles in full, each beginning with the character *p'o*, "to destroy" or "refute."

The introductory portion of *chüan* one begins with four five-character verses: "heretical teachings (*hsieh-fa*) are confused and chaotic, [but] emptiness is free from fetters. If one does not use a key to open up [confusion], where can one escape from birth and death?"

Then follows, "to benefit both self and others, on behalf of bodhisattvas both clerical and lay, this text refutes heresy and makes realization [truth] manifest," after which there is a section expressing gratitude for the kindness of emperors and officials, the various Buddhas, and Hsuan-tsang (here called the "T'ang monk") who brought back scriptures from India. At the end of this introduction emperor and officials are promised Buddhahood and unending merit if they "protect the Buddhist dharma (*hu Fo fa*)." The first section begins with prose quotations from the *Diamond sūtra* and the *Sūtra of Complete Enlightenment*. After eight lines of prose the dominant pattern of ten-character verse begins, arranged in two sets of three characters, with one of four. This alternates with occasional sections of verse in two seven-character lines. The other sections follow this basic pattern of several lines of prose at the beginning, followed by ten-character verse.

My other edition of the *P'o-hsieh* text is a commentary edition in four *chüan*, with the complete text. It begins directly with title and table of contents; each chapter heading is followed by an explanatory ode. The chief object of criticism

[22] Overmyer, "*Pao-chüan*," pp. 15–24. See also Richard Hon-chun Shek, "Religion and Society in Late Ming: Sectarianism and Popular Thought in Sixteenth and Seventeenth Century China" (Ph.D. diss. University of California, Berkeley, 1980), pp. 155–251.

[23] Overmyer, "*Pao-chüan*," pp. 20–24; Overmyer, "Boatmen and Buddhas," pp. 285–287; and Overmyer, *Folk Buddhist Religion*, pp. 114–129, 232.

is any form of externalized piety that does not understand the fundamental emptiness and unity of all things, and therefore abides in false distinctions, such as that between laity and clergy, (*tsai-chia/ch'u-chia*). Other views attacked are those stressing recitation of Amitāhba's name, quests for immortality or supernatural powers, and so on. Chapter Six criticizes reliance on meditation, and attacks the White Lotus sect for its political ambitions, techniques of "circulating *ch'i*," emphasis on prognostication, rituals of burning paper, and veneration of non-Buddhist deities, including the sun and moon. None of these practices leads to enlightenment and escape from *saṃsāra*.

The thought of the *P'o-hsieh chüan* is based on that of the *Chin-kang k'o-i*, with its emphasis on transcending all dualities. Lo Ch'ing quotes long sections of the earlier text almost verbatim, including some of those translated above. To these he adds supporting material from other books, linked together with his own comments in verse form. This style of composition served to keep Lo close to his orthodox Buddhist sources, and distinguishes his work from earlier texts such as *Chin-kang k'o-i*, which amplify only one scripture.

The primary value of the *P'o-hsieh chüan* is spiritual freedom and independence, *tzu-tsai* (in Sanskrit, *Íśvara*), which Lo combines with the term *tsung-heng* "vertical and horizontal" or "in all directions," for him meaning to move everywhere without spiritual impediment. This freedom in turn is based on the capacity for salvation that all possess in the mind; if one will only turn within to this Buddha mind, then salvation is assured, *saṃsāra* transcended, and all false obstructions and dichotomies left behind. This simple "restoring the mind" (*hui-hsin*)[24] is all that is needed; everything else is misleading activism (*yu-wei fa*). Hence, Lo Ch'ing extols at length a nonactivist approach, *wu-wei fa*, which gained for his sect the name Wu-wei chiao.

All this provides little comfort for those looking through the *P'o-hsieh chüan* for clear-cut ethical injunctions; on the contrary, Lo Ch'ing explicitly and repeatedly denies the validity of conventional ethical distinctions, including that between good and evil. For him, all forms of charity and piety are inferior to enlightenment because they remain within the self/others duality of *saṃsāra*. As Lo affirms in a quotation from the *Chin-kang k'o-i*,

> There is no self and no other; sentient beings accomplish true realization by themselves . . . (1 : 26; section two). You should not settle [reside] anywhere (*ying wu so chu*); be an independent person (*tzu-tsai jen*). You should have no place to reside; manifest the brilliant light [of your true nature]. . . . honor independence (*tu wei tsun*). . . . To reside in anything is the path of *saṃsāra*; you should not be fixed anywhere; [thus you will] cut off birth and death and forever break away from *saṃsāra*. . . . Activist methods are precisely the high road to birth and death. (1 : 48–50; section four)

---

[24] *Hui-hsin* 回心, "to turn the mind around" can mean "to repent," but in Lo Ch'ing's usage indicates returning or restoring the mind to its true nature.

This is so because such methods are oriented toward gaining merit or avoiding demerit, which is still in the realm of concern for self. For Lo Ch'ing, "there is basically no merit at all in doing good and no demerit in doing evil" (1:89; section seven) (*hsiu shan yuan wu kung-te; tso e i wu tsui-kuo*). Lo Ch'ing does not flinch from the radical implications of this position:

> With neither words nor wonderful teachings, be independent (*tsung-heng tzu-tsai*). Turn things upside down, be established by yourself. Only when the good is bad and the bad good does one attain self-sufficiency. Only when white is black and black white is one independent everywhere.... Sweep away the 10,000 phenomena to become independent wherever you are. (1:27; section two)

Lo Ch'ing accepts the orthodox Buddhist teaching that the *devas* (gods) dwelling in the heavens are still tied to *samsāra*, however joyous they may be for a time. Since rebirth in Heaven is an essential part of the conventional merit system, he points out that even for the most exalted beings such rebirth leads nowhere:

> Although all of the *devas* are joyous, they are not liberated; when the merit of the ten kinds of immortals is exhausted, they return to *samsāra*. (1:90; section seven)

All of this leads to repudiation of conventional ethics.

> You yourself are a brilliant light; if you do not preserve it, from heaven above you will be reborn and enter darkness. Those who preserve it of themselves manifest a brilliant light. When you enter birth and death, the light is extinguished. The true precepts of the self are beyond birth and death; if you maintain [the conventional] precepts you will enter into *samsāra*. The five precepts and the ten forms of goodness are the path of birth and death; those who cling to doing good fall into *samsāra*.... The true precepts of the self are the Western Land. (1:40–41; section four)

These same strictures apply to ordinary religious practice, which is lost in the world of sense and form. So, Lo Ch'ing writes of

> pitiful religious practice which knows not the root, so that when birth and death come there is no way to escape. (1:46; section four)

* * *

> How pitiful to love darkness while sitting in meditation; a drunken man who binds himself up is not independent and sits until morning for nothing. (1:79; section six)

So it is with the "fruits of the Way," arduous discipline, leaving the household life, remaining at home, repairing monasteries, reciting scriptures, becoming a Buddha, carrying out rituals, bowing to false images (*pai chia hsiang*).... All are to be rejected because they lead one astray on exterior paths, away from the source of enlightenment within (1:84–85; section six). Thus, ethical values are subordinated to the quest for ultimate deliverance.

As one can see from such material, this rejection of conventional religious practice includes charity, which has been an expression of Buddhist devotion from the beginning. Lo Ch'ing, citing the *Sūtra of Complete Enlightenment* [*Yuan-chueh ching*], writes, "To fill up the 3000 great worlds with seven kinds of precious jewels, and distribute them in charity is not so good as one sentence of wonderful significance" (1:9; section one). The "sentence of wonderful significance" refers to the mind as the foundation of enlightenment. Elsewhere in the *P'o-hsieh chüan* we read,

> To distribute wealth is *samsāra*, not deliverance.... To bestow drink and food saves life for one day; to bestow precious jewels, money and goods supplies the needs of a lifetime, but increases entanglements. To preach salvation is called bestowing the dharma; with this one can cause all living things to escape the way of the world.... To distribute wealth is what ignorant men love; to bestow the dharma is what the wise love. (1:97; section eight)

*   *   *

> One should not abide in material charity. (1:101; section eight)

All this is the case because "the true precepts are the original nature" (1:117; section nine), and this "original nature is precisely the true Three Jewels" (Buddha, dharma, sangha) (1:42; section four). So Lo reminds his readers,

> You yourself are originally old Amitābha. (1:85; section six)

*   *   *

> Recognize that you yourself are heaven. (1:57; section five)

*   *   *

> Recognize that all the Buddhas assemble in oneself; the realms of all the Buddhas are in the mind. (1:42; section four)

Lo Ch'ing was thus convinced that the way to salvation did not lie in external observances of any sort. For him the whole realm of ordinary piety is relative, including maintaining a vegetarian diet and reprinting *sūtras*; all of this is but "manipulating puppets" (1:20; section nine). However, this radical antinomian language is not in the interest of license but of salvation. As Lo writes, "If people are not yet enlightened they should not seize upon these words to act in disorderly ways; [if they do], at death they will certainly see Yama [lord of the underworld] and only with difficulty avoid being boiled in a cauldron and ground up in a mill [punishment in purgatory]" (1:89; section seven).

In other Lo chiao texts, Buddhist ethics are strictly enjoined, particularly vegetarianism, while the Buddhist precepts are correlated with such Confucian virtues as filial piety and cohumanity (*jen*). But even in these sources it is clear that such principles are to be informed by faith and are seen as leading toward the liberation of all beings from *samsāra*. The effectiveness of action depends upon its intention; as we read in the *Cheng-hsin pao-chüan*, "if a fisherman remembers the mind he returns Home; a vegetarian who does not believe in the Buddha returns to fall into *samsāra*."[25]

Lo Ch'ing thus taught an internalization of religion and ethics in a lay sectarian context, where he made available the quest for individual enlightenment long advocated by the Ch'an and Pure Land traditions. It was along these lines that his attack on conventional piety seems to have been understood, with the result that the Lo chiao tradition became known for its communities of earnest religious devotees. For the most part, the radical implications of ethics made relative do not seem to have been drawn; however, I have encountered two brief historical accounts that indicate that some Ming Wu-wei groups rejected image worship and veneration of ancestors.[26] De Groot also indicates that Wu-wei congregations in nineteenth-century Amoy did not use images.[27]

Mahāyāna Buddhist philosophy has criticized conventional piety from the beginning because it is based on the assumption that one can earn one's own salvation as a reward for good deeds. This assumption is ego-centered, and simply replaces attachment to worldly success with attachment to religious practices, both of which miss the point of Buddhism, the attainment of an enlightened and selfless perspective. Buddhist leaders have long supported conventional ritual and ethical teachings as a means of communicating with people at a level they can easily grasp. While it is understood by the intellectuals that this level should be transitional and temporary, in fact it has been the mainstream of popular Buddhism for centuries. Lo Ch'ing's contribution is his insistence within Chinese popular culture that enlightenment can be sought directly, without compromise—that his own followers can attain the highest goals of Buddhism. The universal potential for enlightenment had long been proclaimed by both Confucianism and Buddhism, but discussions of how to attain such enlightenment directly were intended for the most part for an elite

[25] Overmyer, "*Pao-chüan*," p. 23.

[26] The first of these accounts is by Fan Lien 范濂 in his *Yün-men chu mu ch'ao* 雲門據目抄, preface dated 1592, *chüan* 2, p. 7a in *Pi-chi hsiao-shuo ta kuan* 筆記小說大觀 (Taipei: Hsin-hsing shu-chü 新興書局, 1962), vol. 1, p. 1272. "The Wu-wei chiao 無爲敎 puts aside Buddha images and incense offering and does away with them. When parents die, they do not perform sacrifices for them" (*fu-mu chih sang, pu tso chi-hsiang* 父母之喪, 不作祭享). The second reference is from Chu Kuo-chen 朱國禎 (1557–1632) in his *Yung-ch'uang hsiao-p'in* 湧幢小品, introduction dated 1619, 32:13, in *Pi-chi hsiao-shuo ta-kuan*, vol. 2, p. 2120. Chu discusses a Fukien sect leader "whose title was Wu-wei" who ordered people to sell all their possessions in order to offer them to the multitudes. "He said, 'chaos is about to arrive. Their ignorant rustic (*sic*) possessions are all your possessions.'" He prohibited people from sacrificing to ancestors and spirits with a view to breaking their [family] loyalties. They sacrificed only to the sect head."

[27] J. J. M. De Groot, *Sectarianism and Religious Persecution in China* (Amsterdam: Johannes Muller, 1903), vol. 1, pp. 183–185.

of literati and monks. Lo Ch'ing's innovation was to proclaim this old truth in a new social setting. The significance of a statement such as "recognize that you yourself are Heaven" is that here it is directed toward an audience of merchants, artisans, and farmers. The statement promised that at least in the realm of religion they could be masters of their own fate. The problems of anxiety and fear of death that beset them could be solved, because in the perspective of enlightenment there is no self to be threatened by hostile forces, and at death one departs forever from *samsāra* and all its ills.

To represent the third type of *pao-chüan*, I will discuss the values of the *Ku Fo T'ien-chen k'ao-cheng Lung-hua pao-ching* [The Dragon Flower precious scripture, verified by the Old Buddha T'ien-chen], 1654, which Sawada Mizuho calls the "*Lotus Sūtra* of heretical texts."[28] This *Lung-hua ching* is one of the most important sectarian scriptures of the seventeenth century, and later writings derived from it vocabulary and mythological themes. Late Ming texts represent a new and innovative stage of *pao-chüan* development, with a new mythological framework. As I have discussed before, the belief system of these books centers on Wu-sheng lao-mu, the Eternal Venerable Mother, and her children Fu-hsi and Nü-kua, whose union produces mankind. At first, human beings lived in a paradisal condition, but they gradually fell from grace, so that now all but a few are "scattered and lost." This "fall" is conceived of spatially as well: the original and true home of men and women is the Eternal Mother's paradise in the West, but now they live in the "Eastern Land," the "red dust" world of *samsāra*, devoted to avarice and lust, forgetful of their true nature. Wu-sheng lao-mu in her compassion weeps for her children, and sends down gods and bodhisattvas to rescue them. The chief means of this saving message is the *pao-chüan*, which remind men and women of their true origin, and provide the devotional and ritual means to return to their "real home" (*chia-hsiang*). In this mythological context, the *pao-chüan* call upon those who hear them to believe, and become members of the sects to which the texts are related. For this some of them provide membership rituals, stories that tell of sect founders who are among the Eternal Mother's messengers, and assurances that at death those with the proper talismans will be welcomed in Heaven.

This is all given more immediate social relevance by the connection made in some of these texts between the Eternal Mother and Maitreya, the future Buddha, who is described as one of her envoys. Maitreya is in turn related to a three-stage cosmic time scheme of Buddhist origin in which the power of the Buddha's teaching progressively declines. In sectarian mythology, the last period of the "decay of the dharma" is imminent or already upon us, and just at this time Maitreya will appear, bringing with him the promise of a new world. As was true in orthodox Indian Buddhist texts, Maitreya's arrival is intimately

---

[28] Sawada Mizuho 澤田瑞穗, *Kōchu haja shoben* 校注破邪洋辯 ["A detailed refutation of heresies," with corrections and commentaries] (Tokyo: Dōkyō kankō kai 道教刊行会, 1972), p. 164.

associated with the reign of a world emperor. Some Chinese popular sects identified their founder or leaders with both Maitreya and the new emperor, and rose up in the name of this potent combination of beliefs. Sect members were promised comfort, wealth, and office in the new world, if they would but give their allegiance and support now. Thus, adherence to the Eternal Mother cult could offer both individual and communal hope, either at death or in one's own lifetime.

All of this is presented in a Buddhist framework, and with much Buddhist terminology, but in relation to the thought of earlier *pao-chüan* an important transposition has taken place. Deities from Chinese popular religion are mentioned in early texts such as the *Hsiang-shan pao-chüan*, but always in a minor and supporting role that reminds one of the role of Indian gods in the Pali *suttas*. In the *Hsiang-shan* text Buddhist concepts, Buddhas and bodhisattvas are dominant throughout; Shang-ti, the supreme deity, orders gods and animals to aid Miao-shan in the nunnery or manifests himself as an old man to show her the way to Fragrant Mountain, but all of this is to assist a thoroughly Buddhist figure on her way to enlightenment. In the Lo chiao texts, popular deities are mentioned as well, but always in a subsidiary position. In fact, direct appeal to them to meet immediate needs is condemned as heretical.

In the late Ming *pao-chüan*, this relationship between Buddhism and popular religion is reversed, for here it is deities of popular origin that are dominant, particulary Wu-sheng lao-mu. It is she who orders bodhisattvas to descend to the world with her message of deliverance; her paradise in the K'un-lun mountains has absorbed many of the characteristics of Amitābha's Pure Land; chanting her mantra, *chen-k'ung chia-hsiang wu-sheng fu-mu* ("Eternal Progenitor in our real home in the realm of true emptiness") has to a large extent replaced reciting Amitābha's name. In addition, there are references in these and other sources to sectarian practices of meditation, charm writing, and magic, all of popular Taoist origin.[29]

The earliest dateable text known to me that discusses this mythology is the *Huang-chi chin-tan chiu-lien cheng-hsin kuei-chen huan-hsiang pao-chüan* [Precious book of the golden elixir and nine lotuses of the imperial ultimate (which leads to) rectifying belief, taking refuge in the real and returning to the native place]. In the summer of 1981, I found a copy of this text in Peking that was printed in 1523. (See the comments on it by Susan Naquin in this volume). A detailed study of this book must wait for a later time, and in any case, the *Lung-hua ching* describes the Eternal Mother mythology in more detail.

The *Lung-hua ching* is ascribed to a sect leader named Kung Ch'ang, who is understood to be a reincarnation of the Old Buddha, T'ien-chen, in turn a transformation of the Venerable Patriarch Chen-wu, the Buddha of Measureless Life (Wu-liang shou Fo), and Amitābha himself. Kung Ch'ang

---

[29] Overmyer, "*Pao-chüan*," pp. 26–27.

lived in central Hopei Province, in Ts'ao-ch'iao kuan of modern Kao-yang County. Through careful investigation, Sawada Mizuho has determined that Kung Ch'ang founded a sect called the Yuan-tun chiao (Religion of complete and instantaneous enlightenment) in 1624, after receiving instruction from Wang Sen (d. 1619) of Shih-fo k'ou in Hopei, the leader of the Ta-ch'eng chiao (Mahāyāna sect). These were both sects of the "Sūtra recitation" type discussed by Susan Naquin in chapter 9. In the following years, Kung Ch'ang traveled about preaching and gathering disciples, so that by the mid-1630s his sect was well established. During his travels, he collected various religious books, on the basis of which he began to write a scripture for his own sect in 1641. This task was completed by his disciples, who published the *Lung-hua ching* in 1654. Sawada traces this book back in part to a ritual penance text, the *Ku Fo T'ien-chen shou-yuan chieh-kuo Lung-hua pao-ch'an* [The Dragon-flower precious penance, the results of restoring wholeness by the Old Buddha T'ien-chen], which was offered to the throne by a Buddhist monk in 1599.[30]

I have earlier discussed the lengthy extracts from this text included by Huang Yü-p'ien (fl. 1830–1840) in his *P'o-hsieh hsiang-pien* [A detailed refutation of heresies], 1834. My comments here are based on a Japanese description and translation by Sawada Mizuho, who has two copies of the *Lung-hua ching*, reprinted in 1917 and 1929.[31]

The *Lung-hua ching* is in four *chüan* with twenty-four *p'in* (sections). It is composed in a combination of prose and seven- and ten-character verse, and includes a number of invocations for inviting the gods, purifying the mind and body, and so on. An introduction to the text reads in part,

> The Unborn [Mother] says, "This *Lung-hua pao-chüan* is from the time when creative chaos was first divided, before the beginning of things, when the Old Buddha T'ien-chen opened up the precious storehouse of the native place [paradise], took out this *Lung-hua* true scripture and transmitted it to later generations to save both men and gods. [Thus he sought] to recover all the ninety-six myriads of the children of the imperial womb, that they might return home, recognize the patriarchs (*tsu*), penetrate to the origin, return to the source and attain eternal life." (p. 168)

The basic mythological framework of the text is as described above. Section one, "*Hun-tun ch'u-fen*" [Creative chaos first divided], describes how the Old Buddha of the Limitless T'ien-chen first appeared by transformation within creative chaos to establish Heaven and earth. Before the beginning there was no Heaven and earth; no sun or moon; no above, below, or four directions; and no seasons. Then, in an obscure and mysterious way, pure and impure were distinguished, and in a period of 5048 years the true vital force of the prior realm was made complete. With a slight movement, an apex (*chi*: focal point of order)

---

[30] Sawada, *Kōchu*, pp. 192–212.
[31] Overmyer, *Folk Buddhist Religion*, pp. 135–138: Sawada, *Kōchu*, pp. 164–218.

was born as if in an egg; vital force was gathered together and its forms were completed. From within true emptiness, a shaft of brilliant light burned forth, and within this light a golden body appeared. It was the Old Buddha of the Limitless T'ien-chen. Forming an interwoven precious network with inexhaustible transformations, he skillfully established the earth and the universe (p. 169).

A verse at the end of this section reads,

> The Old Buddha T'ien-chen divided the chaotic origin. From within an egg an apex was produced which transformed the prior realm. Mountains and water were joined together; the light was glistening and pure. One vital force flowed throughout, and the myriad phenomena became manifest. (p. 170)

This creation account is continued in section two, where "True Emptiness" (*Chen-k'ung*) is equated with "the Unborn" (*Wu-sheng*). This Wu-sheng as a mother gave birth to a son and daughter, *yang* and *yin*. They were Li Fu-hsi and Chang Nü-kua, the ancestors of mankind.

The Old Buddha T'ien-chen invited Wu-sheng lao-mu, who was in the Tushita palace of the Great Imperial Heaven (a reference to the paradise of Maitreya), to talk with him, and they arranged the marriage of Nü-kua and Fu-hsi.

In their marriage, *yang* and *yin* were incarnated as a man and woman. The woman became pregnant, and gave birth to ninety-six myriads of children of the imperial womb. Wu-sheng lao-mu ordered these numberless children to live in the Eastern Land (the earth):

> The children, receiving the Venerable Mother's decree, went to the Eastern Land, wearing precious gems and crowned with brilliant light. Since they possessed their original divine nature, they freely travelled about [between heaven and earth?] and did not dwell in a fixed place. . . .
>
> Later the Venerable Mother took the light from their heads, withdrew the five colors from their bodies and removed the two wheels from under their feet, and decided that the children would remain in the Eastern Land. Wu-sheng lao-mu in the Native Place looked out on her children, and commanded them saying, "You have gone to the Eastern Land, and act in a negligent way day and night; if you think of your parents, return immediately to Ling-shan of the Native Place and receive blessing in front of the Old Buddha." However, one day the children in the Eastern Land, confused in this dusty world, attached to wine, sex, wealth and material things, forgot their original divine nature, and until today are still drowned in the sufferings of *samsāra*. [Lao-mu] looking on this from afar was unbearably grieved, and called on the people of the origin to awaken. She sent them a letter, calling the children of the Eastern Land to return, to meet together in their Dragon Flower assemblies at their home, to restore the original number of ninety [sic] myriads. (p. 170)

Wu-sheng lao-mu assembled all the gods and Buddhas to decide who would descend to earth with her message of deliverance. The Old Buddha T'ien-chen was chosen, and was reborn as Kung Ch'ang (pp. 170–171). Other deities were sent down as well, for the time was late, and the end of this corrupt age was soon to come. As we read in section eighteen, "The people of the last age" [*Mo-chieh chung-sheng*]:

> One day the Venerable Patriarch Kung Ch'ang was quietly sitting on his meditation bed, and entered *samādhi*. Manifesting his "emptiness body," he went to the Tushita Palace of the Native Place, where he had an audience with Wu-sheng lao-mu. Lao-mu asked Kung Ch'ang, "In the lower world there are omens of coming natural disasters. Are you familiar with them?"
>
> Kung Ch'ang replied that he was not. Lao-mu said, "In the *chia-tzu* year of the lower *yuan* period, disasters will arrive; in the *hsin-chi* year there will be famine, drought and floods. The people of Shantung will starve to death while they eat each other; husbands and wives will not look after each other, and fathers and sons will be divided. When they move to northern Chihli, they will again meet with famine and die."
>
> Kung Ch'ang asked Lao-mu, "When will it become easier to live?" The Mother replied, "In the *jen-wu* year things will be a little better, but again calamities will occur, mountains will shake, the earth will move, the Yellow River will overflow and people will drown. There will be a plague of grasshoppers, a dark rain will fall continually, houses will collapse, and there will be no place to dwell. These disasters of the last age, formed by bad karma accumulated for 500 years, are deserved and brought by people on themselves, so there is no way of escape. In the *kuei-wei* year there will be an epidemic."
>
> Kung Ch'ang asked, "What should one do to be saved from these disasters?" The Mother said, "For people who sincerely believe there will be no calamities; for those who cultivate the Way, there will be no difficulties." (p. 183)

The text goes on to describe spirits who protect the "imperial children," and provides invocations and meditation exercises for warding off danger. It is made clear that only those who adhere to the teachings of this text will be saved from the catastrophes marking the end of the era. The *Lung-hua ching* thus promises aid in this life as well as salvation after death through re-uniting with the Venerable Mother in paradise. Five (sic) "Dragon Flower assemblies" are promised in this text, great eschatological reunions of gods and men, modeled on assemblies of the Buddha Maitreya. At each of these meetings some of the Mother's children return home (pp. 168, 185–186).

Here again, then, the basic value is religious salvation, a new form of life after death, described in mythological terms and accompanied by promises of relief from present dangers. Though *Lung-hua ching* mythology is not in accord with orthodox beliefs, its ethical teachings are a combination of conventional Buddhist and Confucian principles. These teachings are to a large extent presented in a negative way, by listing evils to avoid. We have seen above that attachment to wine, sex, wealth, and material things brings disasters, and that one aspect of the calamities to come will be alienation of family members. Other causes for celestial punishment include ingratitude for kindness, wasting food, cutting up silk gauze, failing to reverence Buddhism, destroying images of gods and Buddhas, being unfilial, not living in harmony with relatives, and despising the good (p. 187). During Kung Ch'ang's quest for enlightenment he saw that, "the people of the world were given to sexual indulgence and competing for fame and profit, and he sighed because they had lost their true nature" (p. 171).

At a more positive level, the ethical values of this text are presented through the image of Ju-t'ung Fo, the "learned youth Buddha," who rides around on horseback preaching Buddhism. This Ju-t'ung Buddha is a reincarnation of Confucius. In the context of advocating the harmony of the Three Teachings, our text has the following to say about this interesting figure:

> When the Sage [Confucius] established his teaching, he proclaimed the Way while travelling about on horseback. Later, the Buddha Ju-t'ung appeared in the world; he was a manifestation of the Sage who travelled about on horseback to preach the Way. Going round to all the states he converted the ignorant, and was considered a worthy. He called on the people of the world to maintain a vegetarian diet and recite the Buddha's name, to reform evil and turn toward the good.
>
> However, it was the last age, and people's minds were evil and deceitful, with all sorts of artifices; there was not one good man in a hundred. So, the gods of heaven became angry, and sent down the three calamities and eight forms of distress; sentient beings were treated cruelly but did not awaken. Now the last age draws closer and closer, and peoples' lives are in danger.
>
> As the Venerable Old Buddha could not bear this, he sent down the Buddha Ju-t'ung to descend to the world, to save all people and reform their formerly wicked minds. Thus, for the first time the wind and rain were harmonious, the nation prosperous, and the people secure, waiting only for the Buddha to come to restore wholeness. The various schools and sects go to the Dragon-flower assembly, and the [teachings of the (?)] patriarchs and teachers of each sect can also be gathered together in the *Lung-hua* book. (p. 184)[32]

This section continues by saying that Lao-chün (Lao-tzu) saves Taoist immortals and priests, Śākyamuni, monks and nuns, and Confucius, lay households. Confucius is assisted in the task of salvation by seventy-two followers, including Tzu-lu, Yen-hui, Tseng-tzu, and Meng-tzu (p. 185).

From this material we can see that the chief implicit value of this text is the restoration of lost unity, in particular the unity of the family of humankind. It is

---

[32] The sectarians did not invent this image of Confucius as an itinerant Buddhist preacher. In the *Hai-lu sui-shih* 海錄碎事, preface dated 1149, by Yeh T'ing-kuei 葉廷珪, there is a reference to a Ju-t'ung p'u-sa 儒童菩薩 (bodhisattva) in a quote from the *Ch'ing-ching fa-hsing ching* 清淨法行經, a Chinese Buddhist text now lost. In this passage we are told that the Buddha sent three disciples to China to preach. The first was the "Ju-t'ung Bodhisattva, otherwise known as K'ung Ch'iu" 孔丘, the second Yen Hui 顏回 (an historical disciple of Confucius), and the third Lao-tzu 老子. The *Ch'ing-ching* text is not dated here, but was clearly in existence by the twelfth century. This reference is in *chüan* 13, first section, pp. 1770–1771 in vol. 3 of a Taipei, 1969 reprint of a 1598 edition of the *Hai-lu*.

a promise of collective paradise and immortality in which the sufferings of this life no longer occur.

The fourth type of *pao-chüan* is characterized by long and complex stories illustrating karmic retribution and the value of religious living. I have thirty-one such texts, all reprinted in the early Republican period. Except for the *Ho Hsien-ku pao-chüan*, which opens with an invocation to Taoist immortals, these texts all begin by invoking the presence of Buddhas and bodhisattvas and promising to the pious blessings and long life. All those that are complete end either with a summary of the moral lessons of the story or with assurances of salvation in Amitābha's paradise. The endings of several include both. These books are all composed with the familiar alternation of verse and prose sections, with the verse in rhyming seven-character lines. Though they may employ some terms derived from sectarian mythology, these story *pao-chüan* do not appear to be sectarian in origin or content, but rather are vehicles of more generalized morality and piety, published for profit by religious book houses, as is discussed above.

The stories in all but four of these texts involve the families of government officials, usually of high rank, or those of wealthy merchants. The tales are set in the distant past, usually the T'ang, Sung, or Ming dynasties, though one purports to go all the way back to the Han. For the most part, the characters are located in time and space, though in a stereotyped and obviously fictional style. Seventeen of these books begin with basically the same story line, that of a wealthy and pious official (or merchant) and his wife, who have everything they want except a child. They proceed to beseech the gods and Buddhas for a child, through both ritual offerings and acts of benevolence. Eventually, as a reward for their faithfulness, the wife, usually beyond normal child-bearing age, is miraculously made pregnant. The resulting child, usually a boy, turns out to be a model of intelligence and responsibility who cares for his parents through becoming a high official. An alternative pattern is for a girl child to become a Buddhist nun who in the end leads her parents to salvation. In some cases the child is in fact the incarnation of a deity or bodhisattva. There can be many obstacles on the path to success, but these stories all have happy endings. They are intended to illustrate that goodness brings its own reward.

Of the remaining fourteen texts, three deal with family situations in which there is only one son or daughter. Here the initial problem is to find a proper wife or husband. Another three stories describe the struggles of orphans to survive, succeed, and continue the family line. Other main characters include a ten-year-old orphan girl, the slave of a wealthy family, an old man who wishes to leave the household life to become a monk, and a crown prince in hiding whose rightful place has been usurped by the son of a rival concubine. Thus, twenty-six of the thirty-one tales are concerned with family life and its preservation. Female protagonists form a significant minority.

The ethical perspective of these books can be illustrated by passages from two of them. First, let us look at a closing summary and exhortation (*ch'üan-shih wen*) from the *Chin Pu-huan pao-chüan*: "The Chin family were old and had no sons; fortunately they did many good deeds, [and] to constantly do good is to save one's life. . . . Heaven does not turn its back on good people, and gave them a son to continue the family line. They had this son when they were fifty years old."

Then follows a list of moral exhortations to ten types of people, each illustrated by a character in the story.

1. Officials: "bring about good order for all the people; do not covet wealth, or injure others."
2. The wealthy: "aid the poor," remembering that the "spirits are three feet above your heads" [and watching what you do].
3. Scholars: "study industriously; there are rooms of gold in books; don't worry about being poor. If you study with all your might for ten years why fear that your name will not appear on the notice board [with the names of those who have passed the civil service examinations]? Look at the son of the Yang family [in the story] who gained great merit and a position at court."
4. Merchants: "be fair in business transactions, and you will become rich. Just devote yourself to your business; doing good does it no harm."
5. Young people: "be filial and obedient to your parents. Filial children always obtain a good reward."
6. Old wives: "if you have children, you must teach them the correct principles of behavior, and must not allow them to idly roam around."
7. Young wives: "record in your hearts the 'three obediences' [to father, husband, and son] and the 'four womanly virtues' [right behavior, proper speech, proper demeanor, proper employment]. Be obedient to your parents and in-laws; you also want to become a mother-in-law. If your husband doesn't act properly, you should urge him [to change his ways]."
8. Unmarried daughters: "read the *Classic of Female Sages* (*Nü-sheng ching*); obey your parents, study needlework, never go outside to stand in front of the gate. Look at the girl in the story who followed these precepts and married the son of the Yang family."
9. The licentious: "never reap any good rewards, but just sorely harm their bodies and minds." [Here the example is given of an evil man in the story who goes to purgatory.]
10. Those who go out to work in the world [lit. "go out the gate"]: "to seek wealth, profit and fame; they just bring calamity on themselves."

The specific moral acts that bring rewards are conveniently listed on the first page of the *Lan-ying pao-chüan*. They are to

- print morality books (*shan-shu*) to exhort the multitudes;
- collect paper with writing on it;
- respect the five grains;
- repair bridges and roads;
- provide vegetarian food for Buddhist monks;
- repair temples;

- give money to the poor;
- buy and release living creatures in the spring;
- provide cold tea for travelers in the summer;
- provide aid for orphan souls in the autumn;
- give wadded clothing in the winter, thus forming good karma;
- maintain a vegetarian diet and diligently recite the Buddha's name;
- concentrate with one's whole mind on attaining Buddhahood or immortality.[33]

A discussion of similar values may be found in Judith Berling's contribution to this volume (chapter 7). We see here a combination of traditional Chinese values with those of popular Buddhism, so that aid for the living and dead not only expresses compassion, but brings saving merit to the donor as well. Most of these injunctions are self-explanatory, but perhaps one should add that releasing living creatures is an old Buddhist practice for demonstrating nonviolence and gaining good karma. Orphan souls in purgatory have no living families to look after them, so ritual offerings on their behalf show compassion, relieve their sufferings, and encourage them not to bother the living. Maintaining a vegetarian diet has, of course, been a Buddhist ideal from the beginning as a symbol of nonviolence, a sign of dedication, and a means of gaining merit. The sense of moral causation in Buddhism gives coherence and direction to ethical actions, so that they benefit both giver and receiver. This combination of values no doubt gave the *pao-chüan* a wider appeal.

The text I have chosen as an example of this type of story text is the *Hui-t'u Liu Hsiang pao-chüan* [The Liu Hsiang *pao-chüan*, illustrated], for which the full title is *T'ai-hua shan Tzu-chin chen liang-shih hsiu-hsing Liu Hsiang pao-chüan ch'üan chi* [A complete edition of the Liu Hsiang *pao-chüan* of Tzu-chin town of Mt. T'ai-hua, (which deals with) two lifetimes of spiritual discipline], two *chüan*, reprinted in Shanghai, 1930. Chou Tso-jen describes an edition printed in 1870 for which the printing blocks were preserved in the Shanghai city-god temple.[34] The summary and excerpts he presents are in accord with the 1930 text. Li Shih-yü lists twenty-one editions of this book, published from 1774 to 1930 or later, all but the first dating from the nineteenth and twentieth centuries.[35] Glen Dudbridge discusses it under the title "A charter for celibacy," as part of a "whole class of *pao-chüan* [which explore the fate of] pious women at odds with their secular destiny." He suggests that such books were closely related to small communities "specially dedicated to the maintenance and welfare of women pursuing a life of celibacy and vegetarianism,"[36] as I discuss in more detail below. Professor Dudbridge also understands Liu Hsiang

---

[33] Overmyer, "*Pao-chüan*," pp. 32–34.

[34] Chou Tso-jen 周作人, *Kua-tou chi* 瓜豆集 (Kowloon: Shih-yung shu-chü 實用書局, 1969; first published in 1937), p. 45.

[35] Li Shih-yü, *Pao-chüan*, pp. 27–28.

[36] Dudbridge, *Miao-shan*, pp. 85–89. Celibacy in Buddhism is a symbol of high dedication to cutting off the sensual desires that bind one to the wheel of rebirth.

nü, the heroine of our text, as part of the tradition of such figures initiated by the story of Miao-shan, which is introduced near the beginning of this essay. Hence, though the *Lui Hsiang pao-chüan* is certainly representative of the type of literary *pao-chüan* that became more popular in the nineteenth century, it derives from an earlier tradition and may have had connections with sectarian groups composed of women.

The book opens with a promise of the blessings that flow from listening to it: "When the *Liu Hsiang pao-chüan* is first opened, the various Buddhas and bodhisattvas all descend and draw near, and as pious men and women everywhere listen sincerely, their blessings and life span are increased, and calamities dissipated."

The story begins as follows:

> It is generally known that the *Liu Hsiang pao-chüan* first appeared in the Shao-yuan reign period of the Sung emperor Chen-tsung (r. 998–1023).[37] In Tzu-chin town of Mt. T'ai-hua in Shantung there was a man named Liu Kuang who from birth was correct and upright, with his mind and nature fair and just. His ancestors from of old were a family of loyal and generous good persons, who provided vegetarian feasts for monks and bestowed alms. In more recent times, because of poverty Liu Kuang's family ... had opened a restaurant, for which they butchered pigs and served wine. It was a business in which they did evil at every turn.
>
> Liu's wife was a very generous and kind woman of the Hsu family, good and compassionate. The two of them lived together in harmony and affection, [yet] though they were close to forty, they had no children. Fortunately an auspicious star drew nigh, and [Liu's] wife became pregnant. In no time ten months passed, and she gave birth to a girl.
>
> At the time of the baby's birth there were many auspicious phenomena, while music and a strange fragrance filled the room.... Her face was like the full moon, her appearance was dignified, and her parents were very happy. They named her Hsiang nü (Fragrance).
>
> *   *   *
>
> By the time Hsiang nü was six or seven years old she understood the need to maintain a vegetarian diet. She was filial and obedient to her parents, who loved her as much as if she were a precious jewel. Time passed quickly; soon she was ten *sui* old, good, generous, modest, peaceful, humane, and filial, not lustful or avaricious. With a compassionate mind she recited the Buddha's name.
>
> Near her home there was a convent for nuns called the Fu-t'ien an. In this convent there was an old nun whose religious name was Chen-k'ung, who meditated every day. She had cultivated her mind and realized the Way. On the first and fifteenth of the month she preached about Buddhist dharma and karma, to convert men and women. Many came to hear her and all who did praised and reverenced her, and were convinced.

[37] There was no Shao-yuan reign period in the Sung dynasty, so this date reference is either in error or deliberately fictional.

One day while sitting in the shop, Fragrance saw a large number of men and women going by carrying incense and candles. She asked her parents where these old gentlemen and ladies were going, and her father replied that they were going to the Fu-t'ien convent to hear the old nun preach. (*chüan* 1, p. 1a)

Fragrance prevails on her mother to take her to the convent, where they hear a powerful sermon about karmic morality, salvation, and the toils of woman-hood. The girl is deeply impressed, and upon returning home convinces her father to become a pious Buddhist, give up butchering, and open a vegetarian restaurant. This new enterprise prospers, time passes, and soon Fragrance is fifteen.

Now, in the town there is a rich and powerful man named Ma Hsin, who has three sons. He is not a Buddhist, and likes to kill things. One day Ma and his sons stop at the restaurant after a hunting trip, and Ma is impressed by Fragrance's beauty. He asks that she be betrothed to his youngest son, Ma Yü, and without thinking, Mr. Liu agrees.

Almost a year later Ma Hsin sends a go-between to draw up a marriage contract. However, Fragrance refuses the gifts she brings, and asks that Ma Yü come in person. This he does, and she says that she will marry him if he agrees to ten moral conditions (described below). He is a good man, and assents.

Soon afterwards, Hsiang nü's parents die of illness, and after a period of mourning she marries Ma Yü. Problems begin as soon as she moves into the Ma household: her two sisters-in-law are jealous of the attention she receives and persistently slander her to their mother-in-law, who is nasty but bides her time.

Fragrance asks her husband what he does with his time, and sharply criticizes him when he replies that he is studying for the civil service exami-nations. She says, "What's the use of reading books? . . . It's better to study the Way; profit lies therein. To be an official for one life is to gain enemies for 10,000 lifetimes. I am pointing out to you the path to the Western Land. I urge you, husband, to take the earliest opportunity to practice spiritual discipline" (*chüan* 1, p. 8b).

When this conversation is reported to Ma Yü's mother she is enraged, and orders her son off to school, forbidden to see his wife. He sadly takes leave of Fragrance, who says he should obey his mother, and thinks to herself that it is appropriate for the husband to study while the wife recites the Buddha's name.

With Ma Yü gone, his mother summons Fragrance, berates her, and orders her henceforth to work in the kitchen. When she refuses to cook game, she is put to tending the stove; this she does, chanting Buddhist tunes all the while. (The song texts are provided.)

Fragrance is twice beaten senseless by her mother-in-law for singing and having a religious influence on the other servants. She is then banished to work in a vegetable garden, but is beaten again for hiding a rabbit from the two older brothers, who were hunting it. Next, she is transferred to live with the family of the clan gravekeeper, but through it all becomes even more devout. The gravekeeper and his wife are soon converted and take her as their religious teacher, just as a kitchen maid had done earlier. In the meantime Ma Yü has been studying diligently and has attained the *hsiu-ts'ai* and *chü-jen* degrees. Each time he returns home, but is denied permission to see his wife. Finally he takes highest honors at the palace examination, and is appointed prefect of Ch'ao-chou Prefecture in Kwangtung.

The Ma family rejoices at the news, but the two sisters-in-law are worried that Fragrance will lord it over them as the wife of an official, so they falsely report that she has had illicit sexual relations. At this she is again beaten by her mother-in-law, her hair is cut off, and she is driven out of the house. By day she begs for food, at night she stays in old temples, all the while chanting Amitābha's name and preaching to those around her. Soon many are converted and become her disciples; several examples are given in some detail. Fragrance even converts two ruffians who try to rape her in an abandoned temple. In sum, she becomes a charismatic religious leader.

When Ma Yü returns home, a loyal maid tells him the whole story, and he rushes out to the graveyard to look for his wife. In his hurry, he knocks himself unconscious on a pillar, which moves the whole family to look for Fragrance. A brother finds her in a country temple, and takes her back to the assembly at the graveyard. There her husband urges her to return home with him, but she refuses, and goes back to her temple. At this the mother-in-law insists that Ma Yü take a second wife to keep up appearances, and after some resistance, he obeys, and marries the daughter of a wealthy family. On the way to Kwangtung, Ma Yü and his number two wife take leave of Fragrance, who gives her blessing, and urges him to be a kind and just official, saying that when they return, all three can practice religion together.

Not long afterwards, the entire Ma family in Tzu-chin dies of food poisoning after eating tainted game at a birthday feast for the mother, a fate ordained for them by the Jade Emperor. Upon hearing the news, Hsiang nü returns home and sends a letter to Ma Yü. He, in the meantime, has suddenly become unconscious while his soul takes a trip to Purgatory. There he sees his whole family weeping in pain and remorse because they had not listened to Fragrance. They plead, "Son, please ask your wife to save us."

After two days, Ma Yü wakes up, just as the letter comes from home telling him that twelve members of his family have died from food poisoning. With his new wife he hastens to Shantung, there to ask Fragrance to save his family from Purgatory. The three of them meditate together, and Fragrance preaches a sermon attended by "a large number of gentry, their wives, monks, nuns, priests and lay persons."

Here my copy of this text ends, but Sawada Mizuho's summary indicates that at the end of the story Hsiang nü's piety does indeed rescue the whole Ma family, and that later she, Ma Yü, and his second wife are welcomed in the

Western Land. There they are blessed by Amitābha, who predicts they will become gods.[38]

The explicitly ethical teachings of the *Liu Hsiang pao-chüan* are those of pious lay Buddhism, well summarized in the old nun's sermon, and in the ten conditions for marriage imposed by Hsiang nü.

The sermon is a summary of karma, the doctrine of moral cause and effect:

> If you want to know what happened in your last existence, look at what you are going through now. What your next existence will be depends on what you do in this life. If you practice religious discipline now, then you will be rewarded. However, if you are not willing to maintain a vegetarian diet, read *sūtras*, and recite the Buddha's name; if you do not reverence Heaven and earth, the gods and Buddhas, but rather do evil, kill living beings, steal goods, beat monks and curse priests, cheat good people, and commit all manner of crimes in disobedience to Heaven, then when your life is ended, your *hun* soul will go to purgatory and [in all of its ten courts] endure a myriad *kalpas* of suffering.
>
> When they have paid for their crimes, some will be reborn as cattle, horses, or other domestic animals. Some will be reborn without eyes, hands, or feet, some as those who are starving and cold, afflicted with all sorts of illness, or punished as animals. All of this is retribution for sins committed in one's previous existence. (*chüan* 1, p. 1b)
>
> If [on the other hand] in one's previous existence one has reverenced and esteemed the Buddhist dharma, monks, and the Three Jewels; if one has gilded Buddha images, repaired bridges and roads, provided vegetarian feasts for monks, bestowed alms, aided the poor, abstained from killing, released living beings, maintained a vegetarian diet, read *sūtras*, and recited the Buddha's name, then in one's next existence one will obtain the rewards of pure blessings, become a Buddha or patriarch or become an official or minister, with wealth, high position, and honor. One will amass gold and jade, have children and grandchildren who are good and filial, and blessings and money as one wishes, with all things as one wills. These are all rewards for accumulated goodness in a previous existence. (*chüan* 1, p. 1b)

Fragrance's ten conditions for betrothal are these:

1. Recite the Buddha's name and reverence Buddhism.
2. Be filial to parents and friendly with fellow villagers.
3. Stop hunting; don't kill living things.
4. Don't be greedy, or injure or cheat others.
5. By no means be lustful or sexually immoral.
6. Do not lie or deceive.
7. Do not act in violent ways, but restrain anger and be peaceful.
8. Do not be greedy for the cup; abstain from wine, meat, and strong smelling vegetables.
9. Be merciful; release living beings and do good.
10. Help the poor. (*chüan* 1, p. 5b)

[38] Sawada, *Hōkan*, p. 156.

These values are reiterated throughout the book. Though the *Liu Hsiang pao-chüan* is still concerned with ultimate salvation, detailed ethical injunctions have a much more prominent place in it than in Ming sectarian *pao-chüan*, which are devoted to doctrine and mythology. This text is a vehicle of a more generalized Buddhist piety, with a strong emphasis on filial devotion. There is a conviction throughout that the best way to repay one's parents is to gain deliverance on their behalf.

The questions "why these values?" and "what do they mean?" of course directly involve a discussion of the larger issue of the role of Buddhism in Chinese culture, a discussion beyond the scope of this paper. The first translations of Buddhist texts expressing many of these values were done in the mid-second century A.D., so by the time these *pao-chüan* were written such principles had been known in China for about seventeen hundred years; they were an established part of what it meant to be a Buddhist. Values such as abstaining from meat, sexual immorality, and hunting were understood as a means of detachment from sensual desires. Actions motivated by such desires have an inevitable reaction or effect, which continues our present stream of existence into another one, beyond death; the quality of our life then is conditioned by what we do now. The ultimate goal of such injunctions is to prepare for a state of complete detachment and desirelessness. In such a state of mind, one's actions no longer produce effects or residues, so that at death one is no longer reborn, but enters the ineffable dimension of Nirvāna. However, such an enlightened condition may take many lifetimes to attain; in the meantime ethical living can produce "good karma," which will ensure a quick passage through Purgatory and a felicitous rebirth thereafter.

The *pao-chüan* support these values because they were produced by persons of a Buddhist frame of mind who wrote for a like-minded audience. But of course, writing, printing, and distributing such books were acts of merit in themselves, so the popularity of these books was not entirely due to the teaching they espouse.

Though the explicit ethical values supported in the *Liu Hsiang pao-chüan* are quite conventional, the chief implicit value is not, because at a basic level this text is devoted to the courage, freedom, and salvation of women. Hsiang nü is a full-scale religious heroine with great strength of conviction and powers of persuasion, just as Miao-shan was. She firmly remonstrates with her social superiors, and eventually brings them all around to her side. She endures the worst insults and beatings and yet remains ready to forgive. She breaks social custom by insisting on her own betrothal agreement, without an intermediary. She opposes that most established of traditional values, obtaining office through the civil service examination system. When she is eventually driven out of her husband's home, she develops her own vocation as a religious preacher and leader. And in the end she succeeds, and all the rest depend on her for deliverance.

From the social point of view, perhaps what is most important is that Hsiang nü never really has a normal marriage. The text does not say that she didn't sleep with her husband in their few days together, but she certainly remained celibate thereafter. What she values is meditation, not sex and children. There is in this text, then, a strong implicit resistance to marriage and all the toil and submission it requires. This is made abundantly clear in the sermon preached by the old nun, which contains a long section on the suffering and dangers of pregnancy and childbirth and other difficulties a wife must endure. To be sure, the point is made that these are all grounds for being filial to one's own mother, and that a woman should be especially pious so as to be reborn a man. But the resentment is strong, and the implication not far off that it is better not to marry at all, as the nun herself had not.

The nun notes that when a boy is born, his mother is joyous, the neighbors all congratulate her, the relatives are happy, and father and mother love the child as if he were a precious jewel. When he grows up he studies books, and perhaps becomes wealthy, honored, and famous throughout the world. When he goes out he is honored; when he returns home his wife diligently looks after him. As a husband he fulfills his aims and honors his ancestors.

However, when a girl is born, everyone hates her, and no one in the household rejoices. "We women (*wo nü tzu*) are despised for troubling our mother's bodies, and for not caring for our parents. When a girl grows up she abandons her parents and is married to another" (*chüan* 1, p. 1b).

By giving birth to children she befouls heaven and earth,
    and offends the river god by washing bloody skirts.
If she is on good terms with her mother-in-law she can visit her mother every year or so.
But if she is not in accord with her mother-in-law's wishes,
    she is never able to return to her mother's home.
She thinks of the pain in the hearts of her parents, and of when she will be able to
    repay their kindness.
No matter how many plans you might have, women have always submitted to
    others and served them.
This is because of serious sins in their former existences. (*chüan* 1, p. 2a)

*   *   *

When a woman is married to a husband for her whole life she is controlled by him. All her joys and sorrows derive from him. After they are married she necessarily suffers the pains of childbirth, and cannot avoid the sin of offending the sun, moon, and stars with a flow of blood. Now I will speak with you in more detail about the sufferings women endure in childbirth. (*chüan* 1, p. 2a)

Then follows a description of ten different forms of childbirth brought on as retribution for past sins, including several forms of birth in which the hands or feet came out first, or which involve entanglement in the mother's viscera, stillbirth, and so on. The theme is repeated that menstrual blood and the blood of childbirth offend the gods. The nun continues:

> Now the suffering of giving birth which I have discussed, the suffering of ten
> months of pregnancy and of three years of nursing, and after birth, the bitter toil
> day and night of exchanging dry and wet [clothing], these are what is called, "in
> loving a child, there is nothing one won't do."

The nun then recites the *Pregnancy pao-chüan* (*Huai-t'ai pao-chüan*), which is a
detailed month-by-month account of the pains and anxieties of pregnancy.
This text expresses the point of view of one who has been through all this; one
wonders if it was written by a woman. It begins:

> At the beginning of the first month of pregnancy, the mother does not yet know
> what is happening inside her abdomen, and is afraid she is becoming ill. Half
> anxious, half joyous, she fears the thickness of her body.

This narration continues by describing such problems as sleeplessness, weak-
ness, and loss of interest in food and appearance.

> In the fifth month the child starts to kick, and she [the mother] can't put on her
> embroidered shoes [because of swollen feet]. When the child is born, the mother is
> happy, but must nurse it, wash its clothing, and worry that it may become ill.
>   In one day a child nurses three times, in three days nurses nine times; but
> a mother's milk is not like the Yangtze river, nor the sap of forest trees. (*chüan* 1,
> p. 3a)

The explicit conclusion the nun derives from all this is that children should
repay the suffering and pain their parents have gone through by "vowing to
bring about their salvation in the Western Land" (*chüan* 1, p. 3a). It seems
reasonable to suggest, however, that such material might have led some women
to question marriage itself, as did those described by Marjorie Topley in her
"Marriage Resistance in Rural Kwangtung." Topley writes,

> Aimed expressly at women was the "precious volume" (*pao-chüan*) which con-
> tained biographies of model women. . . . Many of my informants had "precious
> volumes" . . . which further emphasize that refusing to marry is not morally
> wrong. . . .

These books were read by women who lived in "girls' houses" or joined religious
sects that "stressed sexual equality." Most of these women were involved in
making silk, and hence had independent means of support.[39] Thus, there was

---

[39] Marjorie Topley, "Marriage Resistance in Rural Kwangtung," in *Women in Chinese Society*, ed.
Margery Wolf and Roxane Witke (Stanford: Stanford University Press, 1975), pp. 71–76. For
other discussions by Dr. Topley of these and similar groups see her "Chinese Women's Vegetarian
Houses in Singapore," *Journal of the Malayan Branch of the Royal Asiatic Society* 27.1 : 51–67 (1954);
Topley, "The Great Way of Former Heaven: A Group of Chinese Secret Religious Sects," *Bulletin of
the School of Oriental and African Studies*, 26.2 : 362–392 (June 1963); and Topley and James Hayes,
"Notes on Some Vegetarian Halls in Hong Kong Belonging to the Sect of the Hsien-t'ien tao: The
Way of Former Heaven," *Journal of the Hong Kong Branch of the Royal Asiatic Society* 8 : 135–148 (1968).

a specific social context in which such books as the *Liu Hsiang pao-chüan* made sense, that of religious voluntary associations in which unmarried women played an important or dominant role. It seems reasonable to suggest that the *Liu Hsiang pao-chüan* was related to such a group, but I have not as yet found a specific reference to this effect.

CONCLUDING COMMENTS

In sum, there is a curious duality of values in *pao-chüan* literature. The earliest texts focus mainly on religious deliverance, beside which conventional ethical injunctions are of secondary importance or even without validity. Here the ambivalence is between ordinary piety and the need for the enlightened to go beyond it.

From the late Ming *pao-chüan* on, the split is between explicit conventional values and implicit dissenting ones. In the *Lung-hua ching*, the chief implicit value is the whole structure of sectarian mythology, loyalty, and organization; general ethical teachings are not emphasized. In nineteenth-century texts, ethical principles are described in much more detail, but a certain tension remains between them and the freedom from social restraints demanded by the quest for enlightenment. In addition, in some of these texts there is a powerful undercurrent of empathy for women.

Put in another way, this is a duality between Confucianism and Buddhism, with Buddhism providing the theoretical support for dissent. The *P'o-hsieh pao-chüan* is essentially popularized Mādhyamika, with little comfort for Confucian ethical positivism. The ethical theory in this text is thoroughly radical and relativistic, an understanding that for the most part was directed to enlightenment rather than social reform.

Lung-hua ching mythology is a combination of Taoist and Buddhist themes, with but passing references to Confucian principles. When Confucius is mentioned he is described as a popular Buddhist preacher. The *Liu Hsiang pao-chüan* advocates filial piety, but in a distinctly Buddhist form, and with a strong dash of remonstrance. Here Buddhism reinforces the old ethical-critical dimension of filial devotion, a devotion that popular Confucianism tended to interpret as sheer obedience. We have already discussed the strongly Buddhist orientation and life style of Hsiang nü, much of which an orthodox Confucian could not approve.

From this perspective, Buddhism at the popular level continued to provide an alternative point of view that was institutionalized in religious groups and a long textual tradition. However, in the spirit-writing texts of the nineteenth century much of this residual tension is lost, except in those books that continue the old Wu-sheng lao-mu mythology. From the beginning, most *fu-chi* texts reiterate popular Confucian morality, though with some Buddhist influence still evident.

Ming and Ch'ing *pao-chüan* were produced by and for persons in a middle level of learning and status, neither scholars on the one hand nor illiterate laborers and peasants on the other. These texts are important sources for our understanding of the perspectives and values of this cultural level. In addition, they testify to the piety and moral earnestness of a segment of the Chinese population down through the turmoil of late traditional history. For some, the old values were still strong, and were being expressed in new ways as that history came to a close.

NINE

The Transmission of White Lotus Sectarianism in Late Imperial China

Susan Naquin

WHITE LOTUS HISTORY

By the sixteenth century, a new sectarian religion had appeared in China, an outgrowth of venerable traditions of popular Buddhism and Taoism. The Chinese state labeled it heterodoxy, but the religion survived and grew ever more popular during the next four centuries. Believers and historians have referred to this religious teaching, and to the sectarian organization through which it was perpetuated, by a confusing variety of names; I shall here employ the generic term in most general use, "White Lotus religion" (*Pai-lien chiao*).[1]

The new White Lotus religion was characterized by a belief in a female deity known as the Eternal Mother (*wu-sheng lao-mu*), creator of mankind, and by the

I am grateful to the participants in the Conference on Values and Communication in Ming–Ch'ing Popular Culture, and to the organizers in particular, for their comments and criticisms. I would also like to express my thanks to the curators of the Ch'ing archives in the National Palace Museum in Taipei and of the Ming–Ch'ing Archives in Peking for their invaluable assistance.

Dates used in the notes are given for each document according to the Chinese lunar calendar: year/month/day. The reign periods have been abbreviated as follows: YC, Yung-cheng (1723–1735); CL, Ch'ien-lung (1736–1795); CC, Chia-ch'ing (1796–1820); TK, Tao-kuang (1821–1850).

[1] The term *chiao* 教 meant both "teaching" and "sect." It is this same religious tradition that Daniel Overmyer discusses elsewhere in this volume, although not under the name White Lotus. As a matter of definition, I use the term White Lotus religion to refer only to sectarian activity after 1500 and not before. (This is the second phase of *pao-chüan* development in Overmyer's chronology.) I intend not to deny the religion's complex antecedents, but merely to indicate the decisive transformation I see taking place when the Eternal Mother cosmology and millenarian eschatology were combined with sectarian organization and written scriptures in the sixteenth century.

For a general history of this tradition in English, see Daniel L. Overmyer, *Folk Buddhist Religion: Dissenting Sects in Late Traditional China* (Cambridge, Mass.: Harvard University Press, 1976); for additional sources in Japanese and somewhat more attention to Taoist antecedents, see T. H. Barrett, "Chinese Sectarian Religion" (a review), *Modern Asian Studies* 12:333–352 (1978).

conviction that personal salvation could be found only through adherence to
the teachings transmitted by her emissaries. These beliefs were first articulated
by several preachers[2] who, in the course of the sixteenth century, lectured in

[2] The earliest and best known of these teachers was Lo Ch'ing 羅清 (1443–1527), whose five
books were in print by 1518. Lo Ch'ing's pivotal role in early White Lotus history makes him
somewhat difficult to categorize. His *pao-chüan* do not contain the basic White Lotus cosmology and
eschatology. For this reason, Daniel Overmyer places the Lo texts at the end of his first phase of *pao-
chüan* development. On the other hand, Lo's life as a preacher and author of sacred texts was similar
to that of the White Lotus teachers (named below) who may also have emulated him. Furthermore,
a great many White Lotus believers later came to view Lo Ch'ing (perhaps inaccurately) as a
founder and patriarch of their religion. Many of those who later called their religion the Lo sect (*Lo
chiao* 羅教) had adopted some White Lotus ideas that their patriarch never espoused (at least not in
print). For these reasons, I have preferred to see Lo Ch'ing as the earliest ancestor of White Lotus
sectarianism. For Lo Ch'ing, see Daniel Overmyer, chapter 8, above, and "Boatmen and Buddhas:
The Lo Chiao in Ming Dynasty China," *History of Religions* 17:284–302 (1978); *T'ai-shang tsu-shih
san-shih yin-yu pao-chüan* 太上祖師三世因由寶卷 [Precious scroll explaining the highest patriarch
teacher's three incarnations] (hereafter, *T'ai-shang tsu-shih pao-chüan*), (1875 reprint of 1682 edition;
Li Shih-yü 李世瑜 private collection, Tientsin), part I; Sawada Mizuho 澤田瑞穂, *Hōkan no
kenkyū* 宝巻の研究 [A study of precious scrolls] (Tokyo; Kokusho kankōkai 国書刊行会, 1975),
pp. 101–104; Richard Hon-chun Shek, "Religion and Society in Late Ming: Sectarianism and
Popular Thought in Sixteenth and Seventeenth Century China" (Ph.D. dissertation, University of
California at Berkeley, 1980), pp. 202–251. Evidence on the activities of subsequent teachers and
their relationship to one another is less full. The most important men appear to have been the
unnamed author of the *Chiu-lien pao-chüan* 九蓮寶卷 reprinted in 1523, the earliest dateable text
setting forth White Lotus cosmology and beliefs; Li Pin 李賓, founder of the Huang-t'ien-tao
黃天道 and active in the 1560s northeast of Peking; Patriarch Yin 殷祖, 1540–1582, a follower of
Lo Ch'ing who proselytized in the 1570s in Chekiang; Patriarch Han P'iao-kao 韓飄高, active in
the 1570s–1590s in Chihli, whose activities are described in the texts of the Hung-yang sect 紅陽教;
and Wang Sen 王森 of Luan-chou in eastern Chihli, who had followers at the court of the Wan-li
emperor and was arrested in 1595.

   For the 1523 text, see *Huang-chi chin-tan chiu-lien cheng-hsin kuei-chen huan-hsiang pao-chüan*
皇極金丹九蓮正信皈眞還鄉寶卷 [Precious scroll of the imperial ultimate's golden elixir and nine
lotus (path to) rectifying belief, espousing what is true, and returning to our real home] (hereafter,
Chiu-lien pao-chüan), (1523; Wu Hsiao-ling 吳曉鈴 private collection, Peking). For Li Pin, see *Kung-
chung tang* 宮中檔 [Palace memorial archive], hereafter KCT (Taipei: National Palace Museum)
14593, CL 28/4/1; Li Shih-yü, *Hsien-tsai Hua-pei mi-mi tsung-chiao* 現在華北秘密宗教 [Contem-
porary secret religious sects in North China] (Ch'eng-tu, 1948; reprint ed. Taipei, 1975), pp. 14–17;
Richard Shek, "Millenarianism Without Rebellion: The Huangtian Dao in North China," *Modern
China* 8:305–336 (1982). For Patriarch Yin: *T'ai-shang tsu-shih pao-chüan*, part II. For Han P'iao-
kao, see Sawada Mizuho, "Koyokyō no shitan" 弘陽教の試探 [Preliminary investigation of the
Hung-yang sect], *Tenri daigaku gakuhō* 天理大学学報 24:63–85 (1957); *Wai-chi tang* 外紀檔 [Outer
court record], hereafter WCT (Taipei: National Palace Museum) CC 22/12/21; James Inglis,
"The Hun Yuen Men," *Chinese Recorder* 39:270–271 (1908); *Hun-yuan hung-yang t'an-shih chen-ching*
混元弘陽嘆世眞經 [True sutra of the original chaos red sun lament for the world], (no date,
Ming edition; Peking: Institute of Religion, Chinese Academy of Social Sciences). For Wang Sen,
see *Dictionary of Ming Biography, 1368–1644*, ed. L. C. Goodrich and Fang Chao-ying (New York:
Columbia University Press, 1976), pp. 587–589; Susan Naquin, "Connections Between Rebellions:
Sect Family Networks in North China in Qing China," *Modern China* 8:337–360 (1982). I am
much indebted to Daniel Overmyer, to the Institute of Religion of the Chinese Academy of Social
Sciences, to Li Shih-yü, and to Wu Hsiao-ling for making it possible for me to consult the various
scriptures cited here.

public in the cities of north and central China and whose ideas were subsequently written down and published in "scriptures" (*ching*) and "sacred books" (*pao-chüan*).[3] Believers formed small congregations bound by strands of teacher-to-pupil ties, and met to worship and to read these scriptures together. Some, inspired by their patriarch's predictions that the end of the present cosmic era would be signaled by great catastrophes and by the appearance of a savior sent by the Eternal Mother, rose in rebellion in order to usher in the new world. Although outlawed by the Ming (1368–1644) and Ch'ing (1644–1911) governments for their beliefs, deemed incompatible with official orthodoxy and conducive to violent political action, communities of White Lotus adherents survived and grew in subsequent centuries.

For those who believed, the White Lotus religion provided a process for salvation that did not necessitate reliance on the temples and priests of either popular religion or the state cult, and it offered a community supplementary to those of family, village, market, and bureaucracy. It also held out a unique promise of imminent and direct salvation in the form of divinely guided apocalypse and millennium. In consequence, this religion appears to have had a particular attraction for individuals for whom the normal paths to salvation were unappealing or unattainable or for whom ordinary community structures were unavailable. White Lotus ideas and organizations were appealing, it seems, to those who for all or part of their lives were not completely absorbed by orthodox institutions: men and women who were elderly or without families, monks without temples, migrant laborers and other itinerant workers, urban immigrants, peasants whose village and temple organizations were dominated by others, and so forth.[4]

By the early eighteenth century, a variety of different sects (groups of believers linked by the bonds between pupils and teacher) had appeared, some relying on written scriptures and congregational life, others emphasizing the recitation of mantras and individual yogic meditation. Although uprisings were few, government persecution (arrests of sectarians, confiscation of books, destruction of meeting places) slowly intensified; both congregational and meditational sects nevertheless continued to attract followers. By the 1760s, martial arts had been added to the techniques for circulation of breath and became an increasingly prominent part of the repertory of meditational sects. In the late eighteenth century, a period of population growth and growing social and

---

[3] Books used by White Lotus sectarians commonly had as the final word of their title the terms *pao-chüan* 寶卷 or *ching* 經; in the Ch'ing, believers usually called the books *ching* or *ching-chüan* 經卷. Daniel Overmyer chooses to use the term *pao-chüan*, and thus, because not all *pao-chüan* were sectarian, he places White Lotus books in the larger context of the emergence and development of this genre of popular religious literature. Following Ch'ing usage, I have employed the term "scripture" and occasionally "sutra." I have used "sutra" only when sectarian *ching* were being explicitly chanted like the Buddhist sutras (also called *ching*) on which they were unquestionably modeled. Not all sectarian scriptures, however, were recited like sutras.

[4] The hypotheses set forth in this essay about the social contexts of White Lotus sectarianism are meant to be suggestive but not definitive. Further research is necessary.

economic tensions, White Lotus millenarianism found more and more adherents, and starting with the Wang Lun uprising of 1774, there followed a series of rebellions (especially among meditational sects) that lasted through the next century.[5]

As social order broke down in the mid-nineteenth century and after, sect organizations merged with community structures and entire villages adopted White Lotus leadership and techniques of self-defense. Ming and early Ch'ing editions of scriptures were in short supply and the planchette (*fu-chi*) became popular as a fresh source of religious revelation; new books were dictated by sectarian deities through this technique of spirit writing and became the basis of authority for new sects.[6] These books restated White Lotus eschatology but amplified the doctrine to meet the changed world of the late nineteenth and twentieth centuries. A variety of urban sects of the congregational sort, many with planchette sessions as their primary activity, appeared and flourished in the cities of China and among overseas Chinese. At the same time, the Boxer (1898–1900) and Red Spear (1920s–1940s) movements in the countryside revealed the continued importance of sectarian organization and martial arts in rural North China. By the time of the establishment of the People's Republic in 1949, a wide variety of what the new regime termed "reactionary Taoist cults" with demonstrable White Lotus antecedents could be found all over China. They survive today in Taiwan and Southeast Asia.

In order to examine how the White Lotus religion adapted itself to the political, social, and geographic environment of late imperial China, this essay will concentrate on one segment of this historical development, the middle Ch'ing. Because there is excellent documentation for the eighteenth and early nineteenth centuries, it is my hope that a focus on that period will reveal patterns and dynamics of more general applicability.[7] I shall attempt to show how different modes of communicating and perpetuating basic values made

---

[5] For more on the 1774 and subsequent rebellions, see my *Shantung Rebellion: The Wang Lun Uprising of 1774* (New Haven: Yale University Press, 1981), especially pp. 153–159.

[6] Daniel L. Overmyer, "Values in Sectarian Literature: Mid-Ming to Twentieth Century, Part II, Spirit-writing (*fu-chi* 扶箕) Texts" (unpublished paper, 1981).

[7] The ideas presented in this essay are based on a large corpus of several thousand documents on those White Lotus sects prosecuted by the Ch'ing state in the period 1720 to 1840. (Cases dated before 1720 are few and fragmentary.) I have been able to look at nearly all the documents on White Lotus sects before 1840 preserved in archives in both Taipei and Peking—that is to say, the great preponderance of surviving records. The investigations so documented give information only about sects discovered by the government, not about the entire universe of Ch'ing sects. (The efforts of the state in ferreting out sectarianism varied in time and space; for example, the throne took a less intense interest in sub-Yangtze China, and temporary bursts of arrests elsewhere often followed the discovery of a particularly offensive—usually rebellious—group.) This evidence has suggested the typology presented here, but to cite all the cases I have seen illustrating each generalization would drown the reader in footnotes. I have, therefore, *faute de mieux*, given citations only for specific information mentioned in the paper and cited secondary sources when relevant.

possible the survival of the religion and its dissemination to different constituencies. And in order to contribute to our skimpy knowledge of Ch'ing popular religion more generally, I shall also examine briefly the relationship between popular sectarianism and popular orthodoxy and try to suggest the extent to which White Lotus beliefs and activities may fairly be termed heterodox.

A number of factors affected the ways in which White Lotus religious values were communicated within the changing society of late imperial China. The existence of several sect founders whose teachings were carried on by expanding networks of pupils (and their pupils) fragmented the religion from the outset. The lack of any overall religious organization—no church to regularize doctrine and ritual or to train clergy—only further encouraged diversity. The hostility of the state, moreover, made contact and coordination between believers difficult and hastened subdivision and segmentation.

On the other hand, an identifiably common cosmology and belief system did persist despite organizational fission. At first the survival of this religious doctrine was tied directly to those sacred books produced in the late Ming and to the patriarchs who wrote them. These scriptures became the repository of the religious ideology (just as sutras were to Buddhism and the Classics to Neo-Confucianism); those who owned and could read and understand these texts acquired considerable religious authority. There was thus a felt need to study the old texts, to preserve them carefully, and to make more copies for future believers, an imperative made all the more urgent by the eagerness with which Ch'ing authorities confiscated and destroyed White Lotus scriptures.[8]

This emphasis on mastery, preservation, and reproduction of scriptures, while providing ideological continuity, might also have limited participation in sectarian activities to the relatively literate and well-to-do, but White Lotus teachers did not ignore the possibilities for conversion among the large semiliterate and illiterate population. In order to appeal to poor or uneducated men and women, some teachers quite naturally reduced their reliance on scriptures and tried to popularize doctrine and alter ritual for a nonreading, less affluent audience.

A variety of circumstances thus produced considerable diversity in sect organization and activities by the eighteenth century, yet we can discern within the diversity two analytically distinct modes. Generally speaking, one was characterized by an active congregational life in which recitation of scriptures played a central role, the other by a looser structure and a concentration on meditation and martial arts. The role of written texts, importance of oral transmission, functions of ritual, nature of sect structure, relationship to ortho-

---

[8] The expansion of the printing industry and the increases in education and urbanization during this period may also have helped enlarge the audience for books, even unorthodox ones. See Evelyn Rawski's article in this volume, chapter 1.

dox popular religion, and social background of the membership all varied (relatively systematically) between these two modes. We shall look closely at the dynamics of both continuity and change in each type in order to reach a better understanding of the general processes by which sectarian values were communicated in the Ch'ing period.

SUTRA-RECITATION SECTS

Sutra-recitation sects should be seen as part of the long development of congregational and devotional institutions for pious Buddhist laymen previously described by Daniel Overmyer.[9] Typically, sect members, like monks and nuns, practiced lifelong vegetarianism, made a formal commitment to explicitly Buddhist precepts, and met regularly to engage in the ritual recitation of scriptures. They also performed religious services (especially mortuary rites) for the community at large. When possible, believers met in buildings formally designated for a religious purpose. Congregational activities were emphasized and men and women were allowed to meet together; at the same time, a high value was placed on celibacy. In such groups, horizontal ties among sect members were strong, and the believer's life was usually very much absorbed by religious activities. Vertical connections did exist, however, because like all White Lotus sects, these groups were perpetuated by the transmission of doctrine from teacher to pupil. Each sect traced its teaching back to a patriarch (ideally in the Ming dynasty) and members usually knew the names of past sect masters. Because of the central role of sutra recitation, these sects attracted relatively literate followers, and because the public buildings and printed books necessary to their worship were conspicuous, these groups appear to have prospered in cities and away from areas of active government surveillance. (Those mid-Ch'ing sects that conformed most closely to this sutra-recitation model used the names Lo sect and Hung-yang sect.[10])

Sutra-recitation sects created a quasi-monastic life for their adherents. Sect members made formal, lifelong commitments to a vegetarian diet (as did Buddhist and Taoist clerics) and regarded the "breaking of the vegetarian fast" (*k'ai-chai*) as a serious matter equivalent to leaving the sect. They also formally acknowledged key precepts of the Buddhist faith. The most common ritual procedure for entering such a sect was to pledge adherence to the Buddhist Five Vows (*wu-chieh*), promising not to kill, steal, drink alcohol, lie, or perform immoral sexual acts. Believers also acknowledged the Three Refuges of

---

[9] In addition to other work cited in notes 1, 2, 6, 19, and 80, see his "The White Cloud Sect in Sung and Yuan China," *Harvard Journal of Asiatic Studies* 42:615–642 (1982).

[10] There already exists a substantial scholarly literature on the Lo sect. See Overmyer, "Boatmen and Buddhas," and the works cited therein and David E. Kelley, "Temples and Tribute Fleets: The Luo Sects and Boatmen's Associations in the Eighteenth Century," *Modern China* 8:361–391 (1982). For the Hung-yang sect, see Sawada Mizuho, "Kōyōkyō no shitan."

Buddhism (*san-kuei*), the Buddha, the Dharma (Buddhist law), and the Sangha (religious community).[11] Sect members also imitated monks and nuns by taking religious names (*fa-ming*), with members of one sect or one generation often using a common element to emphasize the role of the community as a surrogate family.

Celibacy, although not required of men and women who wished to enjoy the rewards of a pious life without giving up a family, was still prized. The existence of all-female sects and the creation of halls for residence during celibate periods in the lives of believers (for example, for men living away from home, or for unmarried or widowed women) made a partially monastic life possible.[12] It appears, in fact, that this sort of sect was especially appealing to women, providing them with a supplementary community, new avenues for education and leadership, and an escape from their families.

The assembly (*hui*) was central to the life of members of this type of White Lotus sect. It was the occasion when members met together as a group and was the locus for their congregational devotions. These assemblies also distinguished sectarian worship from that of ordinary popular religion (where such meetings had few counterparts). The frequency of assemblies could vary widely. At their most intensive, sects met twice a month, on the new and full moon (the first and fifteenth day of each lunar month), and then on certain other special days during the year. Some sects imitated monasteries by meeting to take their scriptures outside to be aired (*shai-ching*) every year in the sixth lunar month. In others, a teacher's birthday or deathday might be the occasion for an assembly. To the normal offerings made by the ordinary person to ancestors or to a particular domestic or neighborhood god,[13] White Lotus sects added worship of their own deities; assembling for such worship emphasized their separate community. Regular and frequent sect assemblies promoted solidarity and formalized it through collectively performed rituals. (The possibilities for community life may explain why sectarianism appealed to people who had no immediate family or permanent residence.)

Assemblies would usually take place in the homes of sect members or of a senior teacher, but believers also tried, when possible, to establish separate

---

[11] In his description of a Lung-hua 龍華 sect in Amoy in the late nineteenth century, J. J. M. de Groot gives a lengthy and detailed account of an initiation ceremony in which strong similarities to monastic ordination are pointed out. See *Sectarianism and Religious Persecution in China* (Amsterdam, 1903–1904; reprint ed. Taipei: Ch'eng-wen, 1971), pp. 204–215. Public declaration of these vows was also a common way of proclaiming oneself a devoted lay Buddhist in the twentieth century. See Holmes Welch, *The Practice of Chinese Buddhism, 1900–1950* (Cambridge, Mass.: Harvard University Press, 1967), pp. 317, 358–364.

[12] For an example of an instance when several male believers demonstrated their commitment to celibacy by the extreme gesture of voluntary castration, see WCT, TK 3/12/22.

[13] For daily religious practice, see Stephan Feuchtwang, "Domestic and Communal Worship in Taiwan," in *Religion and Ritual in Chinese Society*, ed. Arthur P. Wolf (Stanford: Stanford University Press, 1974), pp. 107–111.

rooms or buildings for their worship. These places, probably modeled on temples or ancestral halls, were called, variously, "halls for purification" (*chai-t'ang*), "halls of retreat" (*an-t'ang*), or "scripture halls" (*ching-t'ang*). In the absence of government prosecution, there appears to have been a developmental cycle (common to most cults in China) from ordinary rooms in private homes to particular rooms in such homes, to small separate buildings nearby, to large independent halls with endowed property. Separate halls served several purposes. They could be places of temporary or permanent residence for members, and they could house a permanent altar to sect patriarchs and deities. Images of patriarchs were most common; those of the Eternal Mother or of the Buddha Maitreya (the savior to come) were rarer. In these halls, believers could also store objects necessary to their worship: candles, incense, musical instruments, and scriptures. The public nature of any hall, however, constituted a danger for the community. The government knew that the existence of sectarian buildings signaled the presence of a wealthy and numerous White Lotus community and, when discovered, these halls were taken over and either destroyed or converted to public use.[14]

The primary activity at sect assemblies (wherever held) was the collective recitation of sacred scriptures (*sung-ching*). Such chanting was normally combined with the presentation of offerings to sect deities and the consumption of a vegetarian meal by participants. Some sects may have had endowed land that generated a regular income, but usually money had to be contributed for each assembly toward the purchase of incense, offerings, and food.

Detailed descriptions of sutra recitation are rather rare, and there was surely variation from group to group and over time. In most cases, the chanting of sutras by Buddhist monks and nuns appears to have provided the model.[15] When the group met, they bowed to the altar and to the scriptures themselves, lighting incense and offering fruit or tea (as was also done in ordinary worship[16]). Then they sat and chanted the scriptures in unison, simultaneously beating out a rhythm with the tok! tok! of the wooden-fish drum and the ding! ding! ding! of the brass-bowl bell. The length of such meetings probably varied with the leisure time of the participants but typically would have been no more

[14] A particularly intense government campaign to locate and tear down sectarian halls occurred in the mid-eighteenth century. See David E. Kelley, "Sect and Society: The Evolution of the Lo Sect Among Grain Tribute Fleet Boatmen, 1700–1850," paper presented at the Conference on Orthodoxy and Heterodoxy in Late Imperial China: Cultural Beliefs and Social Divisions (Montecito, California, August 20–26, 1981).

[15] For descriptions of recitation of sutras by monks, see J. Prip-Møller, *Chinese Buddhist Monasteries* (Copenhagen, 1936; reprint ed. Hong Kong: Hong Kong University Press, 1967), pp. 365–367; Welch, chap. 3. For White Lotus practice: Overmyer, *Religion*, pp. 186–188.

[16] Ordinary home or temple worship might involve a variety of offerings. See Feuchtwang, pp. 110–111, and Arthur Wolf, "Gods, Ghosts, and Ancestors," in his *Religion and Ritual*, pp. 176–182. By Feuchtwang's criteria, these White Lotus offerings were relatively "pure," characteristic of those presented to the highest gods.

than several hours a day. Sect members described the purpose of sutra recitation only in vague language—"dispelling malevolent influences and attracting good fortune"[17]—but their chanting was surely intended to acquire karmic merit for the reciters and for others to whom they, like Buddhist clerics, could transfer such merit.

As would seem obvious from the central role of sutra recitation, possession of religious books was crucial to the operation of these sects. "If one is not familiar with the scriptures," said one text, "it will be difficult to understand about life and death."[18] Despite the post-sixteenth-century increase in printing in China that made popular literature available to an unprecedented degree, sectarian scriptures were still rare in the eighteenth century. Joining a sect meant gaining an opportunity to see and hold these books, to learn to chant and to read them, and perhaps even to make handwritten copies. Teachers, like monks, may have lectured on the scriptures and taught reading indirectly through character-by-character explications.[19]

The books most commonly found in the possession of sutra-reciting sects in the middle Ch'ing were those associated with two important sixteenth-century teachers later revered as the patriarchs (tsu) of the Lo and of the Hung-yang sects: Lo Ch'ing (fl. 1500) and Han P'iao-kao (fl. 1580). Five texts are attributed to Patriarch Lo, and in the centuries after his death these books were treasured and read by sects using various names. In their original printed editions, these books present the salvationist message of late Ming popular Buddhism, use relatively abstract language ("boundless emptiness is the body of the limitless"), and do not contain the cosmology and eschatology associated with the Eternal Mother.[20] The late Ming scriptures identified with Patriarch P'iao-kao and his teachings,[21] although not the earliest texts to do so, set

---

[17] It is difficult to tell if the generally unsophisticated explanations of religious activities given by believers reflect a shallow understanding of the philosophical underpinnings of the religion or the hostile atmosphere in which depositions were recorded.

[18] T'ai-shang tsu-shih pao-chüan, part II, p. 12.

[19] The fact that commentaries were written on these texts (just as they were on Confucian Classics) suggests that sect teachers were in the habit of explaining texts to students. One commentary on the T'an-shih wu-wei chüan 嘆世無爲卷 [Scroll on nonaction and lamenting for the world], for example, gave the pronunciation of unusual characters. See Overmyer, "Ming Dynasty Popular Scriptures: An Introduction to the Pao-chüan of Lo Ch'ing and His Wu-wei Chiao" (unpublished paper, 1976), pp. 11–12.

[20] Overmyer has analyzed these texts in "Boatmen and Buddhas" and "Ming Dynasty Scriptures." A few pages from these books are illustrated in Fou Si-houa 傅惜華 "Catalogue des Pao-kiuan," Mélanges Sinologiques (Paris: Université de Paris, 1951), p. 46.

[21] Sawada Mizuho lists twenty-one Hung-yang sect scriptures in his "Koyōkyō no shitan"; several of these provide information on Han P'iao-kao himself. At least seven of these titles appear to be clearly distinct scriptures dating from the Ming. See also Huang Yü-p'ien 黃育楩, P'o-hsieh hsiang-pien 破邪詳辯 [A detailed refutation of heresies] (1883), where most of these texts are mentioned or quoted from. Some of these scriptures borrowed the names (and perhaps the content) of Lo Ch'ing's five books, simply adding hung-yang or hun-yüan to the title.

forth the historical vision that shaped the thinking of White Lotus believers: the story of the Eternal Mother's concern for the suffering of her human children, her decision to send a teacher (here, P'iao-kao) who will reveal the path to salvation, and the promise of deliverance by the Buddha Maitreya. (Later books claiming to represent Lo Ch'ing's teachings also incorporated this message.) A number of penance texts (used especially in Hung-yang sects) were important in the performance of funeral rites (of which, more below) and describe how one can be saved from the torments of hell.[22]

Scriptures printed in the late Ming continued to circulate during subsequent centuries. Routine loss, confiscation by the state, an increase in the number of believers, as well as the Buddhist injunction to disseminate and distribute sacred books as an act of piety, all encouraged reprinting and copying. In a Hung-yang scripture reprinted in Shantung in 1697, to cite only one example, the sponsor noted,

> [This edition] follows the Ming dynasty version in the possession of my ancestors. My family and the people in our assembly have together contributed [to this reprinting] as an expression of our hearts' desires. If anyone wishes to reprint [further], please ask for the woodblocks so that this may be carried out.[23]

New books were also produced. Early Ch'ing scriptures often imitated earlier books and retold the lives and teachings of Ming patriarchs, adding similar descriptions of later disciples. The *T'ai-shang tsu-shih san-shih yin-yu pao-chüan* [Precious scroll explaining the highest patriarch teacher's three incarnations], printed in 1682, for instance, contains an account first of Patriarch Lo and then of two followers, Patriarch Yin (1540–1582) and Patriarch Chao (1578–1646), who were allegedly his reincarnations.[24] Ch'ing government records give ample illustration of the desire of sect leaders to create their own

---

[22] Many penance (*ch'an* 懺) texts are discussed in Huang Yü-p'ien. See also, inter alia, KCT 45833, CL 48/9/17; KCT 24036, CL 34/1/22; KCT 15334, CL 28/6/28.

[23] One volume from this printing was discovered in 1817, confiscated, and then burned. *Shang-yü tang fang-pen* 上諭檔方本 [Imperial edict record book, long form], hereafter SYT (Taipei: National Palace Museum) 211, CC 22/12/21. In 1652, two sect members collated, verified, and reprinted the Lo scripture *K'u-kung wu-tao chüan* 苦功悟道卷 [Scroll on enlightenment through religious austerity]; there was another reprinting in 1798 using a printer in Kiangsi and woodblocks from a family of sect members. SYT 255–256, CL 21/2/22; *Sui-shou teng-chi* 隨手登記 [Daily record], hereafter SSTC (Taipei: National Palace Museum) CC 19/5/20; Overmyer, "Ming Dynasty Scriptures," p. 9.

[24] This text makes clear that by the end of the sixteenth century, White Lotus cosmology had been fully accepted into some Lo sects. There is archival evidence for the continuation of this sect into the early nineteenth century. See KCT: Secret society category 秘密結社, hereafter KCT-NM (Peking: Ming–Ch'ing Archives) 461, for documents on the 1814 case of Wu Tzu-hsiang 吳子祥. There we learn how a pupil of Wu's collected between 1000 and 2800 cash from each of his twenty pupils (a total of 20–56 taels) in order to reprint Patriarch Lo's five books. References to the Eternal Mother and to the three cosmic eras and their three buddha-patriarchs are to be found in the lives of patriarchs Yin and Chao but not Lo Ch'ing.

books (both to enhance their own prestige and to supply written materials where lacking), but not many were educated enough for such work. For those who were, the hazards and expenses of printing usually meant that copies had to circulate in manuscript and could not easily be widely distributed. In an atypical case in the 1810s, an ambitious boatman named Fang Jung-sheng composed six books in an astonishing 130 volumes (*ts'e*). All were written out by hand; they were eventually confiscated after Fang's arrest and circulated no further.[25] Occasionally one finds sect leaders who relied on spirit mediums to give added authority to their own pronouncements, but there are few instances of texts transmitted through such an intermediary.[26] (By the nineteenth century, as mentioned above, spirit writing using the planchette became a popular way of creating new texts.) In general, new scriptures lacked the prestige of the old, richly bound, and beautifully printed Ming volumes and rarely became widely known.

It is difficult to estimate the number of White Lotus scriptures in circulation at any one time. In general terms, the number of Ming editions diminished while the number of handwritten books increased. At least two thousand books (nearly four hundred different titles) were seized and destroyed by the government between 1720 and 1840.[27] We will never know how many were not confiscated. At least until the middle of the eighteenth century, texts associated with Lo sects existed in large quantities. In 1734, for instance, the magistrate of Kan county (the seat of Kan-chou prefecture) in Kiangsi arrested a sect member who owned seven copies of the *Lo-ching* (Lo scripture), another man who had forty-seven volumes (*chüan*) of sectarian books, one who had fifty-three, a monk who had six, a widow with six left to her in a trunk, a group of people who owned nineteen between them, and three other men who had six copies each of the *Lo-ching*. Four months later, the same magistrate had located 970 more copies of the *Lo-ching*.[28]

Texts associated with Hung-yang sects, although they turn up throughout this period, were not discovered in such large quantities. Few individuals owned more than one book, and those books were as often handwritten as printed. (This situation seems to reflect a somewhat less affluent and geographically more scattered membership.) Several official investigations into Hung-yang sects in the early nineteenth century reveal, however, that sect teachers occasionally had relatively large supplies. In 1817, a man from a

[25] *Chün-chi-ch'u lu-fu tang* 軍機處錄副檔 [Grand Council copy archive, peasant uprising category 農民戰爭], hereafter CCT-NM (Peking: Ming–Ch'ing Archives) 2764, CC 20/9/13.

[26] The clearest reference to such a practice apparently involved trickery. In 1766, a Hupei man confessed to deceiving others by first writing a book himself, and then giving it to a spirit medium to memorize so that he could pretend to transmit it from a god. CCT-NM Second Supplement (hereafter CCT-NMSS) 54:1, CL 31/5/19.

[27] This figure represents my own calculation from evidence I have seen so far.

[28] KCT 10568, YC 12/7/21; KCT 3445, YC 12/11/20.

county near the Grand Canal in Shantung who counted himself the twelfth-generation disciple of Patriarch Han P'iao-kao had eighty-eight volumes of religious literature. Of these, sixteen books (in twenty-one volumes) were singled out for their sectarian content, but of those sixteen, only four were printed. In another investigation in 1814 in Peking, another sect teacher had nineteen different scriptures—thirty-five volumes—but no more than half of them were clearly sectarian.[29]

These examples are indicative of the quantities of books usually available. They also illustrate that sutra-reciting sects did not limit themselves to White Lotus scriptures but, out of a combination of necessity and perceived compatibility, acquired and chanted more orthodox books such as the *Chin-kang ching* [Diamond sutra], *Hsin ching* [Heart sutra], and *Kuan-yin ching* [Kuan Yin sutra].

To illustrate the content of a single scripture and its survival over time, let us look at an early dateable White Lotus text: the *Huang-chi chin-tan chiu-lien cheng-hsin kuei-chen huan-hsiang pao-chüan* [Precious scroll of the imperial ultimate's golden elixir and nine lotus (path to) rectifying belief, espousing what is true, and returning to our real home], hereafter, *Chiu-lien pao-chüan*. One surviving copy of this book was printed in 1523 and consists of two large (15 by 4 inch) rectangular printed volumes in the accordion-folded style typical of Buddhist sutras, with large-type characters, brocade covers, and woodblock illustrations at the beginning and end of each volume. The text (in twenty-four chapters) describes how a patriarch (called the Imperial Ultimate or Wu-wei Patriarch, but never named) was sent to earth by the Eternal Mother, revealed the path to salvation, left this book, and returned to paradise.

> The true patriarch came quietly into this world,
> Disguising his identity and living among us,
> Secretly teaching the golden elixir path.
> After the three assemblies, we shall all return to our origin.

Much of the text (possibly derived from actual debates during his lifetime) consists of the patriarch's answers to questions posed by individuals seeking to understand his system; White Lotus cosmology and eschatology are thus explained in language that is relatively concrete and straightforward. The patriarch also urges believers to burn a stick of "returning-home incense" and teaches them the Three Refuges and Five Vows and a special technique of meditation that enabled one to travel to see the Eternal Mother in the "heaven

---

[29] WCT, CC 22/12/21; *Chiao-pu tang* 剿捕檔 [Suppression and arrest record book], hereafter CPT (Taipei: National Palace Museum) 435, CC 18/12/21. The best-known confiscation of White Lotus scriptures was carried out by Huang Yü-p'ien, an energetic magistrate of the Tao-kuang period. Serving first in Chü-lu and then in Ts'ang-chou (both in Chihli), Huang collected twenty different *pao-chüan* in 1833 and thirty more (of which only five were duplicated) in 1839. He discussed these books in his *P'o-hsieh hsiang-pien*, a work in which he attempted to demonstrate the implausibility and heterodoxy of the White Lotus religion.

beyond the heavens." The text is full of phrases in which simple terms are invested with a new and special meaning: "recognizing the patriarch and returning to one's roots," "attending the Dragon Flower Assembly," "seeing our Mother, receiving verification, and registering one's name," "securing one's fate and one's nature," "entering the holy womb, never to be reborn."[30] Such phrases recur throughout most White Lotus scriptures.

We know that the *Chiu-lien pao-chüan* dates from at least 1523, but details on later editions are fragmentary. There were reprintings in 1693 and in 1899 (both in Soochow), and another in 1909. No fewer than eight copies of this book were confiscated by the Ch'ing government—in 1775, 1788, 1805 (two copies), 1814, 1816, 1817, and 1823—in widely separated parts of China (Kansu, Shensi, Shantung, Chihli, Honan, Kiangsu, and Kwangsi). Some of these confiscated books were printed, some handcopied. Several other copies survived and found their way into the hands of scholars in the twentieth century. Three of these were two-volume Ming editions; two others were one-volume abbreviations, one with a new preface dictated by planchette.[31]

Sutra-recitation sect members not only chanted sacred books as monks and nuns did, they also acted more generally like religious professionals. Many sects provided mortuary rites for members. One purpose of funeral rites in Chinese society was to expedite the passage of the soul of the deceased person through the underworld (that is, to assure a speedy and better rebirth). Such services ordinarily ranged from the simple to the very elaborate. They were one of the important services that Buddhist and Taoist priests performed for communities and were the main source of their livelihood. By their own admission, sectarians supplemented the orthodox professionals and performed funeral services not only for followers of their religion but for other people who were too poor to afford monks or priests.[32] (The frequent membership of monks in White Lotus sects probably made it easier for believers to acquire these skills.) Such mortuary rites could include recitation of entire sutras (some sectarian, some not) and of shorter penance texts (*ch'an*) that could cancel the bad deeds of the deceased by transferring merit already stored up by others. As White Lotus scripture halls imitated the traditions of monastic Buddhism, so sectarian funeral rites copied other less prestigious but lucrative clerical services.

Some sects provided a more informal (and less conspicuous) service: supply-

---

[30] *Chiu-lien pao-chüan.* The verse comes from chap. 3.

[31] Huang Yü-p'ien 4.23–27; CCT-NMSS 106, CL 39/4/9; KCT 50279, CL 52/2/27; KCT 54485, CL 53/7/9; SYT 49–50, CC 10/5/7; WCT (Peking: Ming–Ch'ing Archives), hereafter WCT-P, 93, CC 19/2*/4; *Na-wen-i-kung tsou-i* 那文毅公奏議 [The collected memorials of Na-yen-ch'eng], hereafter NYC (1834; reprint ed. Taipei, 1968) 42.41–45, CC 20/12/21; SYT 53–56, CC 22/7/9; WCT, TK 3/11/24; CCT-NM 2297:6, CC 10/5/21; KCT-NM 493:1, CC 21/1/10. For surviving copies, see n. 2, above; Fou Si-houa, p. 61; Li Shih-yü, *Pao-chüan tsung-lu* 寶卷綜錄 [A comprehensive bibliography of sacred scrolls] (Peking: Chung-hua 中華, 1961), number 167.

[32] KCT-NM 490:2, CL 40/2/21. For monks, Welch, *Practice of Chinese Buddhism*, pp. 99, 491, and chap. 7. Laymen were not supposed to perform these services.

ing passports (*lu-yin*) that would expedite the soul's passage from the underworld into paradise. These passports probably resembled those made up and
sold by priests and monks.[33] They were single sheets of paper or silk cloth, with
writing on them that invoked the power of sectarian deities, and on which
official-looking seals were usually stamped. Sect members printed up the forms
in bulk, leaving blank spaces for the name of the bearer; then the passports were
sold to individuals or to the relatives of deceased people. The papers would
either be burned or placed in the coffin on the chest of the corpse (two copies
may have been used) so as to be near at hand in the underworld. The *lu-yin*
could be used by anyone, sect member or not.

Similar documents were available for White Lotus adherents exclusively,
documents that attested to membership among the elect and assured exemption
from the cycle of rebirth and entry into the Eternal Mother's paradise. Drawing
on the language of their scriptures, some sects called these documents "contracts" (*ho-t'ung*). New members were given a set of four sheets of paper: two
consisted of religious passages to be chanted, two constituted the *ho-t'ung*. The
contracts were pieces of yellow paper on which the bearer's right to passage
through the underworld was asserted and sect membership guaranteed so that
the bearer "could have his name checked off and then be led to the Golden City,
ferried across [the Sea of Bitterness] on a silver boat."[34] The idea of providing
documentary proof of membership among the elect (*yu-yuan*) was characteristic
of all White Lotus sects, and references to the process of registering one's name
and then, upon arrival in Cloud City to attend the Dragon Flower Assembly,
having one's name compared and checked off (*tui-hao*) are ubiquitous in White
Lotus scriptures.[35] (This approach to salvation also reflects the extent to which
bureaucratic practices pervaded Chinese popular culture.)

The above discussion has set out in general terms the constellation of
characteristics typical of one kind of White Lotus sect. The historical reality
was, of course, not only far more complicated but also constantly in flux. There
were sects that closely resembled the prototype and did so for long periods of
time; others evolved away from it. Preliminary data suggest that "classic"
sutra-recitation sects—the best examples of which are the early eighteenth-
century Lo sects—flourished under certain conditions. An understanding of
these conditions can help explain why these sects had to change if they were to
be successful elsewhere.

Sutra-recitation sects could take their fullest form not only when public
meetings and the construction of buildings for worship were possible but also

[33] There are illustrations of this sort of passport in Henri Doré, *Researches into Chinese Superstitions*
(Shanghai, 1914–1938; reprint ed. Taipei: Ch'eng-wen, 1966), I:69–79.

[34] KCT 47961, CL 49/4/26; KCT 48013, CL 49/5/4; KCT 50279, CL 52/2/27; SYT 292–295,
CL 52/3/2; CCT-NMSS 58:7, CL 18/8/3.

[35] See the *Chiu-lien pao-chüan*, chap. 9 and 19.

when members were literate enough to read and understand the texts, leisured enough to have the time for frequent meetings, and wealthy enough to support the infrastructure of halls, scriptures, and religious objects. And because statutes accumulated banning all White Lotus sects, believers could therefore practice their religion most freely and safely when and where government scrutiny was minimal. Preliminary evidence confirms that well-developed sects of this type were most likely to be found in cities, and particularly in the large and busy cities of Peking and of the Lower and Middle Yangtze. There, sects had large memberships (hundreds or thousands of individuals), many books, and complexes of well-established halls. (In most big cities, with the exception of Peking, government and elite interest in sectarian activities was apparently minimal.)

Members of monastic communities could devote all their time to religious activities because they were free from the concerns of daily life and because they belonged to an institution that gave them both discipline and training. Sutra-recitation sects emulated these conditions but accommodated them to the lay person's life. Their communities were only partially (and intermittently) separate, they had only occasional leisure for their activities, and their religious training was far less intense. Maintenance of this lay devotional life could be difficult and expensive. A government investigation that destroyed scripture halls, confiscated books and objects, and disbanded the community would require that the group renew its commitment and slowly and carefully accumulate new resources in order to recreate the old life. Lo sects located near the southern terminus of the Grand Canal never recovered from the prosecutions of the mid-eighteenth century.

Those sutra-recitation sects located in uncongenial environments found it difficult even to build and then maintain the simplest of infrastructures. Consider the problem faced by nine men from a village in Po-chou, Anhwei, in the late eighteenth century.[36] Several of them had learned about religious books, sutra recitation, and vegetarianism in their youth from older members of their families. As elderly men in 1781, they decided to revive these activities and to hold an assembly. Wang Fu brought a Lo sect scripture and some other material used by his deceased grandfather; Liu P'ei had similar items belonging to his mother; Li Tzu-ching retrieved a Lo scripture from descendents of an acquaintance; Li Shih-teng inherited one volume from a maternal uncle. In these scriptures, we are told, were recorded the Five Vows and words urging people to do good deeds. Then,

> [because] they wanted to dissipate calamities and attract benefits, they went to Wang Fu's house on the new and full moon each month and chanted.

[36] *Ta-Ch'ing li-ch'ao shih-lu* 大清歷朝實錄 [Veritable records of successive reigns of the Ch'ing dynasty], hereafter CSL (Mukden, 1937; reprint ed. Taipei, 1964) 980.10–11, CL 40/4/10; KCT 42617, CL 47/9/29.

Subsequently [five other men, here named], all of whom knew Wang Fu well, came to his house to listen to the chanting. Then they learned to recite the words of the scriptures for themselves.

Two of these converts then sought out copies of books for their own use, one borrowing a volume from a friend, the other obtaining five scriptures from a deceased relative and then copying Wang Fu's *Lo ching*. Thereafter, in addition to the twice-monthly assemblies, if anyone in the household of a member of this group fell ill, all would meet at that person's home to chant the sutras in order to "dissipate this calamity," and then share a vegetarian meal.

This sect was not highly institutionalized to begin with: they had no separate hall or objects of worship. On the other hand, memory of past practices (organizational and ritual), literacy, and the easy availability of texts made it possible for these men to recreate with little alteration the pious activities that had been interrupted by a hiatus of more than twenty years. The ease with which Lo scriptures were obtained was obviously critical to the success of this group.

The case of another sect, this one in P'ing-yuan County in Shantung, illustrates continuity under even more adverse conditions.[37] Since at least the middle of the eighteenth century, members of the Sun family from a village in this county had practiced their sectarian religion. They owned printing blocks, wooden seals, and a trunk full of scriptures that had been handed down for generations. The sect had expanded or contracted its activities in response to the leadership of this family. In the spring of 1822, because sect members had recently been reciting sutras only by memory and at home, Sun Wen-chih (into whose hands the books and other items had been transfered seven years before) decided to revive the regular assemblies of believers that had characterized past practice. He called together two dozen sect members from the vicinity and arranged that each would serve in rotation as an assembly head. Every month they met in one person's home and there made offerings and chanted scriptures brought by Sun. When people in the community at large asked for their services, the group went to funerals or to the home of a sick person to chant. (Some thirty-three people requested such help in a period of twenty months.) Although the Suns had in the past financed the reprinting of a scripture, most members of the group did not own one.

In the two examples given above, sects as a group made money by the performance of funeral rituals. Because both free time to engage in religious activities and the reprinting of books required money, sect members who were not wealthy were led to find ways to generate income. The Ch'ing state regarded such activities as the misuse of religion for deception and personal profiteering; "tricking ignorant countryfolk in order to make a profit for

[37] WCT, TK 3/11/24.

oneself" was an oft-repeated charge against White Lotus adherents.[38] Books, images, and offerings had to be paid for, however, and leisure too was costly. In the cases just described, groups of believers performed services for the public for pay, and individuals donated money and food to their group. These "profits" were thus shared and used to benefit the sect as a whole.

Other, poorer groups undertook different money-making activities, and it is in this context that the other-worldly passports and contracts (described above) printed by some sects and sold on demand can be understood. A particularly expensive silk *lu-yin* was sold in 1769 in Kiangsu for 1.2 taels, a substantial sum; paper passports cost a fraction of that amount but if produced and sold in large quantities represented a considerable income.[39] Enterprising sect teachers, copying the services offered by Buddhist and Taoist professionals, had found new ways to serve their pupils' needs and to recruit among the population at large.

The Sun family sect also illustrates the fact that when large numbers of books were unavailable, the continued existence of a community of believers could be dependent on the leadership and resources of a single teacher and on memory not only of rituals and sect structure but also of the sacred texts themselves. Even without halls or books for everyone, this group was able to re-establish a pattern of assemblies and to generate an income. Fluctuations between participation in and abandonment of religious activities, reliance upon teachers (not the group) as the chief custodians of books and doctrines, and a lower public profile are quite typical of the sutra-recitation sects that were common in North China in the middle Ch'ing. The sect led by the Wang family of Luan-chou in eastern Chihli illustrates this variant; by such modifications it was able to grow without always having the more elaborate institutions one finds in the Hung-yang or Lo sects.[40]

A scarcity of books encouraged teachers to rely on memorization of excerpts from the scriptures, rhymed passages that could be chanted in place of an entire book. Even a member of the Wang family itself, which owned a copy of the *Chiu-lien pao-chüan* (but stored it in a temple some distance from their home), admitted to learning about sect doctrine from oral transmission. He quoted

[38] To my mind, the more important question is not whether sectarian activities generated income, for they did, but if this money was used for the collective purposes of the group or the private pleasures of one individual. Regarding with suspicion all income-generating activities that could not be taxed, the Ch'ing state did not recognize this distinction.

[39] KCT 50279, CL 52/2/27; KCT 54821, CL 53/8/21; KCT 24036, CL 34/1/22.

[40] See the information on Wang Sen in note 2 above and my "The High Road and the Low Road: Lineage Strategies of the Wangs of Yung-p'ing Prefecture, 1500–1800" (paper prepared for the Conference on Family and Kinship in Chinese History, Asilomar, California, January 2–7, 1983). The most readily available collection of documents on the Wang family has been published in *Ch'ing-tai tang-an shih-liao ts'ung-pien* 清代檔案史料叢編 [Archival sources on Ch'ing history] (Peking: Chung-hua 中華, 1979), 3:1–90.

long sections of the text (about the three Buddhas sent by the Eternal Mother to
save the world) but maintained disingenuously, "all this was what my grand-
mother taught me; whether it came from the *Chiu-lien pao-chüan*, I don't
know."[41] Effective memorization required prolonged and intimate relations
between members of the sect (or at least between teacher and pupil). In the case
of the Wang family, male members were continuously on the move, keeping in
touch with their scattered congregations. Books were sometimes copied out by
pupils, but often oral transmission had to suffice. Excerpted passages (or at least
those later revealed to government authorities) did not necessarily concentrate
on radical sectarian themes but often simply restated Buddhist cliches. One
chant exhorted people to break free of evil habits in order to gain long life.

> Wine, lust, avarice, and anger are like four walls,
> The deluded do not recognize them and are trapped within.
> To leap beyond these walls
> Is the prescription for long life and never growing old.

(The original consists of four lines of seven characters each; the first, second, and
fourth lines rhyme.)[42]

The ways in which the desire for access to sacred texts and for a regular
income could combine to generate a larger following among the uneducated
are well illustrated by the case of Tung Min, a man from rural Chihli who lived
in the 1780s.[43] In 1780, a sect member from the southern part of the province
re-established contact with the family of T'ien Chin-t'ai, a well-known sect
teacher from Shansi who had been executed in 1762. He had previously
received from T'ien printed materials to be used for chanting, and wanted to
obtain more. These "songs" (*ko-tz'u*) were apparently rhymed and probably
had their own tunes (as did passages in late Ming White Lotus scriptures);
judging from examples available, they represented condensed versions of real
scriptures. This man learned that T'ien's supply had been confiscated, so on his
own initiative, using his own copies, he had blocks carved, and the song-sheets
reprinted. In order to guarantee the authenticity of these documents, he paid
the surviving grandson of the T'ien family for the right to declare (truthfully)
that the texts had originally come from them. In the next decade, he and a
colleague printed several hundred sets of these song-sheets and then gave them
to their pupils in return for contributions. Tung Min was a member of a sect
that chanted at funerals and for sick people. In 1786 he heard about these song-
sheets and acquired ninety sets, for which he paid five thousand cash. Tung
then made these songs available to members of his own small group, instructing

[41] SYT 333–336, 341–342, CC 20/12/26.
[42] KCT-NM 476:14, CC 21/3/8.
[43] KCT 50279, CL 52/2/27; KCT 50323, CL 52/2/30; SYT 292–295, CL 52/3/2; KCT 51168,
CL 52/6/12. Tung's profit was about thirteen taels. The income he and others gave to the T'ien
family was about ten to twenty taels a year.

them how to read them and asking for contributions in return. The availability of extra song-sheets, the model of Buddhist distribution of pious tracts, and the possibilities for profit clearly also encouraged teachers like Tung to sell these sheets to people who were not sect members. And indeed Tung Min sold sixty-one sets (for between one hundred and five hundred cash each) to women in his neighborhood.

Tung Min's case illustrates the further adaptation of sutra-recitation practices to groups that had no public space and no books and to believers who were poorer and less literate. Other sects simplified the ritual even further and made room for other levels of participation. One group in Shantung, for instance, held assemblies and chanted sutras to the accompaniment of drum and bell, but for those who could not read, it was enough to kneel to present a single stick of incense while the others chanted.[44]

In White Lotus sectarianism, as in Chinese culture generally, the quest for salvation and immortality was closely entwined with the search for good health and long life. In those sects that most closely imitated monastic life, a greater emphasis was placed on accumulating spiritual merit and escaping from the cycle of birth and rebirth, but other sect teachers (such as the Sun, Wang, and T'ien families) tended to physical as well as spiritual needs and thus reached a wider audience. The ability to heal was a sign of spiritual power in China, and for White Lotus members, healing became a way of attracting converts and securing a regular income. Some sects chanted sutras as a group at the bedsides of sick people, some teachers did the same by themselves, without the group.

The above examples show the changes in organization and activities that some sutra-recitation sects underwent. The need for income encouraged professionalism and rewarded entrepreneurial personalities. As horizontal ties between assembly members became weaker, the vertical connections between teachers and pupils became more important. But although rituals and religious ideas were simplified and occasionally supplemented with orthodox texts, written materials conveying sect doctrine remained central and the basic organizational framework was unchanged. Whereas, at one extreme, Lo sect members participated in funeral rites as semiprofessionals, familiar with the chants and rituals and practiced in their performance, at the other extreme, individual sect members performed this sort of service themselves merely by selling song-sheets or passports that could be used by strangers. Sutra-recitation sects thus ranged from close-knit quasi-monastic groups with leisure, halls, images, and fine books, to those who were pressed for income, met in private

---

[44]WCT, TK 3/12/22. The emphasis on special techniques of incense presentation is a characteristic of many White Lotus sects. Ample authority can be found in their scriptures. The *Chiu-lien pao-chüan*, for example, describes the great power of the right incense, with its special fragrance, to attract irresistibly the attention of the gods (chap. 1). The I-chu-hsiang 一炷香 (single stick of incense) sects incorporated this imagery into their name and met sometimes to chant songs but often simply to bow, burn incense, and pray. See KCT-NM 596:2, CC 19/5/28 for one illustration.

homes, relied on song-sheets or their memories, and provided medical as well as clerical services for a larger public. Clientele ranged from literate city dwellers to semi-educated country folk. Considered in this light, meditational sects, which we will discuss below, represent a development even further from the congregational mode.

MEDITATIONAL SECTS

Let us now turn to the second major type of White Lotus group: the meditational sect. These sects were not characterized by the lay monastic practices so far described: they had no halls, no sutras, no vows, no vegetarian diet, no funeral rituals. The act of meditation was the primary focus of religious activity. Meditational chants were transmitted orally and ritual was simple. Martial arts were sometimes passed along together with methods of breath circulation; both were intended to benefit the practitioner in this world as well as the next. Individual sect teachers routinely used healing to attract new converts. The values they taught seemed marked as much by Confucian as by Buddhist influence and emphasized participation in society rather than withdrawal from it. Sects had no single geographic focus, assemblies were not a regular activity, and horizontal ties between members were weak. Because the most important bond was between pupil and teacher, vertical links within long chains of masters and disciples were strong. A well-developed system of formal and regular contributions to teachers strengthened their power and resources. Late Ming patriarchs played no role in the history of these sects, although one family was a focus for millenarian expectations. Members of this type of sect appear to have been rural people with little or no education; the great majority lived in the villages of North China. Sects of this type appear to have emerged in the early eighteenth century (possibly earlier) among the pupils of a single family of teachers, the Liu family of Shan County in southwestern Shantung. Such sects used a variety of names, but most commonly borrowed the name of one of the eight trigrams—symbols derived from *The Book of Changes* and commonly used to represent basic configurations of the universe.[45] (For this reason, I shall here use the terms Trigram sect and meditational sect interchangeably.)

The history of the development of White Lotus meditation is not presently very clear. In her book on Lin Chao-en, Judith Berling has described the rich traditions of Buddhist, Taoist, and Neo-Confucian meditation that Lin used as the basis for his sixteenth-century popularization of meditation as a path to enlightenment.[46] All three of those traditions surely influenced the White

[45] Some information on the Lius may be found in my "Connections" article and in my *Shantung Rebellion*, pp. 51–53.

[46] Judith A. Berling, *The Syncretic Religion of Lin Chao-en* (New York: Columbia University Press, 1980), esp. chap. 5. In the twentieth century, certain monasteries concentrated on meditation (as opposed to sutra recitation); monks meditated in the morning, noon, and evening according to a complex schedule that alternated periods of sitting with periods of rapid circumambulations. See Welch, *Practice of Chinese Buddhism*, chap. 2; Prip-Møller, *Chinese Buddhist Monasteries*, pp. 74–77.

Lotus. In fact, many late Ming White Lotus scriptures devoted considerable attention to meditation as the route to salvation. (The Golden Elixir technique described in the *Chiu-lien pao-chüan* was a special system of meditation.) Nevertheless, it was the Trigram sects, which had no such books, that turned to meditation as their central concern. (Further research on meditation in sixteenth- and seventeenth-century sects is necessary.)

The meditational techniques used in White Lotus sects in the middle Ch'ing have been described at length elsewhere,[47] and I will simply restate the essentials here. Prior to meditation, a believer would perform a few simple acts: making an offering, kneeling while holding a stick of burning incense (to attract the attention of the gods), and kowtowing (kneeling to knock one's head on the ground) a certain number of times. No altar or special place was necessary. There were chants (*chou-yü*) of various lengths to be recited during these rituals, chants that described (and served as a guide to) the actions performed ("a single stick of incense will easily rise up to the heavens," and so forth). Then he (rarely she) sat cross-legged and "circulated the breath" (*yun-ch'i*). One teacher of a Ken Trigram system of meditation was described (in 1820) as follows:

> He practiced an exercise (*kung-fu*) that would nourish one's nature (*hsing*) and one's life store (*ming*). He told people to close their eyes and circulate their vital breath, thus cultivating their virtue (*te*). The *ming* would negotiate the five viscera and emerge; the *hsing* would go through the five gates and then emerge. Thus one could reach our real home in the realm of true emptiness and see the Eternal Progenitor face to face.[48]

On one level, meditation was intended to benefit one's health and lead to long life; on another, it made possible direct contact with the Eternal Mother. In late Ming scriptures, patriarchs are often said to have ascended to heaven through meditational trance, but the average believer in a sect of the sutra-recitation type expected to meet the Eternal Mother only after death. Immediate access to the supreme deity was obviously a more appealing possibility, and promise of such a face-to-face meeting (between "Mother and child") surely increased the relative popularity of meditational sects.

The language of meditational chants borrowed directly from Confucian and Taoist notions that were not only found in White Lotus scriptures but were part of popular culture generally. Some chants emphasized that meditation established basic correspondences between the human, natural, and supernatural worlds and thus created harmony among them:

> Heaven represents the larger heaven,
> Man represents the smaller heaven. . . .

---

[47] Susan Naquin, *Millenarian Rebellion in China: The Eight Trigrams Uprising of 1813* (New Haven: Yale University Press, 1976), pp. 26–29; Overmyer, *Religion*, pp. 188–192. Neither of these books makes a distinction between sutra-recitation and meditational sects.

[48] WCT, TK 1/11/16. For these terms in each of the three meditational traditions, see Berling, *Syncretic Religion*, pp. 37, 43, 95–98. I have used her translation for *ming* 命.

or

As there are eight trigrams in heaven
And eight rivers on earth,
So there are eight mansions in your body....

One chant oriented the human body to physical space (the five directions), to time (the ten stems), and to natural processes (the five phases):

The ear corresponds to the east, to *chia* and *i*, and to wood.
The eye corresponds to the south, to *ping* and *ting*, and to fire.
The nose corresponds to the west, to *keng* and *hsin*, and to metal.
The mouth corresponds to the north, to *jen* and *kuei*, and to water....

This chant then instructed the devotee to "close the four gates and thus nourish your true nature, which is located in the place between your eyebrows." That place, the "dark gate" (*hsuan-men*), was the passage through which one emerged to rise up toward the Eternal Mother.[49]

Meditational chants seem to have usually consisted of no more than fifty characters; the majority were even shorter and thus easier to remember. Most had lines of seven characters each (as did large portions of White Lotus scriptures), often rhymed and with parallel grammatical structures that could also serve as aids to memory. The first few lines could sometimes substitute for an entire passage.

The best known and most popular meditational mantra consisted of eight characters, although longer versions also existed. The first line was "Eternal Progenitor in our real home in the realm of true emptiness" (*chen-k'ung chia-hsiang wu-sheng fu-mu*). This was sometimes followed by a second line, such as "Past, Present, Maitreya-to-Come" (*kuo-ch'ü hsien-tsai mi-le wei-lai*).[50] The two lines referred to the central historical vision of these sects: their belief in the Eternal Mother in her paradise, in the three historical eras into which all time is divided, and in the promise of deliverance by the Maitreya Buddha. The basic eight-character mantra could thus not only refer to visiting the Eternal Mother in trance but encapsulate the more radical message of White Lotus millenarianism.

By contrast, some mantras consisted of simple ethical exhortations and communicated very orthodox moral messages. One popular chant was drawn directly from the Six Maxims (*liu-yü*) of the first Ming emperor. In its simplest six- or eight-character form, it said, "be filial to parents, amicable toward neighbors" (*hsiao fu-mu, mu hsiang-li*). A longer form elaborated, saying that one should be

[49] WCT, CC 23/9/19; KCT 1044, TK 17/6/2; WCT, TK 3/11/24.
[50] WCT, TK 3/12/20.

Reverential toward heaven and earth,
Filial toward father and mother,
Respectful toward elders,
Amicable toward neighbors.[51]

Believers were also told to revere life and kill no living thing, to be benevolent (*jen*), righteous (*i*), polite (*li*), wise (*chih*), and thoughtful (*t'i-t'ieh*), not to be wicked and not to cheat those with more or oppress those with less.[52] This behavior constituted "doing good" (*hsing-hao, hsing hao-shih, hsing-shan*) and brought the merit that would assure salvation. The same hortatory tone found in these chants appears, of course, in Buddhist and Confucian works.[53] We might speculate that just as sutra-recitation sects emphasized pious Buddhist values as part of their public appeal, so meditational sects appear to have readily incorporated more elements from the popular orthodoxy into their teachings. Unorthodox White Lotus ideas could be identified with (or hidden behind) conventional values: the Eternal Progenitor could be presented as one's own father and mother, the "real home in the realm of true emptiness" as one's own village, and so forth. Such seeming similarities could speed conversion by making the sectarian religion taught together with meditation seem less bizarre and frightening.

In their most elaborate forms, the act of meditation and the recitation of mantras, like the repetition of a catechism, were ways in which the individual believer—without any intermediary—reviewed some of the basic tenets of the religion, adjusted the correspondences between human beings and the world so as to assure a spiritually and physically healthy life, and remembered how to live correctly. Sect members phrased these goals as "protecting one's body from illness," "dissipating disaster and extending one's life," "attracting good fortune and avoiding calamity," "preparing for the life to come." For sects without the more formal and detailed discussions of doctrine found in religious scriptures, the chants used in meditational rituals were an important source of continuity, but they also clearly encouraged a simplified understanding of the religion.

[51] The full text of the six maxims is 孝順父母。恭敬長上。和睦鄉里。敎訓子孫。各安生理。無作非爲. In 1652 these exhortations were ordered displayed on stone stele throughout the empire. See *Ch'in-ting ta-Ch'ing hui-tien shih-li* 欽定大清會典事例 (1899), 397.1. White Lotus versions (of which there were many) included the following: from 1815 (KCT 18834, CC 20/6/1), 孝父母。睦鄉里; from 1788 (KCT 54228, CL 53/6/8), 敬大天地。孝順父母。遵敬長上。和睦四鄰. For other versions, see NYC 70.40-47, TK 7/8/10; KCT 41681, CL 47/5/28; WCT, TK 5/12/22; NYC 38.67-72, CC 20/9/6; WCT, TK 1/11/16; CCT-NM 2308, CC 18/12/11; KCT-NM 779:4, TK 16/1/24; CCT-NMS 295:13, CL 51/8/9; KCT-NM 458:11, CC 24/4/26. For official popularizations of Ch'ing sacred edicts, see Victor H. Mair, chapter 11, below.

[52] Naquin, *Eight Trigrams*, p. 47.

[53] See Evelyn Rawski, *Education and Popular Literacy in Ch'ing China* (Ann Arbor: University of Michigan Press, 1979), pp. 136-137, for the similar tone of Confucian primers.

Altars and special halls were not necessary to these Trigram sects. Believers did not worship physical images of the Eternal Mother and usually disguised their references to her. Some sects kowtowed to Heaven (which, they would admit, was the same as the Eternal Progenitor), others to Heaven and Earth. (This term "eternal progenitor" [*wu-sheng fu-mu*] had come into common usage by at least 1724 as a way of referring to the Eternal Mother [*wu-sheng lao-mu*], perhaps because it had a less heterodox sound.) The ostensible object of many meditational-sect rites was the sun (*t'ai-yang*). (I cannot demonstrate that this too was a surrogate for the Eternal Mother.) Some groups addressed the sun as "Venerable Sagely Ruler" (*sheng-ti lao-yeh* or *sheng-chün lao-yeh*) and gave money "to be used for the worship (*chi-ssu*) of the sun." Believers kowtowed facing east at sunrise, facing south at noon, and facing west at sunset, reciting as part of the ritual certain chants that described their actions—"your humble disciple receives and welcomes the Sagely Ruler and begs the Venerable Sagely Ruler to shine forth," and so on.[54]

Entry into one of these sects could mean no more than the transmission of meditational techniques and mantras by a teacher to a new pupil. The level of training in breath circulation could, furthermore, vary a great deal: some believers knew how to go into deep meditation, others did no more than sit quietly and recite mantras. But even when the therapeutic value of regular meditation was not fully realized, new converts were aware that this system could give them access to the Eternal Mother's benefits in the next world as well as this. In many cases, the religious message was no more elaborate than this.

The martial arts that sometimes accompanied training in meditation (possibly influenced by the ritualized circumambulations of meditating monks?) were likewise intended to be beneficial to the health. They were also designed to provide this-worldly protection as well as useful skills during the expected apocalypse. These arts included various sorts of boxing, fencing (with poles or swords), and kicking. Like meditation, the martial arts were ritualized, preceded by offerings of incense, and accompanied by the recitation of chants. In the early 1770s, Wang Lun taught the following lines:

> If a thousand arms impede me, ten thousand arms will intercept them;
> The azure dragon [*yang*] and the white tiger [*yin*] will come to give protection.
> If I call on Heaven, Heaven will assist me;
> If I call on Earth, Earth will give me magical strength.
> Their guns will not fire,
> What men will dare impede me?

The relationship between the meditational and martial arts was theoretically complementary: the former were called "civil" (*wen*) arts, the latter "military" (*wu*). Sect members adopted the assumption common to elite and popular

---

[54] KCT 8014, YC 12/3/24; KCT 54994, CL 53/9/13.

culture in China that *wen* and *wu* were interdependent parts of an integrated system.[55]

In Trigram sects, the millenarian ideas originally set forth in White Lotus scriptures were, like rituals and ethical values, carried in easily remembered chants. A great many short couplets taught believers about the future; it is not yet possible to know if such lines were originally borrowed from scriptures.

> Change the universe, change the world,
> The year of rebellion, the year of the end of the kalpa....

> The seventy-two families will open up the yellow way,
> We wait only for one family to come and return us to the origin....

> If the time of the purple sprouts has not yet arrived,
> The true form will not dare manifest itself....[56]

Brief phrases such as "making known the Way" (*ming-tao*) or "responding to the kalpa" (*ying-chieh*) could also be easily remembered and still evoke visions of millenarian activity. But because of their mysterious language and ambiguous terminology, these phrases actually conveyed little concrete information and in this regard are typical of the way in which meditational sects communicated their religion.

There was among these sects a pervasive concern with what was referred to as the "coming life" or "coming age" (*lai-shih*). The Chinese term meant both the life one might expect after death and the millennium one might experience in this world. Believers repeatedly asserted that the purpose of sect membership was "to pray for protection in the coming life," "to ask for wealth and honor in the coming life," "to prepare through self-cultivation for wealth and honor in the coming life," and so forth. One believer burned incense every day and recited the following chant in order to "prepare for the life to come" (*hsiu lai-shih*):

> Having left the magical mountain and lost our way home,
> We live in this world of suffering and bitterness.
> The Eternal Mother will send a message
> And come especially to invite us to return home.[57]

This kind of language and the links between meditation and contact with the Eternal Mother and between martial arts and the kalpa calamities all suggest that the White Lotus millenarian message was especially close to the surface in these sects. Predictions about the arrival of the Maitreya Buddha, well known to sect members, gave a focus to such ideas.

---

[55] For the battle chant, see my *Shantung Rebellion*, pp. 59–60. For *wen* 文 and *wu* 武, see the same, p. 186.

[56] CSL 980.11–12, CL 40/4/12; Naquin, *Shantung Rebellion*, p. 57; KCT 50279, CL 52/2/27.

[57] CPT 147, CC 5/8/7.

Trigram sects shared the apocalyptic visions of late Ming scriptures and sutra-recitation groups, but appear to have been somewhat more willing to act on them. For leadership in the period of transition to the millennium, they looked to the Lius of Shan County, Shantung. The three historical ages were renamed Former Heaven (*hsien-t'ien*), Middle Heaven (*chung-t'ien*), and Latter Heaven (*hou-t'ien*), paralleling the Ch'ing-yang, Hung-yang, and Pai-yang terminology found in most scriptures. Members of the Liu family were identified as the ones who would be in charge during the last era, and were known as "Patriarchs of Latter Heaven" or "Patriarchs in Charge of the Return to the Origin" (*shou-yuan chih tsu*). Other couplets mentioned the arrival on earth of the Tzu-wei Constellation, a disguised reference to the Maitreya Buddha. Predictions that the long-awaited Maitreya would be found in the Liu family focused attention on them and perpetuated their religious authority.[58]

By contrast with the sutra-recitation sects, very few books were used by these Trigram sects. Government investigators sometimes found registers of names of sect members, handwritten volumes containing the texts of chants or diagrams for charms, and occasionally handcopied scriptures in small booklet form, but although these teachers were obviously literate, they seldom owned printed scriptures or whole books. The chanting of sutras did not have a place in Trigram ritual, and chants such as those discussed above were "passed along by word of mouth and retained in the mind" (*k'ou-ch'uan hsin-shou*). On the other hand, some believers were able to recite long passages of religious material of various sorts, perhaps once derived from written texts (as many as 1800 characters in one case), and there were several simple booklets associated directly with the Liu family.[59]

Like sutra-recitation sects, however, meditational groups were concerned with making sure that their members could be readily identified by the Eternal Mother after death and so find salvation. Their attentions were not, however, focused on the transition of the soul at death, and we seldom find funeral rituals performed by these sects. Believers relied instead upon announcements to the Eternal Mother of their membership to establish their place among the elect.

---

[58] Naquin, "Connections," and *Shantung Rebellion*, pp. 57, 121–122.

[59] For "passed along..." see CSL 1158.7–8, CL 47/69. A Trigram sect member named Liu Chao-k'uei 劉照魁 was arrested and interrogated in 1791. He recited for the authorities three passages taught to him by different teachers, all with the name "Eight Trigram Principles" (*pa-kua li-t'iao* 八卦理條). The first consisted of 1253 characters, irregular verse followed by a prose story about Confucius; the second was 340 characters long and combined verse and prose, recapitulating essential White Lotus eschatology; the third was entirely in verse (150 characters) and urged believers to pious activities. CCT-NMSS 2327:2, CL 56/9/27. Clearly, Trigram sects had a rich oral tradition, even if few shared in it, one that carried essentials of the religion without books.

Two books associated with the Lius were the *Wu-nü ch'uan-tao shu* 五女傳道書 [Book of the five women who transmit the way] and the *Ling-shan li ts'ai-ch'a ke* 靈山禮採茶歌 [Magical mountain ritual tea-picking song]. See CSL 309.42–44, CL 13/2/20; KCT 41883, CL 47/6/24; CSL 900.27–29, CL 37/1/13.

Ideally, such announcements were put in writing (as were most communications with deities in China) at the time of initiation: the teacher copied a facsimile on a piece of yellow paper, filled in the name of the new pupil, and then burned the paper; the pupil then kowtowed to him. In another sect,

> when they made offerings, they took down the name and residence of anyone who had entered the sect and wrote them down on paper and recited them. Those who could not write recited them orally with much sincerity. This was called "paying respects to the membership" (*pai chia-men*).[60]

Flexibility and simplicity in procedure and the willingness to substitute oral for written forms made it possible for teachers and pupils with few material or intellectual resources to perform these rituals readily under almost any conditions.

Organizationally, meditational sects were relatively diffuse and horizontal ties were weak. The crucial links were the ties between teacher and pupil. Yet these ties did not have to be particularly intimate, and the teachings were often very abbreviated. Thus, anyone could be a teacher and many sect generations could be created in a short time. Long, uneven, and rapidly expanded chains of teachers and pupils were most characteristic of Trigram sects. The act of initiation focused on the master–disciple tie and consisted primarily of the new pupil's kowtow before his teacher. Pupils regularly paid ritual obeisance to their teachers, even if the latter were younger or female—that is, the sect hierarchy took precedence over conventional relationships. The ties between teachers and pupils, despite their importance, were sometimes quite fragile, and unless reinforced by frequent contact, the links in the chain could easily snap.[61]

New believers frequently came to a sect because they had previously been cured by a sect member whom they then took as their teacher. The use of healing to generate converts was a very common practice in these sects and probably reflected an accommodation to a clientele for whom narrowly religious concerns were secondary. The desire for health, more than concern about salvation, became a major motive for conversion. The relationship between patient and healer laid the groundwork for the personal tie of disciple to master. Long life was a powerful and venerable ideal in Chinese culture, and in their healing, sect teachers utilized a wide variety of medical techniques (massage,

---

[60] KCT 54669, CL 53/7/28.

[61] For such chains, see Naquin, *Eight Trigrams*, p. 40. One man described the rather fractured (but very typical) history of his sect as follows in 1816: "He had heard that during the Shun-chih and K'ang-hsi periods [1644–1722] some man from Honan named Chang had taught the sect ... but after Chang died, the sect was not continued until 1769 when a Ch'ing-ho County [Chihli] man named Liu revived it.... Liu transmitted it to [this man's teacher] Ts'ui Ta-kung 崔大功 of Chiao-ho County [Chihli].... In 1810–1811 Ts'ui Ta-kung died; in 1813 Liu died. Because Ch'ing-ho County was not near, he had never met Liu and after Liu died, there was no one in the sect to assume responsibility." SYT 301–306, CC 21/2/28.

acupuncture, prescriptions, charms), often learned independently of the sect.[62]

In sutra-recitation sects, collective religious activities were the reason for contact between members. In meditational sects, rituals were more private, and a new member who had learned how to meditate would not necessarily meet with fellow believers on a regular basis. Teachers appear to have been geographically mobile (by previous profession or choice) and to have found their pupils in many separate communities sometimes very distant from one another. (White Lotus sectarianism was not so popular that entire villages readily joined, and it may have been because of the need to travel that we find so few women becoming successful teachers in Trigram sects.) Small groups of sect members might live in the same village but, even for them, regular assemblies were not the norm. Eating together was less significant for people who were not vegetarians, meetings were less convenient for the poor and hard working, and the construction of public buildings was expensive and conspicuous in the countryside. Each person merely meditated and made simple offerings at home every day or twice a month. Boxing groups, on the other hand, were formed by devotees in one area and, because of their more secular appearance and possibly a greater enthusiasm for instruction, met informally to practice their arts. Those groups who did sometimes assemble followed the pattern of the congregational sects. Believers would contribute money in advance for the purchase of supplies, then meet in the evening, burn incense and make offerings, practice reciting chants (without books or music) and meditate, and then share a meal.

In his lifetime, one teacher could witness the rapid transmission of his teachings through a great many generations of pupils living in many places. Because the most frequent meetings of sect members were not for devotional purposes and usually involved only pupil and teacher, these vertical ties were stronger than horizontal ones. It was customary for pupils to make calls (alone or in small groups) on their teacher, no matter how far away he lived. On such occasions, the position of the teacher was highlighted by the ritual of the pupil's kowtow and presentation of a gift. These visits appear to have taken place on ordinary holidays or on the teacher's birthday.[63] In fact, it was the giving of gifts that provided the excuse for regular contact between believers. The presentation of money was ritualized by the use of special terms: "foundation money," "installment money," "wealth-and-honor money." Each gift might range (as I have shown elsewhere) from a few dozen to more than several hundred cash.[64]

---

[62] Naquin, *Eight Trigrams*, esp. pp. 29–31.

[63] For nine years, for example, Chien Ch'i paid a formal visit on his teacher on the latter's birthday and on annual holidays, bringing gifts of food to his home in a nearby village. When the teacher moved farther away, Chien went only once a year, but he did so for another fifteen years. KCT 46730, CL 48/12/7.

[64] See the discussion in Naquin, *Eight Trigrams*, pp. 49–53 and appendix 2 for size of payments. Some Luan-chou Wangs also used special terms for monetary gifts. It is not now clear to me who used such terms first.

Both expectations about "the life to come" and the lack of regular community gatherings probably contributed to the practice of keeping registers (usually called *pu*) that listed names of believers and the amounts of their contributions. These registers, sometimes running to many volumes, helped keep track of sect members and guaranteed that appropriate rewards could later be distributed. Some teachers specifically recorded not only names and gifts but also the ranks and honors of high office, allocated according to the size of contribution, that were expected in the age to come. Keeping such books required minimal literacy, and they were a symbol of the group's power (indeed, evidence for the sect's existence) and a useful if hazardous tool for fund-raising.[65]

The collection of money by each teacher from his pupils and the existence of chains of teachers and pupils many generations long meant that substantial funds could be generated. This income gave teachers the leisure to engage in proselytizing and to cement ties between members on a full-time basis. Each teacher would take out a share of what he had been given and then pass the rest on to his teacher. Wang Jui, for example, had been brought into the Lao-li Assembly by his father (who traced it to the Lius of Shan County). Beginning in 1805, Wang collected about five or six strings of copper cash from his pupils; he kept a few strings for his own use and gave the rest to a member of the senior generation of the sect.[66] Such was the prestige of the Liu family that it was easy for pupils to collect money for them. In 1771, the Lius were found to have 12,400 taels of silver buried at their home and further support continued to arrive in the half-century following that investigation.[67] Money raising not only reinforced vertical solidarity but was the mechanism for re-establishing broken contact between groups.

Perhaps to make up for their infrequent face-to-face contact, Trigram sects used rather elaborate organizational schemes to relate scattered sects to one another. Although texts such as the *Chiu-lien pao-chüan* mention the stems and branches of the patriarchs' pupils and use the language of the eight trigrams, it was the meditational sects that took such ideas and made formal schema an important part of their identity. These followers of the Liu family differentiated themselves according to branches named after different trigrams and used charts to record generational seniority. An investigation in 1817 turned up not only a chart of the assistant chiefs of the K'an Trigram but a one-page Eight Trigram Sect Heads Genealogy (*p'u*) that, like conventional genealogies, listed names and birth and death dates. One aged sect teacher authorized the succession in his sect by writing up and dating in bureaucratic style a piece of paper stating that the right to be head of his K'un Trigram sect was thereby transferred to so-and-so, his chief pupil.[68]

[65] Naquin, *Eight Trigrams*, pp. 24, 84, 130, 294.
[66] WCT, CC 22/12/22.
[67] KCT-NM 508:4, CL 37/5/12.
[68] WCT, CC 22/12/22.

Individuals who belonged to meditational sects usually did not know one another personally. They thought first of their affiliation in terms of such-and-such a trigram sect. The Li and the Chen Trigrams, sects led by two pupils of the Liu family, were the most numerous. They developed (possibly borrowed) systems of secret greetings to allow fellow believers to identify one another. The secret sign was given at the moment when two strangers met and greeted each other: a special positioning of the first two fingers signaled membership in a certain sect. Special questions and answers could achieve the same end. "Which magical mountain (*ling-shan*) have you traveled to?" one would ask, and to reply "the south" meant being in the Li Trigram, "the east" the Chen Trigram, and so forth.[69] Leaders of these branch sects sometimes adopted special titles for themselves, both as a way of borrowing the charisma of the Lius and in order to provide another focus of identification for their pupils. A family named Kao from Shang-ch'iu County in Honan traced their teaching to the Lius but called their branch the "School of the Li Trigram Sect of the Realized Man of the First Hall (*t'ou-tien chen-jen*)" and asserted that members of the family were "Masters of Former Heaven."[70]

Although Trigram sects maintained a very low profile in their home communities, they were still conspicuous. Lacking the aura of piety associated with vegetarianism and sutra chanting and the legitimacy provided by the temples and images of popular religion, the activities of these sects probably seemed somewhat strange. The daily rituals of bowing toward the sun or sky and reciting mantras had few analogues (and may have more resembled Muslim than Chinese practice). It was unusual not to have statues and altars in a culture where gods were normally represented in human form, housed in temples, and treated like powerful people. Sectarian martial arts were probably also greeted with suspicion, if for different reasons. Fighting skills were associated as much with criminal activity as with good health. Furthermore, to train groups of men privately in boxing and fencing was to encroach on the jealously guarded Manchu military monopoly. The rituals of respect between pupil and teacher were modeled after relationships that were the foundation of professional training throughout Chinese society, but in these sects other conventional hierarchies were sometimes disregarded or inverted. The far-flung networks that these ties created were, moreover, not usually congruent with ordinary market- and family-centered associations, and thus represented the grounds for new and potentially unsettling alliances

The contrast between Trigram sects and the Lo sects is marked and seems to reflect a difference in both the resources and goals of the membership. Whereas the latter raised enough funds from a group of people living near one another to

---

[69] WCT, TK 3/11/24; WCT, TK 3/12/20; KCT 48843, CL 51/9/14; KCT 18960, CC 20/6/20.
[70] For the Kaos 郜: SYT 141–142, CC 21/10/24. Another pupil called the Kaos "Realized Men Who Penetrate to Heaven" (*t'ou-t'ien chen-jen* 透天眞人).

finance halls and images and books, Trigram sects generated their more slender resources by collecting small sums from a great many people scattered over a wide area. They based their appeal not on the tangible rewards of congregational life but on the charisma of certain individuals (often demonstrated through healing), the benefits of meditational exercise, and the power of millenarian prophecies. Lacking a geographic focus for their devotions, and without much leisure time, believers engaged in religious activities that were uncomplicated and easily sandwiched into the busy routines of daily life. They did not need books to learn about sect teachings, and individuals who were illiterate could readily join. Belonging to a sect meant having access to the short mantras and longer chants of an oral tradition. Finally, it was the teacher-pupil relationship, not the assembly, that was reinforced by ritual and shaped the structure of the sect community, creating a basis for affiliation with a larger group with whom personal contact was rarely made. Most of the followers of the Lius of Shan County came from the villages of North China. As we have seen, the characteristics of Trigram sects made them well suited to a region of intense state surveillance, and they appear to have appealed directly to a large but poor, rural, and illiterate audience. They did so by providing short encapsulations of doctrine in mantra form, by relieving people's anxieties about physical well being, and by stressing concrete benefits realizable in this world. Teacher-pupil ties, money raising, and millenarian prophecies became more important than congregational rituals and merit making.

Now let us turn to some of the problems faced by sects with few scriptures and formal institutions on which to rely in perpetuating themselves and their teachings.

It is impossible at present to determine the extent to which martial and meditational chants came originally from White Lotus scriptures. It is clear, however, that once an oral tradition was established, there was a tendency for portions to be lost, lines mixed up, and characters misunderstood or changed. The variations in the lines of the two most common chants (the eight-character mantra and the mantra on filiality and neighborliness) show that such changes did occur.[71] Where a similar term was substituted—as when *cheng* ("correct") replaced *chen* ("true")—variations in individual characters shifted emphasis but did not drastically change meaning. But when lines were dropped altogether—as when the second line about the Maitreya-to-come was eliminated entirely from what became the eight-character mantra—then significant ideas could be lost. A preference for the simplest form, one that was easily remembered and likely to appeal to the greatest number of people, did lead to

---

[71] Other variations on the second line include: "Present, future, Maitreya our master," "Present, future, our patriarch to come," and "Present, past, Maitreya-to-come." See WCT, TK 3/12/20; KCT 464, TK 17/1/30; SYT 89–91, CC 21/3/4; KCT 41681, CL 47/5/28; KCT 18152, CC 20/5/27. For the "filiality" chant, see note 51 above.

the reduction of the religious doctrine to a few key ideas and a few simple practices.

Such changes may, however, have reflected as much a devolution on the organizational periphery of the religion as a progressive deterioration over time. After all, sects that had too little religious content were not likely to survive for long as identifiably White Lotus organizations (although they could and did become the frameworks for other social groups[72]), and at the core of the tradition, committed teachers passed on the doctrines faithfully and in elaborate form.

The techniques of meditation and martial arts could be changed without substantially affecting sect doctrine. Capable people who had learned only the rudiments of such arts from their teachers could later devise or discover (and then teach) new and more effective techniques whose purposes were similar. The blossoming of White Lotus martial arts in the nineteenth century surely occurred in this fashion. Similarly, although healing was a manifestation of spiritual power, a great many methods could serve, and if they worked, they too could be perpetuated within the sect framework. As teachers continuously borrowed such techniques of long life from the culture at large, the White Lotus tradition was enriched, not depleted.

Without religious scriptures as a vehicle for the transmission and perpetuation of doctrine and as a source of authority, new sources of legitimacy were created. Trigram sect leaders relied for legitimacy primarily on their claim to be in a direct line of transmission from the Lius of Shan County. Some sect leaders asserted that they had also received authorization directly from the Eternal Mother via spirit mediums. Ts'ui Huan, after his teacher died, wanted to claim leadership of his teacher's other pupils but was "afraid that the people in the sect might be unwilling to respect and believe in me." So he urged a friend who was a medium to go into trance and pretend to deliver a message naming Ts'ui as sect head. Wang Lun, the leader of an uprising in 1774 in Shantung, likewise turned to a friend who was able to "go over to the nether world" (kuo-yin) to claim divine favor for his plans.[73]

Without assemblies to provide a focus for group activities, over time Trigram sects were not so much revived as reconnected. An enterprising believer might seek to re-establish links in the chain of teachers and pupils broken by death or geographic distance. The collection of money to assist one's teacher (and ultimately the Lius) was the most common way of re-integrating the vertical chains that constituted the sect and of expressing a commitment to a larger community of believers. Government investigations in 1748, 1772, 1782, 1786,

---

[72] David Kelley's work shows how Lo sect institutions among grain fleet boatmen were transformed gradually into a primarily secular organization, the Ch'ing-pang 青帮 (so-called Green Gang).

[73] For Ts'ui Huan 崔煥: SYT 141–142, CC 21/10/24. For Wang Lun: Naquin, Shantung Rebellion, p. 39.

1787, 1791, and 1817 all resulted from the renewed sectarian activity designed to aid the Lius.[74] We might look at one instance in detail in order to see the dynamics involved.

K'ung Yü-hsien was the nephew of a K'an Trigram chief who had been executed together with Liu Sheng-kuo (then the senior member of the Shan County Lius) in 1772. In 1783, K'ung learned from two men whose fathers had also been involved in that case that Liu Sheng-kuo's second son, Liu Erh-hung, was poor and hiding in Peking. They decided to "use the excuse of caring for Liu Erh-hung in order to revive (hsing) the old sect." Remembering past prophecies, they declared that Liu Erh-hung was the Maitreya Buddha. K'ung called himself Trigram Chief (kua-chang) and began collecting money. Formerly active members were contacted and new ones converted; each was taught the meditational mantra and asked to help by giving money. Each year, gifts of copper cash were converted to silver bullion and delivered to K'ung Yü-hsien (more than thirty-two taels in three years). But K'ung did not locate and help Liu Erh-hung; instead, he used the money to buy himself some land. (This behavior has the appearance of simple profiteering, but once self-sufficient, K'ung did become a full-time teacher.) Obviously, the mere claim to be helping the Lius had been enough to give new life to the sect.[75]

It is possible that the more volatile millenarianism of Trigram sects in the late eighteenth and early nineteenth centuries was connected not only to the economic and social consequences of population growth but to the difficulty these newly successful sects had under normal circumstances in expressing themselves as a community. Coming together in rebellion may have been, among other things, a kind of substitute for the sect assembly. The registering of names, donations, and rewards directed the attention of the believer toward a community that would be realized only in the "coming life." The knowledge that there were other fellow believers, unrecognized and far away but all children of the Eternal Mother and pupils of the Lius, surely created some desire for union, for greater solidarity with them against nonbelievers. Some sect members tried as individuals to locate and get to know other believers, but for most the realization of a world when "all were in the sect" could not take place until the great kalpa calamities that initiated the millennium. Wang Lun's rebellion in 1774 brought together hundreds of Trigram sect members who lived within several hundred kilometers of one another but had never met as a group until Wang predicted the time of the "return to the origin" and all left home to join him. In 1813, Lin Ch'ing drew together sect groups of both the meditational and sutra-recitation types, promising them an unprecedented

---

[74] SYT 215–218, CC 22/8/26; CSL 309.42–44, CL 13/2/30; CSL 1382.23–27, CL 56/7/13; KCT 41883, CL 47/6/24; CSL 1261.18–21, CL 51/7*/21; SYT 322–324, CL 52/3/5; Naquin, *Shantung Rebellion*, pp. 52–53.

[75] KCT 50189, CL 52/2/14; SYT 322–324, Cl 52/3/5.

opportunity for solidarity and union. "Be of one spirit with me, never to be separated, always at peace," read one of his rebel banners.[76]

Between the sixteenth and early nineteenth century, an extensive repertory of sectarian activities had been developed. The Trigram sects may represent an evolution out of the sutra-recitation sort in which, as we have suggested, first meditation and then martial arts were emphasized instead of group chanting in order to appeal to a different audience. In time, some sects concentrated exclusively on fighting skills. Premillenarian activities, on the other hand, were found in both types of sects, as was the readiness of believers to take violent action to greet the new era, and both witnessed an increase in popularity in the half-century before the Opium War.[77] And yet the more popularized forms did not automatically supplant other types, for their audiences were in part very different. Furthermore, when sectarian content was too far reduced, secular purposes replaced religious ones altogether; when visions of the millennium were acted upon, sects rebelled and were destroyed by the state. Thus, in the late Ch'ing, we still find a broad range of sectarian types active and successful, serving men and women of different strata from all over China, yet all passing along in their various ways the central vision of salvation through the teachings of the Eternal Mother.

HETERODOXY AND ORTHODOXY

Having seen the constraints under which all White Lotus sects operated and still survived, we should remind ourselves of the limitations on the institutional development of popular religion generally in the Ch'ing period. Both sectarians and their neighbors were poorer and less literate than the elite, both had difficulty finding leisure time and could not readily finance the apparatus of high culture, and both felt the restrictions of state control of religion. Although the government bore down on suspicious sects with particular vigor, it also banned unseemly or unorthodox (by its definitions) books and plays, attempted to register and restrict the number of religious professionals, and actively discouraged large religious gatherings of any sort. A disdain for vulgar (*su*) practices pervaded the rhetoric of the Ch'ing elite and government and encompassed the rituals performed by Buddhist monks, Taoist priests, and village spirit mediums, as well as White Lotus teachers. On the other hand, it is important to remember that members of the elite participated in the state cult as officials, usually patronized local temples, hired Buddhist and Taoist pro-

---

[76] Naquin, *Eight Trigrams*, pp. 152, 330.

[77] There are many explicit references to the worship of Maitreya in sutra-recitation sects, and there were collective actions in Fukien in 1725 and 1748. See KCT 11268, YC 3/6/2; CSL 309.38–41, CL 13/2/30. The first uprising to achieve any measure of success was that led by Wang Lun 王倫 (in the Liu family tradition) in 1774, and most of the rebellions (or would-be rebellions) in the next half-century were led by Trigram sects. See Naquin, *Shantung Rebellion*, pp. 154–158.

fessionals, and generally shared the cosmology and value system of their less privileged neighbors. White Lotus sects, although originally patronized by members of the late Ming court,[78] found most of their adherents not among the ruling elite but among the people at large. A major difference between orthodox popular religious institutions and sectarian ones was that the former could bridge the gap between state and society in ways that White Lotus sects were unable to do (at least not until the millennium).

By the eighteenth century, White Lotus sects were part of a continuum with the popular religion from which they had emerged, and they differentiated themselves from it to varying degrees. As we have seen, some sects considered themselves to be quite orthodox. Pious sutra reciters took monks and nuns as their models, and suspicious officials were frequently convinced that there was nothing heterodox about them. Meditational sects cured illness, taught techniques for good health and long life, and espoused some of the ethics of Confucian familism. Sects incorporated gods from the popular hierarchy into their pantheon, making them minions of the Eternal Mother, and they disguised references to their deities by borrowing the names of more orthodox ones. Statues to Kuan Yin, for example, were not uncommon among sutra-recitation sects, and their scriptures made frequent reference to her. Similarly, Confucius and Lao-tzu are mentioned routinely in sectarian texts, oral and written. In terms of daily life, furthermore, it does not appear that there was a clearly articulated, radically different White Lotus ethic in either type of sect. On the other hand, nowhere in White Lotus materials have I yet seen a single reference to that foundation of orthodox social relations, the Three Bonds (*san-kang*, between ruler and subject, father and son, husband and wife), and further research on this topic is much needed.[79]

One reason for the close connection between sectarian practice and conventional religion may have been that the one could substitute for the other. The success of White Lotus sectarianism may indeed have varied indirectly with the effectiveness of orthodox religious institutions. Not only did sects provide, as Daniel Overmyer has suggested, an alternative to popular religion,[80] they may also have tried to provide the same services. Thus, where religious professionals (such as monks, priests, and spirit mediums) were unavailable, experienced sectarians performed their functions.

[78] See sources on Wang Sen in n. 2, above. There was also court patronage of the Hung-yang sect (Li Shih-yü, personal communication, 1981).

My thoughts on the general question of heterodoxy and orthodoxy have benefited from discussions at the 1981 Conference on Orthodoxy and Heterodoxy in Late Imperial China.

[79] For a discussion of this issue and some examples of Ming dynasty White Lotus sects that *did* reject ancestor worship, see Richard Shek, "Ethics and Rituals of the Ming–Ch'ing Religious Sects," paper for the Conference on Orthodoxy and Heterodoxy, 1981.

[80] Overmyer, "Alternatives: Popular Religious Sects in Chinese Society," *Modern China* 7:153–190 (1981).

The contrast with indigenous Chinese Christianity, also banned by the Ch'ing state as a form of heterodoxy, is instructive in this regard. Intending to demonstrate the difference between Christian and orthodox values, an official (writing in 1811) also highlighted how in many ways sectarians were relatively "unheterodox."

> Christians [he wrote] do not respect heaven and earth, do not worship ancestors, do not show filial piety toward father and mother, do not fear punishment, ... do not seek to make money, and do not urge people to do good deeds. ...[81]

On the other hand, further along the continuum, there *were* sects that diverged from the norm rather more dramatically. Certain tensions between White Lotus doctrine and prevailing orthodoxies could be muted but not eliminated. The state seldom lost sight of the implicit rejection of the communities of family, village, and state in favor of the heterodox community founded on voluntary commitment to a new religion. The discovery of books in which an entirely unorthodox deity wielded supreme power, the uncovering of sects in which female members played prominent roles independent of their husbands, the periodic millenarian uprisings in which state authority was rejected outright, all added to the general suspicion with which the Chinese government viewed any religious institution and served to remind the ruling class of the fundamentally heterodox (*hsieh*) nature of the sectarian religion and to blind them to distinctions among sects. Moreover, just as some sects were more heterodox than others, so was it possible for a sect to transform itself slowly or rapidly in either direction. Whereas one group might deliberately make itself more acceptable, another might be persuaded by a daring leader to adopt temporarily a more radical style.

It is thus inaccurate to label all White Lotus sects either heterodox or orthodox; most were both. Indeed, even the definition of heterodoxy (as set by the state) was very fluid. The Ming and Ch'ing governments drew the line in different places at different times. A sect ignored one year as no more than a group of innocent Buddhists might be prosecuted later as a seditious society. And even though the statutes and substatutes banning sects accumulated steadily, the ability and desire of the government to prosecute also rose and fell. We must bear in mind both the fluidity of the definitions and the fluidity of the social reality if we are to understand the place of White Lotus sectarianism in Chinese culture.

The purpose of this essay has been to look at the ways in which the White Lotus religion was perpetuated and adapted in the late imperial period. By differentiating between types of sect activity, I have also tried to show that this religion was neither unchanging nor a confusing blend of miscellaneous prac-

[81] WCT-P 85, CC 16/4/19.

tices. It was a living tradition, with systematic variations within it, one that responded to the times and to the changing nature of the communities where it found adherents.

In the course of nearly five centuries, this White Lotus religion slowly created its own integration among different social groups and different areas of China. Although never united in a single social movement, these fellow believers shared a language, historical vision, and form of community organization that had an identifiable consistency across time and space. Moreover, even as they borrowed from elite and popular traditions to enlarge their own, White Lotus sectarians in turn influenced the culture around them. The central role of sectarianism in the development of popular religious literature is beginning to be demonstrated, but sectarian contributions to folk medicine, martial arts, and folklore have yet to be studied. Certainly the heritage of White Lotus millenarianism has affected the attitudes of Chinese of every social class and may even have been important in creating a receptivity to the message of the Communists. Once we understand the origins and development of the White Lotus religion, we will have to look also at its cultural legacy.

TEN

Standardizing the Gods:
The Promotion of T'ien Hou
("Empress of Heaven")
Along the South China Coast,
960–1960

James L. Watson

It can be argued that, in comparison with many other peasant societies, late imperial China had a remarkably high level of cultural integration. Of course, important variations existed at the local level with respect to kinship, ethnicity, and economic organization. Nonetheless, one need only read Eugen Weber's account of nineteenth-century France to appreciate just how integrated Chinese society was during the late imperial era.[1] Like their French counterparts, Chinese political leaders had great difficulty converting the peasantry to an ideology based on modern nationalism. But, unlike the French, Chinese leaders did *not* have to forge a new national culture based on urban models that were alien to the mass of rural people.

In China most villagers already identified themselves with an overarching "Chinese culture," an abstraction they had no difficulty understanding. The general peasantry did not need urban leaders to remind them that they shared a grand cultural tradition. This was true in spite of the fact that the Chinese spoke mutually unintelligible dialects (or languages) and were linked closely to their regional cultures—a pattern that would seem to parallel that described by Weber. An important difference between nineteenth-century France and late imperial China was that the regional elites played contrasting roles in the two societies. In France, if I understand Weber's thesis correctly, indigenous leaders became the champions of pluralism and did everything in their power to resist Parisian cultural imperialism. In China, by contrast, local elites shared a common cultural tradition (fostered by a standardized educational curriculum[2]) and were anxious to participate in the affairs of state. They could, in

[1] Eugen Weber, *Peasants into Frenchmen: The Modernization of Rural France, 1870–1914* (Stanford: Stanford University Press, 1976).

[2] Evelyn S. Rawski, *Education and Popular Literacy in Ch'ing China* (Ann Arbor: University of Michigan Press, 1979); see also her chapter in this volume.

the process, retain their regional identities as long as they were loyal to the idea of a unified whole. Chinese national-level authorities were themselves likely to have strong ties to kinsmen in the countryside and, hence, allegiance to the center did not necessarily preclude loyalty to one's region. In this sense China may have been unique.

The present paper examines one aspect of China's tradition that played an important role in the standardization of culture—namely, the promotion of "approved" deities by state authorities. At first sight, it is easy to gain the impression that Chinese temple cults are a manifestation of cultural anarchy rather than integration. Literally thousands of deities were worshipped in temples of every conceivable description throughout the empire. In most parts of China religious activities were not organized by a professional clergy. Local people built their own temples, installed their own deities, and ran their own festivals. On closer examination, however, it becomes apparent that the state intervened in subtle ways to impose a kind of unity on regional and local-level cults. The mass of peasants were seldom even aware of the state's intervention. A surprisingly high degree of uniformity was attained through the promotion of deities that had been sanctioned by the Imperial Board of Rites and recognized by the emperor himself.

Local elites, defined here as literate men with interests in land and commerce, were eager to cooperate with state authorities in the standardization of cults. Assisting in the construction of an approved temple was one of the many ways that an educated gentleman could "gentrify" himself and his home community. The unsanctioned, purely local deities gradually disappeared as new, recognized ones were installed in these temples. Local gods were never completely eradicated, of course, and it is still possible to find cults dedicated to deities known only to the residents of one or two communities.[3] Nevertheless, the promotion of state-approved cults in South China was so successful that, by the mid-Ch'ing, local gods had been effectively superseded by a handful of approved deities.

This paper focuses on the cult dedicated to the goddess T'ien Hou (T'in Hau in Cantonese), also known as Ma Tsu. Her temples are found all along the South China coast from Chekiang to Kwangtung, including Taiwan. She will be known to many readers as the patron goddess of fisherpeople, sailors, and maritime merchants. The study of this cult is particularly interesting because T'ien Hou was originally a minor deity that emerged on the coast of Fukien during the tenth century. For a number of reasons to be discussed below, the state found it expedient to adopt her as a symbol of coastal pacification in the twelfth century and, by virtue of imperial sponsorship, she eventually became

---

[3] Minor deities of this nature are found in villages throughout Kwangtung and Fukien. See, for example, Keith Stevens, "Three Chinese Deities," *Journal of the Hong Kong Branch of the Royal Asiatic Society* 12 : 169–195 (1972).

the leading goddess in South China. T'ien Hou's rise to pre-eminence is
conveniently marked by a progression of illustrious titles conferred on her by
grateful emperors (*T'ien Hou* itself is a title Western observers often translate as
"Empress of Heaven"). Not surprisingly, the elevation of T'ien Hou and the
promotion of her cult are paralleled by the gradual rise of state authority over
China's southern coastal region.

In this paper I examine the T'ien Hou cult from two perspectives. First I look
at the southern coastal region as a whole and chart the spread of her cult in
geographical and historical terms. I then concentrate on two small districts
(*hsiang*) on the Kwangtung coast and show how T'ien Hou cults were organized at the local level. This study is thus an attempt to address one of the
central themes set out by the editors of this volume. In what ways did the ideas
and symbols of China's bureaucratic elite "penetrate" to the local level? And
how were these symbols interpreted by the peasant masses? Here we have an
interesting case of a minor deity that was adopted by the state, transformed in
important ways, and then reimposed on local communities as an officially
recognized goddess. The flow of ideas was both up and down the hierarchy of
power.

These concerns are not always evident in the literature devoted to Chinese
temples and their cults. As I argue below, most anthropologists have under-
played the power dimension and focused instead on the collective activities of
cult participants. Chinese cults are thus seen as expressions of community
values (i.e., cooperation, solidarity, social equality); the shadow of Émile
Durkheim looms large in this literature.[4] As demonstrated below, the
Durkheimian approach glosses over some important aspects of temple organization and makes it difficult to trace changes over time. The analysis that
follows is explicitly historical in the sense that it charts the transformations of
two local cults from their foundation in the early Ch'ing to the present.

I begin with the assumption that people at all levels of the social hierarchy in
China try consciously to align themselves with temples that best represent their
own interests. This means that participants in the T'ien Hou cult were (and
are) aware of the symbolic messages conveyed by their deity. The pantheon of
Chinese deities, together with the symbols they invoke, can thus be viewed as
the basic elements in a complex system of communication. The exploration of
two local cults demonstrates how deities mean different things to different
people, depending on their position in the hierarchy of power. To the boat
people, for instance, T'ien Hou promised mastery of the seas and protection
from storms; to the landed elite she symbolized territorial control and social
stability; to Ch'ing authorities she represented the "civilizing" effects of approved culture. The physical attributes of the cults (i.e., the temples and the

---

[4] The "Durkheimian approach" to religion stresses the integrative aspects of ritual. This
approach, first developed in Émile Durkheim's *The Elementary Forms of Religious Life* (1912; reprint
ed., Glencoe: Free Press, 1954), has had a profound influence on Anglo-American anthropology.

images of the deities themselves) are usually—but not always—controlled by literate males near the top of the social hierarchy. Local elites kept a firm grip on their own cult organizations (including temple lands), but state authorities were ultimately responsible for deciding which deities would be sanctioned by the emperor.

The study of religious cults thus provides an opportunity to determine how values and symbols are transformed as they cross social boundaries. In the following pages the transformation of T'ien Hou as a religious symbol is traced through several links in the power hierarchy of traditional China. The analysis begins with state bureaucrats and passes down to the local elite, then to educated peasants, illiterate tenants, and finally to illiterate women and boat people.

ORIGINS OF THE T'IEN HOU MYTH

The goddess we now know as T'ien Hou was first recognized as a deity by the coastal people of Mei-chou, P'u-t'ien hsien in Fukien Province, during the late tenth century. Like many Chinese deities, T'ien Hou is in fact the spiritual representation of a living person who attained special notoriety in her home district. According to most accounts, the woman in question was born into a Mei-chou seafarer's family (surname Lin) in A.D. 960 and died in 987.[5] In childhood, it is said, she never cried or showed any emotion and, as an adult, she did not marry. She was, in short, an unusual person who did not fit any of the stereotyped roles set aside for women in Chinese peasant society. Toward the end of her brief life, local people were convinced that she had supernatural powers that allowed her spirit to guide seafarers safely home through storms. The first hint of this came when she dreamt of saving her brothers at sea, only to learn upon their return that they had in fact been aided by a mysterious female spirit. Soon after her death, seafarers along the Fukien coast began to report similar incidents, which they attributed to "Aunt Lin," Lin Ta-ku[6] (ta-ku is an honorific title that peasants confer on illustrious women; it derives from the kinship term for father's elder sister). Later, as we shall see, the Lin goddess was to be recognized by the imperial court and known by other titles. However, for the first two centuries after her death, the goddess of Mei-chou appears to have been treated like any other local deity capable of supernatural feats, of which there were thousands in China. It was, I would contend, the intervention of the state that ultimately transformed the local worthy "Aunt Lin" into the nationally prominent "Empress of Heaven" (T'ien Hou).

The account presented above gives only the bare outline of the T'ien Hou

[5] A reliable summary of these accounts is provided by J. J. L. Duyvendak, "The True Dates of the Chinese Maritime Expeditions in the Early Fifteenth Century," *T'oung Pao* 34:341–412 (1939).

[6] Jen Yu-wen, "The Southern Sung Stone Engraving at North Fu-t'ang," *Journal of the Hong Kong Branch of the Royal Asiatic Society* 5:65–68 (1965).

myth. There are, of course, many lengthy versions of the myth, which differ with respect to the circumstances of the Lin woman's life and the nature of her spiritual exploits after death. Some of these are preserved in written records that have been standardized over the centuries.[7] Others are passed on orally and, hence, even today the goddess's story is undergoing transformation. The study of myth in China thus presents a special problem to anthropologists who draw their inspiration from the structuralist tradition of Lévi-Strauss and his followers. Most structuralist theories of myth derive from research on nonliterate people and, as such, the problem of competing written versions does not arise. Those anthropologists who do work on written myths have, for the most part, focused on classical traditions (e.g., ancient Greek or Hebrew texts) that are extinct and thus no longer undergoing oral transformation.[8] Chinese myths like that of T'ien Hou are difficult to analyze systematically because they are very much alive—at least in the area under study here. Later in this paper I attempt an analysis (although not necessarily a "structural" one) of the T'ien Hou myth, showing how different sets of people choose to emphasize certain elements of the goddess's story and downplay others. Those at the top of the social hierarchy accept the standard written version of the myth as "true" or "correct," while those at the bottom, notably boat people and illiterate women, are oblivious to any but the oral versions.

David Johnson has worked on similar problems in his study of the myth of Wu Tzu-hsu,[9] a Chinese minister-hero who lived during the fifth century B.C. T'ien Hou and Wu Tzu-hsu were both, according to their myths, paragons of virtue and both were recognized as deities after death—but here the similarities end. It is Johnson's method of analysis, rather than the parallels between the two mythic characters, that warrants our attention here. According to Johnson, the records of such characters are preserved at many levels in Chinese society, primarily by the literate elite but also by the unsophisticated peasantry. In the Wu Tzu-hsu case, the written documents tend to incorporate aspects of the myth from numerous sources, and thus, after several centuries, it becomes difficult to distinguish those elements that were once part of the oral tradition. This blending of oral and literary traditions is complicated by the fact that the authors of published accounts do not always write for the same audience.[10]

---

[7] See for example Wen Pao-chai 文寶齋, comp., *T'ien Hou pen-chuan* 天后本傳 (Foochow, 1816). This booklet, an inexpensive tract typical of its type, appears to have been compiled largely from an earlier edition of the Fukien provincial gazetteer. Other evidence of standardization is found in the broadsheets handed out at T'ien Hou temples and published in annual festival booklets. Several of these popular texts are in my possession. One, collected at the Lukang (Taiwan) Ma Tsu temple (see n. 32, below), and another, collected in one of Hong Kong's leading temples (near Yuen Long), are almost identical in their rendering of the T'ien Hou myth. (See also James Hayes's essay, chap. 3 above.)

[8] See, for example, Edmund Leach, *Genesis as Myth and Other Essays* (London: Cape, 1969).

[9] David Johnson, "The Wu Tzu-hsü *Pien-wen* and Its Sources," *Harvard Journal of Asiatic Studies* 40:93–156, 465–505 (1980).

[10] Ibid., pp. 97–103.

Similar problems exist when one examines oral and written versions of T'ien Hou's life and death. As we shall see, these variations in the basic mythic structure are important because they allow people of all social stations to claim T'ien Hou as one of their own and, hence, their patron goddess. It is notable that the literate elite made use of T'ien Hou's story to enhance its own position by ensuring that the written versions stress her "worthy" social origins in the family of a virtuous official of low rank. The elite versions also tend to ignore the fact that the woman who was to become T'ien Hou lived to be 27 and did not marry, deviating from the norm of her era and place. T'ien Hou's death is also glossed over in the written versions and little is said about it except that she was freed to become a spirit and rose on a cloud to Heaven.

In contrast to the written versions, the goddess emerges as the daughter of a poor fisherman among the peasants of Taiwan.[11] When asked, illiterate people in the New Territories usually replied that the goddess was the seventh child of a *shui shang jen* (a castelike category of boat people often referred to as "Tanka", an ethnic slur). Many of the oral versions of T'ien Hou's myth contain strong hints that, in addition to her services to male seafarers, she had a special relationship with spinsters and other unmarried women. In some accounts, for instance, she refused to marry and became notable as a seer or medium.[12] One oral account from Taiwan reports that she voluntarily ended her life with a total fast.[13] A number of women in the New Territories maintained quite firmly to me that T'ien Hou killed herself rather than marry an older man chosen by her parents. Duyvendak, in his study of this cult, gives an indirect hint that suicide may have been accepted as the means of death in other versions of the T'ien Hou myth. After her death, he notes, the goddess often appeared in a red dress.[14] Although Duyvendak offers no explanation, the appearance of a female spirit in a red gown is an unambiguous symbol of suicide in Chinese peasant society. Women who have reached the end of their patience sometimes commit suicide in a red wedding gown. This extra measure gives the deceased's spirit awesome powers.[15]

Whatever the circumstances of her life and the means of her death, the

[11] Michael Saso, *Taiwan Feasts and Customs* (Hsinchu, Taiwan: Chabanel Language Institute, 1968), p. 41.

[12] C. K. Yang, *Religion in Chinese Society* (Berkeley: University of California Press, 1961), p. 73; and Lewis Hodous, *Folkways in China* (London: Probsthain, 1929), p. 105.

[13] Saso, *Taiwan Feasts*, p. 42.

[14] Duyvendak, "True Dates," p. 344.

[15] The red wedding dress symbolizes the liminality of a woman as she is transferred between two families; see Rubie S. Watson, "Class Differences and Affinal Relations in South China," *Man* 16:593–615 (1981). Suicide in this liminal state creates an uncontrollable ghost, one without ties to any kin group. On suicide in traditional China, see Margery Wolf, "Women and Suicide in China," in *Women in Chinese Society*, ed. Margery Wolf and Roxane Witke (Stanford: Stanford University Press, 1975) and Wolfram Eberhard, *Guilt and Sin in Traditional China* (Berkeley: University of California Press, 1967), pp. 94–116. To my knowledge, at least two women in the New Territories village of San Tin committed suicide while wearing their wedding dresses in the late 1960s. In each case the house in which the suicide took place was abandoned and has not been occupied since.

written versions of the T'ien Hou myth show a certain degree of uniformity
concerning the charitable characteristics of the deity. The heroic deeds for
which she is noted concern seafarers who were threatened by storms or freak
waves. The most popular written records[16] of these exploits present T'ien Hou
as a universalistic deity who saves everyone in need, from the emperor's
favorite official to the poorest sailor in the realm. Written versions of the myth
always make a point of crediting the goddess with the suppression of pirates and
other "opportunists" (reading between the lines this can only mean boat
people) who take advantage of disorder along the coast. As outlined in more
detail below, this view of T'ien Hou as a queller of social disorder is not stressed
in all oral versions of her myth, particularly those told by fisherpeople. Among
landed peasants in South China, however, T'ien Hou is revered primarily for
her ability to tame the sea and bring order to the coast.

Before proceeding to a consideration of the state's involvement in this cult,
something needs to be said about the goddess's relation to other Chinese deities.
It is by now commonly accepted that the so-called folk traditions of religion in
China cannot be understood with reference only to the three Great Religions
(Buddhism, Taoism, and Confucianism).[17] Nonetheless, the special characteristics of T'ien Hou as a savior and a guardian spirit have led some observers
to speculate that she is grounded primarily in the Buddhist faith and is, in fact, a
transformation of earlier deities.[18] The impression is further strengthened by
the proliferation of tracts dedicated to T'ien Hou and written in the style of
Buddhist incantation manuals.[19] Other commentators maintain with equal
resolve that T'ien Hou is a Taoist deity consciously created to "offset" the
popular Buddhist deity, Kuan Yin.[20] Another theory of T'ien Hou's origin is
presented by Wolfram Eberhard in his study of South China's aboriginal
cultures. According to Eberhard,[21] T'ien Hou is often identified with, or
confused with (the distinction is difficult to unravel), a set of female water
deities that predate Han Chinese settlement of the south. One of these deities,
associated with river transport and rice transplantation, was known as Lin-shui

---

[16] Abbreviated broadsheets and festival booklets referred to in note 7.

[17] This problem is treated at length in the conference volume *Religion and Ritual in Chinese Society*,
ed. Arthur P. Wolf (Stanford: Stanford University Press, 1974).

[18] Hodous, *Folkways*, pp. 104ff., argues that T'ien Hou is a female transformation of earlier
male Buddhist deities.

[19] A booklet of this nature, entitled *Hung-jen p'u-chi T'ien Hou sheng mu ching-ch'an (hai t'ien huo-fo)*
弘仁普濟天后聖母經懺(海天活佛), can be found in the library of the School of Oriental and
African Studies. The book, compiled by Fang Hsing-shen 方行愼 and published in 1722, gives a
long list of Buddhist-style incantations for various problems. It is written in highly sophisticated
literary language.

[20] See, for example, V. R. Burkhardt, *Chinese Creeds and Customs* (Hong Kong: South China
Morning Post, 1953, 1955), vol. I, p. 13, and vol. II, p. 105; and John Shryock, *The Temples of Anking
and Their Cults* (Paris: Paul Geuthner, 1931), p. 79.

[21] Wolfram Eberhard, *The Local Cultures of South and East China* (Leiden: Brill, 1968), pp.
402–403.

fu-jen (lit. "Near Water Lady") and originated in the same Fukien coastal district as T'ien Hou (whose surname, Lin, is an exact homophone of the term *lin*, "near"). It is entirely possible, therefore, that T'ien Hou may have originated as a Chinese (i.e., ethnic Han) transformation of a non-Chinese (aboriginal) water deity. Although this line of enquiry is interesting, I do not propose to pursue it in this paper. Suffice it to note that T'ien Hou eventually became one of the leading deities of the Chinese "folk tradition" and, as such, it is difficult, if not impossible, to chart her origins with any degree of precision. We are on firmer sociological grounds when we deal with the uses to which this deity was put in the services of cultural integration.

STATE INTERVENTION: THE CREATION OF AN "APPROVED" DEITY

The process of incorporating a Chinese deity into the state-approved pantheon was, like the validation of saints in the Catholic church, governed by well-established bureaucratic procedures. It began with an imperial decree citing the deity for some special service to the nation. These citations took the form of honorific titles conferred by the grateful emperor. The first of T'ien Hou's many titles, Ling-hui fu-jen (lit. "Divine Kindly Lady"), was granted in 1156 in response to a request by an imperial emissary. The goddess had, it was claimed, guided this official and his fleet safely through a storm. Soon afterwards (1192), she received a slightly higher title, Ling-hui Fei (adding the designation *fei*, "Imperial Concubine").[22] These minor titles were important at the time, but the guardian of maritime travelers did not attain national prominence until the Mongol era. In 1278, Kublai Khan himself singled out the goddess for meritorious service to the state and conferred upon her the title T'ien Fei ("Celestial Concubine").[23] A series of related titles followed in the fourteenth and fifteenth centuries, including a particularly revealing one in 1409: Hu-kuo pi-min chih T'ien Fei ("T'ien Fei who Protects the Nation and Defends the People").[24] The goddess became even more important to the state as the Ch'ing emperors sought to tighten their grip on the southern coastal region. The founder of the Ch'ing (1644–1662 reign) attributed his own deliverance from a storm to T'ien Fei and granted her the illustrious title T'ien-shang sheng-mu (lit. "Heavenly, Saintly Mother"). And, finally, in 1737 the Ch'ien-lung Emperor elevated her to the exalted position of T'ien Hou, "Empress of Heaven."[25]

[22] Duyvendak, "True Dates," p. 344. See also Von Bodo Wiethoff, "Der staatliche Ma-tsu Kult," *Zeitschrift der Deutschen Morgenländischen Gesellschaft* 116:311–357 (1966), for a discussion of the chronology of imperial titles.

[23] Clarence B. Day, *Chinese Peasant Cults* (Shanghai: Theological Press, 1940), p. 84.

[24] Duyvendak, "True Dates," p. 344.

[25] Saso, *Taiwan Feasts*, pp. 45–46, gives this date for the T'ien Hou title but adds that the goddess was popularly known by the title as early as the Ming. Laurence G. Thompson maintains that the

Once T'ien Hou was recognized by the court, her cult fell under the jurisdiction of the Imperial Board of Rites, which saw to it that the goddess was treated according to the rules and regulations of the *ssu tien* (Register of Sacrifices). As C. K. Yang notes, this system of state sponsorship created a distinction between unrecognized cults and state-approved cults.[26] Many of the latter enjoyed special privileges, including the construction—at state expense—of elaborate temples in centers of government throughout the empire.

An excellent example of the promotion of approved cults is found in Harry Lamley's study of Taiwanese urban development. When Ch'ing authorities first took over the administration of the eastern Taiwan region of Ko-ma-lan, they discovered that the inhabitants (Chinese fisherpeople and farmers) did not have temples for any of the deities in the state pantheon. One of the first things the officials did was sponsor the construction of three new temples in the city of I-lan, the region's administrative center. Images of T'ien Hou, Kuan Ti (God of War), and Kuan Yin (Goddess of Mercy) were brought from the mainland and installed in I-lan. The officials in charge saw temple construction as an integral part of the government's mission to "civilize" the Taiwanese frontier.[27]

Official temples like the ones described by Lamley were used by government functionaries, but common people were expected to follow their lead. The highest ranking bureaucrat in every administrative center in China was charged with the duty of worshipping the deities in the state pantheon twice each year, during the spring and autumn festivals.[28] These occasions were prescribed by the Board of Rites and were normally at odds with the deities' popular festival dates (the so-called "birthdays" of the gods, or *tan*). For instance, T'ien Hou's annual festival falls on the twenty-third day of the third lunar month, while the dates set aside for her worship in the state-supported temples do not correspond with any major celebrations in her honor. This system of separate worship meant that many Chinese cities had two major temples dedicated to T'ien Hou, one administered by the bureaucratic elite and another controlled by local businessmen. The distribution of Ma Tsu (T'ien Hou) temples on Taiwan shows this process very clearly. In Taipei, for example, the official

---

T'ien Hou title was conferred in 1683, see *Chinese Religion* (Belmont, Calif.: Wadsworth, 1979), p. 61. The process of recognition did not end with the fall of the Ch'ing. In 1929, for instance, the Republican government issued an order that T'ien Hou temples throughout the country were to be kept in good order; see Chen Ta, *Emigrant Communities in South China* (Shanghai: Kelly and Walsh, 1939), p. 239.

[26] On the distinction between official and popular cults see Yang, *Religion in Chinese Society*, pp. 145–146; on the *ssu tien* see Stephan Feuchtwang, "School-Temple and City God," in *The City in Late Imperial China*, ed. G. William Skinner (Stanford: Stanford University Press, 1977), pp. 584–596.

[27] Harry Lamley, "The Formation of Cities: Initiative and Motivation in Building Three Walled Cities in Taiwan," in Skinner, *The City*, p. 195.

[28] Yang, *Religion in Chinese Society*, pp. 145–146.

temple was built inside the old walled city[29] but it did not become the primary focus of popular worship. Another temple outside the city is commonly regarded as northern Taiwan's leading center of devotion to Ma Tsu.[30] The pattern of dual temples is even clearer in the Taiwanese city of Lukang. Here the official Ma Tsu temple is a magnificent stone building; government officials spared no expense in its construction. Yet, from the day of its inauguration in the eighteenth century to the present, it has hardly been used by local people. Lukang's unofficial Ma Tsu temple is located only a few streets away and, in striking contrast to the state temple, it has become one of Taiwan's leading pilgrimage centers.[31]

On the face of it, the unpopularity of official temples in Taiwan's cities would appear to contradict one of the central propositions set forth in this paper— namely, that state authorities played a leading role in the propagation of the T'ien Hou cult. The question here is whether the state *led* or *followed* the masses in the promotion of specific deities. Did officials impose their own set of religious symbols on the Chinese people or did they simply respond to local pressure by aligning the state with deities that were already popular with the masses? This problem is pursued in more detail below, but it would appear that in the case described by Lamley state authorities led the masses, while in the port city of Lukang their efforts to "co-opt" the deity did not succeed. It is important to note, however, that religious cults in Taiwan developed under a special set of historical circumstances. The island was settled very late by Chinese standards (seventeenth and eighteenth centuries) and the pioneers came mostly from coastal Fukien, the original home of the T'ien Hou cult. In effect, these settlers brought the goddess with them when they emigrated to Taiwan. In Taipei and Lukang, therefore, the Ma Tsu (T'ien Hou) cult was well established by the time Ch'ing authorities made their presence felt.[32] There was little likelihood

---

[29] Stephan Feuchtwang, "City Temples in Taipei Under Three Regimes," in *The Chinese City Between Two Worlds*, ed. Mark Elvin and G. William Skinner (Stanford: Stanford University Press, 1974), p. 281.

[30] Philip C. Baity, *Religion in a Chinese Town* (Taipei: Orient Cultural Service, 1975), pp. 25–27.

[31] Based on personal observations in 1978, with the aid of a guided tour by the director of Lukang's folk museum. The famous temples of Lukang are the subject of two excellent essays by Donald R. DeGlopper, "Religion and Ritual in Lukang," in *Religion and Ritual in Chinese Society*, ed. Arthur P. Wolf (Stanford: Stanford University Press, 1974), and "Social Structure in a Nineteenth-Century Taiwanese Port City," in Skinner, *The City in Late Imperial China*.

[32] The oldest Ma Tsu temple in Taiwan is the unofficial one in Lukang; see DeGlopper, "Religion and Ritual," pp. 50–51. The local committee for this temple claims that it was built during the early Ming (pamphlet entitled *Lu-kang T'ien Hou kung*, 1977). This date, however, is probably exaggerated and a late Ming foundation is more likely (personal communications, W. S. Atwell and H. Lamley). The earliest Ma Tsu temple in northern Taiwan dates from 1661, when a monk brought her statue from the home temple in Mei-chou, Fukien, and built a shelter for it at Kuantu, on the Tanshui River (see Baity, *Religion in a Chinese Town*, p. 67). The important Ma Tsu temple in An-ping, Taiwan, is dated 1688 (see Lin Ho-t'ing 林鶴亭, "An-ping T'ien Hou kung chih 安平天后宮志," *T'ai-wan feng-wu* 台灣風物, 26:37–71 [1976]; I am grateful to Harry Lamley for drawing my attention to this interesting article).

that the offical temples would be viewed by local people as anything other than unambiguous symbols of state control. Unofficial temples, on the other hand, are to this day identified with the indigenous political and cultural interests of Taiwan.[33] "Branches" of these unofficial temples have been founded in villages throughout the island.[34]

The glaring opposition between official and unofficial Ma Tsu temples in Taiwan's major cities may thus be a consequence of the island's unique settlement history. Nonetheless, the Taiwanese pattern of dual temples does illustrate one of the main themes developed in this essay: T'ien Hou, like most Chinese deities, symbolized different things to different people. Government officials (most of whom were born outside Taiwan) promoted her as a symbol of imperial pacification and "approved" culture, while the Taiwanese people accepted her as the embodiment of their own independence. In this respect, it is significant that the goddess is known by her familiar name, Ma Tsu, in Taiwan and *not* by her imperial title, T'ien Hou. The historical circumstances were quite different in the region where I did my own field research. Official and unofficial temples also appeared in Kwangtung's major cities,[35] but they evolved *together* over a six-hundred-year period; hence, the distinction did not carry the same emotional charge that one finds on Taiwan. And, perhaps as a consequence, Cantonese fisherpeople and farmers have always referred to the goddess by her imperial titles, first T'ien Fei and later T'ien Hou.

Although space does not permit a full discussion of the subject, it is necessary to mention the geographical distribution of the T'ien Hou cult and its close identification with Chinese maritime interests. The earliest known T'ien Hou temple (dated 1122) is located in her home district on the Fukien coast.[36] From there the cult seems to have spread up and down the coast. The oldest temple in the Hong Kong region is dated 1266.[37] If the claims made for Lukang's unofficial Ma Tsu temple are to be believed (see note 32), the cult reached

[33] Personal observations in Lukang and elsewhere. Emily Ahern presents a similar argument for the local "earth gods" that have become the focus of Taiwanese cultural nationalism. See her "Thai Ti Kong Festival" in *The Anthropology of Taiwanese Society*, ed. Emily Ahern and Hill Gates (Stanford: Stanford University Press, 1981), pp. 397–425.

[34] "Branch temples" are formed by transferring ashes from the major temple's incense pot to smaller temples. Ma Tsu branches are found in the villages studied by Burton Pasternak, *Kinship and Community in Two Chinese Villages* (Stanford: Stanford University Press, 1972), pp. 111–112; Bernard Gallin, *Hsin Hsing, Taiwan: A Chinese Village in Change* (Berkeley: University of California Press, 1966), pp. 251–252; David Jordan, *Gods, Ghosts, and Ancestors: The Folk Religion of a Taiwanese Village* (Berkeley: University of California Press, 1972), p. 8; and Stuart Thompson, "Ch'ing Han Village, Yun Lin Hsien, Taiwan," Field Report, School of Oriental and African Studies (University of London, 1981).

[35] John H. Gray, *Walks in the City of Canton* (Hong Kong: De Souza, 1875), pp. 172–177, notes that there are at least two major T'ien Hou temples in Canton. It appears that, in contrast to the Taiwanese pattern outlined in the text of this paper, the temples in Canton developed together over a longer period of time.

[36] Eberhard, *Local Cultures*, p. 403.

[37] Jen, "Southern Sung," p. 67.

Taiwan in the early Ming (1370s or 1380s). T'ien Hou temples were found as far north as Weihaiwei on the Shantung coast from at least the fifteenth century.[38] The cult was not confined to the coastal fringe of China, however. Generations of Fukien emigrants adopted T'ien Hou as their patron goddess and built temples for her in Thailand, Java, and California—to name only a few overseas extensions.[39]

By the mid-Ming, T'ien Hou had become closely identified with Chinese commercial interests from Fukien to the Malayan peninsula and beyond. This was due, in part, to the testimonials of merchants and government officials who attributed their success to the goddess's divine intervention. Perhaps the most influential of T'ien Hou's many supporters was Cheng Ho, the imperial eunuch who became famous for his maritime adventures. Cheng Ho claimed that the goddess was responsible for guiding him through uncharted seas, thereby allowing the Ming court to extend its commercial empire far beyond the shores of China. Upon returning from his first expedition, in the early fifteenth century, he built a temple to T'ien Fei (as she was then known) near the city of Ch'ang-lo, Fukien. This temple became the rallying point for Cheng Ho's later expeditions.[40]

T'ien Hou also became the patron goddess of several merchant guilds that drew their members from cities on the southern coast. In Taipei, for instance, one of her major temples was the headquarters of the Amoy guild[41]; a similar arrangement was found in Anking, Anhwei, where the T'ien Hou temple doubled as the Fukien guild hall.[42] This is not to imply that T'ien Hou was monopolized by merchants from her home province. Doolittle notes that the largest T'ien Hou temple in what was then Fukien's leading city (Foochow) was in fact built by traders from Ningpo, Chekiang Province.[43]

As we have seen, T'ien Hou was a multifarious deity in the sense that she symbolized many things. It should not be surprising that maritime merchants and imperial officials chose to portray her as a queller of disorder on the seas. The sea was, in fact, the last frontier; disorderly elements (pirates, Ming loyalists, smugglers) could always find temporary refuge somewhere along South China's vast stretch of coastal estuaries and islands. Government and

---

[38] R. F. Johnston, *Lion and Dragon in Northern China* (New York: Dutton, 1910), pp. 385–386.

[39] G. William Skinner, *Chinese Society in Thailand* (Ithaca: Cornell University Press, 1957), p. 84; Chen Ta, "Emigrant Communities," p. 240; Eberhard, *Local Cultures*, p. 403. Skinner notes that, in Southeast Asia, the worship of T'ien Hou is an ethnic marker and is closely associated with Hokkien migrants from the Chang-Ch'uan (Amoy) region (personal communication).

[40] This sequence of events was confirmed in the 1930s by the discovery of a stone tablet in the Ch'ang-lo temple; dated 1431, the stone carries Cheng Ho's seal (see Duyvendak, "True Dates," pp. 342–345). Interestingly enough, Cheng Ho himself became the object of a cult and is deified by the Chinese in Java and elsewhere: see Stevens, "Three Chinese Deities," pp. 192–195, and D. E. Willmott, *The Chinese of Semarang* (Ithaca: Cornell University Press, 1960), pp. 213–217.

[41] Feuchtwang, "City Temples," p. 274.

[42] Shryock, *Temples of Anking*, p. 26.

[43] Justus Doolittle, *Social Life of the Chinese* (New York: Harper and Brothers, 1865), I: 262.

commerce could not be expected to survive for long in an unstable frontier. Cheng Ho, the Ming emissary referred to above, expressed these sentiments in a tablet detailing T'ien Hou's services to the imperial court. The goddess, it was claimed, had a "calming" and "civilizing" effect on the sea peoples encountered by the Ming expeditionary forces. Those who resisted were either killed or captured. The tablet concludes that "the sea route was cleansed and pacified" with T'ien Hou's assistance.[44] This vision of the goddess as a guardian of stability and order was later to be adopted by the powerful, landowning lineages that emerged along the coast of Kwangtung.

TWO LOCAL TEMPLES: THE ECONOMIC AND SOCIAL BACKGROUND

In the following sections, two specific T'ien Hou temples and their local cults are examined in detail. These temples are situated in the northwest corner of Hong Kong's New Territories, near the Anglo-Chinese border. Both are closely identified with powerful lineages that have dominated this region for at least three centuries. One temple, called Tung Shan Miao ("Eastern Mountain Temple"), is located in the village of San Tin—home of the Man lineage.[45] The other, Sha Chiang Miao ("Sand River Temple"), faces a stretch of coastline claimed by the Teng lineage. The Teng were the first to settle in this part of southern Kwangtung and now inhabit five major villages in the New Territories. Sand River Temple is controlled by a branch of this Teng higher-order lineage located in the village of Ha Tsuen.[46] As Chinese lineages are already so well documented in the anthropological literature,[47] I do not propose to outline the internal structure of the Man or Teng lineages in any detail here. Suffice it to note that these two lineages are representative of the landowning collectivities that dominated much of rural Kwangtung and Fukien prior to the Communist victory in 1949.

The Man and the Teng each control a *hsiang* of approximately twelve square miles surrounding their home communities. Ha Tsuen *hsiang* is one of the largest in the New Territories and incorporates a four-mile stretch of open coast that fronts on Deep Bay. San Tin *hsiang* is also located along the coast, but the Man

[44] Duyvendak, "True Dates," pp. 345, 350.

[45] A general study of the Man lineage is presented in J. L. Watson, *Emigration and the Chinese Lineage* (Berkeley: University of California Press, 1975).

[46] An account of Ha Tsuen's history can be found in Rubie S. Watson, "The Creation of a Chinese Lineage: The Teng of Ha Tsuen, 1669–1751," *Modern Asian Studies* 16:69–100 (1982).

[47] Besides the above, see Hugh Baker, *Sheung Shui: A Chinese Lineage Village* (Stanford: Stanford University Press, 1968); Maurice Freedman, *Lineage Organization in Southeastern China* (London: Athlone, 1958) and *Chinese Lineage and Society: Fukien and Kwangtung* (London: Athlone, 1966); Jack Potter, *Capitalism and the Chinese Peasant* (Berkeley: University of California Press, 1968); Rubie S. Watson, *Inequality Among Brothers: Class and Kinship in South China* (Cambridge, Eng.: Cambridge University Press, 1985).

and their clients have reclaimed thousands of acres of saline marsh over the centuries and the sea front has long since been encased by brackish-water paddies and fish ponds.[48] The people of Ha Tsuen developed a fresh-water ecosystem, but they could not rely on local fields to feed everyone in the community. From at least the 1750s until the 1960s, nearly half of the farming households in Ha Tsuen engaged in subsidiary occupations associated with oyster production, shellfish collection, and shore fishing. Wealthier Teng developed a number of lucrative industries that produced lime, cement, oyster sauce, and salted fish. Teng middlemen also nurtured patron-client relationships with full-time fisherpeople (*shui shang jen*) who anchored regularly in Ha Tsuen's territory. As members of a landed lineage, however, the Teng were always careful to keep the *shui shang jen* at arm's length; there was no intermarriage between the groups and social relations were restricted to the conduct of business. There is evidence that the Teng engaged in salt production, besides processing fish and oysters, from a very early date—beginning in the Southern Sung and lasting until the mid-Ch'ing. Salt pans were maintained on the tidal flats that once surrounded Ha Tsuen's present site.[49] The pans are said to have been owned by a wealthy Teng merchant who involved himself in Ming loyalist activities and consequently fled the village in the 1640s, never to be heard from again.

The people of Ha Tsuen, therefore, were heavily dependent on coastal products. A steady supply of oysters, fish, salt, and lime is what made the difference between commercial success and economic obscurity. Among the Man, reliance on the coastal environment was even more essential. The people of San Tin had no fresh-water paddies to fall back on and were completely dependent on the brackish-water reclamations. In addition to producing a single crop of red rice every year, they could manipulate the reclamations to trap large quantities of shrimp, crabs, and fish. The Man built stake nets along the outer perimeter of the dikes and leased these to boat people who lived in nearby anchorages. All of these activities were regulated by San Tin's main ancestral hall, which, in fact, owned some of the largest reclamation projects.

The Man and the Teng were dependent on the sea in other ways as well. Both lineages operated coastal ferries that plied between the area's major markets and population centers. The San Tin Man monopolized much of the boat traffic to and from Sham Chun, a leading market town. The Teng concentrated on the route to the Ch'ing administrative center at Nam Tao and the market in Yuen Long. By the 1850s, several landlord-merchant families in Ha Tsuen had also diversified into the coastal shipping business. They owned

[48] On the technology of land reclamation in the San Tin area see J. L. Watson, *Emigration*, pp. 31–42.

[49] On salt production in this region see Lin Shu-yen, "Salt Manufacture in Hong Kong," *Journal of the Hong Kong Branch of the Royal Asiatic Society* 7:138–151 (1967). This topic is discussed in the study mentioned in n. 58.

flat-bottomed freighters that carried local products (sugar, salt, fish, preserved vegetables, and the like) to markets throughout the Canton Delta region. These freighters were staffed primarily by members of the Teng lineage.

As an expression of territorial claims, the Man and Teng chose to build their T'ien Hou temples near the piers that serviced this coastal traffic. San Tin's Eastern Mountain Temple stands on what was once the high-water mark above the original beach. Lineage tradition has it that this was also the location where the Man established their first pier. Over the centuries, this pier has been moved several times to accommodate the lineage's massive reclamation projects. Today, Eastern Mountain Temple is located nearly a mile from open water, but the local people are still very much aware of its historical significance. T'ien Hou is seen as the guardian of the reclaimed fields. In Ha Tsuen *hsiang*, the T'ien Hou temple still faces the open sea; the oyster beds have not altered the basic ecology of the tidal lands along this expanse of coast. Sand River Pier, which stood nearby, is listed in the 1819 edition of the region's gazetteer[50] as an important communication center for Hsin-an *hsien*. Although this original pier was supplanted in the 1930s by another Teng-owned facility two miles down the coast, Sand River Temple is still perceived as the guardian of Ha Tsuen's commercial territory. T'ien Hou presides over the coast and, according to Teng elders, "she has a special relationship with those of us who are the original settlers (*pen-ti jen*) in this place."

T'IEN HOU AS A SYMBOL OF COASTAL PACIFICATION

The origin of the T'ien Hou cults in San Tin and Ha Tsuen can be traced to the turbulence that marked the Ming–Ch'ing transition. The collapse of the Ming and the early efforts to establish Manchu control over the South resulted in a period of unparalleled chaos for the coastal peoples of Kwangtung and Fukien. There is good evidence that the ancestors of the Teng had settled in Hsin-an perhaps as early as the Southern Sung (twelfth century); the Man also maintain that they have local roots dating from the twelfth and thirteenth centuries, but their claims are more difficult to substantiate. In any case, the pre-Ch'ing social structure of the region under study was nearly obliterated during the period from approximately 1640 to 1670. The local gazetteer presents a grim picture of the first two decades of Manchu rule, with famine and disorder combining to devastate the local population.[51] But the most important watershed of this chaotic era was the Great Evacuation of the southern coast ordered by the K'ang-hsi emperor in the year of his enthronement, 1662.[52] The people who

[50] *Hsin-an hsien-chih* 新安縣志 (Canton, 1819; reprint ed. Taipei: Ch'eng-wen 成文, 1975), pp. 258–259.

[51] Ibid., pp. 270, 364–373.

[52] On the Great Evacuation see R. Watson, "Creation," and Hsieh Kuo-ching, "Removal of Coastal Population in the Early Tsing Period," *Chinese Social and Political Science Review* 15: 559–596 (1932).

lived along a strip of land up to 50 *li* (approximately 17 miles) from the coast were driven inland and the area was sealed off by imperial troops. The evacuation was undertaken to deprive Ming loyalists of sanctuaries among local inhabitants. The oral history of the Teng is replete with stories of the suffering experienced by their ancestors during this period of disruption. (Significantly, the Man of San Tin do not have a corpus of myth relating to the evacuation, leading me to suspect that they did not settle in the region until the 1670s.) Finally, in 1669 the emperor relented and permitted the recolonization of the coastal strip. The Teng, Man, and other lineage groups rushed into southern Hsin-an to stake new claims and to reclaim old territory.

In the aftermath of the evacuation, I would argue, T'ien Hou was embraced by coastal settlers as a symbol of social stability and tranquility. We have seen how the goddess already embodied these qualities in the cults fostered by maritime merchants and imperial emissaries. There is no evidence that the many T'ien Hou temples built by landed interests in the New Territories predated the Great Evacuation. There were, as I have noted, earlier temples dedicated to the goddess in the Hong Kong region, but these were controlled primarily by fisherpeople and merchants who catered to the floating population; pre-Ch'ing T'ien Hou shrines are *not* associated with the major lineages. Sand River Temple was built by the Ha Tsuen Teng during the early 1670s, and the bell, installed during its first major renovation, is dated 1707.[53] Eastern Mountain Temple in San Tin also dates from the 1670s or 1680s, as does the T'ien Hou temple in the village of Kam Tin, Hong Kong's wealthiest lineage community.[54] The same pattern of postevacuation construction is found in many other temples controlled by landed lineages in the New Territories.[55] It would appear that there was a major boom in the popularity of the T'ien Hou cult along the coast of Hsin-an in the decades immediately following the evacuation.

At this point we must pause for a moment and ask an important question: Why T'ien Hou? There were, of course, dozens of deities from which to choose. One lineage in the region selected Pei Ti as their main patron deity, while another chose Hung Sheng.[56] And yet six major lineages in Hong Kong promoted T'ien Hou as their patron, together with at least four other

[53] *Hsia ts'un hsiang-yueh shih-nien t'ai-p'ing ch'ing-chiao* 厦村鄉約十年太平清醮 (Ha Tsuen, 1974), p. 36, and personal observation at Sand River Temple.

[54] Sung Hok-p'ang, "Legends and Stories of the New Territories: Kam Tin," *Journal of the Hong Kong Branch of the Royal Asiatic Society* 14:160–185 (1974), p. 184; and inscription evidence in San Tin.

[55] For example, the T'ien Hou temple at Tun Mun (controlled by two lineages) was erected on its present site in 1698, according to a stone inscription. The bell in the T'ien Hou temple at Sheung Shui (Liao lineage) is dated 1721 (see Baker, *Sheung Shui*, p. 103) and the bell in Yuen Long Old Market's temple is dated 1716 (personal observation). Bell dates do not always correspond to the actual foundation of the temples concerned; in the New Territories temple bells were usually installed during the first major renovation, when the local people had become more affluent.

[56] The Pang lineage at Fan Ling and the Teng lineage at Kam Tin respectively.

lineages—to my knowledge—just across the border in that part of Hsin-an
County that remained in Chinese territory after the 1898 lease. It is not T'ien
Hou's association with the sea as such that made her appeal to so many coastal
lineages; both Hung Sheng and Pei Ti are categorized by the local people as sea
deities. The best clue to T'ien Hou's overwhelming popularity with landed
interests can be found in the written documents distributed by temple committees during the goddess's annual festival. Following are some highlights of a
broadsheet collected at Sand River Temple (it is almost identical to the
documents distributed at other lineage-controlled temples). The sheet begins
with a standardized version of T'ien Hou's origin and her services to the state; a
long list of pacification incidents is then enumerated.

> During the Sung, pirates caused troubles along the coast and T'ien Hou ma-
> terialized to make a storm which overturned their boats, killing them all.... [In
> another incident] T'ien Hou appeared at the mouth of a pirate's island cave and
> kept him captive until imperial troops arrived.... [Incident] T'ien Hou poisoned
> the drinking water of a pirate fleet, killing them all in their sleep.... [Incident]
> During the early Ch'ing, T'ien Hou helped the emperor vanquish pirates who
> raided the coast....[57]

The broadsheet continues with many more examples of the goddess's involvement in the suppression of disorderly elements.

T'ien Hou in this guise is an active, aggressive deity whose wrath is visited on
the enemies of order. Note that she not only suppresses pirates but acts as the
agent of their extermination. Here, for the first time, we learn that T'ien Hou is
capable of creating storms as well as quelling them. It is not hard to see how this
image of the goddess as a champion of social stability appealed to the founders
of the landed lineages that emerged in the chaotic aftermath of the evacuation.
Those who settled nearest the coast were never safe from the pirate gangs that
roamed the Canton Delta. The history of piracy, banditry, and kidnapping in
the two *hsiang* under study are explored elsewhere,[58] but it should be noted that
delta pirates raided Man and Teng territory well into the 1940s. To the people
of San Tin and Ha Tsuen, it is not a mystery why T'ien Hou was chosen as the
patron deity for their respective lineages. As one elder put it to me, "Our
ancestors needed all the help they could get."

No doubt there were other, more practical reasons why so many lineages
erected temples to T'ien Hou. The local elites that emerged during the postevacuation period were aware that the adoption of approved deities would give
their lineages certain advantages. The state did not actually underwrite the

---

[57] Broadsheet collected in 1978; the selections offered here are rough translations of relevant
sections.
[58] J. L. Watson, "The Protection of Privilege: Self Defence Corps and Local Politics on the South
China Coast," manuscript.

construction costs of these unofficial temples, but it did offer recognition in the form of wooden plaques (bearing T'ien Hou's imperial titles) that hung above the altars. The most important aspect of recognition, however, was the listing of approved temples in the hsien gazetteers. In effect, the editors of gazetteers had the power to censure lineages that failed to comply with state guidelines concerning the promotion of approved cults. Communities such as San Tin and Ha Tsuen stood to gain nothing by fostering the unrecognized deities that they inherited from pre-Ch'ing inhabitants (see below). The construction of a T'ien Hou temple, on the other hand, placed the community in the mainstream of "civilized" society and —perhaps more to the point—served notice to state authorities that the local elite was not involved in heterodox cults. As we have seen, the coastal people of Kwangtung suffered greatly because of government suspicions that they were involved in Ming loyalist activities (which, in fact, may have been true for some of the Ha Tsuen Teng). Adopting T'ien Hou as their patron goddess was one way the leaders of powerful lineages could signal that they were prepared to cooperate with Ch'ing authorities.

The boom in temple construction coincided with a campaign to re-establish government control over the major sea routes leading to and from Canton. During the K'ang-hsi emperor's reign (1662–1727), a string of forts and cannon stations were built along the shores of Deep Bay.[59] Two of these were located at strategic points near Ha Tsuen and San Tin.[60] Partly as a consequence of this pacification campaign, the Man and the Teng (along with other lineages in the area) enjoyed more than a century of prosperity beginning in the 1670s and 1680s.[61] The lineages expanded their populations and consolidated their hold on the regional economy during this period. Some of the newfound wealth was used to construct the T'ien Hou temples owned by these powerful kin groups. The elaborate multichambered temples that one finds in the New Territories today are a consequence of that golden era.

Not everyone who rushed into southern Hsin-an in the aftermath of the Great Evacuation fared as well as the Man and the Teng. There were many losers in the scramble for land. Some of these less fortunate pioneers, together with migrants who arrived in subsequent decades, became tenants of the major lineages. The postevacuation period saw the emergence of a dual-ownership system of land tenure, with tenants holding hereditary rights over the "surface" (*ti p'i*) of fields while landlords—in this case, ancestral estates of the major lineages—paid the land taxes and thereby claimed ownership of the "subsoil" (*ti ku*). These hereditary tenants congregated in smaller "satellite villages" in

---

[59] See for example Siu Kwok-kin, "The Fat Tong Mun Fort," *Journal of the Hong Kong Branch of the Royal Asiatic Society*, 18:209–210 (1978).

[60] *Kuang-tung t'u shuo* 廣東圖說 (Canton, 1862; reprint ed. Taipei: Ch'eng-wen 成文, 1968), pp. 156–157. See also *Hsin-an hsien-chih*, pp. 350–359.

[61] See R. Watson, "Creation."

the hinterland of San Tin and Ha Tsuen.[62] More will be said about the satellite village system later in this essay. Although hereditary tenants played an important role in the region's T'ien Hou cults, their view of the goddess was quite different from that held by members of the landlord lineages.

THE PROCESS OF RELIGIOUS STANDARDIZATION

A closer look at the T'ien Hou temples in San Tin and Ha Tsuen gives some insight into the process of religious standardization in China. T'ien Hou, in her local manifestation, was a jealous and—at times—vindictive goddess who did not tolerate rivals. The oral traditions of the Man and Teng make this very clear. In 1977–1978, I spent a considerable amount of time attempting to reconstruct the microhistories of various cults in the two *hsiang* under study. One of the more interesting findings was that, according to informants, T'ien Hou actually ate, or ingested, earlier deities when she rose to preeminence during the postevacuation era. The myths relating to T'ien Hou's "conquest" of the coast are vivid in their imagery; we will begin with Sand River Temple near Ha Tsuen.

The Teng claim that an earlier deity, Sha Chiang Ma (Sand River Mother), once presided over the strip of coast now governed by T'ien Hou. Sand River Mother is a parochial goddess who is not recognized outside Ha Tsuen *hsiang*. The accounts of this goddess and her demise are part of the region's oral tradition and, as such, they must be treated like any other body of myth. It is not the historical veracity of the Sand River Mother stories that should preoccupy us here. My own interest in analyzing local myths is to find clues to the way local people *think* about their deities. According to most informants, Sand River Mother was the patron of the original inhabitants who lived along the Ha Tsuen coast prior to the arrival of the Teng. Some time in the misty past, so the story goes, a cone-shaped stone was dredged up by a fishing net. The stone was taken to be the representation of a deity and installed in a shrine near the place where a small stream (Sand River) emptied into the sea. This minor deity, it is said, was worshipped by fisherpeople and itinerants who lived along the coast—sedentary farmers (i.e., "proper people" in the Teng's own conceptual scheme) were not involved in the cult. When the Teng returned to the region after the evacuation, they built a temple to T'ien Hou on the same spot and took possession of Sand River Mother's stone representation. Rather than discarding the stone, they used it as the foundation for the Teng's own molded statue of T'ien Hou. At this point in the story, local people maintain that T'ien Hou "ate" (Cantonese *shik*), or "digested" (Cantonese *siu-fa*), Sand River Mother. As evidence that their version of the story is correct, numerous informants—

---

[62] The satellite village system is outlined in J. L. Watson, "Hereditary Tenancy and Corporate Landlordism in Traditional China: A Case Study," *Modern Asian Studies* 11 : 161–182 (1977).

Teng and non-Teng alike—pointed to what appears to be a pumice stone core near the base of T'ien Hou's image in today's temple. In my view it is largely irrelevant whether or not Teng ancestors actually used the original stone as the foundation for this statue; the important point is that local people believe they did.

Sand River Mother may have been ingested by T'ien Hou, but she did not disappear entirely. Once every ten years, during Ha Tsuen's *ta chiao* festival (discussed below), Sand River Mother materializes for a brief time along with other obscure local deities. All the deities known to have existed in Ha Tsuen *hsiang* are gathered together in a special shrine to witness a five-day opera performed during this festival. Most of the deities, like Sand River Mother, no longer have statues or even stones to represent them and, hence, their names are written on slips of red paper. They appear on the altar as rows of small placards, along with the portable images of major deities and the tablets of founding ancestors. In my experience, this is the only time it is possible for the fieldworker to collect a complete list of deities that play a role in the local pantheon. During ordinary times, the people of San Tin and Ha Tsuen worship only a handful of deities that appear in the region's temples, but as many as a hundred obscure gods and goddesses may be "invited" to attend important rituals. Elders explained that they dare not risk offending even the most insignificant of deities during the critical *ta chiao* rituals. This is the only context in which Sand River Mother retains a separate identity.

Here we see, in its most elementary form, the process by which a state-recognized cult is formed at the local level. Sand River Mother is only one case in point. A similar set of myths surround the installation of T'ien Hou in San Tin's Eastern Mountain Temple. The Man also claim to have taken possession of a fisherpeople's shrine and "raised" (*ch'i*) a T'ien Hou temple on the same spot. There are also hints that the T'ien Hou statue in San Tin incorporates a stone representation of another deity. In every case that I have investigated in the New Territories (seven in all), T'ien Hou has superseded a parochial deity and become the leading cult figure of the *hsiang*. It will be noted, however, that she does not actually destroy or obliterate the original incumbents. Rather, in the words of one informant, T'ien Hou takes on the spiritual essence, or "steam" (Cantonese *ching hei*), of those she assimilates and "grows stronger every time she eats a local deity like Sand River Mother." As I hope to show in the next section, T'ien Hou's spiritual conquest of the Kwangtung coast can be seen as a metaphor of political domination in the real world.

T'IEN HOU AS A SYMBOL OF LINEAGE HEGEMONY

In most parts of China, T'ien Hou is identified primarily as a guardian of seafarers and a defender of the coast. However, in the two *hsiang* under study, the goddess has taken on an additional representation as a symbol of lineage hegemony. By adopting her as a patron deity, the Man and Teng converted T'ien Hou into a territorial deity with jurisdiction over land as well as sea. T'ien Hou's role as a guardian of lineage territory is clearly expressed in the recurrent rituals performed in her honor. Space does not permit a full discussion of these rituals but the most important is a purification ceremony (*ta chiao*) held every ten years to placate lost souls that may cause trouble for the living.[63] Traditionally, every *hsiang* in Hsin-an had a recurrent *ta chiao* supported by everyone in the territory concerned (the Teng of Ha Tsuen sponsored a spectacular *ta chiao* in 1974 and plan another in 1984; the Man have not held a proper *ta chiao* since the 1940s). The *ta chiao* rites as such are extremely complex and last for five days and six nights, during which the local population is entertained by an opera troupe. T'ien Hou, as the *hsiang* patron, is physically transferred from her temple to the seat of honor in a special shelter near the opera site (she is represented by a small statue). Here the goddess presides over the rites and, according to informants, enjoys the opera. For the purposes of this discussion, the most important aspect of the *ta chiao* sequence is a procession of men who carry a pot of burning incense (also pronounced *hsiang*) around the boundaries of their *hsiang*. The procession, known as *hsing hsiang* ("walking the *hsiang*" or, alternatively, "walking the incense"), is thought to purify the territory controlled by the lineage and mark out T'ien Hou's domain.

The processions have all the attributes of a military operation. Only men are allowed to participate; women stay in the village and attend to domestic rituals. In Ha Tsuen, upwards of two thousand men take part. Until the 1950s, when colonial police began to patrol such events, *ta chiao* processions sometimes led to violent confrontations between neighboring lineages. Rivals used the occasion to claim bits of disputed territory for their own lineages. Another important feature of the processions was that tenants who lived in the *hsiang* were "encouraged" to participate along with members of the dominant lineage. The route always passed through satellite villages controlled by the landlord lineage and, if tenants or other dependents did not show proper deference, trouble was certain to follow.

The political dimensions of the T'ien Hou cult are even more salient in the rituals performed during the goddess's annual festival, her so-called "birthday" (*tan*) on the twenty-third day of the third lunar month. T'ien Hou *tan* is celebrated in this part of Kwangtung by a colorful and exciting competition. Small associations, known as *hua p'ao hui* ("flower cannon societies"), gather at major temples and young men fight over lucky coins shot from small cannon. The prizes are elaborate altars, made of bright paper, brought to the temple by participating associations (every altar is numbered and thereby ranked in order of "luckiness"). The associations are composed of neighbors and work mates

---

[63] On *chiao* ceremonies see Michael R. Saso, *Taoism and the Rite of Cosmic Renewal* (Pullman: Washington State University Press, 1972).

from hamlets or commercial enterprises in the *hsiang*; every satellite village has at least one such association. Should a village choose not to participate in the annual festival, this is tantamount to a declaration of independence and is viewed as such by members of the dominant lineage.

The territorial exclusivity of the T'ien Hou cult is illustrated by the regional organization of these annual festivals. Among land people in Kwangtung, T'ien Hou *tan* is observed on the same day in every *hsiang*. It is impossible for a Man or a Teng (or their clients) to attend more than one festival. The local cults are thus mutually exclusive and temples are not linked together in a hierarchical fashion, as one finds on Taiwan. Furthermore, the landed peasants of Hsin-an do not engage in regular pilgrimages to T'ien Hou temples outside their own *hsiang*. This, more than anything, explains why T'ien Hou is perceived by the local people as a jealous and vindictive goddess. Her festivals are arranged in such a manner that local people are forced to make a clear and unambiguous statement of their territorial loyalties once every year.

This does not appear to be true for the fisherpeople who live on boats along the Kwangtung coast. T'ien Hou festivals that cater primarily to the floating population are often staggered to allow devotees to attend *hua p'ao hui* celebrations in several locations. In the Hong Kong region, these observances sometimes occur two or three weeks after T'ien Hou's accepted *tan* date. If a pilgrimage complex devoted to this goddess does exist in Kwangtung, therefore, it is largely associated with boat people.[64] Boat people occasionally observe the festivals associated with lineage-controlled temples, but, as they are not considered to be permanent residents of the *hsiang*, they are not expected to bring an altar. Once they settle on land, however, the fisherpeople are treated like any other group of clients and they are encouraged to pay allegiance to the local T'ien Hou temple. More will be said about the boat people's vision of the goddess later in this paper.

THE ORGANIZATION OF LOCAL CULTS: LEADERSHIP AND CONTROL

The T'ien Hou temples associated with major lineages were (and are) managed by a handful of wealthy men and not by members of a professional clergy. Full-time keepers (*miao chu*) were sometimes employed but they were not involved in decision making. Temple records[65] show that managers were the same individuals who served as trustees for the lineage's ancestral estates. As rep-

---

[64] Two T'ien Hou temples located on islands in Hong Kong waters have become pilgrimage centers for the region's boat people. The annual festival at one of these temples, Tsing Yi Island, is held a week after T'ien Hou *tan*; see Graham Johnson, "From Rural Committee to Spirit Medium Cult," *Contributions to Asian Studies* 1 : 123–143 (1971), p. 142.

[65] Handwritten accounts and records dating from 1910.

resentatives of the region's landlord-merchant class,[66] these men had attended schools in Canton, Nam Tao, and Hong Kong. Ordinary members of the lineage progressed no further than the three to five years of elementary tuition offered in local ancestral halls. Most adult males in San Tin and Ha Tsuen were "semiliterates," to use Rawski's designation,[67] because they could not read or write beyond an elementary level. Nonetheless, this modicum of learning set them apart from hereditary tenants and other clients who, almost without exception, were totally illiterate. Local women (as outlined in more detail below) were also largely illiterate, irrespective of class or social background.

Landlord-merchants were the only men in the *hsiang* capable of handling the complex accounts and sophisticated records required for the smooth operation of temple organizations. Although the members of this class constituted an "elite" in the sense that they dominated the region's economic and political life, few attained the status of imperial degree holders. The Hsin-an gazetteer lists only three men from Ha Tsuen (and none from San Tin) who passed low-ranking exams—and they did not serve in government posts.[68] James Hayes has argued that the merchants who lived in Hong Kong's island districts were quite capable of managing local affairs without help from degree holders and imperial officials.[69] With certain qualifications,[70] Hayes's generalization also applies to the lineage-dominated *hsiang* on the Kwangtung mainland.

The T'ien Hou temples controlled by the Man and Teng were endowed with property to help defray expenses. In San Tin, for instance, Eastern Mountain Temple owned 1.49 acres of land in 1905.[71] The property concerned is located in one of the *hsiang*'s commercial centers and generates a considerable income in shop rents. The most important sources of income, however, are the contribution drives held to support temple renovations and decennial *ta chiao* festivals. Temples in this part of China are renovated, at great expense, approximately once every 70 to 100 years. The renovations are organized by committees of up to 30 men who live in the *hsiang*.[72] Every community in the catchment area of the temple, including satellite villages, has at least one representative on the

---

[66] For a discussion of the local class system, see R. Watson, "Class Differences and Affinal Relations."

[67] Rawski, *Education and Popular Literacy*, pp. 3ff.

[68] *Hsin-an hsien-chih*, pp. 442, 449. A larger number of local men purchased degrees.

[69] James Hayes, *The Hong Kong Region, 1850–1911* (Hamden, Conn.: Shoe String Press, 1977), pp. 181–193.

[70] There is evidence that some lineages in the region under study were heavily influenced by degree-holding gentry. The economic success of the Teng lineage at Kam Tin, for instance, is due in large part to the work of one ancestor, Teng Pao-sheng, the only *chin-shih* to have lived in the area that is now the New Territories. He was responsible for building at least one T'ien Hou temple at Yuen Long Old Market during the immediate postevacuation period.

[71] Land records, 1905, held at the Yuen Long District Office, New Territories.

[72] Evidence that such committees existed from at least the 1840s can be found in stone inscriptions at major temples. For a case study of one temple renovation see J. Watson, *Emigration*, pp. 141–143.

committee. It is taken for granted, however, that the key decisions are made by members of the landlord-merchant class.

Contributions are collected by the self-defense corps (*tzu wei tui* or, alternatively, *hsun ting*), a body of men drawn from the less advantaged sections of the dominant lineage. The history and organization of these local security forces are described elsewhere (see note 58) but, in the context of the present discussion, it is important to note that one of their primary functions was to enforce a kind of religious orthodoxy in the territory controlled by their lineage. This was accomplished by "encouraging" hereditary tenants and other dependents to attend the T'ien Hou festivals at Sand River Temple and Eastern Mountain Temple. Satellite villages that failed to present an altar at the annual gatherings ran the risk of collective punishment (i.e., the loss of livestock and the burning of property—including homes). Corpsmen also saw to it that clients of the dominant lineage participated in the decennial *ta chiao* processions. Colonial police put an end to many of these bullying tactics in the 1950s, but corpsmen still make the rounds of every household in their territory to collect donations for renovations and *ta chiao* celebrations. Residents of satellite villages deeply resent these intrusions, but they continue to pay rather than incur the wrath of their powerful neighbors.

Prior to the 1950s, the security forces of dominant lineages also made certain that minor temples (of which there are more than twenty in each *hsiang*) did not become the foci of independence movements. Many satellite villages had their own cults dedicated to deities other than T'ien Hou, but they remained small and did not compete with the *hsiang*'s central cult. Until British authorities interceded, the Man and Teng did not permit satellite villagers to hold processions on the *tan* dates of minor deities. In recent years, a number of satellite villages have made feeble attempts to promote independent processions, but the routes have never extended beyond the immediate boundaries of the communities concerned. Residents of these small villages are very conscious that their actions are interpreted as an intrusion into T'ien Hou's traditional domain and, by implication, the processions constitute a direct challenge to Man and Teng hegemony. Satellite villagers are, therefore, always careful not to push their former landlords too far. Corpsmen from dominant lineages are still capable of making life difficult for anyone living in the *hsiang*.

PERCEPTIONS OF T'IEN HOU: A STUDY IN CONFLICTING REPRESENTATIONS

As I have demonstrated in the previous section, T'ien Hou is generally perceived by land people in rural Hong Kong as a jealous goddess who reigns over an exclusive territory. In many areas she has become a symbol of lineage hegemony and participation in her cult is enforced by coercive means. How does this picture of local organization fit the image of temple cults presented in the general literature on Chinese religion? The most common view is that temple activities serve to reinforce feelings of social solidarity; periodic festivals are often seen as the concrete expression of collective values. This approach is summarized by C. K. Yang in his important book *Religion in Chinese Society:*

> In such communal events [i.e., temple festivals] the essential function of religion was to provide a collective symbol that would transcend the divergence of economic interests, class status, and social background, so as to make it possible to coalesce a large multitude into a community. People from all walks of life thus could tread the common ground of popularly accepted cults.
>
>   *   *   *
>
> ... the temple was a visible expression of the community and its collective interests, and public worship in it represented the periodic mustering of the community for the demonstration of common beliefs and common interests.[73]

The influence of Durkheim is readily apparent in these passages. Yang's view of temple cults is supported by many other anthropologists, especially those who have worked in Taiwan. Jordan found that "religious allegiances" centered on temples were the primary means of organizing and unifying Taiwanese rural society.[74] Diamond, in her study of a Taiwanese fishing community, states that the local temple was the "strongest organizing force in the village."[75] A similar view is presented for one of the villages studied by Pasternak; the interesting point about the latter's analysis, however, is that he demonstrates that not all village cults in Taiwan are expressions of collective values.[76]

Turning to the Hong Kong region, Brim argues that collective rituals at major temples serve the function of maintaining political alliances. Ritual, in his view, thus solves the "latency problem" that organizers of these alliances have in ensuring that local people will always be ready to defend their territory.[77] Brim's analysis does not hold true for all the cults included in his study but, in one respect, it does correspond to the publicly expressed views of local elites. One must bear in mind, however, that not all categories of people in the "village alliance systems" described by Brim share the same set of values and expectations. The Durkheimian view of Chinese cults, as expressed in the work of many anthropologists, seems better suited to multisurname communities in areas where powerful lineages did not dominate the political scene.[78]

[73] Yang, *Religion in Chinese Society*, pp. 81, 96.

[74] Jordan, *Gods, Ghosts, and Ancestors*, p. xvii.

[75] Norma Diamond, *K'un Shen: A Taiwanese Village* (New York: Holt, Rinehart and Winston, 1969), p. 77.

[76] Pasternak, *Kinship and Community*, pp. 111–112, 125–126.

[77] John A. Brim, "Village Alliance Temples in Hong Kong," in Wolf, *Religion and Ritual*, p. 102.

[78] See also Marjorie Topley, "Chinese Religion and Rural Cohesion in the Nineteenth Century," *Journal of the Hong Kong Branch of the Royal Asiatic Society* 8:9–43 (1968), p. 19, and James Hayes, "Chinese Temples in the Local Setting," in *Some Traditional Chinese Ideas and Conceptions in Hong Kong Social Life Today* (Hong Kong: Royal Asiatic Society, 1966), pp. 92–93. Eugene Anderson also notes that the Durkheimian approach is useful when analyzing many of the T'ien Hou cults which serve Hong Kong's boat people (personal communication).

Although the approach adopted in this paper is different from that espoused by C. K. Yang and others, I would not contend that my findings necessarily contradict those of earlier fieldworkers. Rather, I prefer to think of the two approaches as complementary. It is possible, for instance, to attend a T'ien Hou festival at Eastern Mountain Temple and gain the impression that everyone present shares an identical set of collective values. When asked about their role in the local cult, people in all walks of life express such views as the following: "We all work together to run this festival," or "Eastern Mountain Temple belongs to everyone in this *hsiang* and T'ien Hou helps us all." If the fieldworker is willing to restrict the analysis to publicly expressed values, the two cults under study do indeed serve the needs of everyone concerned. However, on closer inspection, it becomes apparent that these public expressions of solidarity conceal more than they reveal.

The best way to approach this problem, I discovered, was to ask people to tell me their own versions of the T'ien Hou myth. In particular, I asked informants from every settlement in the two *hsiang* to explain how they and their ancestors related to the goddess. When the results were compared, I found that every category or class of people had a different representation of T'ien Hou. These findings are not unique to the area under study. Arthur Wolf has argued, for instance, that a common feature of Chinese peasant religion is that "it mirrors the social landscape of its adherents. There are as many meanings as there are vantage points."[79] Wolf's insight helps explain how religious cults like the ones under investigation can incorporate people from such diverse backgrounds. As long as tenants or clients participated in the public rituals and professed an allegiance to T'ien Hou, they were free to develop their own representations of the goddess. Those at the top of the regional and national hierarchies (i.e., local elites and government officials) were only concerned with actions, not beliefs.

In earlier sections of this paper I argued that T'ien Hou was promoted by imperial authorities because, to them, she represented "civilization" and approved culture. This view of the goddess is projected in official documents that circulated at the national level. Government functionaries may have had private beliefs regarding T'ien Hou but these did not find public expression. At the local level, members of the landlord-merchant class had their own reasons for promoting T'ien Hou cults. Being literate, men in this category related more easily to the vision of T'ien Hou presented in government publications. The goddess appealed to them primarily as a symbol of coastal pacification but she carried other, "deeper" messages as well. In effect, by building temples to T'ien Hou the local elite signaled that they wished to join the mainstream of Chinese culture. Educated men who lived in the countryside were anxious to have their temples, and by implication their lineages, mentioned in the hsien gazetteers. The vision of T'ien Hou as a bearer of "civilization" and a guardian of social

---

[79] Wolf, "Gods, Ghosts, and Ancestors," in Wolf, *Religion and Ritual*, p. 131.

order thus appealed primarily to literate decision makers at all levels of the political hierarchy in China.

When one looks at other categories of people, the pattern is rather different. For ordinary, semiliterate members of the landowning lineages T'ien Hou is perceived as a symbol of territorial control. Since the foundation of the local cults in the postevacuation period, most people in San Tin or Ha Tsuen have been unable to read the documents pertaining to T'ien Hou's exploits. This does not mean that they are unaware of the goddess's associations with the imperial court, but rather that they choose not to dwell on these points in their own renditions of the T'ien Hou myth. When asked, men in this category (the views of women are discussed later) refer almost exclusively to the goddess's ability to quell pirates in the nearby delta and her conquest of parochial deities such as Sand River Mother. T'ien Hou's assistance to lineage ancestors is the most common theme of these stories.

In many respects, ordinary members of the lineage have taken on the religious attitudes of their educated kinsmen. The local elites are keenly aware that "uncivilized" behavior lowers the status of the entire lineage. This, I would argue, is one reason why spirit possession, flagellation, and self-immolation play no role in the local T'ien Hou cults. The Man and Teng do have female mediums who communicate with the spirits of deceased people, but these activities have not evolved into cults as such.[80] It is significant that males in San Tin and Ha Tsuen do not themselves act as mediums. This concern for "proper" behavior (in their own terms) sets lineage members apart from many of their clients and neighbors in the surrounding countryside. During my stay in San Tin (1969–1970), I attended a spirit medium session held by Teotiu immigrants in the city of Tsuen Wan. When I returned to the village with photographs of flagellation and tongue cutting, my neighbors were horrified, and yet fascinated. They had heard of such behavior but had never actually witnessed anything like it themselves. Their reactions were revealing: "How can anyone who calls himself 'Chinese' act like such a barbarian."

In contrast to what I have seen in other parts of Hong Kong and Taiwan, the temple festivals in San Tin and Ha Tsuen are remarkable for their utter lack of religious fervor. The *hua p'ao hui* competitions sometimes dissolved into brawls and the *ta chiao* processions occasionally led to organized violence, but the religious content of the two T'ien Hou cults under study is understated in the extreme. Nor is the efficaciousness of the local T'ien Hou temples a matter of great concern. In my discussions with Man and Teng (male) elders, it became apparent that T'ien Hou's divine intervention on their behalf is perceived in generalized, abstract terms. The goddess is thought to have assisted their ancestors but she is not credited with specific miracles in living memory. Women, as demonstrated below, have a different vision of T'ien Hou, but local

[80] On female mediums see Jack M. Potter, "Cantonese Shamanism," in Wolf, *Religion and Ritual*.

males are not particularly concerned with the spiritual powers of their patron deity. For men who belong to powerful lineages, she is, above all else, a symbol of territorial hegemony.

Moving down the hierarchy of power, we must consider the residents of satellite villages. Until recently, people in these small communities had little choice but to participate in the T'ien Hou cults. Although they are no longer tenants as such,[81] many remain clients of their former landlords and continue to play a subordinate role in local politics. Being clients, they cannot, of course, accept T'ien Hou as a symbol of territorial control; to do so would mean that the goddess would represent their own oppression. Accordingly, most satellite villagers have reinterpreted the T'ien Hou myth to "explain" their position in the social hierarchy and to gloss over the fact that they play such a minor role in cult activities. This method of ideological self-justification is common among oppressed minorities who find it difficult, if not impossible, to affect a change in their political circumstances.[82] If asked, therefore, people in smaller villages deny—often aggressively—that there is an exploitative dimension to the T'ien Hou cults. They do not hide their resentment of the local security forces but, they argue, this has nothing to do with their relationship to the goddess.

Clients of dominant lineages were traditionally illiterate (this is still true for those over 45) and, as a consequence, their myths and legends were never recorded in writing. In collecting T'ien Hou myths from satellite villagers, I found that their versions all have one thing in common: the Man and Teng are presented as usurpers who are unable to harness the power of the deity. An interesting, and revealing, myth was told to me by elders in Sa Kong Wai ("Sand River Village"), a satellite of Ha Tsuen. As the name implies, residents of this community claim a special relationship to Sand River Temple. In their version of local history, the founders of Sa Kong Wai arrived on the scene prior to the Teng and were responsible for starting the T'ien Hou cult. The Teng took control of the temple after they had destroyed Sa Kong Wai's favorable *feng shui* ("wind and water," geomantic influences) and usurped the land in Ha Tsuen *hsiang*. To this day, however, the goddess will not help the Teng and will only respond when she is approached by a descendent of the people who first installed her in Sand River Temple. Once every ten years, according to the story, Teng elders bribe a male resident of Sa Kong Wai to initiate the casting of lots required for the selection of ritual leaders who preside over the *ta chiao*. The goddess will not "cooperate" unless someone from Sa Kong Wai starts the procedure, supposedly under the cover of darkness to hide his actions from fellow villagers. In punishment for tricking the goddess, however, the man who breaks ranks and accepts the Teng bribe is said to die before the next *ta chiao*. No

[81] In 1905, colonial officials gave full ownership rights to sitting tenants, but these rights were largely unenforceable until the 1950s.

[82] A similar theme is explored by Barrington Moore, Jr., *Injustice: The Social Bases of Obedience and Revolt* (New York: Random House, 1978).

one has actually witnessed any of these events, of course, but the people in Sa Kong Wai are convinced that the goddess is really their patron and not the Teng's. This is only one of the ways that satellite villagers use myth to justify their participation in the local T'ien Hou cults.

The discussion to this point has concentrated almost exclusively on local males. Women, as indicated earlier, have a very different vision of T'ien Hou from that held by any category of men—so different, in fact, that one begins to wonder if we are dealing with the same deity. Women play no role whatsoever in the formal organization of the temple cults, not even to the extent of forming a women's auxilliary to complement the activities of their husbands or fathers. For women the worship of T'ien Hou is usually defined in personal or family terms. Wives appear at the annual festivals with individual sets of offerings, which they present to the goddess on behalf of their households. Men never make these prestations, as they are said to be "too busy" attending to the collective rituals associated with the cult.

In considering the religious conceptions of village women, one must bear in mind that until recently all but a handful were totally illiterate.[83] Most women over 45 are not even able to recognize the characters for common surnames or the names of their own villages. It is not surprising, therefore, that they know little about the traditions of T'ien Hou preserved in writing. And, yet, I was amazed to discover that women's conceptions of the goddess did not seem to reflect their own (or their husbands') position in the social hierarchy. The myths told to me by women varied somewhat in content, but the underlying messages were basically the same: T'ien Hou is a personalized deity who, if approached properly, will answer individual pleas for help. Women usually refer to the goddess as T'ien Hou Niang Niang, adding a feminizing suffix that (in the local dialect) carries maternal connotations. In this guise, T'ien Hou is perceived primarily as a fertility goddess and her efficaciousness is very much at issue. Land women (I cannot comment on the views of boat women) bring their gynecological and childbearing problems to the goddess and make personal appeals for divine intercession. In anthropological terms, a dyadic contract is established between supplicant and deity[84]; should T'ien Hou keep her side of the bargain, the woman presents a special offering in repayment. These individual arrangements have nothing to do with the formal structure of the T'ien Hou cults and the prestations are made at times other than the goddess's annual festival. Men, at least those I am familiar with, do not make individual contracts with the deity; they rely on their mothers or wives to handle this aspect of religious life. Thus, the women's personalistic vision of T'ien Hou is

[83] R. S. Watson found only five women in Ha Tsuen over the age of 45 who were literate. These women belonged to the wealthiest family in the village. I did not discover any literate women over 45 in satellite villages.

[84] George M. Foster, "The Dyadic Contract: A Model for the Social Structure of a Mexican Peasant Village," *American Anthropologist* 63:1173–1192 (1961).

not necessarily opposed to the various male representations outlined above. Nonetheless, the differences are so striking that I am led to speculate that village women and men inhabit separate conceptual worlds—at least in respect to religion.

Before concluding, one further category of people remains to be considered—namely, the *shui shang jen* ("people on the water").[85] Many observers of the Hong Kong scene assume that T'ien Hou originated in this region as a boat people's goddess and that land people began to worship her only after the cult had become popular. As I have tried to illustrate in earlier sections of this essay, the historical origins of the T'ien Hou cult are difficult to trace and, although the deity has always been associated with the sea, she was not monopolized by a single category of people. In the two *hsiang* under study, boat people play a very minor role in temple activities. Only twice in twenty-nine months of fieldwork did I encounter boat people worshipping in the local T'ien Hou temples. I overheard one of the women concerned ask the keeper for permission to worship the goddess because, as she put it, "this temple does not belong to us." (Women from the dominant lineages, in contrast, worship whenever they please and treat the keepers like servants.) Even those boat people who maintain regular anchorages in Ha Tsuen *hsiang* rarely use Sand River Temple. They prefer to worship at temples located on Hong Kong's smaller islands where the local population is more receptive to boat people (see note 64).

My own research among people who call themselves *shui shang jen* has been restricted to the inhabitants of two client settlements (actually shanty towns built from the remnants of boats) along the Ha Tsuen and San Tin coast. These people no longer rely on boats, but they continue to fish from the shore and work in oyster fields. Nonetheless, it is doubtful that they can still be categorized as boat people and it is unclear (to me) whether their views are representative of those who live on boats and make their living at sea. The residents of these small communities have been co-opted into the T'ien Hou cults controlled by the Man and Teng in the sense that they are expected to present altars at the annual festivals. However, they also pay regular visits to the temples that cater to the floating population. In my talks with sedentary fishermen (not women), it became clear that their vision of T'ien Hou had very little in common with the representations held by land people. For these men the goddess symbolizes

---

[85] On Cantonese boat people see Eugene N. Anderson, Jr., *Essays on South China's Boat People* (Taipei: Orient Cultural Service, 1972) and *The Floating World of Castle Peak Bay* (Washington: American Anthropological Association, 1970); and Barbara E. Ward, "A Hong Kong Fishing Village," *Journal of Oriental Studies* 1 : 195–214 (1954) and "Varieties of the Conscious Model: The Fishermen of South China," in *The Relevance of Models for Social Anthropology,* ed. Michael Banton (London: Tavistock, 1965). Barbara Ward's article "Varieties" is particularly relevant to the theme of this paper because she deals with the boat people's own conceptions of their place in Chinese society.

mastery of the sea; she appealed to them primarily for her ability to quell storms—not disorderly elements. In fact, the myths presented by my informants (all, incidentally, illiterate) had nothing to do with social stability or coastal pacification. Their stories dealt primarily with T'ien Hou's divine intervention on behalf of people who make their living at sea.

In a real sense, therefore, boat people and land people in this part of China have diametrically opposed representations of a religious symbol that, on the surface, would appear to unite them. They both claim T'ien Hou as their patron deity, but this does not mean that they are part of the same "moral community." In this respect, there are some intriguing hints that, among sea peoples, the goddess is associated with pirates and other entrepreneurs of violence who operated along the South China coast. Many researchers claim to have found a connection between T'ien Hou temples and pirate outposts, particularly in the islands of the Canton Delta. Da Silva notes, for instance, that the famous eighteenth-century pirate Chang Pao-tzu was a lavish contributor to the T'ien Hou temple on Lantau Island—according to local tradition, at least.[86] Lo also argues that two of Hong Kong's island temples were associated, in legend, with pirates; a stone tablet, dated 1752, in one of these shrines commemorates Cheng Lien-ch'ang, a "notorious pirate," who paid for the temple's renovation.[87] It is quite possible that T'ien Hou, in her guise as a mistress of the seas and a queller of storms, could have been adopted by pirates as their patron deity. The ultimate irony is that the landed elites of the Kwangtung coast worshiped the same goddess, and accepted her as their own special patron, precisely because she was—for them—a symbol of coastal pacification and an enemy of pirates.

CONCLUSION

In concluding, I return to the problem of cultural integration in late imperial Chinese society. The literate elite, I have argued, played an important role in the standardization of culture by ensuring that religious cults conformed to nationally accepted models. The question remains, however, whether the state led or followed the masses in the promotion of specific deities. Were Chinese peasants "easy material for ideological molding," as Kung-chuan Hsiao has suggested,[88] or were they detached and self-confident enough to resist those

[86] Armando M. Da Silva, "Fan Lau and its Fort: An Historical Perspective," *Journal of the Hong Kong Branch of the Royal Asiatic Society* 8:82–95 (1968), pp. 87–88.

[87] Lo Hsiang-lin, *Hong Kong and Its External Communications Before 1842* (Hong Kong: Institute of Chinese Culture, 1963), pp. 129–130 and plate 34. On the pirate connection see also S. F. Belfour, "Hong Kong Before the British," *Journal of the Hong Kong Branch of the Royal Asiatic Society* 10:134–179 (1970) and Dian Murray, "Sea Bandits: A Study of Piracy in Early Nineteenth Century China," Ph.D. diss., Cornell University (1979), pp. 159–160.

[88] Kung-chuan Hsiao, *Rural China: Imperial Control in the Nineteenth Century* (Seattle: University of Washington Press, 1960), p. 225.

who attempted to change their religious traditions? The answer, of course, lies somewhere in between. The state both led the masses and responded to popular pressure; it both promoted and co-opted deities. T'ien Hou is an excellent case in point. As outlined in the first part of this paper, she began as an obscure, parochial deity on the Fukien coast and rose to become one of the luminaries of the imperial pantheon. Obviously, a transformation like this could not have occurred without state intervention. But it is equally true that imperial officials did not have the power, or the resources, to impose an unpopular deity on the masses.

Rather than relying on coercion, therefore, the state exercised control over the religious lives of ordinary people by more subtle means. For instance, it was made "advantageous" for local elites to promote deities that were represented in the imperial pantheon. Recognized deities such as T'ien Hou carried all the right messages that literate decision makers wished to convey about their communities: civilization, order, and loyalty to the state.

One's perception of cultural uniformity in late imperial Chinese society depends entirely upon perspective. At the highest level of abstraction, the acceptance of religious symbols such as T'ien Hou does indeed indicate unity and integration. Although I have not made a complete survey, a glance through Fukien and Kwangtung gazetteers reveals that literally thousands of local cults were dedicated to three or four state-approved deities. State officials might have accepted this as evidence that they had had a "civilizing" effect on the masses and that they had succeeded in their efforts to introduce a standard form of religion. Members of the national elite preferred not to probe too deeply into the religious beliefs and conceptions of ordinary people. Herein lies the genius of the Chinese government's approach to cultural integration: the state imposed a structure but not the content. The actual organization of temple cults devolved to local elites who had a vested interest in maintaining good relations with state officials. The system was flexible enough to allow people at all levels of the social hierarchy to construct their own representations of state-approved deities. Put another way, the state promoted symbols and not beliefs.

The fact that deities such as T'ien Hou represented different things to different categories of people does not in itself make the Chinese pattern of cultural integration particularly unique. One need only consider how a primary symbol of Christendom (the Virgin Mother) is variously interpreted in European peasant societies. Nevertheless, one characteristic of the Chinese political system that does set it apart from other traditions is that state authorities did not try to legislate beliefs. As long as proper ritual forms were observed, including the worship of approved deities, the state did not intervene. The educated elite at all levels of the national and regional hierarchies thoroughly understood the rules of acceptable behavior. By observing proper forms, therefore, the local elites cooperated with state authorities in the construction of a national culture that appeared—on the surface—to be remarkably integrated, especially when compared to the cultural systems of other premodern societies.

The conflicting and at times contradictory representations of T'ien Hou must be understood in this national context. The cults dedicated to the "Empress of Heaven" were like microcosms of Chinese culture. They incorporated people from a wide variety of social backgrounds, all with their own visions and beliefs regarding the deity. But, to the outside observer, a T'ien Hou temple symbolized respectability and "civilization." The ambiguity of fundamental symbols was thus an important element in the creation of a unified cultural tradition in China.

ELEVEN

Language and Ideology
in the Written Popularizations
of the *Sacred Edict*

Victor H. Mair

> *"So that the correct doctrine may be*
> *known to every family and household"*
> (chia yü hu hsiao).
> —*Stock expression of orthodox propagandists*—

"Ouang-iu-p'uh
on the edict of K'ang-hsi
in volgar' eloquio taking the sense down to the people."
—*Ezra Pound*—[1]

TEXTS

From its promulgation in the latter part of 1670 until the end of the Ch'ing dynasty, the hortatory *Sacred Edict* (*Sheng-yü*) of the K'ang-hsi emperor was widely recognized as the most concise and authoritative statement of Confucian ideology. At the time he issued the *Sacred Edict*, K'ang-hsi was sixteen years old and in the ninth year of his reign. The edict consisted of sixteen maxims, all seven characters in length and possessing an identical grammatical structure that is evident even in translation:

1. Esteem most highly filial piety and brotherly submission, in order to give due importance to the social relations.
2. Behave with generosity toward your kindred, in order to illustrate harmony and benignity.
3. Cultivate peace and concord in your neighborhoods, in order to prevent quarrels and litigations.
4. Recognize the importance of husbandry and the culture of the mulberry tree, in order to ensure a sufficiency of clothing and food.
5. Show that you prize moderation and economy, in order to prevent the lavish waste of your means.

---

[1] *The Cantos of Ezra Pound* (New York: New Directions, 1975), canto 98, p. 688. For studies of Pound's extensive knowledge and application of the *Sacred Edict*, see Caroll F. Terrell, "The Sacred Edict of K'ANG-HSI," *Paideuma* 2.1:69–112 (Spring 1973); David Gordon, "Thought Built on Sagetrieb," *Paideuma* 3.2:169–190 (Fall 1974); and David Gordon, "Pound's Use of the Sacred Edict in Canto 98," *Paideuma*, 4.1:121–168 (Spring 1975). I am grateful to Achilles Fang for this information.

6. Give weight to colleges and schools, in order to make correct the practice of the scholar.
7. Extirpate strange principles, in order to exalt the correct doctrine.
8. Lecture on the laws, in order to warn the ignorant and obstinate.
9. Elucidate propriety and yielding courtesy, in order to make manners and customs good.
10. Labor diligently at your proper callings, in order to stabilize the will of the people.
11. Instruct sons and younger brothers, in order to prevent them from doing what is wrong.
12. Put a stop to false accusations, in order to preserve the honest and good.
13. Warn against sheltering deserters, in order to avoid being involved in their punishment.
14. Fully remit your taxes, in order to avoid being pressed for payment.
15. Unite in hundreds and tithings, in order to put an end to thefts and robbery.
16. Remove enmity and anger, in order to show the importance due to the person and life.[2]

Here were, so to speak, the bare bones of Confucian orthodoxy as it pertained to the average citizen. It was not long, however, before the need was felt to flesh them out. Within a few years of the issuance of the *Sacred Edict*, adaptations, commentaries, paraphrases, and exegeses began to appear. What is most interesting about these derivative works is that many of them were written in the colloquial language. Who wrote these versions and why? Who read them? And what significance did they have for Chinese society in the eighteenth and nineteenth centuries?

The tradition of explicating classical texts in written colloquial versions seems to have grown up during the Yuan period.[3] Hsu Heng (1209–1281) wrote a *Chih-shuo Ta-hsueh yao-lueh* [Directly expounded essentials of the *Great Learning*], a *Ta-hsueh chih-chieh* [Direct explanation of the *Great Learning*], and a *Chung-yung chih-chieh* [Direct explanation of the *Doctrine of the Mean*]. These were still a bit bookish, and served as lecture outlines for the Mongol emperors. After Hsu Heng and inspired by him, in the year 1308, Kuan Yun-shih (1286–1324) prepared a *Hsiao-ching chih-chieh* [Direct explanation of the *Classic of Filial Piety*]. This was written in fluent colloquial and, according to its preface, was intended to educate the masses. But there also seems to have been a close connection between the appearance of the *Direct Explanation of the Classic of Filial Piety* and the presentation to the Mongol princes of copies of the *Classic of*

---

[2] Slightly modified from James Legge, "Imperial Confucianism," *The China Review* 6.3 : 150a–b (1877).

[3] This is not the place to go into such forerunners of popular *oral* education in China as the Han institution of the "Three Elders" (*san-lao*), Six Dynasties and T'ang Buddhist lectures for laymen (*ch'ang-tao* and *su-chiang*), or Sung village association (*hsiang-yueh*) instructional methods.

Filial Piety itself the year before.[4] Another Yuan work of this type is Wu Ch'eng's (1255–1330) *Ching-yen chin-chiang* [Lectures presented by the interpreter of the classics]. During the Ming, Chang Chü-cheng (1525–1582) wrote a *Ssu-shu chi-chu chih-chieh* [Direct explanation of the *Four Books* and collected commentaries] and a *Shu-ching chih-chieh* [Direct explanation of the *Book of Documents*].[5] Aside from the fact that these colloquial-language explications constitute a clear precedent for the various popularizations of the *Sacred Edict* in the Ch'ing, it is noteworthy that all of them were written by members of the elite.[6]

An even more explicit model for the Ch'ing popularizations is Chung Hua-min's *Sheng-yü t'u-chieh* [Illustrated explanation of the *Sacred Edict*], dated 1587.[7] Chung, whose choice of personal name is conspicuous since it means "transforming the people," was the *ch'a-ma ssu* ("tea and horse administrator") for Shansi and elsewhere. The *Sacred Edict* referred to here was not K'ang-hsi's but the Ming *Liu-yü* [Six maxims], usually ascribed to the emperor T'ai-tsu. It may be translated as follows:

> Be filial to your parents.
> Be respectful to your elders.
> Live in harmony with your neighbors.
> Instruct your sons and grandsons.
> Be content with your calling.
> Do no evil.

Chung's work consisted of the following parts: (1) a moral precept in classical Chinese; (2) a prose development on the precept that varies from highly colloquial to easy classical; (3) a poem ("song") on the same theme in language more purely classical; (4) a picture with a caption; and (5) a story

[4] See *Yuan-shih* 元史 [History of the Yuan] (Kaiming 開明 ed.), *chüan* 22, p. 6184, col. 1, and *Hsin Yuan-shih* 新元史 [New history of the Yuan] (Kaiming ed.), *chüan* 160, p. 6927, col. 2.

[5] Lü K'un (1534–1616), an important Ming scholar-official, was noted for his popularizations of classical texts. Cf. Joanna F. Handlin, "Lü K'un's New Audience: The Influence of Women's Literacy on Sixteenth-Century Thought," in *Women in Chinese Society*, ed. Margery Wolf and Roxane Witke (Stanford: Stanford University Press, 1975), pp. 13–38 and 277–283.

[6] Most of the information in this paragraph is drawn from Ōta Tatsuo 太田辰夫, *Chūgoku rekidai kōgobun* 中國歷代口語文 [Colloquial Chinese texts from successive dynasties] (Tokyo: Kōnan shoin 江南書院, 1957), pp. 70–71. Wm. Theodore de Bary discusses Hsu Heng's vernacular interpretations of basic Confucian texts in his *Neo-Confucian Orthodoxy and the Learning of the Mind-and-Heart* (New York: Columbia University Press, 1981), pp. 137, 141–144.

[7] Ed. Chavannes, "Les saintes instructions de l'empereur Hong-wou (1368–1398); publiées en 1587 et illustrées par Tchong Houa-min," *Bulletin de l'École Française d'Extrême-Orient* 3:549–563 (1903). In 1901–1904, when Berthold Laufer led an expedition to China for the American Museum of Natural History (New York), the original stela was still located in the Confucius Temple at Sian. See entry no. 1066 in Hartmut Walravens et al., eds., *Catalogue of Chinese Rubbings from Field Museum*, Fieldiana Anthropology, n.s., No. 3 (Chicago: Field Museum of Natural History, November 30, 1981), p. 256. Monika Übelhör, who provided me with the reference to Chavannes's article, has also kindly read and commented on an earlier version of this paper.

about the picture in vernacular Chinese with a slight admixture of classical. It will be well to remember this format, because we shall see elements of it cropping up in the Ch'ing popularizations. We should be particularly mindful of the incorporation of materials written in different language levels, because it is typical of the later efforts to make the message conveyed accessible to people of varying degrees of literacy. Also pertinent is the obvious effort of Chung to make his *Illustrated Explanation* widely available, ideally to every household in the empire. According to its inscription, the stele on which the *Illustrated Explanation* was cut was meant to serve as a huge lithographic printing block from which copies could be taken. These were to be distributed to magistrates having administrative responsibility for *chou* (subprefectures or departments) and *hsien* (counties or districts). The local officials were in turn directed to make blocks from which to print additional copies. These would be distributed to each family (ten sheets per tithing [*chia*]). The elders of each district and the heads of the village associations (*pao*) were to lecture on the maxims twice a month (on the first and the fifteenth). It is clear that the broadest possible exposure of the maxims throughout the populace was envisaged, though we cannot be certain that these measures were faithfully executed in all areas.

Around the beginning of the K'ang-hsi reign period, presumably in connection with the 1652 promulgation, a *Liu-yü yen-i* [Elaboration of the hortatory edict of six maxims][8] was composed by Fan Hung of Li-ch'eng in Honan. The village lecture system described in the postface was not yet highly formalized. Fan Hung suggests that his book be used for discussions among brothers, officials, village association members, and so on. Furthermore, it is important to note that, at this time, heterodoxy is not really an issue, being referred to only in passing. Fan's attitude toward Buddhism and Taoism, particularly the former, is that they have their legitimate place.[9]

The language of the *Elaboration* is decidedly colloquial but embraces many classical elements (e.g., the use of *tz'u* instead of *che*[a] for "this," *yun* instead of *shuo* for "say," *wei*[-*ts'eng*] instead of [*ts'ung-lai*] *mei*[-*yu*] for "have/has not/never," *ho* instead of *shen-me* for "what," *che*[b] instead of *te* as nominalizer, the frequent use of *erh* as an adversative, etc.). There is, furthermore, an unvernacular tendency toward a four-six prose rhythm and other classical cadences. The treatment of each maxim includes extensive quotations from the Ch'ing legal code in classical language and concludes with twelve lines of heptasyllabic verse rhyming AABACADAEAFA.

---

[8] I have used the text reprinted in Ogaeri Yoshio 魚返善雄, ed., *Kago kanbun Kō-ki kōtei Sei-yu kōkun* 華語漢文康熙皇帝聖諭廣訓 [Classical and vernacular versions of the amplified instructions on the *Sacred Edict of the K'ang-hsi Emperor*] (Osaka: Yagō shoten 屋號書店, 1943). The edition I have used is available in *Chin-tai Chung-kuo shih-liao ts'ung-k'an hsu-pien* 近代中國史料叢刊續編 [Materials for the study of recent Chinese history, continuation], seventh series, no. 61, pp. 139–205.
[9] See his discussion of the sixth maxim.

Thus, by the time of the K'ang-hsi emperor, there already was a well-established tradition for the popularization of imperial apothegms. It is not surprising that the vulgarizers soon directed their attention to the *Sacred Edict*. Throughout the Ch'ing period, they issued a constant stream of exegetic and metaphrastic texts based on it. The first of these works to consider is the *Sheng-yü ho lü chih-chieh* [Direct explanation of the *Sacred Edict* in combination with the laws]. This was published in 1679, just nine years after the appearance of the *Sacred Edict* itself. The *Combination* was compiled from extant glosses (*yen-shuo*) and edited by the Manchu governor of Chekiang, Ch'en Ping-chih, who had copies printed and distributed to villages throughout the empire.[10] Provided with prefaces by the lieutenant-governor of Chekiang, Li Shih-chen, and another high official, Ch'eng Ju-p'u, the work was divided into two sections: a general survey of the *Sacred Edict*, and discussions of each of the sixteen maxims with examples of applicable legal guidelines. The following extract from the first section will give an idea of Ch'en's approach:

> Since taking up our post, we have observed that, among you commoners, there are quite a lot who are good but there are also not a few who are bad. You have a penchant for litigation and like to get in quarrels. This is ruinous for local customs. Since it is true everywhere, the village lectures that have been held must not be concrete and detailed enough. Now we shall take these sixteen maxims of the Imperial Edict as the text of our lecture. We shall begin with a brief overview of the gist of the sixteen maxims for you to listen to carefully.

The language used throughout is natural and familiar. A rather polished style of the vernacular, it still would have been easily understood by the average listener. There can be little doubt that the explanations in the *Combination* were meant to be delivered orally at the official semimonthly lectures on the *Sacred*

[10] Suerna 素爾納 (18th c.) et al., comp., *Ch'in-ting hsueh-cheng ch'üan-shu* 欽定學政全書 [Imperially commissioned complete book of the directorate of education] (1774), reprinted in the *Chin-tai Chung-kuo shih-liao ts'ung-k'an* 近代中國史料叢刊 [Materials for the study of recent Chinese history], thirtieth series, no. 293, 74.3a; *Ta Ch'ing hui-tien shih-li* 大清會典事例 [Precedents for the combined regulations of the great Ch'ing Dynasty] (1899 lithograph), 397.3ab, under the year 1679. The *Combination* appeared together with Wei Hsiang-shu's (1617–1687) *Liu-yu chi chieh* [Collected explanations of the *Hortatory Edict of Six Maxims*] as *Shang-yü ho lü hsiang-yüeh ch'üan-shu* [Complete book of the village lectures on the *Imperial Edict* in combination with the laws). The *Combination* was also referred to in various prefaces (dated 1670, 1679) and in a postface (dated 1678) to this edition as a "direct explanation" (*chih-chieh*) or an "annotated explanation" (*chu-chieh*). It was reissued during the year 1693 under the same title in a crudely printed edition of one fascicle without Wei's *Collected Explanations*. In their stead, we find three pieces of moral encouragement (on agriculture, general diligence, and the proper behavior of women) by Wang Tseng-yuan, the county magistrate of Han-tan County in Kuang-p'ing Prefecture of Chihli Province. Wei's *Collected Explanations*, provided with a 1678 postface by the magistrate of Hai-ning County in Hangchow Prefecture, Hsu San-li, is particularly interesting because of the musical notations provided for the songs that end the treatment of each maxim. I have used a copy of the 1679 edition of the *Combination* kept in the library of the Institute of Oriental Culture, University of Tokyo (Tōkyō Daigaku Tōyōbunka Kenkyūjo).

Edict. Ch'en repeatedly states that he and his representatives are "lecturing [on the maxims] for you to hear" (*chiang yü ni-men t'ing che*). The prefaces and postface are also very clear on this point. A sizable proportion of the material for presentation consists of songs with word-by-word indication of musical notes. Ch'en displays no particular animus against Buddhism and Taoism, and even goes so far as to admit that they thoroughly illuminate the mind and personality. His emphasis in the discussion of the seventh maxim (a scant two and one-half pages long in contrast to his seven-and-one-half-page lecture on the first maxim) is on the positive qualities of orthodox Confucianism. But Ch'en is wary of unrecognized sects (*tso-tao*) and says in the general survey that they are "most hateful." [11] His greatest effort seems to go into explaining in apprehensible language how the laws work. Accordingly, he devotes fourteen and one-half pages to the eighth maxim.

Two years after the appearance of Ch'en Ping-chih's *Combination*, in 1681, the *Sheng-yü hsiang-chieh* [Illustrated explanations of the *Sacred Edict*], a large work in twenty fascicles, was published by the magistrate of Fan-ch'ang County in Anhwei, Liang Yen-nien. The original edition probably did not circulate much beyond the confines of Liang's own district but, more than two hundred years later, it was twice reprinted by one En-shou and, as I shall show below, was broadly disseminated.

The *Illustrated Explanations* adopts the following format: (1) citation of the maxim; (2) a straightforward explanation of it in easy classical language with punctuation; (3) a finely engraved picture; (4) a caption description of the picture in classical Chinese; and (5) a discussion of the maxim in relation to the picture written in a semiclassical style (i.e., midway between classical and colloquial). Altogether there are 248 pictures, most of them based on well-known personalities and incidents from history. Liang Yen-nien's "General Principles" (*fan-li*) declare that the pictures were intended to stimulate those who did not know how to read. It is possible that the pictures may have been shown to small groups of onlookers. The format of the original edition, retained by Yeh Chih-hsien (b. 1779) of Han-yang (Hupei) in his 1856 reprinting, is quite large: 6 1/4″ × 9 3/8″ for the printed portion of each page (as opposed to 4 7/8″ × 7 1/8″ for the editions published by En-shou). The following quotation from Liang's discussion of the thirteenth maxim shows that it was probably meant to serve as the basis for an actual lecture:

> Think of it yourselves, O people. Where can you best enjoy repose,—in the sandy desert of the frontier regions, or in the village in the country amid its ancestral trees? Which is more comfortable,—to dine on the wind and sleep beneath the rain, or to get up in the morning and go to bed at night in your own homes? Which is the more pleasant, to be supporting your aged and leading your young as they trudge along the weary road, or to know that you have plenty with which to serve

[11] *Combination*, 4a.

the former class and to nourish the latter? Which is the preferable life,—to hear your wives weeping and you and your children wailing or to be free from all trouble and embarrassment? Even if the runaways were your own relations and acquaintances, you ought sternly to repel them; for even a fool would not plunge after another into a deep well to try to rescue him; and how can you involve yourselves and your neighbours, and run such risks for worthless parties, whom you know nothing about?[12]

Liang Yen-nien and his associates definitely saw themselves as operating in a long tradition of popularization. In his preface, Kung Chia-yü (1622–1685) records that

> [of] old, when Feng K'ang (744–809) was administering Li-ch'üan, he wrote *Yü meng shu* [A book of parables for beginning learners] in fourteen chapters. In it, he taught the people to devote themselves to the fundamental occupation of agriculture. As a result, Li-ch'üan was well governed. When Chang Tsai (1020–1077) was administering Yun-yen, on the first of every month he would prepare wine and food and invite the villagers to a meeting in his court, where he instructed them in the principles of caring for parents and serving elders. As a result, Yun-yen was well governed.[13]

The author of the *Illustrated Explanations* is not opposed to Buddhism and Taoism as such but to the abuse of their doctrines. Writing in 1681 or earlier, he is not at all preoccupied with heretical sects. This is in stark contrast to the later paraphrasts, whose chief concern is often the suppression of heresy ("discrepant doctrines" [*i-chiao*]). Indeed, as we shall see below, individuals responsible for the publication of various versions of the *Sacred Edict* after the eighteenth century often view it as being in direct competition with religious movements.[14]

En-shou twice reprinted the *Illustrated Explanations*, once while he was the governor of Kiangsu and a second time while he was the governor of Anhwei. As stated in his "General Principles," he reprinted the *Illustrated Explanations* following the original edition of Liang Yen-nien. There were no revisions or modifications—except in the one transcription that was presented for imperial

---

[12] James Legge, trans., in "Imperial Confucianism," *The China Review* 6.6:365b (1878).

[13] *Illustrated Explanations*, 2a.

[14] The religious dimensions of the village lecture system were present from its inception. In a fascinating article pointed out to me by Evelyn Rawski after I had completed this study, Ōmura Kōdō 大村興道 shows how the aim of the village lectures gradually changed from being one of prompting cooperation among the local people during the Sung to that of propagating the teachings of the emperor during the Ming and Ch'ing. The ritualistic, incantatory aspects of the lectures also became increasingly evident, especially during the Ch'ing. It is significant that, in some early Ch'ing lectures on the *Sacred Edict*, the presence of Buddhist monks and Taoist priests was required. "Mei-matsu Shin-sho no senkō zushiki ni tsuite" 明末清初の宣講図式について [A study of the figures of Xüan jiang at the turning point of the Ming and Ch'ing], *Tōkyō gakugei daigaku kiyō* 東京学芸大学紀要 [Bulletin of the Tokyo University of Arts], 2, Jinbun kagaku 人文科学 [Humanistic sciences], 30:193–203 (1979).

inspection. Even the original typographical errors were repeated. En-shou specifically states that this procedure was adopted to ensure the rapid completion of the project. All that was done to improve the original was to append a list of eleven errata in the 1902 edition (it is omitted from the 1903 edition).

En-shou had submitted to the throne a copy of the *Illustrated Explanations* with a memorial requesting that it be reprinted and distributed throughout the land. Both the memorial and the imperial response are recorded at the beginning of the 1902 edition. The imperial rescript recognizes that the *Sacred Edict* is "the basis for transforming the people and reforming customs. Every household throughout the land, whether of scholars or commoners, surely already knows it." The rescript further recognizes that the simple and clear language of the explanations that accompanied the pictures was "calculated to allow all women and children to understand easily and thoroughly. It is indeed a worthy supplement to the *Sacred Edict* for educating the ignorant and the benighted." Following the suggestion of En-shou's original memorial, the decision was made—from the throne itself—to reprint the book by lithography and to send copies to each of the provinces. There the governors-general and the governors would instruct their subordinates in the prefectures, subprefectures, departments, and counties to see that it was made available in each school.

En-shou's memorial had been prompted by repeated directives from the empress dowager to take some active steps with regard to the system of education that would stop the rampant spread of heterodoxy. It was agreed that there was an urgent necessity to influence the students during the initial stages of the learning process so that they did not stray onto unwelcome paths.

The *Illustrated Explanations*, En-shou claims, is even more effective in reaching the people than were Li Hsi-yü's *Chung hsiao t'u* [Pictures of loyalty and filial piety], written during the T'ang, or the *Wai-p'ien* ("Outer Chapters") of Chu Hsi's *Hsiao-hsueh* [Minor learning], written during the Sung. Unfortunately, the work has had only limited circulation and minimal influence. Consequently, En-shou proposes that three thousand copies of the book be lithoprinted and distributed to all primary and middle schools throughout the country. His proposal was approved and this lengthy work was consequently reprinted in a run of three thousand copies. We cannot say with any certainty how many copies were made of the 1903 edition, for it simply reprints all of the prefatory materials of the 1902 edition without adding any new information.

One of the most prolific popularizers of the *Sacred Edict* was Li Lai-chang (1654–1721), a native of Hsiang-ch'eng in Honan. He became a provincial graduate (*chü-jen*) in 1675. After having been involved with several academies in his home province, both as lecturer and administrator, he was assigned to the magistracy of Lien-shan (literally, "connected mountains") County in Kwangtung. It took him more than four months to reach the place, so isolated and distant was it. The county included a population of approximately ten thousand Yao tribesmen as well as a lesser number of the Han race (seven villages consisting of two thousand individuals). The Yaos lived together in clusters ranging from five to less than twenty families. It was a mountainous district with dangerous paths and very little arable land (one-tenth, by Li's estimate). Moved by the difficult environment, Li is reported to have said,

"Though the Yao are a different type of people, they possess a human nature. I ought to treat them with sincerity." Whereupon, following the legacy of Wang Yang-ming of the Ming period, he daily received the elderly and inquired about the sickness and suffering of the people. He summoned to him those who were deserters, encouraging them to open up new lands, and lessening their taxes. Furthermore, he went straight into their hovels and engaged teachers for them, impressing them with his utter sincerity. He founded the Lien-shan Academy and wrote its academic rules. He had the people come to him daily so that he could teach them. The superior members of the Yao tribes, too, responded to this opportunity for learning. The sound of people reciting books filled the precipitous valleys.[15]

Judging from this brief sketch of a part of Li Lai-chang's life, it would have been quite in character for him to provide texts that would facilitate the dissemination of the ideals of the *Sacred Edict* among even the lowest levels of society.

There are three works by Li Lai-chang dealing with the *Sacred Edict*. They are the *Sheng-yü t'u-hsiang yen-i* [Illustrated elaboration of the *Sacred Edict*] in two fascicles, the *Sheng-yü yen-i san-tzu-ko su-chieh* [Vernacular explanation of the *Trimetrical Song* from the elaboration of the *Sacred Edict*] in one fascicle, and the *Sheng-yü hsuan-chiang (hsiang-pao) i-chu/t'iao-yueh* [Regulations/Usages for lectures on the *Sacred Edict* (by village elders)] in one fascicle.[16] Some copies were given away at government expense to inhabitants of Lien-shan County who Li thought could profit from them personally or, more often, could use them to teach others. In all of Li's popularizing, there is an evident wish to contribute to the sinicization of minority peoples.

The *Illustrated Elaboration*, preface dated December 22, 1704, treats each of the sixteen maxims with the following apparatus: (1) a picture; (2) an elaboration in stilted Mandarin; (3) examples of suitable behavior in the same style; (4) pertinent extracts from the Ch'ing code in legalistic classical language; (5) a "popular" song; and (6) instructions for the Yao written in easy classical with some colloquial elements. Li claims that he did not devise this arrangement

[15] Kuo-fang yen-chiu-yuan *Ch'ing-shih* pien-tsuan wei-yuan-hui [Editorial Committee for the *Ch'ing History* of the National Defense Research Institute], ed., *Ch'ing-shih* (*Ch'ing History*) in *Erh-shih-liu shih* [Twenty-six histories] (Taipei: Ch'eng-wen ch'u-pan-she, reprint of 1961 ed.), *chüan* 479, p. 5152a. The compilers of the *Ch'ing History* have drawn heavily on Li's own prefaces in writing his biography; most of the statements made here about the education of the Yao are corroborated in them.

[16] All of these are preserved in Li's collected works, which are poorly printed and on bad paper. *Li-shan yuan ch'üan-chi* 禮山園全集, vols. 25–26, 27, and 28 respectively.

himself but was following earlier examples. He further states in the preface that he has "used the literary language with an admixture of the local dialect, the elegant and the vulgar presented together." Li declares that he wrote the *Illustrated Elaboration* because he feels that the teachings of the sages are so deep that not even learned scholars can be sure to understand them fully. He basically treats his auditors as children. His attitude toward Buddhism and Taoism is that they confound the people, are replete with useless customs, and hence are "not to be believed in overly much." But heretical sects are a menace to society, a genuine source of chaos and are "not to be believed in mistakenly." [17]

The *Trimetrical Song*, patently an attempt to duplicate the popularity of the famous and influential *Trimetrical Classic*, was written within the first year of Li's arrival in Lien-shan County. He then made it a part of the *Illustrated Elaboration* but has here printed it separately with a colloquial commentary, without which it would be virtually unintelligible to the average citizen. In his preface, dated the summer of 1706, Li justifies his use of the vernacular by referring to the practices of the Sung Neo-Confucians. He states that his *Illustrated Elaboration* was so successful in the semimonthly lectures on the *Sacred Edict* that he was prompted to extract the song portion of it and provide it with annotations and explications "in the local dialect." The commentary, however, is written neither in Yao nor in Cantonese but rather in slightly pompous Mandarin. What Li must have meant is that, during the lecture, the Mandarin text was extemporaneously rendered into the local dialect. There is an occasional tendency for the text, which is punctuated, to lapse into the four-six rhythm of parallel prose. Li maintains that he wants "to make it as thoroughly understandable as daily speech." Indeed, the song is fully interpreted for the reader, very little being left to the imagination. There are even a few pronunciation notes for difficult words in the song. Each maxim of the *Sacred Edict* has forty-eight lines of verse devoted to it, and these are commented upon a quatrain at a time. Here is the first of the twelve quatrains on the first maxim, together with its commentary:

> [To be] freed [from] bosom's care,
> [They] must [wait] three years;
> [The] kindness [of] father [and] mother,
> [Is] equal [to] Vast Heaven.

These four lines say: after a father and a mother give birth to a child and for the next one or two years, how concerned they are about feeding and nursing him! In the winter months, they only fear he will be cold; in the summer months, they only fear he will be hot. And, even when they go to work in the fields or gather firewood, they strap him on their backs and take him along with them. They are unwilling to leave him alone in the house. How hard it is! Only after three years,

[17] Maxim 7.

when he can talk and walk, are they freed somewhat from the labor of caring for him in their bosoms. The great kindness of a father and mother is as that of Heaven Above. "Vast Heaven" means "Heaven Above."[18]

The *Regulations for Lectures on the Sacred Edict*, bearing a preface dated 1705 and newly recut in that year, was printed from blocks kept in the Lien-shan County *yamen*. It offers complete instructions on how to carry out a lecture ceremony on the *Sacred Edict*: where to hold the lecture (different in city, town, and country); how to purify the site; where to place the incense, candles, and flower vases; how to wrap and store the *Sacred Edict*; where various groups of the auditors are to stand; what furniture is required; when the musicians are to play; what is the appropriate time for the cantor's singing; when the drums and clappers should be hit; and when the auditors should kneel, bow, kowtow, and so on. There can be no doubt that Li and others like him were attempting to provide a ritualistic setting for the liturgical text embodied in the *Illustrated Elaboration*. As a matter of fact, Li stipulated in the *Regulations* that a copy of the *Elaboration* was to be kept on the altar during the *Sacred Edict* lecture service. Four record books were to be placed on the altar as well. As Li traveled from village to village to lecture on the *Sacred Edict*, he would order the local headmen to record the behavior of the villagers in these four registers or ledgers.[19] In the books were recorded instances of good behavior (subdivided good, better, best), bad behavior (likewise subdivided bad, worse, worst), repentance for misdeeds leading to improved behavior, and amicable settlement of conflict through arbitration by respected members of the community. Li would use these records to gauge the effectiveness of his preaching and would also give rewards or mete out punishment where appropriate. Li says that, after he had published and distributed the *Regulations*, they were widely used as the basis for the twice-monthly lectures on the *Sacred Edict* in all parts of his county, no matter how remote. This represented a deliberate attempt to extend the *Sacred Edict* lecture system beyond the towns and cities, where it was a simple matter to organize because of the presence of centrally appointed personnel, into the villages and countryside.

Li Lai-chang's complex apparatus for lectures on the *Sacred Edict* described in his *Regulations* and presented in his *Illustrated Elaboration* would seem to have allowed for ready adjustment to different types of audiences. We know that other officials from around this time who were actively engaged in popularizing

---

[18] *Sheng-yü yen-i san-tzu-ko su-chieh*, 1a. The translation is deliberately crude. Cf. *The Chinese Repository* 1 : 244–246 (May 1832 – April 1833), where it is incorrectly stated that these songs are taken chiefly from Wang Yu-p'u's paraphrase. This is impossible, since the *Trimetrical Song* was written at least twenty-two years before the *Discussion and Explanation* (see below).

[19] Compare the Ming "Ledgers of Merit and Demerit" discussed by Tadao Sakai in his "Confucian and Popular Educational Works," pp. 342–343 of *Self and Society in Ming Thought*, ed. Wm. Theodore de Bary (New York: Columbia University Press, 1970), pp. 331–366.

the *Sacred Edict* did take into account the level of sophistication of their audiences. While Chang Po-hsing was governor of Fukien (1707–1710), he used one
version of the *Sacred Edict* "embellished with classical allusions for the literati,
one illustrated with popular sayings for those of medium intelligence and
scholarly ability, and one with memorable jingles for the simple country
folk." [20]

In the second year of his reign (1724), the Yung-cheng emperor issued the
Sheng-yü kuang-hsun [Amplified instructions on the *Sacred Edict*], consisting of
approximately ten thousand characters. He was evidently concerned that the
K'ang-hsi emperor's sixteen maxims were so concise as to be incomprehensible
to the common man. Yung-cheng's preface begins with a justification by
ancient example: " 'Every year in the first *month* of spring, the herald with his
wooden-tongued bell goes along the roads, proclaiming. . . .' " [21] It is clear that,
within the confines of the literary language, he was aiming at lucidity: "Our
text attempts to be clear and precise; our words, for the most part, are direct and
simple." [22] The prose is easily understandable for someone with a modicum of
training in the literary language.

A statistical study of the frequency of graphs in the *Amplified Instructions* in
comparison with a standard list for classical Chinese is revealing. [23] There is a
close correlation for most of the graphs, particularly those that function as
grammatical particles. It is striking, however, that the *Amplified Instructions* has
such an extraordinarily high number of occurrences for "people" (*min*) and
"soldiers" (*ping*). These two graphs do not occur until much farther down on
the standard list. Conversely, the standard list has "Heaven" (*t'ien*) and "ruler"
(*chün*) among the first twenty graphs, but they are not so prominent in the
Amplified Instructions. It is obvious to whom the Yung-cheng emperor was
directing his remarks. Unfortunately, his intended audience was unable to
comprehend him because he wrote in a language that was alien to its members.
Yung-cheng's failure to communicate with the bulk of his subjects and the

[20] Jonathan Spence, "Chang Po-hsing and the K'ang-hsi Emperor," *Ch'ing-shih wen-t'i* 1.8: 3–9
(May 1968), esp. 5; quoted in Evelyn Sakakida Rawski, *Education and Popular Literacy in Ch'ing China*
(Ann Arbor: University of Michigan Press, 1979), p. 15.

[21] *Book of Documents*, Hsia-shu, 4.3, trans. James Legge, *The Chinese Classics*, vol. 3, pt. 1 (London:
Trübner, 1865), p. 164. Fan Hung had also quoted this sentence in his postface to the *Elaboration of
the Hortatory Edict of Six Maxims*.

[22] My translation follows that of A. Théophile Piry, trans. and annot., *Le Saint Édit: Étude de
littérature chinoise* (Shanghai: Bureau des Statistiques, Inspectorat Général des Douanes, 1879), p. 7.
William Milne, trans. and annot., *The Sacred Edict, Containing Sixteen Maxims of the Emperor Kang-he,
Amplified by His Son, The Emperor Yoong-ching; Together with a Paraphrase on the Whole by a Mandarin*
(London: Black, Kingsbury, Parbury, and Allen, 1817; second ed. by American Presbyterian
Mission Press, 1870), p. xxii, is mispunctuated.

[23] Based on data supplied by a chart in Piry, *Le Saint Édit* and from the classical lists in E. Bruce
Brooks and A. Taeko Brooks, *Chinese Character Frequency Lists* (Northampton, Mass.: SinFac Minor,
1976), pp. 6–7.

urgent necessity his officers felt in seeing that he did so led to the repeated vernacular paraphrasis of his *Amplified Instructions.*

The *Amplified Instructions* was eventually also issued in a Manchu version.[24] A trilingual (Chinese, Mongolian, Manchu) edition of the text, the *San-ho Sheng-yü kuang-hsun*, was published no later than the Ch'ien-lung period.[25]

By far the most influential and best known popularizations of the *Sacred Edict* are a series of related texts emanating from Wang Yu-p'u (1680–1761), who, when he composed the original work on which they are based, was serving as assistant salt controller in Shensi Province. Wang Yu-p'u was a man of Tientsin. He attained the advanced scholar (*chin-shih*) degree in 1723 and subsequently became a Bachelor in the National Academy. The highest rank he achieved was first-class subprefect of Lu-chou prefecture.[26]

It seems odd that Wang chose not to mention the paraphrase in his autobiography, especially since he is best known for having written it, although he did have a minor reputation as a scholar of the *Book of Change*. Wang completed the autobiography on March 9, 1761, not long before he died, clearly waiting for his end and using the autobiography to assess the course and import of his life. He stated that, in writing it, he would "hide nothing, whether good or bad."[27] He also gave a fairly complete list of his writings. Why, then, did he avoid the paraphrase altogether? The answer is, quite probably, that he simply did not wish to be remembered for this work of *basse vulgarisation*. Nor did his biographers in the *Gazetteer of Tientsin Prefecture*[28] and the *Ch'ing History*[29] think the paraphrase worthy of mention. They were wrong; Wang Yu-p'u's place in

[24] Translations are available in Russian and in Italian. A. Agafonov, trans., *Manzhurskago i Kitaiskago Khana Kan'siya Kniga* ... (St. Petersburg, 1788; reissued in 1795 with a different title) and Lodovico Nocentini, trans. and annot., *Il santo editto di K'añ-hi, e l'amplificazione di Yuñ-ceñ*, 2 vols. in one (Florence: Successori Le Monnier, 1880–1883). For various editions of the Manchu text, see Wang Yun-wu 王雲五, ed., *Hsu-hsiu ssu-k'u ch'üan-shu t'i-yao* 續修四庫全書提要 [Continuation of abstracts of the complete collection of books in four categories] (Taipei: Taiwan Commercial Press 臺灣商務印書館, 1971), vol. 10, pp. 1048, 1050–1052, including one work that significantly dealt exclusively with the seventh maxim (against heterodoxy).

[25] Ogaeri, *Kago* (cited n. 8), p. 6.

[26] Wang Yu-p'u's autobiography (the *Chieh-shan tzu-ting nien-p'u* 介山自定年譜), in one fascicle, is available both in his collected works (the *Shih-li t'ang ch'üan-chi* 詩禮堂全集, also called *Wang Chieh-shan hsien-sheng ch'üan-chi* 王介山先生全集, published in 1751) and in a Republican period reprint series published by Chin Yueh 金鉞 (*Ping-lu ts'ung-k'e* 屏廬叢刻, 1924). The same is true of his *Shih-li t'ang tsa-tsuan* 詩禮堂雜纂 [Compilation of miscellaneous materials], in two fascicles, which has been useful in determining Wang's own views on a number of matters touched upon in his famous paraphrase of the *Sacred Edict*. Chin Yueh's interest in Wang Yu-p'u was due largely to the fact that he, too, was a native of Tientsin. The *Ping-lu ts'ung-k'e* consists of materials that had been brought together by the bureau charged with the compilation of the Tientsin gazetteer.

[27] *Autobiography*, preface, 1a.

[28] Shen Chia-pen 沈家本 and Hsu Tsung-liang 徐宗亮, comp., *T'ien-chin fu-chih* 天津府志 (Taipei: T'ai-wan hsueh-sheng shu-chü, 1968 rpt. of 1899 ed.), 43.14b (p. 3840).

[29] *Ch'ing shih lieh-chuan* 清史列傳 [Biographies from the Ch'ing history] (Taipei: Chung-hua shu-chü 中華書局, 1962), 68.25b.

history is assured for no other reason than that he was ultimately responsible for the most widely circulated vernacular paraphrase of the *Sacred Edict*.[30]

Wang Yu-p'u's paraphrase has a rather complicated history. It was originally written in 1726, just two years after Yung-cheng issued the *Amplified Instructions*. The original title of the work would appear to have been *Chiang-chieh Sheng-yü kuang-hsun* [Discussion and explanation of the *Amplified Instructions on the "Sacred Edict"*].[31] When it was republished, with minor modifications, by various officials here and there throughout the empire, it came to be known as *Sheng-yü kuang-hsun yen* [Elaboration of the *Amplified Instructions on the "Sacred Edict"*]. This is also the title it bears in Wang Yu-p'u's *Collected Works*.[32] Later, when the text was subjected to major changes and distributed still more widely, it was entitled *Sheng-yü kuang-hsun chih-chieh* [Direct explanation of the *Amplified Instructions on the "Sacred Edict"*].

Baller's translation[33] of Wang Yu-p'u's *Direct Explanation* went through no

---

[30] Wang Yu-p'u was by no means the only person to write a "direct explanation" of the *Amplified Instructions*. One Lü Shou-tseng also wrote a work entitled *Sheng-yü kuang-hsun chih-chieh* [Direct explanation of the *Amplified Instructions of the Sacred Edict*] in one fascicle. This is mentioned in Liu Chin-tsao 劉錦藻, comp., *Ch'ing-ch'ao hsu Wen-hsien t'ung-k'ao* 清朝續文獻通考 [Continuation of the comprehensive examination of documents relating to the Ch'ing Dynasty] (Commercial Press, Wan-yu wen-k'u ed.), 269.10129b.

[31] Ogaeri, *Kago* (cited n. 8), postface, p. 3.

[32] Outside of the *Collected Works*, the oldest extant copy of the *Elaboration* known to me is that consisting of four volumes printed in Canton (after 1808) from crudely cut blocks. It is available in the typeset edition of Ogaeri, *Kago*, pp. 1–101. I have also used a rare copy of this text, in one volume, that is kept in the University of Pennsylvania Van Pelt Library. There are a few small differences between the Canton text of the *Elaboration* and that appearing in Wang's *Collected Works* (vols. 37–38). One of the most noticeable is the consistent use of "His Majesty" (*wan-sui-yeh*) to refer to the Yung-cheng emperor in the former as opposed to "Epochal Progenitor" (*Shih-tsung huang-ti*) in the latter. The *Elaboration* continued to be reprinted as late as 1876, when it was recut at the request of the Censor of Yunnan Circuit, Wu Hung-en. In his postface, Wu states that he used a "presentation copy" of the Ying-chou (in Anhwei) Prefectural Director of Schools, Hsia Hsing, as the basis for his reprinting.

[33] F. W. Baller, *The Sacred Edict with a Translation of the Colloquial Rendering* (Shanghai: American Presbyterian Mission Press, 1892; later editions published in Shanghai by the China Inland Mission and issued in London, Philadelphia, Toronto, and Melbourne by the Religious Tract Society of London). The citations in this study are to the sixth edition (1924). Baller also published a lengthy study aid entitled *A Vocabulary of the Colloquial Rendering of the Sacred Edict* (Shanghai: American Mission Press, 1892). It is somewhat unfortunate that Baller chose the *Direct Explanation*, which was usually issued in two volumes, as the basis for his English translation. The choice was unfortunate, as we shall see below, because the *Direct Explanation* was a slightly classicized adaptation of the *Elaboration*, which was written in unadulterated colloquial. Milne (cf. note 22), working in Malacca toward the end of 1815, did follow the *Elaboration* in his English translation of Wang Yu-p'u's paraphrase. Since Baller's rendition of the *Direct Explanation* is commonly known and widely available in this country, however, it will be convenient to refer to it in many cases instead of to the *Elaboration*. Furthermore, Baller provides the Chinese text of both the *Amplified Instructions* and the *Direct Explanation* whereas Milne's translation, itself rare and difficult to obtain, includes neither. I have also examined three Chinese editions of the *Direct Explanation*. The first is a rare edition from the Yung-cheng period printed by movable wooden type. The second is a block print of 1850 and

less than six editions between the years 1892 and 1924. It was sold widely in general bookstores and had a sizable influence. The original purpose for bringing out this publication was to provide authentic material for the study of Mandarin by Protestant missionaries. Yet, in the end, the work had a much deeper impact upon the foreign community than its sponsors could have imagined. The British magistrate in Weihaiwei, for example, was fond of citing the *Direct Explanation* "in delivering judgments in both civil and criminal cases."[34] He vigorously defended this practice in spite of the fact that a local missionary pointed out to him that he could have found a "far more appropriate text" for his purpose in the Bible.

My impression is that roughly half of the *Direct Explanation* was taken over intact from the *Elaboration* and much of the rest of it follows closely. But there are telling differences, partly due simply to the persistent classicizing tendency in the *Direct Explanation* to avoid prolixity and partly due to a harsher, more condescending attitude toward its audience. Where Wang Yu-p'u tells the people that the government collects taxes to pay the officials who "take care of your affairs," the *Direct Explanation* says that it does so to "control you, the populace."[35] There are also fewer explicit references in the *Direct Explanation* to the solicitude of the K'ang-hsi emperor for the people. Where the *Direct Explanation* simply tells its auditors to use the money they have left over from paying taxes "to buy some things," the *Elaboration* has the more solicitous "to buy some nice things."[36] Yung-cheng had advised the scholars that "the books which you read should all be proper." Wang Yu-p'u displays a keen sense of the real state of affairs when he counsels that "what you read must all be proper books. Don't look at so much as a single line of those lewd lyrics and short stories." The editors of the *Direct Explanation* bring the admonition back more closely to Yung-cheng's formulation with the dull "you must read some proper books."[37] In an attempt to pare down Wang Yu-p'u's smoothly flowing, expansive prose, the *Direct Explanation* editors sometimes construct ungrammatical sentences. For example, they rewrite *Chei-ke ch'ien-liang tsui shih yao-chin-te* ("This tax revenue is most important") as *Che ch'ien-liang tsui shih yao-chin.*[38] The

---

the third a reprinting of 1865 with an added preface dated 1876. Many other editions of the *Direct Explanation* were published. Legge, "Imperial Confucianism" (cited n. 2), p. 149a, states that the *Direct Explanation* was sold everywhere in China. One edition was printed entirely in vermilion ink by the archivist of Soochow Prefecture sometime during the Kuang-hsu reign period (1875–1908). See Ogaeri, *Kago*, plate 6.

[34] R. F. Johnston, *Lion and Dragon in Northern China* (New York: E. P. Dutton, 1910), p. 123. It is possible that Johnston knew of the *Direct Explanation* apart from Baller's rendering because one passage he quotes from it (about fellow-villagers quarrelling) is in his own distinctive translation (cf. Baller, *Sacred Edict*, p. 31).

[35] Ogaeri, *Kago*, p. 82; Baller, *Sacred Edict*, p. 149.

[36] Baller, *Sacred Edict*, p. 151; Ogaeri, *Kago*, p. 83.

[37] Baller, *Sacred Edict*, p. 193; Ogaeri, *Kago*, p. 33; Baller, *Sacred Edict*, p. 65.

[38] Ogaeri, *Kago*, p. 82; Baller, *Sacred Edict*, p. 149. Current usage would prefer *Chei-ke ch'ien-liang shih tsui yao-chin-te.*

Direct Explanation has a greater tendency to use monosyllabic nouns and verbs than does the *Elaboration*, and its handling of colloquial particles and complements is less fluent and assured. The *Elaboration* is an almost flawless masterpiece of natural, colloquial prose. The *Direct Explanation*, on the other hand, is awkward in many instances where it departs from the *Elaboration*. There are other subtle distinctions between the two texts. The *Elaboration* relies more on persuasion to cajole and coax the people, while the *Direct Explanation* is somewhat peremptory and threatening. Both texts are condescending to their auditors but the *Direct Explanation* is more so. It calls the people "stupid," "doltish," "ignorant," "idiotic," "dullards," and "imbeciles." [39] The *Direct Explanation* cites large segments of the Ch'ing code in classical Chinese but the *Elaboration* does not.

There is little doubt that both the *Elaboration* and the *Direct Explanation* were intended to be read aloud *to* the people. There are frequent direct addresses to a listening audience: "You masses of the people," "you soldiers and civilians," "I ask you," "you look," "you just think," "you who are sons," and so on. Rhetorical questions abound: "Do you mean to say ...?" "Is it not ...?" "Examine yourselves—how can you do it in all conscience?" "What is filial piety?" "Since you know the kindness of your parents, why are you not filial to them?" and so forth. The recurrence of the words "lecture" (*chiang*) and "hear" (*t'ing*) is another indication of the purpose of these texts. Both also display a fondness for proverbs and popular sayings that would have been an effective element in public lectures.

The *Direct Explanation* and the *Elaboration* are explicit in identifying their intended auditors: "Although these remarks are addressed to the soldiers and civilians, we still wish you country squires, men of rank, elders well up in years, graduates in letters, and leading men in the community, first of all to set an example of concord: then you will be able to educate the ignorant people." [40]

It would, admittedly, have been impossible for an official in Canton or Fukien, say, simply to read off Wang Yu-p'u's Mandarin (Chihli) paraphrase and expect the local denizens to comprehend it. This difficulty was obviated by the fact that, "in reading, the orator deviates considerably from the printed copy; supplying what he thinks needful to render the sense perspicuous to the hearers, and altering the phraseology to suit it to the idiom of the spoken language of that particular province, or district." [41] This, of course, is premised upon the ability of the orator to speak the local dialect. In many cases, the centrally appointed officials were not linguistically equipped to speak to the people in the districts they administered.

[39] See, for example, Baller, *Sacred Edict*, pp. 85, 93, 95, 137, 153, 177, and *passim*.
[40] Baller, *Sacred Edict*, p. 38, cf. p. 48; Ogaeri, *Kago*, p. 17.
[41] William Milne, "Bibliotheca Sinica," *The Chinese Repository* 16:504 (1847). For sample translations of the *Amplified Instructions* into various dialects, see S. Wells Williams, *A Syllabic Dictionary of the Chinese Language*, rev. ed. (Tung Chou: North China Union College, 1909), pp. xlii–xlvii.

The problem of language barriers comes up again in a report of Wang Chih (Advanced Scholar, 1721), like Wang Yu-p'u, also from Chihli. While serving as magistrate of Hsin-hui in Kwangtung Province, Wang Chih wrote a *Shang-yü t'ung-su chieh* [Popular explanation of the *Imperial Edict*]. Although Wang Chih refers to the work he paraphrased as the *Imperial Edict*, because of his mention of the *Amplified Instructions*, it is clear that he means the *Sacred Edict*. He explains how he had come to write this work in the following words:

> Formerly I had developed a method of explaining the *Imperial Edict*, using colloquial language to paraphrase the text of the *Amplified Instructions*. I ordered the lecturers to preach in the native dialect. Listeners were able to understand and appreciate quite well. The Overseer of Hsin-ning, Wang Chün-sung, whenever he lectured on one of the maxims himself, would [make the people] understand by going over it again and again. Because my accent was not right, I could not do that.
>
> Upon arriving at the place where the village lecture was to be held, I ordered elderly inhabitants over eighty or ninety to sit behind the gentry. All were served tea; but none [of this privileged group of listeners] was permitted to report on public affairs. Commoners were ordered to stand and listen during the village lectures.[42]

The frank admission of a language barrier is revealing; Wang Chih was unable to address the people of the county in which he was the highest ranking government officer. Wang Yu-p'u reveals his own ambivalence toward colloquial speech when he speaks derogatorily about the "local dialects in the various parts of China."[43]

Several of the editors and publishers of Wang Yu-p'u's famous paraphrase have provided helpful information about how they came to know of it and why they decided to undertake the responsibility for making it available to others. Shortly after 1808, the acting viceroy of the province of Canton, Han Feng, was shown a copy of the *Discussion and Explanation* (i.e., the *Elaboration*) by Wang Hsun-ch'en, the superintendant of land revenue. "Having received and read the explanation," he confesses, "I couldn't help liking it. Therefore, I ordered the officer in charge of instruction to select, from among the fourth class of the literary candidates, four persons whose teeth and mouth were formed for clear and distinct utterance; that on the first and fifteenth of each moon, they might proclaim the original text in the Canton dialect." It is obvious that oral interpretation was an essential part of the presentation, for it would have been impossible simply to read off Wang Yu-p'u's northern dialect *Elaboration* in

---

[42] Hsu Tung 徐棟, comp., *Mu-ling shu chi-yao* 牧令書輯要 [Compilation of essential documents relating to the shepherds of the people], ed. Ting Jih-ch'ang 丁日昌 (Kiangsu shu-chü 江蘇書局, 1868 rev. and printed, preface 1838), 6.18a. Cf. Kung-chuan Hsiao, *Rural China: Imperial Control in the Nineteenth Century* (Seattle: University of Washington Press, 1960, second printing, 1967), p. 619, n. 51.

[43] Baller, *Sacred Edict*, p. 83; Ogaeri, *Kago*, p. 41.

Cantonese. Apparently it was easier to interpret orally from the *Elaboration* than to translate directly from Yung-cheng's classical *Amplified Instructions* into Cantonese. Han Feng, not without exaggeration, declares that the lectures were a success and then goes on to describe his instructions to subordinate officials:

> I accordingly distributed it throughout the districts; gave it to the local officers, the pastors of the people, ordering that they should widely proclaim the Edict; and not leave a single person, even in the huts thinly scattered along the shores of the ocean, ignorant and disobedient. Should we at a future time receive your imperial order to remove to other places, we will teach the same in the dialects of those places to all the people....[44]

Judging from these and other remarks, the publication and distribution of vernacular paraphrases of the *Sacred Edict* were dependent upon the individual initiative of officials outside the capital.

In the statement of the Canton editor of the *Elaboration*, Wang Hsun-ch'en, we find the following passage:

> From the time that your Imperial Majesty began to reign until now, you have earnestly commanded all statesmen and officers to hold lectures in accord with precedent so as to encourage and guide the ignorant villagers. We, your ministers, have not failed, each in the vulgar dialect of his own district, by various methods, to lead on the people to the knowledge of the *Edict*. But our lectures are only occasional and we fear that they may not reach everyone. Hence I have searched out the *Discussion and Explanation of the [Amplified] Instructions on the Sacred [Edict]* published by the Assistant Salt Controller of Shensi, Wang Yu-p'u.[45]

Wang Hsun-ch'en would seem to believe that publication of the *Discussion and Explanation* would allow the *Sacred Edict* to reach a greater audience than he and his colleagues could in the course of their own lectures. But he does not entertain any serious expectation that the common people would actually read the *Sacred Edict*, even in this popularized form. He simply thinks it his duty as an official to make it more widely available, probably to local literates, because "the sense of the discussions and explanations is easily understood and is truly beneficial to the ignoramuses who *hear* them."[46] With this in mind, he "accordingly re-printed Yu-p'u's text and distributed it to the prefectures and counties so that it might be known to every family and household and that they would comment on and explain it to each other."[47] Wang Hsun-ch'en's statement closes with a challenge to the "good civil authorities" to animate and encourage the people without wearying and by a variety of methods.

---

[44] Translations of this and the preceding quotation (with slight alteration) are by Milne, *Sacred Edict*, pp. xxvii–xxviii.

[45] Ogaeri, *Kago*, p. 100; cf. Milne, *Sacred Edict*, p. xxv.

[46] *Elaboration* (cited n. 32 above), italics mine.

[47] Ogaeri, *Kago*, p. 100.

On June 21, 1815, the judicial commissioner of the province of Shensi, Chi-ch'ang (a Manchu bannerman who had become a provincial graduate [*chü-jen*] in 1800), finished his *Sheng-yü kuang-hsun yen-shuo* [Glosses for the *Amplified Instructions on the "Sacred Edict"*].[48] It is obvious that this text is an abridged adaptation of the *Direct Explanation*. Entire sentences and even paragraphs are left out, while others are rearranged and rewritten. The language, though still fluent colloquial Mandarin, is less assured than that of the *Direct Explanation*, not to mention the *Elaboration*. It is also less graphic and earthy. In short, *Glosses* is an assiduous but unsuccessful attempt to camouflage wholesale plagiarism from its famous predecessor. But it is more than just that, for *Glosses* also evinces a different attitude and tone. Where the *Elaboration* and *Direct Explanation*, in decrying the growth of heretical sects, declare that such sects are prone to "do bad things,"[49] *Glosses* warns that they "do rebellious things until they are discovered, exposed, and attacked from all sides by soldiers and officials."[50] *Glosses* is more threatening than the *Direct Explanation*, partly through greater emphasis on specific punishments cited from the Ch'ing code,[51] partly through increased insistence on the necessity for individuals to "mind their own busi-ness" (*shou pen-fen*), as it were.[52] There is also more frequent reference to the "stupidity" and "ignorance" (*yü-mei, wu-chih*) of the people.[53]

The most telling indication of Chi-ch'ang's intentions in issuing this para-phrase, however, is to be found in the conclusion to his own postface:

> Fearing that the stupid men and women are not fully acquainted with the profound meaning of [the Emperor's] writing [in the *Sacred Edict*] and still cannot completely comprehend it, I have respectfully elaborated the royal words in common language. Thus the twice-monthly explications in the various prefec-tures and counties as well as the propagandizing (*hsuan-ch'uan*) by instructors in each village and community will be intelligible to the ear of women and children while the recalcitrant and the craven alike will be moved with enthusiasm. It is hoped that the officials who guide the people will carry out these orders without being remiss. They will be endlessly supportive and protective[54] in order to

[48] I have used a rare copy preserved in the Gest Library of Princeton University. It is bound together with a standard edition of the *Amplified Instructions* published by Chu Hsun (from Kiangsu), the Governor of Shensi, a post he assumed in 1813. The two texts retain their separate paginations, 1a–54a for the *Amplified Instructions* and 1a–93b plus 1a–2b (postface) for the *Glosses*. On the cover is a seal indicating that the bound volumes were once owned by a Wang I-ch'ang 王義昌.

[49] Ogaeri, *Kago*, p. 43; Baller, *Sacred Edict*, p. 84.

[50] *Glosses*, p. 36a.

[51] E.g., pp. 5B–6a, 36b–37a; cf. Ogaeri, *Kago*, pp. 6–7, 42–43, and Baller, *Sacred Edict*, pp. 16–17, 85–86.

[52] See, for example, p. 39a, and contrast Ogaeri, *Kago*, p. 45 and Baller, *Sacred Edict*, p. 88.

[53] See pp. 6b, 33a, 34a, 34b; cf. Ogaeri, *Kago*, pp. 7, 37, 38, 39, and Baller, *Sacred Edict*, pp. 18, 74, 76, 78.

[54] Based on a passage in the *Book of Change* 易經. See *Shih-san ching chu-shu* 十三經注疏 (Taipei: I-wen yin-shu kuan 藝文印書館, 1965 reprint of 1815 [1896] ed.), 3.7a (p. 59a).

achieve for our country the blessing of peace and harmony and in order to assist the sage Son of Heaven in the task of enlightening the people through emulating his ancestors and making them submit for all time. May this be of some assistance.[55]

Toward the end of the Tao-kuang reign period (1821–1850), heretical sects were proliferating wildly. It was thought that a large part of the responsibility for this unrest lay with the local officials, who were supposedly too lax in combating them. Consequently, study of the *Sacred Edict* in all schools and academies was required as a corrective. The editor of the 1850 edition of the *Direct Explanation* expresses a deep concern about the increasingly overt activities of illicit religious groups:

> Recently, heterodox doctrines have been transmitted to all the provinces and are spreading across them. At first, it was only a matter of burning incense, collecting money, and stirring up doubt in the minds of the stupid people. Gradually, we have come to a situation where crowds gather and disturbances are incited. This is all because the local officials are ineffective in their daily guidance of the people. Furthermore, the seniors and leaders among the people are unable to teach and enlighten them from time to time so that the ignorant might be governable and fear punishment and, hence, not be confused by heterodox pronouncements.

Not wanting to be blamed as an irresponsible official, the editor chose to reprint the *Direct Explanation* as his contribution to the struggle against heresy.

The same concerns inform the preface of the 1865 edition of the *Direct Explanation*, which I quote in full:

> Of old, the people were made up of four classes; now there are six classes of people. Of old, there was but a single doctrine; now there are three.[56] The more these doctrines diverge, the more confused people become. Divergence multiplies upon divergence until the oppression of the masses caused by these heterodox pronouncements exceeds that of Yang-tzu, Mo-tzu, Buddha, and Lao-tzu.[57] The damage they cause cannot be told in words.
>
> Our Sacred Ancestor, the Benevolent Emperor [K'ang-hsi], himself having been given great authority by Heaven, was disposed to display his sympathy for the benighted. He expressly promulgated the *Sacred Edict* composed of sixteen items to constitute forever a method of indoctrination. Our Epochal Progenitor, the Exemplary Emperor [Yung-cheng], in turn, composed the *Amplified Instructions* in ten thousand words. He also instituted study halls and lectures on the first and fifteenth of each month.
>
> The Plans of the Sages are far-reaching and bright as the sun and the moon. Now the Son of Heaven, at a moment when the empire's fate turns, brings about

[55] *Glosses*, 2ab.

[56] The four classes are scholars, farmers, artisans, and merchants; the six classes are these four plus monks and priests. The single doctrine is, of course, Confucianism; the three doctrines are Confucianism, Buddhism, and Taoism.

[57] Representing Hedonism, Universal Love, Buddhism, and Taoism, respectively.

restoration by diligently seeking order. The Silken Words of the Emperor repeatedly disseminate clear explanations as he lectures on the essentials of the old statutes. Truly this is an important way to transform the people and to reform custom. However, his language is literary and his purport is deep. The learned doctors who proclaim his words and elaborate upon them may perhaps not fully elucidate their meaning. The dull and slow-witted people of the villages and lanes cannot fathom the instructions of the classics nor can they apprehend their profundity, so they do not fully see the intent of the Sages. This is not the way to propagate the Supreme Doctrine.

Formerly, when I was serving as an official in the capital, I heard that in Kiangsi, Hupei, and other provinces, there had been printed a book called the *Direct Explanation*. The authorities, out of respect for the Excellent Teaching of the Court, probably hoped that thereby a part of it might be known in every household. I regret that before I had had a chance to see it, I went to fill a post in Anhwei. It so happened that military matters were quite pressing and I was no longer able to think of the *Direct Explanation*. Today, fortunately, the ravages of the soldiers have abated somewhat.

I deeply maintain that, in order to inculcate the doctrine of propriety, we must cause the eyes and ears of the people to be steeped in it so that it is easy for them to know and follow. By chance, in a conversation with the former Commissioner of Education, the Academician Ma Yü-nung, the subject of this book came up. He brought out from a chest a copy that he owned and showed it to me. I read it carefully and savored its details. This book respectfully adheres to the *Amplified Instructions on the Sacred Edict* by explaining its import in language that young and old among the people can understand and hence become thoroughly conversant with its message. Going over them again and again renders the instructions perspicuous and makes them clear as speech. This causes the auditors to take them to heart actively without wearying of them. For the ignorant and the uneducated, it is quite beneficial. So, having borrowed the book, I took it back to my own place. There I copied it down and re-edited it with the intention of broadening its circulation.

Perhaps someone might say, "When there is great disorder in society, one must first alleviate suffering. Before you have been able to rescue the people from the clutches of death, what leisure have you to cultivate ceremony and righteousness?"[58] What are you doing with these writing materials?" He who asks this does not realize that great disorder in society arises in the hearts of men. If the hearts of men are not changed, the disorder in society will not soon abate. Today the area south of the Yangtze is somewhat settled and the people are gradually being relieved of their distress. Everybody is saying, "Peace and order have already been achieved!" Yet those who employ violence presume on their harsh threats; those who are accustomed to cunning abuse others with opportunistic tricks; those who work at being unconventional detest ceremony and law; those who insist upon obstinacy unleash their obtuseness. What is there to be happy about? With

---

[58] This is based on *Mencius*, 1.7. Cf. James Legge, *The Chinese Classics*, vol. 2 (London: Trübner, 1861), p. 24: "In such circumstances they only try to save themselves from death, and are afraid they will not succeed. What leisure have they to cultivate righteousness?"

words becoming confused and affairs disorderly, once again unfounded heretical pronouncements incite the people. The flames leap higher and higher, as though there were a blazing fire, until they become worrisome indeed.

The printing of the *Direct Explanation* is for the very purpose of elaborating and spreading the fine civilizing influence of the *Amplified Instructions on the Sacred Edict* so as to bring rectitude to the hearts of men. Accordingly, I have brought forth this book to be distributed in the various prefectures and counties. Each of our officials and outstanding citizens ought in all sincerity to do his best to realize this measure. May they daily have the young and the old come to them so that they can instruct them in the meaning of filial piety and subordination, disseminating the Virtues of the Ruler among his subjects. Thus, to a degree, the laws may be restored, the people renewed, and the evils of heresy not arise. Is this not the basis for assisting China to be greatly distinguished in the Way for eons? Is this not the basis?

> —*Autumn, ninth month, 1865.*
> *Respectfully inscribed by Ho Ching,*
> *Financial Commissioner of Hupei,*
> *retained as Acting Financial*
> *Commissioner of Anhwei.*

The *Sacred Edict* and two separate *Amplified Instructions* are mentioned in the introductory essay of Huang Yü-p'ien's well-known antiheretical work, *P'o hsieh hsiang-pien* [A detailed refutation of heresies, preface 1834]. The date given for the first *Amplified Instructions* is 1724, so this is obviously Yung-cheng's original text. The date given for the second is 1797. From the description provided by Huang, it would appear that the text in question is one or another edition of the *Direct Explanation*[59]: "Written completely in everyday colloquial language of the people to set forth and comment upon [the *Amplified Instructions*]. All local officials, on the first and the fifteenth of each month, respectfully use it for lectures so that the ignorant people too can understand thoroughly and with ease. The rectification of the laws and the renewal of the people lie in this." In the preface, Huang writes of his own work: "Because the ignorant people in the villages who recognize characters are few, it is hoped that the gentry in each village read this book [i.e., *Disputation*] until they are thoroughly familiar with it and then transmit it extensively to the broad masses."[60] Presumably, a similar process of transmission was used for the *Amplified Instructions*. The purpose of the *Direct Explanation* thus would have been to provide the gentry or other responsible individuals with a ready-made

---

[59] Ogaeri, *Kago*, p. 15 of postface, mentions a one-volume edition of the *Direct Explanation* that was labled on the outside simply as *Sheng-yü kuang-hsun* [Amplified Instructions on the *Sacred Edict*]. On the title page, it carried the additional annotation, "with appended citations from the legal code."

[60] Sawada Mizuho 澤田瑞穗, ed. and annot., *Kōchū Haja shōben* 校注破邪詳辯 [A detailed disputation against heterodoxy, with collocations and commentaries] (Tokyo: Dōkyō kankō-kai 道教刊行會, 1972), p. 8 and preface, p. 7. I am indebted to Professor C. K. Wang of National Taiwan University for this reference and for the citation in note 88.

lecture in the colloquial language that they could adapt to their own needs and tastes.

Who the purchasers of these texts were might be partially deduced from the prices asked for them. In 1847, the *Elaboration*, on good paper, could be bought in Canton for the equivalent of two shillings and sixpence.[61] In Canton, this amount of money, in the same year, could have bought about 40 pounds of rice or a pair of trousers and a jacket.[62] This was surely within the realm of possible purchase by the literati but it would have been a luxury for the common man. Perhaps there were cheaper editions available, although I do not know what their price might have been. Even at half the price, buying this text would still have been a big investment for the average person.

A most curious production is the small volume called *Sheng-yü ch'u-yen* [Plain talk on the *Sacred Edict*], by Chien Ching-hsi. This work would appear to be the product of a local group of intellectuals who gave themselves quaint names (Chien, for example, styled himself "The Woodcutter of Cassia Village" [*Kuei-ts'un ch'iao-che*]). The production also seems to have had a limited budget and, hence, limited circulation, perhaps because it did not receive any official backing. The printing on the pages of the text is close set, as though the intention was to save space and hence paper. The carving is clear but by no means distinguished. While not an expensive publication, it has manifestly been lovingly and carefully executed. I have used the 1893 recutting done at Yü-shan, Chekiang. The two prefaces, dated 1887, are in the neat calligraphy (one regular script, one cursive) of two of the sponsors of the publication and are helpful in understanding the origins and purpose of the *Plain Talk*. The prefaces are full of amusing self-congratulatory sentiments. Chien, it would seem, was a rather successful lecturer on the *Sacred Edict*. He was probably a member of the gentry who had been tapped by a county magistrate for this purpose.[63] Some of his friends who read his lectures in written form were so delighted with them that they decided to publish and distribute them. In his preface, one of Chien's friends, Huo Chen, makes rather grand claims about the extent of the influence they hope it will have ("everyone within and without the Four Seas will know how to establish the Way").

The *Plain Talk* may be said to be "plain" only in the sense that it provides straight exegesis of the *Amplified Instructions*. It is insipid and dull; without considerable embellishment, it could hardly have stirred its auditors to follow the teachings of the sages. After quoting each maxim, it mechanically begins

[61] William Milne, "Bibliotheca Sinica," *The Chinese Repository* 16:502 (1847).

[62] Computed from figures available in *The Chinese Repository* 16:56, 297, 318 (1847), and Osmond Tiffany, Jr., *The Canton Chinese: or, The American's Sojourn in the Celestial Empire* (Boston: J. Munroe, 1849), p. 222.

[63] In some localities, respected members of the gentry were called upon to help in expounding the *Sacred Edict*. See Chung-li Chang, *The Chinese Gentry: Studies on Their Role in Nineteenth-Century Chinese Society* (Seattle: University of Washington Press, 1955), pp. 15, 65.

with the words "The *Sacred Edict* of the August One Above would have us ..." or a similar formulation. Each section ends with a sentence to the effect that "The _____th maxim of the *Sacred Edict* means precisely this." The author is quite condescending to the people, calling them by such endearing epithets as "inferior ignoramuses." On the other hand, he servilely flatters the emperor. He is strongly against secret societies and "religious bandits" but would appear to have no overt quarrel with Buddhism and Taoism. Huo Chen's preface claims that when Chien used his *Plain Words* to lecture on the *Sacred Edict*, he made "the resplendent, imperial language of the *Amplified Instructions* suitable for women and children." But he could not have done so without utilizing some mechanism of oral interpretation, for, although the *Plain Words* does not employ arcane allusions, only an audience with several years of training in the classical language could have understood the text were it read aloud.

The *Sheng-yü kuang-hsun chi-cheng* [Collected verifications of the *Amplified Instructions on the Sacred Edict*], in two fascicles, bears an inscription by Shih Chih-mo[64] of Yang-hu in Kiangsu dated the sixteenth day of the eleventh month of the year 1878. The blocks for the edition I have used were recut in 1900 and kept at Wu Yin-sun's place in Kiangsu. Wu was from I-cheng County, also in Kiangsu, and brought out the *Yu-fu tu-shu-t'ang ts'ung-k'e* [Good fortune library series] of which the *Collected Verifications* is the first title. In his preface, Wu says that his family owned more than seven thousand books. Of these, 50–60 percent were trade publications and 40–50 percent were old or rare editions. The Wus were obviously avid collectors and they frequently had interesting titles, some still in manuscript form, sent to them. They were also publishers and keenly aware of the intense competition in the reprint-series field. Wu had several times begun to publish a series but soon stopped in each case because he was uncertain of its potential success. He emphasizes that he had to think of some distinctive theme for the series. Ultimately, he decided to choose *easy-to-understand* works of solid moral content that had been overlooked by other publishers. We thus have the Wu family's entrepreneurial spirit to thank for the preservation of the *Collected Verifications*. It is also significant that a market for this type of material existed and that it was sufficiently large to attract competing publishers.

The nature of the market may, to a certain extent, be understood by examining the *Collected Verifications*. This book consists of stories illustrating the maxims that had been used by lecturers on the *Sacred Edict*. The treatment of each maxim conforms to the following pattern: a general introduction, illustrative stories, and a recapitulation. The latter section often effectively compares and contrasts the moral issues raised by the illustrative examples. A number of

---

[64] Shih Chih-mo must be the brother or cousin of Shih Chih-kao 史致誥 (d. 1854), also of Yang-hu in Kiangsu. For the latter, see Ch'en Nai-ch'ien 陳乃乾, comp., *Ch'ing-tai pei-chuan wen t'ung-chien* 清代碑傳文通檢 [Finding-list for texts of stele biographies] (Peking: Chung-hua shu-chü 中華書局, 1959), p. 36.

the stories are from the Shanghai area but a few come from as far away as Shansi. Some of the stories are historical but most are contemporary. To lend veracity to the accounts, the compiler supplies dates and places, with the result that the reader almost begins to feel that the *Collected Verifications* represents a species of reporting. On the one hand, as might be expected in such a situation, sensational tales of murder are vividly recounted but, on the other hand, there are also a couple of charming stories about animals (the filial calf and the filial kitten). Surprisingly, the compiler has been able to link up such disparate items into fairly coherent and persuasive arguments.

Linguistically, the *Collected Verifications* is a hodgepodge of styles. The first sentence of each section is in the classical language but there is often a gradual shift into an impure colloquial (*chih* for *te*, *ch'i* for *t'a*, *hu* instead of *ma*, *tz'u* for *che*[a], and so on). Some stories are entirely in simple classical and this leads me to suspect that the compiler may merely have been following his sources without making any serious effort toward stylistic unity.

Buddhists are said to be "only preoccupied with purity and cleanliness, calmness and extinction," while Taoists "let things take their natural course so that no harm will come to the people."[65] Elsewhere, the compiler displays a certain sympathy for such Buddhist concepts as retribution and reincarnation. But the millenarian cults are an entirely different matter. Like all the other literati popularizers, he is completely opposed to the ideas and activities of such groups.

LECTURES

To give some idea of the institutional setting in which the Ch'ing popularizations of the *Sacred Edict* appeared, it may be helpful to provide a brief chronology of related government actions. In 1652, the *Six Maxims* were promulgated throughout the land.[66] Following Ming precedent, an imperial directive was issued in 1659 establishing a system of village lectures (*hsiang-yüeh*) to elucidate the *Six Maxims* in plain and simple language on the first and fifteenth of each month.[67] It was this system that was carried over subsequently for use by lecturers on the *Sacred Edict* and continued, with varying degrees of vitality, to the end of the Ch'ing dynasty.[68] Kung-chuan Hsiao refers to it as a method of popular indoctrination.[69] Pei Huang states that later, during the

---

[65] *Collected Verifications*, 1.18b.

[66] Suerna, *Complete Book* (cited n. 10), 74.1a.

[67] Ibid., 74.1ab.

[68] The *Six Maxims* continued to play an important role in the village lectures alongside the *Sacred Edict* during the first half of the Ch'ing.

[69] *Rural China*, p. 185. Hsiao devotes an entire chapter, which he entitles "Ideological Control: The *Hsiang-yüeh* and Other Institutions" (pp. 184–258), to this subject. T'ung-tsu Ch'ü also considers the lectures on the *Sacred Edict* to be a form of indoctrination. See his *Local Government in China under the Ch'ing* (Cambridge, Mass.: Harvard University Press, 1962), p. 162.

Yung-cheng period, "all the variant forms of intellectual restriction . . . were channeled toward the same end—the enforcement of orthodox ideology." There was a determined attempt to make this orthodoxy the pattern for the political behavior of everyone within the empire, not just the ideological standard for the literati.[70] Numerous official measures relating to the propagation of the maxims of the *Sacred Edict*, including successive refinements of the village lecture system, were an integral part of this ideological enforcement. Chung-li Chang agrees that the purpose of the semimonthly lectures on what he calls the "politico-moral maxims" of the *Sacred Edict* was "to indoctrinate the masses with the official ideology."[71]

In 1729, it was decreed that, in all larger towns and villages where there were dense concentrations of people, places for lectures on the Yung-cheng emperor's *Amplified Instructions* were to be established.[72] The following year, Yung-cheng agreed to sanction special educational procedures for the children of aboriginal peoples in remote parts of Chien-ch'ang prefecture (Szechwan) who had submitted to Chinese rule but were unacquainted with Chinese notions of propriety. It was decided that village tutors (*shu-shih*) ought to be invited to instruct them. The problem was that these children did not understand Mandarin (*kuan-yü*) while the tutors were not at ease in the local language.[73] In order to overcome this difficulty, it was suggested that exemplary first-degree licentiates from Szechwan be hired to establish training centers on the model of the free schools in Han areas. The aboriginal children were to be sent to schools not far from their own homes together with Han children so that gradually the culture of the latter would rub off on them. The first text mentioned for study was the *Amplified Instructions on the Sacred Edict*. Only after this work was thoroughly mastered would they turn to the recitation and study of the classics. A similar procedure was suggested in 1732 for instructing the children of the Miao people in six villages of the Yung-sui area.[74] For the instruction of the Li and Yao peoples in Kwangtung Province, the emphasis was on securing linguistically talented teachers and, as in the Miao case, the selection and advancement of the most capable aboriginal children for further

---

[70] *Autocracy at Work: A Study of the Yung-cheng Period, 1723–1735* (Bloomington: Indiana University Press, 1974), p. 188. Cf. John R. Watt, "The Yamen and Urban Administration," in G. William Skinner, ed., *The City in Late Imperial China* (Stanford: Stanford University Press, 1977), pp. 353–390, esp. pp. 361–362.

[71] *The Chinese Gentry*, p. 65. Perhaps the most extensive treatment of the *Sacred Edict* in English is to be found in Leon E. Stover, *The Cultural Ecology of Chinese Civilization: Peasants and Elites in the Last of the Agrarian States* (New York: Mentor, 1974). Stover has structured much of his discussion around the *Sacred Edict* in a way that is pertinent to many of the papers in this book.

[72] Suerna, *Complete Book*, 74.4a.

[73] See ibid., 74.10b–11a for the need to translate the *Amplified Instructions* and parts of the Ch'ing legal code into aboriginal languages. It was recommended that interpreters accompany officials into the aboriginal settlements expressly for this purpose.

[74] Ibid., 73.4ab.

study. There were also the obligatory semimonthly lectures on the *Amplified Instructions* and explanations of the legal code.[75] Reading through the government regulations on the subject, one gains the clear impression that the problem of the education of non-Han subjects represented but an extreme form of the difficulties inherent in transmitting the values of the elite to the rest of the population. It is noteworthy that, in both circumstances, the *Sacred Edict* was considered to be the best vehicle for the transmission of these ideals.

By 1736, measures were taken to extend the lecture system to all villages without restrictions on size.[76] Additional measures were to be taken in following years to ensure that copies of the *Amplified Instructions* and abridged legal codes would be available to chief and assistant lecturers throughout the empire. Furthermore, these lecturers were not to look upon their task of speaking on the *Amplified Instructions* and the legal code as a mere formality but were to take it with the utmost seriousness. In 1737, it was specifically stipulated that the main provisions of the imperial code be explained at the end of each lecture session on the *Sacred Edict*.[77] This order had a direct impact on authors and editors of written popularizations of the *Sacred Edict*, who began increasingly to append relevant passages from the code to their discussions of the maxims. In 1753, the emperor ordered that officials be strongly encouraged, in addition to giving the regular semimonthly lectures on the *Sacred Edict*, to instruct the villagers in Confucian moral precepts whenever they could, employing local dialects and colloquial speech so that those present might understand what they were hearing.[78] A directive of 1758 declared that "it would do no harm to explain [the *Amplified Instructions*] clearly in local dialects and with common sayings."[79] This directive was especially concerned with bringing a halt to the spread of heterodox sects. The laws forbidding such doctrines were to be printed and posted widely. By the time of the Tao-kuang emperor (r. 1821–1850), the government seems to have become almost paranoid about the activities of secret and unsanctioned religious groups. Considering the events of the second half of the nineteenth century, however, perhaps their fears were justified. At any rate, from about 1750 on, there is always a close connection between the village lecture system and the suppression of heresies. The increasing emphasis during the Ch'ing on the prevention of socially disruptive behavior and unlawful conduct can be seen clearly by comparing the *Six Maxims* with the *Sacred Edict* and the *Sacred Edict* with the *Amplified Instructions* and its commentaries.[80]

One account of the prescribed ritual for lecturing on the *Sacred Edict* is as follows:

[75] Ibid., 73.4b–5a.
[76] Ibid., 74.5a–6a.
[77] Hsiao, *Rural China*, p. 190.
[78] Ibid., p. 186.
[79] Suerna, *Complete Book*, 74.11ab.
[80] Hsiao, *Rural China*, p. 188.

Early on the first and fifteenth of every moon, the civil and military officers, dressed in their uniforms, meet in a clean, spacious, public hall. The superintendent or Master of Ceremonies (*li-sheng*) calls aloud, "Stand forth in files." They do so, according to their rank: he then says, "Kneel thrice, and bow the head nine times." They kneel, and bow to the ground, with their faces towards a platform, on which is placed a board with the Emperor's name. He next calls aloud, "Rise and retire." They rise, and all go to a hall, or kind of chapel, where the law is usually read; and where the military and people are assembled, standing round in silence.

The Master of Ceremonies then says, "Respectfully commence." The orator (*ssu-chiang-sheng*), advancing towards an incense-altar, kneels; reverently takes up the board on which the maxim appointed for the day is written, and ascends a stage with it. An old man receives the board, and puts it down on the stage, fronting the people. Then, commanding silence with a wooden rattle which he carries in his hand, he kneels, and reads it. When he has finished, the Master of Ceremonies calls out, "Explain such a section, or maxim, of the *Sacred Edict*." The orator stands up, and gives the sense.[81]

The following extract from a letter, dated Shanghai, September 23, 1847, and written by a foreign resident gives a perhaps truer picture of the manner of proclamation of the *Sacred Edict*:

I have just returned from hearing *Chinese preaching*, or what answers to preaching better than anything else I have yet seen among the Chinese. You know that on the 1st and 15th of every month, the local officers throughout the empire are required to repair to the municipal temples, and then, after having worshiped the deity enshrined therein, and the emperor, are there to have the Sacred Edict brought out in state, and read to the assembly of the people and soldiers. This ceremony I have just had an opportunity of seeing.

At a quarter past 5 o'clock this morning, in company with some friends, I started for the *Ching-hwáng miáu* [i.e., *ch'eng-huang miao*], the residence of the tutelary god of Shánghái. Entering the city by the Little South gate, and by the way calling for three other gentlemen, we all reached the temple some time before six o'clock. A multitude of devout idolaters had already collected, and most of them were busily engaged in performing their religious rites—making prostrations, offering incense, &c., &c. The officials not having arrived, we strolled through the different apartments of the temple, upstairs and downstairs, among all sorts of shrines and images. This temple is not only the largest in Shánghái, but has the reputation of being inferior to none of the kind in the whole empire.

In a little while the chief magistrate arrived with his retinue, and was soon followed by the colonel, accompanied by three subalterns, who all repaired

---

[81] Adapted from Milne, trans., *The Sacred Edict*, pp. ix–xi, who has based his account on a local gazetteer from Kwangtung province. Most other gazetteers include a similar description. For one such elaborate account, see Sun Hao 孫灝, et al., *Honan t'ung-chih* 河南通志 [General gazetteer of Honan] (1882), 10.4a. Huang Liu-hung 黃六鴻 has provided a wealth of detail on the prescribed method for reading and expounding the *Sacred Edict* in his 1699 *Fu-hui ch'üan-shu* 福惠全書, tr. by Djang Chu as *A Complete Book Concerning Happiness and Benevolence: A Manual for Local Magistrates in Seventeenth-Century China* (Tucson: University of Arizona Press, 1984), pp. 530–35.

immediately to the presence of the presiding divinity, in the centre of the great hall, and on their hassocks went through with the three kneelings and nine knockings of head. As soon as they had retired into a side apartment, a broad yellow satin curtain was suspended in front of the god whom they had worshiped, and under it, projecting forward, a small altar was erected upon a table. Before this little altar, a small yellow satin screen was placed, designed, as I suppose, to hide from vulgar eyes something intended to represent imperial majesty. In front of the small yellow screen were placed pots of burning incense, and close behind them was a small box. These things being arranged, the same was duly announced to the officers, who returned and repeated the ceremonies which they had already performed. Then, while they were still standing before the representatives of imperial power, an aged man, dressed in official robes, came forward, and with all becoming gravity took up the little box from the table, raised it as high as his chin in both hands, and then turned and carried it out of the temple, and laid it on an elevated table in front of the great hall. Another man now came forward, mounted the platform, opened the box, and took out a small volume. This was the *Sacred Edict*, and he the appointed orator for the morning. He commenced and read on most unconcernedly, the officers having retired and a rabble gathered around, attracted evidently more by the presence of half a dozen foreigners than by the eloquence of the orator, or the importance of his subject.

... Anxious to see and hear, and imitating the forwardness of the Chinese, I mounted the low platform and took my position close behind the orator, and the man who bore the little box—both of whom were standing. In this position I had a good opportunity of hearing and witnessing the *effects* of the eloquence. It was *reading*, and nothing more, in a rapid and distinct, but not very elevated tone of voice. The number of listeners could not have exceeded sixty, though the temple and court in front of the hall were thronged.

Neither the officers, nor their principal attendants were present to *hear* the reading, but were enjoying themselves with tea and tobacco in one of the side apartments. The five classes—scholars, soldiers, farmers, merchants, and mechanics—were all in turn addressed by the orator, for so it was written in the book; but few or none of them were present. The audience consisted almost wholly of vagrants, idle people who were loitering about the place, beggars, and truant boys. The sentence selected for this morning was the tenth, ... Mind your-own business, to settle the people's will: or, in other words, "let each one attend to his own profession, so that the minds of the people may be fixed, and each one remain quiet and contented in his own sphere." Reading the paraphrase on it occupied the orator about ten minutes, when the book was closed, put in the box, and that replaced again on the table before the little screen; the officers in attendance immediately took leave of each other, and returned to their chairs, we at the same time making our exit.[82]

Another report, from the year 1832, corroborates the impression that the official reading of the *Sacred Edict* had already fallen into desuetude by that time: "At present the public reading of the Sacred Edict is kept up in the 'provincial cities,' but is neglected in the country towns, or *heen* [*hsien*] districts. The people

[82] *The Chinese Repository* 17 : 586–588 (1848).

rarely attend this *political* preaching of the 'mandarins.'"[83] Indeed, the consensus of all foreign observers is that, by 1850, the official lectures on the *Sacred Edict* were largely meaningless exercises.[84] This is partially borne out by the following notice from the *Canton Court Circular* for April 30, 1836, which was the fifteenth of the third lunar month: "Their excellencies went early in the morning to the temple of the god of war, and offered incense; and then repaired to the 'hall of ten thousand years' (consecrated to the worship of the emperor), and there attended to the reading of the Sacred Edict. Seven criminals were brought in for the assizes."[85] The reading of the *Sacred Edict* here seems to have become a rather routine part of government business.

Apart from the officially sanctioned twice-monthly lectures, there were also Confucian-minded performers whose oral renditions of didactic tales illustrating the *Sacred Edict* must have been truly entertaining. In Kuo Mo-jo's autobiography, we find the following extraordinary description:

> Lecturers on the *Sacred Edict*, who told stories about loyalty, filial piety, and fidelity from the morality books (*shan-shu*), often came to our village. These morality books were for the most part made up of folktales. The form of the narration was a combination of spoken and sung passages, making it seem a lot like that of "strum lyrics" (*t'an-tz'u*, i.e., ballads with string accompaniment), yet it was not exactly the same. If someone had been willing to collect these things and then put them in order and spruce them up, he could probably have produced some ready-made folk literature.
>
> At a street corner, they would set up a dais composed of three square tables, one placed atop the other two. On the dais, incense and candles were lit as offerings to the plaque of the *Sacred Edict*. On top of the right-hand table was placed a chair. If two people performed together, then a chair was placed on each of the side tables.
>
> When it came time for the lecturer on the *Sacred Edict* to preach, he, dressed as though going to have an audience with the emperor, would knock his head audibly on the ground four times as he faced the plaque of the *Sacred Edict*. Then he would stand up again and, drawing out his voice, would recite the ten [*sic*] maxims of the *Sacred Edict*. After that, he would get back up on the platform and start telling stories. His method of delivery was to chant the text[86] in a very simple

---

[83] Review of Milne, trans., *The Sacred Edict*, in *The Chinese Repository* 1 : 299–300 (1832).

[84] S. Wells Williams, *The Middle Kingdom: A Survey of the Geography, Government, Education, Social Life, Arts, Religion, &c., of the Chinese Empire and Its Inhabitants* (New York: John Wiley, 1859, 4th ed.; 1st ed., 1848), vol. 1, p. 554, and Thomas Francis Wade, *Hsin ching lu* (Hong Kong, 1859), p. 47.

[85] *The Chinese Repository* 5 : 47 (1837).

[86] Literally, "to intone according to a text" (*chao pen hsuan-k'o* 照本宣科). The phrase *chao pen* implies that these lecturers ultimately based their oral renditions of stories on written texts. Whether or not they actually referred to a book during performance is problematic, though it would have been effective as a prop in any case and would have lent an air of authority to the proceedings. *Gwoyeu tsyrdean* 國語辭典 [Dictionary of the national language] clearly defines the expression *hsuan-k'o* (q.v.) as the chanting or intoning of priests or scholars. This and other aspects of Kuo's characterization suggests that the *Sacred Edict* storytellers he heard as a boy were wont to assume the persona of Confucian officiants.

manner. Whenever he came to a part that was to be sung, he would draw out his voice as he sang and, especially when there was something sad, it would be tinged with the sound of weeping. Some of the lecturers would accompany themselves with bells, fish-shaped woodblocks, bamboo clappers, and the like to help their tunes along.

This type of simple storytelling was a form of entertainment that people in the villages liked to listen to very much. They would stand before the platform of the *Sacred Edict* and listen for two or three hours. The better storytellers could make the listeners weep. It was easy to make the villagers cry; all you had to do was draw out your voice a bit at the sad parts and add a few sad sobs.

Before I had begun my schooling, I was already able to understand the morality books of these lecturers on the *Sacred Edict*.[87]

This account indicates that preaching on the *Sacred Edict* had given rise to a form of popular entertainment that was probably detached from the semi-monthly system of lectures described above. Kuo's lecturers on the *Sacred Edict* actually were more akin to storytellers. Furthermore, it should be noted that they may very well have been itinerants, since they are said to *come* to the village and not to live there. In fact, there is strong confirmation for Kuo Mo-jo's description in the observation of F. R. Eichler for Canton in the early 1880s:

The *Sacred Edict* is preached nearly every day, yet at many places the orthodox Confucian preacher, under the pretext of expounding the Shing-yü to the people, tells them all kinds of stories that are likely to captivate their fancy, or at the best, betakes himself to the history of the empire in order to entertain the crowd.[88]

That the *Sacred Edict* was "preached nearly every day" shows conclusively that this type of performance was no longer a part of the official twice-monthly ceremonies. In my estimation, the individuals described by Kuo and Eichler were operating at the level of the cultural facilitators and brokers whom James Hayes discusses in chapter 3 of this volume. There can be no doubt that the diffusion of Confucian ideals was far more efficiently accomplished through this type of grass-roots activity than through the pompous, ritualistic, and often lifeless ceremonies presided over by local officials.[89]

[87] *Shao-nien shih-tai* 少年時代 [The time of my youth], in *Mo-jo wen-chi* 沫若文集 [Collected works of Kuo Mo-jo], vol. 6 (Shanghai: Hsin wen-i ch'u-pan-she 新文藝出版社, 1955; originally published in 1947 by Hai-yen shu-tien 海燕書店 of Shanghai), pp. 29–30. I am grateful to Milena Doleželová-Velingerová for bringing this passage to my attention; cf. her article, "Kuo Mo-jo's Autobiographical Works," in *Studies in Modern Chinese Literature*, ed. Jaroslav Průšek (Berlin: Akademie Verlag, 1964), pp. 45–75, esp. pp. 52–53. David Johnson went out of his way to send me a copy of the original Chinese text and kindly pointed out a number of interesting features about it.

[88] "The K'uen Shi Wan or, the Practical Theology of the Chinese," *The China Review* 11.2:94–95 (1882).

[89] It cannot be denied, however, that the government actively and repeatedly encouraged frequent explanation of the *Sacred Edict*. This is evident from numerous edicts preserved in *Precedents for the Combined Regulations of the Great Ch'ing Dynasty*, fascicles 397 and 398. Note particularly the exhortations to use local dialects and homely proverbs (398.9a, in 1746; 398.9b, in 1758).

TABLE 1.   Interpretations and Paraphrases of the *Sacred Edict*

	Attitude	Tone/Style	Method	Language
Sacred Edict 1670	Imperious	Sententious	Commands	Highest classical
Combination 1679	Benign	Straightforward	Instructs	Cultivated colloquial
Illustrated Explanations 1681	Advisory	Expository	Describes	Mixed
Illustrated Elaboration 1704	Magisterial	Methodical	Stipulates	Mixed
Trimetrical Song 1706	Pedagogic	Terse verse, verbose prose	Teaches	Classical verse, vernacular commentaries
Amplified Instructions 1724	Paternal	Laconic	Demands	Classical
Elaboration 1726	Avuncular	Diffuse	Reasons	Colloquial
Direct Explanation c1729	Judicial	Admonitory	Exhorts	Colloquial
Glosses 1815	Bureaucratic	Peremptory	Declares	Colloquial
Verifications 1878	Raconteurial	Rambling	Explains	Jumbled
Plain Talk 1887	Seignorial	Patronizing	Dictates	Classical

CONCLUSIONS

We have examined a number of interpretations of the *Sacred Edict*. Table 1 brings them together for easy comparison. The one-word characterizations are naturally inadequate and are intended only to call to mind other facets of these texts. Essentially, the message in all is the same: be good and dutiful subjects. The individuals who wrote and published these interpretations had a real stake in the maintenance of order and public security. Distasteful as it may have been for them to address *hoi polloi*, there were compelling reasons for doing so. They were both responsible for and stood most to benefit from the inculcation of Confucian values in the populace. Every written popularization of the *Sacred Edict* known to me was the work of a member of the literati. The people themselves were neither equipped nor motivated to undertake such an endeavor. This is a clear case of the bearers of high culture consciously and willfully trying to mold popular culture.

It is remarkable that, without a single exception, all prefaces and postfaces to every version of the *Sacred Edict* mentioned in this study were written in the literary language. If these texts were truly addressed to a popular *reading* audience, what would be the point of providing them with prefaces and postfaces that were impenetrable? The prefaces and postfaces, on the contrary, are always addressed to fellow scholars and officials or other educated individuals who were able to read the literary language, never to a presumed mass reading public.

There were various motives for publishing these texts. The *Collected Verifications* was part of a commercial venture; there was a group of moderately literate persons who enjoyed reading the didactic stories it presented and who were willing to pay for the opportunity to do so. The *Plain Talk* was issued by and for local gentry who were peripherally involved in the lectures on the *Sacred Edict*. The *Amplified Instructions* was obviously directed only at the elite; it was up to them to convey its message to those who were not conversant with the classical language. Those popularizations of the *Sacred Edict* written entirely in the demotic language, ironically, were not meant to be read by the common man. A constant refrain in these texts and in their prefaces is that they are to be presented *orally* to the ignorant populace. They were essentially guidebooks for literate specialists that told them not only *what* to say to the people but, more importantly, *how* to say it. Their own ideological predispositions made the first function somewhat superfluous. The distancing effects of social and linguistic stratification made the second function a necessity if there was to be any meaningful communication between the rulers and the ruled. It is for this reason that the vernacular versions of the *Sacred Edict* were such a tremendous boon to local authorities.

In spite of the fact that the *Sacred Edict* and its interpretations cannot be shown to have been read by the vast majority of the populace, their impact was nevertheless considerable. This was accomplished by making the written *Sacred Edict* or one of its amplifications available to virtually everyone who could read and, further, by strongly encouraging this literate segment of society to verbalize its teachings for the nonliterate or semiliterate. In one form or another (including examination essays, school texts, and lecture handbooks as well as boards, strips, and placards to be displayed in public places, etc.), the *Sacred Edict* must have been written down or printed hundreds of thousands of times during the Ch'ing dynasty. The remarkably prolonged stability of the eighteenth-century reigns may, in some measure, be attributed to the effectiveness of formal lectures and informal homilies on the *Sacred Edict* in propagating a uniform ideology. It is noteworthy, as I have pointed out, that this system had largely begun to collapse by around 1850. Yet, even as late as the 1870s, it was possible for anti-Christian forces in Canton to mobilize against the preaching of missionaries by founding a society to hold lectures on the *Sacred Edict* in various meeting halls.[90] Giles was of the opinion that the widespread dissemination

[90] Legge, "Imperial Confucianism," p. 148a. The same spirit was exhibited by the famous general Tso Tsung-t'ang when he was sent in 1868 to control Islamic unrest in Chinese Turkestan. Tso firmly believed that distribution of a Uighur version of paraphrases on the *Sacred Edict* would help to restore order. See Chu Wen-djang, *The Moslem Rebellion in Northeast China, 1862–1878: A*

throughout China of the *Sacred Edict* "proved a serious blow to the immediate spread of Christianity."[91] In *The Gallant Maid*, a novel in Peking dialect written during the Tao-kuang period by a Manchurian bannerman, the *Sacred Edict* is referred to in a manner that indicates it had indeed become a household word. It is used in an oath to convince another person of one's honesty: "By the resplendent *Sacred Edict*, how could I tell you a lie?"[92]

The local units of the Ch'ing government at the end of the dynasty included 214 prefectures, 75 independent departments, 54 independent subprefectures, 139 departments, 57 subprefectures, and 1381 counties.[93] With 3000 books available from the 1902 printing of the *Illustrated Explanations*, each unit could theoretically have been issued at least one copy, though we cannot assume that this actually happened. If the 1903 printing also amounted to 3000 copies, each of the 1920 local units of government or schools within their jurisdictions could have received three. In its many editions, the *Direct Explanation* must surely have been issued in far greater numbers. And, as I have shown, numerous other popular versions of the *Sacred Edict* were published on a local or regional scale. Taken all together, there can be little doubt that—from about 1750 to the close of the dynasty—the guardians of the people were saturated with handbooks for proclaiming the *Sacred Edict* to their charges in comprehensible language. Still, there is very grave doubt that the common people themselves ever acquired these books in significant numbers. I have found no evidence indicating that the vernacular versions of the *Sacred Edict* and the *Amplified Instructions* were read by the common people on their own initiative (if at all, except in a few government-sponsored schools), whether out of duty, for pleasure, or for edification. These texts are popular or vernacular chiefly in their level of literacy.

Study of Government Minority Policy, Central Asiatic Studies, V (The Hague: Mouton, 1966). Albert von le Coq obtained several copies of this book during his early twentieth-century archeological expeditions in the area. One of these is edited and translated by him as "Das Lī-Kitābī," *Körösi Csoma-Archivum*, 1:439–480 (1921–1925). A Russian translation of *Lī Kitābī* was made by Nikolai Fedorovich Katanov and published in Saint Petersburg in 1902. Wolfram Eberhard also saw a copy at the Türkiyat Enstitüsü in Istanbul. His observations on the text may be found in "Bemerkungen zum 'Li Kitabi,'" on pp. 123–127 of his *China und seine westlichen Nachbarn: Beiträge zur mittelalterlichen und neueren Geschichte Zentralasiens* (Darmstadt: Wissenschaftliche Buchgesellschaft, 1978).

[91] Herbert A. Giles, *Confucianism and Its Rivals*, The Hibbert Lectures, second series (London: Williams and Norgate, 1915), p. 254.

[92] Wen K'ang 文康, *Erh-nü ying-hsiung chuan* 兒女英雄傳 [The gallant maid] (Shanghai: Ya-tung t'u-shu-kuan 亞東圖書館, 1932, fourth ed.), chap. 18, p. 29. Widespread familiarity with the *Sacred Edict* is also evidenced by the fact that many of the early attempts to create an alphabet for Chinese used it as a sample text. For examples, see the reproductions on the outside back covers of *Shin Tarng*, 2 (January 1983), *Shin Tarng*, 3 (April 1983), and *Xin Talng* 4 (November 1984).

[93] H. S. Brunnert and V. V. Hagelstrom, *Present Day Political Organization of China*, rev. by N. Th. Kolessoff, trans. from the Russian by A. Beltchenko and E. E. Moran (Shanghai: Kelly and Walsh, 1912; reprint ed. Taipei: Ch'eng Wen, 1971), p. 426. For earlier periods, when the numbers were slightly smaller, see T'ung-tsu Ch'ü, *Local Government in China under the Ch'ing*, p. 2.

But they are actually pseudovernacular or pseudopopular[94] in terms of their social standing, for their origin did not lie in any segment of the masses, but rather rested squarely with the ruling classes.

Admittedly, large numbers of the populace were exposed to and, in some cases, thoroughly familiarized with the *Sacred Edict* through the village lecture system. Expositions of the *Sacred Edict* were, however, by no means limited to the officially sanctioned semimonthly lectures. In the hands of talented storytellers who operated outside that system, oral renditions of the *Sacred Edict* were a welcome form of entertainment for certain segments of the populace. There is an enormous gulf between the exalted, sententious maxims of the K'ang-hsi emperor and the minds of the peasants and soldiers for whom they were ultimately intended. The transfer of doctrine from the one level to the other was an exceedingly complicated process and involved many different types of people. Most of the individuals involved in this process of transmission were able to perceive, however dimly, the close interconnections among language, ideology, and politics. Their perceptions of these matters determined, to a great extent, the nature of the written popularizations of the *Sacred Edict*.

---

[94] Cf. Charles J. Wivell, "The Chinese Oral and Pseudo-oral Narrative Traditions," *Transactions of the International Conference of Orientalists in Japan* 16:53–65 (1971).

TWELVE

The Beginnings of Mass Culture: Journalism and Fiction in the Late Ch'ing and Beyond

Leo Ou-fan Lee and Andrew J. Nathan

The Ming–Ch'ing civilization portrayed in the preceding essays was marked by active local and long-distance trade, cosmopolitan cities, frequent travel, and extensive communication across regions and among social groups. It was a highly integrated society by traditional standards. We have been shown a complex, diverse, changing popular culture, one that served both to express the particular concerns of regional and class groups and to weave these groups into one Chinese culture with common myths and festivals, values and habits.

In the twentieth century, the homogeneity of Chinese culture and the national culture's penetration among the people was greatly intensified. Through economic development, social dislocation, war, and political revolution, virtually the entire populace was eventually mobilized into a unified nationwide pattern of social and political organization. The instruments of communication were gathered into a few hands, the mass media thrust into the remotest corners of the countryside, and the duty of attending to them imposed on every citizen. Popular culture was overlaid with and to some extent displaced by mass culture—that is, culture that is nationwide, universal to all classes, and consciously engineered and controlled from above. Among many mass cultures in the world today, China's may rank highest in all these characteristics.

As profound as the twentieth-century revolution was, in cultural terms it was as much a development as a break with the past. The media, genres, styles,

Leo Lee wishes to thank the National Endowment for the Humanities for a fellowship in the academic year 1979–1980, which enabled him to do initial research on the topic of late Ch'ing popular literature. Andrew J. Nathan gratefully acknowledges financial support from the John Simon Guggenheim Memorial Foundation, the Joint Committee on Contemporary China of the Social Science Research Council and the American Council of Learned Societies, and the East Asian Institute of Columbia University.

tastes, and beliefs, and the cultural problems and dilemmas of the Ming and Ch'ing in many ways shaped what became the "cultural politics" and "cultural policy" of the twentieth century. Our task in this essay is to describe the process of transition and to trace elements of continuity and change in that process.

In the first few decades of the great awakening that began about 1895, political information and new ideas came to the people almost exclusively through the press. Until the 1950s, electronic media were rare and there were few newsreels to inform people about politics. There was little tradition of village or clan elders discussing national affairs in tea houses or in front of young people. Politicians did not come to local villages and wards to electioneer for votes, and the government did not push roads, electricity, and bus services into the countryside as a way of building popular support. Instead, the quickening of political and cultural life was achieved to an extraordinary degree by a single medium.[1] Hence the first section of our essay describes the rise of the modern periodical press, with special attention to the development of its characteristic role and voice in the formative period from 1895 to 1911. The second section traces the rise of the mass public, sketching the stages by which the modern media's audience grew eventually to encompass the whole nation.

Even before a mass public or a concept of "the masses" was fully developed, late Ch'ing and early Republican critics and theorists were discussing what were in effect the problems of designing and imposing a mass culture. The third section of this essay discusses some of these theories and the dilemmas they reveal, focusing on the crucial medium of fiction. It explores in particular the perennial problem of all didactic, manipulative forms of culture, the tension between what the cultural leaders wish to convey to the people and what the people find attractive. The capacity of popular culture to resist efforts to replace it with an officially approved culture posed a sharp problem for cultural leaders throughout the century. The conclusion draws our themes together in a discussion of some of the reciprocal effects of mass culture and politics.

THE LATE CH'ING PERIODICAL PRESS: RISE, ROLE, AND VOICE

So striking was the growth of the periodical press after 1895 that we may be tempted to exaggerate the sharpness of the break with the past.[2] China has been a highly mobile, integrated society for at least three centuries. People wrote home and sent money through private letter-carrying companies and banks. Government officials communicated with the capital through an elaborate

---

[1] In this respect China differed from countries that modernized during the postwar era of electronics and universal suffrage, as described in the classic work of Daniel Lerner, *The Passing of Traditional Society: Modernizing the Middle East* (New York: Free Press, 1958).

[2] The first two parts of this essay as well as the conclusion draw on Andrew J. Nathan, "The Late Ch'ing Press: Role, Audience and Impact," *Proceedings of the International Conference on Sinology: Section on History and Archeology* (Taipei: Academia Sinica, 1981), vol. III, pp. 1281–1308.

system of posts. In the village, government policy was announced by posters and notices read aloud to the illiterate. Technical innovations in agriculture were spread by printed illustrated manuals and in conversations at local periodic markets.

To a limited extent, traditional periodicals contributed to the flow of communication. The several Peking gazettes (all called *Ching pao*), which copied central government memorials and edicts, had an aggregate circulation through the empire of several tens of thousands, presumably mostly government officials—who also subscribed to local gazettes emanating from provincial capitals. Popular news sheets appeared irregularly in the cities when there was sensational news to report, and apparently were bought by clerks and small businessmen primarily for entertainment. For very limited circulation, local guilds published price circulars.

To these traditional forms of periodicals nineteenth-century missionaries and a few pioneer Chinese journalists added "modern"-style newspapers and magazines, published on a regular basis and containing news and essays. By the early 1890s, perhaps a dozen Chinese-language newspapers were being published in the major treaty ports. Of these the largest was Shanghai's *Hu pao*, with a circulation of ten thousand, and the *Shen pao*, with a circulation of fifteen thousand; the circulation of their major local competitor, the *Hsin-wen pao*, was well under five thousand. In Canton the *Hsun-huan jih-pao* and in Hong Kong the *Chung-wai hsin pao* and *Hua-tzu jih-pao* were longer established but more modest in sales. These dailies were supplemented by a handful of monthly missionary-sponsored magazines with circulation of a few hundred or a few thousand (notably the *Wan-kuo kung-pao* and *Ko-chih hui-pien*).[3]

To be a commercial success, a Chinese-language newspaper of the late nineteenth century had to stress commercial news, for its potential readers were mainly treaty-port Chinese businessmen. The Shanghai *Hsin pao* stated in its founding issue in 1861,

> In general what is valuable for the conduct of commerce and trade is the circulation of reliable information. In printing this new paper (*hsin pao*), we will not fail to carry all national government or military intelligence, [news of] marketplace advantage or disadvantage, business prices, and the coming and going of ships and cargo. In a place like Shanghai people from all over are mixed together. This creates obstacles to doing business, such as the inability to manage one another's dialects and the failure to hear about news. By glancing at this new paper, you can learn that a certain cargo is to be sold on a certain day, and on the day you can personally inspect the cargo and negotiate the price. Thus you can

---

[3] Roswell S. Britton, *The Chinese Periodical Press, 1800–1912* (Shanghai: Kelly and Walsh, 1933; reprint Taipei: Ch'eng-wen, 1966), pp. 1–85; Tseng Hsu-pai 曾虛白, *Chung-kuo hsin-wen shih* 中國新聞史 [History of Chinese journalism] (Taipei: Kuo-li cheng-chih ta-hsueh hsin-wen yen-chiu so 國立政治大學新聞研究所), pp. 94–100, 125–157.

avoid endless delay and procrastination by agents or making a bad purchase on speculation.[4]

The treaty-port commercial papers introduced a series of innovations in content, format, and circulation methods to expand their sales and profitability. *Hsin pao*, for example, introduced headlines in 1870 in lieu of what had previously been unchanging section titles. *Shen pao* accepted contributions of poems and literary essays. It offered a lower price-per-copy for bulk orders and encouraged people outside Shanghai to subscribe by post. In 1882, *Shen pao* made use of the new Tientsin-Shanghai telegraph line to publish the first telegraphic dispatch in Chinese journalism, and in 1884 it raised its circulation with on-the-scene war correspondence reporting the French naval attack on Ningpo. The *Hu pao* featured exclusive Chinese translations of Reuters dispatches, published the same day they were printed in the parent newspaper, the *North-China Daily News* (other papers could pirate the dispatches only the next day). With the rise of the telegraph, the major papers competed to carry telegraphic dispatches from around the country, headlining each with heavy type and sidelining each word of the dispatch with emphatic punctuation. Newspapers also carried slower, mailed dispatches, and competed to have the quickest, most complete service of excerpts from newspapers in other cities. All these papers took readability as a goal, although they achieved it with differing degrees of success. Without going so far as to publish in *pai-hua* (*Shen pao* set up a separate *pai-hua* newspaper in 1876), they wrote in a plain style known as "easy *wen-li*" and took the lead in improving layout and punctuation so that busy readers could scan more easily.[5]

As a matter of policy, the late Ch'ing commercial papers avoided political advocacy or controversy. They did not wish to offend readers of varying persuasions or to invite government harassment such as the denial of post office and telegraphic privileges.[6] "When you open one," Liang Ch'i-ch'ao noted,

> the page is clogged with words like "Bureaucratic Bustle in Shanghai," "Official's Spouse Coming South," ... "Robbery Plan Fails," ... "Willing to Die for Love." All the articles are alike. ... As for the editorials, if it isn't "An Examination of How Western Learning Originated in China," then it's "China Should Urgently Plan for Wealth and Power." They plagiarize from one another over and over. When you read it you are only afraid of falling asleep.[7]

The crisis of 1895 spurred dramatic growth in periodicals. China's defeat in the war with Japan and the signing of the Treaty of Shimonoseki—which granted Japan a 200 million tael indemnity, the right to open new treaty ports

---

[4] Quoted in Tseng, *Hsin-wen*, p. 142.

[5] Tseng, *Hsin-wen*, pp. 142–155; Britton, *Periodical*, pp. 82–83.

[6] Tseng, *Hsin-wen*, pp. 287–288; Britton, *Periodical*, pp. 81–82.

[7] *Yin-ping shih wen-chi* 飲冰室文集 [Collected essays from the Ice-Drinker's Studio] (Taipei: Chung-hua shu-chü 中華書局, 1960), vol. III, *chüan* 6, p. 52 (hereafter *YPSWC* III:6:52).

and establish factories and businesses in China, and control over Formosa and the Liaotung Peninsula—persuaded many Chinese that their nation was in literal danger of extinction. Such fears greatly stimulated the appetite for news and political discussion. The experience of the young Pao T'ien-hsiao in Soochow was typical:

> Our country and Japan were warring over Korea, and the Shanghai newspapers carried news about it every day. Previously young Chinese readers paid no attention to current events, but now we were shaken. I often went out and got Shanghai newspapers to read, and I began to understand bits and pieces about current events. I began to discuss them, and I accounted myself as pro-reform. . . . [After the loss of the war and the establishment of a Japanese concession in Soochow], most educated people, who had never before discussed national affairs, wanted to discuss them: why are others stronger than we are, and why are we weaker?[8]

The standard commercial papers, however staid, carried sought-after news about the war and subsequent peace negotiations, and their circulations shot up—that of the Shanghai *Hsin-wen pao*, for example, went from five thousand in 1895 to twelve thousand, largest in the nation, in 1899.[9] Even more important, however, was the emergence and rapid growth of a kind of newspaper new in China—the political journal, devoted largely to essays of political dispute and advocacy.

The new political press started inconspicuously. The harbinger, Liang Ch'i-ch'ao's *Chung-wai chi-wen* (1895), bore a close resemblance to traditional gazettes. Avoiding editorial polemic, it limited itself to retailing proreform memorials and edicts and translating foreign materials conducive to reform thinking. Like gazettes, it was 6 inches high and 3 inches wide, bound in Chinese-book form in yellow covers. This gazettelike appearance was explained partly by the fact that the magazine was printed in the shop of one of the gazette companies. Also, the intended audience was higher Peking officialdom: the journal was distributed free to some three thousand subscribers to the real Peking gazette.

However small its beginnings, the new political press quickly surpassed the pre-1895 press in numbers, circulation, and political liveliness. The historian Ko Kung-chen identified 216 newspapers and 122 magazines that were published in the few years after 1894. Many of them were short-lived, so that in 1901, for example, Liang Ch'i-ch'ao counted only 80 newspapers and 44 magazines being published—still a considerable increase over the dozen or so journals of the early 1890s. While many journals had circulations of only a few hundred, the more popular ones broke records. Liang Ch'i-ch'ao's *Shih-wu pao*

---

[8] Pao T'ien-hsiao 包天笑, *Ch'uan-ying lou hui-i lu* 釧影樓回憶錄 [Reminiscences of the Bracelet Shadow Chamber] (Hong Kong; Ta-Hua ch'u-pan she 大華出版社, 1971), pp. 135, 145.

[9] Tseng, *Hsin-wen*, p. 153.

achieved an unprecedented circulation of twelve thousand in 1896, and his
Hsin-min ts'ung-pao claimed a circulation of fourteen thousand in 1906.[10]
The "reform propagandists," as Don Price calls them,[11] drew on a long,
complicated tradition. It was of course an ancient function of Chinese government to educate the people in their duty of obedience. Traditionally, such
education had been achieved through the moral example of the emperor and
his magistrates, conspicuous punishment of criminals, and promotion of
Confucian ethics. Private citizens occasionally sponsored publication of moral
tracts designed for the edification of the common people.[12] The early
nineteenth-century Protestant missionaries, who were barred from direct proselytizing in China, introduced the use of the periodical press as a medium of
public education. The earliest modern periodical in Chinese, the *Ch'a-shih-su
mei-yueh t'ung-chi-ch'uan* (1815–1828), was published by the English missionary
William Milne in Malacca for distribution in China. "To promote *Christianity*
was to be its *primary* object," Milne said. "Other things, though they were to be
treated in subordination to this, were not to be overlooked. Knowledge and
science are the hand-maids of religion, and may become the auxiliaries of
virtue...."[13]

While none of the missionary periodicals appears to have been widely read in
China, they laid seeds in the minds of some historically important Chinese.
Liang Ch'i-ch'ao, the most influential figure in Chinese journalism and one
of modern China's major political thinkers, was briefly associated with missionary publisher Timothy Richard in Peking in 1895–1896.[14] The pioneer
journalist Wang T'ao, founder of the Hong Kong *Hua-tzu jih-pao* in 1864,
worked with James Legge in Hong Kong during the 1860s.[15] So did Hung Jen-
kan, later a Taiping revolutionary leader.[16] In a proposal to the Heavenly
King in 1859, Hung suggested the establishment of newspapers (*hsin-wen kuan*)

[10] Figures variously taken from Britton, *Periodical*, pp. 74, 90–91; Tseng, *Hsin-wen*, pp. 106–107,
192, 198, 205; Ko Kung-chen 戈公振, *Chung-kuo pao-hsueh shih* 中國報學史 [History of Chinese
journalism] (1927; reprint ed. Taipei: Hsueh-sheng shu-chü 學生書局, 1964), pp. 145–150.
Liang's list (reprinted by Tseng, pp. 233–237) seems to include some Chinese-language papers
printed overseas. For additional lists of periodicals illustrating growth after 1895, see Chang Ching-
lu 張靜廬, *Chung-kuo chin-tai ch'u-pan shih-liao* 中國近代出版史料 [Historical materials on modern
Chinese publishing] (Shanghai: Shanghai ch'u-pan she 上海出版社, 1953–1954), vol. I, pp.
77–97, 97–103, 103–110; and vol. II, pp. 276–297, 297–300.

[11] Don C. Price, *Russia and the Roots of the Chinese Revolution, 1896–1911* (Cambridge, Mass.:
Harvard University Press, 1974), p. 27.

[12] See the chapters in this volume by James Hayes and Daniel Overmyer.

[13] Quoted in Britton, *Periodical*, pp. 18–19.

[14] Chi-yun Chen, "Liang Ch'i-ch'ao's 'Missionary Education': A Case Study of Missionary
Influence on the Reformers," *Papers on China* 16:86 (December 1962).

[15] Paul A. Cohen, *Between Tradition and Modernity: Wang T'ao and Reform in Late Ch'ing China*
(Cambridge, Mass.: Harvard University Press, 1974), pp. 57–61 and elsewhere.

[16] Britton, *Periodical*, p. 36; Cohen, *Between Tradition*, pp. 52–55.

as a means for, among other things, keeping the people informed of their legal and moral duties:

> Newspapers will be useful in carrying out education to obey the laws, distinguish between good and bad, encourage a moral sense, and teach loyalty to sovereign and parents. When education is carried out the law is clear; when the law is clear then [people] know their duty to the sovereign—so much so that people will warn one another [to obey the law], talent and virtue will emerge daily, and popular customs will constantly improve.[17]

In Ch'ing government circles too—although later than in Taiping revolutionary circles—the idea took hold that the government could use periodicals to promote wider enthusiasm for its policies. In 1851 the emperor had emphatically rejected a proposal for an official government gazette with the implication that to allow all officialdom to know what was going on in its various parts was only to encourage people to meddle in what did not concern them.[18] In 1896, however, in the aftermath of the defeat by Japan, the Tsungli yamen was allowed to print two gazettelike journals, which carried selected memorials and edicts as well as translations of foreign materials bearing on reform topics. Although lacking editorials, these journals' purpose was to promote reformist ideas among officials.[19]

The Tsungli yamen's two journals were short-lived, but in the aftermath of the Boxer debacle official gazettes were established in great numbers by various regional and provincial offices and central government organs. In 1911, the government decided to have all new laws and regulations take effect from the date of publication in the official gazette (at that time renamed the *Nei-ko kuan-pao*). In the course of fifty years, the government had moved from disdain of gazettes to official sponsorship and finally to reliance upon them to give force to the law.

The reform propagandists' idea of the press grew out of this background. At first, they gave an account of the role of the press similar to that of the official sponsors of gazettes. In 1896, Liang Ch'i-ch'ao argued that "newspapers are beneficial to the state" because they increase solidarity between above and below and enable people and government alike to be better informed about commerce, technology, foreign affairs, and all other topics important to strengthening the state.[20] But this view belonged to the period when Liang still hoped to gain a hearing for his ideas in Peking. With the failure of the Hundred Days reform and his flight to Japan, he began to develop a notion of the press as mobilizing the people against or in spite of the regime. His first essay written in Japan, "Preface and Regulations to the *Ch'ing-i pao*," set down the aims of a new

---

[17] Translated from Tseng, *Hsin-wen*, pp. 101–102.
[18] Ibid., p. 104.
[19] Ibid., pp. 106–107.
[20] *YPSWC* I : 1 : 100–103.

reform journal that was to propagandize for reform from outside the country, since the government had proscribed all reformist newspapers at home.[21] Of course, this did not mean that Liang abandoned the belief that newspapers could help invigorate the public cooperation of citizens and government when a right-thinking government was in office.[22] But he had ceased to pretend that propaganda activities did not threaten the regime.

The press as a propaganda instrument independent of the state could be used to promote many different kinds of ideas. Whatever these were, the primary responsibility of a propaganda journal was to persuade people to accept the argument it promoted. As Liang put it, unknowingly echoing Marx, "One must intend to use one's words to change the world. Otherwise, why utter them?"[23] On another occasion he argued,

> Once a journalist has fixed on a goal, he should press it with the most extreme arguments possible. Even if he is somewhat biased or somewhat overexcited, it is not a flaw. Why? ... if we concede to one another and speak accommodating, ambiguous words, then all over the country people's nerves will be calm and democracy will stagnate. For it is human nature to be comfortable with the familiar and startled with the unfamiliar. What we must do is make the startling become familiar; only thus can people's knowledge advance....[24]

The voice of the press, in short, must be polemical, even at the cost of extremism and polarization. It was a notion born of the high ambition that the press could serve as "the citizens' alarm clock, a wooden clapper for civilization."[25] But it could easily degenerate to the level of such captive organs as the "newspaper set-ups" (*t'ao-pan pao*) of the 1920s—ordinary four-page newspapers with most of their contents lifted from *Shen pao* and *Hsin-wen pao*, but with three sections left blank—the newspaper title, the editorial column, and the column of "important news." For a few hundred *yuan* a warlord's agent had these three sections typeset as he wished, and a few hundred copies of the journal run off to give the backing of "public opinion" to the warlord's latest maneuvers.[26] When propaganda for high purposes gave way to huckstering for petty advantage, audiences became wary, bequeathing a skepticism about political claims that is still a notable feature of Chinese public life today.

Yet Liang's example also showed that well-written propaganda with a compelling point to make could have a strong public impact. One reader

[21] *YPSWC* II:3:29–31.
[22] For such an argument see *YPSWC* III:6:47–57.
[23] *YPSWC* IV:11:47.
[24] *YPSWC* IV:11:38.
[25] Cited in Lai Kuang-lin 賴光臨, *Liang Ch'i-ch'ao yü chin-tai pao-yeh* 梁啓超與近代報業 [Liang Ch'i-ch'ao and modern journalism] (Taipei: Shang-wu yin-shu kuan 商務印書館, 1968), p. 46.
[26] Chao Hsiao-i 趙效沂, *Pao-t'an fu-ch'en ssu-shih-wu nien* 報壇浮沉四十五年 [Forty-five years' ups and downs in the newspaper world] (Taipei: Chuan-chi wen-hsueh ch'u-pan she 傳記文學出版社, 1972), p. 26.

recalled that the publication of Liang's *Shih-wu pao* in 1896 was "like the explosion of a large bomb, which woke many people from their dreams. . . . It wasn't just that Liang Ch'i-ch'ao's writing was good; it was also that what he said seemed to be just what we had stored in our hearts and wished to express ourselves."[27] And Huang Tsun-hsien wrote to Liang about his magazine, *Hsin-min ts'ung-pao*, in 1902,

> It alarms and moves people, each word like a thousand precious coins. In a style no one can match you say what everyone thinks, so that even men of stone or iron must be moved. Since ancient times, the power of the word has never been so great.[28]

THE RISE OF THE MASS AUDIENCE

The late Ch'ing press was concentrated in a few treaty ports and overseas cities, as illustrated in the postal statistics reproduced in Table 1. Shanghai was the great newspaper-exporting city[29]; Peking and Tientsin exported newspapers and, as the homes of many commercial and political "sojourners," also provided large markets for newspapers imported from other districts and overseas. A city such as Canton appears to have done most of its newspaper trade locally, through vendors rather than the post office. Ningpo was typical of most cities, in that it imported many times more newspapers than it exported.

The political, technical, and cultural reasons for the press's urban concentration are obvious. To avoid government repression, which on Chinese territory was virtually unconstrained by legal guarantees for the press,[30] political and also commercial journals sought registration in treaty-port concessions, often in the name of foreign agents. (The famous *Su pao* case was an example of how this worked: the publishers were brought to trial, but only after time-consuming legal procedures by the Chinese government to cause the International Settlement authorities to arrest and try them.) Modern printing machines, which are essential to rapid production of a large number of copies of a periodical, were available only in large treaty ports, as was the imported paper that these machines required.[31] Culturally, of course, the cities thrived on the

[27] Pao, *Hui-i lu*, p. 150.

[28] Ting Wen-chiang 丁文江, *Liang Jen-kung hsien-sheng nien-p'u ch'ang-pien ch'u-kao* 梁任公先生年譜長編初稿 [Draft chronological biography of Liang Ch'i-ch'ao, long version], 2 vols. (Taipei: Shih-chieh shu-chü 世界書局, 1962), vol. I, p. 150.

[29] The tenfold surge in newspapers received in 1908 is unexplained; it may have been due to increased imports of publications from overseas.

[30] Lee-hsia Hsu Ting, *Government Control of the Press in Modern China, 1900–1949* (Cambridge, Mass.: East Asian Research Center, 1974), pp. 27–48.

[31] Ho Sheng-ting 賀聖鼐, "San-shih-wu nien lai Chung-kuo chih yin-shua shu" 三十五年來中國之印刷術 [Chinese printing techniques in the last thirty-five years] (1931), reprinted in Chang, *Chin-tai ch'u-pan*, vol. I, pp. 257–285.

TABLE 1.   Newspapers and Printed Matter Received and Despatched,
Selected Districts, 1907 and 1908

District	Received		Despatched	
	1907	*1908*	*1907*	*1908*
Peking	1,398,550	2,198,853	1,159,140	3,647,555
Kaifeng	627,693	2,756,758	745,257	829,014
Manchuria	422,122	667,853	237,709	239,272
Tientsin	3,596,222	3,262,137	1,942,159	2,155,840
Tsinan	254,520	404,690	76,591	107,508
Other North China	489,209	792,563	71,080	109,559
Hankow	2,079,912	3,656,659	152,257	904,110
Kiukiang	1,030,308	195,804	11,712	17,976
Other Central China	692,767	1,256,024	54,443	87,389
Nanking	735,407	1,650,505	149,760	794,871
Chinkiang	1,295,552	2,068,812	28,139	43,577
Shanghai	1,069,486	10,595,024	10,961,464	16,656,127
Soochow	1,190,509	2,052,244	8,935	12,631
Ningpo	397,180	1,016,444	6,125	15,657
Other lower Yangtze	555,229	902,697	45,887	194,460
Foochow	384,414	864,298	38,361	104,220
Canton	155,070	321,074	159,841	215,332
Other South China	708,547	1,055,116	83,990	265,933
Total	17,082,697	35,717,555	15,932,850	26,401,031

SOURCES: China, Imperial Maritime Customs, *Report on the Working of the Imperial Post Office*, 1907 and 1908
editions (Shanghai: Inspectorate General of Customs, 1908 and 1909).

NOTE: Periodicals probably constituted about 69 percent of "newspapers and printed matter." Roughly half
or less of periodical circulation was by post; the rest was by vendors and bookstores within the city of
publication. More items were "received" than "despatched," presumably because of publications
from overseas. Certain anomalies in the table are unexplained: e.g., the great rise in items received in
Kaifeng from 1907 to 1908, and the decline in Kiukiang. The possibility that some of them are
typographical errors seems reduced by the fact that the totals of the columns add to the sums given.
The prose sections of the postal reports often refer to large changes in the volume of business in a single
year, responding to changes in the number of postal establishments or of newspapers in a district,
political disturbances, economic cycles, the transfer of business from native postal *hongs* to the
Imperial Post Office, and like factors. See Andrew J. Nathan, "The Late Ch'ing Press; Role,
Audience, and Impact," in *Proceedings of the International Conference on Sinology: Section on History and
Archaeology* (Taipei: Academia Sinica, 1981), vol. III, pp. 1301–1305.

self-reinforcement of their size and centrality: in this respect after Shanghai the
biggest late Ch'ing Chinese publications center was probably Tokyo, with its
several tens of thousands of students and exiled politicians publishing probably
a score or more of journals.

Thanks partly to new roads and railroads, the growing and increasingly efficient Chinese Post Office and a spreading network of bookstores, and partly to traditional letter-carrying hongs (*min-hsin chü*), riverine paddle-boats and the like, the urban-centered press achieved wide distribution throughout the nation. Ts'ao Chü-jen recalls,

> *Hsin-min ts'ung-pao* was published in Tokyo, Japan, but its distribution was so wide that it reached into poverty-stricken villages and remote places.... It took a month to reach our family village, 400 *li* from Hangchow, by post, yet my late father's thought and writing style were influenced by Liang Ch'i-ch'ao; as far away as Chungking and Chengtu, the *Hsin-min ts'ung-pao* leapt over the "three gorges" [of the Yangtze River] and penetrated, changing the perceptions of the gentry.[32]

Tsou Lu describes a bookstore in the *hsien* town of Ta-p'u, Kuangtung, about 1902:

> At a Confucian temple near our house a bookstore was established. This bookstore not only had material of the reformers and modern Europe and America, but also bits and pieces of the rarely seen writings of the revolutionaries. I frequently went there to read....[33]

Hu Shih recalls students going home for vacation from school in Shanghai smuggling the banned *Min pao* into the interior sewn into their pillows.[34] There are many more anecdotes about newspapers from Shanghai or Tokyo reaching such distant places as Manchuria, Kansu, and Szechwan.[35] Cities had long been cultural centers, but now a smaller number of them became foci of influence over a nationwide audience whose cultural experience was increasingly similar from one region to another.

How large was this nationwide audience in the late Ch'ing? The answer will give us a starting point from which to trace the growth of the mass audience through the century. There are several ways to arrive at this figure. To begin with, fluctuating and unreliable figures exist for numbers of periodicals published and for claimed per-periodical circulations. On this basis one can estimate that there were about a hundred substantial periodicals being published at any given time in the Ch'ing's last decade, and that on the average each

---

[32] Ts'ao Chü-jen 曹聚仁, *Wen-t'an wu-shih nien, cheng-pien* 文壇五十年, 正編 [Fifty years in literary circles, vol. I] (Hong Kong: Hsin wen-hua ch'u-pan she 新文化出版社, 1976), p. 32.

[33] Tsou Lu 鄒魯, *Hui-ku lu* 回顧錄 [Memoirs], reprint ed. (Taipei: Tu-li ch'u-pan she 獨立出版社, 1951), vol. I, p. 11.

[34] Hu Shih, "An Autobiographical Account at Forty," chap. IV, William A. Wycoff, trans., *Chinese Studies in History* 12. 2:27 (Winter 1978–1979).

[35] *Hsin-hai ko-ming hui-i lu* 辛亥革命回憶錄 [Reminiscences of the 1911 revolution] (Peking: Chung-hua shu-chü, 1961–1963), vol. V, pp. 442, 486; Mabel Lee, "Liang Ch'i-ch'ao (1873–1929) and the Literary Revolution of Late Ch'ing," in A. R. Davis, ed., *Search for Identity: Modern Literature and the Creative Arts in Asia* (Sydney: Angus and Robertson, 1974), pp. 205–206.

published about three thousand copies per issue, for a national circulation of three hundred thousand.[36]

Analysis of postal figures produces a similar result. Table 1 shows that in 1908 upwards of 35 million items of "newspapers and printed matter" were "received" by the post office for delivery. Using a ratio of 69 percent (derived from later postal figures when newspapers were distinguished from other printed matter), we estimate that nearly 25 million of these printed items were periodicals. If half or fewer of all periodicals were delivered through the mail, this suggests a total annual circulation of somewhat more than 49 million. Since some Ch'ing periodicals were published daily, some weekly, some on ten-day schedules and some monthly or less frequently, we must divide this estimate in turn by an average periodicity, weighted for the relatively high average circulations of the daily press. Data are lacking for a reliable solution to this problem. But if we assume for the purposes of argument that daily publications contributed two-fifths of the annual flow of periodicals and weekly, ten-day, and monthly publications one-fifth each, then the weighted average periodicity would have been 166 issues per year. Divided into the estimated annual flow of 49-million-plus issues, that represents approximately 295,000 subscriptions.

But each circulated issue had many readers. Some proscribed but popular periodicals, such as Liang Ch'i-ch'ao's Hsin-min ts'ung-pao and Hsin hsiao-shuo, were reprinted ten or more times after they were smuggled into China.[37] Each copy of a magazine was passed from person to person. Agnes Smedley tells the story of the young Chu Teh, a student at Chengtu's Higher Normal College in about 1906, finding a copy of the Min pao "which someone had slipped under his pillow in the dormitory. The paper had passed through so many hands that much of its print was obliterated. . . . Chu read and reread the little sheet, then slipped it in the bed of another student." [38] In 1904, when Pao T'ien-hsiao was serving as a school principal in Ch'ing-chou-fu, Shantung, the Shanghai Hsin-wen pao was received in the prefectural yamen, then after several days passed on to the school.[39] An American observer reported even more extensive multiple

---

[36] See Nathan, "The Late Ch'ing Press," pp. 1297–1299. The publication and circulation figures consulted are in the following sources: Kaji Ryūichi 嘉治隆一, Shina ni okeru shimbun hattatsu shōshi 支那に於ける新聞發達小史 [Short history of the development of newspapers in China], annex to Keizai shiryō 經濟資料, 12.3 (March 20, 1927); Ko, Pao-hsueh; Ōtsuka Reizō 大塚令三, "Shanhai no shōhō ni kansuru ichi kōsatsu" 上海の小報に關する一考察 [An investigation of Shanghai mosquito newspapers], Mantetsu Shina gesshi 滿鐵支那月誌 6.3:63–73 (December 15, 1929); Gaimushō seimukyoku 外務省政務局, Shina ni okeru shimbunshi ni kansuru chōsa 支那ニ於ケル新聞紙ニ関スル調査 [Investigation into newspapers in China], 1913 and 1914 editions; and Tseng, Hsin-wen.

[37] Liang Ch'i-ch'ao, Intellectual Trends in the Ch'ing Period, trans. Immanuel C. Y. Hsü (Cambridge, Mass.: Harvard University Press, 1959), p. 102.

[38] Agnes Smedley, The Great Road: The Life and Times of Chu Teh (New York: Monthly Review Press, 1956), pp. 72–73.

[39] Pao, Hui-i lu, pp. 299–300.

readership, although this was in the 1920s and in the highly developed Yangtze Valley region:

> The daily paper first goes to the city people, and after they have read it, the paper is given the various country boat lines for distribution in country towns from which it is passed on to the villages. On occasions there are gatherings at which a good reader reads, in a very dignified manner, to an audience. A further method used for spreading news is that of posting the paper on a wall or board where passers-by may read it.[40]

It is not surprising that a specialist like Chang P'eng-yuan estimates the per-copy readership of some late Ch'ing periodicals at ten to twenty persons.[41]

If readership averaged fifteen persons per copy, then our circulation figure of three hundred thousand suggests an audience on the order of 4.5 million. But some people may have read many periodicals, and others may have seen only an occasional copy. If we assume for the sake of discussion that the average periodical reader regularly read two periodicals,[42] then we would have to divide our audience figure in half to reach an estimated audience of 2.25 million. No doubt it would be more precise to say that there was a core audience whose members read several periodicals regularly and a peripheral audience of those who could obtain only a few copies a year, but it would be hard to say how large each group was. In any case, the rough estimate for the total audience remains in the neighborhood of 2 to 4 million.

This figure is not out of line with demographic information. G. William Skinner estimates China's population (excluding Taiwan and Manchuria) as 394 million in 1893 and suggests that the urban population was 6 percent, or 23.5 million. Roughly 63 percent of these were age 16 or over, and of these slightly over one-half were men.[43] Thus the urban adult male population was about 7.4 million. An observer of the early 1890s states, "What in 1881 was the exception is now the rule in all good families in Chinkiang as well as in the interior—that is, for every intelligent adult to take a glance at the Chinese daily

[40] Charles Frederick Hancock, "Introduction and Influence of Modern Machinery in China," M.A. thesis, University of Texas, 1926, p. 82. Citation courtesy of Thomas Rawski.

[41] Chang P'eng-yuan 張朋園, *Liang Ch'i-ch'ao yü Ch'ing-chi ko-ming* 梁啓超與清季革命 [Liang Ch'i-ch'ao and revolution in the Ching period] (Nankang: Chung-yang yen-chiu yuan chin-tai shih yen-chiu so 中央研究院近代史研究所, 1964), p. 320. For a similar estimate for the 1920s, see Kaji, *Shina ni okeru*, p. 43.

[42] Although in 1896, Liang Ch'i-ch'ao observed that few readers could obtain copies of more than one periodical; *YPSWC* II : 2 : 55.

[43] G. William Skinner, "Regional Urbanization in Nineteenth-Century China," in *The City in Late Imperial China*, ed. Skinner (Stanford: Stanford University Press, 1977), pp. 225–226. Urban is defined here as central places with populations of 2000 or more. Age and sex ratios from Evelyn Sakakida Rawski, *Education and Popular Literacy in Ch'ing China* (Ann Arbor, Michigan: University of Michigan Press, 1979), p. 183.

paper brought here from Shanghai."[44] But how many "good families" and "intelligent adults" (presumably meaning literate males) were there in the cities? Evelyn Rawski has suggested that literacy was quite widespread in late imperial China, especially among urban males.[45] If one-quarter of them were occasional periodical readers, then the urban audience would have numbered about 1.85 million. If literates living in the countryside provided an audience of roughly equal size, the total readership would have numbered about 3.7 million.

Another benchmark can be derived from Chung-li Chang's numerical analysis of the gentry.[46] He sets the post-Taiping gentry at 1,443,900. This includes only those of *sheng-yuan* and *chien-sheng* rank or higher. There were also 2 million *t'ung-sheng* (registered students) who had studied for a decade or so and were more than sufficiently literate to read newspapers. There were unknown numbers of literate tradesmen, women, and ex-students formerly registered for the examinations. While some of the 3.5 million registered students and gentry may have been too absorbed in their classical studies to give any time to current events, they might have been roughly compensated for by readers in other social categories.

Such figures are extremely rough, and the results are sensitive to the assumptions used in the calculations. But the fact that each kind of evidence (urban population, gentry size, circulation information, and postal statistics) points to the same rough audience size of 2 to 4 million tends to confirm the assumptions used and lend plausibility to the common result. The audience's order of magnitude, at least, seems fairly clear—it would be hard to support the view that it was less than 1 million or more than 10 million. It was, in short, 1 percent—more or less—of China's population in the last decade of the Ch'ing.

In about a decade the modern press had created the largest, most far-flung audience in Chinese history. But the audience still consisted of the highly literate minority. In a country in which perhaps 30 to 45 percent of males and 2 to 10 percent of females had basic literacy and in which literacy had many important social and economic uses,[47] in which the press in large part sang the praises of democracy and popular mobilization, and in which as we shall show the problems of mass culture were already being widely discussed, the "masses" were not being reached by modern media.

---

[44] Report of Commissioner F. Hirth, *Decennial Reports, 1882–1891* (Shanghai: Inspectorate General of Customs, 1893), p. 315, cited in Ying-wan Cheng, *Postal Communication in China and Its Modernization, 1860–1896* (Cambridge, Mass.: East Asian Research Center, 1970), p. 49; quotation corrected to conform to original source.

[45] Rawski, *Education*, pp. 10–13, 140–146.

[46] Chung-li Chang, *The Chinese Gentry: Studies on Their Role in Nineteenth-Century Chinese Society*, paperback ed. (Seattle: University of Washington Press, 1967), pp. 10, 92, 97, 111, 165; cf. the discussion by David Johnson, pp. 58–59 above.

[47] Rawski, *Education*, p. 23 and *passim*.

In the next few decades, the audience was greatly enlarged, thanks in part to widening education, the growing mobility of laborers, and the enlargement of urban population. The figures in Table 2, although incomplete and unreliable, give some sense of this growth. Even if only one-third of those who entered elementary school each year went on to complete a substantial part of the seven-year course, then by 1940 the schools would have added roughly 13 million medium-literates to the population.[48] And thanks to the vernacular movement, a middle-school education was no longer necessary to read most periodicals, as it had been in the late Ch'ing. There were now many papers for the working class. The Shanghai *Li pao*, a popular tabloid of the 1930s, had three supplements aimed at different classes: the "Forest of Words" for "cultural circles," the "Fruit and Flower Mountain" for "upper and middle classes, the professions and commercial circles," and the "Little Teahouse" for "the ordinary working class."[49] In Shanghai there were also a hundred or more "mosquito" tabloids sold for a few cash on street corners, which stung with gossip of politics and the entertainment world.[50] Thirty-two of fifty-eight working-class families studied by Olga Lang in Peiping in the 1930s included men who read newspapers (there were women readers in only two).[51]

There were now correspondingly larger circulations. The largest claimed in the last decade of the Ch'ing was twenty thousand (achieved by both the *Hupei kuan-pao* in 1903 and the revolutionary *Min-li pao* in 1910); in the 1930s, the biggest Shanghai papers claimed circulations of one hundred and fifty thousand and more.[52] Postal statistics suggest the curve of growth (Table 3): newspapers posted doubled every few years from 1908 to 1936, before declining during the war. We cannot conclude that the audience grew at exactly the same rate, however, since conditions such as percentage of papers posted, periodicity and multiple readership may have changed.

Radio came to China in 1922. By 1937 there were ninety-three broadcasting stations, of which almost half were in Shanghai, which had an estimated one

---

[48] We arrived at this figure in the following way. We took the enrollment figures given in Table 2 as well as those for other years contained in the same sources and interpolated arithmetically to estimate enrollment for the missing years. For each year we divided elementary enrollment by 7 to reach the estimated size of the entering class. We estimated that one-third of the class completed enough schooling to learn to read a vernacular newspaper. Finally, we added the numbers of such medium-literates produced each year from 1907 through 1940. This estimate is conservative for at least two reasons. First, because of a high dropout rate the entering class must have been larger than one-seventh of each year's student body. Second, despite the high dropout rate, it is plausible that more than one-third of elementary school students managed to attain enough literacy to read a vernacular paper before leaving school.

[49] Pao, *Hui-i lu*, vol. II, p. 39.

[50] Ōtsuka, "Shanhai no shōhō . . . ."

[51] Olga Lang, *Chinese Family and Society* (1946), reprint ed. (n.p.: Archon Books, 1968), p. 85.

[52] Tseng, *Hsin-wen*, pp. 117, 215, 355.

TABLE 2. Elementary and Middle School Enrollments,
Selected Years

Year	Elementary	Middle
1907	918,586	31,682
1909	1,532,746	85,689
1912	2,795,475	103,045
1916	3,843,454	111,078
1918–20	5,031,687	132,432
1922	6,601,802	182,744
1930	10,948,979	514,609
1944–45	17,221,814	—
1945	—	1,394,844

SOURCES: 1907: Ch'en Ch'i-t'ien 陳啓天, *Tsui-chin san-shih nien Chung-kuo chiao-yü shih* 最近三十年中國教育史 [History of Chinese education in the last thirty years] (1930, reprint ed. Taipei: Wen-hsing shu-tien 文星書店, 1962), pp. 97, 114.

1909: Taga Akigorō 多賀秋五郎, ed., *Kindai Chūgoku kyōikushi shiryō* 近代中国教育史史料 [Historical materials on modern Chinese education] (Tokyo: Nihon gakujutsu shinkōkai 日本学術振興会, 1973–1977), vol. I, pp. 103–106.

1912, 1916, *Ti-i-tz'u Chung-kuo chiao-yü nien-chien* 第一次中國教育年鑑 [First Chinese education
1922, 1930: yearbook], Chiao-yü pu 教育部, comp. (Shanghai: K'ai-ming shu-tien 開明書店, 1934), part IV, pp. 133, 172–173.

1918–1920: Shu Hsin-ch'eng 舒新城, ed., *Chung-kuo chin-tai chiao-yü shih tzu-liao* 中國近代教育史資料 [Materials on the history of modern Chinese education] (Peking: Jen-min chiao-yü ch'u-pan she 人民教育出版社, 1961), vol. I, p. 377.

1944–1945: *T'ung-chi yueh-pao* 統計月報, 113–114:39–40 (January–February, 1947).

NOTE: Elementary includes girls' half-day, nursery, and lower, middle, and higher elementary schools; middle includes normal schools, middle-level industrial schools, and middle schools. A sizable number of students in traditional schools are not counted (see Evelyn Sakakida Rawski, *Education and Popular Literacy in Ch'ing China* [Ann Arbor: University of Michigan Press, 1977], p. 163). Different sources often give slightly different figures for the same year.

hundred thousand receiving sets.[53] There were about three hundred movie theaters with an aggregate seating capacity of three hundred thousand, likewise concentrated in Shanghai and a few other large cities.[54] But the coming of the war set back the radio and movie industries as it did the print media.

It was not until after 1949 that a truly mass audience was created. The new regime concentrated first on print media—by 1956, of course, entirely under party and government control. Through mobilization in small groups and mass movements, the party evidently achieved wonderful efficiency for its newspapers and magazines despite the continued existence of substantial functional

[53] Chu Chia-hua, *China's Postal and Other Communications Services* (London: Kegan Paul, Trench, Trubner, 1937), pp. 192–194; also see Rudolf Löwenthal, "Public Communications in China Before July, 1937," *The Chinese Social and Political Science Review* 12.1:56–57 (April–June, 1938); Tseng, *Hsin-wen*, pp. 601–621.

[54] Löwenthal, "Public Communications," pp. 47–48.

TABLE 3.   Newspapers Posted, Selected Years

Five-Year Intervals	Other Years	Number of Items
—	1908	24,645,112[a]
—	1919	47,437,161[a]
1920	—	56,318,904[a]
—	1923[b]	80,720,326
1925	—	107,665,723
—	1927	114,543,288
—	1928	124,410,600
1930	—	163,083,300
1935	—	208,946,500
—	1936	235,144,600
—	1937	124,589,700
—	1938	95,854,400
—	1939	87,180,410
1940	—	131,880,600
1945	—	98,120,227
—	1947	171,723,007
—	1948	160,679,323

SOURCES: 1908:   China, Imperial Maritime Customs, *Report on the working of the Imperial Post Office*, 1908 edition (Shanghai: Inspectorate General of Customs, 1909), p. 21.

Other: *Yu-cheng t'ung-chi hui-chi* 郵政統計彙輯 [Compilation of postal statistics] (Taipei: Chiao-t'ung pu yu-cheng tsung-chü 交通部郵政總局, 1966), pp. 120–121.

[a]Figures derived by taking 69 percent of "newspapers and other printed matter" when this category was not further broken down.
[b]First year when statistics give a separate category for newspapers.

illiteracy (38.1 percent of the population illiterate or semiliterate in 1964, 23.5 percent in 1982).[55] In an innovative study, Paul Hiniker estimated that in about 1962, Chinese newspapers had 9 readers per copy and magazines 11.5 readers per copy, so that 62 percent of the adult population were exposed to magazines and 39 percent to newspapers.[56] In the last few years, the periodical press has enjoyed further substantial growth. By official report, China in 1979 had more than eighteen hundred magazines, newspapers, and other periodicals with a combined circulation of more than 150 million copies.[57] There are reports of plans to increase the circulation of the central party newspaper, *Jen-min jih-pao* [People's Daily], from 5.3 million to 50 million by the year 2000.[58]

[55]"The 1982 Census Results," *Beijing Review* 45:20 (November 8, 1982).

[56]Paul James Hiniker, "The Effects of Mass Communication in Communist China: The Organization and Distribution of Exposure" (Ph.D. diss., Massachusetts Institute of Technology, 1966), pp. 162, 165, 205, 206.

[57]*Beijing Review* 47:31 (November 23, 1979); Xinhua report of 8 September 1980 in Foreign Broadcast Information Service: *Daily Report: People's Republic of China*, 18 September 1980, p. L 19.

[58]Tokyo Kyodo in English, 19 April 1980, in Foreign Broadcast Information Service, *Daily Report: People's Republic of China*, 21 April 1980, p. L 12.

In the last decade or so, the party has also moved to exploit the potential of electronic media. By 1974, wired loudspeakers reached 90 percent of production brigades and teams and 65 percent of peasant homes; by 1982, according to a Chinese sample survey, there were 50.5 radios in use for each 100 rural families. In 1979 a film audience of more than 20 billion was reached through one hundred and ten thousand movie houses and film production teams.[59] Most recently China entered the age of television. In 1980, a national audience of 200 million could supposedly be reached through 7 million TV sets—an amazing watchers-per-set ratio reflecting the fact that most receivers are owned by production units rather than families. Domestic production of new sets was 2.2 million in 1980, and officials predicted there would be 20 million sets in use by 1985, 200 million by the end of the century.[60] Some of the most popular printed media now deal with the consumerism of electronic media, including the popular-science magazine *Wu-hsien tien* [Radio], with a circulation of 1.3 million; the cinema magazine *Ta-chung tien-ying* [Popular Cinema], with a circulation of 8 million; and the weekly television guide, *Tien-shih chou-pao*, with a circulation of 1 million.[61]

The growth curve of China's audience has been sharp—from roughly 1 percent of the population in the first decade of this century to near universality now that radio and television are widespread. But most of the growth was achieved only recently. It may even be that the bulk of the population has been reached with regularity only in the last fifteen years or so, after the spread of electronic media. In this sense, China's mass audience is a recent creation despite its century-long gestation. Yet, thanks to the structure of the contemporary Chinese media—tightly centralized, mutually reinforcing, working in concert with cadre and activist "face-to-face" communicators—this newest of the world's mass publics may also be among the most efficiently and intensively reached.

The media were not unassisted in their work of cultural proseletyzing and homogenization. The wars and migrations of the twentieth century mixed

[59] Radio and loudspeakers: Godwin C. Chu, *Radical Change Through Communication in Mao's China* (Honolulu: University Press of Hawaii, 1977), p. 31; Jack Craig, "China: Domestic and International Telecommunications, 1949–1974," in *China: A Reassessment of the Economy*, Joint Economic Committee of the Congress (Washington, D.C.: U.S. Government Printing Office, 1975), pp. 304, 307; *Beijing Review* 20:8 (May 16, 1983); Alan P. L. Liu, *Communications and National Integration in Communist China* (Berkeley: University of California Press, 1971), pp. 118–129. Movies: "Huang Chen Press Conference on Cultural Work," Beijing Xinhua in English, 27 September 1979, in Foreign Broadcast Information Service, *Daily Report: People's Republic of China*, 28 September 1979, p. L 18; Liu, *Communications*, pp. 157–167.

[60] Craig, "Telecommunications", pp. 304–307; *U.S.-China Relations: Notes from the National Committee* 11.1–2:1–2 (Spring-Summer 1981); ibid. 10.1:3 (Spring 1980).

[61] *Wu-hsien tien*: Beijing Xinhua in English, 4 March 1979, in Joint Publications Research Service No. 73085, *Translations on People's Republic of China* 500:50 (26 March 1979); *Ta-chung tien-ying: Chinese Literature* (June 1980), p. 130; *Tien-shih chou-pao: Beijing Review* 10:27 (March 9, 1981).

people together; the spread of manufactured goods to some extent reduced local differences in clothing, food, housing, transportation, and tools. Post offices and banks, trains, buses, and bicycles all increased the circulation of ideas and people. However, because of China's low economic growth in this century, such processes have been relatively slow to work and many parts of the countryside remained culturally isolated as late as the early 1950s. It may have been a peculiarity of Chinese development that, both before and after the change of regime in 1949, political change and the media spread farther and faster than material change. As a result, cultural homogenization is probably less far advanced than a media-based and politically focused view of China would lead one to expect.[62] Moreover, because the party abused its monopoly of the media by propagating lies and contradicting itself, cynicism is apparently widespread. People have learned to get information from alternate channels of communication, especially rumor and foreign radio broadcasts.[63] Traditional popular literature remained popular even during the time the regime tried to proscribe it. In recognition of this, the government recently launched a national monthly magazine, *Min-chien wen-hsueh* [China Popular Literature] to carry condensations of such works as the *Tale of the Three Kingdoms* and *Water Margin* as well as new works written in the same vein.[64] Another new journal carries stories to be read aloud in a contemporary version of the storyteller's arts.[65]

LATE CH'ING FICTION: IDEOLOGY AND PRACTICE

With the emergence of the periodical press as a powerful instrument of communication in the late nineteenth century and with the beginning of the evolution of a mass audience, a new set of issues arose. What should be the purpose of the press? How should its writers effectively reach the people? What should they try to do for and to their readers? What kind of cultural diet should they provide for the mass audience? The problem became, in short, the creation of a new ideology, which, though still reflecting the elitist attitudes of traditional scholar-officials, nevertheless represented something more specifically geared to the needs of the populace. Intellectuals who became involved in the periodical press as writers and editors found themselves adopting a somewhat different role—no longer that of the state-oriented scholar-official, but that of a

[62] The *People's Daily* reported in June 1981 that dialects staged a comeback against standard spoken Chinese during the "ten years' upheaval" of the cultural revolution. See Editorial, "Let Every One of Us Strive to Make Our Language Refined and Healthy," *Jen-min jih-pao* 人民日報, June 19, 1981, in Foreign Broadcast Information Service, *Daily Report: People's Republic of China*, July 2, 1981, p. K 5.

[63] Both these statements are based on a series of interviews on media participation habits in the People's Republic of China that Nathan carried out in 1978–1981.

[64] Beijing Xinhua in English, 12 March 1981, in Foreign Broadcast Information Service, *Daily Report, People's Republic of China*, 13 March 1981, p. L 16.

[65] The journal, *Ku-shih hui* 故事會, is announced in *Wen-hui pao* 文滙報, July 13, 1980, p. 1.

"popular" spokesman for society. The figure who epitomized this subtle transformation was Liang Ch'i-ch'ao.

A noteworthy feature of Liang's journalistic activities and, as a result of his seminal influence, of the late Ch'ing periodical press, was the prominent position accorded to "fiction" (*hsiao-shuo*). Why fiction? Why did Liang choose this traditionally disreputable literary genre and reinvest it with a new sociopolitical significance?[66]

When we examine the initial statements by Liang and his colleagues on the subject, it is clear that their original purpose was loftily political: they wanted to use fiction to reform contemporary Chinese society and government and to inculcate in their readers their new political conception of modern nationalism. The source of their inspiration came from Japan and the West: Liang became aware that a kind of "political fiction" (*seiji shōsetsu*) had been in fashion that in turn the Japanese had borrowed from Western countries. As with the periodical press, this new fictional model could prove to be another powerful medium for political education of the "people." Thus Liang's 1898 "Preface to the Published Series of Translations of Political Fiction"—which was to be serialized in his newspaper *Ch'ing-i pao*—highlighted the example of Western fiction as an illustration of his view that a new fiction could exert a shaping influence on all spheres of a nation's life: morality, religion, manners and mores, learning and the arts, as well as the character of the people. The prerequisite for renovating the people of a nation, Liang asserted, lay in renovating fiction. In a similar statement ("Announcing Our Policy to Publish a Fiction Supplement" in the *Kuo-wen pao* of Tientsin), Yen Fu and Hsia Tseng-yu likewise emphasized the need to re-educate the Chinese people with the new kind of fiction that had done wonders in Japan and the West as a vehicle of social reform and intellectual enlightenment.[67]

Finally, in the *locus classicus* of late Ch'ing theories of "New Fiction," Liang's celebrated essay published in 1902, "On the Relationship between Fiction and Popular Sovereignty," the significance of fiction as the primary medium for political education was affirmed beyond question. Liang pinpointed four basic "powers" of fiction: its power to "incense" (*hsun*), to "immerse" (*ch'in*), to "goad" (*tz'u*), and to "uplift" (*t'i*) the reader. Liang attached the greatest

---

[66] As used in this period, the term *hsiao-shuo* 小說 still had its broad connotations from traditional times as a mixed category of miscellaneous writings that fell outside the domains of classical poetry and prose. As understood by the late Ch'ing practitioners, the *hsiao-shuo* comprised all forms of popular narrative literature—the classical tale, the novel, the *t'an-tz'u* 彈詞, and even drama. But of these variegated forms, the serialized novel emerged as definitely the major form of late Ch'ing popular literature.

[67] For a discussion of their theories, see C. T. Hsia, "Yen Fu and Liang Ch'i-ch'ao as Advocates of New Fiction," in *Chinese Theories of Literature from Confucius to Liang Ch'i-ch'ao*, ed. Adele Rickett (Princeton: Princeton University Press, 1978), pp. 221–257. Leo Lee has also briefly discussed the topic in his chapter for the *Cambridge History of China* (Cambridge: Cambridge University Press, 1983), vol. 12, part 1, "Literary Trends I: The Quest for Modernity (1895–1927)," pp. 454–457.

value to fiction's last power—its capacity to lift the reader to a higher plane of the hero and to persuade him to emulate the hero's exemplary behavior. Together with Yen and Hsia, Liang managed to elevate fiction to a position of unprecedented intellectual respectability in China.

But the intellectual and moral high-mindedness of their intention as manifested in these theoretical formulations was coupled with a more practical concern. While attempting to justify their ideas of New Fiction, these elitist intellectuals nevertheless wished to capitalize on the proven popularity of an old genre: they did not altogether lose sight of the fact that traditional Chinese fiction had had an enormous appeal for the "masses" long before the introduction of New Fiction from foreign countries. While they uniformly denigrated the artistic quality of traditional Chinese fiction and bemoaned the generally negative effect on the audience of its "incitement to robbery and lust," they were also compelled to address a different, and less lofty, set of questions: What made "people of shallow learning" addicted to traditional novels? What made fiction truly "popular" and how could they use this popular medium to popularize their reformist ideas?

At the end of their erudite announcement of the establishment of a fiction supplement, Yen Fu and Hsia Tseng-yu discussed, although in a condescending manner, the issue of why some types of historical writing were more widely circulated than others. They weighed five variables that determined why some written sources were more easily transmittable than others. They concluded that genres that used the familiar language of the day close to the living vernacular, and that described subjects familiar to readers, circulated more widely among the Chinese people even if they were unreliable accounts of historical fact. This was why fiction and unofficial history enjoyed more popularity than the official twenty-four histories. Liang Ch'i-ch'ao was even more responsive to the demands of popularity than his two colleagues.[68] His own essays were definitely written to reach a wide audience. In his 1902 essay on "Fiction and Popular Sovereignty," his designation of the "four powers" of fiction was, for all its serious intent, directed at helping New Fiction reach the largest possible audience. Hence Liang's concern with the power of fiction led naturally to a concern with reaching a large audience.

Liang also accounted for the popularity of fiction by citing its ability to "transport people to roam in a different realm," and to express the familiar in a more profound fashion. According to Liang, these two functions of fiction were the sources of the two major traditions of fantasy (idealism) and realism.[69] This

[68] Liang reportedly advised Yen to adopt a more vernacular language, which Yen refused to do. See Ah Ying 阿英, "Wan-Ch'ing hsiao-shuo ti fan-jung" 晚清小說的繁榮 [The flourishing of fiction in the late Ch'ing] in Chang, *Chin-tai ch'u-pan*, vol. I, p. 201.

[69] Ah Ying, *Wan-Ch'ing wen-hsueh ts'ung-ch'ao: Hsiao-shuo hsi-ch'ü yen-chiu chüan* 晚清文學叢鈔 小說戲曲研究卷 [Collection of late Ch'ing literature: volume of researches on fiction and drama] (Shanghai: Chung-hua shu-chü, 1960), pp. 15–16.

concern with the powers of fiction became more pronounced in a host of articles published shortly afterwards by other theorizers of lesser intellectual stature. A writer under the pen name of Ch'u Ch'ing, for instance, closely followed Yen and Hsia's five variables in a 1903 essay discussing the relative audience appeal of the following varieties of literary technique: depictions of the past versus depictions of the present, implicitness versus explicitness, elegant versus vernacular style, and reality versus fantasy. In his view, fiction often possessed the latter qualities of these polar pairs. Ch'u Ch'ing made a special plea on behalf of the vernacular language (the fourth quality) by stating that, as Liang Ch'i-ch'ao had once told him, the popularization of the vernacular language was crucial to the progress of literature and was an inevitable result of literary evolution.[70] (These pioneers anticipated Hu Shih's major tenet of the 1917 Literary Revolution by more than a decade.)

Perhaps the most revealing is an essay published in 1908, entitled "My Views on Fiction," by Chueh Wo, an editor of the magazine *Hsiao-shuo lin* [Forest of fiction]. Contrary to Liang's view, Chueh Wo argued that fiction was a product rather than a progenitor of society. It reflected tendencies of existing society as it combined art with life in order to meet the demands of readers. Chueh Wo presented a series of statistics on the basis of his own surveys: 80 to 90 percent of the works published in the previous year were translations. Fiction written in *wen-yen* sold better than that in *pai-hua* because "ninety percent of those who purchased fiction were persons from a traditional background who were later exposed to new learning" and "those truly educated in the [new] schools who had ideas and talent and welcomed new fiction constituted no more than one percent."[71] On the basis of the sales record of his own magazine, he observed that of the various categories of fiction, detective stories sold best, love stories next, works on social mores and funny incidents next, and works on military affairs, adventure, science, and personal ambitions and commitment (*li-chih*) last. While Chueh Wo deplored such tastes, he nevertheless argued that the sales price for fiction should be lowered and its readership broadened. Students, military men, businessmen, and women should be sought as readers, and efforts should be made to accommodate their tastes. In the case of female readership, for instance, Chueh Wo pointed out that works designed for them should be "roughly the same in format, subject-matter, language, and value as those for businessmen readers. But such items as *t'an-tz'u*, poetry and songs, riddles, drinking games, painting, music, and others of an aesthetic nature should also be added," presumably to teach them a wide-ranging array of civilized habits.[72]

Whether intended or not, the implications of Chueh Wo are inescapable:

[70] Ibid., pp. 27–31.
[71] Ibid., p. 46.
[72] Ibid., p. 49.

popularity of the medium takes precedence over seriousness of intention; only after the medium can reach the widest possible audience can the communicative potential of fiction be fully realized. In Chueh Wo's view, the reform of fiction involves more medium than message. And his attention to sales promotion betrays more than a hint of compromise with commercialism.

Chueh Wo's article proved both typical and prophetic, for in a brief span of a few years, late Ch'ing fiction reached unprecedented popularity as a new commercial product. The ideological seriousness of the reform-minded intellectuals was gradually lost amidst the half-hearted rationalizations and sales pitches of the later practitioners and promoters of New Fiction. Its increasing commercial popularity triggered in turn a flurry of strong reactions against it couched largely in traditional terms. The reformist thrust was buried in an outburst of moral conservatism. Huang Mo-hsi, another editor of *Hsiao-shuo lin*, warned that though China remained underdeveloped in such areas as popular sovereignty, educational reform, science, and industry, fiction seemed overdeveloped—so much so that "one could, in fact, regard the civilization of our country today as a fictional civilization." [73] The unintended pun in this statement underscores the degree of unreality in the popular practice of fiction. Huang pointed to the irony that whereas fiction had been downgraded in the past, it was now overemphasized. Another critic, writing anonymously in the magazine *Yueh-yueh hsiao-shuo* [Monthly Fiction] in 1906, remarked bitterly on the alarming tendency among fiction writers to resort to such vapid parroting of the original slogans as to make a mockery of their serious intentions:

> As for works concerned with the meaning of popular sovereignty, I don't dare say that there aren't any. But of bizarre and ridiculous works, unlearned and unsmooth translations, I have seen quite a number . . . . They have nothing to do with the so-called popular sovereignty, yet they proclaim with aplomb: "we shall reform society, we shall aid in the progress of popular government." How ridiculous is this empty echoing devoid of authenticity! [74]

Predictably, the author, who was probably the editor of the magazine, announced that he would put an end to that bad tendency and "rechannel fiction into the realm of morality." He wished to serve as an educator through fiction and he warned prospective contributors that he would not publish anything—not even stories of love and romance—unless it "conformed to the orthodox way." [75]

However, neither this nor other moral admonitions served to stem the tide. The process of commercialization continued unabated. In the next year, a writer in the same magazine lamented,

[73] Ibid., p. 59.
[74] Ibid., pp. 152–153.
[75] Ibid., p. 154.

Fiction writers of today not only fail to promote morality, but their influence is such that one fears they will destroy morality altogether. The author does not ask himself: how can I henceforth awaken my countrymen? How can I henceforth benefit society? Rather, he asks: how can I cater to the taste of the times? how can I make a lot of money? With intentions like these, their possible benefit is beyond comprehension. After a work is published, he advertises it in the newspapers with pomp and circumstance: how perfect is the work's content, how rich its material, how elegant its style. He would rather fool a thousand people in order to obtain profit for himself. For his own pocket, he wastes other people's time and money, and doesn't care. If we entrust the responsibility of fiction to men of such character, how can we expect to achieve good results? . . . If we want to save our country today, we cannot but begin with fiction and with reforming fiction.[76]

It must have saddened the originators of the New Fiction to be confronted with this outcome—a testament, ironically, to their success. Only a few years after the New Fiction came into being, its initial purpose was cast to the winds and a new cycle of reform had to be urged. What had gone wrong? How can this sorry state of affairs be accounted for? The answer may have as much to do with the urban audience as with the writers or works themselves.

As we read late Ch'ing fiction—both original works and translations of Western fiction—we find that Liang Ch'i-ch'ao's worries were not groundless: "robbery" and "lust" were indeed hallmarks of the genre. In the former category one might include such popular subgenres as murder and detective stories, "black curtain" (*hei-mu*) exposés of scandal filled with lurid sensationalism, and stories of banditry and adventure. In the latter category belong popular romances of the "scholar-meets-beauty" (*ts'ai-tzu chia-jen*) variety, and accounts of courtesans and their lifestyles. In the opinion of Chinese literary historians—notably Hu Shih, Lu Hsun, and Ah Ying[77]—these were all degraded and decadent offshoots of the once serious fiction of social criticism, such as Li Pao-chia's *Kuan-ch'ang hsien-hsing chi* [Exposé of officialdom], Wu Wo-yao's *Erh-shih nien mu-tu chih kuai hsien-chuang* [Bizarre phenomena witnessed in the last twenty years], and Liu E's *Lao Ts'an yu-chi* [Travels of Lao Ts'an]. In these best specimens of late Ch'ing fiction, the authors' critical perceptions of society and politics also involved a subjective awareness of their own feelings. Often, the social and sentimental strains were combined to create a heightened emotional intensity and to justify the author's seriousness of purpose. However, as commentators on the contemporary scene, these journalist-littérateurs also realized that their own livelihood depended on the very people they exposed: government officials, "foreign affairs" experts, compradors in the treaty ports, merchants, status-hungry *nouveaux-riches*, and decadent scions of rural landlords

[76] Ibid., p. 38.
[77] See Lu Hsun, *A Brief History of Chinese Fiction* (Peking: Foreign Languages Press, 1964), chaps. 27–28; Ah Ying, *Wan-Ch'ing hsiao-shuo shih* 晚清小說史 [History of late Ch'ing fiction], reprint ed. (Hong Kong: T'ai-p'ing shu-chü 太平書局, 1966).

who migrated to the cities for fun and pleasure. Reading through endless vignettes of satire, we cannot fail to perceive the authors' self-mockery and ambivalence. The modish trends of *yang-wu* ("foreign affairs") and *wei-hsin* ("reform"), which they satirized, also served to make their works popular. And they themselves "degenerated" on account of their popularity. Wu Wo-yao, perhaps the most prolific novelist of the period, is a case in point. The author of the devastating *chef-d'oeuvre, Erh-shih nien mu-tu chih kuai hsien-chuang*, became also an expert in detective stories (*Chiu-ming ch'i-yuan* [The strange case of nine lives]) and sentimental romances (*Hen hai* [Sea of sorrow] and *Chieh-yü hui* [Ashes after catastrophe]). He wrote ethically lofty prefaces for his sentimental novels, but the true reason for their popularity lay elsewhere. A plot summary of *Chieh-yü hui* can serve as an illustration.

> The hero, a young man named Ch'en Keng-po, and the heroine, a young woman named Chu Wan-chen, are betrothed. The young man goes to the provincial capital and succeeds in passing the civil service examination. But an evil uncle has secretly sold him into slavery, and has lured his fiancée to Hong Kong where she is sold to a brothel. Chu Wan-chen resists, is repeatedly beaten by her madam, but finally manages to plead her case to the local magistrate who happens to be a friend of Ch'en's father. The magistrate rescues her and sends her back on a boat. Mid-way, the boat capsizes. After floating in the river for a long time, she is rescued by another official, who wants her to be his concubine. She resists and is beaten to death. But she does not exactly die. The sound of torrential rain beating on her coffin, which had been abandoned in a deserted place, revives her, and she escapes to a nunnery. There, however, she becomes seriously ill. The doctor who is summoned to treat her disease turns out to be a true knight-errant. He not only cures her but voluntarily escorts her to her home town. Meanwhile, the young man's father is looking for his son. The evil uncle, who has been imprisoned for another crime, falsely tells the father that Ch'en Keng-po has died of an epidemic disease in Hong Kong. The father believes him and Chu Wan-chen, as her name suggests, remains faithful to her fiancé and finally marries him (his spirit). A few years later, Ch'en Keng-po returns: he has apparently escaped from slavery and married another woman. The whole family eventually decide that both women should be his wives, and they live happily ever after.[78]

A careful reading of the novel would surely reveal a large number of formulaic devices in characterization and narrative structure derived from traditional Chinese fiction. But the above outline already indicates that the author easily combines a *ts'ai-tzu chia-jen* formula with a melodramatic plot full of implausible twists and turns. The elements of murder, detection, knight-errantry, and adventure are also present, and the implications of sex and violence are obvious. The novel certainly offers little of "redeeming social value" (aside from some indirect criticism of the treatment of Chinese coolies in America). Its main appeal to the average reader of the day must have stemmed

---

[78] Ah Ying, *Wan-Ch'ing hsiao-shuo shih*, pp. 174–175.

from the author's clever manipulation of the trials and tribulations of the virtuous heroine (a Chinese equivalent of Eliza's escape in *Uncle Tom's Cabin*, or "The Perils of Pauline"?). The formula can be found in many traditional Chinese stories (the boat and nunnery rescue episodes recall the plots of several stories in the *San-yen* collection), which likewise offer happy endings.

The novel's indebtedness to traditional conventions raises a central issue concerning the modes of expression in late Ch'ing popular culture. The formulas obviously evoke a familiar frame of reference for the audience, rather than any sense of novelty. As Robert Warshow once observed of American popular literature, "It is only in an ultimate sense that the type appeals to its audience's experience of reality; more immediately it appeals to previous experience of the type itself: it creates its own field of reference." [79] If Warshow's observation seems to fit a novel like *Chieh-yü hui*, it also points to the discrepancy between a popular work's avowed purpose, which can be lofty, and its visceral appeal to readers. In the late Ch'ing context, this means that from the beginning the advocates of New Fiction were caught in a dilemma: on the one hand, political considerations dictated that they champion realism and a realistic assessment of contemporary society; on the other, past precedents of audience taste dictated that they pay some attention to entertainment, escapism, and fantasy. Ironically, Liang's insight that fiction has the power to "transport people to roam in a different realm" was borne out by his followers, but the fictional realm turned out to be not Liang's intended political utopia as described in his incomplete novel, *Hsin Chung-kuo wei-lai chi* [The future of China], but rather the familiar terrain of traditional popular fiction. Can we then fault practitioners such as Wu Wo-yao for their failure to live up to Liang's high standards because of their preoccupation with audience appeal? Are not Liang's own four "powers" of fiction also concerned more with the possible effect on the reader than with the quality of the writer or the literary text?

We are suggesting, in sum, that Liang may have misjudged the effect of popularization. For all his proselytizing zeal, he was basically more concerned with "elevation" (*t'i-kao*) than "popularization" (*p'u-chi*), to use Mao Tse-tung's celebrated formulation of a half-century later. Liang's followers, being untrained noncadres, had not followed his intention to spread the political message to the people but had chosen to follow "popularity" on its own commercial path. In other words, Liang may have misrepresented the link between the seriousness of purpose that accompanied his popular ideology and the masses' own culture—their tastes in genre, subject matter, and style.

Liang may likewise have underestimated the entertainment side of late Ch'ing literary journalism, which formed an essential part of its practice from the very beginning. As the foremost literary historian of the period, Ah Ying,

---

[79] Quoted in John Cawelti, *Mystery, Adventure, Romance* (Chicago: University of Chicago Press, 1976), pp. 9–10.

has shown, the earliest literary journal, *Ying-huan so-chi* [Tidbits of the world],
first published in 1872, with its contributors drawn from the staff members of
the *Shen pao*, comprised a collection of items ranging from commentary on
current affairs to poetry, folk verses, unofficial biographies of historical figures,
and fragments of a translated novel from England.[80] Serious and frivolous
contents existed side by side. This precedent was followed by most late Ch'ing
literary journals. Moreover, Ah Ying has also shown that late Ch'ing journalism begot not only high-minded newspapers but also "small tabloids" (*hsiao-
pao*) designed solely for the amusement of their readers. They bore such self-
explanatory titles as *Yu-hsi pao* [Playful news], *Hsiao-pao* [News for laughter], and
Hsiao-hsien pao [News for leisurely entertainment]. Featured prominently in
them were serialized novels. While we are not able to establish their average
circulation figures, their mushrooming numbers (Ah Ying counted thirty-two
in Shanghai around 1905) testify to the obvious popular demand for them.[81]
    A detailed study of the fictional material included in late Ch'ing journals and
tabloids would constitute another research project. But a preliminary look into
the most famous compendium of the period—the *Shuo-pu ts'ung-shu* [Collection
of fiction] published by the Commercial Press—gives some interesting clues.
The majority of the works collected are Chinese translations of Western fiction,
in which the preponderant themes are adventure, romance, and popular
history. They include such well-known works as Lin Shu's translations of Rider
Haggard's novels of adventure as well as translated or imitative fiction featur-
ing the famous English detective Sherlock Holmes (Fu-erh-mo-ssu) and his
French counterpart, Arsene Lupin (Ya-sen Lo-p'in). Perhaps Yen Fu and
Liang Ch'i-ch'ao did not expect this "popular" dimension: the New Fiction
from the West, which was capable of renovating the people in those countries,
also served to entertain them and, after translation, proved equally popular
with the Chinese audience as well.
    In 1915, Liang was so exasperated as to issue the following curse:

> Alas! All you self-styled fiction writers, I have nothing to tell you but to make you
> aware of the everlasting and unalterable fact of retribution.... If you continue to
> produce monstrous works to ingratiate yourselves with society, thus directly
> trapping the youths of the whole country in a bottomless hell and indirectly
> dooming our nation to ineradicable catastrophe, you must realize that heaven
> and earth are ultimately just and you yourselves will receive full retribution—if
> not in your own bodies, surely on your offspring; if not in this age, certainly in the
> ages to come.[82]

---

[80] Ah Ying, *Wan-Ch'ing wen-i pao-k'an shu-lueh* 晚清文藝報刊述略 [Brief accounts of late Ch'ing
literary periodicals] (Shanghai: Ku-tien wen-hsueh ch'u-pan she 古典文學出版社, 1958), pp.
7–8.

[81] Ibid., pp. 53–89. For a more detailed discussion of the rise of the fiction press, see Perry Link,
Mandarin Ducks and Butterflies: Popular Fiction in Early Twentieth-Century Chinese Cities (Berkeley:
University of California Press, 1981), chap. 3.

[82] Ah Ying, *Wan-Ch'ing wen-hsueh ts'ung-ch'ao*, p. 21.

Was Liang's expression of personal rage an acknowledgment of defeat? Did he and his intellectual colleagues fail in achieving their goals? His charge of the subversion of the New Fiction's serious purpose by commercial vulgarization makes him sound as elitist and morally conservative as some detractors of this popular genre. In a sense, the criticism of one detractor, Huang Mo-hsi, mentioned earlier, was justified: New Fiction suffered from "overemphasis." Reformist intellectuals took fiction so much more seriously than ever before in Chinese history that they lost sight of the intended educational effect. After all, the popular appeal of sex and violence has been perennial in Chinese literature—and, for that matter, in literatures everywhere. To fall back on the tried-and-true formulas of sex and violence in order to enhance the salability of a novel, as Wu Wo-yao apparently did in his work *Chieh-yü hui*, was nothing new. It was the leaders and theoreticians, not the followers and actual practitioners of New Fiction, who did not have a realistic sense of what the popular audience wanted. Being "populist" in their proclaimed orientation did not make them seasoned "popularizers" of their own cause. In fact, it was the followers, some of whom shared to a large extent the outlook of the leaders, who were instrumental in spreading the gist of the leaders' reformist message, however simplified and vulgarized.

On the other hand, one is tempted to argue that the popular practitioners of late Ch'ing fiction were much less hypocritical than their high-minded theoretical leaders in seeing through the facade of reformist rhetoric and in portraying a more authentic reality. This reality was a counterpart of the "Other Victorians" in nineteenth-century England: high-ranking officials or high-sounding intellectuals of the reformist persuasion who, in private, were addicted to "decadent" traditional pursuits (smoking opium, frequenting brothels, etc.) and enjoyed them in spite of their consciousness of sociopolitical crisis. The realistic depictions of this phenomenon in a much lauded serious novel—a *roman-à-clef* titled *Nieh-hai hua* [Flower in a sea of retribution]—as well as sensationalistic exposés in the so-called black-curtain novels seem to indicate that there was a big market for socially masochistic literature—a literature that revealed the "glamor" of the rottenness of the very society to which the readers belonged. Perhaps the sociopolitical crisis caused such a feeling of demoralization that the pursuit of sex and violence became a necessary psychological diversion. Or perhaps the entire reformist ideology was always seen by the largely traditional audience, who did not go through a transformation of ideas as Liang Ch'i-ch'ao had expected, as a hypocritical facade that veiled such perennially favorite subjects as crime and its detection, and scholar-meets-beauty in a world beyond "reform." In a crisis-ridden society on a trajectory of decline, "robbery" and "lust" seemed to assume heightened fascination.

These conjectures of audience response by no means approach an accurate description of the *mentalité* of the average urban reader in late Ch'ing China. More research is needed in order to unravel the mystery of this nebulous, thorny, yet significant problem. However, on the basis of the above discussion, we can still tentatively conclude that late Ch'ing fiction presented a certain "divided" quality, mirroring the "divided selves" of its writers and readers—serious and flippant, harshly realistic and harmlessly escapist, conscientious and degenerate, elitist and popular. The two sides, though divided, were "closely intertwined in publications throughout the late Ch'ing period," according to Perry Link, "becoming more clearly stratified only in the 1910s." [83]

The subsequent history of Chinese popular culture may be seen as further development of this dual legacy. There was on the one hand the more serious ideology of popular culture, which sought to redefine the nation in terms of the "people," to carry out mass education, and to uplift the people through culture sponsored from above. This is the legacy that persisted in the May Fourth and Yenan periods, as exemplified in the discussions of "proletarian literature," "mass education," and Mao Tse-tung's "Talks at the Yenan Forum." This ideology was accompanied by the less serious, but perhaps more pervasive, legacy of popular culture and literature as diversionary and escapist enjoyment, which was castigated by most May Fourth thinkers as "traditional" or "traditionalistic." This legacy is admittedly more problematic to assess but, in the opinion of most Chinese literary historians, led directly to the ascendancy of the "Mandarin Duck and Butterfly" school of popular urban fiction in the 1910s and 1920s. It also provided the justification for another "revolution"—the May Fourth Movement, in which the importance of reaching and edifying the people through serious literature was again championed with great fanfare.

The two currents continued to interact with each other throughout the first half of the twentieth century: the serious intellectual "crest" ran over the less serious "undercurrent" of "popularized" literature—which was a commercialization and vulgarization of the very values of the "crest" culture. A detailed portrait of this fascinating phenomenon remains to be done; however, we can attempt a brief profile here with a view to encouraging further research.

As Perry Link has brilliantly demonstrated, the vitality of the "Mandarin Duck and Butterfly" school of fiction, which, beginning in the 1910s, carried on the entertainment side of late Ch'ing fiction, continued unabated throughout the heyday of the May Fourth Movement. Link attributes its popularity to "the impulse in Butterfly fiction to keep Westernization at arm's length and to 'protest' against its deviations from proper values." [84] From the perspective of Butterfly fiction writers, the May Fourth "literary renaissance" was a highly elitist movement. Its seriousness of purpose and its Western orientation in championing a new literature recalled Liang Ch'i-ch'ao's arguments for New Fiction. Yet by and large, the May Fourth Movement was a success: by the early 1930s some of its major tenets had been legitimized by the government

---

[83] Link, *Mandarin Ducks and Butterflies*, p. 143.

[84] Link, "Traditional-Style Popular Urban Fiction in the Teens and Twenties," in *Modern Chinese Literature in the May Fourth Era*, ed. Merle Goldman (Cambridge, Mass.: Harvard University Press, 1977), p. 345.

(the adoption of the vernacular in textbooks) and accepted by urban society. In the literary sphere, such cherished May Fourth values as individualism, romantic love, and personal emancipation had evolved into catchy slogans and glamorous lifestyles, much in the way that reformism and "foreign affairs" had been popularized in the late Ch'ing. Thus we find in post-May Fourth literature such erstwhile elite writers as Chang Tzu-p'ing and Chang I-p'ing crossing over to the "popular" camp, and by catering to the prurient tastes of their audience, eliciting negative criticism from former colleagues and ensuring for themselves a bad name in the moralistic pages of most literary histories. But when we examine some of their works, it is clear that they managed successfully to capitalize on their reputation as May Fourth writers and injected pet ideological themes into old literary formulas. Chang Tzu-p'ing's stories of love triangles and pornography, in particular, are reminiscent of the *ts'ai-tzu chia-jen* fiction of both the late Ch'ing and Butterfly writers, except that Chang's protagonists are all presumably "new-thinking" types of a more recent (May Fourth) vintage. This popularization of the May Fourth ethos was effected, ironically, with the aid of the Butterfly fiction: without the comfort of old formulas in which to depict modern-style romances, Chang's works would not have proved so commercially viable. Does this mean that these popularized versions of "new literature" served to pre-empt the more traditional-style Butterfly fiction?

Link has argued that the latter maintained its popularity throughout the 1920s and 1930s. In fact, the two traditions—one modern, the other more traditional—seemed to exist side by side in the urban literary marketplace. The reason for the eventual decline of Butterfly fiction may have been the Sino-Japanese war: as the eastern and lower Yangtze cities were quickly lost to the Japanese invading forces, modern Chinese literature was forced to move into the countryside and the hinterland. In this crucial respect, it was not Butterfly fiction, which had always been an urban literature, but "the patriotic wartime plays and stories of the developing May Fourth tradition" that finally reached the larger audience of peasantry.[85] In the Communist revolutionary base of Yenan, as is well known, this rusticated May Fourth tradition was further politicized by Mao Tse-tung and directed to serve the masses of peasants, workers, and soldiers. The leftist heirs of May Fourth literature became "the first writers in modern China to achieve what may be properly called a 'mass' audience."[86]

Did urban popular literature of the Butterfly variety recede from the scene forever? Did "mass literature" become by definition "revolutionary literature" or "proletarian literature"? From a latter-day Chinese Communist perspective, the answer is naturally in the affirmative. However, recent research by

[85] Ibid., p. 348.
[86] Ibid.

Western scholars has shown that the war years saw, at least in Japanese-occupied areas, a resurgence of traditional forms of escapist popular literature. Swashbuckling tales continued to find a wide audience, and one of the most popular of this genre was a novel, first serialized in a Tientsin newspaper in 1937, titled *Shu-shan chien-hsia chuan* [Swordsmen of the hills of Shu] by a writer under the pseudonym of Huan-chu Lou-chu.[87] In Shanghai (and, to some extent, in Chungking as well) the modern commercial theater grew to proportions unprecedented in China. Most of the plays performed were not seriously concerned with the war effort; rather, they consisted of costume dramas on historical themes, adaptations from Western plays, and comedies on love and marriage. According to Edward Gunn, a play called *Ch'iu-hai-t'ang* [Begonia] broke all performance records with a continuous run of 135 days from December 1942 to May 1943 at Shanghai's famous Carlton Theater, and was later made into a film.[88] The story revolves around a modern-style woman who is forced to become the concubine of a warlord and forms an illicit liaison with a Peking opera actor. An abundance of sex and violence can be found among the plot twists of lust, revenge, and reunion. Interestingly, the play was based on a novel by Ch'in Shou-ou, an unknown author who seems to have come from the Butterfly tradition, but it was adapted for the stage by three consummate artists of a more "modern" background—Huang Tso-lin, Ku Chung-i, and Fei Mu.

This conjuncture of the traditional and the modern was due largely to political circumstances: censorship in Japanese-occupied Shanghai forbade overt expressions of anti-Japanese nationalism. But, despite these constraints, some of the first-rate "elite" writers were able to create works that were both artistic and popular. Among the many examples Gunn has collected, we can mention two names: the novelist Chang Ai-ling (Eileen Chang) submitted in 1943 two long stories to a Butterfly magazine, *Tzu-lo-lan* [Violet], and received high commendation from its editor. Her modern sensibilities and Western technique did not prevent her from employing some of the rhetorical devices drawn from traditional *ts'ai-tzu chia-jen* fiction ("The Golden Cangue" is an obvious and most successful example). The playwright Yang Chiang wrote some of the most sophisticated comedies in modern Chinese literature, which contained ironic critiques of May Fourth romanticism while maintaining a veneer of harmless entertainment. A third name, not included in Gunn's study of wartime literature in Shanghai and Peking, belonged to a writer who preferred to call himself "Nameless" (Wu-ming-shih) and who wrote a series of novels with such strange titles as *Woman from the Tower* (*T'a-li te nü-jen*), *A Romantic Portrait from the North Pole* (*Pei-chi feng-ch'ing hua*) and *From Russia with*

---

[87] Edward M. Gunn, *Unwelcome Muse: Chinese Literature in Shanghai and Peking, 1937–1945* (New York: Columbia University Press, 1980), p. 109.

[88] Ibid., p. 113.

Love (Lu-hsi-ya chih lien).[89] Their unusual mixture of decadence and vitality, exoticism and traditionalism, impressionistic art and mystical philosophy, apparently made the author something of a cult figure with a large following. It is difficult to categorize him as either a serious or a commercial writer. But more than anyone else he popularized the May Fourth ethos of romantic individualism and at the same time carried it to an esthetic extreme.

Wu-ming-shih's popularity and fame have persisted since 1949, mostly in Hong Kong and Taiwan, where a host of "popular writers," less gifted than he, have apparently followed in his footsteps and developed a lucrative "pulp fiction" of love and romance set against the middle-class commercialism of Taipei or Hong Kong. The most popular of them all is a woman writer, Ch'iung Yao, whose two or three dozen novels together with their film versions have made her a millionaire.[90]

On the mainland since 1949, on the other hand, the new "mass literature" of socialist realism is a far cry from the popular romanticism of Ch'iung Yao and Wu-ming-shih. But here too the dilemma of "elevation" versus "popularization" remains unsolved. Mao's classic formulation of these two concepts had, of course, a political purpose. But although Mao placed the proletariat on an ideological pedestal as the model for emulation by all other classes, he and his followers in art and literature seem to have failed to elevate the political consciousness of the people themselves. After a decade of socialist realism, writers and critics in the early 1960s began to debate whether to include "middle characters" (whose political standpoint could be wavering or "blank") in order to represent, more realistically, some segments of the non-politicized people and, by extension, to appeal to the reading interests of these "middle" groups. In the late 1960s and early 1970s, however, the ideological radicalism of the Cultural Revolution prompted the creation of "model works," with characters painted in unambiguous colors of black and white. We now know that such works, however laudable in political intent, failed to attract an audience. The most popular genre of literature during the last years of the Cultural Revolution, according to several insiders, was storytellers' oral renditions of "spy" and "counterspy" (*fan-t'e*) tales, which describe Chinese special agents fighting Kuomintang or American spies.[91] Some of the stories were later recorded by anonymous authors and circulated in handcopied or mimeographed form. One such story, which combined spying with romance

---

[89] Wu-ming-shih's complete works have been republished recently in Taipei by the Yuan-ching 遠景 Publishing Company. Aside from a few journalistic articles, there is no scholarly study of this fascinating figure in any language.

[90] See Leo Ou-fan Lee, "'Modernism' and 'Romanticism' in Taiwan Literature," in *Chinese Fiction from Taiwan*, ed. Jeannette Faurot (Bloomington: Indiana University Press, 1980), pp. 21–30.

[91] See Lee, "Dissident Literature from the Cultural Revolution," in *Chinese Literature: Essays, Articles, Reviews* 1.1 : 78–79 (January 1979).

and science, surfaced from the underground after its author was jailed and later rehabilitated, and was published officially in 1979 under the title *The Second Handshake* (*Ti-erh tz'u wo-shou*) and became an instant best-seller. Perry Link has pointed out the novel's indebtedness to its traditional predecessors such as Butterfly fiction and he also reports that a handcopied version of Wu-ming-shih's novel *Woman from the Tower* was found in Canton in 1980 that had gone through at least eight copyists.[92] This amazing discovery, plus the continuing popularity in translation of such Western works as *The Count of Monte Cristo*, leads us to believe that despite successive waves of ideological transformation—from the May Fourth to Yenan to the various campaigns since the 1950s—the serious ideological "crest" culture has not suppressed the genuinely popular "undercurrent"—be it late Ch'ing detective fiction and stories of courtesans, or Butterfly fiction, or the spy and counterspy stories during the Cultural Revolution. Perhaps the popular desire for diversion and escape became all the more desperate precisely because of the heightened atmosphere of excessive politics in the period of the Cultural Revolution. This renewed fascination with "robbery" and "lust" in the Cultural Revolution seems almost a replay of the late Ch'ing situation. But the scale of suffering and crisis in real life was much larger. If Butterfly fiction could afford its readers a way to hold Westernism at arm's length, the appeal of this new type of underground literature can only be its ability to relieve the reader, at least temporarily, of the increasing burden of the chaos of revolution itself. In this sense, it can be regarded as a form of "remedial protest" against Mao's politics.

CONCLUSION: THE POLITICS OF CULTURE AND THE CULTURE OF POLITICS

Our surveys of journalism and fiction from the late Ch'ing to the present yield several lessons. For one thing, the populist ideologies taken up by waves of elite intellectuals hoping to shape the mentality of the people have not entirely achieved their objectives. There remains a gap between populist ideologies and popular practices: in other words, populism remains at a considerable remove from popularity. The pressures of modernization in many ways invigorated rather than crushed popular culture. One way to deal with the anxieties of change, as we have seen in some of the popular fiction described above, was to create for both writer and reader a fictional buffer zone between them and outside reality, and even an escapist haven when that reality became unbearable. The modern mass media gave the fiction-reading and movie-going public greater access than ever to this kind of solace.

But the rise of the periodical press and the growth of a mass audience over the course of nine decades have also done much to change the culture of politics and of everyday life. For one thing, the intensification of communication gradually

<hr>

[92] Link, *Mandarin Ducks and Butterflies*, p. 238.

altered China's sense of space and time. More and more Chinese learned of a larger China and a wider world, if only by reading popular novels or newspapers for entertainment. They saw their region as part of a nation, their nation as a fragile entity in a threatening world, their civilization as only one among many, and not self-evidently the best. Intellectual and psychological disorientation created an urgent need for new world views, which Liang Ch'i-ch'ao and his colleagues and rivals undertook to meet.

As news came to readers more quickly, time moved faster. Ts'ao Chü-jen observed,

> We can no longer say like Mencius that five hundred years pass like a breath. From Ch'in and Han on, a historical cycle occurred every three hundred years or so. In modern times sixty years was considered an era. Still more recently people would speak of thirty years as a generation; after that period of time it was out with the old and in with the new, another renewal in human affairs. And nowadays ... it seems one must consider each decade a distinct phase.[93]

In earlier centuries, an argument of political philosophies might have taken a generation or more to unfold. In Tokyo in 1906–1908, the literary duel between reformers and revolutionaries flashed back and forth over the course of a few years.[94] And this was a polemic known not just to a group of court officials or to members of a local scholarly society, but to a nationwide audience. So in the 1890s Chinese began to suffer that uniquely modern experience, a world that moved too fast to keep up with.

In directing their voices to the masses to try to change their world views, the elite changed their own political culture as well. No longer a genteel mandarinate, in political debate the elite became extremist, ideological, and rabble-rousing. They disagreed with one another more profoundly and expressed their disagreements more sharply than in the past. Disputes were flaunted and even exaggerated for the edification of distant publics.

Ideological polarization and extremism were spurred by the press's self-image as a political instrument serving its masters at any cost to the truth. The press did not become a unified propaganda instrument until after 1949. From 1895 through the 1940s, thousands of papers were founded to serve diverse causes. They were not expensive to produce and often received subventions from political factions or foreign powers. Representing political factions, the press kept stirring up the "sheet of loose sand" of Chinese politics. The strong regime built after 1949 tried to turn the press into a force for unity by allowing no dissenting journalism.

---

[93] Ts'ao, *Wen-t'an, cheng,* p. 83. Ts'ao's reference is to literary events but it applies more broadly as well.

[94] Ch'i Ping-feng 亓冰峯, *Ch'ing-mo ko-ming yü chün-hsien ti lun-cheng* 清末革命與君憲的論爭 [The late Ch'ing debate over revolution versus constitutional monarchy] (Nankang: Chung-yang yen-chiu yuan chin-tai shih yen-chiu so, 1966), pp. 145–151.

The era offered new roles to writers. One could be a professional journalist (a rare breed with uneasy professional identity), a revolutionary or other committed propagandist using the mass media for a higher goal, or what most Chinese saw as a mere entertainer. The most vigorous and honored of these roles was the writer as propagandist, because it implied political commitment. The authorities' response to agitation was censorship. Together, propaganda and censorship created modes of discourse—the Aesopian, the ironic, the inflammatory, and the dissident—which dominated the public arena throughout the twentieth century.

The public responded accordingly. They read the news much as they read fiction, for gossip and sensationalism. Their own political history as it occurred was perceived by many as a tale of duplicity and revenge no different from the ancient legends of the Three Kingdoms or *Water Margin*.[95] Such detachment from and cynicism about politics, combined with a lively voyeuristic interest in it, was an unintended consequence of the press's efforts to mobilize the people, one that paradoxically made it more difficult to mobilize them and delayed the creation of the unified public will that all Chinese political leaders thought necessary for national progress. The problem survived the revolution and must have been exacerbated by recent exposures of lies and distortions allegedly propagated by the media under the "fascist dictatorship of the Gang of Four."

Chinese literati had always conceived of a gap between high and low cultures, but the twentieth century developed a sharper sense of their differentiation, verging on estrangement. The interaction of city and countryside declined. Urban intellectuals replaced the landed literati and speculated about the peasant mind as if the villages were on another planet. After 1949, the system of residential registration legally tied the peasants to the land. People from the cities resisted being sent to the countryside and if they were sent there tried to get back. Increasingly throughout the century, the actual culture of the people was seen by city-based cultural reformers as "backward" and "feudal," an obstacle to progressive ideas, a source of bad hygiene, a matrix of irrational agricultural practices, a bedrock of superstitious resistance to modern science (Lu Hsun's "Medicine"), and—after about 1960—a seedbed of "petite bourgeois" and "revisionist" political values. The proposed new culture by contrast was to be designed and directed by politicians to introduce modern and rational values, promote scientific ways of thinking, and prepare people by stages for democracy (Sun Yat-sen's idea, recently resurrected by the

---

[95] See the *yen-i* 演義 -style treatment in the popular, often-reprinted work, Ts'ai Tung-fan 蔡東藩, *Min-kuo t'ung-su yen-i* 民國通俗演義 [Popular epic of the Republic], 8 vols. (Shanghai: Hui-wen t'ang hsin-chi shu-chü 會文堂新記書局, 1936). The approach is not much different in a serious work of history, such as T'ao Chü-yin 陶菊隱, *Pei-yang chün-fa t'ung-chih shih-ch'i shih-hua* 北洋軍閥統治時期史話 [History of the period of rule of the northern warlords], 7 vols. (Peking: San-lien shu-tien 三聯書店, 1957–1959). There are myriad biographies, reminiscences, and exposés in the same vein, including many published in the magazine *Chuan-chi wen-hsueh* 傳記文學.

Communist Party in its plan for introducing direct election of people's congresses one level at a time).

What were formerly cultural givens became policy questions—language (vernacularization, the attempt to spread a national language, simplification of characters), costume (the Sun Yat-sen suit), music (from Liang Ch'i-ch'ao's call for patriotic songs to the PLA's 1980 campaign for singing songs of the four modernizations). To solve these questions the government needed a Ministry of Culture, a Propaganda Department of the Central Committee, a "line on literature and art" (*wen-i lu-hsien*). What values to promulgate, what models to present, what genres to develop, and—especially—which people would control the "instruments of propaganda" (*hsuan-ch'uan kung-chü*) became prime political issues, perhaps indeed the hottest issues of the 1960s and 1970s.

But, as we have argued, well before there was a real mass audience the cultural reformers had identified the central problem of cultural engineering, the conflict between the "elevation" of taste and content that is the commissar's goal and the need to accommodate to existing popular tastes and values in order to achieve a wide audience. The failure of the Cultural Revolution and its "model revolutionary works" showed once again that it is harder to create mass culture than the cultural designers from Liang Ch'i-ch'ao to Mao Tse-tung admitted. In crucial respects, popular tastes seem to have changed little through decades of reform and elevation. The mass culture that the elites designed has consistently been too polemical, too idealistic, too propagandistic, and too simplistic for an audience who wanted variety, excitement, and fun. At the end of the 1970s, the brief emergence of "underground fiction" and "people-managed periodicals" challenged both the official monopoly of the mass media and the narrowness of the culture they had been used to transmit, prompting in turn a wave of self-criticism in the press and a fragile Party-sponsored "thaw" that aimed to enrich culture without losing control of it. How to design a wholesome culture for the masses was again the topic of writers' congresses and official speeches. In that sense, the agenda of cultural issues for the remainder of the century bore a remarkable resemblance to the agenda of the late Ch'ing.

PART III

Concluding Perspectives

THIRTEEN

Problems and Prospects

Evelyn S. Rawski

Research, prolonged discussion, and revisions extended over several years have left those of us who participated in the 1981 conference "Values and Communication in Ming-Ch'ing Popular Culture" with a clearer sense both of the problems that still confront us and of the new topics that will amply reward study in the next phase of our investigation of Chinese popular culture.

Aside from introductory surveys of the socio-economic context of late imperial culture and the complex stratification that cut across graduated categories of literacy, the papers focus on several key areas in the formation and transmission of values. Most treat topics that straddle the boundary between written and oral realms: for example, the papers on popular religion treat *pao-chüan* that were read aloud, White Lotus sects that did not rely on written doctrine, and the ambivalent meanings of the T'ien Hou cult among citizens of South China. Our papers on the organization and functions of local drama treat a vital area of culture that by its nature could not be completely or even wholly captured in a written text. Victor Mair's work on the *Sacred Edicts* points to the critical stage, which was oral recital, and James Hayes concludes his survey of written materials by pointing to the cultural intermediaries, the specialists who informed villagers about the cultural norms of the larger culture. These papers fill out our reconstruction of a culture that included oral and written communications.

LANGUAGE AND MEANING

The boundary between the oral and written realms on which we focused led us quickly to the question of language. Language is of critical importance in cultural transmission, and David Johnson discusses the problems created by the gap between a diverse spoken and a unified written language, the first serving to express regional, ethnic, and social differentiation, the second acting as a major force for cultural integration.

Discussion of each of these facets of Chinese revealed great complexities that defied quick generalization. In written Chinese, the question "What is easy and what is difficult to read" proved impossible to answer simply. On the one hand, linguists pointed out that a written vernacular is always easier than classical language for a native speaker to learn, but in China use of a vernacular style in written materials was curtailed by the restricted circulation such materials could achieve because of the proliferation of dialect areas. The splintering of the cultural unity found in Europe with the growth of nation states was absent under China's bureaucratic empire. The orthodox educational curriculum stressed reading ability in the classical style, or *wen-yen*. The popular primers, which even peasants used in late imperial times—this is clear in Hayes's account and other studies—were written in *wen-yen*, and they were read by persons belonging to all social strata. *Wen-yen* was the prestige language, the language read by educated persons. The *Sacred Edicts* had to be written at least initially in *wen-yen*: an emperor could not address his subjects in vernacular prose. Officials on stage in Kwangtung plays spoke in *kuan-hua* (official dialect) for the same reason: the point was not comprehension but the function of language as a social marker. Missionaries discovered this popular perception in the nineteenth century when their efforts to communicate the Gospels in vernacular texts were sometimes rejected as vulgar.[1]

Cultural context is thus the second important factor we must consider when attacking the ease or difficulty of written Chinese styles. *Wen-yen* novels were probably easier for less educated readers than the vernacular novels; proverbs and the New Year's couplets pasted on house doors everywhere were also in *wen-yen*.

Writing has always served to codify, standardize, and preserve knowledge, while the oral tradition was more changeable in the information being transmitted. During late imperial times, expanding educational access probably promoted cultural transmission through written materials, but since the majority of the population remained illiterate, the point at which the written and oral traditions interacted remained very important. Susan Naquin's analysis of how social, geographical, and economic conditions helped shape the organization and religious activities of White Lotus sects, for example, illustrates how written and oral modes could be flexibly combined in response to the political situation, literacy skills, and economic status of believers. Naquin's points are reinforced in J. J. M. de Groot's study of another White Lotus sect, the Lung-

---

[1] Charles Hartwell, "Remarks on the Early Distribution and Preparation of Christian Literature," in the *Ninth Annual Report and Catalogue of the N. Fuhkien Tract Society for the Year ending Dec. 31, 1901* (Foochow: Anglo-Chinese Methodist Book Concern, 1902), pp. 7–13; *Chinese Recorder* 25:329–336 (1894).

hua movement in Fukien, which admitted illiterates as well as literate believers, stipulating different religious disciplines for the two groups.[2] Oral transmission of written materials, cited by Naquin and Daniel Overmyer, is also evident in the transmission of the *Sacred Edicts* and in some cases in transmission of popular fiction as well.

The study of language and modes of transmission is complex, but the search for meaning proves to be even more difficult. We have first of all the problem cited by Johnson and others: since we do not know the identity of the readership for novels and other works, how can we make statements about values and beliefs from analysis of texts? A second level of discourse introduces the notion of multivalence. Clifford Geertz has observed that the search for culture always betokens a search for meaning or the "structures of signification."[3] That the object being studied—novels, plays, rituals, or patterns of behavior—yields multiple meanings and social implications is obvious but difficult to resolve in historical research. We believe that Arthur Wolf's statement about Chinese religion, "There are as many meanings as there are vantage points,"[4] can be extended to cover secular phenomena as well. If the audience for a play is socially varied, we can assume divergent levels of knowledge and education among the spectators, divergent attitudes toward authority and the status quo, and hence variant meanings assigned to the drama. Fiction introduces the added complication that materials need not always be read but can be read aloud to groups. If by "the audience of a work" we mean the public that was exposed to it, we may have to speculate on both the social characteristics of different audiences and the meanings assigned by these audiences to a given work or event. We must discard the assumption that participants in a culture understood everything or nothing, or that they all understood in the same degree and the same way.

As academics we may also err in our assumption that participants in a culture seek to understand everything they see or hear. Many spectators only partially comprehend many cultural events, if by "comprehend" we mean gain textbook knowledge. As Barbara Ward shows, playgoers in the New Territories seek the glamor and excitement of the event and only vaguely understand the plots without trying to know every detail. Others go to gamble, to see friends, or for myriad other reasons only tangentially related to the play itself. It is irrelevant that few if any understand or attend the opening and closing religious segments of the theatrical performance: all know that the play is staged for the gods. Likewise, religious problems elicited demands for specialists. One hired

[2] J. J. M. de Groot, *Sectarianism and Religious Persecution in China* (Amsterdam: Johannes Müller, 1903), vol. I, pp. 197–241.

[3] Clifford Geertz, "Thick Description: Toward an Interpretive Theory of Culture," in Clifford Geertz, *The Interpretation of Cultures* (New York: Basic Books, 1973), p. 9.

[4] Arthur Wolf, "Gods, Ghosts, and Ancestors," in *Religion and Ritual in Chinese Society*, ed. Arthur Wolf (Stanford: Stanford University Press, 1974), p. 131.

exorcists and priests whose esoteric knowledge gave them spiritual powers and protection from dreaded supernatural forces. What counted was the widespread perception that such specialists had efficacious skills, not any lay understanding of precisely how the other-worldly phenomena were manipulated.

Multivalence works in yet another way. In an ideal world educated people may be perfectly rational, but in real life this is seldom the case. The late imperial era shared with all pre-industrial societies an awareness of the great uncertainties that governed men's lives. Belief in ghosts could co-exist with extremely sophisticated perceptions on other topics in educated men such as the eighteenth-century poet Yuan Mei. Educated men were not necessarily creative intellectuals, and many must have adhered to beliefs in what we call the popular realm. We close a potentially important area of inquiry if we draw a sharp line between educated and uneducated that correlates with belief systems. Geomancy, the pseudoscience of manipulating primal forces in topographical features, was pursued by educated and unlettered Chinese alike. Taoist cults of immortality attracted men from a wide range of educational levels. James Watson's study of T'ien Hou presents a deity whose multivalence is mirrored in the fact that she is worshipped both by pirates and by those who seek protection from piracy, by degree-holding members of the dominant lineage and by the subject tenants who live in their locality. T'ien Hou was also a symbol of native-place loyalties, and the nineteenth-century official Lin Tse-hsu went to worship her at the Fukien *hui-kuan* (*landsmannschaft*) on his tour of duty in Canton.[5]

COMPARATIVE MODELS

Values and beliefs do not exist in isolation. The traditional society of late imperial times appeared increasingly complex as we tried to analyze its components. We were struck by the ways in which values expressed the dynamism of a changing society and economy—ambition, faith in the potential for social mobility—while simultaneously expressing fears and anxieties generated by the rising personal insecurity that such times also evoke. If the morality books with a "bookkeeping mentality" speak for the calculating spirit of the marketplace that was penetrating more rural regions with economic growth, the millenarian vision of all men as children of the Eternal Mother is an equally eloquent voice for the security of a familial society that those precariously situated on the margin of society longed to recapture. Our understanding of

[5] Arthur Waley, *Yuan Mei: Eighteenth Century Chinese Poet* (Stanford: Stanford University Press, 1970), chap. 5; Maurice Freedman, *Chinese Lineage and Society: Fukien and Kwangtung* (New York: Humanities Press, 1966), chap. 5; on Taoism, see Wei-ming Tu, *Neo-Confucian Thought in Action: Wang Yang-ming's Youth (1472–1509)* (Berkeley: University of California Press, 1976), pp. 42–54; on Lin Tse-hsu, who was "much given to pious observances," see Arthur Waley, *The Opium War Through Chinese Eyes* (Stanford: Stanford University Press, 1968), pp. 20, 40.

basic historical trends in late imperial society clearly influenced what we found in Chinese culture.

It is for this reason that evaluation of comparative models and identification of both the differences and similarities among different premodern cultures become important. We discovered from the responses of Eugen Weber that China's late imperial society differed in some significant ways from pre-industrial societies in Western Europe, and specifically France. That evaluation prompted a rethinking about the ways in which European models could be useful for analysis of Chinese popular culture, and a pin-pointing of elements on the Chinese scene deserving of greater emphasis and study.

In comparison with France, China in the late imperial era experienced a much higher degree of cultural integration. This was due in part to a much greater diffusion of literacy skills through various social groups in China. French popular culture was basically illiterate, and as Weber himself has shown, unification of a national culture was not completed until French penetrated the various dialect regions in the course of the late nineteenth century. By contrast, Chinese illiterates lived within a literate culture that influenced their lives in manifold ways, as James Hayes shows in his paper. The persistence of illiteracy among large segments of the French rural population was partially the product of the class structure, and is eloquently depicted in Pierre-Jakez Hélias's account of his boyhood in Brittany, where learning French was a part of the process of upward mobility that separated him from Breton culture. By contrast, the Chinese system's emphasis on merit rather than birth had produced a society in which downward mobility was very much a fact of life for the degree-holding elite, whose sons had to succeed in the civil service examinations or fall in status. Even though the majority of degree-winners came from families who had produced literati before, the turnover of persons caused by the examination system produced a popular perception of the possibility of social mobility that was extremely important in shaping family strategies. Other contrasts can be cited: the separation of town and village was much more profound in early modern France than in late Ming and early Ch'ing China. This separation was reinforced by gaps in the trading network and by the persistence of dialects and class-stratified language, and it was supported by the constraints of French premodern transport. Especially in the fourteenth to seventeenth centuries, France's political system was less effective than the unified bureaucratic Chinese state in overcoming the many forces working for localism.[6]

As G. William Skinner has observed elsewhere, China also differs signifi-

---

[6] Eugen Weber, *Peasants into Frenchmen: The Modernization of Rural France, 1870–1914* (Stanford: Stanford University Press, 1976); Pierre-Jakez Hélias, *The Horse of Pride: Life in a Breton Village*, trans. and abridged by June Guicharnaud (New Haven: Yale University Press, 1978); Natalie Z. Davis, "Printing and the People," in her *Society and Culture in Early Modern France* (Stanford: Stanford University Press, 1975), pp. 189–226.

cantly from the Meso-American peasant societies studied by many anthropologists. Skinner used local systems analysis to examine the mechanisms underlying the relative integration of urban and rural traditions in late imperial society. Chinese culture is a product of high geographical and social mobility, modified by the attachment of elites to their native place. During periods of peace and prosperity (phases of "openness" in the temporal cycle), Chinese peasants were "exposed to diverse customs, alien values, and exogenous norms." The Redfield model of the Great and Little Traditions does not work in such a context. Chinese local culture might have introspective periods marked by resistance to external forces, but these were temporary intervals during phases of closure, generally at periods of dynastic decline.[7]

China was thus different in very important respects from premodern societies in France and Meso-America. The history of Chinese popular culture must take note of these structural divergences and pursue areas of inquiry such as the role of the Chinese state in cultural matters, and the role of the elite in shaping local cultures. While the European model cannot supply us with ready answers for our dilemmas, it can provide clues to questions that those studying China should also address. We will consider these questions when we turn to topics for future research.

CULTURAL INTEGRATION AND DIFFERENTIATION

The theme of cultural integration as a major process in late imperial China raises several questions. Modern Chinese historians will find that this theme contradicts their own work, which sees a rural-urban gap as an important aspect of the twentieth century, reflecting different attitudes, access to power, and participation in the westernized culture evolving in Shanghai and some other large cities. Our scrutiny of Ming and Ch'ing suggests that a rural-urban gap was a product of the late nineteenth and early twentieth centuries, when Chinese society began to adopt new modes of education and new values. That such a gap persists to the present, in ironical reversal of the expectation that modernization lessens rather than heightens rural-urban difference, and the effect of this phenomenon on contemporary culture remain tantalizing subjects for further study.

Cultural integration and differentiation are highly abstract terms that were examined fairly intensively in the course of our deliberations. By cultural integration we refer primarily not to the phenomenon of "sameness" that Durkheim identified as the "mechanical solidarity" characteristic of early and relatively simple societies, but rather to new forms of solidarity that emerge with economic advance, seen for example in the blossoming of native-place

---

[7] G. William Skinner, "Chinese Peasants and the Closed Community: An Open and Shut Case," *Comparative Studies in Society and History* 13.3: 270–281 (1971).

consciousness during the late Ming and early Ch'ing, as market advances stimulated expansion of regional sojourners into China's large urban centers, where new forms of solidarity along class lines also began to emerge. Economic opportunity also stimulated lineage consciousness: lineage organization increased during the late seventeenth century in response to Ch'ing rehabilitation of the war-torn economy, but also as an organizational tool in competition among local groups for rural dominance. Ethnic and subethnic consciousness rose too, as the early Ch'ing stimulated widespread rural migration that disrupted the settled social order and brought groups into conflict over water and land rights. Aboriginal uprisings in the Lingnan, Yun-Kwei, and Middle Yangtze regions join the communal feuds (*hsieh-tou*) found in the Southeast Coast and Lingnan as examples of the escalating violence born out of the eighteenth century economic expansion.[8]

Differentiation and interdependence form the backdrop against which improved communication between towns and villages led to greater uniformity of cultural norms. In the late imperial period all Chinese shared a common social vocabulary based on acceptance of orthodox cultural models concerning the family. The lineage form of organization was known throughout the empire, even in North and Northwest China where lineages never appeared in their elaborate South Chinese form. The major form of marriage was acknowledged even by groups who practiced other customs such as adoption of daughters-in-law. A Soochow merchant, Hupei peasant, and high official in Peking would all have subscribed to values asserting the primacy of the family and of its drive to prosper and perpetuate itself.

If Chinese specialists agree on the universality of Chinese values concerning the family, investigation of commonalities in other areas of culture produces sharp differences visible in the papers in this volume. This difference can be seen in analysis of religious symbolism. What did the Lotus Sutra and a proverb derived from it by some long process of adaptation have in common? Barbara Ward suggests that it is relatively easy to identify ideas and beliefs that are widely shared by Chinese of different social strata, while James Watson argues that symbolic structures such as religious symbols necessarily mean different things to different people and in an important sense are not shared at all. As we delve further into the study of Chinese values and ideas, we can expect to encounter challenging complexities against which we must refine our notions of the core content of Chinese culture.

---

[8] G. William Skinner, "Urban Social Structure in Ch'ing China," in *The City in Late Imperial China*, ed. G. William Skinner (Stanford: Stanford University Press, 1977), pp. 540–545; Liu Yung-ch'eng 劉永成, "Lun Ch'ing tai ku-yung lao-tung" 論清代僱用勞動 [Wage labor in the Ch'ing], *Li-shih yen-chiu* 歷史研究 4: 104–128 (1962); Rubie Watson, "The Creation of a Chinese Lineage: The Teng of Ha Tsuen, 1669–1751," *Modern Asian Studies* 16.1: 69–100 (1982); Harold Wiens, *China's March Toward the Tropics* (Hamden: Shoe String Press, 1954), chaps. 6, 8; Harry Lamley, "Hsieh-tou, the Pathology of Violence in Southeast China," *Ch'ing-shih wen-t'i* 3.7: 1–39 (1977).

The process of cultural integration itself deserves close analysis. Above we cited underlying economic and social changes that helped shape late imperial culture. We have not studied at all the subject of patterns of childrearing, despite its obvious importance for socialization. If we were to produce a Chinese counterpart of Philippe Ariès' *Centuries of Childhood*, what generalization would it contain concerning Chinese concepts of childhood?[9] What alterations in childrearing norms would we identify as significant? Would we find, as in the European case, that adolescence did not exist? Was the onset of adulthood marked by marriage only, or was the capping ceremony for males as significant? In at least the realm of education, we would point to different trends as Europe from the late seventeenth century moved toward a class-stratified system while China continued to have a unified curriculum open in theory to all who could afford schooling.

These are questions for future research. In this volume we focus on the two major conscious agents working for cultural integration, the government and the literati. Victor Mair's paper underlines the important role played by the government in creating and transmitting orthodox culture, a role that grew as the government's power to intervene directly in local affairs diminished. Perhaps the greatest testimonial to the success of the official program is found in Susan Naquin's analysis of the outlawed White Lotus sects, which incorporated the six maxims of the Hung-wu emperor into mantras chanted by illiterate Trigram members. A similar synthesis of imperial and Buddhist values was promulgated by the Lung-hua, a White Lotus sect in the Southeast Coast.[10]

Sinological literature on the role of the state in cultural control cites the importance of the civil service examinations as a means of indoctrinating the literati and winning their allegiance, of the accommodation of Manchu emperors to Chinese expectations of how a Confucian ruler should behave, and of the adroit manipulation of Lamaist symbols by these emperors in the management of foreign affairs with the Mongols and Tibetans living along China's inland borders. As Buddhist patrons, Ch'ing emperors restored some of China's most famous monasteries, temples, and pilgrimage sites, while keeping close watch over monastic communities and regulating ordination. The government promoted its own cult of Heaven, and tried to tame unruly local cults by incorporating them into the official system of temples.[11]

The elite, whose spatial dispersion and attachment to native place were

[9] Philippe Ariès, *Centuries of Childhood: A Social History of Family Life*, trans. Robert Baldick (New York: Vintage, 1962).

[10] de Groot, *Sectarianism and Religious Persecution*, vol. I, pp. 197–241.

[11] Harold L. Kahn, *Monarchy in the Emperor's Eyes: Image and Reality in the Ch'ien-lung Reign* (Cambridge, Mass.: Harvard University Press, 1971), chap. 1; David M. Farquhar, "Emperor as Bodhisattva in the Governance of the Ch'ing Empire," *Harvard Journal of Asiatic Studies* 38.1 : 5–34 (1978); Arthur Stanley, "Putoshan: A Draught at the Well-springs of Chinese Buddhist Art," *Journal of the North China Branch of the Royal Asiatic Society* 46 : 1–18 (1915); Kenneth Ch'en, *Buddhism in China: A Historical Survey* (Princeton: Princeton University Press, 1964), chap. 16; C. K. Yang, *Religion in Chinese Society* (Berkeley: University of California Press, 1967), chaps. 7, 8.

important factors promoting their activities in cultural transmission, did not necessarily promote the interests of the state in their locales. James Watson's paper on the T'ien Hou cult demonstrates that dominant lineages could appropriate an official cult to support their rural power. From the seventeenth century we have a virtual literati tradition of ennui with Chinese government and the sordid realities of an official career, which is expressed in Judith Berling's study of *The Romance of the Three Teachings*. Intellectual alienation from traditional literati career patterns went hand in hand with a fervent renewal of Confucian commitment, and the flowering of the arts to which many educated men now devoted their energies. The privatization of Confucian activities was also an unintended consequence of the major Ch'ing school of evidential research, which began with an attitude of severe skepticism concerning the validity of the Neo-Confucian orthodoxy sponsored by the state. As local power holders and as the heirs of China's intellectual traditions, literati in the eighteenth century found that their relationship with the state was marked by considerable tension and ambivalence.[12]

Watson and Mair's papers illustrate another point concerning the interaction of elite and state efforts to promote cultural norms on the one hand and cultural stimuli emanating from other social groups on the other. T'ien Hou, after all, began as a folk cult before the state adopted the goddess and promoted her worship. In the case of the *Sacred Edicts*, a Japanese scholar has suggested that the state deliberately incorporated certain religious rituals into the ceremony attending the rural lectures in order to enhance the reading of the imperial maxims with a supernatural aura.[13] Officials, rulers, and ordinary citizens must have shared deep-seated beliefs in the efficacy of locational forces, for to this day the old men of Peking exercise on the north-south axis linking the Altar of Heaven to the Hall of Prayer for the Harvest to tap the powers flowing through the site. Both elite and state efforts to propagate and sustain cultural norms succeeded in part by accommodating and incorporating diverse traditions. Cultural influence was most definitely a two-way process.

The Watson and Mair papers raise another extremely important question: what precisely did the state try to control? The work of Kung-chuan Hsiao and others declares that the Chinese state tried to impose ideological control, control of thought and values.[14] Watson, by contrast, asserts that the govern-

---

[12] Willard Peterson, *Bitter Gourd: Fang I-chih and the Impetus for Intellectual Change* (New Haven: Yale University Press, 1979); Robert Hegel, *The Novel in Seventeenth-Century China* (New York: Columbia University Press, 1981); Benjamin Elman, *In Search of Evidence: The Lower Yangtze Academic Community in Late Imperial China*, in manuscript, n.d.

[13] Ōmura Okimichi 大村興道, "Minmatsu Shinsho no senkō zushiki ni tsuite" 明末清初の宣講図式について [A study of lecture diagrams in late Ming and early Ch'ing] (Tokyo gakugei daigaku) *Dai nibumon jimbun kagaku kiyō* (東京学芸大学) 第 2 部門人文科学紀要 20:193–203 (1979).

[14] Kung-chuan Hsiao, *Rural China: Imperial Control in the Nineteenth Century* (Seattle: University of Washington Press, 1960), chap. 6; Chung-li Chang, *The Chinese Gentry: Studies on Their Role in Nineteenth-Century Chinese Society* (Seattle: University of Washington Press, 1955), pp. 197–202.

ment tried to regulate behavior and ignored beliefs. When we examine the list of imperial maxims discussed in Mair's study, we see that they too focus on appropriate behavior much more than on beliefs. Does this mean that the Chinese authorities were uninterested in controlling thought?

The officials and literati who wrote about the virtues of spreading education among the people openly linked values and behavior in the process of moral transformation. "When a boy understands righteousness he can transform the elders of his household, and can transform a neighborhood." Inculcation of the right values leads to correct action. Unity of knowledge and action, established in the Neo-Confucian thought of Wang Yang-ming, was assumed: that was precisely why education was such a powerful tool for social control. When we come to the predominant emphasis on behavior as expressed in the Ch'ing *Sacred Edicts*, however, we must ask this question: If behavior is correct, does that mean that the appropriate values have been successfully inculcated? The answer seems to be yes. Donald Munro's analysis of Chinese concepts of man cites the antiquity of the faith in role models. The Chinese assumed that the most effective way to teach any attitude or conduct was to establish a model that people could emulate. We have here an emphasis on external action that comes close to Watson's point, but models were seen as "principle in action." If correct thought led to correct behavior, the reverse process was also assumed to take place.[15]

RELIGION AND DRAMA

Our survey of late imperial culture reinforced our sense of the vital importance of work in two key areas. The first is religion. Despite modern scholarly disclaimers that traditional Chinese society was secular, religion dominated Chinese life for reasons similar to those cited by Keith Thomas for Europe: the uncertainty of life, coupled with absence of scientific, rational methods for controlling the future, encouraged recourse to the supernatural. Jack Potter has noted that this manipulation of the gods in no way detracts from the work ethic, which remains extremely strong, but individuals feel that hard work alone will not bring good fortune. For that, the gods must be on one's side.[16]

Chinese religion was intertwined with all other aspects of life. It was the basis on which the Chinese state was founded, and the relationship of the emperor to the cosmic order was reaffirmed in imperial sacrifices and other state rituals.

---

[15] Evelyn S. Rawski, *Education and Popular Literacy in Ch'ing China* (Ann Arbor: University of Michigan Press, 1979), pp. 34–35; for the conceptual foundations of the Chinese view, see Donald J. Munro, *The Concept of Man in Contemporary China* (Ann Arbor: University of Michigan Press, 1977), pp. 26–37, 93–97, 135–138.

[16] Keith Thomas, *Religion and the Decline of Magic* (New York: Scribner's, 1971), chaps. 1–2; Jack M. Potter, "Wind, Water, Bones and Souls: The Religious World of the Cantonese Peasants," *Journal of Oriental Studies* 8:139–153 (1970).

Guilds were organized around the worship of a patron deity, lineages around worship of a focal ancestor, cities worshipped the city god, and villages had their earth god (*t'u-ti*) shrines. Religion provided a basis for organizing the calender of events: the great festivals were religious in nature.

Popular religion bore the unmistakable imprint of the bureaucratic government that had long ruled China. The other world as seen by peasants was a mirror image of this world, with a spiritual bureaucracy whose lowest ranking member, the stove god, presided over every hearth. The stove god reported on household affairs to his superior, the local earth god, and so on up the hierarchy. Prayers addressed to the gods were written in the form of memorials, and naturally the gods replied in imperial form with edicts. As in this world, so in the next: Chinese bribed the stove god during the New Year to make a good report; they burned paper money to ease the way in the underworld for the deceased, who could bribe the clerks to alter their account books and perhaps lighten their punishment. Arthur Wolf has observed, "The greatest power the peasant can imagine does not escape the impress of the imperial bureaucracy on his thought," and concluded that, assessed in terms of its impact on popular consciousness, the Chinese state "appears to have been one of the most potent governments ever known, for it created a religion in its own image."[17]

Religion was always potentially subversive, even when sponsored by the state. Conversely, Chinese religions were rarely (perhaps never) completely subversive of societal norms even when they were branded by the state as heterodox. The studies by Overmyer and Naquin suggest that the dichotomy between the orthodox and heterodox was not as sharp as has sometimes been assumed. According to Overmyer, the late Ming *pao-chüan* texts express explicit conventional and implicit dissenting values: there is a duality between Confucianism and Buddhism, with the latter providing support for dissent. Naquin shows that the membership and activities of White Lotus sects also revealed a complex and by no means antithetical link to orthodox popular religious groups. As Overmyer has noted elsewhere, sectarian associations responded to needs that were not met by orthodox religion, providing assurance of religious salvation; transmitting ethical and religious discipline, hope of a new social and political order, assurance of personal worth, and opportunities for upward social mobility; and raising the status of women.[18] Sects were a permanent feature of late imperial society. To call them heterodox should not lead us to ignore the ways in which their adherents conformed to majority ethical norms, and the manifold interactions of ideas that cut across the orthodox-heterodox boundaries.

The religious texts studied by Overmyer contain a strong undercurrent of

---

[17] Wolf, "Gods, Ghosts, and Ancestors," pp. 142, 145.

[18] Daniel L. Overmyer, "Alternatives: Popular Religious Sects in Chinese Society," *Modern China* 7.2 : 153–190 (1981).

dissent. Celibacy, a positive value in orthodox Buddhism, was accepted by pious men and women despite the fact that it contradicted the familial values of mainstream culture.[19] The emphasis in a text like *Liu Hsiang pao-chüan*, however, went beyond the normal expression of celibate orientations to focus on the woman's point of view. Its heroine is a strong religious leader who frees herself from normal social constraints. The text describes in graphic detail the pains of pregnancy, sufferings of childbirth, and pollution of menstruation and childbirth. We are reminded of Watson's observation that the goddess T'ien Hou was known by some as a woman who remained celibate, a woman who may have killed herself rather than marry. Clearly, these views of marriage and childbearing were at odds with male-dominated cultural norms. They indicate to us the potential for learning more about the culture of women through study of popular religious texts and religious associations.

The creation of major cults such as the one studied by Watson is another potentially rewarding area for future work. Kuan Kung (Kuan Yü, Kuan Ti), one of the most popular deities of the late imperial period, is an obvious choice. Here is a god, derived from history, popularized by the Ming novel *San kuo chih yen-i* [Romance of the three kingdoms], who appears in countless dramatic episodes as the personification of loyalty. The God of War, Kuan Yü was adopted by merchants who regarded him as a god of wealth and fidelity in business transactions: he was installed by the Shansi/Shensi merchants in their *hui-kuan* in the major markets of China. The Kuan Yü cult was approved by the state, but the deity also served as a model for the antistate secret societies.[20] How do such cults expand, and how do they relate to the social structure? To what extent do fiction, drama, and religion interact in the propagation of the cult?

Another area much studied by anthropologists but neglected by historians concerns ritual. Ritual pervaded Chinese life from the bottom up. An individual's passage through life was marked by appropriate ceremonies at each critical juncture, the most important being birth, marriage, and death. Death and death ritual have appeared in Chinese materials from Shang times

[19] See items 118, 167–171 in Chu-hung's *Record of Self-Knowledge*, in Chün-fang Yü, *The Renewal of Buddhism in China: Chu-hung and the Late Ming Synthesis* (New York: Columbia University Press, 1981), pp. 250, 252–253; Holmes Welch, *The Practice of Chinese Buddhism, 1900–1950* (Cambridge, Mass.: Harvard University Press, 1967), pp. 116–119, 357, 365–366. Celibacy was an issue when Buddhism first came to China, and it is the leading theme in the Miao-shan legend concerning a princess who defies her father by refusing to marry, is martyred, and eventually leads her father to salvation: see Glen Dudbridge, *The Legend of Miao-shan* (London: Ithaca Press, 1978). According to Dudbridge, the legend originated in Sung times at a monastery in southern Honan, which became a pilgrimage center for the goddess Kuan-yin.

[20] C. K. Yang, pp. 159–161; Ho Ping-ti 何炳棣, *Chung-kuo hui-kuan shih lun* 中國會館史論 [A historical survey of *landsmannschaften* in China] (Taipei: Hsüeh-sheng shu-chü 學生書局, 1966), pp. 68–69.

on, and were strengthened by the ancestral cult. What was the historical development of this cult, and its associated rituals? Were there systematic variations in Chinese mortuary rites that corresponded to regional, ethnic, or class differences? Historians can learn a great deal about Chinese society through a close analysis of the Chinese way of death.[21]

Drama is another extremely important vehicle for understanding late imperial culture, far more so than fiction, because it reached out to virtually every segment of Chinese society, the illiterate as well as those who could read. The origins of Chinese drama were intimately linked with religion, and this connection persisted into modern times. As Barbara Ward reminds us, drama is not merely or even predominantly text: it is performance, and we must look at it in context if we are to appreciate its role in popular culture.[22]

Drama with human actors, the subject of papers by Issei Tanaka and Ward, was of course only part of China's theatrical tradition. The drama performed in the women's quarters of well-to-do households may as frequently have been the less expensive puppet drama, which was also performed in the streets. Indeed, the puppet theater is probably older, and we would profit by comparative analysis of extant repertory and texts in these two traditions.[23]

We clearly need to know a great deal more than we now do about the cultural messages being transmitted in plays. As Tanaka shows, this entails studying local drama, the historical movement of essentially regional forms from one area to another, and research on popular perceptions of famous plays and heroes. Wolfram Eberhard's work on divination slips reinforces Ward's observation that ordinary people knew a lot about plays and plots. When did such knowledge spread so widely? We must also consider the implications of a medium that was not the creation of the government, which tried at various points to repress performances. Who shaped the repertory? According to Tanaka, landlords and gentry dictated which plays would be presented, but he also shows that other types of drama, which did not fit the elite mold, were well known. Ward disputes Tanaka's contention that drama was significantly stratified by class. She also notes that drama was the illiterate man's textbook, his

[21] James L. Watson, "Of Flesh and Bones: The Management of Death Pollution in Cantonese Society," in *Death and the Regeneration of Life*, ed. Maurice Bloch and Jonathan Parry (Cambridge: Cambridge University Press, 1982), pp. 155–186.

[22] Barbara Ward, "Readers and Audiences: An Exploration of the Spread of Traditional Chinese Culture," in *Text and Context: The Social Anthropology of Tradition*, ed. Ravindra K. Jain (Philadelphia: Institute for the Study of Human Issues, 1977), pp. 181–203, and her "Not Merely Players: Drama, Art and Ritual in Traditional China," The Jane Ellen Harrison Memorial Lecture delivered at Newnham College, Cambridge, February 11, 1978.

[23] William Dolby, "The Origins of Chinese Puppetry," *Bulletin, School of Oriental and African Studies* 41.1 : 97–120 (1978); Kristofer M. Schipper, "The Divine Jester: Some Remarks on the Gods of the Chinese Marionette Theater," *Chung-yang yen-chiu so, Min-tsu hsueh-yuan yen-chiu so chi-k'an* 中央研究所, 民族學院研究所集刊 21 : 81–96 (1966); Alan L. Kagan, "Cantonese Puppet Theater: An Operatic Tradition and Its Role in the Chinese Religious Belief System," Ph.D. diss., Music, Indiana University, 1978.

source of knowledge about China's culture and history. To what extent did drama support orthodox values, and where did it deviate from these values?[24]

Religion, drama, and even fiction transmitted cultural values that sometimes supported and sometimes contradicted the values presented in the educational curriculum. We must look at common themes that cut across two or more of these media in order to see and compare treatment of central issues. What are the key problems being addressed? How do they relate to life conditions and the material environment? What are the role models presented? How is deviance identified, and how is it handled? What can we learn of the "flash points" of the Chinese psyche from analysis of the content of cults, plays, novels, and primers?

These questions might be pursued by studying themes that appear in a large number of works in different genres, such as those concerning the White Snake or those on Yueh Fei. George Hayden's study of Judge Pao shows how a historical figure, in this case an eleventh-century official, becomes the hero of oral tales, is elevated into the supernatural pantheon as a judge (of the Court of Prompt Retribution), and subsequently develops as the central figure of courtroom drama. Hayden states that the Judge Pao plays are about justice, which is a principle integrating the human world with the celestial and subterranean spheres. The detective hero, Judge Pao, is simultaneously a secular official and a deputy of Heaven. Religious motifs, secular entertainment, and adherence to common philosophic frames of reference are thus to be found within these plays.[25]

OTHER TOPICS FOR RESEARCH

James Hayes's paper introduces the subject of specialists, who were clearly important agents in the transmission of cultural norms. The specialists he describes fall into two categories: professionals, who had access to knowledge denied to laymen and who earned an income from their service; and informal specialists, whose acquired experience or talents enabled them to aid fellow villagers. Geomancers, physicians, litigation specialists, professional letter writers, monks, priests, and shamans were all professionals who tended to live in central places above the village level and serve a fairly large territory. Informal specialists tended to reside in the village. Levels of education frequently varied between the two groups and tended to be correlated with social recognition. Both kinds of specialists and the spatial contexts within which they worked need to be further studied.

---

[24] Wolfram Eberhard, "Oracle and Theater in China," in his *Studies in Chinese Folklore and Related Essays* (Bloomington: Indiana University Press, 1970), pp. 191–199.

[25] George A. Hayden, *Crime and Punishment in Medieval Chinese Drama: Three Judge Pao Plays* (Cambridge, Mass.: Council on East Asian Studies, 1978).

Women's culture and the role of women in cultural transmission are other noteworthy subjects for research. Women's culture was in some major respects deviant from Chinese majority culture, reflecting the marginal position of women in a society oriented to male descent. Women were half-persons: they appear in genealogies only as wives and mothers, and after death were in some areas remembered only on the domestic altar. The low place of women was reflected in ritual division of labor in South Chinese mortuary rites. Women dealt with the dangerously polluting corpse, which was thought to represent the *yin* or female element, and men monopolized the ancestral rites for the bones (*yang* element) of their male ancestors.[26]

Women were, of course, expected to be sexually chaste before marriage and in widowhood, but statistics from Taiwan for the Chinese population in the early twentieth century suggest that bastardy was a much more common phenomenon among widows than the Confucian norms would lead us to anticipate. We are reminded that the largest single category of cases in the Ch'ing compendium *Hsing-an hui-lan* [Conspectus of penal cases] involved a husband killing his wife's paramour. The few studies of such topics for Ming and Ch'ing provide lurid details of sexual peccadilloes: a young bride is raped and killed by her mother-in-law's lover, and her own family bribed to keep silent; Mrs. Wu, a widow in nineteenth-century Kiangsi, marries her paramour to avert scandal, then turns her son out of the family farm; an illicit sexual liaison between a nephew and his uncle's wife leads to their murder by kinsmen. Then there are the women who committed suicide as an ultimate act of revenge on domineering mothers-in-law and husbands.[27] There seem to be ample examples of a world that is passionate, violent, and quite deviant from the harmonious Confucian family model.

Women were also important bearers of culture, as they are in every society. Their very position as brides following Chinese rules of surname exogamy dictated that this would be the case. Unlike sons, daughters almost always left their natal families to marry. In the Southeast Coast and Lingnan regions, where single-surname villages are common, brides had to be sought from outside villages, and if contemporary rules concerning marriage held true in the late imperial period, these brides came from families of lower socio-economic

---

[26] James L. Watson, "Of Flesh and Bones," pp. 178–180.

[27] Richard E. Barrett, "Short-term Trends in Bastardy in Taiwan," *Journal of Family History* 5.3:293–312 (1980); Derk Bodde and Clarence Morris, eds., *Law in Imperial China* (Philadelphia: University of Pennsylvania Press, 1973), pp. 162–164; Shōji Tadashi 庄司荘一, "Ki Yū-kō itsuji— Chōjo jiken o megutte" 帰有光逸事— 張女事件をめぐって [The affair of woman Chang through Kuei Yu-kuang's *I-shih*], *Chūgoku bunshitetsu gakuronshū* 中國文史哲学論集, 1979:793–818; Alan R. Sweeten, "Women and Law in Rural China: Vignettes from 'Sectarian Cases' (Chiao-an) in Kiangsi, 1872–1878," *Ch'ing-shih wen-t'i* 3.10:49–68 (1978); Margery Wolf, "Women and Suicide in China," in *Women in Chinese Society*, ed. Margery Wolf and Roxane Witke (Stanford: Stanford University Press, 1975), pp. 111–141.

status than the families into which they married. There were thus always differences in local cultures involved in a marriage.

Women played the major role in childrearing as mothers and grandmothers. Not only was this the result of household division of labor, but the product of family dynamics, which dictated that the father be a distant authoritarian figure toward his sons after they passed the age of six or seven. The mother-son bond was further strengthened by the wife's psychic isolation within the household. As Margery Wolf has pointed out, from a Chinese woman's point of view family is not the male line of descent but the uterine family created by herself and her mother. A woman's loyalties are thus not identical with the interests of the male-centered family unit.[28] How does the Chinese system ensure that socialization of males will not be subverted by women? Not only as mothers but as nurses and servants in well-to-do households, women were intimately linked with the upbringing of children. How did they influence what children learned?

European social history also provides us with important questions for future inquiry. The *Annales* scholars have demonstrated that material culture supplies a key to understanding historical societies and human mentalities. Sinologists for the most part have failed to synthesize the available information on physical features of life, so there are many gaps in our knowledge of material culture in late imperial times.

What did villages look like? How were they arranged spatially? We know about contemporary variations in settlement patterns by region—had these changed over time? Does domestic architecture provide us with insights useful for social history? We know that China's public buildings—its palaces, government offices, and ritual sites—were carefully planned to express notions of the relationship between the spiritual and secular realms and displayed many symbolic and numerological features. A survey of domestic architecture shows us that here too was an underlying plan, transmitted through an artisanal tradition, whereby emphasis was placed on the spatial layout. The largest and most important room in the house, which was usually the tallest as well, was the central room where the altar to the ancestors and gods was located. This room was also the reception room for guests, the "bright" (*ming*) room in opposition to the "*an*" (dark) sleeping rooms opening off it. Chinese houses tended to have an enclosing wall, separating the house from the outside world. Life was organized around a central courtyard, where informal visitors were admitted. The spatial arrangement of the house permitted graduated differentiation of public and private space to accommodate visitors of different degree and to

---

[28] Margery Wolf, *Women and the Family in Rural Taiwan* (Stanford: Stanford University Press, 1972), chap. 3, and her "Child Training and the Chinese Family," in *Family and Kinship in Chinese Society*, ed. Maurice Freedman (Stanford: Stanford University Press, 1970), pp. 37–62.

provide women privacy from outsiders. The links between domestic architecture and the Chinese family system are obvious.[29]

What about furniture and food? What can we learn from clothing, not in terms so much of the textiles used (although each had its social connotations) but the symbolic significance of color, design, and occasion? We know that the Manchus imposed their national dress on the Chinese bureaucracy of the Ch'ing period, so that the queue and court robes (*chi-fu*) were both visual reminders of conquest. We suspect that there was a finely graded vocabulary of hairstyle and dress providing information on age, ethnicity, and occupation or status, but we have not done much close analysis of the materials and have not yet linked these elements of material culture with broader patterns of social life: patterns of work and leisure, seasonal and annual rhythms, and life-cycle rituals.

Then there is the ethnic factor. The Ming and Ch'ing saw widespread contact between Han Chinese and aboriginal tribespeople in China's south and southwest, between Han Chinese, Chinese Muslims, and Central Asian Muslims, Mongols, and Tibetans. The history of the Northwest China region is incomplete without an understanding of the many ethnic groups who resided there. As Chinese Muslims became sinicized in the seventeenth and eighteenth centuries, they became a distinct group, separated from their brethren in the Central Asian oases by the adoption of Chinese dress, names, and speech, yet separated from Han Chinese by their religion and refusal to eat pork. As Skinner has noted, ethnic markers can be deliberately raised (or lowered) in response to the environment. The early Ch'ing was a period of economic opportunity that stimulated intense competition, frequently along ethnic and subethnic lines. Conflict among groups such as the Hakka and other local residents of the Southeast Coast and Lingnan sharpened as the Hakka expanded their territorial range and moved into new regions, both in the mountain environment that had been their traditional habitat and in the rich Canton Delta, challenging the dominant Punti groups. Distinctive in their speech and customs, the Hakka awareness of living in a hostile environment can be seen in the unique multistoried houses in which they dwelled for collective security.[30]

Travel was another important means of cultural interchange. We who live in the twentieth century find it amazing that Ming and early Ch'ing travelers

[29] Liu Tun-chen 劉敦楨, *Chung-kuo chu-chai kai-shuo* 中國住宅概說 [A study of Chinese domestic architecture] (Peking: Architectural and Engineering Press, 1957); Nelson I. Wu, *Chinese and Indian Architecture: The City of Man, The Mountain of God, and the Realm of the Immortals* (New York: George Braziller, 1963), chap. 3; Andrew Boyd, *Chinese Architecture and Town Planning, 1500 B.C.—A.D. 1911* (London: Alec Tiranti, 1962), chap. 3.

[30] Myron Cohen, "The Hakka or Guest People: Dialect as a Sociocultural Variable in Southeast China," *Ethnohistory* 15.3:237–292 (1968); Liu Tun-chen, *Study of Chinese domestic architecture*, pp. 44, 47–50, 113–114, 121–126.

covered the enormous distances recorded in a travel diary such as Hsu Hsia-
k'o's, yet his experience does not seem to have been very unusual.[31] Officials
journeyed frequently and far as they were rotated from post to post; merchants
and peddlers had their regular routes, as did coolies, sailors on the Grand
Canal, and shippers in the riverine and coastal junk trade. Soldiers, whether
volunteers or conscripts, and peasants fleeing famine or war were also moving
outside the confines of their standard marketing area. There was seasonal
migration of peasants from one rural area to another, migration of workers from
villages to cities, and migration between cities. The devout went to monasteries
to learn from Buddhist or Taoist masters, traveled to visit branches of sectarian
cults, or flocked to pilgrimage sites. As we trace geographical patterns of
mobility and identify different types of mobility, we will be better able to fit this
component into our perception of the mechanisms that stimulated cultural
diffusion.

SOURCES AND MATERIALS

The fairly ambitious agenda set forth in the previous pages awaits the hand of
the researcher. How should we proceed and with what tools? It seems to us that
the very breadth of the topics subsumed under the heading "popular culture"
demand interdisciplinary cooperation and tolerance of multiple approaches
and analyses.

Anthropologists will urge historians to use the storehouse of knowledge we
possess from fieldwork in twentieth-century Chinese societies to supplement
often sparse historical data. There is much merit in this recommendation,
provided we can successfully avoid its inherent dangers: the error of assuming
without proof that current conditions prevailed in earlier times, or that observations of regional cultures in Hong Kong and Taiwan can be used to generalize
for other regions or for all of China. Contemporary studies have a richness of
detail derived from direct observation that historians cannot recreate but can
learn from. These studies help us identify key points in social organization or
cultural forms that can be pursued in historical records, and they also provide a
model for comparison with earlier phenomena.

Historians, it seems, must learn from anthropologists and begin to use
contemporary analyses as a starting point for their pursuit of historical reality.
For their part, anthropologists might link the specific village studied to China's
long cultural tradition by reading pertinent historical texts, sharpening their
historical sensitivity while raising their sights to encompass the whole society of
which the village was a part. Philosophers and literary specialists contribute to
our broader understanding as they look at lesser works as well as the master-

---

[31] *The Travel Diaries of Hsü Hsia-k'o*, trans. Li Chi (Hong Kong: Chinese University of Hong
Kong, 1974).

pieces and analyze ideas that have come to be so much a part of the culture that they are no longer questioned. Pursuit of popular culture challenges us all to become more interdisciplinary in our orientation.

A rich body of primary sources exists for the investigation of popular culture in late imperial China. The voluminous collection of government documents in the Ming–Ch'ing archives on Taiwan and in Peking have not been extensively explored for research of the kind we have described. Other collections of government documents emanating from lower levels of administration are scattered throughout China.[32] Large collections of essays (*pi-chi*) written by literati contain information on local customs; so do the numerous local gazetteers. We have collections of dialect literature; of folk poetry; of set phrases (*ch'eng-yü*); modern collections of ethnographic data, folklore, and stele inscriptions as well as oral histories that can be used to supplement other kinds of records. We have almanacs, technical handbooks, travel guides, contracts and all the other kinds of written materials produced by a literate culture: museums house paintings that tell us a great deal about clothing styles, garden designs, domestic interiors, and city plans. For the Ming and Ch'ing, we still have extant monuments, buildings, tools, clothing, and other artifacts. In view of the wealth of potential sources, social historians face the problem of indigestion rather than starvation as they evaluate the research possibilities that lie ahead.

Finally, we must cast our vision backward and forward in time for the longer historical view. We cannot fully gauge the significance of Ming developments without knowing more than we do now about the dynamics of Sung and Yuan society. Many scholars now think that it was in the Sung that China's family and lineage institutions achieved the forms we see in the late imperial period. Urbanization, printing, drama—these also have their roots in the Sung and Yuan.

As Leo Lee and Andrew Nathan indicate, the late nineteenth and early twentieth centuries saw the emergence of mass culture that departed in fundamental ways from the traditional pattern. Contemporary mass media and the culture they create exist in symbiosis with much older cultural vestiges. We can advance our understanding of the long-term changes in the development of Chinese culture by overriding the disciplinary fences separating the late imperial from modern periods. We must investigate the alterations and continuities in Chinese popular culture as it developed in the twentieth century and as it is developing today.

---

[32] *Ming and Qing Historical Studies in the People's Republic of China*, ed. Frederic Wakeman, Jr. (Berkeley: Center for Chinese Studies, 1980), pp. 45–60, 63–72; Beatrice S. Bartlett, "An Archival Revival: The Qing Central Government Archives in Peking Today," *Ch'ing-shih wen-t'i* 4.6:81–110 (1981).

CONTRIBUTORS

Judith A. Berling is an associate professor in the Department of Religious Studies, Indiana University, Bloomington, Indiana 47405.

James Hayes is a member of the Administrative Grade, Hong Kong Civil Service and Honorary Research Fellow at the Center of Asian Studies, University of Hong Kong.

Robert E. Hegel is an associate professor in the Department of Chinese and Japanese, Washington University, St. Louis, Missouri 63130.

David Johnson is an associate professor in the Department of History, University of California, Berkeley, California 94720.

Leo Ou-fan Lee is a professor in the Department of Far Eastern Languages and Civilizations, University of Chicago, Chicago, Illinois 60637.

Victor H. Mair is an associate professor in the Department of Oriental Studies, University of Pennsylvania, Philadelphia, Pennsylvania 19104.

Andrew J. Nathan is a professor in the Department of Political Science and a member of the East Asian Institute, Columbia University, New York, New York 10027.

Susan Naquin is an associate professor in the Department of History, University of Pennsylvania, Philadelphia, Pennsylvania 19104.

Daniel L. Overmyer is a professor in the Department of Asian Studies, University of British Columbia, Vancouver, British Columbia, Canada V6T 1W5.

Evelyn S. Rawski is a professor in the Department of History, University of Pittsburgh, Pittsburgh, Pennsylvania 15260.

Tanaka Issei is a professor in the Institute of Oriental Culture, Tokyo University, Tokyo, Japan.

Barbara E. Ward was Fellow, Newnham College, Cambridge, and Reader in Anthropology, Chinese University of Hong Kong.

James L. Watson is a professor in the Department of Anthropology, University of Pittsburgh, Pittsburgh, Pennsylvania 15260.

GLOSSARY-INDEX

Academies, 5, 22. *See also* Schools
Agriculture, x, 4, 6, 26, 78, 362
Ah Ying 阿英, 383, 385, 386
Almanacs: publication of, 22, 23, 28, 65; description of, 78, 82–83, and magic, 106n; official, 98n
America, 303, 404. *See also* West, the
Amitābha, 224–225, 226, 233, 235, 238, 243, 248, 249
Amplified Instructions on the Sacred Edict. See *Sheng-yü kuang-hsun*
an 暗 [dark], 414
Ancestor worship: and genealogies, 79, 80; ritual for, 100, 410, 413; and drama, 145–146; and Lo sect, 236; and White Lotus sects, 261, 289n, 290; and local gods, 311; and lineages, 409
"Announcing Our Policy to Publish a Fiction Supplement" (Yen Fu and Hsia Tseng-yu), 379
an-t'ang 菴堂 [halls of retreat], 262
Ao t'ou tsa tzu 鰲頭雜字 (Tseng Ch'u-ch'ing), 149
Architecture, *See* Buildings
Ariès, Philippe, 406
Arkush, R. David, 57
Astrology. *See* Divination
Atwell, William, 4
Audiences: women as, xv, 65, 86, 113, 177, 374, 381; actual, 34–35, 114; reflected in texts, 40, 41, 112–142; intended, 42, 113; and social status, 43, 67–69, 401; for inexpensive books, 65; for opera, 161–187; for *The Romance of the Three Teachings*, 188; for Religion of the Three Teachings, 196; for *pao-chüan*, 228–231; for White Lotus sects, 288; for *Sacred Edict*, 335–336, 339–342; for mass media, 367, 370–378, 392–395; for popular fiction, 380, 381, 383, 385, 386, 387–388, 401. *See also* Uneducated audiences
Avalokiteśvara, 199n
Avatámsaka sutra. See *Hua-yen sutra*

Ballads: audiences for, 63, 65, 67, 68, 79, 88–89; and values, 107; themes of, 182. *See also* Oral tradition; *t'an-tz'u*
Baller, F. W., 338
Bilingualism, 35, 44. *See also* Dialects
Births, 82, 101, 251–252, 320
Board of Rites, 83, 293, 300
Boat people, 78n, 81, 305, 310; and T'ien Hou, 294–298 passim, 307, 313, 321
Bodhidharma, 223
Book of Changes. See *I Ching*
Book of Documents. See *Shu Ching*
Book of History. See *Shu Ching*
Book of Poetry. See *Shih Ching*
Book production costs. *See under* Publishing
Boxer rebellion, 258, 366
Brim, John A., 316

35–40, 399; and elites, 46, 66, 120; variations within, 57, 67, 68; and women, 62–63, 67; and written texts, 121, 122n, 124n, 125, 138, 400–401; in religious sects, 259, 271–272, 274, 280, 281, 285; and T'ien Hou cult, 296, 297, 310; and education, 326n; and *Sacred Edict*, 329–330, 340–341, 359. *See also* Popular culture; Storytellers; Uneducated audiences

Orthodoxy: and *Sacred Edict*, xvi, 349–350; in popular literature, 191, 201, 215; in sectarian texts, 221, 230, 241, 409; Buddhist, 223, 227, 233, 234, 250, 253; and White Lotus sects, 257, 259, 276, 277, 288–290; and T'ien Hou, 309, 315; and cultural integration, 405; and drama, 412. *See also* Censorship; Indoctrination

Outlaws of the Marsh. See *Shui-hu chuan*

Overseas Chinese, 90n, 185, 258, 303

pai chia hsiang 拜假像 [bowing to false images], 234

Pai chia hsing 百家姓 [Hundred names], 29–30, 83, 85

pai chia-men 拜家門 [paying respects to the membership], 281

pai-hua 白話 [vernacular], 363, 381. *See also* Vernacular language

pai-lien chiao 白蓮教 (*tsung* 宗). *See* White Lotus sects

Pai-p'ao chi 白袍記, 148n, 149

Pair Shift Allegiance to the T'ang, A. See *Shuang t'ou T'ang*

Pai-t'u chi 白兔記, 148, 149n, 151

Pai-yang 白陽 sect, 280

Pai-yueh t'ing 拜月亭, 150n, 151

Pa Kao 巴高 [Reaching High], 213

pa-kua li-t'iao 八卦理條 [Eight Trigram Principles], 280

Pan Chao 班超, 149n, 151

P'an Ching-jo 潘鏡若, 188, 189–192, 217

P'an-t'ao chi 蟠桃記, 148

Pao Cheng 包拯 or Pao Kung 包公 [Judge Pao], 65, 114, 412

pao-chia 保甲 [police security] system, 12, 205, 328

pao-chüan 寶卷 [precious scrolls], xv, 65, 148n, 192, 219–254, 399, 409; and White Lotus sects, 255n, 256n, 257. *See also* Scriptures; *names of individual works*

Pao-kuang 寶光 [Precious Ray], 197

pao-kuan wen-chüan 包管文卷 [written guarantee], 215

Pao T'ien-hsiao, 364, 371

Pao T'ing-po 鮑廷博, 22

pao-t'ou jen 包頭人 [promoters], 143

pao-tzu 包子, 204, 205

Paper, 18–19, 204, 205, 368

Parker, E. H., 79

Partible inheritance, 9, 215

Pasternak, Burton, 316

Patriarchs (*tsu*), 239, 256, 257, 259–264, 266, 274, 280. *See also* Teachers

Peasants: dependency of, 50–52; and elites, 71n, 72, 394, 404; and drama, 145, 159, 160, 168; culture of, 291–293, 294, 296, 400; and T'ien Hou, 295, 298; and fiction, 389. *See also* Popular culture; Uneducated audiences; Villages

Pei-chi feng-ch'ing hua 北極風情畫 [A romantic portrait from the North Pole] (Wu-ming-shih), 390

Pei Huang, 349

Pei Ti 北帝, 307, 308

Peking, 112n, 168, 193, 269, 368, 369; printing in, 24, 25n, 26, 27. *See also* Opera, Peking

Peking gazette. See *Ching pao*

P'eng P'ai, 71n

Pen-hsu 本虛 [Originally Void], 195

pen-ti jen 本地人 [original settlers], 306. *See also* Punti

pen-ti pan 本地班 [local troupes], 146

People's Daily. See *Jen-min jih-pao*

Perry, Elizabeth, 51

Peterson, Willard, 13

pi-chi 筆記 [essays], 417

pien-wen 變文 stories, 39

Pi-fu 鄙夫 [Niggardly], 195

p'i-huang hsi 皮黃戲. *See* Opera, Peking

ping 兵 [soldiers], 336

ping 丙 [stem], 276